The Changing World of School Administration

Edited by
George Perreault
Fred C. Lunenburg

A SCARECROWEDUCATION BOOK

The Scarecrow Press, Inc.
Lanham, Maryland, and Oxford
2002

A SCARECROWEDUCATION BOOK

Published in the United States of America
by Scarecrow Press, Inc.
A Member of the Rowman & Littlefield Publishing Group
4720 Boston Way, Lanham, Maryland 20706
www.scaroweducation.com

PO Box 317
Oxford
OX2 9RU, UK

British Library Cataloguing in Publication Information Available

Library of Congress Cataloging-in-Publication Data

The changing world of school administration / edited by George
Perreault, Fred C. Lunenburg.
    p. cm.
"A ScarecrowEducation Book."
Includes bibliographical references and index.
  ISBN 0-8108-4482-6 (hardcover : alk. Paper)
  1. School management and organization—United States. 2. Educational
leadership—United States. 3. Educational change—United States. I.
Perreault, George Michael. II. Lunenburg, Frederick C.
  LB2805 .C4734 2002
    371.2'00973—dc21
2002006301

∞™   The paper used in this publication meets the minimum requirements of
American National Standard for Information Sciences—Permanence of
Paper for Printed Library Materials, ANSI/NISO Z39.48-1992.
Manufactured in the United States of America.

NCPEA OFFICERS FOR 2001–2002

President

Paul M. Terry, *University of Memphis*

President-Elect

Elaine L. Wilmore, *University of Texas, Arlington*

Past President

Judith Adkison, *University of North Texas*

Executive Director

Theodore Creighton, *Sam Houston State University*

Executive Board

2002

Genevieve Brown, *Sam Houston State University*
Helen Ditzhazy, *Eastern Michigan University*

2003

Jim Berry, *Eastern Michigan University*
Dwain Estes, *McNeese State University*

2004

Angus MacNeil, *University of Houston*
Michael "Mick" Arnold, *Southwest Baptist University*
Jesse J. McNeil, *University of Texas, Arlington*

NCPEA HONOR ROLL OF PRESIDENTS, 1947–2001

1947	Julian E. Butterworth, *Cornell University*
1948	William E. Arnold, *University of Pennsylvania*
1949	Russell T. Gregg, *University of Wisconsin*
1950	Clyde M. Campbell, *Michigan State University*
1951	Dan H. Cooper, *Purdue University*
1952	Walter K. Beggs, *University of Nebraska*
1953	Robert S. Fisk, *University of Buffalo*
1954	Van Miller, *University of Illinois*
1955	Harold E. Moore, *University of Denver*
1956	Walter A. Anderson, *New York University*
1957	A. D. Albright, *University of Kentucky*
1958	Jack Childress, *Northwestern University*
1959	Richard C. Lonsdale, *Syracuse University*
1960	William H. Roe, *Michigan State University*

1961	Howard Eckel, *University of Kentucky*
1962	Daniel E. Griffiths, *New York University*
1963	Kenneth McIntyre, *University of Texas*
1964	Luvern Cunningham, *University of Chicago*
1965	William H. Roe, *Michigan State University*
1966	Willard Lane, *University of Iowa*
1967	Harold Hall, *California State University, Los Angeles*
1968	Kenneth Frasure, *SUNY, Albany*
1969	Samuel Goldman, *Syracuse University*
1970	Malcolm Rogers, *University of Connecticut*
1971	Paul C. Fawley, *University of Utah*
1972	Gale W. Rose, *New York University*
1973	Anthony N. Baratta, *Fordham University*
1974	John T. Greer, *Georgia State University*
1975	C. Cale Hudson, *University of Nebraska*
1976	John R. Hoyle, *Texas A&M University*
1977	J. Donald Herring, *SUNY, Oswego*
1978	Charles Manley, *California State University, Northridge*
1979	Jasper Valenti, *Loyola University of Chicago*
1980	Max E. Evans, *Ohio University*
1981	Lesley H. Browder Jr., *Hofstra University*
1982	John W. Kohl, *Montana State University*
1983	Bob Thompson, *SUNY, Oswego*
1984	Donald L. Piper, *University of North Dakota*
1985	Robert Stalcup, *Texas A&M University*
1986	Robert O'Reilly, *University of Nebraska, Omaha*
1987	Donald Coleman, *San Diego State University*
1988	Charles E. Kline, *Purdue University*
1989	Larry L. Smiley, *Central Michigan University*
1990	Frank Barham, *University of Virginia*
1991	Paul V. Bredeson, *Pennsylvania State University*
1992	Rosemary Papalewis, *California State University, Fresno*
1993	Donald Orlosky, *University of South Florida*
1994	Paula M. Short, *University of Missouri, Columbia*
1995	Maria Shelton, *NOVA Southeastern University*
1996	Clarence Fitch, *Chicago State University*
1997	Clarence M. Achilles, *Eastern Michigan University*
1998	Robert S. Estabrook, *Stephen F. Austin State University*
1999	Cheryl Fischer, *California State University, San Bernadino*
2000	Michael Martin, *University of Colorado, Denver*
2001	Judith Adkison, *University of North Texas*
2002	Paul M. Terry, *University of Memphis*

Contents

Part II: Leadership Preparation

Part III: Leadership in Practice

Contributing Authors

C. M. Achilles, *Eastern Michigan University*
Ramon Alaniz, *Texas A&M International University*
Margaret Andrews, *Southern Illinois University*
Robert Beebe, *Youngstown State University*
Robert J. Bell, *University of Kentucky*
Lars G. Björk, *University of Kentucky*
Lynn K. Bradshaw, *East Carolina University*
James Coaxum III, *Rowan University*
Patrick Cosiano, *Baldwin-Wallace College*
Chris Cox, *Alvin Independent School District, Alvin, Texas*
Theodore B. Creighton, *Sam Houston State University*
Charlene Crocker, *Stephen F. Austin State University*
John M. Decman, *University of Houston, Clear Lake*
Gini Doolittle, *Rowan University*
Harry Eastridge, *Cuyahoga County Educational Service Center*
Fenwick W. English, *University of North Carolina at Chapel Hill*
J. D. Finn, *State University of New York, Buffalo*
Lance D. Fusarelli, *Fordham University*
Margaret Grogan, *University of Virginia*
Steven J. Gross, *Temple University*
D. Keith Gurley, *University of Kentucky*
Sandra Harris, *Stephen F. Austin State University*
John E. Henning, *University of Northern Iowa*
Michael H. Hopson, *Stephen F. Austin State University*
Sandy Hutchinson, *Central Missouri State University*
Dorothy James, *Southern Illinois University*
Judy A. Johnson, *Sam Houston State University*

Lawrence T. Kajs, *University of Houston, Clear Lake*
Theodore J. Kowalski, *University of Dayton*
Linda Lambert, *California State University, Hayward*
Sharon Shockley Lee, *Southern Illinois University, Edwardsville*
Fred C. Lunenburg, *Sam Houston State University*
Martha M. McCarthy, *Indiana University*
Martha Ovando, *University of Texas, Austin*
George J. Petersen, *University of Missouri, Columbia*
Joy C. Phillips, *University of Texas, Austin*
Brianne Reck, *Hanover County (Virginia) School District*
Victoria Robinson, *University of Northern Iowa*
Connie Ruhl-Smith, *Bowling Green State University*
Edith A. Rusch, *Rowan University*
Seymour B. Sarason, *Yale University*
Joan Poliner Shapiro, *Temple University*
James M. Smith, *Bowling Green State University—Firestone*
Karolyn J. Snyder, *University of South Florida*
Scott R. Sweetland, *Ohio State University*
Paul M. Terry, *University of Memphis*
Linda C. Tillman, *Wayne State University*
Louis Trenta, *University of Akron*
Edward Willman, *Texas A&M International University*

Review Board

Preface

As we begin the 21st century, those of us who work in education find that, more than ever, perhaps, we occupy contested ground. Numerous critics assail public schools, laying much of the blame for their perceived failures and shortcomings upon those who occupy positions of leadership and influence. That such critics find little common ground and that the proposals for reform are so discordant doesn't seem to matter—something must be changed. Change, of course, is inevitable, although progress is optional and highly dependent upon one's view of the purpose of education, which is to say that ultimately all arguments about social concerns are grounded in axiology. It is fitting, therefore, that the NCPEA yearbook presents a look at pressing issues from a variety of philosophical perspectives.

In part 1, for example, two of the invited chapters deal directly with one of the most contentious issues of the day, standardized testing, yet the authors reach very different conclusions. The impact of market forces on public education is the focus of one chapter, and another reports on the implementation of zero tolerance disciplinary policies. Several of the pieces in this section, though, take a look at educational leadership in a broader way, critiquing it from postmodernist, feminist, and communitarian approaches. And finally, one of the more acute observers of American society offers a global overview of the current crisis in public education.

The two remaining sections of the yearbook contain chapters that were chosen through a blind review process. For each contribution, a minimum of four reviews were conducted, and a variety of pieces were selected which address issues related to the preparation of school leaders and the challenges they will face in practice. Not surprisingly, given the current focus on accountability, two chapters deal directly with student testing and the use of such data in making leadership decisions. A number of chapters address the issue of diversity, in terms both of gender and of ethnicity, and several authors describe specific changes made to administrator preparation programs. Foci also include both the principalship and the superintendency.

It would be easy, of course, to predict (and bemoan) that divergent points of view on educational matters would be inevitable in today's climate, but this overlooks a fundamental feature of American culture—our social contract is not about a precise definition of the truth; it is, instead, about the areas in which ongoing arguments will take place. That is, the American premise is that dialogue should occur, and from this will arise spaces in which ultimately we can all set roots, grow, and flower. The authors in this yearbook have, in elaborating upon their experience and insights, contributed to that effort and are to be commended.

Naturally, a book of this scope cannot be completed without the assistance of a great many people. I would like first to thank the authors and reviewers who are listed at the front of the book, as well as the NCPEA Publications Committee, for their professional contributions. In addition, special thanks are due to the following individuals: Professor Fred C. Lunenburg who provided numerous suggestions for improvement of the book, including expansion of the invited chapters; Professor Theodore Creighton, executive director of the NCPEA, who gave ongoing technical support to the project; Professor Theodore Kowalski who has proven to be a wonderful colleague over the past two years; and my graduate assistant, Gwen Shonkwiler, who handled many of the difficult tasks associated with completion of the book and did so with remarkable efficiency and unfailing grace.

GEORGE PERREAULT
MARCH 2002

I

INVITED CHAPTERS

President's Message

Professors and Practitioners:
Building Bridges through Leadership

Paul M. Terry

Never in the history of education has the accountability bar been as high as at the start of the 21st century. It appears that every entity interested or involved in education has an opinion on what and how to teach, how to organize programs and align curriculum, and even what should be the color scheme on the walls of the local schools. Whatever the opinions are, they are grounded in finding fault with what exists.

The theme of the 55th Annual Conference, "Professors & Practitioners: Building Bridges through Leadership," was chosen because educators can no longer play the "blame game." Unfortunately, it has become standard operating procedure for elementary educators to blame parents and society for problems that must be addressed prior to being able to focus attention on teaching in the classroom. Likewise, middle school educators and high school educators blame those below them for any short-falls students may have when moving up. University educators continue the blame game by pointing the finger at the public school systems for not producing students prepared to deal with the rigor of university work and in need of remedial courses at the entry to higher education. Further, many university graduate programs are being closely scrutinized and challenged to consider alternative criteria for admissions other than the standard GRE or MAT scores in order to ensure more equitable procedures for an increasingly diverse demographic population. Throughout the entire system, what has traditionally been accepted as the norm may no longer be appropriate. But educators at all levels can no longer continue the blame game; we must work in tandem to build stronger bridges for more effective communication among all vested parties. As Gandhi stated, "Leadership at one time meant muscle; but today, it means getting along with people."

Unfortunately, one of the paradigms of education is still to pay deference to the group with the most muscle and clout to influence educational policy and practice.

Paul M. Terry, University of Memphis

Whether the groups are from the K–12 public education arena, the higher education system, or the policymakers, it is crucial that stronger alliances be built to address common concerns and issues in education. It is in the building of this bridge of communication that the future of our nation, indeed of our world, can be found.

The foundation and future of our nation is built on a strong education system. The United States prides itself on being a nation of freedom and rights, and for years each political party vying for strength and political clout has touted the fundamental tenet that "all children have a right to learn—all children must have access to a quality education." At the start of the public school movement, Horace Mann envisioned schools as the great equalizer of the classes, and certainly increasing attention must be paid to socioeconomic status, rather than race, as having the greatest impact on a broad array of issues leading to access and equity in public education. No one could disagree with the philosophical basis of this statement. However, public perception has determined that the nation is in an educational crisis, and education has become seen, not as the solution to problems but as the "whipping post"—the cause of low standards, low achievement, low productivity, and inept leadership across the entire society.

Education, indeed all of society, is in a mode of change. Changing times require caring, competent, and astute leaders who can envision the future without losing sight of the past. While using the past as a benchmark and guiding principle is acceptable, university preparation programs can no longer afford to live in the past and train potential administrators using outdated paradigms. Higher education must have educational administration programs designed to recruit and develop 21st-century leaders who can serve with vision and integrity to enhance the notion of effective leadership for organizational, managerial, but mainly instructional skills for positive differences in the lives of young people, adults, families, and communities (Veir, 2002).

There are already more than 80,000 principals in the United States, and according to the Bureau of Labor (2001), there will be a more than 10 percent increase in openings for principals in the next six years. And that does not include principals needed for new schools in the five most populated states, nor does it include administrators in other positions in school districts. With only a few more than 500 universities having administration preparation programs, one must pose the question, are we in higher education truly ready and able to train even the 8,000 principals needed in the next five years? I think not! And given new competition from alternative programs sponsored by local school districts, state departments of education, and regional educational service centers, higher education must rethink leadership development programs (Veir, 2002). For the educational administration profession to stay at the forefront in leadership preparation, we must build stronger bridges between professors and practitioners.

STONE, WOODEN, OR STEEL BRIDGES?

Historically, there were stone bridges because they were solid and it was thought they would last forever. However, as the nation moved into the industrial and agricultural age, with changes in the uses and needs for bridges, wooden bridges became more prevalent. In this era, bridges were constructed from strong hardwoods and they too were expected to last forever. But after some time, with weather and use, much of it brought on by automobiles, bridge slats begin to wear out and were in need of repair and replacement. Later, following further experimentation and many new inventions, it was discovered that constructing bridges of steel would yield yet a longer life. Steel bridges were stronger and more substantial, making the span between two bodies of land much easier and safer. The analogy to be gleaned from this metaphor is that perhaps university educators, who originally built bridges to K–12 from hardwood, have failed to realize that many of these bridges are now old and still using outdated materials; they are in desperate need of repair or replacement with newer and much stronger materials to operate efficiently and effectively. Additionally, I would purport that there are several boards on these wooden bridges that have just rotted away with the rapidly changing times. Many of the bridges of communication are so splintered that there is no link spanning educational administration and K–12 practitioners— there is no leadership development for serving the changing expectations and needs of the schools.

In the 21st century, universities can no longer afford to simply repaint, repair, or replace rotten boards in the current bridges. If our leadership programs are to survive, they must build newer and more solid bridges between universities and K–12 programs. These bridges must be built of a material flexible enough to stand in the winds of change, and yet strong enough to endure as a foundation for the future. These are the challenges universities face; these are the paradigms that must be built. As we enter this new century, these are the challenges that are placed before those of us charged with the daunting task of leadership development. What materials will *you* choose with which to build your bridge?

REFERENCES

United States Bureau of Labor. (2001). *Bureau of Labor Statistics*. Washington, DC: Author.
Veir, C. (2002, March). Reinventing leadership development for the 21st century: Leading in a culture of change. Paper presented to the meeting of the International Academy of Educational Leaders, Atlanta, Ga.

Cocking Lecture

Improving Student Achievement: Some Structural Incompatibilities

Fred C. Lunenburg

Beginning in the mid-1980s, the "excellence movement" was launched, which challenged educators to improve the academic performance of America's schools. The reform movement is now more than a decade old. There are numerous reports that demonstrate that it is possible to find effective public schools where administrators, teachers, and parents collaborate to produce high achievement for all students. But these successes occur in only a small number of schools. We still cannot account for the fact that some students master academic content and many others do not. Most schools and school systems are not organized to effectively support and encourage learning.

The answer to this problem is to determine how to improve teaching and learning in whole school districts instead of merely in isolated schools (Elmore, 2000; Fullan, 2000a). The mantra the "school is the unit of improvement" was based on the misguided belief that individual teacher professionalism would produce excellent schools. The most recent literature suggests that we need to modify that belief (Elmore, 1995, 2000; Fullan, 1999, 2000a, 2000b; Louis, Toole, & Hargreaves, 1999). The school will always be the primary unit of intervention, but without a supportive policy environment and resources outside the school, the chances of enduring change and improvement are limited. Similarly, research suggests that unless improvement efforts penetrate the classroom and affect individual teachers directly, we will continue to find far more variance within and between schools (Elmore, 1997; Elmore & Burney, 1999; Louis & Kruse, 2000; Louis, Toole, & Hargreaves, 1999; Tye, 1987).

My purpose in this chapter is to examine the incompatibility between the structure of organizations and efforts to improve student learning. I develop this analysis in four parts. I begin with a few ideas about why school improvement is so problematic.

Fred C. Lunenburg, Sam Houston State University

Then I make a case for the incompatibility between the structure of schools and the demands for school improvement. Two frameworks are useful here: Parsons' (1960) levels of organization and Weick's (1976) loose coupling. Next, I introduce a new leadership framework, the purpose of which is to rebuild a new school structure, which may better accommodate the demands for school improvement. Finally, I discuss one state's successful experience with school improvement, which I believe is compatible with the new leadership structure I propose.

THE PROBLEM OF SCHOOL IMPROVEMENT

School improvement has been well studied over the past decade, but change in schools has been problematic for several reasons. First, successful change occurs in only a small number of schools; that is, these reform efforts have not been widely replicated from one school context to another. Second, there is no guarantee that the change will last. Put another way, there has been strong adoption and implementation of change and improvement, but not strong institutionalization; that is, the innovation did not become integrated into the school system's mission and organizational structure. Third, and equally problematic, is the impact of the change. Has the change reached the classroom? Have students been positively and significantly affected by the change?

Of these problems, one of the most perplexing continues to be how to make changes in the "substantive core of teaching and learning"—what it is teachers actually do in their classrooms and what it is that students learn (Elmore, 1995; Fullan, 1997; Louis, Toole, & Hargreaves, 1999; Tyack & Cuban, 1995). There is a great deal of school improvement activity that is ultimately unconnected to any improvement in student learning (Lunenburg & Ornstein, 2000).

The main reason for the failure of these reforms to endure and penetrate the classroom is that many of the principal structures and roles of schooling remain remarkably stable over time, despite repeated efforts to change them (Ogawa, Crowson, & Goldring, 1999). Reform is more likely to be altered to "fit" existing structures than to result in major organizational restructuring. That is, many changes remain at the organizational periphery rather than penetrate to the "deep structure" of schooling (Cuban, 1988, 1992; Tye, 1987). Both local school development and a supporting infrastructure surrounding the school are critical for lasting success and penetration into the technical core of teaching and learning.

If school improvement efforts are bent to fit comfortably into schools as they are currently structured—and this has been the typical pattern of every major reform in the 20th century—improvement efforts will be weakened and unrecognizable by the time they reach the classroom. In this case, a strong basic education for all students will be diminished. But it is also possible that public schools will find a way to initiate and sustain a major organizational restructuring. If successful, the organizations that emerge will probably not look anything like the current ones, but a strong basic education system is more likely to endure and flourish (Elmore, 2000, 2001).

THE THEORY OF LOOSE COUPLING

Talcott Parsons (1960) delineated a framework which describes three fundamental levels of an organization—technical, managerial, and institutional. In education, the technical level is concerned with the teaching-learning process. The managerial level refers to the administration and organization of schooling. The institutional level is concerned with the relations between the school and its external environment—both close relations, such as those with school boards and their representative functions in the local community, and more distal relations, such as those with the state and other economic, political, and social dimensions of society.

The belief that educational systems may be designed to articulate efficiently and effectively across these organizational levels is questionable. Decisions made at the state or school board may have little impact on the "real work" of school administrators (superintendents and principals), much less in the classroom (teachers and students). For example, the relations between state policymaking toward school reform and instructional improvement practices in schools "rarely make broad or close contact with instruction" (Cohen & Spillane, 1992, p. 11). Two kinds of structural fragmentation typically occur. First, state-district-school articulation is not well connected. Second, the articulation across levels of organization is complex: the responsibility for organizational implementation is fragmented and given to a variety of individuals, each of whom has little interaction with the others (Spillane, 1998).

Organizational analysts who study the structure of organizations have coined a term for the way our schools are organized: "loose coupling" (Meyer & Rowan, 1992; Rowan, 1990; Weick, 1976). Derived from organizational sociology, this view, in brief, suggests that the "technical core" of education—detailed decisions about what should be taught, how it should be taught, what students should be expected to learn, how students should be grouped for instruction, how they should be required to demonstrate their knowledge, and how their learning should be evaluated—resides in individual classrooms, not in the organizational infrastructure that surrounds them.

To reinforce this view, a "grammar of schooling" has been well institutionalized in our schools composed of subjects, specialized subjects, grades, grade levels, and individual teachers in their classrooms forming a foundation of organizational stability. The combination of these characteristics can balkanize schools into isolated units that only sporadically communicate between and among classrooms, schools, and levels of organization. Thus, many structural innovations have not effected substantive changes in the core of teaching and learning (Elmore, 1995, 2000, 2001).

The administrators who manage our schools do not manage the way its basic functions are carried out. Put another way, school administrators have little to do with the technical core of education—teaching and learning. Teachers' work is guided more by inherited practices than by any clear and common view as to what is to be taught, how it is to be taught, why it is to be taught, and how learning is to be evaluated (Cohen & Spillane, 1992; Lunenburg, 1995), and in many cases there is no support from the organizational infrastructure that surrounds them. Furthermore, the knowledge base that guides the teachers' classroom decisions is not formalized or even agreed upon. Moreover, there is a lack of clearly defined success criteria. Social myths of teacher professionalism and teacher autonomy help to "buffer" the classroom and its instructional activities from the uncertainties of close evaluation and inspection by the external environment (Elmore, 2000, 2001).

School administrators, then, do not manage instruction. They manage the infra-structure surrounding the technical core of teaching and learning. They "buffer" to protect their core technologies. Superintendents and principals hold strong organizational allegiances and seek distancing from their clients to protect their autonomy. They perform ritualistic tasks, such as planning, organizing, budgeting, and dealing with disruptions inside and outside of the system. These rituals help to maintain the legitimacy of the organization as a social reality to their constituents, what organizational theorists call a "logic of confidence," and furthermore help the organization to persist by "decoupling" the technical core from environmental uncertainty.

Ignoring student achievement indicators is possible and is, in fact, standard operating procedure in many school districts, because the assessment of a "good" superintendent is made primarily based on his or her political shrewdness and skill on managerial-type indicators, such as financial stability, clean buildings, and well-behaved students. Rowan and Miskel (1999), referencing Meyer and Rowan's study (1977), described this type of judgment of superintendent ability as being based on how close the superintendent is able to bring the school district to widely shared organizational norms of "good schooling." Rowan and Miskel further assert that adherence to these norms was actually more important for the survival of school districts during pre-accountability times than was fulfilling the "technical core" mission of the school district—educating students—and that this allowed school leaders to ignore information that showed that the "technical core" mission was not being fulfilled:

> A logic of confidence and good faith develops in organizations as administrators deliberately ignore and discount information about technical activities and outcomes [such as teaching and learning] in order to maintain the appearance that things are working as they should be, even if they aren't. In this way, organizations continue to mobilize support and resources simply by conforming to externally-defined rules, even when such rules do not promote technical efficiency. . . . The legitimacy of schooling as an enterprise depend[s] crucially on maintaining the public's confidence . . . and this require[s] educators (and the public) to ignore obvious variations in classroom activities and student outcomes that occur within standardized forms of schooling. (p. 363)

Teachers work in isolated classrooms and manage the technical core. This school system hierarchy has continued relatively unchanged throughout most of the 20th century (Elmore, 2000).

Elmore (2000, 2001) suggests that the theory of loose coupling explains much about the strengths and weaknesses of public schools. According to Elmore, it explains why most innovations in schools occur in the structures that surround teaching and learning, and only peripherally in the actual process of teaching and learning. Most innovation is about maintaining the logic of confidence between the public and the schools. The theory of loose coupling explains why schools continue to promote structures that are not productive for learning. They include extraordinarily large high schools that are impersonal and alien to many students; rigid tracking systems that stereotype students according to academic ability; athletic programs that limit participation to only a few students; grouping practices in elementary schools that provide less stimulating curriculum to some students; special programs that remove students from regular instruction; and site-based governance structures that engage in decision making about everything but the conditions of teaching and learning.

Proponents of restructuring note that most innovations emphasize changes in governance and management, not changes in curriculum and instruction (Murphy, 1991). Others document the limited impact that restructuring has had on the instructional practices of teachers (Elmore, Peterson, & McCarthey, 1996). Because teachers and administrators buffer the technical core and because articulation among the levels of organization—technical, managerial, institutional—is complex, innovations are not connected to any larger goal or mission belonging to the school system. And because teachers work in isolated classrooms, instructional improvement is a matter of individual initiative. This leads to innovations that are highly personal and thus tend to be adopted in only a few classrooms and schools.

Loose coupling explains the unsuccessful quest for school administrators to act as instructional leaders. Theories of leadership in loose coupling structures stress the role of leaders as buffers, coalition-builders and brokers among diverse interests, custodians of organizations, and manipulators of symbols (Elmore, 2000, 2001). None of these theories of leadership captures the imperative for sustained districtwide instructional improvement, because none of them postulates a direct relationship between the work that leaders do and the technical core functions of the school district.

Loose coupling explains the unstable conditions of politics and leadership in most large school systems. The governance structure is designed to support the logic of confidence between the public and the schools, not to provide direction to the improvement of student achievement. Since politics is not about the technical core but about the logic of confidence between the schools and the community, all policy decisions are essentially about consolidating political constituencies. Superintendents come and go based on their capacity to maintain a working majority of an unstable elected board, rather than on their capacity to focus the school district on the technical core—teaching and learning (Elmore, 2000, 2001). This leads to frequent turnover of superintendents resulting in an unstable environment for sustained districtwide school improvement (Lunenburg & Ornstein, 2000).

It is not difficult to see why school improvement is so hard to institutionalize, maintain, and replicate. It conflicts with the way public schools are currently organized. This incompatibility is not likely to be resolved in the usual way by bending the innovation until it fits into the existing organizational structure. School improvement must penetrate into the instructional core of teaching and learning. This requires the creation of a new framework of instructional improvement and a new leadership to manage it.

THE NEW FRAMEWORK

Policymakers are sending a clear message to school systems that their main focus should be to improve teaching and learning (Elmore, 2000, 2001). Will they be able to respond to the demand? In an ideal system, school improvement efforts focus educational policy, administration, and practices directly on teaching and learning. This will require districtwide leadership focused directly on learning. School leaders can accomplish this by (1) clarifying purpose, (2) encouraging collective learning, (3) aligning with state standards, (4) providing support, and (5) making data-driven decisions. Taken together, these five dimensions provide a compelling framework for accomplishing sustained districtwide success for all children.

Clarifying Purpose

The school district and the administrators and teachers who work in it are accountable for student learning. This assertion has strong economic, political, and social appeal; its logic is clear. What teachers teach and students learn is a matter of public inspection and subject to direct measurement (Elmore, 1995, 2000, 2001). Superintendents need to develop a practical rationale for school improvement. Clearly and jointly held purposes help give teachers and administrators an increased sense of certainty, security, coherence, and accountability (Conley, Dunlap, & Goldman, 1992; Hargreaves, Earl, & Ryan, 1996; Louis, Toole, & Hargreaves, 1999; Rosenholtz, 1989). Purposes cannot remain static for all time, however. They must be constantly adapted to changing circumstances and the needs of the system. Few really successful schools lack purpose (Louis & Miles, 1990).

In their studies of "successful school restructuring" in over 1,500 schools, Newmann and Wehlage (1995) found that successful schools focused on "authentic" pedagogy (teaching that requires students to think, to develop an in-depth understanding, and to apply academic learning to important realistic problems) and student learning. They achieved this in two ways: greater organizational capacity and greater external support. The most successful schools, according to Newmann and Wehlage, were those that functioned as professional communities. That is, they found a way to channel staff and student efforts toward a clear, commonly shared purpose for learning. Moreover, they found that external agencies helped schools to focus on student learning and to enhance organizational capacity through three strategies: setting standards for learning of high intellectual quality; providing sustained schoolwide professional development; and using deregulation to increase school autonomy. In short, dynamic internal learning communities and their relationships with external networks made the difference. Evidence on the critical combination of internal and external learning is mounting (see, for example, Elmore & Burney, 1999; Fullan, 2000a; Louis & Kruse, 2000; Spillane, 1998).

There are instructional strategies that can help teachers increase student learning. In research recently completed at the Mid-continent Research for Education and

Learning (McREL) Institute, Marzano, Pickering, and Pollock (2001) identified classroom practices that generally increase student achievement: identifying similarities and differences; summarizing and note taking; receiving reinforcement for effort and recognition for achievement; doing homework and practicing; using nonlinguistic representations; learning cooperatively; setting objectives and testing hypotheses; and using cues, questions, and advance organizers. Regardless of whether or not teachers teach to standards, these classroom practices work well.

Encouraging Collective Learning

A key task for school administrators is to create a collective expectation among teachers concerning the state's accountability criteria. That is, administrators need to raise the collective sense of teachers about state standards. Then administrators must work to ensure that teacher expectations are aligned with the state's accountability criteria (Adams & Kirst, 1999). Furthermore, administrators need to eliminate teacher isolation so that discussions about state standards become a collective mission of the school and school district.

"The key to student growth is educator growth" (Joyce & Showers, 1995, p. xv). In a collective learning environment, teachers become generators of professional knowledge rather than simply consumers of innovations (Hopkins, 1993; Louis & Kruse, 2000; Schon, 1984). Innovations are built around the system rather than using prepackaged school improvement models (McLaughlin, 1990). Changing mental models replaces training educators in new behaviors (Senge, 1990). Continuous instruction-embedded staff development replaces one-shot non-instruction specific professional development events (Hall & Hord, 2001). Single-loop, linear learning that monitors whether a system is reaching its goals is replaced by double-loop learning where systems are able to revisit whether goals are still appropriate and then recycle as needed (Argyris, 1990).

School administrators must develop and sustain school structures and cultures that foster individual and group learning. That is, administrators must stimulate an environment in which new information and practices are eagerly incorporated into the system. Teachers are more likely to pursue their group and individual learning when there are supportive conditions in the school and school district, such as particularly effective leadership (Leithwood, 1994; Leithwood & Atkins, 1995; Leithwood & Jantzi, 1997; Leithwood & Louis, 2000). Schools where teachers collaborate in discussing issues related to their school improvement efforts are more likely to be able to take advantage of internally and externally generated information (Louis & Kruse, 2000; Murphy, 1991). Teachers can become willing recipients of research information if they are embedded in a setting where meaningful and sustained interaction with researchers occurs in an egalitarian context (Huberman, 1993).

Aligning with State Standards

Some critics believe that the emphasis on high-stakes testing narrows the curriculum and prevents teachers from using good teaching practices (see, for example, Gordon, 2000; McNeil, 2000; Orfield & Wald, 2000; Panta, 2001). However, teaching a common body of essential knowledge and skills need not narrow the curriculum or inhibit good teaching practice (Lunenburg, 1995). When they are well constructed and implemented, state standards and tests can change the nature of teaching and learning. They can lead to a richer, more challenging curriculum. They can foster discussion and collaboration among teachers within and across schools. They can create more productive conversations among teachers and parents. And they can help focus stakeholders' attention on increasing student achievement (Lunenburg & Ornstein, 2000).

For standards to have an impact on what happens in classrooms, they must be clear. A few years ago, standards were left vague in deference to local control of the curriculum. The state set broad goals and left the curriculum to local schools and educators (Lunenburg & Irby, 1999). But this is a mistake. When school districts, administrators, and students are held accountable for results, more specificity is needed in implementing the standards. In a high-stakes accountability environment, teachers require that the standards contain enough detail and precision to allow them to know what the students need to learn.

Most states are attempting to align their tests with their standards. Gandal and Vranek (2001) encourage states to consider three principles in this endeavor. First, tests not based on the standards are neither fair nor helpful to parents or students. States that have developed their own tests have done a good job of ensuring that the content of the test can be found in the standards. That is, children will not be tested on knowledge and skills they have not been taught. This is what Fenwick English and Betty Steffy (2001) refer to as "the doctrine of no surprises." However, the same is not true when states use generic, off-the-shelf standardized tests. Such tests cannot measure the breadth and depth of each state's standards. Second, when the standards are rich and rigorous, the tests must be as well. Tests must tap both the breadth and depth of the content and skills in the standards. Third, tests must become more challenging in each successive grade. The solid foundation of knowledge and skills developed in the early grades should evolve into more complex skills in the later grades.

If one accepts the premise that tests drive curriculum and instruction, perhaps the easiest way to improve instruction and increase student achievement is to construct better tests. Critics argue that many state-mandated tests require students to recall obscure factual knowledge, which limits the time teachers have available to focus on critical thinking skills (Ad Hoc Committee on MCAS, 1998; McNeil, 2000; Panta, 2001; Smith, 1991; Smith & Rottenberg, 1991; Yeh, 2001).

According to Yeh (2001), it is possible to design force-choice items (multiple-choice test items) that test reasoning and critical thinking. Such tests could require students to *use* facts, rather than *recall* them. And test questions could elicit content knowledge that is worth learning.

To prepare students to think critically, teachers could teach children to identify what is significant. Teachers could model the critical thinking process in the classroom, during instruction, through assignments, in preparing for tests, and in the content of the test itself. By aligning test content with worthwhile questions in core subject areas, it may be possible to rescue testing and instruction from the current focus on the recall of trivial factual knowledge. Test items could be created for a range of subjects and levels of difficulty. Then there would be little incentive for teachers to drill students on factual knowledge.

Providing Support

One of the biggest challenges in advancing state standards and tests, and the accountability provisions tied to them, is providing teachers with the training, teaching tools, and support they need to help all students reach high standards. Specifically, teachers need access to curriculum guides, textbooks, or specific training connected to state standards. They need access to lessons or teaching units that match state standards. They need training on using state test results to diagnose learning gaps. Teachers must know how each student performed on every multiple-choice item and other questions on the state test. And training must be in the teachers' subject areas. Only then can teachers be prepared to help students achieve at high levels on state-mandated tests.

In addition to professional development for teachers, all schools need an intervention and support system for students who lag behind in learning the curriculum. Some states require schools to provide additional help to students who lag behind in core subjects, either in school, after school, on weekends, or during the summer. Some states supply the financial resources to fulfill this mandate.

School administrators need to broker the resources required to improve teachers' abilities to teach the state standards. This involves acquiring materials, information, or technology; manipulating schedules or release time to create opportunities for teachers to learn; facilitating professional networks; and creating an environment that supports school improvement efforts.

Higher state standards usually mean changes in curriculum, instruction, and assessment—that is, changes in teaching and learning. The history of school reform indicates that innovations in teaching and learning seldom penetrate more than a few schools and seldom endure when they do (Elmore, 2000, 2001; Elmore, Ablmann, & Fuhrman, 1996; Fullan, 2000a). Innovations frequently fail because the individuals who make it happen, those closest to the firing line—classroom teachers—may not be committed to the effort or may not have the skills to grapple with the basic challenge being posed (Adams & Kirst, 1999; McLaughlin, 1990). Teachers are motivated to change when their personal goals are aligned with change, when they are confident in their ability to change, and when they feel supported in attempting the change (Lunenburg, 1995; Lunenburg & Ornstein, 2000). To gain commitment of teachers and students to pursue school improvement efforts, school administrators must promote school cultures that reward achievement.

Making Data-Driven Decisions

How can school districts gauge their progress in achieving high state standards? Three factors can increase a school district's progress in meeting state standards (Sclafani, 2001). The primary factor is the availability of performance data connected to each student, broken down by specific objectives and target levels in the state standards. Then schools across the district and across the state are able to connect what is taught to what is learned. The state standards should be clear enough to specify what each teacher should teach. And a state-mandated test, aligned with state standards, will indicate what students have learned. Also, teachers need access to longitudinal data on each student in their classroom. With such data, teachers are able to develop individual and small-group education plans to ensure mastery of areas of weakness from previous years while also moving students forward in the state-mandated curriculum.

The second factor is the public nature of the measurement system. Assuming the school district has a system of rating schools, annually the district should publish a matrix of schools and honor those schools that have performed at high levels. This provides an impetus for low-performing schools to improve their performance. It also provides role models for other schools to emulate. At the school and classroom levels, it provides a blueprint of those areas where teachers should focus their individual education plans and where grade levels or schools should focus their professional development plans. The public nature of the data from the accountability system makes clear where schools are. Assuming the state disaggregates its data by race/ethnicity and socioeconomic status, performance of each subgroup of students on state-mandated tests makes the school community aware of which students are well served and which students are not well served by the school district's curriculum and instruction.

The third factor in gauging progress toward meeting state standards is the specifically targeted assistance provided to schools that are performing at low levels. Before the advent of state accountability systems, it was not evident which schools needed help. The first step is to target the schools in need of help based on student performance data. Each targeted school is paired with a team of principals, curriculum specialists/instructional coaches, and researchers to observe current practices, discuss student performance data with the staff, and assist in the development and implementation of an improvement plan. The targeted schools learn how to align their program of professional development to the weaknesses identified by the data. They learn how to develop an improvement plan to guide their activities and monitor the outcomes of the activities, all of which are designed to raise student performance levels.

DOING THE RIGHT THINGS

Considering the magnitude of the task posed by high-stakes accountability for school districts and schools, there is little research on organizational design and practice in exceptionally high-performing school districts (Elmore, 2000, 2001; Rowan, 1990). The available documentation does point to some common themes that high-performing school districts possess, but the knowledge base on which to offer advice to school districts and administrators on the design of sustained districtwide improvement processes is limited.

Within the past 5 years, however, a few examples of sustained districtwide academic success of children have begun to emerge in the research literature. These examples have appeared in states that have highly developed, stable accountability systems, such as New York, North Carolina, and Texas (see, for example, Elmore & Burney, 1999; North Carolina Department of Public Instruction, 2000; Ragland, Asera, & Johnson, 1999; Skrla & Scheurich, 2001). Preliminary research in some of these districts found evidence of common strategic elements in the way these districts managed themselves. Superintendents in high-performing districts exhibited a much greater clarity of purpose, along with a much greater willingness to exercise tighter controls over decisions about what would be taught and what would be monitored as evidence of performance. They used data on student performance to focus attention on problems and successes; they built district accountability systems that complemented their own state's system; and they forged strong relationships with their school boards around improvement goals. They created a climate in which teachers and principals were collectively responsible for student learning and in which the improvement of instruction was the central task. Incentive structures in these districts focused on the performance of all students, not just on average school performance. Superintendents realigned district offices in these school districts to focus on direct relationships with schools around instructional issues; and they focused more energy and resources on content-specific professional development (Elmore, 2001; Koschoreck, 2001; Ragland, Asera, & Johnson, 1999; Skrla & Scheurich, 2001).

The particular configuration of the Texas accountability system has changed the fortunes of students, especially minority students, in dramatic ways. As such, the Texas accountability system stands out from among the variety of state accountability systems insofar as it disaggregates data on the basis of race, ethnicity, and economic status. Additionally, it stipulates performance levels for all identified groups at both school district and school levels, and it ensures compliance by legislatively imposing rewards and sanctions.

The Academic Excellence Indicator System (AEIS) in Texas represents an integrated accountability system that includes an exceptional demand for racial and socioeconomic equity by requiring equal levels of performance for all disaggregated groups (including African American, Hispanic, White, and economically disadvantaged). Unlike other accountability systems that measure success against a group norm, the testing used in the accountability system in Texas is criterion referenced; hence, by insisting on equal performance levels for all disaggregated groups, the system has built into it an orientation toward equity. The multiple indicators built into the design of the accountability system are noteworthy. Since 1994, three types of performance indicators have been used: base, additional, and report only (Texas Education Agency, 1996). The base indicators—which include Texas Assessment for Academic Skills (TAAS), dropout rates, and attendance rates—are used to determine school and district performance ratings. Additional indicators, although not employed specifically to assign performance ratings, may determine whether the district or school will receive acknowledgment for exceptional achievement. These additional indicators include average college admissions test performance, percentage at or above criterion on college admissions tests, percentage of students tested on college admissions tests, and percentage of students passing the Texas Academic Skills Program (TASP), a college-readiness test. Finally, report-only indicators include such things as numbers of students exempt from TAAS, percentage of students completing advanced courses, and percentage of students taking and passing end-of-course exams in algebra, biology, U.S. history, and English II.

Some critics claim that accountability systems harm children of color and children from low-income homes (see, for example, Anderson, 2001; Gordon, 2000; Haney, 2000; Klein, Hamilton, McCaffrey, & Stecher, 2000; McNeil, 2000; Orfield & Wald, 2000; Parker, 2001). Others argue that accountability systems drive educational improvements for these students (see, for example, Fuller & Johnson, 2001; Grissmer & Flanagan, 1998; Grissmer, Flanagan, Kawata, & Williamson, 2000; Johnson, Treisman, & Fuller, 2000; Koschoreck, 2001; Reyes, Scribner, & Paredes Scribner, 1999; Scheurich, 1998; Scheurich, Skrla, & Johnson, 2000; Skrla, Scheurich, & Johnson, 2000, 2001; Sclafani, 2001; Sebring & Bryk, 2000; Skrla & Scheurich, 2001; Skrla, Scheurich, Johnson, & Koschoreck, in press). Few state accountability systems have been in place long enough to sort out the negative and positive commentary on accountability policy's equity effects. However, the Texas public school accountability system has been in place for several years, providing a useful case for analyzing the impact of accountability systems on student achievement. Additionally, Texas is a useful case study because of the wealth of disaggregated student achievement data available through the state education agency.

The current accountability system in Texas began in 1994 through a testing program known as the Texas Assessment of Academic Skills (TAAS). The TAAS is currently given in reading and mathematics in grades 3 through 8 and 10, writing in grades 4, 8, and 10, and science and social studies in grade 8. Students in regular and bilingual education are included in the testing in either English or Spanish, depending on their language of instruction. As of 2000, students in special education also are included if they are working at grade level. Students in special education who are working below grade level are tested on off-level or alternative tests. In addition, recent immigrants who are not literate in English or Spanish are exempted from testing for one year.

In 1997, the state moved to raise the bar on what students know and are able to do. It adopted Texas Essential Knowledge and Skills (TEKS), which specify what the student must know and be able to do at each grade level in each core subject (Texas Education Agency [TEA], 1997). A new, more rigorous test (TAKS) will be implemented in 2003. In addition to more rigorous assessments at grades 3 through 8, the state has added assessments in grades 9 and 11 and has changed the 10th-grade assessment to reflect 10th-grade-level work. The exit-level TAKS, given at 11th grade starting in 2003, will require mastery of algebra and geometry, integrated physics and chemistry and biology, American and U.S. history, and two years of English. No student will receive a high school diploma unless he or she passes all four sections of the exit-level test.

Improvements in TAAS Performance in Texas Public Schools

Where is Texas now? School districts have made significant progress over the past decade due to the stability of the current Texas accountability system, which began in 1994. Students have made real gains on both TAAS and National Assessment of Educational Progress (NAEP) results. In fact, African American, Hispanic, and economically disadvantaged students in Texas have made the greatest gains.

In 1994, 74 percent of all students tested (including those in special education) passed the TAAS reading assessment (see table 1). Even more (85 percent) White students tested passed the assessment, yet only 58 percent of African American students and 63 percent of Hispanic students passed the reading assessment. Among students categorized by the state as economically disadvantaged, 61 percent passed the reading assessment. Among students with limited English proficiency, only 39 percent passed.

By 2000, TAAS reading assessment results had improved considerably. In that year, 87 percent of all students tested passed the reading test. Furthermore, 80 percent of all African American students and 81 percent of Hispanic students passed the assessment, compared with 94 percent of White students, 80 percent of students from low-income homes, and 60 percent of students with limited English proficiency. Performance on the writing assessment showed similar gains.

There was even more dramatic improvement in mathematics on TAAS over the same time period. In 1994, only 57 percent of all students tested passed the mathematics

Table 1. Percentages of Students Passing the Texas Assessment of Academic Skills (TAAS)-English Version

	1994	1995	1996	1997	1998	1999	2000	Gain (in points)
All students								
Reading	74	76	77	80	83	86	87	13
Writing	76	79	79	82	84	88	88	12
Math	57	63	70	76	80	85	87	30
African American								
Reading	58	61	64	70	74	78	80	22
Writing	63	68	69	72	76	81	82	19
Math	36	42	52	60	66	72	76	40
Hispanic								
Reading	63	65	67	75	80	81	87	18
Writing	67	71	71	77	83	82	88	15
Math	45	50	60	73	80	83	87	38
White								
Reading	85	86	86	89	91	93	94	9
Writing	85	87	87	89	90	93	94	9
Math	70	76	81	85	88	92	93	23
Economically Disadvantaged								
Reading	61	64	65	70	74	78	80	19
Writing	65	69	69	72	75	81	81	16
Math	43	49	58	66	71	78	81	38
Limited English								
Reading	39	42	43	49	54	59	60	21
Writing	44	48	47	51	54	60	60	16
Math	30	35	44	53	59	68	69	39

assessment, whereas 87 percent passed in 2000. The percentage of African American students passing the mathematics assessment increased from 36 percent in 1994 to 76 percent in 2000. The percentage of Hispanic students passing increased from 45 percent in 1994 to 83 percent in 2000. The percentage of students meeting low-income criteria who passed increased from 43 percent in 1994 to 81 percent in 2000. Additionally, the percentage of students with limited English proficiency who passed the mathematics section of TAAS increased from 30 percent in 1994 to 69 percent in 2000 (TEA, 1994, 2000, 2001).

For students in grades 3 through 6, schools may choose to administer a Spanish version of TAAS. To be consistent, I have reported only the TAAS English version results here. All other accountability data reported later in the chapter are offered in English only. Nevertheless, statewide results from both English and Spanish administrations of TAAS show improvements in student achievement (TEA, 1994, 2000, 2001).

Improvements in NAEP Performance in Texas Public Schools

The National Assessment of Educational Progress (NAEP), often referred to as the nation's "report card," is the only assessment that provides state-by-state comparisons in core subject areas. NAEP is administered at 4th grade and 8th grade at various points in time. Both public and private school students in grades 4 and 8 are sampled and assessed on a regular basis. The NAEP tests are developed nationally by teachers, curriculum experts, and the public. The NAEP is authorized by Congress and directed by the National Center for Education Statistics of the U.S. Department of Education.

NAEP Mathematics

In mathematics, the NAEP was administered to 4th-grade students in 1992, 1996, and 2000 and to 8th-grade students in 1990, 1992, 1996, and 2000. Each student demographic group in each state achieves a scale score that ranges from 0 to 500. Thus, one can use NAEP scale scores to compare the performance of various demographic groups both within and between states.

Based on the rankings of states' average scale scores (see table 2), Texas students have made tremendous progress in their mathematics knowledge and skills as mea-

Table 2. Texas Grade 4 and 8 NAEP Mathematics Ranking

Year	All Students/ Participating States	African American/ Participating States	Hispanic/ Participating States	White/ Participating States
1992	18/42	9/36	12/42	12/42
1996	6/44	1/37	6/44	1/44
2000	5/43	1/36	1/43	1/43
1990	22/36	16/28	10/35	12/36
1992	21/42	15/36	11/42	14/42
1996	21/44	4/37	8/44	9/44
2000	21/43	9/36	5/43	7/43

sured by NAEP. This is especially true for Texas 4th-grade students. Indeed, Texas African American, Hispanic, and White 4th graders rank 1st in the nation. In addition, Texas 4th-grade students had the greatest increase in overall mathematics scale scores, whereas African American, Hispanic, and White 4th graders had 2nd, 3rd, and 1st greatest increase in scale scores, respectively (National Center for Education Statistics, 2001a).

Texas 8th-grade mathematics achievement on the NAEP is somewhat less impressive than the 4th-grade mathematics achievement. Texas8th graders ranked 21st out of 43 participating states on NAEP mathematics achievement. However, when analyzing sub-populations, Texas African American, Hispanic, and White 8th graders rank 9th, 5th, and 7th in the nation. Texas 8th-grade students had the 2nd greatest increase in overall mathematics scale scores, whereas African American, Hispanic, and White 8th graders had the 9th, 10th, and 3rd greatest increase in scale scores respectively (National Center for Education Statistics, 2001b).

Comparing Texas with other large states is illuminating. The test-taking populations of the four most populous states (Texas, California, Florida, and New York) are quite similar. However, the test results are strikingly different (see tables 3 and 4). Texas 4th and 8th-grade students perform far better than their peers in other large, diverse states. Texas African American, Hispanic, White, and Title I students rank 1st in the nation on the NAEP 4th-grade mathematics test. Texas African American, Hispanic, White, and Title I students rank 9th, 5th, 7th, and 10th on the 8th grade mathematics test (National Center for Education Statistics, 2001a, b).

NAEP Reading

Texas reading achievement on the NAEP is less impressive than the mathematics achievement on NAEP. Texas 4th-grade students had an average scale score slightly above the national average and the 13th greatest scale score among all participating states. When the data are disaggregated, however, Texas African American, Hispanic, and White students had average scale scores that ranked 7th, 6th, and 2nd, respectively (see table 5). In addition, each of these scores was above the national average for the respective demographic group, especially for African American and Hispanic students. The NAEP reading performance of Texas 8th-grade students ranked 18th in the nation. When the data are disaggregated, however, Texas African American, Hispanic, and White students had scale scores that ranked 11th,

Table 3. Rankings of Four Largest States on 2000 NAEP Grade 4 Mathematics

Student Subgroups	Texas	California	Florida	New York	# Participant States
AA	1	36	32	12	37
H	1	39	22	30	44
W	1	41	26	8	44
TI	1	42	22	26	44

Note. AA = African American, H = Hispanic, W = White, TI = Title I Participants.

Table 4.   Rankings of Four Largest States on 2000 NAEP Grade 8 Mathematics

Student Subgroups	Texas	California	Florida	New York	# Participant States
AA	9	24	25	10	37
H	5	23	17	26	44
W	7	21	23	14	44
TI	10	22	26	29	44

Note. AA = African American, H = Hispanic, W = White, TI = Title I Participants.

2nd, and 6th, respectively (see table 5) (National Center for Education Statistics, 1999).

NAEP Science

The only administration of the NAEP science assessment was in 1996 for grade 8 students; thus, no comparable data are available to discern a trend. Unlike mathematics and reading, science achievement in Texas is only about average on the NAEP. Overall, Texas average scale scores in science were slightly below average, although there was no statistical difference between the Texas and the U.S. score. The state ranking in Texas was 26th out of 40 participating states. The disaggregated data, however, provide a slightly more positive picture for Texas students. Specifically, Texas grade 8 African American, Hispanic, and White students ranked 7th, 19th, and 10th, respectively. Texas African American scores were statistically greater than the national average, whereas the Texas scores for Hispanic and White students were not statistically different from the national average (National Center for Education Statistics, 1997).

NAEP Writing

As with science, there has only been one state-level NAEP administration at grade 8 in writing. Thus, again, it is impossible to discern a trend. Overall, Texas average scale scores in writing were 3rd in the nation and statistically greater than the national average. Again, the disaggregated data provide an even more positive picture for Texas students. Specifically, grade 8 Texas African American, Hispanic, and White students ranked 1st, 2nd, and 2nd, respectively. All of the scores were statistically greater than

Table 5.   Texas Grade 4 and 8 NAEP Reading Ranking

Year	All Students/ Participating States	African American/ Participating States	Hispanic/ Participating States	White/ Participating States
1992	21/**35**	9/**31**	11/**35**	11/**35**
1994	23/**35**	9/**30**	9/**35**	5/**35**
1998	13/**41**	7/**36**	6/**40**	2/**41**
1998	18/**41**	11/**36**	2/**40**	6/**41**

the national average. Clearly, Texas students excelled in writing compared with their peers from across the country (National Center for Education Statistics, 1999).

In sum, critics claim that accountability systems harm children of color and children from low-income homes. The data set forth above seem to refute such claims. In Texas there have been substantial increases in the percentage of students from all population groups (African American, Hispanic, White, and economically disadvantaged) who pass the statewide assessment, known as TAAS. In addition, all population groups in Texas have performed well on a national test, the NAEP. Some of the most impressive gains have occurred among African American, Hispanic, and economically disadvantaged groups. Gaps between the performances of different racial/ethnic/socioeconomic groups of students on TAAS and NAEP still remain, but the gaps have diminished over time.

Other Indicators of Improvements in Texas Student Performance

TAAS and NAEP are appropriate indicators of improvements in Texas student performance. Other indicators of academic performance include the number of Texas students taking advanced placement examinations, the number of African American and Hispanic children taking advanced placement examinations, and the performance of students on college entrance examinations such as the SAT or ACT test.

Some critics of the Texas accountability system contend that minority students are tracked in TAAS remediation classes rather than college preparatory classes. The available data on advanced-placement test taking refute this contention. The percentage of African American and Hispanic juniors and seniors taking at least one advanced-placement examination has increased dramatically from the year before the adoption of the accountability system (1992–1993) to the year 2000. The percentage of African American students in Texas taking at least one advanced-placement examination has increased 423.3 percent since the 1992–1993 year. This is more than four times the rate of increase for all other states. The percentage of Hispanic students taking at least one advanced-placement examination has increased 306.1 percent since the 1992–1993 year. This is almost twice the rate of increase for all other states (see, for example, College Board and Educational Testing Service, 1993a, 1994a, 1995a, 1996a, 1997a, 1998a, 1999a, 2000a). The data refute the assertion that high-stakes accountability in Texas has decreased the number of minority students who are accessing more rigorous courses.

Performance on the SAT and ACT are common indicators of the quality of education. Since not every high school graduate takes these college entrance examinations, comparison of schools or states based on SAT/ACT scores is difficult. However, we can analyze the trends in the number of students who take the SAT in Texas as well as the average SAT score in Texas. Most graduating seniors in Texas take the SAT rather than the ACT. According to College Board data, the number of Texas public school seniors who take the SAT increased by 30 percent from 1993 to 2000 (see, for example, College Board and Educational Testing Service, 1993b, 1993c, 1994b, 1994c, 1995b, 1995c, 1996b, 1996c, 1997b, 1997c, 1998b, 1998c, 1999b, 1999c, 2000b, 2000c). The data are presented in table 6.

Table 6.   Increase in Students Taking the SAT

| | Percentage Increase in the Number of College-Bound Seniors | | Percentage Increase in Number of Texas |
	United States, Without Texas	Texas	Texas
All Students	19	30	3
African American	15	34	2
Hispanic	23	35	4
White	7	14	2
Other	59	92	16

Over the same time period, Texas Education Agency data show the number of 12th-grade students increased by just 3 percent. Thus, a far greater percentage of Texas public school students took the SAT in 2000 than in 1993, the year before the accountability system was implemented. Furthermore, the increase in percentages of students taking the SAT from 1993 to 2000 exceeded the increase in test takers nationally for all demographic groups of students (TEA, 2001).

CONCLUSION

The new framework for leadership that I have described here provides a powerful and useful model for achieving school success. The framework is indeed compelling. Essentially it serves to lend coherence to an otherwise loosely coupled system incapable of articulating effectively across levels of organization. Sustained districtwide school improvement is not possible without a strong connection across levels of organization and a recoupling of the system. Internal school development is necessary, but school improvement cannot occur unless each school is supported by a strong external infrastructure, stable political environments, and resources outside the school, including leadership from the superintendent and school board as well as leadership from the state.

What occurs as the three levels of organization coalesce is a fusion of three powerful forces—the technical core, the managerial core, and the institutional core. The purposeful interactions that happen within and across these levels of organization serve to mobilize commitments and energies to pursue school improvement efforts on a scale never before witnessed. Such mobilization is powerful, so as to increase capacity to overcome obstacles that are bound to surface in a school district attempting to "do the right things"—to educate *all* children and to persist in this mission. The Texas accountability system was used as a model for sustained districtwide academic success of *all* students. The most impressive gains in student achievement were made by children of color and children from low-income homes on both state and national tests.

REFERENCES

Adams, J. E., & Kirst, M. V. (1999). New demands and concepts for educational accountability: Striving for results in an era of excellence. In J. Murphy & K. S. Louis (Eds.), *Handbook of research on educational administration* (2nd ed., pp. 463–489). San Francisco: Jossey-Bass.

Ad Hoc Committee on MCAS. (1998). *Educators criticize new Massachusetts comprehensive assessment system (MCAS) exams.* FairTest. Retrieved from www.fairtest.org/pr/mcaspr.htm

Anderson, G. L. (2001). Promoting educational equity in a period of growing social inequities: The silent contradictions of Texas reform discourse. *Education and Urban Society, 33*(3), 320–332.

Argyris, C. (1990). *Overcoming organizational defenses.* Boston: Allyn and Bacon.

Cohen, D. K., & Spillane, J. P. (1992). Policy and practice: The relations between governance and instruction. In G. Grant (Ed.), *Review of research in education* (vol. 18, pp. 3–49). Washington, DC: American Educational Research Association.

College Board and Educational Testing Service. (1993a). *1993 AP Texas and national summary reports.* New York: Author.

College Board and Educational Testing Service. (1993b). *1993 college-bound seniors: National report.* New York: Author.

College Board and Educational Testing Service. (1993c). *1993 college-bound seniors: Texas report.* New York: Author.

College Board and Educational Testing Service. (1994a). *1994 AP Texas and national summary report.* New York: Author.

College Board and Educational Testing Service. (1994b). *1994 college-bound seniors: National report.* New York: Author.

College Board and Educational Testing Service. (1994c). *1994 college-bound seniors: Texas report.* New York: Author.

College Board and Educational Testing Service. (1995a). *1995 AP Texas and national summary reports.* New York: Author.

College Board and Educational Testing Service. (1995b). *1995 college-bound seniors: National report* New York: Author.

College Board and Educational Testing Service. (1995c). *1995 college-bound seniors: Texas report.* New York: Author.

College Board and Educational Testing Service. (1996a). *1996 AP Texas and national summary.* New York: Author.

College Board and Educational Testing Service. (1996b). *1996 college-bound seniors: National report.* New York: Author.

College Board and Educational Testing Service. (1996c). *1996 college bound seniors: Texas report.* New York: Author.

College Board and Educational Testing Service. (1997a). *1997AP Texas and national summary reports.* New York: Author.

College Board and Educational Testing Service. (1997b). *1997 college-bound seniors: National report.* New York: Author.

College Board and Educational Testing Service. (1997c). *1997 college-bound seniors: Texas report.* New York: Author.

College Board and Educational Testing Service. (1998a). *1998 AP Texas and national summary reports.* New York: Author.

College Board and Educational Testing Service. (1998b). *1998 college-bound seniors: National report.* New York: Author.

College Board and Educational Testing Service. (1998c). *1998 college-bound seniors: Texas report.* New York: Author.

College Board and Educational Testing Service. (1999a). *1999 AP Texas and national summary reports.* New York: Author.

College Board and Educational Testing Service. (1999b). *1999 college-bound seniors: National report.* New York: Author.

College Board and Educational Testing Service. (1999c). *1999 college-bound seniors: Texas report.* New York: Author.

College Board and Educational Testing Service. (2000a). *2000 AP Texas and national summary reports.* New York: Author.

College Board and Educational Testing Service. (2000b). *2000 college bound seniors: National report.* New York: Author.

College Board and Educational Testing Service. (2000c). *2000 college-bound seniors: Texas report.* New York: Author.

Conley, D., Dunlap, D., & Goldman, P. (1992). The "vision thing" and school restructuring. *OSSC Report, 32*(2), 1–8.

Cuban, L. (1988). A fundamental puzzle of school reform. *Phi Delta Kappan, 70*(5), 341–344.

Cuban, L. (1992). Managing dilemmas while building professional communities. *Educational Researcher, 21*(4), 4–11.

Elmore, R. F. (1995). Structural reform and educational practice. *Educational Researcher, 24*(9), 23–26.

Elmore, R. F. (1997). Accountability in local school districts: Learning to do the right things. In P. W. Thurston & J. G. Ward (Eds.), *Improving educational performance: Local and systemic reforms* (pp. 59–82). Greenwich, CT: JAI Press.

Elmore, R. F. (2000). Building a new structure for school leadership. *American Educator, 23*(4), 6–13.

Elmore, R. F. (2001). *Building a new structure for leadership.* New York: The Albert Shanker Institute.

Elmore, R. F., Ablmann, C. H., & Fuhrman, S. H. (1996). The new accountability in state education reform: From process to performance. In H. F. Ladd (Ed.), *Holding schools accountable: Performance-based reform in education* (pp. 65–98). Washington, DC: The Brookings Institution.

Elmore, R. F., & Burney, D. (1999). Investing in teacher learning. In L. Darling-Hammond & G. Sykes (Eds.), *Teaching as the learning profession: Handbook of policy and practice* (pp. 263–291). San Francisco: Jossey-Bass.

Elmore, R. F., Peterson, P. L., & McCarthey, S. J. (1996). *Restructuring in the classroom: Teaching, learning and school organization.* San Francisco: Jossey-Bass.

English, F., & Steffy, B. (2001). *Deep curriculum alignment.* Alexandria, VA: Association for Supervision and Curriculum Development.

Fullan, M. (1997). Emotion and hope: Constructive concepts for complex times. In A. Hargreaves (Ed.), *Rethinking educational change with heart and mind: The 1997 ASCD Yearbook* (pp. 216–233). Alexandria, VA: Association for Supervision and Curriculum Development.

Fullan, M. (1999). *Change forces: The sequel.* London: Falmer Press.

Fullan, M. (2000a). The return of large scale reform. *Journal of Educational Change, 1*, 1–23.

Fullan, M. (2000b). The three stories of education reform. *Phi Delta Kappan, 81*(8), 581–584.

Fuller, E. J., & Johnson, F. (2001). Can state accountability systems drive improvements in school performance for children of color and children from low income homes? *Education and Urban Society, 33*(3), 260–283.

Gandal, M., & Vranek, J. (2001). Standards: Here today, here tomorrow. *Educational Leadership, 59*(1), 7–13.

Gordon, B. M. (2000, Autumn). On high stakes testing. *Division Generator*, 1–4.

Grissmer, D., & Flanagan, A. (1998). *Exploring rapid achievement gains in North Carolina and Texas.* Washington, DC: National Education Goals Panel.

Grissmer, D., Flanagan, A., Kawata, J., & Williamson, S. (2000). *Improving student achievement: What state NAEP tests tell us.* Santa Monica, CA: RAND.

Hall, G. E., & Hord, S. M. (2001). *Implementing change: Patterns, principles, potholes.* Boston: Allyn and Bacon.

Haney, W. (2000). The myth of the Texas miracle in education. *Education Policy Analysis Archives, 8*(41) [Online]. Retrieved from http://epaa.asu.edu/epaa/v8n41/

Hargreaves, A., Earl, L., & Ryan, J. (1996). *Schooling for change: Reinventing education for early adolescents.* Philadelphia: Falmer Press.

Hopkins, D. (1993). *A teacher's guide to classroom research* (2nd ed.). Philadelphia: Open University Press.

Huberman, M. (1993). Linking the practitioner and researcher communities for school improvement. *School Effectiveness and School Improvement, 4*(1), 1–16.

Johnson, J., Treisman, U., & Fuller, E. J. (2000). Testing in Texas. *The School Administrator, 57*(11), 20–27.

Joyce, B., & Showers, B. (1995). *Student achievement through staff development.* New York: Longman.

Klein, S. P., Hamilton, L. S., McCaffrey, D. F., & Stecher, B. M. (2000). *What do test scores in Texas tell us?* (Issue Paper No. 202). Santa Monica, CA: RAND.

Koschoreck, J. W. (2001). Accountability and educational equity in the transformation of an urban district. *Education and Urban Society, 33*(3), 284–304.

Leithwood, K. (1994). Leadership for school restructuring. *Educational Administration Quarterly, 30*(4), 498–518.

Leithwood, K., & Atkins, K. A. (1995). *Making schools smarter: A system for monitoring school and district progress.* Thousand Oaks, CA: Corwin Press.

Leithwood, K., & Jantzi, D. (1997). Explaining variation in teachers' perceptions of principal's leadership: A replication. *Journal of Education Administration, 35*(3–4), 213–231.

Leithwood, K., & Louis, K. S. (2000). *The learning school and school improvement: Linkages and strategies.* Lisse, The Netherlands: Swets and Zeitlinger.

Louis, K. S., & Kruse, S. (2000). Creating community in reform: Images of organizational learning in urban schools. In K. Leithwood & K. S. Louis (Eds.), *Organizational learning and strategies.* Lisse, The Netherlands: Swets and Zeitlinger.

Louis, K. S., & Miles, M. B. (1990). *Improving the urban high school: What works and why.* New York: Teachers College Press.

Louis, K. S., Toole, J., & Hargreaves, A. (1999). Rethinking school improvement. In J. Murphy & K. S. Louis (Eds.), *Handbook of research on educational administration* (2nd ed., pp. 251–276). San Francisco: Jossey-Bass.

Lunenburg, F. C. (1995). *The principalship: Concepts and applications.* Englewood Cliffs, NJ: Prentice Hall.

Lunenburg, F. C., & Irby, B. J. (1999). *High expectations: An action plan for implementing Goals 2000.* Thousand Oaks, CA: Corwin Press.

Lunenburg, F. C., & Ornstein, A. O. (2000). *Educational administration: Concepts and practices.* Belmont, CA: Wadsworth/Thomson Learning.

Marzano, R. J., Pickering, D. J., & Pollock, J. E. (2001). *Classroom instruction that works.* Alexandria, VA: Association for Supervision and Curriculum Development.

McLaughlin, M. W. (1990, December). The RAND change agent study revisited: Macro perceptions and micro realities. *Educational Research, 11–16.*

McNeil, L. M. (2000). *Contradictions of school reform: Educational costs of standardized testing.* New York: Routledge.

Meyer, J. W., & Rowan, B. (1977). Institutionalized organizations: Formal structure as myth and ceremony. *American Journal of Sociology, 83,* 340–363.

Meyer, J. W., & Rowan, B. (Eds.). (1992). *The structure of educational organizations, organizational environments: Rituals and rationality.* Newbury Park, CA: Sage.

Murphy, J. (1991). *Restructuring schools.* New York: Teachers College Press.

National Center for Education Statistics. (1997). National Assessment of Educational Progress state performance report [Online]. Retrieved from http://nces.ed.gov.nationsreportcard/site/home.asp

National Center for Education Statistics. (1999). National Assessment of Educational Progress state performance report [Online]. Retrieved from http://nces.ed.gov.nationsreportcard/site/home.asp

National Center for Education Statistics. (2001a). National Assessment of Educational Progress state performance report [Online]. Retrieved from http://nces.ed.gov.nationsreportcard/site/home.asp

National Center for Education Statistics. (2001b). National Assessment of Educational Progress state performance report [Online]. Retrieved from http://nces.ed.gov.nationsreportcard/site/home.asp

Newmann, F., & Wehlage, G. (1995). *Successful school restructuring*. Madison, WI: Center on Organization and Restructuring of Schools.

North Carolina Department of Public Instruction. (2000). Improving student performance: The role of district level staff. *Evaluation Brief, 2*(4) [Online]. Retrieved from www.dpi.state.nc.us/accountability/evaluation/evalbriefs/vol2n4–role.pdf

Ogawa, R. T., Crowson, R. L., & Goldring, E. B. (1999). Enduring dilemmas of school organization. In J. Murphy & K. S. Louis (Eds.), *Handbook of research on educational administration* (2nd ed., pp. 277–295). San Francisco: Jossey-Bass.

Orfield, G., & Wald, J. (2000, June 5). Testing, testing. *The Nation* [Online]. Retrieved from www.thenation.com/issue/000605/0605orfield.shtml

Panta, S. J. (2001, March 11). KHSD chief blasts exit test. *Californian, 1–2.*

Parker, L. (2001). Statewide assessment triggers urban school reform: But how high the stakes for urban minorities. *Education and Urban Society, 33*(3), 313–319.

Parsons, T. (1960). *Structure and process in modern societies*. Glencoe, IL: Free Press.

Ragland, M. A., Asera, R., & Johnson, R. F., Jr. (1999). Urgency, responsibility, efficacy: Preliminary findings of a study of high-performing Texas school districts. Austin, TX: Charles A. Dana Center.

Reyes, P., Scribner, J. D., & Paredes Scribner, A. (1999). *Lessons from high performing Hispanic schools: Creating learning communities*. New York: Teacher College Press.

Rosenholtz, S. J. (1989). *Teachers' workplace: The social organization of schools*. New York: Longman.

Rowan, B. (1990). *Commitment and control: Alternative strategies for the organizational design of schools*. Newbury Park, CA: Sage.

Rowan, B., & Miskel, C. G. (1999). Institutional theory and the study of educational organizations. In J. Murphy & K. S. Louis (Eds.), *Handbook of research on educational administration* (2nd ed., pp. 359–383). San Francisco: Jossey-Bass.

Scheurich, J. J. (1998). Highly successful and loving, public elementary schools populated mainly by low-SES children: Core beliefs and cultural characteristics. *Urban Education, 33*(4), 451–491.

Scheurich, J. J., Skrla, L., & Johnson, J. F. (2000). Thinking carefully about equity and accountability. *Phi Delta Kappan, 82*(4), 293–299.

Schon, D. (1984). *The reflective practitioner: How professionals think in action*. New York: Basic Books.

Sclafani, S. (2001). Using an aligned system to make real progress for Texas students. *Education and Urban Society, 33*(3), 305–312.

Sebring, P. B., & Bryk, A. S. (2000). School leadership and the bottom line in Chicago. *Phi Delta Kappan, 81*(6), 440–443.

Senge, P. (1990). *The fifth discipline*. New York: Currency Doubleday.

Skrla, L., & Scheurich, J. J. (2001). Displacing deficit thinking in school district leadership. *Education and Urban Society, 33*(3), 235–259.

Skrla, L., Scheurich, J. J., & Johnson, J. F. (2000). *Equity-driven achievement-focused school districts*. Austin, TX: Charles A. Dana Center.

Skrla, L., Scheurich, J. J., & Johnson, J. F. (2001). Toward a new consensus on high academic achievement for all children. *Education and Urban Society, 33*(3), 227–234.

Skrla, L., Scheurich, J. J., Johnson, J. F., & Koschoreck, J. W. (in press). Accountability for equity: Can state policy leverage social justice? *International Journal of Leadership in Education.*

Smith, M. L. (1991). Put to the test: The effects of external testing on teachers. *Educational Researcher, 20* (5), 8–11.

Smith, M. L., & Rottenberg, C. (1991). Unintended consequences of external testing in elementary schools. *Educational Measurement: Issues and Practice, 10*(4), 7–11.

Spillane, J. (1998). State policy and the non-monolithic nature of the local school district: Organizational and professional considerations. *American Education Research Journal, 35*(1), 33–63.

Texas Education Agency. (1994). *Academic Excellence Indicator System 1994 state performance report* [Online]. Retrieved from www.tea.state.tx.us/perfreport/aeis/94/state.html

Texas Education Agency. (1996). *The development of accountability systems nationwide and in Texas* (Statewide Texas Educational Progress Study Report No. 1). Austin, TX: Author.

Texas Education Agency. (1997). *The development of the Texas Essential Knowledge and Skills [TEKS]* (Statewide Texas Educational Progress Study Report No. 2). Austin, TX: Author.

Texas Education Agency. (2000). *Academic Excellence Indicator System 2000 state performance report* [Online]. Retrieved from www.tea.state.tx.us/perfreport/aeis/99/state.html

Texas Education Agency. (2001). *Snapshot: 1994–2000 school district profiles* [Online]. Retrieved from www.tea.state.tx.us/perfreport/snapshot/99/index.html

Tyack, D., & Cuban, L. (1995). *Tinkering toward utopia: A century of public school reform.* Cambridge, MA: Harvard University Press.

Tye, B. B. (1987). The deep structure of schooling. *Phi Delta Kappan, 69*(4), 281–284.

Weick, K. E. (1976). Educational organizations as loosely coupled systems. *Administrative Science Quarterly, 21*, 1–19.

Yeh, S. S. (2001). Tests worth teaching to: Constructing state-mandated tests that emphasize critical thinking. *Educational Researcher, 30*(9), 12–17.

Standardized Testing and Educational Standards: Implications for the Future of Emancipatory Leadership in U.S. Schools

James M. Smith and Connie Ruhl-Smith

There can be little doubt that educational standards and standardized testing are two of the most prominent themes that pervade current educational journals, as well as related mainstream magazines and newspapers. Seldom does a day pass without some attention given to one of these topics. Although much attention is offered to these issues, it seems obvious to us that this coverage is often woefully inadequate in terms of both breadth and depth. Given all that is published with respect to standards and standardized testing, there is seldom an intellectual discussion of the differences between these two topics; concomitantly, even less frequently can a factually based discussion of issues surrounding accountability and student learning be uncovered. In this chapter we propose to carefully examine the four aforementioned issues, utilizing both the context of P–12 schools and higher education.

Critical theorists and Marxist scholars have long questioned the disparity of educational options in the United States. Cries for emancipatory pedagogy and the evaluation of socially conditioned practices that hinder the free development of individuals have garnered, in limited circles with small audiences, tremendous discussion. However, the basic acceptance of the cries of these theorists and scholars has gained little attention in the educational mainstream. Words like those of Charles Reitz (2000), although tremendously powerful, have not been widely disseminated:

> Through collective emancipatory struggle we equip ourselves with a comparative and critical view of the multidimensional experience of being human and being oppressed. We learn outside as well as inside of these institutions of domination, often in spite of them. But we must come to understand the history of competing warrants for knowledge claims, moral judgments, and political goals. In dialectically theorizing the supersedure

James M. Smith, Bowling Green State University, Firestone
Connie Ruhl-Smith, Bowling Green State University

of our alienated lives and labor, we find the central criteria that are indispensable if social and educational theory are to be emancipatory. (p. 262)

Reitz is not, by most accounts, a mainstream scholar. His study of the works of
Herbert Marcuse would often be categorized as obscure. Likewise, in many political
circles, his research would be labeled as insignificant. However, to reinforce his
words, it is rather simple to draw upon the thoughts of John Dewey, a far more accepted (i.e., mainstream) educational scholar. Dewey, in an essay dedicated to the
generalized problems with public acceptance of life in a laissez-faire society, discusses the basic reactions of middle- and upper-class citizens to the existence of
slums in the United States. As Dewey states:

> We are mostly satisfied with . . . ugly slums, and oftentimes with equally ugly places.
> We do not "naturally" or organically need them, but we want them. If we do not demand
> them directly we demand them none the less, effectively. For they are necessary conse-
> quences of the things upon which we have set our hearts. In other words, a community
> wants . . . either education or ignorance, lovely or squalid surroundings, railway trains
> or oxcarts, stocks and bonds, pecuniary profit or constructive arts. (1984, p. 301)

So, precisely what does the struggle for emancipatory education and the acceptance of ghetto dwellings in the United States have to do with standards, standardized testing, accountability, and student learning? It seems to us that issues of eman-
cipation and the consideration of the dominant view of success in U.S. society have
everything to do with these topics. Reitz and Dewey call upon us to look more
broadly at what we teach and who we are. These authors seem to urge all educators,
P–12 and beyond, to reconsider what we do in the name of education/schooling in
hopes that this type of introspection will create reforms that bring about changes that
empower all students, not just those of privilege. Quite possibly, Oakes, Quartz,
Ryan, and Lipton (2000) have stated this best:

> The dominant order of concern about schooling has been that if my own child does well,
> the community will do well (not . . . my own child will only do well in a strong com-
> munity). The century's end has brought the ascendance of policy makers and social the-
> orists who argue that only a reemergence of individual morality, accountability, and vol-
> unteerism can mitigate the hard edges of self-interest. How far this is from collective
> work to create educative, socially just, caring, and participatory schools to raise all of
> the community's children! . . . We think it will take something else to fan the flames of
> the nation's civic soul. (p. 325)

STANDARDIZED TESTING

At the center of most discussions concerning standards and standardization is the
importance given to standardized testing. Legislators, local politicians, and myriad members of the educational community argue that an increased focus on academic measurement will produce positive results with respect to student achievement. Educational consultants, like Schmoker (1999), argue that standardized
testing can be properly aligned with instructional actions and student practice, thus

producing increased levels of student performance. Schmoker contends that such efforts are a "promising development" in education (1999, p. 74). This point of view is clearly becoming the dominant one in the United States. Books, articles, and monographs on instructional alignment, teaching to the test, and aligning instructional activities with test bank questions pervade the educational landscape. Some authors even contend that the alignment of teaching and testing will, once and forever, end the belief that race, poverty, and other social issues hamper overall opportunities for educational success (Gorman, 1999).

As many politicians and educational consultants move forward with their support of the teaching and testing alignment movement, others forcefully question the efficacy of such actions (Jones, 2001; Kohn, 2000, McNeil & Valenzuela, 2000; Nevi, 2001; Popham, 2001, Smith & Ruhl-Smith, 2000). A 1998 study indicated that students in states with mandatory high school graduation tests performed less effectively on a neutral measure of academic performance than did students from states with lower-stakes assessment systems (Neill & Schaeffer, 1998). Furthermore, these same examinations are under fire for their inability to produce the results that the test construction experts claim to be the only purpose for said test. In the case of the SAT, the College Board claims that this test is designed solely to predict students' first year college grades. However, men continue to outscore women on the SAT, while women continue to outpace men on grade reports during the entirety of their college experience (National Center for Fair and Open Testing, 2000a). With nearly 1.75 million young people taking the SAT each year, is it a concern to the U.S. public that this test does not produce the results that are claimed by the test construction experts? Obviously, the answer is a resounding "no." Just a short time ago, the Hudson Institute commissioned a report entitled, *On Shaky Ground*. This report is basically a diatribe against all that is done in public P–12 educational institutions in Indiana (Bracey, 2000). The report, authored by Garber, Heet, and Styring (2000), repeatedly provides reference to the importance of using the SAT to make comparisons between students in Indiana and their counterparts throughout the country. In one instance, the report includes a graphic of SAT scores reported by average family income; the authors then chose to make the following assertion based on the graphic provided: "Indiana's public education system fails students everywhere, whether their trip to school winds through the newest suburbs in an SUV or through cornfields in a pick-up truck or through urban streets on public buses" (Garber, Heet, & Styring, 2000, p. 21).

Obviously, the fact that the SAT does not offer the predictive validity that the test construction specialists maintain it should is of little or no consequence to the authors of the report. Furthermore, the fact that the test is designed solely to predict first year college success seems to be unobserved by the Hudson Institute authors. Possibly the real concern for those involved with the creation and distribution of *On Shaky Ground* was the fact that the following phenomena, as reported by Berliner and Biddle (1995), were not observed:

> at present the average SAT score earned by students goes down by fifteen points for each decrease of $10,000 in family income. This means, of course, that whenever colleges

use the SAT for making admissions decisions, they are also discriminating against students from poorer homes. And it means that aggregate SAT scores will also fall when more students from poorer families choose to take the test. (p. 19)

How is it that such a large percentage of the U.S. public seems to endorse the use of standardized testing even though these tests do not offer the intended results? First, one must take into account the immediate access to the media held by those voices speaking in favor of standardized tests (e.g., politicians, state superintendents, and corporate leaders). Second, it must be noted that the powerful presentation of ideas by pedagogical conservatives like E. D. Hirsch Jr. and Diane Ravitch has allowed the political right to link U.S. culture with phrases such as efficient, effective, and necessary school reform. Third, a considerable number of neoliberal educators have accepted such testing practices as a means of assuring equal opportunity, diversity, and progressive modes of curricular and instructional practice. Furthermore, neoliberals have, in many cases, accepted this standardization process as a means of precluding noneducators from taking total control of U.S. schools (Vinson, Gibson, & Ross, 2000).

This odd mix of neoliberal, conservative, and mainstream political power bases has allowed a few major corporations to flourish because the U.S. public has been led to believe that testing is, indeed, an efficient and effective way of assessing what is truly occurring in modern U.S. schools. We believe it is of the utmost importance to display for the reader the tremendous financial results that this skewed collective perception has provided for certain corporate entities. According to Sacks (1997), Harcourt General Incorporated is now a $3 billion dollar per year company; the Houghton Mifflin Company recently recorded $529 million dollars in sales of testing materials; the Educational Testing Service, from 1980 to 1996, grew in overall sales by 256 percent, recording a current sales volume of $380.6 million (triple that of the 85 percent rise in consumer prices over the same period). Without question, testing in the United States is a huge business. Upon the backs of children and adolescents, corporate executives, members of their boards, and the respective corporate shareholders to whom they report, have made huge profits. Schools and school districts have invested heavily in this standardized testing phenomenon. However, the simple question of testing to what end seems to be so frequently overlooked. As Glasser powerfully notes in a section of his landmark work, *The Quality School* (1990), teachers can and do facilely articulate the dissatisfying paradox that this national obsession with standardized testing reifies for them on a daily basis. The following words of a classroom teacher epitomize the thoughts of hundreds of thousands of educators across the country:

> If I teach conceptually and challenge them to think and defend their ideas, which is the way I know is right, my students have a chance to succeed in learning something worthwhile, but they may not do well on the tests that measure fragments and I will be labeled a troublemaker and a failure. On the other hand, if I teach the way I am told, my students will fail to learn anything that I, and most of them, believe is worthwhile, but I will be praised as a successful team player and they will be blamed as incompetent. (Glasser, 1990, p. 23)

Why do the thoughts of teachers, like those expressed above, so often fail to be reported by the mainstream media or discussed in statehouses from Maine to Hawaii? Is it because, as Audrey Thompson (1996) believes, political pragmatism is such an interwoven aspect of our culture that politicians are incapable of examining the educational system in new and different ways? Has this type of political pragmatism become so ingrained in our everyday lives that we can accept only solutions that appear to revert back to the status quo? Do we simply accept race, gender, and socioeconomic power indicators as "the way things must be" and, thus, continue to search for sorting mechanisms that reify the hegemonic needs of our preconceived notions? We are troubled by these questions because it seems virtually impossible to reject the darkness that surrounds the many answers that these questions evoke. Possibly, the words of the late Paulo Freire can best be used to objurgate those who simply fail to recognize the nonproductive and counterproductive outcomes of this national obsession with standardized testing. As Freire (1970) has defined the banking concept of education, we would urge the reader to extend this concept to the banking notion of testing:

> [schooling] turns students into "containers," into "receptacles" to be "filled" by the teacher . . . The more completely [the teacher] fills the receptacles, the better a teacher she is. The more meekly the receptacles permit themselves to be filled the better students they are . . . Education becomes an act of depositing, in which the students are the depositories and the teacher is the depositor . . . the scope of action allowed to the students extends only as far as receiving, filing, and storing deposits. (p. 53)

To overcome this banking notion of testing, education professionals must work to create environments that promote thoughtfulness, critical inquiry, and discussions of the establishment of agencies that actually create spheres of civic virtue (Oakes, Quartz, Ryan, & Lipton, 2000). In so doing, though, teachers will no longer be forced, permitted, or even encouraged to conduct Advanced Placement classes as semester-long test-preparation exercises that leave little time for class discussion or review of experiences that promote and engender student interest or thought (Berliner & Biddle, 1995). Educators will be encouraged to begin creating classroom environments that are enveloped with the notion of emancipatory pedagogy—moving teaching beyond the basic skills and engaging students in critical reflection about realities that constantly surround them (King, 1993). The struggle for civic virtue, the engagement in broad-based intellectual thought, and the creation of environments that live an emancipatory message are some of the essentials that will allow education to be both real and meaningful to the 21st-century student. However, these are clearly educational constructs that will never appear as part of a multiple-choice format. Therefore, the authors of this work must ask—is there support for real educational reform or are we forever mired in the Frederick Winslow Taylor notion of schools as places of standardized effectiveness, efficiency, and order?

ACCOUNTABILITY AND STUDENT PERFORMANCE

As has been discussed in previous sections of this chapter, much confusion seems to exist with respect to the topics of standardized testing, professional accountability, and student performance. Given the apparent seamlessness that the media utilize to portray a direct correlation between standardized test scores and teacher accountability, there can be little wonder why considerable confusion exists both within and outside the educational community. Authors such as Wiggins (1994) exacerbate this problem when they posit notions such as the following: "It is not [standardized] tests per se but the failure of classroom teachers . . . to be results focused and data driven" (pp. 17–18). Again, this type of statement would lead the average reader to believe that results-focused and data-driven educators must utilize standardized tests in order to be successful in their quest for overall increases in student performance. However, authors like Wiggins certainly must have failed to read and understand the words of Cornell West (1993) and the earlier words of Carter Godwin Woodson (1933) that urge educators to consider the relevance of Eurocentric schooling in relation to the Black experience in the United States. If standardized tests measure only isolated elements of the Eurocentric curriculum, and if Eurocentric schooling is at best irrelevant to Blacks and at worst a lie and a cheat to their children, why would professional educators want to rely on such tests to make data-driven decisions? As a colleague once said at a gathering of test and measurements experts:

> If you measure dog dung deposited on my front lawn and, in turn, develop the most sophisticated measurement techniques in order to report the mass and density of said deposits, please do not forget that you have continued only to measure dog dung. (B. A. Lotven, personal communication, 1990)

As the National Center for Fair and Open Testing states, "No test is good enough to serve as the . . . primary basis for important educational decisions" (2000b).

Although no test is powerful enough to serve as the primary basis for educational advancement considerations, it appears that many are indeed extremely powerful disincentives for student retention. A feature article in the *Columbus Dispatch* portrayed students who had, of late, decided to discontinue high school attendance as uninterested, bored, and of the general belief that they were not "learning anything [new and] different" (Glenn, 2001, A1). A counseling supervisor, employed by Columbus (Ohio) City Schools, further cited the district's problems with holding power (i.e., the 9th worst ranking for retention of all urban schools in the U.S.) as being directly related to students "failing the state's required graduation proficiency test" (Glenn, 2001, A2).

The question of accountability with respect to racial fairness and relevance is only one segment of the debate that is seldom unearthed by the mainstream media. Another significant element of this debate can be found in the area of curricular narrowness. In response to worries of educators from rural communities to urban cities, teachers have been urged to adjust their instructional focus to test items and the concomitant test formats that will be thrust upon their students. As was reported by the classroom teacher (cited earlier in this work), who described the situation as a dissatisfying paradox and was uncomfortable with the belief that teaching and testing alignment would result in anything but increased student scores, many other educators have simply acquiesced in order to be seen as good modern educators and fine team players. Possibly, these team players do not understand nor have they internalized the thought-provoking words of William Ayers in the first edition of his text, *To Teach: The Journey of a Teacher*:

> Standardized tests can't measure initiative, creativity, imagination, conceptual thinking, curiosity, effort, irony, judgement, commitment, nuance, good will, ethical reflection, or a host of other valuable dispositions and attributes. What they can measure and count are isolated skills, specific facts and functions, the least interesting and least significant aspects of learning. (1993, p. 59)

Furthermore, the results of these team players' actions, often powerfully presented under the guise of accountability, can clearly bring about tragic consequences in the classroom. Testing specialist George Madaus describes the results of these behaviors in the following manner:

> When you have high-stakes tests, the tests eventually become the curriculum. It happened with the Regents exams in New York. Items that are not emphasized in the test are not emphasized in school. That's a fundamental lesson that cuts across countries and across time. Teaching has not changed that much; it's an art form. Given basically the same set of circumstances, teachers will behave in much the same way . . . But if you go to Europe, to the British Isles, or to Australia and look at comparable literature, [concerns about] the external achievement exams . . . appear often . . . they write about cramming, about how they prepared for the exams. They write about how, after taking the exams, they purged their minds of the answers that they had learned. (1989, p. 644)

Berliner and Biddle (1995) question the belief that most citizens of the United States are interested in accepting and promoting an education system that results in instruction directed specifically toward "learning that is narrow, test-specific, standardized, superficial, and easily forgotten" (p. 197). This doubt for prevailing support of such testing has been cited, although not widely quoted, in works like *Choosing Excellence* (Merrow, 2001). Here popular journalist John Merrow documents, through results of a national survey, that 68 percent of all respondents and 71 percent of public school parents opted for "classroom work and homework" rather than standardized "test scores" (p. 44) as evidence for overall learning. Given these data, why, then, would politicians so anxiously accept standardized tests as the panacea for educational ills and the cornerstone for accountability? Could it be that we are again seeing members of the dominant society and the educational elite vigorously striving to maintain their positions of power and prestige? As Patricia Kusimo (1999) notes in her essay, "Rural African Americans and Education: The Legacy of the Brown Decision," it seems more than coincidental that in the 623 counties in 11 Old South states (Alabama, Arkansas, Florida, Georgia, Louisiana, Mississippi, North Carolina, South Carolina, Tennessee, Texas, and Virginia), where some of the highest percentages of African Americans reside, more than half (54 percent) of all Black adults, age 25 or older, do not possess a high school diploma. Further evidence of this nature is offered by Hill, Campbell, and Harvey (2000):

In the largest cities over 30 percent of all children live in poverty, compared to less than 20 percent elsewhere. Teacher salaries are seldom as high as in wealthier suburbs, so city schools often lose their best teachers. As a result, schools in the lowest-income neighborhoods are often staffed by shifting casts of new and provisionally certified teachers. City children are more likely than children elsewhere to have teachers who lack field-specific training, and the discrepancies are greatest in the most challenging fields, mathematics and science. (pp. 10–11)

Like the conservative and neoliberal politicians, Darling-Hammond and Goodwin (1993) obviously are willing to accept the narrowness and inappropriate nature of standardized tests in order to bring teachers together as a profession. In a 1993 publication, these authors portray the belief that teachers will never gain a true professional status in U.S. society if they do not accept some form of "accountability, including the relationship that exists between practitioners and their clients and between practitioners and the society at large" (p. 22). Darling-Hammond, in an earlier work, notes that educational leaders often move forward with standards' attainment by "supplying concrete goals and using both carrots and sticks to move educators to pursue them" (1990, p. 287). It seems that these leaders have not only failed to intellectually assimilate much of the research presented throughout this work, they have also failed to internalize research on organizational change and school reform. Suggestions that accountability can be thrust upon teachers by use of carrots and sticks fit perfectly into the organizational change strategies that Robert Owens (1998) describes as power-coercive strategies. The words of Owens, regarding this type of change strategy, should prove to be particularly instructive to all of us:

based on the use . . . of sanctions to compel the organization to change. For example, a state education department might require each school district to draw up and implement a program of competency-based instruction in accordance with specific guidelines. This could be accompanied by specific required timetables, forms of reporting, and other techniques for monitoring compliance. Problems often encountered with this strategy include the problem that public school systems . . . are—at best—composed of relatively loosely coupled components, through which it is difficult to transmit precise orders and from which it is difficult to extract compliance. As I have described, satisficing is commonplace in organizational decision making: that is, adopting workable responses to demands (sufficient to avoid sanctions) but not seeking maximally effective responses when faced with an array of conflicting demands. (p. 329)

What must educators do, then, to be accountable, but likewise professionally responsive, in their quest for accountability? Many outstanding educators would argue that they are accountable each and every day they walk into the classroom. These individuals are accountable to their students. They are accountable to their principals. They are accountable to their professional colleagues. They are accountable to curriculum directors who, in collaboration with other teaching professionals, create the curriculum guides that are the essence of their daily instructional activities. These men and women passionately teach the curriculum assigned to them. They test in accordance with that curriculum. They design units that expand the basic curriculum and create opportunities for in-depth discussions and far-reaching experimentation. They design both simple and complex measures of student success. They report these successes (and the corresponding failures) to their students and to parents and guardians of these students. These men and women have the ability to design, on a localized basis, extremely robust measures of student success. As Berliner and Biddle (1995) note:

> Given commitment, leadership, and support, many teachers are quite capable of designing creative, authentic assessment programs; and when such programs are explained to parents, many parents will choose them over standardized multiple-choice tests. Traditional, standardized tests are clearly hampering efforts to improve the schools. If we are to hasten change we must develop and experiment with more performance tests. Performance and portfolio assessment are not yet in widespread use, largely because they are so different from past visions of what assessment ought to be. But they are surely an important part of the school-improvement effort. As our vision of curricular aims are expanded to promote greater thoughtfulness, self-awareness, and competence in students, we will also need a lot more testing procedures that are authentic, performance oriented, and locally evaluated. (p. 320)

The next phase of this discussion will revolve around the following basic but important question: How will efforts of this nature be funded? The simple answer to this query rests with a rather elementary accounting analysis of the dollars spent on statewide and national test endeavors. If the Educational Testing Service was documented as producing a sales volume of $380.6 million in 1996, greater sales magnitudes certainly exist today; informal conversations have indicated that the new sales volume for this one testing construction organization easily exceeds $500 million (L. McNeal, personal conversation, 2001). Schools and school districts are, without question, contributing heavily to such increases in sales and the accompanying increases in corporate wealth. If the outflow of such dollars were kept locally (i.e., in districts or multi-district collaboratives), many of the authentic assessment measures noted above could easily be developed. Furthermore, dollars could be redirected from the governmental largess back to educational professionals employed within a specific state or regional area. Clearly, examples like that found in the state of Mississippi indicate that this redistribution could and should prove more reasonable in both a real-use and real-outcome sense:

> Mississippi . . . signed a $4.4 million contract with McGraw Hill/CTB, partly on the strength of the company's promise to deliver test results in early July, two months after the first test [was to] be given. That would allow low performing schools to regroup, to change their practices, to retrain teachers . . . But then McGraw Hill/CTB announced that it would not be able to provide test results until mid-November, long after the window for making changes had closed, and only five months before the second round of testing. Did the state leadership take into account and postpone the high-stakes decision . . . In a word, no. Mississippi was determined to hold educators accountable, even if it

. . . [meant] not giving them a chance to use what they learned from the first round's results . . . the public was hell-bent for "accountability." (Merrow, 2001, pp. 32–33)

This redistribution of state dollars could move testing beyond the banality of the aforementioned example and, concomitantly, would allow for increased opportunities for teachers to extend the restricted nature of their professional contracts (i.e., beyond the current nine- or ten-month barrier). Likewise, these redistributed funds could provide the opportunity for the creation of authentic measures that would actually serve as benchmarks for genuine accountability. Organizational actions of this type would move beyond the power-coercive strategies that have been outlined above and would, conversely, incorporate much of the best elements of professional empowerment, as described below:

> Empowerment involves the sense people have that they are at the center of things, rather than the periphery. In an effectively led organization, everyone feels he or she contributes to its success. Empowered individuals believe what they do has significance and meaning. Empowered people have both discretion and obligations. They live in a culture of respect where they can actually do things without getting permission first from some parent figure. Empowered organizations are characterized by trust and system-wide communication. (Bennis, 2000, p. 29)

In closing this section of the chapter, we believe it is of paramount importance to share a recently published statement, regarding accountability, as articulated by a former North Carolina teacher of the year, an individual now employed by the elite Phillips Academy in Andover, Massachusetts. James Rogers offers the following insights into the U.S. accountability movement:

> I have a unique experience in that I taught in a public school and now I teach in a private school. We talk about standards and accountability. No one comes and asks us, "What did you do in that class?" We give our test, and our students come out of those classes. We have a reputation: If you come to our school, you're going to get a good education. And so the public has nothing to say about it. I don't worry about meeting someone else's standards in my classroom. I have standards. The whole history department has standards. (Henry, 2000, p. D5)

If this type of conceptualization and/or interpretation of accountability is acceptable in one of the most elite high school academies in New England, is it not possible to replicate that same belief in public school environments throughout the 50 states? Would educational reformers, like Darling-Hammond, be equally as comfortable and seemingly as confident in describing James Rogers as one who has not yet attained professional status? These questions are obviously small but essential elements of the overall accountability discussion. Regardless of the size or the magnitude, queries of this nature are, undoubtedly, not the typical accountability questions that are presented in journals, magazines, newspapers, or television commentaries. Quite possibly, educators at private academies are given greater levels of freedom and autonomy to define standards and standardization for themselves; thus, creating a more meaningful definition and more aligned outcomes—students with the ability to think and perform academic tasks in powerful and appropriate ways.

STANDARDS FOR PROFESSIONAL PREPARATION

Given the research presented throughout this chapter, many readers will assume that we must hold an equally dismissive attitude toward professional standards. Such is not the case. Standards are benchmarks. They are useful and necessary elements of any professional endeavor. Just as hospitals have carefully developed and modified "standards of care," educational professionals must work collaboratively to determine standards for student performance, teacher performance, and administrator performance. Standards must, likewise, be determined for the preparation of teachers, counselors, and administrators. No institution of higher education should prepare professional educators in an environment equivalent to that of a postsecondary vacuum. However, as has been articulated throughout this chapter, all successful organizational activities must be accomplished through the use of collaborative teams and collaborative sharing of different perspectives on the topic at hand. National standards can and should be developed for all specialty groups in the field of education. It is, however, the duty of the faculty and the university administrative team to determine what elements of those standards will be taught; how they will be taught; where in the curriculum such instructional activities might occur; what types of technological methodologies can be applied to the classroom environment (i.e., two-way telecommunications, Web-based course delivery); how experiential and field-based courses will be sequenced and presented; and how and when the learning process will be assessed. No set of professional standards can be unmitigatedly imported into the university curriculum—the concept of university governance will always circumvent such actions. As Birnbaum (1988) notes, the concept of governance as applied to virtually every segment of higher education requires:

> a shared responsibility and joint effort involving all important constituencies of the academic community, with the weight given to the views of each group dependent on the specific issues under discussion. In particular, while recognizing the legal authority of the board and the president, [we must identify] the faculty as having primary responsibility for the fundamental areas of curriculum, instruction, faculty status, and the academic aspects of student life. (p. 8)

Having accepted standards as both valuable and important, we would like to present a sample set of standards that can be utilized for graduate offerings throughout the field of educational leadership. These standards are generic in nature; therefore, they will require a significant degree of modification in order to properly "fit" within the context of various university settings and with the operational procedures of differing states. These sample standards exist without a corresponding national or state standardized test for assessment of the essential elements contained within each of the eight proposed standards. Obviously, it is our hope that such instruments will never be created to correspond with the standards outlined below. And, finally, these standards exist based on myriad theoretical and practical knowledge bases that exist within the field of educational leadership (Beyer & Ruhl-Smith, 2000; Council of Chief State School Officers, 1996; Hoyle, English, & Steffy, 1985, 1998; National Commission for the Principalship, 1990; Thomson, 1993). These eight standards, for both principal and superintendent preparation, are:

1. School administrators must assist in the creation of a school or district vision that ensures a learning climate that focuses on success for all students and recognizes the cultural context that surrounds the power of those opportunities for success.
2. School administrators must assist in the development and continuation of democratic forms of governance that focus on grassroots empowerment, shared policy development, internal and external agency collaboration, and open inquiry.
3. School administrators must be equipped with the skills and abilities to promote internal and external community relations and to engender broad-based community support for the successful transition of students from preschool to high school graduation.
4. School administrators must provide leadership throughout all elements of the organization and, concomitantly, must use appropriate data to assist teams in making proper decisions with respect to curricular and financial success, expansion and maintenance of facilities, and proper evaluation of all organizational resources (i.e., people, places, and things).
5. School administrators must be willing and able to lead curricular reform efforts throughout all phases of the organization. Educational leaders must offer assistance in the development and delivery of a research-based curriculum that addresses the needs of students from all population bases. Leaders must understand the potential power of oppression that exists within society and must aggressively work to eliminate all overt and covert forms of educational oppression.
6. School administrators must create an environment that promotes instructional systems that are exciting, relevant, and engaging to students. These systems must include proven, innovative instructional strategies. Assessment strategies for these instructional systems must be relevant, creative, and authentic in nature. Teachers must be encouraged and rewarded for creating high quality, locally produced, assessment tools.
7. School administrators must be willing and able to provide comprehensive staff evaluation, personnel leadership, and professional development in order to assure that students are given the utmost opportunity to succeed academically, aesthetically, athletically, socially, and personally.
8. School administrators must demonstrate ethical and personal integrity and model that behavior throughout all interactions in order to serve as exemplars

for students, faculty, and staff. Ethical behaviors must include an understanding of issues such as fairness, equity, personal responsibility, personal causality, efficacy, and civil disobedience.

CONCLUSIONS

We have attempted to review critical issues related to four extremely complex educational concerns. These issues have been difficult to fully consider in a work of this size and scope—obviously, more data exist than could have been presented to give even greater credence to the claims noted throughout this chapter. Nonetheless, the topics of standardized testing, accountability, student performance, and standards have been examined and discussed in a manner that attempts to look beyond the simplistic drivel that often is dispensed with respect to each of these issues. Facts have been presented with regard to the hazards of relying on standardized tests to make assertions about any significant degree of educational success/attainment. Furthermore, claims have been presented that negate the traditional views of accountability and student performance. Finally, a set of standards has been offered for review that utilizes the best of the research available in the knowledge base arena in order to allow university faculty the opportunity to consider principalship and superintendent preparation as part of a larger movement that can, indeed, make a difference in the transformation of schools.

These data have been presented with several overarching themes. First, the reader can find a simple theme based on the premise that all children can succeed in a properly constructed educational environment. The second theme encourages the collaborative redevelopment of P–12 and postsecondary curricula that, when redeveloped, attends to the voices and experiences of the nondominant groups found in modern U.S. society. Third is a focus on the theme that less is never more—to attempt to reduce student success to simple mathematical indicators will always be unsuccessful. The fourth theme deals with educational professionalism; here the reader is presented with the belief that such professionalism must be constructed and reified in schools and school districts, not in offices of politicians or university theoreticians who have little or no knowledge of the daily struggles of children and adolescents. A very contemporary example of such illogical and indifferent thought can be found in Rep. John A. Boehner's recently enacted opt-out clause for the National Assessment of Educational Progress. Here students are assured that they cannot be forced to take the test and, concomitantly, must be excused from the testing rigors for any expressed reason—thus, providing fertile ground for myriad concerns regarding overall credibility in test standardization. Fifth, and finally, is the theme that colleges and universities can have a significant role to play in the development of leaders that know, understand, and are able to implement elements of the preceding four themes. Although some members of our own profession and their hackneyed and uninspired practitioner colleagues will not accept such assertions, it is our belief that change can be made in schools via genuine collaboration with universities. To believe less would assuredly require a reselection of professional careers for those presenting this work.

In closing, as these data and the conclusions generated by these data are considered, discussed, and hopefully implemented, the reader must keep in mind that struggles will, without question, ensue. Those who posit an alternative paradigm are often personally and professionally castigated and excoriated. To ask those with a dominant perspective to consider their roles and responsibilities as progenitors of the failure that exists all around them is a disquieting and tumultuous experience. As this tumult ensues, it appears both beneficial and important to heed the words of one of today's most influential organizational theorists:

[a] pervasive emphasis on harmony does not serve organizations particularly well. Unanimity leads rather quickly to stagnation, which, in turn, invites change by nonevolutionary means. The fact that the organizational deviant, the individual who "sees" things differently, may be the institution's vital and only link with, for lack of a better term, some new, more apt paradigm does not make the organization value him [or her] any more. Most organizations would rather risk obsolescence than make room for the nonconformists in their midst. This is most true when such intolerance is most suicidal, that is, when the issues involved are of major importance (or when important people have taken a very strong or a personal position). On matters such as whether to name a new product "Corvair" or "Edsel," or whether to establish a franchise in Peoria or Oshkosh, dissent is reasonably well tolerated, even welcomed, as a way of insuring that the best of all possible alternatives is finally implemented. But when it comes to war or peace, life or death, growth or organizational stagnation, fighting or withdrawing, reform or status quo—desperately important matters—dissent is typically seen as fearful. Exactly at that point in time when it is most necessary to consider the possible consequences of a wide range of alternatives, public show of consensus becomes an absolute value to be defended no matter what the human cost. (Bennis, 2000, p. 256)

REFERENCES

Ayers, W. (1993). *To teach: The journey of a teacher*. New York: Teachers College Press.

Bennis, W. G. (2000). *Managing the dream: Reflections on leadership and change*. Cambridge, MA: Perseus.

Berliner, D. C., & Biddle, B. J. (1995). *The manufactured crisis: Myths, fraud, and the attack on America's public schools*. Reading, MA: Addison-Wesley.

Beyer, B., & Ruhl-Smith, C. (2000). Research and collaboration as keys to improved performance. *Journal of the Intermountain Center for Education Effectiveness, 1*(2), 35–40.

Birnbaum, R. (1988). *How colleges work: The cybernetics of academic organization and leadership*. San Francisco: Jossey-Bass.

Bracey, G. W. (2000). *From shaky ground into the quicksand: The Hudson Institute's flawed, dishonest report*. Unpublished manuscript.

Council of Chief State School Officers. (1996). *Interstate school leaders licensure consortium: Standards for school leaders*. Washington, DC: Author.

Darling-Hammond, L. (1990). Achieving our goals: Superficial or structural reforms? *Phi Delta Kappan, 72*, 286–295.

Darling-Hammond, L., & Goodwin, A. L. (1993). Progress toward professionalism in teaching. In G. Cawelti (Ed.), *Challenges and achievements of American education* (pp. 19–52). Alexandria, VA: Association for Supervision and Curriculum Development.

Dewey, J. (1984). The democratic state. In J. A. Boydston (Ed.), *John Dewey: The later works, 1925–1953* (vol. 2, pp. 282–303). Carbondale, IL: Southern Illinois University Press.

Freire, P. (1970). *Pedagogy of the oppressed.* New York: Continuum.

Garber, M. P., Heet, J. A., & Styring, W. (2000). *On shaky ground.* Indianapolis: Hudson Institute.

Glasser, W. (1990). *The quality school: Managing students without coercion.* New York: Harper & Row.

Glenn, D. (2001, January 23). Schools lack good reasons for staying, teens say. *Columbus Dispatch,* pp. A1–A2.

Gorman, L. (1999). An end to educational racism. *Independence Institute: Independence Feature Syndicate* [Online]. Retrieved from http://i2i.org/SuptDocs/OpEdArcv/Gorman/AnEndtoEducationalRacism.html

Hill, P. T., Campbell, C., & Harvey, J. (2000). *It takes a city: Getting serious about urban school reform.* Washington, DC: Brookings Institution Press.

Henry, T. (2000, May 15). Educators stand and deliver: Top teachers provide the lesson plan for improving schools. *USA Today,* p. D5.

Hoyle, J. R., English, F., & Steffy, B. (1985). *Skills for successful school leaders.* Arlington, VA: The American Association of School Administrators.

Hoyle, J. R., English, F., & Steffy, B. (1998). *Skills for successful 21st century school leaders.* Arlington, VA: The American Association of School Administrators.

Jones, A. C. (2001). Welcome to Standardsville. *Phi Delta Kappan, 82,* 462–464.

King, S. (1993). The limited presence of African-American teachers. *Review of Educational Research, 63*(2), 115–149.

Kohn, A. (2000). *The case against standardized testing.* Portsmouth, NH: Heinemann.

Kusimo, P. S. (1999). *Rural African Americans and education: The legacy of the Brown decision.* Charleston, WV: ERIC Clearinghouse on Rural Education and Small Schools. (ERIC Document Reproduction Service No. ED 425 050).

Madaus, G. (1989). New ways of thinking about testing: An interview with George Madaus. *Phi Delta Kappan, 70,* 642–645.

McNeil, L., & Valenzuela, A. (2000). The harmful impact of the TAAS system of testing in Texas. Beneath the accountability rhetoric. *The Civil Rights Project: Harvard University* [Online]. Retrieved from www.law.harvard.edu/civilrights/conferences/testing98/drafts/mcneil_valenzuela.html

Merrow, J. (2001). *Choosing excellence: "Good enough" schools are not good enough.* Lanham, MD: Scarecrow Press.

National Center for Fair and Open Testing. (2000a). Gender bias in college admissions tests. *Fairtest* [Online]. Retrieved from http://fairtest.org/facts/genderbias.html

National Center for Fair and Open Testing. (2000b). How standardized testing damages education. *Fairtest* [Online]. Retrieved from http://fairtest.org/facts/howharm.html

National Commission for the Principalship. (1990). *Principals for our changing schools: Preparation and certification.* Fairfax, VA: Author.

Neill, M., & Schaeffer, B. (1998). High-stakes testing fails to improve student learning. *Fairtest Press Release* [Online]. Retrieved from www.fairtest.org/pr/naeppr.html

Nevi, C. (2001). Saving standards. *Phi Delta Kappan, 82,* 460–461.

Oakes, J., Quartz, K. H., Ryan, S., & Lipton, M. (2000). *Becoming good American schools: The struggle for civic virtue in education reform.* San Francisco: Jossey-Bass.

Owens, R. G. (1998). *Organizational behavior in education* (6th ed.). Boston: Allyn & Bacon.

Popham, W. J. (2001). *The truth about testing: An educator's call to action.* Alexandria, VA: Association for Supervision and Curriculum Development.

Reitz, C. (2000). *Art, alienation, and the humanities: A critical engagement with Herbert Marcuse.* Albany: State University of New York Press.

Sacks, P. (1997). Standardized testing: Meritocracy's crooked yardstick. *Change, 29*, 24–31.

Schmoker, M. (1999). *Results: The key to continuous school improvement* (2nd ed.). Alexandria, VA: Association for Supervision and Curriculum Development.

Smith, J. M., & Ruhl-Smith, C. (2000). Internalizing and institutionalizing what we know about at-risk students. *The Journal of At-Risk Issues, 7*(1), 4–5.

Thompson, A. (1996). Political pragmatism and educational inquiry. *Philosophy of Education Yearbook* [Online]. Retrieved from http://x.ed.uiuc.edu/EPS/PES-Yearbook/96_docs/thompson.html

Thomson, S. D. (Ed.). (1993). *Principals for our changing schools: The knowledge and skill base*. Fairfax, VA: National Policy Board for Educational Administration.

Vinson, K. D., Gibson, R., & Ross, E. W. (2000). *High stakes testing and standardization: The threat to authenticity* [Online]. Retrieved from www.pipeline.com/~rgibson/HighStakesTesting.htm

West, C. (1993). *Keeping faith: Philosophy and race in America*. New York: Routledge.

Wiggins, G. (1994). None of the above. *The Executive Educator, 16*, 14–18.

Woodson, C. G. (1933). *The mis-education of the Negro*. Washington, DC: The Associated Publishers.

The Fateful Turn: Understanding the Discursive Practice of Educational Administration

Fenwick W. English

Educational preparation programs are made up of courses, curricula, and texts, as well as the expectations and experiences of the professors who teach and prepare educational leaders. Professors' biographical field experiences help mold their ideas of initiatives and responses which are appropriate and possible in leadership contexts in the schools. These "real world" contexts are powerful arbiters between beliefs and actions. Their conceptualization does not exist in some sort of neutral-free zone. Rather, the context which comprises the conversation about educational administration float on assumptions, ideas, concepts, or *theories* which direct, shape, and support them. Theories are simply types of stories or narratives which give meaning to actions in a professional practice. They provide the context to interpret why educational leaders should do some things and not others. Implicit in answering these questions are layers of values which establish priorities. The rhetoric of educational administration departments and programs is that they prepare school leaders. Indeed as a department or program title, leadership has replaced administration and supervision in many college and university programs. Figure 1 shows the generally accepted relationship between educational leadership programs and the leaders they ostensibly produce.

THE DISCURSIVE PRACTICE OF EDUCATIONAL ADMINISTRATION
What professors do, talk, and write about are structured within a system of written rules and unwritten norms. This system has been called a "discursive practice" (Foucault, 1972, p. 46). The current discursive practice of educational administration consists of a system of heuristics (discovery procedures and rules). The rules may not be written, though they may have initially assumed written form. Figure 2 illustrates some of the hidden heuristics and rules of the prevailing discursive practice of

Fenwick W. English, The R. Wendell Eaves Distinguished Professor of Educational Leadership, University of North Carolina at Chapel Hill

Figure 1.   The assumption that educational leaders are the result of educational leadership.

educational administration. The nodes which are visible on the surface show the "theory-practice gap"; the discussion about the "nature of science" which have been dominant in conversations regarding postmodernism (English, 1997, 1998; Willower, 1998); the theory movement in educational administration (Culbertson, 1988); and the substitution of management for leadership (Rost, 1991).

The rules of a discursive practice form boundaries and govern the inclusion/exclusion of content:

> that must be put into operation if such and such an object is to be transformed . . . such and such a concept be developed whether metamorphosed or imported, and such and such a strategy be modified—without ever ceasing to belong to this same discourse. (Foucault, 1972, p. 74)

The rules govern what texts (documents, claims, descriptions, verifications, etc.) are considered "right," "correct," and "truthful." The term "texts" is broadly conceived to stand for all kinds of statements (Anderson, 2001).

The current discursive practice contains three simultaneous "fields" (see figure 3) according to Foucault (1972):

- *a field of presence*—all statements in a discourse "acknowledged to be truthful, involving exact description, well-founded reasoning" (p. 57). These statements may be accepted because they possess "experimental verification, logical validation,

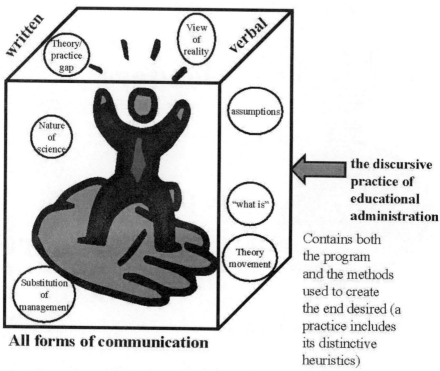

the discursive
practice of
educational
administration

Contains both
the program
and the methods
used to create
the end desired (a
practice includes
its distinctive
heuristics)

Figure 2.   A siscursive practice from Foucault (1972).

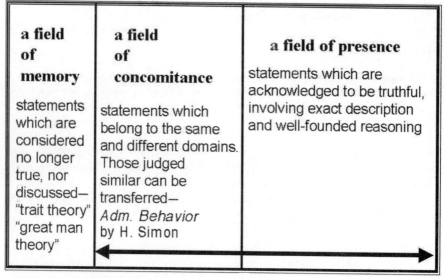

a field of memory	a field of concomitance	a field of presence
statements which are considered no longer true, nor discussed— "trait theory" "great man theory"	statements which belong to the same and different domains. Those judged similar can be transferred— *Adm. Behavior* by H. Simon	statements which are acknowledged to be truthful, involving exact description and well-founded reasoning

Figure 3.   Foucault's three fields which form a discursive practice.

mere repetition . . . justified by tradition and authority, commentary, a search for hidden meanings, [or] the analysis of error" (p. 57);

• *a field of concomitance*—statements which belong to the same and different domains of objects. Those considered to be similar can be transferred to other contents. If all administrative writing (from business and/or public administration) is similar it can be transferred into educational administration (p. 58);

• *a field of memory*—"statements which are no longer accepted or discussed, and which consequently no longer define a body of truth or a domain validity" (p. 58). Concepts relegated to this category in educational administration include "trait theory" (Getzels, Lipham, & Campbell, 1968, p. 1); "the great man theory" (Stogdill, 1974, p. 17); and "scientific management" (Hoy & Miskel, 1982, pp. 1–3). The current discursive practice has relegated to the conceptual/intellectual junk pile a whole host of documents from the humanities as non-scientific and unworthy of serious use (English, 1995, pp. 203–223).

THE FATEFUL TURN

The idea of a "turn" in linguistics means that there is a new understanding based on a different interpretation of an idea, concept, an event. There are two kinds of *turnings* possible. The first *turning* is the more conservative. It means a "turning away from." The ancient Greeks called it *apostrophic*. The second kind of *turning* is more radical. It is the notion of *overturning*. The Greek word for this idea is *catastrophic* (Rapaport, 1989, p. 195).

It is my contention that "the fateful turn" in educational administration occurred in November of 1957 when 50 professors from 20 leading universities gathered at the University of Chicago to partake of a seminar entitled, "Administrative Theory in Education" (Culbertson, 1995, p. 34). It is also my contention that this seminar was *catastrophic* for the field of education administration, leaving an enduring legacy which persists to this day. It is similarly my view that the legacy forms a major obstacle to change, particularly in proposing leadership studies. The impact of the "fateful turn" is shown in figure 4.

The "fateful turn" produced ideas concerning what constituted "the field" of educational administration. It is important to note that current texts in the field were not the subject of the debate. This is true anytime the boundaries of a field are in dispute. In this case the critical texts are those which portend boundary changes or lie in their continuation. When boundary arguments are going on, the key texts which motivate those seeking changes are not located within what the old borders included. This situation was the case in 1957 when key texts outside the field were cited as pivotal to altering it. Among those were texts produced by the Vienna Circle and some in other fields such as public administration.

According to Culbertson (1995) the Chicago seminar was instrumental in advancing the following premises for education administration:

• An embrace of the tenets of logical positivism, as advanced by the Vienna Circle, which eschewed theological and metaphysical thinking in favor of

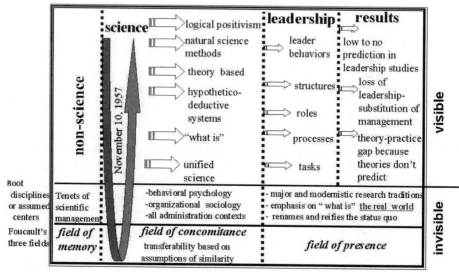

Figure 4.   The fateful turn and the current discursive practice of educational administration.

"positivistic thinking" which would produce "laws" (p. 35). Such laws would be the product of "deductive reasoning" (Culbertson, 1995, p. 41).

- Imagination must be subordinated to observation.
- Natural science methods should be applied to social and human phenomena (Culbertson, 1981, p. 29).
- Since theory was a polyvalent term, the concept of "hypothetico-deductive system" was substituted to clarify what was meant. Two domains were then joined: mathematics and the "real world" of experience (Culbertson, 1995, p. 36).
- A true science would focus on "what is" and not "what should be" or in the words of Neal Gross as cited by Andrew Halpin (1958), "Theory must be concerned with how the superintendent *does* behave, not with someone's opinion of how he *ought* to behave" (p. 3). This emphasis reinforced the "is-ought" dichotomy and led to the current "theory-practice gap" in which the problems of practice have been downgraded and are not considered a sound source upon which to conduct research (Culbertson, 1995, p. 244).
- The goal of science was to produce a "unified field" or a "unified science" (Culbertson, 1995, p. 37). Such a field in educational administration must rest on "all fields of administration" (Thompson, 1958, p. 31). This premise accounts for the extraordinary influence of a work in public administration, *Administrative Behavior* (1947) by Herbert Simon on the discourse of educational administration. Simon's work held up as "science" the doctrine of efficiency and so-called objective statements as opposed to ethical assertions (Culbertson, 1995, pp. 38–93; English, 1994, pp. 204–208; Greenfield & Ribbons, 1993, pp. 137–138). Simon's work emphasized *economic man* as the basis for rational de-

cision making. A similar emphasis was placed on humans when they came under the sway of total quality management (TQM) and its slogan of "continuous improvement." The fundamental contradiction regarding the assumption that all administration is the same is, then, how does one maintain the disciplinary boundaries of the field of educational administration as a distinct discipline?

- The dominance of behavioral psychology and organizational sociology were established as the principal root disciplines supporting educational administration. Such emphases led to organizations "freed" from human irrationality in which the primary emphasis was placed on arguments pertaining to "structure" and "systemic change" which ignored individuals as powerful or important (Steffy & English, 1996). Resistance to change from these perspectives is almost always conceptualized as irrational. The current emphasis on "re-structuring" is seen as the key to educational reform and is epitomized in the ISLLC standards. One does not change schools by changing the beliefs of the people who populate them, but by changing the "structure" in which they work.

THE FALLOUT: THE TRIUMPH OF ADMINISTRATIVE SCIENCE AND THE ABANDONMENT OF LEADERSHIP

Leadership does not require an organization. It does require followers and it implies there is a relationship between them. Wills (1994) indicates that the third leg of the leader/follower triumvirate is the presence of shared goals as the "glue" which binds them together.

> It is also the equalizer between leader and followers. The followers do not submit to the person of the leader. They join him or her in pursuit of the goal. The goal must be shared, no matter how many other motives are present that are not shared. (Wills, 1994, pp. 17, 19)

Wills' definition of a leader is: "one who mobilizes others toward a goal shared by leader and followers. In that brief definition, all three elements are present, and indispensable" (1994, p. 17).

Contrast this idea of leadership with that of Andrew Halpin's (1966), one of educational administration's key architects of the current discursive practice surrounding leadership. Halpin (1966) disliked even the concept of leadership indicating that it portended some "inherent capacity" (p. 40). He much preferred the idea of "leader behavior" (p. 41) and warned that "every concept which is thinking about administrator behavior must be defined, and operational definitions must be employed wherever possible" (p. 23). This was because "theory . . . refers to theory as defined in science, a hypothetico-deductive type of theory to be distinguished from value-theory as the latter is conceived in philosophy" (p. 23).

Consider now the criticism of Halpin's views by Johnson (1996):

> Leadership is a moral issue. As such it requires that we make use of the methods and conceptual tools that have always been the special concern of the humanities in general, and philosophy in particular. We need to develop a philosophy of leadership which sets moral theory at the center of things. (p. 41)

Born (1996) discusses the presence of "anti-intellectualism" in some leadership circles where too much academic work (scholarship) is scoffed at. Academic work must be augmented by so-called real-world experience with "hands-on" learning. Born avers that such rhetoric "proves most attractive to students and teachers averse to the rigors of scholarly activity" (p. 48). Then Born stakes out a claim to what he sees as the future of leadership studies:

> if leadership . . . is to have any enduring shelf life, if it is to avoid the fate of becoming one more academic fad, that endurance will only accrue through sober and rigorous scholarship that seeks to create a lasting body of work and through empirical forms of assessment that demonstrate unequivocally that students in leadership programs indeed perform in ways superior to their peers . . . at . . . colleges which lack such leadership programs. (p. 48)

We see the presence of "real world" concerns emanating from the Vienna Circle in which there is a clear bias towards "what is" instead of "what ought to be" and the proclivity towards experience as opposed to "philosophizing." That same bias has been represented today in the form of criticisms of educational administration programs that are "too removed from school problems and realities, too abstract and theoretical, and insufficiently embedded in school settings" (Imig, 2001, p. 2). A whole array of concepts is at work in this rancor, a discursive practice that sanctions "hands on" work over everything else and sees hard academic study as "too theoretical."

More hours in schools prepare administrators to function effectively within current schooling borders. Insisting that future educational leaders spend most of their time in "real world settings" is a rationale for re-creating what currently exists in them. It is indicative of a profound fear of change. The definition of "real world" is the world as most of us know it, that is, *the status quo.* An idea, a scheme, a concept is evaluated on how well it fits into what exists. This is one of the major tenets of logical positivism. What is "real" is the immediately observable, the here and now.

The early emphasis of the theory movement was founded on role and structure. It is a perfect framework to duplicate the status quo. The "range of possibilities" is evaluated by what currently exists and what currently "would fit" what exists. The ultimate arbiter of what is "practical" is what we do now. Programs that are grounded on "what exists" are the subject of management whose chief concerns are with efficiency. In the rush to provide realistic internships in real settings, educational administration programs are interested in preparing technically competent managers who can work within real (actual) settings. Thus the ISLLC standards perpetuate the idea of the primacy of the status quo, particularly by the creation of the scoring rubrics based on the norms of professional consensus. Such a consensus must utilize as its yardstick "what will work in current schools" as its principal criterion (see also Anderson, 2001).

Management is first and foremost concerned with maintaining an organization. Without organization there are no roles. Without roles there are no managers. The study of roles and structure is another name for management. What management is, is embedded in itself. For this reason Barrows Dunham (1964) wisely observed that the first task of management (leadership) was the creation and extension of organizational unity:

> It is therefore part of the strategy of leadership and part of the politics of organizational life to regard doctrines not merely as true or false but as conducive to unity or disruptive of it. In this second pair of alternatives lies the distinction between orthodoxy and heresy. For a doctrine is orthodox if it helps unite the organization; it is heretical if it divides. (p. 18)

A manager's first responsibility is to preserve the organization. If he or she must choose between change and unity, unity will almost always prevail. Acceptable change, therefore, lies within current capacity. If leadership involves going beyond current organizational boundaries and the division of authority and power, the risks may be too great for the unity of the organization and role of the leader. For this reason, an emphasis on management science involves essentially conservative doctrine. There is little that is democratic with management science; although there is a lot of "sharing" and "empowerment" rhetoric in contemporary educational administration discourse as exemplified in the ISLLC standards, there is very little actual equalization of power or fundamental role changes that would lead to the "deprofessionalization" of the role of authority of the school administrator (Anderson, 2001, p. 204).

When leadership is confined to schools it becomes management because:

1. Leadership has been confined only to observable behaviors by the dominant discursive practice, eliminating all of the so-called subjective elements, including beliefs which lead to motivation, morality, and choices which are value based.
2. "Observable behaviors" fit nicely into organizations, task delineations, and various forms of analyses centered on roles and structures. A discussion of leadership outside this framework is difficult to apply and analyze quantitatively. Behaviors, tasks, roles, and structures lend themselves to more "objective" (i.e., quantitative) forms of measurement, even though historically they don't account for much of the variance in leadership. The sociology of organizations becomes preeminent in such studies and remains so to this day.
3. In this discursive research practice the "ought to be" is rarely addressed. The "is" often assumes a normative quality because it is the only data set allowed to be counted. Graduate students often mistake theories of organization which are descriptive in nature as the way they "are" in some "natural state" instead of partial portraits of historically constructed and contextually confined snapshots which have been rigorously filtered and hence "warped."

Most leadership preparation programs are aimed at implanting one view of reality (the so-called scientific one which is either logical positivism or a derivative version) and giving candidates the requisite management skills. One does not find with much regularity the presentation of multiple versions of reality in programs that focus on leadership outside schools or organizations. The current discursive practice has accentuated a form of scholarship based on inductive approaches that has failed to match the scientific norms it desired, leading to the so-called theory-practice gap.

HEGEMONIC MODERNISM: THE FOCI OF CONFLICT

Once again we are witnessing a current challenge to the boundaries of the discursive practice in educational administration. The metaphor of the "big tent" was adopted by Donmoyer (1999) in his review of the trends in educational administration, especially in the efforts of those dealing with knowledge base issues to retain their own primacy while including some of the emergent perspectives (p. 31). The "tent," a metaphor for modernism and its traditions, has been expanded to "make room" for alternatives. The result is greater diversity, but "a very balkanized environment" (p. 34).

It is my position that Kuhnian (1996) paradigmatic monism or "hegemonic modernism" contains within it the seeds of the conflict which are currently manifest in the debates regarding the propriety of the boundaries and content of educational administration. Here are several definitions of modernism:

> I will use the term *modern* to designate any science that legitimates itself with reference to a metadiscourse . . . making an explicit appeal to some grand narrative, such as the dialectics of Spirit, the hermeneutics of meaning, the emancipation of the rational or working subject, or the creation of wealth. (Lyotard, 1997, p. xxiii)

In a review of relevant theoretical literature, Magnus (1999) indicates that modernism is supported by presuppositions of certain foundational tenets of philosophers of the 16th, 17th, and 18th centuries. Among these tenets are:

* essentialism, realism, and foundationalism;
* transcendental arguments;
* an accurate representation of knowledge;
* the correspondence idea of truth as being congruent to "reality" [out there];
* canonical descriptions and final vocabularies;
* principles, distinctions, and descriptions that are unconditionally binding for all times, persons, and places;
* the employment of grand narratives (meta-narratives) as in dialectical materialism; and
* the idea of a complete, unique and closed explanatory system upon which to rest any of the above tenets typically supported by binary oppositions. (p. 725)

The "anti-paradigmatic" or oppositional stance(s) to modernism embrace a critique or denial of one or more of these positions (Magnus, 1999):

* the neutrality or sovereignty of reason encompassing a gendered, historical, and ethnocentric focus;
* the concept of a social construction of "word-world mappings";

- a proclivity to embrace historicism ["the view that the history of anything is a sufficient explanation of it, that the values of anything can be accounted for through the discovery of its origins, that the nature of anything is entirely comprehended in its development" (Feibleman, 1984, p. 142)];
- the "ultimate status of a contrast between epistemology" and "the sociology of knowledge";
- the idea of an autonomous, rational subject;
- the notion of a difference or differential between the divisions of labor in knowledge acquisition and production; and
- elevation and enshrinement of the Enlightenment and its ideology (Magnus, 1999, p. 725).

The "anti-paradigm," if the counter-position may be called that within the ideology of modernism, is not a coherent body of propositions (Woods, 1999, pp. 23–24). The critique has been a broad-based front beginning with Dewey's opposition to positivism, Kuhn's writings, and "Wittgenstein's insistence on the language-game character of representation" (Magnus, 1999, p. 726). It also involves the scholarship of Michel Foucault and Jacques Derrida, as well as the feminist works of Judith Butler and Helene Cixous. Loosely combined into the "anti-paradigm" it has been called *postmodernism* (Magnus, 1999, p. 726)

Kuhn (1996) unsettled the scientific world by positing that science did not engage in change in the way it was often portrayed, that is, via the Baconian method embodied in rational discourse, which in its purest form was "theory free" (p. 28; Lakatos, 1999, p. 161). Rather, change was only grudgingly conceded under certain conditions. Kuhn conceptualized the work of scientists as proceeding from organized centers, or master discourses, which contained and defined problems within context. Although he never used the term "paradigm shift" (Horgan, 1997, p. 43), he did describe the extreme reluctance of scientists to accept them. He opined that "normal science" represented periods of time when one paradigm attained complete dominance or hegemony, a concept designated "hegemonical modernism" in this chapter.

The function of *paradigm* domination was to create a monistic mental box in which the acceptable problem was contained within it. The paradigm in use not only defined the problem and provided the web of possible solutions, scientists could also design the apparatus "able to solve the problem" (Kuhn, 1996, p. 27). None of these particulars were independent. Rather, they were interdependent. "No part of the aim of normal science is to call forth new sorts of phenomena," remarked Kuhn (1996); "indeed those that will not fit the box are often not seen at all. Nor do scientists normally aim to invent new theories, and they are often intolerant of those invented by others" (p. 24).

Kuhn's (1996) views about change were thoroughly modernistic (English, 2001c). Specifically, these positions stand out:

- Change occurs with a process of re-centering monistic mental boxes or *paradigms* (he never considers the possibility of a non-center or the need for a discourse which requires one).

- Change is viewed chronologically and periodized. Periodization is one of the distinguishing hallmarks of modernism (Carroll, 1997). It requires a beginning point by which something can be traced. It thus is compatible with historicism, which is also evident in Kuhn's work;
- While Kuhn (1996) is critical of the disciplinary aspects of working within paradigms—they serve to regulate the mental activities and conduct of those working within them, (p. 37)—his conceptualization of scientific activity never questions their underlying legitimacy nor primacy as a master hegemonic discourse.

Three current scholars in educational administration have chosen to characterize research and scholarship in a similar fashion as Kuhn (1996): Jack Culbertson, Don Willower, and Joe Murphy. We see rather clearly with Jack Culbertson and his work in the 1988 *Handbook of Research on Educational Administration* the prism of hegemonic modernism. He divides the work of scholars into periods chronologically and from the perspective of pre-science and science, or "scientific management," 1901–1925; "management science," 1926–1950; and "administrative science," 1951–1966. Culbertson (1988) never leaves the idea of science. His last chronological period he labels, "administrative science as an embattled concept, 1967–1985" (p. 18). He never calls into question the legitimacy of the so-called scientific perspective itself. The master discourse of modernism thoroughly shapes his characterization of the conceptual activities in educational administration (see also English, 2001).

The second author is the late Don Willower (1998) who formed his metaphorical vision about educational administration similarly within the tradition of the social sciences and "scientific norms" (p. 7). He admitted to two challenges to the traditional social science models, Marxism (and Neo-Marxism or critical theory) and something he called "subjectivism" which he laid initially at the feet of T. B. Greenfield (p. 6). "Subjectivism" was Willower's (1998) catch-all category that included "phenomenology, existentialism, and most forms of idealism" (p. 11) and "other forces" which included postmodernism (p. 15). Willower's critique of alternatives to the traditional social science models did not include recognition that those same models were replete with transcendental arguments, final vocabularies, the notion of a supportable foundationalism upon which the distinction between science and non-science could be established, and the corollary that certain principles, distinctions, and descriptions were unconditionally binding for all times, persons, and places. With the exception of postmodernism, which is "anti-paradigmatic," all of the positions Willower critiqued including Marxism are also modernistic. So, from a thoroughly Kuhnian perspective regarding modernism, all of them involve "shifting centers" but no real change otherwise.

Joe Murphy's work employs the same prism of paradigmatic modernism, first in his presentation of the "field's" metaphors (1993) and secondly in his 1999 AERA and later UCEA monograph, *The Quest for a Center*. Murphy's disdain for any conceptual alternatives to hegemonic modernism is clearly evident in his choice of descriptors for alternatives, such as "bridges to nowhere" (p. 48) and "academic trophy hunting" (p. 48) (as noted in English, 2000a, p. 456).

In all three of these examples (Culbertson, Willower, and Murphy) the admonition by Lakatos (1999) is prescient:

> One must never allow a research programme to become a Weltanschauung, or a sort of scientific rigour, setting itself up as an arbiter between explanation and non-explanation, as mathematical rigour sets itself up as an arbiter between proof and non-proof. (p. 68)

In all three of the scholars cited, it is my contention that they set themselves up as arbiters employing a hegemonically modernistic perspective. Their views are normative and disciplinary (regulative). Their objective is to portray what is "normal" and what is a "deviation" and to remind us that the deviations are either not appropriate (not "science") or not fruitful ("subjective").

THE CONFLICT WITHIN MODERNISM AS THE HARBINGER OF CHANGE

The current challenge to the modernistic discursive practice of educational administration is occurring on a broad front. The idea of leadership for social justice contains many intellectual and conceptual probes which are sharply critical of our past traditions. Among them is that modernism is a "master signifier" (Usher & Edwards, 1996, p. 77); that is, it creates an identity which is defined by its own existence. It is its own epistemological justification and arbiter.

> Knowledge as the master signifier of science . . . is emotionally invested and therefore unquestioned and unquestionable . . . we have noted on a number of occasions, science claims that it can know everything, that it is progressively coming to know and more, that what it knows is valuable in itself. In the discourse of the university scientific knowledge knows no bounds and no limitations. It is a self-perpetuating system of knowledge which is its own end and justification. (Usher & Edwards, 1996, p. 77)

The absolute centrality of perspective, albeit incorporating some shifting centers, maintains the primacy of the modernistic perspective. It is as a master signifier, whether expressed in the form of traditional social science methods, critical theory, or phenomenology, that is *the essence* as to whether or not a reconciliation is possible. That prospect represents the path to the future. However, as long as modernists insist on hegemony, making the tent larger is not a solution to the problem. But the issue of the tent itself, the issue of whether there is a *master signifier,* is the fulcrum on which the issue of *hegemony* and any restoration of harmony rests.

In order to make what may appear as a fairly ethereal matter more tangible, it should be remembered that the current hegemonic modernistic frame undergirds:

- the legitimacy of an academic field of study at the university;
- the manifestation of that legitimacy in the creation and maintenance of a *knowledge base* which identifies the boundaries of exclusivity and privilege in the university and larger society;

- the *knowledge base* represents the political power of those charged with maintaining it via teaching, research, and licensure. The creation of that political power is incorporated into Foucault's (1980) *apparatus* of interlocking agencies with a vested interest in perpetuating their own hegemony. (p. 132)

The hegemonic modernistic frame presents an image of a compelling singularity, a unity that broaches no serious competition or conceptual alternatives. Such a unitary singularity is supported by an epistemological foundation which provides epistemological stability (and finality) to *the field, the knowledge base, practice,* and *licensure;* even though the particulars within each may not be constant over time, their boundaries remain enduring.

The notion that such unity is simply a convention based on a make-believe foundationalism is unthinkable to most modernists. The idea that there is no such identity possible, and in fact may consist of multiple identities, is the equivalent of "madness" (Usher & Edwards, 1996, p. 78). The unthinkable alternative is that there may be *fields, knowledge bases,* and *practices* (English, 2001a).

A GLIMPSE OF THE FUTURE

The first task in trying to create a new future for educational administration is to extricate oneself from the necessity of seeing every choice as dualistic "either-or" menu options. The modernistic mind-set forces one to see the future in binoculars that produce reactions and defensiveness because there must always be a winner or a loser. A postmodern perspective is that the boundaries are more open than that. A postmodern view is that there ought to be competing views present *without* any being pushed to the side as less than worthy ("less than science"). Alternative epistemologies ought to be welcome, subjected to examination, and held to some agreed-upon norms.

It is this task to which I now turn. The theory movement was in pursuit of a science. However, those doing the pursuing defined science in such a way as to produce theories with little to no predictive power. Part of the problem was the method by which their theories were constructed, that is, inductively. What is needed are more broad brush, deductive theories which when subject to testing, reveal some predictive power, and which if pursued over a long time period, lead to some stunning and novel findings. The strength of a theory is not what they confirm about themselves (correlate) but rather what they anticipate. On this notion, I am drawing heavily on the ideas of Imre Lakatos (1999) in describing a scientific research program. As long as theories in educational administration lag behind practice, that is, as long as they fail to be predictive instead of merely correlative, we will have a continuing "theory-practice" gap. The solution to the "theory-practice gap" is not to move the university into the field, as many have supposed or proposed, but to change the way theories are created and verified. In that respect theories will be ahead of and predict the impact of practice. The "gap" is part and parcel of the heuristics we have employed to inquire about leadership.

Lakatos calls Kuhn's (1996) notion of *normal science* (p. 24) in which one paradigm comes into dominance simply a convenient *monopoly* and warns:

> The history of science has been and should be a history of competing research programmes . . ., but it has not been and must not become a succession of periods of normal science; the sooner competition starts, the better for progress. Theoretical pluralism is better than theoretical monism: on this point Popper and Feyerabend are right and Kuhn is wrong. (Lakatos, 1999, p. 69)

The creation of new leadership theories which may have the characteristics of prediction are not likely to come about under the rubric of present courses and curriculum in most educational administration programs. The theory movement and its vestiges are far from dead in their continuing influence. We are still infatuated with the idea of management science. There are still no rigorous theories of leadership in schools which have not been recast in behavioral and structural forms, the most recent being the ISLLC standards. The theory-practice gap is as real as ever, with increasing criticism about the so-called lack of reality in preparation programs (Imig, 2001).

Gaining a new perspective on leadership studies begins by examining the existing discursive practice of educational administration. Foucault (1972) makes it clear that tackling the "ideological functioning of a science" means first interrogating it "as a discursive formation" and questioning neither its propositions nor contradictions, but rather "the system of formation of its objects . . . concepts, its theoretical choices," treating it simply as one practice among many possible (p. 186). That attitude alone will be a significant breakthrough in erasing the 40-year "fateful turn" in the field that has substituted management for a substantive discussion of leadership (English, 2000a). The irony is that while many of us work in programs of educational leadership, the methods we have embraced to create our content have obliterated the essence of what we believe we should be doing. Educational leadership has been transformed into management and a preoccupation with behaviors, tasks, roles, processes, and structures. The best that can be said is that we occasionally graduate a leader, but most of our students are preparing to be technicians within the existing bureaucracy (English, 2001b).

The current discursive practice of educational administration is under intensive interrogation. While various facets of it have been dropped or modified, it remains the dominant structure in which most university-based preparation programs still function. Field practice is firmly in its intellectual and conceptual thralldom. It is a myth of the most pernicious sort that substantive reform of schools or the leaders in them will ever emerge solely from the field. Practitioners practice what they have learned in the university. Often what they have been taught does not appear in the formal texts, but lies in the unwritten rules, assumptions, and pre-suppositions to which they have been thoroughly exposed in their course work and which has been reinforced in their internship experiences. These places have shown themselves not to be the breeding grounds for any radical change in the schools. The overarching posture of organizational sociology is stability. As long as the ethos of this academic discipline permeates educational administration, both field practice and the academic boundaries of the field will reflect this same preoccupation. Any discussion of leadership ends up *inside* schools and perpetuating the status quo, albeit with new names.

Substantive change in educational administration depends upon changing its content, but that is dependent on altering its borders. One is connected to the other. Doing both means confronting the entire discursive practice of educational administration. It is not a search for the impossible dream. It happened in 1957. It is about to happen again.

REFERENCES

Anderson, G. (2001). Disciplining leaders: A critical discourse analysis of the ISLLC national examination and performance standards in educational administration. *International Journal of Leadership in Education: Theory and Practice, 4*(3), 199–216.

Born, D. (1996). Leadership studies: A critical appraisal. In P. Temes (Ed.), *Teaching leadership* (pp. 45–72). New York: Peter Lang.

Carroll, N. (1997). Periodizing postmodernism. *Clio: A Journal of Literature, History and the Philosophy of History, 26*(2), 143–165.

Culbertson, J. (1981). Antecedents to the theory movement. *Educational Administration Quarterly, XVII*(1), 25–47.

Culbertson, J. (1988). A century's question for a knowledge base. In N. Boyan (Ed.), *Handbook of research on educational administration* (pp. 3–26). New York: Longman.

Culbertson, J. (1995). *Building bridges: UCEA's first two decades.* University Park, PA: University Council for Educational Administration.

Donmoyer, R. (1999). The continuing quest for a knowledge base: 1976–1998. In N. Boyan (Ed.), *Handbook of research on educational administration* (pp. 3–34). New York: Longman.

Dunham, B. (1964). *Heroes and heretics: A social history of dissent.* New York: Alfred A. Knopf.

English, F. (1994). *Theory in educational administration.* New York: HarperCollins.

English, F. (1995). Toward a reconsideration of biography and other forms of life writing as a focus for teaching educational administration. *Educational Administration Quarterly, 31*(2), 203–223.

English, F. (1997). The cupboard is bare: The postmodern critique of educational administration. *Journal of School Leadership, 7,* 4–26.

English, F. (1998, September). The postmodern turn in educational administration: apostrophic or catastrophic development? *Journal of School Leadership, 8,* 426–447.

English, F. (2001a). Hegemony or harmony? A conceptual and methodological quest to end the paradigm wars in educational administration. Unpublished symposium paper. American Education Research Association, Seattle, WA.

English, F. (2001b). You say you saw what? Which veil did you lift? *Education Leadership Review, 2*(2), 22–27.

English, F. (2001c). What paradigm shift? An interrogation of Kuhn's idea of normalcy in the research practice of educational administration. *International Journal of Leadership in Education: Theory and Practice, 4*(1), 29–38.

Feibleman, J. (1984). Historicism. In D. Runes (Ed.), *Dictionary of philosophy* (p. 142). Totowa, NJ: Rowman & Allanheld.

Foucault, M. (1972). *The archaeology of knowledge and the discourse on language.* New York: Pantheon Books.

Foucault, M. (1980). *Power/knowledge: Selected interviews and other writings.* (C. Gordon, Ed.). New York: Pantheon Books.

Getzels, J., Lipham, J., & Campbell, R. (1968). *Educational administration as a social process: Theory, research, practice.* New York: Harper and Row.

Greenfield, T., & Ribbons, T. (1993). *Greenfield on educational administration: Towards a humane science.* London: Routledge.

Halpin, A. (1958). The development of theory in educational administration. In A. W. Halpin (Ed.), *Administrative theory in education* (pp. 1–19). New York: Macmillan.

Halpin, A. (1966). *Theory and research in administration.* New York: Macmillan.

Horgan, J. (1997). *The end of science. Facing the limits of knowledge in the twilight of the scientific age.* New York: Broadway Books.

Hoy, W., & Miskel, C. (1982). *Educational administration: Theory, research and practice.* New York: Random House.

Imig, D. (2001). Holding the line on school leader preparation. *AACTE Briefs, 22*(11), 2.

Johnson, P. (1996). Antipodes: Plato, Nietzsche, and the moral dimension of leadership. In P. Temes (Ed.), *Teaching leadership* (pp. 13–44). New York: Peter Lang.

Kuhn, T. (1996). *The structure of scientific revolutions.* Chicago: University of Chicago Press.

Lakatos, I. (1999). *The methodology of scientific research programmes.* Cambridge, UK: Cambridge University Press.

Lyotard, J. (1997). *The postmodern condition: A report on knowledge.* Minneapolis: University of Minnesota Press.

Magnus, B. (1999). Postmodern. In R. Audi (Ed.), *The Cambridge dictionary of philosophy* (2nd ed., pp. 726–727). Cambridge, UK: Cambridge University Press.

Murphy, J. (1993). Ferment in school administration: Rounds 1–3. In J. Murphy (Ed.), *Preparing tomorrow's school leaders: Alternative designs* (pp. 1–18). University Park, PA: University Council on Educational Administration.

Murphy, J. (1999). *A quest for a center: Notes on the state of the profession of educational leadership.* Columbia, MO: University Council for Educational Administration.

Rapaport, H. (1989). *Heidegger and Derrida.* Lincoln: University of Nebraska Press.

Rost, J. (1991). *Leadership for the twenty-first century.* Westport, CT: Praeger.

Simon, H. (1947). *Administrative behavior.* New York: Macmillan.

Steffy, B., & English, F. (1996). The conceptual limitations of systemic reform in the United States. *International Studies in Educational Administration, 24*(2), 67–82.

Stogdill, R. (1974). *Handbook of leadership.* New York: The Free Press.

Thompson, J. D. (1958). Modern approaches to theory in administration. In A. Halpin (Ed.), *Administrative theory in education* (pp. 20–39). New York: Macmillan.

Usher, R., & Edwards, R. (1996). *Postmodernism and education.* London: Routledge.

Willower, D. (1998). Fighting the fog: A criticism of postmodernism. *Journal of School Leadership, 8*(5), 448–463.

Wills, G. (1994). *Certain trumpets: The call of leaders.* New York: Simon and Schuster.

Woods, T. (1999). *Beginning postmodernism.* Manchester, UK: Manchester University Press.

The (Un)Changing World of School Leadership: A Journey from Discourse to Practice

Edith A. Rusch

A large brown shoe dominated the cover. The caption read, "Big Shoes, Big Shortage." It caught my eye! Now I must admit, I love shoes. Some friends will tell you that I never met a shoe I didn't like. A challenging moment in my life was when my feet grew a full size and I had to let go of 56 pairs of beloved footwear. I actually use a bag of favorite shoes as props in a professional presentation to illustrate key concepts on change. As you can tell, I'm not the kind of person who would get upset about a shoe on the cover of a professional journal. But that was before I saw *the big brown shoe*.

The shoe in question was a traditional brown wingtip shoe, held up by a white male figure. Located on the cover of a recent issue of *School Administrator*, a publication of the American Association of School Administrators, the illustration was meant to depict the current shortage of school administrator candidates and it appeared again in the feature article, "The Changing Face of Leadership Preparation" (Murphy, 2001, p. 14). Perhaps the face of preparation was changing, but the illustration indicated that the face of *who* was being prepared hadn't changed at all. The contradictions within the journal issue became more prominent as I read the articles, which included multiple viewpoints about the "big shoe" problem. For example, one article reported a study that found higher interest on the part of females than males in high school administrative positions. The authors' conclusions included the observation that,

> there remains a substantial degree of sex-role stereotyping that limits the perceived fit of women for certain administrative positions. These perceptual biases may be causing school district leaders and board members to fail to identify highly qualified candidates who don't look like their predecessors. (Pounder & Merrill, 2001, p. 21)

Edith A. Rusch, Rowan University

I wondered how an editor could include that blunt statement and somehow not connect the cover design with the concept of "sex-role stereotyping." Another article in the issue stated that "institutionalized obstacles limit women's entry and advancement in school administration" (Tallerico & Tingley, 2001, p. 23). I wondered how the editor understood the construction and perpetuation of "institutionalized obstacles" that either supported or inhibited women's advancement in school leadership. I found myself increasingly upset by *this big brown shoe*!

After years of advocating for women in school leadership, I'd come to the place of celebrating progress, of tempering my critiques, of believing that traditional white male role definitions were fading. Statistics suggested the world was changing. Currently, women are the majority of candidates in administrative preparation programs. While there is a dearth of good statistics about who occupies administrative chairs in our public schools, we do know that elementary principals are primarily women, that there are increasing numbers of women in secondary principalships, and that in the last decade, the percentage of women superintendents has shifted from 6 percent to 12 percent. Women are also becoming a more prominent force in the professoriate of many leadership preparation programs. My perception of this changing data led me to focus my professional energy more on understanding gendered dynamics in the workplace than issues of entry into the leadership roles in the workplace. But then I saw *that shoe*!

To be fair, the American Association of School Administrators has been a supporter of equity and advancement for women in leadership. The organization has sponsored numerous studies highlighting the status quo. In the past few years *School Administrator* has prominently featured research on women in superintendencies, articles by women researchers, and articles about and by women superintendents. The association also sponsors an annual Women Administrator's Conference and a special session for women administrators at the annual national convention. So why couldn't I get beyond this shoe? It may have had something to do with the editor's response to an objection by a female colleague on AASA's staff—a framed alternate cover featuring a red high heel. Looking at the framed fake cover, I knew that the world had not changed at all for some practicing and aspirant school administrators. The red heel was gorgeous; the message it conveyed was devastating.

How does this shoe and my consternation over its inherent messages connect to the world of professors of school administration? In keeping with the theme of the NCPEA Yearbook, *The Changing World of School Administration*, this chapter focuses on the subtle and not-so-subtle barriers to a changed world of school administration. Readers are invited to go on a hike with me through a thicket of issues that continue to provoke me. After a great deal of agonizing over the brown shoe, I've concluded that, to a large segment of the administrative aspirant population, the world of school leadership is still inaccessible, unattainable, undesirable, or operating in a climate akin to Antarctica. To support my conclusion, I will journey through a series of theories that reframe the questions of equity and access. As the journey progresses, I will use data from previous and current studies to highlight the signposts which women, men, and people of color find in their quest for leadership positions. Finally, attending to the intended message of the brown shoe story, I will explore how professors of educational leadership might construct a discourse of school administration that leads to a more engaging profession for women and men.

THE FAULT LINE

My journey to the question of the social construction of school leadership began at a time when my life was "littered with other people's words" (Rusch, 1990). A doctoral student at the time, my living space literally was a maze of texts that represented the genealogy of leadership from philosophical, management, historical, sociological, feminist, biographical, and narrative perspectives. As I tenuously worked my way through this intellectual labyrinth, I encountered Dorothy Smith's "line of fault" (1987, p. 52), which she described as the moment of rupture when personal experience breaks away from the discourse. As women, Smith noted, we learn to work inside a discursive world that rarely includes a woman's perspective and therefore, often, does not feel like ours. She described this world as "a landscape in which women are strangers" (p. 52). More importantly, Smith noted that the discourse actually defines knowledge from a male perspective for both males and females (Smith, 1990). In her view, once a perspective gained power and privilege within the discursive world, and that discursive world was manifested in general practice over time, the potential to problematize the practices would be limited.

Smith's viewpoint was a defining moment in my journey to deepen my understandings of leadership. As an experienced female school administrator, I seldom found myself in any of the texts or classroom discourses about leadership. If I did find discourse about women, gender, diversity or equity, it typically was in the last chapter of the text and the course was never long enough to get to the last chapter! Classroom conversations, when they occurred, tended to short and tense even though my professors were not narrow minded and maleocentric individuals. In fact, many were actively engaged in equity and diversity work; yet I was not experiencing a proactive dialogue that challenged the complex relations of ruling within our school systems or the possibilities for changing that system. Smith's theory (1987, 1990) exposed my line of fault, there was nothing intellectual about it, and for me, the earthquake had just begun.

Probing the Silence

My values and beliefs about schooling had long been influenced by Dewey's notions of the dialectical relationship between school and society. To me, that relationship represented a mobius strip—an illusory one-sided pattern that perpetuates itself. In other words, what and how we learned and what and how educators taught, constructed and reconstructed a social world. If habits of mind were perpetuated that did not promote openmindedness, the society would continue to be embedded with routines and ruts that sustained stratification and inequity (Dewey, 1916). As I pondered the silences about diversity, equity, and gender issues in my formal administrative education, I discovered Anderson's study of school administrators who "could not or would not see" social inequalities that deeply affected the lives of children in their schools (Anderson, 1990, p. 41). Anderson's empirically supported argument was based on Ralph Ellison's description of himself as an invisible man because individuals he encountered had a "construction of the inner eye" that allowed them not to see him. While Anderson focused on practicing school administrators, noting how school leaders are "carriers of social interchange vertically (up and down the hierarchy) and horizontally (among peers and between the school and community)" (p. 47), for me, his examples clarified the inherent power of discourse in educational leadership classrooms. I recognized that if our professional learning experiences did not purposefully include attention to issues of equity, diversity, and plurality, then the construction of our "inner eye" had limited potential for multiple perspectives to emerge and challenge the social realities that fostered inequities and marginalization.

The "textbook" of careers in my doctoral cohort was rich with experiences for pondering. My own administrative practice spanned a time that included the introduction of affirmative action, the development of multicultural education, and dramatic demographic changes in the racial and ethnic populations of our schools. I'd been part of a feminist struggle to gain voice and position in school administration. I'd grappled with men and women who couldn't understand the need for a special organization to mentor women and I'd also struggled with the dualistic experience of attaining position and disguising my feminist commitments so I could achieve status within the traditional organization. I'd observed the struggles of male administrators who'd bravely supported women colleagues and adapted personal behaviors when faced with disruptions to what they "knew." I'd known sincere and conscientious administrators who took early retirement because the emerging challenges of equity and pluralism were too hard. I was an expert at single parenting and I knew the frustrations of not being able to successfully communicate with an increasingly diverse constituency. I was only one page in a classroom filled with "texts" of equity and diversity, but no one was turning our pages. The lack of open conversations related to the challenges of leading in democratic ways confounded and frustrated me, and Anderson's findings on the construction of the inner administrative eye heightened my distress. My line of fault was only getting longer.

The Embedded World of Leadership

A friend, spotting my distress, agreed to join me on the line of fault. Asking similar questions from the standpoint of a higher education administrator, Penny Poplin Gosetti was examining how social constructions of privilege informed constructions of leadership. She found little attention to the concept in leadership literature. Sociological explanations included defining privilege as a function of power (Lenski, 1966). Lenski maintained that the means by which privilege was attained (force, fraud, and inheritance) and maintained explained why silence surrounded the concept. Lenski (1966) cited Mosca who argued in 1939 that a dominant group assures the maintenance of its status by embedding its privilege in the culture's value and belief systems through the development of theories. We wondered if that explained why "despite the increasing number of women and minorities in school leadership positions, feminist theoretical perspectives, multi-ethnic viewpoints, and gendered standpoints were rarely included in preparation and professional development of school administrators" (Gosetti & Rusch, 1995, p. 20).

Understanding the theory and practices that led to embeddedness was our next challenge. Gosetti drew on Bourdieu's definition of embeddedness as "méconnaissance," translated as misrecognition, "the process whereby power relations are perceived not for what they objectively are but in a form which renders them legitimate in the eyes of the beholder" (Bourdieu & Passeron, 1977, p. xiii). We were also influenced by McIntosh (1986), who argued that members of a highly organized, theoretically justified, and occasionally indulgent dominant culture are taught to view their lives as "morally neutral, normative . . . average, and . . . ideal" (p. 4). These perspectives led us to the same position of most critical theorists, that once a structure or a pattern of power relations became deeply embedded within leadership theories, the assumptions and values upon which the theories were originally based became invisible. For example, even though researchers (Shakeshaft, 1989; Acker, 1992) have built strong empirical cases for the inherent bias in the Ohio Leadership Studies and the Hawthorne Studies, a singular and traditional perspective of this research appears frequently in textual and classroom discourse.

The easy transfer of classroom discourse to practice took on new meaning when Ferguson (1984) put forth the notion of "language having people." She argued that our "participation in speech consists in joining an already existent flow of activity rather than initiating new activity" (p. 60). Ferguson confirmed our proposition that the invisibility of the privilege was fostered by a recursive power/knowledge relationship between the discourse and the practice in the field. Going beyond Ferguson, we concluded that

> the texts, conversation, writings and professional activities that construct our knowing and understanding of leadership come from an embedded privileged perspective which largely ignores issues of status, gender, and race and insidiously perpetuates a view of leadership that discourages diversity and equity. (Gosetti & Rusch, 1995, p. 12)

Exposing Privilege in Discourse

Using our practitioner experience in K–12 and higher education administration, Poplin Gosetti and I worked to locate and name the embedded notions of privilege manifested in symbolic and literal forms of our profession. We examined the traditional discourse of educational leadership found in textbooks, knowledge base documents, and practitioner journals. "Invisibility of the issues" was our observation after a comprehensive review of the discourse (Rusch & Gosetti, 1994, p. 29). For example, we reviewed a 10-year history (1983–1992) of eight practitioner journals to gain insights into the ongoing discourse about equity and diversity. Our findings showed a seriously limited discussions of the issues for practicing professionals, leading us to conclude that "the silences loudly communicated a privileged view" (Rusch & Gosetti, 1994, p. 14). In our view, the "dialectical relationship between discourse and practice, [or] what Anderson (1990) called the 'construction of the inner eye' appeared to promote wearing blinders" (Gosetti & Rusch, 1993, p. 15).

Further investigation of the proliferation of privilege in leadership and administrative discourse led to a partnership with Catherine Marshall (Marshall & Rusch, 1995; Rusch & Marshall, 1995, 1996). Our investigations were framed by Van Nostrand's (1993) theory of territorial sexism which, "at its most extreme . . . allows no space at all for one gender—a form of bias by omission" (p. 38). Similar to theories that defined privilege, territorial sexism, according to Van Nostrand (1993) controlled or relinquished territory that governed who could participate and to what degree they would have influence. Once more, I revisited the data from practitioner journals, looking specifically at how the content and accompanying illustrations in published articles limited or enlarged the space for participation and influence of women and people of color. The analysis of article content differed little from earlier findings (see table 1). In addition, during that decade, photographs accompanying articles about the principalship, powerful leadership, or unusual leadership opportunities were typically of men. Photographs that use mixed groups of people never showed women taller than men, nor did they show men looking up to women. Articles about shared decision making, collaboration, participatory management, or job sharing most often include a photo or sketch of women, suggesting that more democratic and inclusive practices were "women's ways of leading." The lack of attention to professional discourse and lack of balanced gender images in journals were powerful examples of Van Nostrand (1993) territorial sexism. While the findings date back to the early 1990s, if we consider that a pipeline to school administration develops over time, these data offer one explanation of today's shortage of people to fill "big shoes."

Exposing Privilege in Leadership Practices

The issue of equity for women and people of color seemed intractable. Despite decades of research, policy adjustment, and legislation, privilege seemed to govern so many aspects of school administration. Evidence of how the "construction of the inner eye" (Anderson, 1990) affected women, girls, and people of color included

Table 1. Analysis of Content in Educational Journals, 1983–1994

Journal	Articles published	Articles focused on gender equity or diversity	Content challenges, territorial sexism
Educational Leadership	1,740	60	16
Executive Educator	825	31	8
NASSP Bulletin	944	46	8
Phi Delta Kappan	1,600	82	31
Principal	522	18	1
School Administrator	527	41	5

From: Rusch & Marshall, 1995, p. 11.

lower math and science scores, unequal access to competitive sports, skewed hiring and promotion practices in school administration and the academy, and biased content and pedagogy in classrooms. In an effort to understand to how women and men actually negotiated gender issues in administrative relationships, Marshall and I decided to reanalyze data from our earlier work. Our analyses eventually led to a construct we called "gender filters" (Marshall & Rusch, 1995; Rusch & Marshall, 1995, 1996). In our view, the filters operated as enabling behaviors and were used by women and men to manage gendered dynamics. The data suggested that many of these filters mediated the contradictions between conscience and conduct in gendered relationship, but most often, the filters appeared to reify the traditions of gender inequity, thus protecting the privilege of profession as a dominant white-male culture. The filters also served to silence ideas and people that might disrupt the privileges of dominance. While the work focused on gender, we found indications that the filters were used in similar ways for navigating racial and ethnic dynamics.

As noted in earlier writings, some filters we identified contributed to the reproduction and reification of privilege and tradition in administration. These included:

- Anger with Challengers Filter: This filter manifested itself in cold stares, impatience, and labels of deficiency and had the effect of silencing or undermining open dialogue about gender equity and diversity.
- Denial Filter: The Denial Filter appeared as gender blinders, with people espousing that the professional culture is gender-neutral. Any references to gender equity or gendered perspectives were treated as irrelevant and time-wasting.

Other filters were subtler. The privilege inherent in these responses was less visible and or was contradictory. They included:

- Posturing and Intellectualizing Filter: People who used the Posturing and Intellectualizing Filter seldom had actions that match the words, but they garner attention from colleagues and feminist educators by vocalizing a divergent value position.
- Uncomfortable Comfort Filter: These educators supported engaging in dialogue about equity issues. However, when faced with critical and personal equity questions, the individuals remained silent and usually retreated from the previously espoused support positions.
- Rose Colored Filter: Individuals who used this filter did not deny or obviate gender equity issues, but they were filled with uncertainty about the origins of the gendered behaviors. They tended not to reflect deeply on the meaning of complex gendered interactions or were confused about what they should think about them.

We found one set of filters individuals used in attempts to modify conduct and disrupt privileged and traditional perspectives. They included:

- Defining Moment Filters: Individuals using this filter took advantage of teachable moments, using incidents to move colleagues from a filter that supported limited awareness to a filter that opened their eyes to gender inequity.
- Caring and Counseling Filter: This filter was found among women who worked to understand Denial and Anger in male colleagues, while at the same time holding ground for equitable treatment.
- Outsiders-Within Filter: This filter was more prevalent among people who consciously avoided belonging to the privileged administrative inner circle. They were viewed as individuals who understood and navigated gender issues and were usually engaged with and respected by their peers. The difference was that they when confronted with equity issues, these educators actively represented congruence between conscience and conduct in ways that positively influenced their peers and their organization. (Rusch & Marshall, 1996)

Locating Privilege in Leadership Programs and Departments

The study of gender filters included findings that led the conversation directly back to university classrooms. Interviewees described their graduate classroom experiences as filled with shock, anger, and frustration because their professors seemed not to have adequate knowledge of or value for equity and diversity. Students reported "no real discussions" that critiqued law and policy for equity perspectives and a persistent reification of research that ignored gender as a problematic. Informants viewed racial lines as uncrossable, and argued that equity related to gender and race should be a standard part of their educational experience. According to one student, the professoriate should:

> [not be] afraid to say and call the conversations what they are—the way that it is . . . if you can articulate a true situation—areas of gender in the workplace and not be emotional when you state the obvious facts, people will listen to you after a while. They'll recognize those kinds of things. It annoys me when we sit in educational settings and dance around the issues and talk out of context. (Rusch & Marshall, 1996)

Annoyance with the educational leadership professoriate continues to be documented. Researchers have accused educational leadership programs of perpetuating myopic views of equity and justice in schools, of developing minimal understanding of democratic practices, and of treating equity issues as "no problem" (Anderson, 1990; Grundy, 1993; Kempner, 1991). More recent charges include "a lack of coursework related to diversity (Herrity & Glasman, 1999); a lack of faculty commitment to the critical aspects of educating minority children (Parker & Hood, 1995, p. 171); a lack of skill in relating to the experiences of black children (Delpit, 1995); and a lack of understanding of the nuance of poverty and school failure" (Grogan, 1999, parentheses added). Rapp's (2001) recent study of women doctoral students revealed "codes of silence, lies, and secrets whereby doctoral students of underrepresented groups must deculturize, defeminize, and basically desensitize in order to 'successfully' complete their degrees and attain more powerful administrative positions" (p. 281). The lack of inclusion of gendered perspectives or gender issues in traditional coursework was verified by Shakeshaft (1989). McCarthy (1999) noted that "in general, faculty teach what they know" (p. 126).

Echoing Dewey's notions of the dialectical society, Björk and Ginsberg (1995) went so far as to compare the failure to educate aspiring administrators for diverse populations as tantamount to failing the nation's children. Evidence of the failure came in a recent nationwide study of principals who verified that equity and diversity were not primary issues for them. "Few principals made reference to equity as a vexing problem, whether for students, for teachers or for administrators. Race was rarely discussed, and only one individual was open about sex discrimination in her workplace" (Rusch, 1999, p. 42). At the same time, numerous studies report that school boards still see women as unqualified to lead a school district (Glass, 2000; Logan, 1999).

EXPOSING PRIVILEGE IN PROGRAMS, DEPARTMENTS, AND CLASSROOMS

After a decade of research and study on my line of fault, it was time to look inward. Had the world of school administration changed? After a study of 15 UCEA department chairs, Logan (1999) concluded recently that "it is time for educational administration departments to reassess, adjust, and activate gender equity strategies" (p. 7). In an effort to investigate the nature of the adjusted discourse in school administration, I recently completed a study which asked professors at 61 doctoral degree granting institutions to evaluate program, departmental, and individual faculty actions and values for gender and race issues related to leadership. Respondents were also asked to identify supports and barriers, changes in the past five years, and examples of learning experiences that increased knowledge of equity and diversity.

Gender and Race Discourse among faculty

Educational leadership faculty (n = 114 educational administration faculty at 56 of 61 institutions) reported that the construction of an "inner eye" that purposefully attends to gender and race is focused primarily on program goals and individual classrooms. Respondents indicated that departmental and programmatic discourse on topics of gender and race is limited at best and when it does take place, the talk is frequently awkward and is experienced quite differently by women and men. In fact, women reported less clearly articulated program goals, less frequent faculty discussions, and less recruitment of a diverse student body. The most troublesome result was that a majority of the respondents did not perceive a curriculum infused with knowledge and experiences related to gender and race. Faculty also reported that curriculum was only "occasionally or seldom" evaluated for content related to gender and race. One of the few minority respondents wrote, "Most faculty either do not recognize the significance or are uncommitted to ensuring the significance is reflected in the dialogue about and structure of the program."

Faculty were asked to describe the frequency of department discussions on issues of gender and race as they relate to leadership education using descriptors of "often," "occasionally/seldom," and "never." In addition, faculty were asked to assess the

Table 2. Assessment of Faculty Talk about Race and Gender by Faculty Who Perceive Such Talk as Occurring *Often*

Perceived quality of faculty discourse	Women n = 15/52 (29%)	Men n = 35/61 (57%)
Open, thought provoking	67%	71%
Problem finding, problem solving	60%	57%
Uncomfortable, stilted	13%	6%
Contentious, personalized	13%	0%
Intellectual, but not practical	20%	11%
Involves most faculty	33%	40%
Involves a select few	20%	13%

quality of such discussions within their department (see table 2 and table 3). Data sorts by gender and specific response revealed that twice as many men as women experienced conversations about gender as occurring "often" and men generally perceived the dialogue as open, problem solving and involving most of the faculty. Women, on the other hand, had a different experience (table 2). It may be when a discourse has been silenced over time, any opening of the dialogue can be perceived as a major event to those who are less affected by the issue.

For almost half the faculty who responded to this inquiry, talk about gender and race related to leadership education occurred only "Occasionally or Seldom." Once again, the data suggested men and women were in the same, different conversation together (table 3). Compared with male respondents, less than half of the female respondents experienced the conversation as open and problem solving. Women perceived the conversation as more contentious, less practical, and more uncomfortable than their male counterparts.

Few experienced a discourse that involved everyone. One respondent observed,

There are "politically correct" conversations all the time—nonetheless, there is no real evidence that any attention is being directed to substantive issues. . . . Male faculty receives lots more support (symbolic and economic) than do females in the department. The one racial minority faculty is usual left on his own to make sense of things.

Table 3. Assessment of Faculty Talk about Race and Gender by Faculty Who Perceive such Talk as Occurring *Seldom/Occasionally*

Perceived quality of faculty discourse	Women n = 28/52 (54%)	Men n = 35/61 (41%)
Open, thought provoking	29%	52%
Problem finding, problem solving	29%	52%
Uncomfortable, stilted	32%	20%
Contentious, personalized	14%	12%
Intellectual, but not practical	21%	20%
Involves most faculty	10%	36%
Involves a select few	54%	40%

Gender and Race Discourse in Classrooms

The data implied that women faculty experienced far more classroom discussions about gender and race than their male counterparts. Once again, there were marked differences between the two groups, particularly in the percentage of women and men who reported discussions as occurring "often." Men in this group experience the nature of the dialogue as a productive, problem-solving discourse that involved more students. Women, on the other hand, reported having more conversations but experiencing less comfort, more contentiousness, and less involvement of the entire class. Comments described challenges similar to those described in faculty discussions. "Some are involved, while others feel guilty" or "we are starting to see a backlash of conservative students who are starting to speak out against our inclusion of such curriculum." Many respondents reported an increasingly diverse student body which, in turn, led to more discomfort in the classroom as students tried to cross racial and gendered boundaries. One professor noted,

> Actually there is tension, some good, some not so good, surrounding race. The white students and faculty feel bad and put in tough positions by some African American students in the classes who take tight racial lines. They also have a problem with the Latino perspective.

Barriers to Gender and Race Discourse

In all fairness, equity is not an easy subject. Talk about equity demands debate about emotional and value-laden issues such as privilege, meritocracy, affirmative action, gender, race, ethnicity, and sexuality. Over 19 pages of single-spaced comments revealed explanations, descriptions, frustrations, criticisms, and blunt labeling that coded into very clear and consistent categories. The emergent themes included perceived value for the discourse, the actual knowledge base to engage in the discourse, the emotional nature of the discourse, the bias of individuals as they engaged in a discourse, and the actual time available to actually have a discussion.

Value

One respondent spoke for many when he said, "There is more talk than substance to any claims made by our department with respect to diversity issues." Phrases such as: "lip-service," "not part of reward system," "in written mission, but not much apparent," "lack of willingness," and "simply is not discussed" were common remarks. Respondents often judged the values of individuals. "Diversity is not valued by our chair or the dean"; "Individual professors are not open-minded about equity"; "Some do not believe these issues are important or even relevant." One male professor said, "The lack of comfort is due to the importance faculty put on these issues. There are those who take it too seriously." Another male Caucasian professor wrote, "Sorry about this, but our men don't talk or behave as if they value it and derail or absent themselves from discussion. We can't get to the tough stuff."

Emotions

Discourse about gender and race is an emotional subject. Another prevalent set of comments revealed the fear of saying incorrect or offensive things, the discomfort experienced when the conversation became awkward, and the challenges of conflict within the faculty group. Emotional words jumped off the pages of the instruments. Remarks included "uncomfortableness between the races," "anger and whites are quiet," "victimology and personal attacks," "bitter divisions," "aggressive behavior on the part of individuals." Reference to "political correctness" came primarily from white male professors in the upper age categories. One said, "There is an obsession with current expectations of Political Correctness and related hypocrisy." Another observed, "Minority sensitivity is the biggest barrier. Another is the institutional bias toward politically correct policies." A unique insight came from one female Caucasian assistant professor:

> Politically correct speech actually dampens honest thought-provoking discussions. I have lived in a multicultural relationship for 30+ years. My husband, a person of color, can speak out on this issue in public. I cannot because I am of Eurasian-American [sic] heritage. How sad that we have come to this defacto gag rule. In order to grow we must talk. Yet, I cannot speak freely in public.

A minority respondent within this specific group was more specific:

> People are afraid of participants making the racial issue personal and afraid that the discussion may get out of hand, hurting rather than helping. Also, people on the right side of the issue don't want to do anything in the real world as far as possible.

The sense that a discussion would get out of hand was very prominent in this set of comments. The "fear of saying something stupid," or "people don't want to look stupid and they are afraid of offending others and creating a conflictual situation," and "people are so worried about hurting other people that they are not sharing in discussions or asking questions."

Knowledge Base

The lack of sharing in discussions and asking questions was also attributed to a lack of knowledge about the subjects. Responses to questions about attendance at conferences and seminars that focused on topics of gender and race related to leadership suggested that women and men in educational leadership faculties seldom take advantage of or have value for learning opportunities that might enhance their ability to participate in the dialogue. Comments were very specific about faculty and student constituents. Some indicated as one respondent wrote, "Ed. Admin faculty have limited knowledge about diversity." Another noted "suburban educators' ignorance of urban school settings or inequities in school resources." Many more comments mirrored the view of one female associate, "Superficial understanding and interest in diversity issues." One female assistant professor suggested the biggest barrier was a "misrecognition that race/gender are no longer an issue."

Bias/Privilege

Most expressions of bias were related to loss of privilege of position or perspective. Comments ranged from: "There is too much attention on hiring and retention, which makes everyone paranoid" to "Narrow perspectives—i.e. females thinking only of gender issues or Native Americans willing only to examine NA issues, some faculty's tendency to use class as a bloody pulpit." One male Caucasian professor stated:

> As long as we see ourselves as different, we will treat each other as such. People should be judged on the basis of character, skills, attitudes, and knowledge, not on the basis of something they can't control. Special emphasis on "cultural awareness" is silly and counterproductive.

An opposite viewpoint was expressed by a female Caucasian associate professor:

> [A barrier is] the power structure within the discipline. Those in privileged positions— no matter how well intended—are not likely to willingly make changes that result in the loss of privilege. Equally important—perhaps—is that most white men have no "felt understanding" of what it is like to be "different," "the other." They don't understand that the world is normed by and for them.

Supports for Gender and Race Discourse

Professors reported that the addition of women and people of color to their faculties was the clearest indicator of a commitment to diversity. Recruiting and hiring practices were described as much more diverse and equitable than in the past. One respondent noting "the employment of women, Native Americans, and faculty of color," added, "many of these new faculty do their research and writing in these areas." Respondents reported retirements of older, entrenched faculty, often adding a follow-up notation similar to one: "we hired 3 minority faculty to replace Caucasians." Several respondents reported that increasingly diverse institutional leadership was a factor, and some also indicated that women were now the dominant group in their departments. The data included encouraging signs that equity issues were being infused into programs and many respondents indicated that classroom talk was much more prevalent since women and people of color had been hired. However, there were an abundance of comments indicating that equity work was being assigned to specific faculty who, most often were new, female, and/or non-white. Numerous comments indicated a tacit expectation that the new faculty held primary responsibility for race and gender topics and issues. One said, "Gender issues are definitely left up to the women in the department." Another noted, "Only faculty from ethnic minorities believe this is crucial and actually do it."

The data highlighted a few institutions where all responding faculty perceived an active discourse; their responses provided insights into supports for equity dialogues. Faculty wrote about diversity within the context, "the multicultural nature of our city," diversity within the faculty, diversity of the student body, and a commitment to the dialogue. "We have a diverse faculty. Whites are in the minority as students and faculty." Multiple comments within this group addressed faculty commitment and an open atmosphere. "We talk about race a lot," noted one respondent. "We have a shared commitment," noted another. One individual referred to the centrality to a strategic mission, adding, "We are particularly focused on equity, access, and quality outcomes for all." Quite a number of respondents within this group indicated in comments that diversity and equity issues were actually university or college-level strategic directives that, in turn, framed the department policies and practices. A few indicated that the strategic directives and concomitant policies were actually affecting course designs and course materials. Administrators such as presidents, deans, and directors of graduate studies were credited with "providing an open atmosphere for discussion." In the case of several reporting institutions, the university had committed resources for programs and faculty development related to diversity and equity issues.

WHAT IS THE LEADERSHIP WORK REQUIRED
TO CHANGE THE WORLD OF SCHOOL LEADERS?

The writing of this chapter has been a challenging and satisfying intellectual exercise. Fortunately for the readers who have indulged me this far, my teacher/mentor always insisted that I focus on the "so what?" question. Why is this shoe important? In what way does the "line of fault" (Smith, 1987, 1990), "the construction of the inner eye" (Anderson, 1990), embedded privilege (Gosetti & Rusch, 1995), gender filters (Marshall & Rusch, 1995; Rusch & Marshall, 1995), and faculty discourse (Rusch & Harris, 2001) support or inhibit changing the face of educational leadership in the world?

I conclude this chapter with an attempt to refocus the problem of the big brown shoe. I propose that we reframe the discursive practices in ways that might make educational administration a more attractive and inclusive profession. Once again, I ask readers to envision a mobius strip as a metaphor for the unconscious perpetuation of an unchanging practice. In his discussion of the relationship between discourse and practice, Foucault (Lemert & Gillan, 1982) talked about a body of anonymous rules, that he called the "rules of right," which govern what sort of talk can be taken seriously and thus, limit power. As I review the journey I've taken, the rules of right that appear to govern educational administration, the limits individuals still experience in this profession, and the frustrating inequities experienced by our children in schools make Foucault's perspective seem particularly appropriate. He observed, "people know what they do; they frequently know why they do what they do; but what they don't know is what, what they do, does" (Foucault in personal communication to Dreyfus & Rabinow, 1983, p. 187). As Smith (1990) observed, once a perspective gains power and privilege in a discursive world and that world is manifested in practice over time, it is very hard to problematize the practice. What I propose is to create some new "rules of right" and I challenge the profession, at all levels, to think about leadership work that might actually change the world of school administration.

Reframing the Discourse of Leadership

The privilege to select the images and symbols of the norms is a critical factor in sustaining bias. Privilege is also the silencer that, according to McIntosh (1988), limits thought about equity by making it a taboo subject. Inequity can be generated in multiple ways within the academy. In the case of educational leadership classrooms, professors have the power and the privilege to reproduce and reify whatever discourse they choose in classrooms and in research. After her review of similar issues in teacher education classrooms, Cochran-Smith (1995) concluded that one of the

> most potent informal influence[s] on prospective teachers [is] the ways that teacher educators talk about "others," include or ignore multiple perspectives. . . . What we show them about the "norm" or the taken-for-granted point of view is a powerful subtext about teaching and about the boundaries of race and teaching in schools and larger educational systems. (p. 522)

The task is no less potent in a school administration classroom, but the talk about and study of equity must become an essential part of the norm. Currently the data support Grogan's contention, that "research on women's lived experience as leaders is not encouraged" (1999, p. 523). Women and men are actually discouraged by professors from pursuing studies using feminist perspectives or concentrating on issues of equity (Rapp, 2001). According to McGee Banks (2000), "Little is known about the employment experiences of women and people of color within the dynamics of race and gender in schools" (p. 245). Her review of dissertations that explored the intersections of race and gender found studies with narrow foci, limited scope, and little attention to the interactions of variables. Once again, privilege is a powerful determiner of what counts as important knowledge. By limiting studies that would advance our knowledge and understanding of these complex issues, professors of school administration may be unconsciously perpetuating a "landscape in which women are strangers" (Smith, 1990, p. 52).

The silencing of research on leadership issues related to women, people of color, and gender issues translates to silence in our classrooms and lack of emphases in our programs. The external effects of this silence creates institutional cultures that, in turn, "submerge talk about those things that are potentially most controversial and potentially most important" (Darling-Hammond, 1992, p. 23). Honest talk is the only successful way to break defensive routines, according to Argyris (1993). He promotes talk-based valid information and a persistent practice of reflective inquiry as strategies that break the silence, and lead to honest communication and feedback about issues people would prefer not to discuss. Honest talk among faculty and between faculty and students is critical if we are to "stop dancing around the issues" and "behaving like the issues don't exist" (Rusch & Marshall, 1996).

The perpetuation of a narrow discursive practice is not limited to school administration classrooms. The privilege to determine perspective also resides in the publications of the profession. If we want to modify access to the profession, I believe we must examine how some persistent messages "construct the inner eye" of potential and practicing school administrators. One example is the emphasis on coaching as an access point to administration. According to Glass (2000), "athletic coaching and assignments such as band directorships often provide teachers an opportunity to demonstrate skills in leadership, management, and an ability to work with community members" (p. 29). Glass also points out that these assignments are primarily for high school and middle school teachers, thus increasing their access points to administration. Without denying the leadership experience inherent in coaching and band director roles, I suggest that the work of classroom teaching requires equivalent, or in some cases, more leadership, management, and ability to work with community members. The notion that coaching provides a unique leadership opportunity is one example of how a perspective gains power and privilege in a discursive world and comes to be viewed as a norm. That norm, in turn, has led to a pool of aspirants who are predominately male. Reframing the talk, both in practice and in research, can recenter the norm.

Another example of a flawed, but well-entrenched, perspective is that secondary administrative experience is the best pathway to the superintendency. Murphy (2001) points out that effective leadership today requires "caring and humanistic concerns," the traditional domain of elementary and middle school educators. Still another is that elementary and central office curriculum administrators have limited experience with personnel and budget. In truth, I know of few line or staff positions where fiscal management is not a critical skill. I would also suggest that personnel management in a central office position is more dependent on collaboration, coordination, and relationship building—skills essential to the political aspects of leading school communities. While there is always an element of truth in these oft-stated perspectives, we must begin to ask how we are perpetuating a practice through our discourse that limits the landscape for women and men.

Reframing the Profession

The actual landscape of school administration, I believe, is a major factor in the growth of the big shoe problem, and I further contend that to address that problem, the entire profession must work to make visible "what, what we do, does" (Foucault in personal communication to Dreyfus & Rabinow, 1983, p. 187). There is an extraordinary amount of information that describes the landscape of school administration as a less-than-desirable professional aspiration. Onerous time demands are noted by many. Pounder and Merrill (2001) described "such extensive workdays that it is difficult for them to have a life beyond their work" (p. 19). According to AASA's Paul Houston (2000), "school leaders find the jobs leave little time or energy for personal lives" (p. 1). A 50- to 80-hour workweek is not uncommon for today's school administrator, much of it in evening hours. A recent survey of New Jersey teachers showed few interested candidates for the principalship. "Too many hours that adversely affect the quality of life" was the most common reason given for a lack of interest (Stein, 2002, p. 1). While some have proposed job redesigns that would minimize the unattractive elements of the job (Pounder & Merrill, 2001), I suggest that the discourse must take a much more dramatic turn. Essentially, I believe that our current discourse perpetuates an embedded landscape of a profession with roles, institutional structures, values, and traditions that support a practice more related to life in the middle of the last century. Bem (1993), who looked at gender polarization, argued that the historical construction of management at the turn of the 20th century required individuals (men) who were distanced from roles of intimate caregivers. In her view, it was predictable that men would construct institutions based on privilege and separation. The unintended consequences are administrative roles that are disconnected from caregiving, are dependent on separation from family, and are embedded with a societal expectation that school leaders will avoid both. The result is a big shoe problem.

We currently live in a world of dramatically revised gender relations. Men no longer distance themselves from caregiver roles or expect to be separate from their family life. A federal Family Relief Act supports time off work for women and men who need to give care to a newborn or an elderly relative. Dual career couples are a fact of life, in large part because of a successful feminist movement, a changing economy, and modified cultural standards for a good living. Magazines and journals identify family-friendly companies, and family members connected to our schools seek jobs in companies that promote family friendly policies. Parents campaign for alternative teacher conference times, breakfast programs, extended day care programs, and more before and after school programs in order to expand their own experience of a "family-friendly environment." The missing part of the conversation is about the life of the tradition bound school administrator who must manage all these family friendly elements at the expense of his or her own personal well being or time with her or his family. At what point will members of this profession initiate an honest discourse with school communities to restructure an outdated work model for school administrators, rather than preparing administrators to survive increasing complex school communities?

Grogan (1999) is one of few researchers who highlights the contradictions between the traditional organizational structures and the rhetoric of "family oriented schools." She notes, "Family concerns must remain in the background and must not be seen to interfere with the business at hand." She also makes a strong case for "questioning approved administrative practices to discover who they benefit and who they limit," arguing for a "critical inquiry into educational administration, into the sources of knowledge and claims to authority." Without that Grogan predicts that "any efforts to transform the field will fail" (p. 525).

CHALLENGES TO CHANGING THE WORLD

I still aspire to the disappearance of that line of fault, to a transformed profession for women and men. Sadly, many provocative questions remain after my decade-long journey. I still wonder who will foster a discourse that asks the public to re-examine the structures embedded in the institution we call school? Who will challenge a deeply embedded culture of leading based on 20th-century norms? Who will hold up the mirror to the lives of school administrators and help community members understand the sacrifices of the position? Who will help our governing bodies and policymakers understand that the administrative roles they are trying to fill no longer match the majority of lives in the community? What actions will lead to a transformed social structure for men and women aspiring to and participating in the leadership of American schools?

Leadership, according to Foster (1986), calls for "transformative practices which change social structures and forms of community." He challenges us to debate and discuss the direction of the society exercising leadership "as a form of communal life concerned with how lives should be lived, not how they should be controlled" (p. 57). If the world of school administration is to change, I conclude that our profession, at all levels, must engage in a leadership committed to transforming the views of a community about the world and work of school leaders. If professors and practitioners make a commitment to rethink what we say and do, "Rethinking may rejuvenate commitment to conventional discourse-practices or it may lead to something quite different" (Cherryholmes, 1988, p. 153). Perhaps if we collectively begin to work on the "something quite different," the big shortage will disappear and who fills the shoes will reflect equitable access. Perhaps, if we collectively work to construct new inner eyes and challenge ourselves to rethink our embedded privilege, the world of school administration will begin to reflect our diverse community. Then, and then only, will this profession reflect change.

REFERENCES

Acker, J. (1992). Gendering organizational theory. In A. Mills & P. Tancred (Eds.), *Gendering organizational analysis.* pp. 249–260. Newbury Park, CA: Sage.

Anderson, G. L. (1990). Toward a critical constructivist approach to school administration: Invisibility, legitimization, and the study of non-events. *Educational Administration Quarterly, 6*(1), 38–59.

Argyris, C. (1993). *Knowledge for action: A guide to overcoming barriers to organizational change.* San Francisco: Jossey-Bass.

Bem, S. L. (1993). *The lenses of gender.* New Haven, CT: Yale University Press.

Björk, L., & Ginsberg, R. (1995). Principles of reform and reforming principal training: A theoretical perspective. *Educational Administration Quarterly, 31*(1), 11–37.

Bourdieu, P., & Passeron, J. C. (1977). *Reproduction in education, society and culture* (R. Nice, Trans.). London: Sage.

Cherryholmes, C. (1988). *Power and criticism.* New York: Teachers College Press.

Cochran-Smith, M. (1995). Color blindness and basket making are not the answers: Confront the dilemmas of race, culture, and language diversity in teacher education. *American Educational Research Journal, 32*(3), 493–522.

Darling-Hammond, L. (1992). Reframing the school reform agenda. *The School Administrator, 4*(9), 22–27.

Delpit, L. (1995). *Other people's children: Cultural conflict in the classroom.* New York: The New Press.

Dewey, J. (1916). *Democracy and education.* New York: Macmillan.

Dreyfus, H., & Rabinow, P. (1983). *Michel Foucault: Beyond structuralism and hermeneutics.* Chicago: The University of Chicago Press.

Ferguson, K. (1984). *The feminist case against bureaucracy.* Philadelphia: Temple University Press.

Foster, W. (1986). *Paradigms and promises.* Buffalo: Prometheus Books.

Glass, T. (2000). Where are all the women superintendents? *School Administrator, 6*(57), 28–32.

Gosetti, P. P., & Rusch, E. A. (1993). *The lens of privilege: Reexamining educational leadership.* Paper presented at the annual meeting of the American Educational Research Association, Atlanta, GA.

Gosetti, P. P., & Rusch, E. (1995). Re-examining educational leadership: Challenging assumptions. In D. Dunlap & P. Schmuck (Eds.), *Women leading in education* (pp. 11–35). New York: State University of New York Press.

Grogan, M. (1999). Equity/quality issues of gender, race, and class. *Educational Administration Quarterly, 35*(4), 518–536.

Grundy, S. (1993). Educational leadership as emancipatory practice. In J. Blackmore & J. Kenway (Eds.), *Gender matters in educational administration and policy* (pp. 165–180). London: Falmer.

Herrity, V., & Glasman, N. (1999). Training administrators for culturally and linguistically diverse school populations: Opinions of expert practitioners. *Journal of School Leadership, 9*(3), 235–253.

Houston, P. (2000). Not a great job, but a wonderful calling. *School Administrator*, Executive Perspective. Retrieved from www.execperspec_2000_06.htm

Kempner, K. (1991). Getting into the castle of educational administration. *Peabody Journal of Education*, 104–123.

Lemert, C., & Gillan, G. (1982). *Michel Foucault: Social theory as transgression.* New York: Columbia University Press.

Lenski, G. (1966). *Power and privilege: A theory of social stratification.* New York: McGraw-Hill.

Logan, J. (1999). An educational leadership challenge: Refocusing gender equity strategies. *The AASA Professor, 22*(4), 1–8.

McCarthy, M. (1999). The evolution of educational leadership preparation programs. In J. Murphy & K. S. Louis (Eds.), *Handbook of research on educational administration* (2nd ed., pp. 119–139). San Francisco: Jossey-Bass.

McGee Banks, C. (2000). Gender and race as factors in educational leadership and administration. In *The Jossey-Bass reader on educational leadership* (pp. 217–256). San Francisco: Jossey-Bass.

McIntosh, P. M. (1989). Curricular re-vision: The new knowledge for a new age. In C. S. Pearson, D. L. Shavlik, & J. G. Touchton (Eds.), *Educating the majority: Women challenge tradition in higher education* (pp. 400–412). New York: American Council on Education.

Marshall, C., & Rusch, E. (1995). Gender filters in the deputy principalship. In B. Limerick & B. Lingard (Eds.), *Gender and changing educational management* (pp. 79–94). Rydalmere, NSW: Hodder Education.

Murphy, J. (2001). The changing face of leadership preparation. *School Administrator, 10*(58), 14–17.

Parker, L., & Hood, S. (1995). Minority students vs. minority faculty and administrators in teacher education: Perspectives on the class of cultures. *The Urban Review, 27*(2), 159–174.

Pounder, D., & Merrill, R. (2001). Lost luster. *School Administrator, 10*(58), 18–22.

Rapp, D. (2001). The implications of raising one's voice in educational leadership doctoral programs: Women's stories of fear, retaliation, and silence. *Journal of School Leadership, 11*(4), 279–295.

Rusch, E. (1990). *The white spaces of leadership.* Unpublished manuscript. University of Oregon.

Rusch, E. (1999). The principal as a piñata. In F. Kochen, B. Jackson, & D. Duke (Eds.), *A thousand voices from the firing line: A study of educational leaders, their jobs, their preparation, and the problems they face* (pp. 29–43). Columbia, MO: University Council for Educational Administration.

Rusch E., & Gosetti, P. P. (1994). *Diversity and equity in educational leadership: Missing in theory & in action.* Presented at the annual meeting of American Educational Research Association. New Orleans, LA.

Rusch, E., & Harris, K. (2001). *Gender, race, and leadership: Faculty perceptions of a complex discourse.* Paper presented at the Fall Conference of the University Council for Educational Administration, Cincinnati, OH.

Rusch, E., & Marshall, C. (1995). *Gender filters at work in the administrative culture.* Paper presented at the annual meeting of the American Educational Research Association, San Francisco.

Rusch, E., & Marshall, C. (1996). *Troubled educational administration.* Interactive paper symposium presented at annual meeting of the American Educational Research Association, New York.

Shakeshaft, C. (1989). *Women in educational administration.* Newbury Park, CA: Corwin Press.

Smith, D. (1987). *The everyday world as problematic: A feminist sociology.* Boston: Northeastern University Press.

Smith, D. (1990). *The conceptual practices of power.* Boston: Northeastern University Press.

Stein, C. (2002). *The search is on for school principals.* Retrieved from www.njsba.org

Tallerico, M., & Tingley, S. (2001). The leadership mismatch: An alternative view. *School Administrator, 10*(58), 23–27.

Van Nostrand, C. H. (1993). *Gender responsible leadership.* Newbury Park, CA: Sage.

Leadership as a Form of Learning: Implications for Theory and Practice

Linda Lambert

Leadership, both in its definition and practice, has been an elusive idea. For hundreds of years we have been fascinated with leadership, yet we still have few shared understandings about what it is. We are often preoccupied with the "heroes" of leadership—those charismatic creatures who have dominated the landscape—both as powerful models of values in action and as anti-heroes. We seem to understand that our failures as a global community to address the confounding questions of civilization—poverty, illiteracy, conflict, inequity—are failures of leadership. Our homes and schools are the birthplaces of these problems. We have not educated children to be broadly literate, to access their places in the world economy, to mediate conflict, and to value and practice equity. Yet we keep looking for those answers in the same places through the same archaic lens.

I would suggest that we have been looking in the wrong places—and using the wrong lens. These lenses have familiar signposts, similar assumptions. Timeworn assumptions have persuaded us that leader and leadership are one and the same. Therefore, if only we can find the right qualities and characteristics of the leader, we will have found the answer to the problems of leadership. When we assume that leadership lies in an individual, we look for the dispositions, skills, understandings, and personality features that will make this person effective. Then, of course, goes the legend, if we teach these skills and characteristics to others, they too will be effective. This premise drove the effectiveness movement; it is not an adequate lens for today's world.

Familiar paths are seductive. They coax us into moderate novelty, to tinkering with the present, to a failure to step back and think outside the box. We must depart from the familiar if we are to redefine leadership for the new millennium. Such a definition must look beyond the individual, beyond a discrete set of skills, and into

Linda Lambert, Professor Emeritus, California State University, Hayward the very context and culture in which leaders find themselves. I define leadership as *the reciprocal learning processes that engage community participants in the creation and enactment of a shared purpose.*

The most vital aspect of this definition lies in its relationship to learning. It is not new to connect leadership to the creation of a learning organization; it is not new to connect leadership to the transformation of followers; it is not new to envision a community of leaders. These movements have paved the way for some new assumptions about leadership. I would suggest that those assumptions might include:

1. Leadership may be understood as the reciprocal learning processes that involve participants in a community to create and enact a shared purpose.
2. Everyone has the right, responsibility, and capability to be a leader.
3. The adult learning environment in the school and district is the most critical factor in evoking leadership actions.
4. Within that environment, opportunities for skillful participation top the list of priorities.
5. How we define leadership frames how people will participate.
6. Educators yearn to be more fully who they are—purposeful, professional human beings. Leadership is an essential aspect of a professional life.
7. Educators are purposeful . . . leading realizes purpose.

CONSTRUCTING THE RELATIONSHIP
BETWEEN LEADERSHIP AND LEARNING

We have struggled with an acknowledgment of the relationship between leading and learning for some time. Leading is often now seen as guiding, directing, or facilitating the learning process. I would advocate that we need to go a step further and see *leading as a form of learning.* How would this alter our previous understandings? If leading is a form of learning, it is not so much a separate causal factor, but the entity itself. Leading *is learning*, a form of learning together purposefully in community. Leading as a form of learning transforms both leading and learning. Leading learns itself through purposeful enactment of the organization's values and mission.

A closer examination of this premise might begin with what we now know about the nature of learning. Constructivist understandings have enabled us to apply these features to learning together in schools (Lambert, 1995, 1998, 2002; Lamert, Collay, Dietz, Kent, & Richert, 1997). We acknowledge that humans bring to the process of learning personal schemas that have been formed by prior experiences, beliefs, values, sociocultural histories, and perceptions. When new experiences are encountered and mediated by reflection, inquiry, and social interaction, meaning and knowledge are constructed. Learning takes place, as does adult development. When actively engaged in reflective dialogue, adults become more complex in their thinking about the world, more tolerant of diverse perspectives, more flexible and open toward new experiences. Personal and professional learning require an interactive professional culture if adults are to engage with one another in the processes of growth and development.

Such learning in schools or other organizations might involve what I refer to as the "reciprocal processes of community learning":

1. *Surface the values, assumptions, experiences and prior knowledge* of a school staff. This can be powerfully evoked through stories, dialogue, reflective writing. Howard Gardner describes leadership as:

> a process that occurs within the minds of individuals who live in a culture—a process that entails the capacities to create stories, to understand and evaluate these stories, and to appreciate the struggle among stories. Ultimately, certain kinds of stories will typically become predominant—in particular, kinds of stories that provide an adequate and timely sense of identity for individuals who live within a community or institution. (1995, p. 22, cited in Sergiovanni, 2000, p. 169)

For Gardner, the stories that we tell epitomize the leadership journey. By surfacing these stories we can infer values, beliefs, and previous practices that inform our current world. If we leave out this learning step in our work together, we are doomed to relive the unedited stories relentlessly.

2. *Inquire into practice* by posing questions of practice and gathering observations, evidence and data, and new theories and strategies. The inquisitive stance enables us to hold new evidence in juxtaposition to prior assumptions in order to invite cognitive dissonance. Such inquiry evidence might come from action research, observations, examination of student work and other data regarding student performance, and the existing research literature. Inquiry constitutes our discovery process in the world around us. It is what challenges prior beliefs and assumptions. Without inquiry, prior bias and behaviors are doomed to repeat themselves endlessly without adequate regard for progress.

3. *Make sense of the dissonance* by comparing current assumptions, beliefs, and experiences with new evidence through dialogue. (What does the pattern of results mean?) Dialogue is the most powerful form of group interaction, since we seek to listen and to understand. The process of constructing meaning requires an openness of mind so that new patterns can form in our schema. Other forms of conversation, like discussion, can actually get in the way of meaning by prematurely solidifying interpretations of dissonance and declaring them as truth. New patterns are the result of the divergent consideration of possibilities.

4. *Frame actions that embody new behaviors and purposeful intentions*—the most practical aspect of the reciprocal processes. Such activities may include establishing new criteria, planning different approaches, identifying emerging goals and outcomes, implementing new actions, evaluating progress, and redesigning or reframing the actions in response to the information generated by the process. These are the specific actions that emerge from the conversations. These are the actions to be enacted.

Let us assume that the constructivist process described above *is* leading—suggesting that as we learn we alter how we think, and strengthen our commitments to a community of learners as well as to the results of our learning. Such learning is engaging, synergistic, directional, and creates momentum toward shared purpose. These endeavors can be a risky, vulnerable venture. It occurs in a community of practice.

THE NATURE OF SCHOOL AS COMMUNITY

"Community" is a term that has entered our school vocabulary without clear meaning. It has almost come to mean any gathering of people in a school or other social setting. But community asks more of us than gathering together. Community assumes focus on a shared purpose; community assumes mutual regard and caring; community insists on integrity and truthfulness. Therefore, to elevate our work in schools to that of community takes the energies and attention of its members to something greater than themselves.

Two perspectives on community serve us well: an ecological community (ecosystem) and a community based on moral virtue. These perspectives interact in dynamic ways that draw the systemic qualities from ecology and moral virtue from the communitarian view (Etzioni, 1998).

The first perspective asks us to understand that communities are ecosystems. To understand that leadership is embedded in the patterns of relationships and meaning making in a social organization is to notice that everything is connected. The system is dynamic, interdependent in its learning processes. The learning of each participant is dependent upon the learning of the other and of the whole. This ecological portrait can change our schemas about social systems.

Fritjof Capra, author of *The Tao of Physics* (1975), *The Turning Point* (1982), and *The Web of Life* (1996), has given his attention during most of the past decade to the application of the principles of ecology to work with whole-school cultural change and social transformation. This work is called "ecoliteracy," meaning literacy in environmental principles and practices; by "ecology" is meant the guiding principles informing the development of all organisms and systems. In translating the concepts of ecology into social systems, Capra synthesized the tradition of Gregory Bateson in psychology and anthropology; Bruce Joyce, Elliott Eisner, John Goodlad, and C. A. Bowers in education; Robert Kegan in psychology; Robert Bellah in philosophy and political science; and Theodore Roszak in political and environmental philosophy. The principles of ecology are described by Capra (1996) as involving interdependence, sustainability, ecological cycles, energy flow, partnership, flexibility, diversity, and co-evolution.

A composite narrative of a social ecological community might be interpreted in this way: A community is an interconnected and complex web of reciprocal relationships sustained and informed by purposeful actions. Complexity is manifest in the diversity of the system—the more diverse, the more rich and complex. Such communities are flexible and open to information provided through feedback spirals, as well as unexpected fluctuations and surprises that contain possibilities. The co-evolution, or shared growth, of the participants in this community is propelled by, and emerges from, the joint construction of meaning and knowledge and involves continual creation and adaptation (Lambert et al., 1997).

The work of the new communitarians focuses primary concern on "the balance between social forces and the person, between community and autonomy, between the common good and liberty, between individual rights and social responsibilities" (Etzioni, 1998, p. x). These communities, Etzioni contends, are webs of social relations that encompass shared meanings and shared values. Unlike biological systems (that are fundamentally value-free), these social communities are deeply moral, driven by shared values that encompass reciprocity, equity, and democracy. Educational communities of this character concurrently attend to the professional development needs of the individual, to the professional culture of the group, to the engagement with the broader community, and to the outcomes of the students. Such educational communities have coherence, a wholeness and an integration that characterize sense-making.

When we learn and act together in a moral, ecological community toward a shared purpose, we are creating an environment in which we feel congruence and worth. A fundamental belief in this view of leadership is that all of us are capable of leadership, all are capable of this form of learning. Leading is a form of learning in community.

CREATION AND ENACTMENT OF SHARED PURPOSE

It is the creation and enactment of a shared purpose that extends learning in community into leadership. Learning substantiates and evokes purpose; learning together establishes the purpose as shared.

Purpose arises from values, experience, constructed meaning, and passion. Another way to understand this relationship is that meaning is attributed to the integrated field of values and experience and propelled into action by passion (Lambert, 1983). Shared purpose creates "synergy" or the cooperative interaction of peoples and groups that create an enhanced combined effect greater than the sum of the individual effects. When school staff members surface and explore their values in dialogue, participants are energized by the process. Asking what children would be thinking and producing if these values were realized can ground participants in the dailiness of practice. This is how purpose—often manifest as vision and mission statements—is kept vibrant and sustainable.

The mutual search for purpose and complementary action performed in a learning community for students and adults contributes to the growth and development of all participants. If participants are constructing their own meanings and knowledge, how can we be assured that the shared purpose of schooling will entail such a moral commitment? This confidence arises from a faith in ecological communities as enabling their participants to coevolve morally. As this coevolution takes place, caring, equity, and justice tend to surface as guiding values (Gilligan, 1982; Kohlberg, 1976). Poplin and Weeres (1993) reported in the work *Voices from the Inside* that the process created shared meanings that led to larger moral purpose—teachers reconnected with their reasons for going into teaching.

There resides in each of us a deep yearning for community and purpose. When individuals share a common experience of growth in an educational community, they experience an increased responsibility for others. We become committed to a cause greater than ourselves. Within the context of these lived experiences, diversity opens up possibilities, helping us to see the multiple perspectives and world views of others and to transcend the faultlines of difference. This faith in the transformational capacities of communities continues to be echoed by others in Toronto schools; Seattle, Kansas City, and Winnipeg high schools; the National Writing Project network; and leadership preparation programs built around learning communities (Grossman, Wineburg, & Woolworth, 2000; Lambert et. al., 1997; Lieberman & Wood, 2001; Norris, Barnett, Basom, & Yerkes, 2002).

The enactment of purpose suggests movement, direction, momentum, an energy flow derived from meaning and constructed knowledge. "Enactment" may be defined as a set of reciprocal interactions among participants within the skillful performance of leadership tasks situated within a school or organization. It is what people learn and do together, rather than what any particular leader does alone, that creates the fabric of the school. Spillane and Halverson (1999) refer to the performance of these mutual tasks in context as "task enactment," a useful expression for understanding the interaction patterns that are at the heart of the leadership capacity of a school.

Leadership as a form of learning suggests that learning is a constructivist, purposeful, and communal experience. Enactment is the public evidence that such learning is and has been occurring. When schools surface their working assumptions and experiences, discover and try new approaches for student learning, seek evidence of effectiveness, reflect upon this progress, and refine its implementation— leadership as a form of learning has been realized. Leadership realizes purpose.

LEADERSHIP AND LEADERSHIP CAPACITY

"Leadership Capacity" means broad-based, skillful participation in the work of leadership (Lambert, 1998). The "work of leadership," as conceived in this chapter is a form of learning, or the work of attending to the learning of self, others, and the school as an organization. Leadership capacity is the organizational framework for sustainability. A school that can boast high leadership capacity has the structures, processes, and relationships in place to form a strong fabric or learning community, a fabric that can resist unraveling when a principal or key teacher leader leaves. These structures, processes, and relationships involve:

- The principal, teachers, as well as many parents and students are skillful leaders.
- Shared vision results in program coherence.
- Inquiry-based use of information informs decisions and practice.
- Roles and actions reflect broad involvement, collaboration, and collective responsibility.
- Reflective practice consistently leads to innovation.
- Student achievement is high or steadily improving.

School leaders who understand leading as learning and leadership capacity as the framework for improving and sustaining school improvement have learned to lead by performing a few vital understandings, skills, and behaviors.

IMPLICATIONS FOR SCHOOL LEADERS: WHAT DO LEADERS DO?

Let us take an individual case, the case of Jennifer, a four-year veteran at Belvedere Middle School. Jennifer became skillful in the work of leadership. She brought "a leadership perspective" to the task of learning to be a leader. Such a perspective requires an initial formulation of what is meant by leadership—in this case, the realization that leading is a form of learning with, contributing to, and influencing colleagues. Further, such a perspective means continually watching and "codifying" behaviors that she would classify as leading behaviors; for instance, noticing the questions that are asked and the effect of those questions, design features that are suggested and the intended outcome of those features, feedback that is given and the purpose and influence of such feedback. These observations are translated into understandings through the processes of reflection and dialogue. This is the stance of a learner with a leadership perspective.

How was it that Jennifer learned to be a leader? Jennifer watched intently as the principal and teacher leaders practiced leading. She participated in several modes of interaction—leadership team meetings and retreats, faculty meetings, study groups, an action research team. During this participation, she tried out her emerging skills, sometimes as facilitator, process observer, critical questioner, involved participant. Increasingly, it became a habit to design meetings thoughtfully and to reflect upon and debrief them afterwards. She found this to be very much like lesson planning. Her study group read and discussed *Building Leadership Capacity in Schools* (Lambert, 1998), followed by *The Adaptive School* (Garmston & Wellman, 2000), a sourcebook that includes detailed descriptions of the processes of leading and learning. Coaching became a regular feature of the school, both instructional and leadership coaching. Jennifer found coaching to be a mutual process (realizing that each time she was coached, she was coaching as well). Reflection was built into the life of the school through coaching, questioning, and journaling. She and others arranged for workshop sessions for the whole faculty, using constructivist approaches to inquiry and dialogue. In the fall of 2000, Jennifer entered the nearby university to seek formal preparation in educational leadership and secure an administrative credential. She found that the cohort arrangement at the university, the access to multiple sources of knowledge, and the deepening of theory underlying good practice accelerated her learning and moved her to decide that she would pursue a principalship (Lambert, in press).

Jennifer *gave attention to her learning* at Belvedere, meaning that she was alert to what others were doing and thinking, as well as what she was thinking and experiencing. The principal had drawn her attention to a leadership perspective and often coached her by asking what she was noticing and experiencing about her emerging role as a leader. Such attention is an essential way of thinking in what is now termed "job-embedded" professional development, or leadership task enactment. Learning occurs in the process of performing the work of leadership. She participated in experiences that called on her to think in new ways about working with colleagues: teaming, designing, facilitating, analyzing, and debriefing. She experienced coaching from a new perspective, one of mutuality and reciprocity—respecting that learning came from many directions. She studied new thinking in the study groups and in the university. These ideas were mediated with her current knowledge and made sense of in her ongoing dialogues, giving rise to new behaviors. She and her colleagues also recognized that some understandings and skills needed direct instruction because they were relatively new to the school and could be more efficiently learned through training. Reflection in, on, and about practice enabled her to weave these learnings into a new whole.

ACTS OF LEADERSHIP

Leaders like Jennifer understand leadership as a form of learning, and the manifestation of leadership as "acts of leadership." An act of leadership, as distinguished from role leadership, is the performance of actions (behaviors plus intention) that enable participants in a community to evoke potential within a trusting environment, to inquire into practice thereby reconstructing old assumptions, to focus on the construction of meaning, or to frame actions based on new behaviors and purposeful intention. Anyone in the school community can perform an act of leadership. Leadership is an inclusive field of learning processes in which leaders do their work.

Those who perform acts of leadership need:

- A sense of purpose and ethics, because honesty and trust are fundamental to relationships;
- Facilitation skills, because framing, deepening, and moving the conversations about teaching and learning are fundamental to constructing meaning;
- An understanding of constructivist learning for all humans;
- A deep understanding of change and transitions, because change is not what we thought it was;
- An understanding of context so that communities of memories can be continually drawn on and enriched;
- An intention to redistribute power and authority, for without such intention and action, none of us can lead; and
- A personal identity that allows for courage and risk, moderate ego needs, and a sense of possibilities.

These understandings, skills, and characteristics create the larger context in which school leaders perform their work. Table 1 describes the behaviors that school leaders need to understand, be able to do, and enable others to do in order to build leadership capacity. These behavior patterns assume that leadership is a form of learning; therefore, attention is given to the learning of self and others. In order to translate these beliefs and acts into the fabric of sustainable school improvement, school leaders need to understand, be able to do, and enable others to perform in ways that realize leading in a learning community. School leader understandings and

Table 1.   Competencies for School Leaders

School leaders need to understand, be able to do, and enable others to:

- Clarify their own values and engage others in forming and adhering to a shared vision about the role of schooling in society, student learning, and the community commitment.
- Design and implement multiple participation patterns and groups (e.g., study groups, leadership teams, action research teams, parent councils, student focus groups) so that all participants can be part of vibrant learning communities.
- Facilitate conversations and dialogue leading to shared vision and actions designed to implement and sustain the vision.
- Provide opportunities for others to learn and practice leadership skills—including modeling, coaching, involvement, and conversations.
- Invite others into leadership roles and actions.
- Engage educators, students, parents and community members ("participants") in a "cycle of learning" that involves reflection, dialogue, inquiry, construction of meaning, and action.
- Engage participants in authentic and shared decision-making processes.
- Pose questions that focus attention on what is of most importance (the vision of student, adult, and community learning).
- Share, develop, and invite open information. Create information systems that continually cycle throughout the school community.
- Facilitate communication among participants about the shared vision of the school, continually reinterpreting, deepening, and creating indicators of progress toward that vision.
- Seek to broaden and reinforce roles that involve multiple levels of responsibility: classroom, school community, district, profession, and society.
- Create and facilitate patterns of relationships that attend to reciprocal learning. Refuse to be the only "clearinghouse" for ideas, conflict, and communications.
- Promote collective responsibility (internal accountability), involving others in determining criteria for success and taking responsibility for progress—or lack of progress—toward success for all children, particular those who are underperforming.
- Encourage and support individual and group initiative, innovation, and entrepreneurship by providing multiple resources (time, monies, personnel, and outside networks).
- Work with the school community and district to establish standards and benchmarks that challenge all students, yet provide the flexibility for unique interests and talents to arise.
- Design professional development opportunities directed toward state-of-the-art instruction, assessment, and guidance for students.
- Establish assessment programs that involve formative and summative student and parent reflection on products and performance.
- Ensure that guidance programs address resiliency needs in students: the presence of caring adults; problem-solving and goal-setting skills; social networking; opportunities for participation and contribution; and high expectations.
- Know and use strategies and tools that advance leadership as a form of learning.

skills differ from other descriptions in a number of ways. First, they are undertaken with both a conceptual framework and self-knowledge in mind. They are vertically and laterally aligned with purpose and learning. They occur in community, collaboratively engaged. Participation in leadership is broad-based—educators, students, parent, and community members. Responsibility, breadth of commitment (across boundaries and contexts), and accountability are interconnected, arising from collective responsibility for all children and undertaken with evidence and best practice in mind. These understandings are leading us to a new leadership story.

A NEW LEADERSHIP STORY

What did Gardner have in mind when he suggested that the stories that occur in the minds of individuals, the stories that gain prominence in a community, carry the meaning of leadership? Are the stories changing? And, if so, in what ways? There are a few new story elements:

- The leading characters now share the stage with multiple participants within the community.
- The relationships among characters—once hierarchical and linear—are now reciprocal, patterned, and more complex.
- The plot or story line emerges from the learning process, rather than from targeted, pre-set objectives and assumed outcomes.
- The drama is the quest for understanding and action that involves current beliefs and assumptions, found evidence, dissonance and dialogue, and the framing of new approaches.
- The climax of the story—the point of greatest intensity, culmination—is now in process. This climax is the dialectic being played out between traditional views that are being challenged by newer conceptions of leadership.
- The *denouement,* or the final resolution of the story, is yet to come.
- The moral of the story is, in and of itself, moral—based on shared purpose.

The emerging stories are beginning to sound like this:

Today, leaders attend to the learning of all members of the educational community. Together, they explore current practice, beliefs, and assumptions that serve as a basis for posing inquiry questions. These questions are the signposts in the hunt for evidence and the struggle with dissonance. Dissonance is tackled in dialogue, thereby lowering defenses and increasing shared understanding. This journey results in new approaches to student and adult learning, internal school accountability and shared responsibility, and a commitment to the decisions made for school improvement.

This new story is becoming a dominant narrative, or mental schema, of school leaders throughout this hemisphere, England, and Australia. The news is spreading; certain elements of story are becoming shared knowledge about the ways in which leaders and schools perform. Multiple reform communities and networks (e.g., Annenberg Initiatives, Basic Schools, Accelerated Schools, Baldridge, Coalition of Essential Schools, the National Writing Project) are converging around these understandings as well. Administrative standards need to be reexamined in order to challenge dusty narratives that have lost their fluidity and relevance. Leadership as a form of learning is the new story.

REFERENCES

Capra, F. (1975). *The tao of physics.* Boston: Shambhala.

Capra, F. (1982). *The turning point.* New York: Simon & Schuster.

Capra, F. (1993). *Guide to ecoliteracy.* Berkeley, CA: Elmwood Institute.

Capra, F. (1996). *Web of life.* New York: Anchor Books.

Etzioni, A. (Ed.). (1998). *The essential communitarian reader*. Lanham, MD: Rowman & Littlefield.

Etzioni, A. (Ed.). (1999). *Civic repentance*. Lanham, MD: Rowman & Littlefield.

Gilligan, C. (1982). *In a different voice: Psychological theory of women's development*. Cambridge, MA: Harvard University Press.

Grossman, P., Wineburg, S., & Woolworth, S. (2000, April). In pursuit of teacher community. Paper presented at the annual meeting of the American Educational Research Association, New Orleans, LA.

Kohlberg, L. (1976). Moral stages and moralization: The cognitive developmental approach. In T. Likona (Ed.), *Moral development & behavior* (pp. 31–53). New York: Holt, Rinehart & Winston.

Lambert, L. (1983). *A critical analysis of the assumptions held by researchers, policy makers, and staff developers about adult learning*. Unpublished doctoral dissertation. University of San Francisco.

Lambert, L. (1995). *The constructivist leader*. New York: Teachers College Press.

Lambert, L. (1998). *Building leadership capacity in schools*. Alexandria, VA.: ASCD.

Lambert, L. (in press). Developing sustainable leadership capacity. Alexandria, VA: Association for Supervision and Curriculum Development.

Lambert, L., Collay, M., Dietz, M. E., Kent, K., & Richert, A. E. (1997). *Who will save our schools? Teachers as constructivist leaders*. Thousand Oaks, CA: Corwin Press.

Lieberman, A., & Wood, D. (2001). *The work of the National Writing Project: Social practices in a network context*. Palo Alto, CA: Carnegie Foundation.

Norris, C., Barnett, B., Basom, M. R., & Yerkes, D. M. (2002). *The learning community: A model for developing transformational leaders*. New York: Teachers College Press.

Poplin, M., & Weeres, J. (1993, April). *Voices from the inside*. Claremont, CA: Institute for Education in Transformation at the Claremont Graduate School.

Sergiovanni, T. (2000). *The lifeworld of leadership*. San Francisco: Jossey-Bass.

Spillane, J. P., & Halverson, R. (1999). *Distributed leadership: Toward a theory of school leadership practice*. Paper presented at the annual meeting of the American Educational Research Association, Montreal, Canada.

The Changing Environment for School Leaders: Market Forces

Martha M. McCarthy

School leaders face rapidly changing conditions both in the external environment (e.g., demographic shifts) and within the educational leadership field (e.g., standards-based licensure). Many of these conditions pose formidable challenges, and this chapter addresses a few of the environmental developments that have significant implications for American education and how schools are organized and led. The discussion focuses on selected consumer-based models of schooling—voucher plans, charter schools, corporate school management, and home education. Commercial activities in schools and use of technology in providing instruction are also discussed, because commercialization is part of the school privatization movement, and new technologies often enable schools to become more competitive. Taken together, developments in these areas portend a very different context for school leaders and those preparing them.

CONSUMER-BASED MODELS OF SCHOOLING

By World War I, universal schooling was an accepted goal in the United States, and the public school was viewed as the appropriate vehicle to inculcate democratic values and ensure an educated citizenry, thus assuming some functions previously reserved for families and churches (Spring, 1997; Tyack & Hansot, 1982). Compulsory education for students between specified ages became the norm, but states differed in enforcing these mandates.

Although a few states in the early part of the 20th century attempted to compel *public* schooling, the Supreme Court recognized in 1925 that parents have a constitutional right to select private education for their children (*Pierce v. Society of Sisters*, 1925). Accordingly, parents cannot be forced to send their children to public schools to satisfy compulsory education laws, but the government has the authority

---

Martha M. McCarthy, Chancellor's Professor, Indiana University to regulate private education to ensure an educated citizenry for our democracy. The nature and degree of such regulations have varied greatly across states, and recent state regulatory activities have tended to focus on outcome measures (student performance on standardized tests) rather than on curriculum and personnel requirements for private schools. Notwithstanding some controversies over government relationships with private education, private and public schools have generally coexisted with minimal friction in our nation, partly because private education has not served more than 12 percent of elementary and secondary students in the United States since education became compulsory (National Center for Education Statistics, 1999).

This situation may change, however, because consumer-based models of schooling are becoming more popular as a strategy to improve education. Marketplace strategies can be placed on a continuum from purely public options (e.g., magnet schools with a particular focus, such as fine arts, within public school districts) to public-private partnerships that might involve more private schools (e.g., voucher plans that permit state funds to be used to purchase private education for specific students) (see Metcalf, Muller, & Legan, 2001). Allowing the market to dictate which schools will remain in existence has significant implications for education in our nation and for the roles of school leaders.

Although different approaches entail varying degrees of government oversight, all strategies involving consumer-driven education focus on competition among schools. This represents a departure from the near monopoly that government-run schools have enjoyed for more than a century in our nation. Moreover, under marketplace models, the common school can no longer be relied on to transmit fundamental democratic values to the next generation of citizens. Schools will always inculcate values, but in a market-based system, not necessarily shared values across schools.

There is some sentiment that consumer control of education may be the natural next phase in the evolution of school governance, replacing professional control, which prevailed throughout most of the twentieth century (Katz, 1992; Murphy, 1999). If so, school leadership may change dramatically, not only in these new types of schools but also in public schools that must vie for their share of the student constituent base. Leadership preparation programs will need to place more emphasis on political acumen, marketing and promotion skills, development activities, and other business aspects of schooling that will be essential for school leaders in a consumer-driven system. This does not mean that instructional leadership will decline in importance, but other activities formerly left to central office personnel or not considered integral to the educational enterprise will need to be addressed in preparing school leaders for building and district administrative roles.

Furthermore, it is increasingly important for preparation programs to expose future school leaders to the values guiding various strategies to make schooling more competitive and to provide parents more educational options. School leaders need to investigate how these values compare with those undergirding the notion of the American common school (Spring, 1997). Understanding the basic assumptions of marketplace initiatives and their ramifications is important so that informed individuals participate in discussions and decisions about these school improvement strategies.

Many of the justifications offered for allowing other government services to be market-driven are also used to support marketplace models of education, such as encouraging entrepreneurial activity and individual advancement in a free enterprise system and expanding individuals' choices (Nathan, 1996). Proponents of consumer-based education contend that the competitive environment will cause public schools to improve or go out of business. They also assert that focusing accountability on the school rather than the school district will enhance student performance and parental involvement, promote the efficient use of school funds, and provide incentives to change an education system that has been stymied by years of government overregulation (see Buechler, 1996; Chubb & Moe, 1990; Fuller, 2000; Katz, 1992).

Critics fear that opening education to the marketplace will doom the American common school with its democratizing function and will intensify economic and racial segregation (see Berliner, Farrell, Huerta, & Mickelson, 2000; Fowler, 1991; Goodlad, 1997). They contend that middle-class parents will flee public schools, leaving the disadvantaged and special-need students in public education, and that the participation of religious schools in some marketplace models will unconstitutionally entangle church and state (see McLaughlin, 1995; Molnar, 2001).

Selected strategies to infuse market forces in education are briefly described below. The intent here is not to defend or condemn these practices but rather to explore their implications for education generally and for the roles of school leaders.

Voucher Systems

A basic voucher system allocates a specified amount of state funds that parents can redeem at public or private schools of their choice. Several New England states with small school districts have had de facto voucher systems for years; instead of operating their own high schools, the districts have provided tuition grants for high school students to attend public or private schools outside the districts. Currently, various voucher proposals are being considered in almost half of the states, and a few limited voucher programs are being implemented, usually targeting economically deprived children or those attending public schools judged as inferior. As the number of voucher programs increases and competition for students becomes the norm, the environment for which we are preparing leaders will change in rudimentary ways. Some administrators will be leading voucher schools, and those still seeking careers in public schools need to be knowledgeable about implications of marketplace models for education in our nation.

Despite sound defeats for voucher proposals that have been submitted to the voters, there has been renewed interest in voucher programs since the mid-1990s. In 1999, Florida became the first state to adopt a statewide voucher plan that includes religious schools (Sandham, 1999). Under the Florida program, students attending public schools that are rated as deficient (based on test scores, attendance, graduation rates, and other factors) are entitled to state vouchers that can be used in qualified public or private schools of their choice. More limited publicly funded voucher programs have been adopted in Milwaukee and Cleveland for low-income, inner-city children. And recently enacted federal legislation calls for students who have been attending public schools that have failed to provide high-quality education over time to be furnished other options at state expense (*No Child Left Behind Act,* 2002). Also, a number of cities are experimenting with privately funded voucher plans for disadvantaged youth, under which parents can send their children to private schools through vouchers supported by donations. The Children's Educational Opportunity Foundation of America, founded in 1991, has distributed millions of dollars across more than half of the states for such vouchers/scholarships during the past decade ("Supporters of Privately Financed Vouchers," 1998).

There are numerous testimonials but no hard evidence establishing that student achievement has improved in the limited voucher programs in operation to date. Studies of the student achievement in the Cleveland and Milwaukee programs have not been conclusive (see Fuller & Caire, 2001; Greene, Peterson, & Du, 1997; Metcalf, 1999; Molnar, 2001; Rouse, 1998; Witte, Sterr, & Thorn, 1995). Some contend that recent student performance gains have been greater than expected in Florida schools threatened with losing students through the voucher program targeting "failing" schools (Greene, 2001), but hard data linking improvements to the voucher program are not available.

In a 2001 Rand Corporation report, *Rhetoric Versus Reality: What We Know and What We Need to Know About Vouchers and Charter Schools,* several dimensions of voucher and charter schools were investigated, including academic achievement; access to low income, minority, and special-needs students; impact on racial and ethnic segregation; and impact on civic socialization (Gill, Timpane, Ross, & Brewer, 2001). Finding only a few studies of high technical quality, the Rand researchers concluded that many of the significant questions have not yet been answered and conclusive student achievement comparisons have not been produced. Also, the report did not find evidence documenting the positive or negative impact of voucher programs on students electing to remain in public schools.

Since many of those motivated to conduct research on school vouchers have strong positions on the merits of such programs, ideological clashes have been evident in the debates over the research findings. Those preparing to be school leaders need to become astute consumers of this research so they can separate philosophical arguments from data on the impact of vouchers and other consumer-based approaches.

Because courts will play a significant role in determining whether public funds can be used to support private education, school leaders also need to be familiar with the state and federal constitutional issues raised by voucher plans. A case currently before the Supreme Court addresses whether voucher systems that allow public funds to be used for sectarian education abridge Establishment Clause restrictions (*Simmons-Harris v. Zelman,* 2001). The Sixth Circuit Court of Appeals struck down the Cleveland voucher program as advancing religion in violation of the Establishment Clause, because 99 percent of the students receiving vouchers attended sectarian schools. The Supreme Court's decision, expected in the summer 2002, may have significant implications for the future of some marketplace models of education across states. The Supreme Court could curtail voucher plans that include religious schools by finding an Establishment Clause violation in the Cleveland program, or it could provide an impetus for voucher plans to expand if it finds no such constitutional infraction.

Those contending that voucher systems should be upheld are encouraged by the Supreme Court's decision in *Mitchell v. Helms* (1999) in which the Court rejected an Establishment Clause challenge to using federal aid to purchase instructional materials and equipment for student use in sectarian schools. Justice Thomas, speaking for the Supreme Court plurality in *Helms*, reasoned that religious indoctrination or subsidization of religion cannot be attributed to the government when aid, even direct aid, if distributed based on secular criteria, is available to religious and secular beneficiaries on a nondiscriminatory basis and reaches religious schools only because of private decisions.

Even before *Helms*, several Supreme Court rulings reflected an accommodationist posture by allowing more governmental aid to flow to religious schools than had been true in the 1970s. These cases support the contention that state aid benefitting religious schools because of the parents' private choices would satisfy the Establishment Clause (*Agostini v. Felton*, 1997; *Mueller v. Allen*, 1983; *Witters v. Washington Department*, 1986; *Zobrest v. Catalina Foothills School District*, 1993). A voucher proposal that aids religious institutions might also be viewed as religiously neutral legislation because parents—not the government—make the decisions that channel state funds to religious schools.

However, lower court rulings on voucher plans are mixed. The highest courts in Florida, Ohio, and Wisconsin have found no Establishment Clause violation in allowing religious schools to participate in government-funded voucher programs (*Bush v. Holmes*, 2000; *Jackson v. Benson*, 1998; *Simmons-Harris v. Goff*, 1999). The Supreme Court of Arizona also upheld a tax benefit program for citizens' contributions to private school scholarships (*Kotterman v. Killian*, 1999). In contrast, the First Circuit Court of Appeals held that Maine's program, authorizing school districts without high schools to pay tuition for secondary students to attend public or nonsectarian private schools outside their districts, would run afoul of the Establishment Clause if it included religious schools (*Strout v. Albanese*, 1999). The Vermont Supreme Court reached a similar conclusion in rejecting payments for parochial school tuition based on the state constitution's prohibition against compelling citizens to support religious worship (*Chittenden v. Vermont*, 1999).

As noted above, the Sixth Circuit Court of Appeals in 2000 became the second federal appeals court to find an Establishment Clause violation in a voucher program involving religious schools (*Simmons-Harris v. Zelman*, 2001). Given the mixed lower court opinions, considerable attention is focused on the Supreme Court's deliberations in the Cleveland case. Of course, even if the Supreme Court concludes that voucher plans involving sectarian schools do not implicate the Establishment Clause, individual state courts could still find specific voucher programs in violation of state constitutional provisions that prohibit the use of public funds for private purposes.

Assuming that state-supported voucher plans withstand federal and state constitutional challenges, they still face a significant barrier in terms of their fiscal impact
on state coffers. Almost 12 percent of all students are currently supported by their
parents in private schools or home education programs, and they would be eligible
for tax support under a basic voucher program. The fiscal consequences may keep
states from adopting large-scale voucher plans, similar to the fate of most proposed
legislation to provide state tax benefits for educational expenses incurred by parents
in sending their children to private schools. Economic concerns may be one reason
that voucher programs adopted to date have targeted a small portion of children and
why other strategies, such as charter schools, seem more palatable to the electorate
than do voucher systems.

Charter Schools

In contrast to the reluctance of states to adopt voucher systems to fund education,
most states have enthusiastically embraced charter school legislation during the past
few years, and the federal government has provided some support for planning and
creating charter schools (see *No Child Left Behind Act,* 2002). State legislators seem
more receptive to charter schools because they remain public schools, even though
they operate outside many state requirements and must compete for students. In
1993, only two states—Minnesota and California—had passed charter school legislation. By 2001, 39 states had such laws, and more than half a million students were
attending the 2,372 operational charter schools (Task Force, 2002). Chris Pipho
(1995) observed several years ago that charter schools seem to have taken on "the
aura of a 'silver bullet'—a magical solution to a variety of problems" (p. 742), and
this statement still rings true today.

Given that charter schools represent one of the fastest growing school improvement strategies, school leaders need to understand the various approaches to charter
schools across states, the research available on these schools, and the implications of
moving to a system in which charter schools dominate education in our nation. A
new breed of school leaders may emerge to lead these schools, and all school administrators will be affected by the charter school movement.

The intent of charter school legislation is to reduce government constraints and
give schools more flexibility to adopt instructional innovations, although specifica-
tions and government regulations vary across states. Usually the charter can be rene-
gotiated after a specified period, with continuation depending on assessments of student performance. Charter schools are accountable to their sponsors, most often the
local or state board of education, but sponsors in some states can be other agencies,
such as public universities. Of course, the bottom line is that charter schools are directly answerable to consumers (i.e., parents and students), who can select other
schools if dissatisfied.

Charter schools tend to be smaller than public schools, and they are more likely
to be established at the elementary rather than secondary level. They often have a
specific philosophical orientation, such as a focus on strict discipline. Some charter

schools are being created to serve special populations, such as court-placed delinquent youths, professional sports hopefuls, and previously home-schooled students. There are also worksite charter schools to accommodate parents and charters that focus on preparing students for particular occupations (Brockett, 1998). Most charter school legislation pertains to individual schools, but a few states are experimenting with charter school districts that are released from compliance with many state rules and regulations (Lockwood, 2001). Also, about 30 cyber charter schools exist, and as discussed later, these schools have been controversial (Trotter, 2001).

Advocates and critics cite some of the same advantages and disadvantages for charter schools as they do for voucher plans. For example, it is asserted that charter schools skim off the most involved and talented families, which has a negative impact on other public schools (Cobb, Glass, & Crockett, 2000). Critics also allege that charter schools discourage enrollment of children with special needs or low achieving students, which exacerbates various types of segregation. Advocates counter that charter schools are more cost-efficient, responsive to parents, and innovative, which provides models to improve traditional public schools (Fuller, 2000; Manno, Vanourek, & Finn, 1999).

Some contend that charter schools capitalize on the strengths of both the private and public sectors, providing "an appropriate compromise between the current public education system, with little or no market accountability, and a voucher system with little or no accountability to the public at large" (Buechler, 1996, p. 3). Critics, however, are concerned that charter school legislation is a disguised strategy to fund private schools, which ultimately will shift the private/public school ratio in our nation and jeopardize public education (see Berliner et al., 2000; Task Force, 2002).

An increasing trend is for those interested in starting charter schools to turn to for-profit companies for assistance, perhaps because of the difficulties associated with creating and operating schools. Murphy (1999) has referred to private management as the second wave of the charter school movement. Under some state laws, for-profit companies cannot charter schools but they can subcontract with nonprofit entities that actually negotiate the charters.

As with voucher programs, evaluation data are just beginning to be gathered to assess whether charter schools do a better job of educating students and whether the competition provides incentives for regular public schools to improve (Gill et al., 2001). Many questions remain unanswered, partly because consensus has not been reached regarding how the success of charter schools should be measured. This is particularly troublesome for schools designed to be very innovative and nontraditional (Schnaiberg, 1998). When there were only a handful of charter schools nationally, accountability concerns perhaps did not seem as pressing as they do now that the number of charter schools is expanding rapidly. Also, implications of the charter school movement for the preparation of school leaders have not yet been fully explored. It is clear, however, that the next generation of school leaders will be affected by charter schools, whether leading them or competing with them.

Private Contractors

The involvement of private companies in managing public schools and offering instructional services has steadily increased in recent years, especially since corporations can run charter schools in some states. Such involvement of private companies
in public education has been extremely controversial. Illustrative were developments
in the 1990s pertaining to Educational Alternatives Incorporated (EAI) and its
aborted efforts to run schools in Baltimore and Hartford (Green, 1997; Walsh, 1996;
Williams & Leak, 1996). The company, which subsequently changed its name to
Tesseract Group and moved from Minnesota to Arizona, has continued to struggle
(Molnar, Morales, & Wyst, 2000).

The most influential school management firm was conceptualized by entrepreneur
Chris Whittle and launched as the Edison Project in 1992. Originally, Whittle envisioned a national chain of private schools, but due to economic reasons the focus
shifted to managing public schools, primarily charter schools. Now called Edison
Schools, the company's intent is to provide radically different experiences from traditional schools (e.g., multi-age grouping, differentiated staffing, longer school day
and year, extensive use of computers and other technology, etc.). The Edison Project
spent an estimated $40 million in development before opening its first school in
1995 (Walsh, 1998).

In 2001, 136 Edison Schools served more than 75,000 students, and the company
recently acquired LearnNow that operates a number of urban charter schools. Edison's most ambitious undertaking to date is its bid to play the leadership role in managing Philadelphia's public schools, which were taken over by the state in an agreement signed by the governor and mayor in December 2001. Edison's role in
Philadelphia remains controversial, and the company faces stiff opposition from
unionized employees and some community groups ("Philadelphia Mayor," 2002).

In addition to Edison and EAI (Tesseract), other companies managing charter
schools include Mosaica Education, Advantage Schools, and Beacon Education
Management (Walsh, 2001). Also, numerous companies are seeking more limited
contracts with public schools to address student performance in targeted areas. For
example, Sylvan Learning Systems, which has established private tutoring centers
nationwide, has contracts in a number of large school districts to provide remedial
reading and math programs (Walsh, 1995, 1996). In contrast to the controversy surrounding corporate management of public schools, Sylvan has not attracted much
media attention or been targeted by teachers' unions as a significant threat. Rather
than making school budgetary decisions, Sylvan is simply being paid to provide specific instructional services. Other companies offering intensive tutoring or targeted
instruction include Kaplan Educational Centers, Voyager Expanded Learning Corporation, Huntington Learning Centers, Berlitz Language Schools, Britannica
Learning Centers, and Ombudsman Educational Services. The prevalence of high
stakes testing has provided a boon to some of the companies, like Kaplan, that have
programs to assist students and teachers in mastering the tests.

Companies seeking contracts to provide targeted instructional services seem to
face fewer obstacles than do those trying to manage schools and districts (McCarthy,

2000). School boards are becoming more receptive to the idea that they do not have to provide all instructional services themselves as long as they ensure that the private vendors are fulfilling their contracts. Indeed, financially strapped school districts that are under extensive pressure to improve student learning often feel that they have little to risk with a company that will guarantee results and forgo payment unless students satisfy specified performance standards. Additional companies may decide that targeted instructional services hold the greatest promise for tapping the lucrative education market in the near future.

However, critics fear that the corporate concern for realizing profits may result in short cuts that reduce the quality of educational services and downplay important educational activities that are beyond the limited measures included in the company's contract—usually student performance on reading and math tests. School leaders and policymakers need to carefully investigate these corporate relationships and weigh the tradeoffs involved in turning over portions of the instructional program or perhaps management of entire schools to private companies. Also, as corporate involvement in education increases, leadership preparation needs to give additional attention to investigating contract language, relationships between teachers' unions and corporate managers, and application of civil rights mandates and state education accountability provisions in schools managed by private corporations.

Home Schooling

Home education has steadily increased since the 1980s, and the current availability of commercial materials over the Internet has made home instruction much easier to provide. Recent estimates indicate that more than 850,000 children are being educated at home (see Dare, 2001), and this figure may be low because registration of home-schooled students with state agencies is difficult to monitor and enforce. The most common reason for parents to undertake home education is because they do not want their children exposed to content that conflicts with their religious beliefs, but some parents are dissatisfied with public school academic standards, fearful for their children's safety, or simply want to be more involved in their children's learning experiences (McCarthy, 2001). Other families undertake home schooling due to geographic isolation. Paul Houston, executive director of the American Association of School Administrators, has commented that home schooling is putting pressure on public education "because it's personalizing education . . . and changing the use of time, and those are fundamental differences from the assembly-line models of schools" (Keller, 2001).

All states now allow home education; 31 states have statutes specifically addressing home schooling (Dare, 2001). Some features of these laws have generated legal controversies, and most courts have upheld requirements that home instruction be substantially equivalent to public school offerings. A few courts, however, have found challenged "equivalency" requirements too vague to impose criminal liability on parents for noncompliance (see McCarthy, Cambron-McCabe, & Thomas, 1998).

Although the judiciary has recognized states' authority to regulate home schooling, the clear legislative trend for several decades has been toward reducing curricular requirements and standards for home tutors. The Home School Legal Defense Association has reported that about three fifths of the states have eased restrictions on home education programs since the early 1980s when almost half of the states specified that home tutors had to be licensed (Klicka, 1998). Some courts have also ruled that state licensure requirements for home tutors unconstitutionally abridge parents' rights to direct the education of their children (see *Michigan v. Bennett*, 1993), and no state currently requires home instruction to be provided by licensed teachers (Dare, 2001). But courts have upheld requirements that students educated at home be tested to ensure mastery of basic skills (see *Murphy v. Arkansas*, 1988). Also, when home-schooled students attempt to enter (or re-enter) the public school system, school personnel can test the students and use other assessment criteria for placement purposes.

In some public school districts, school leaders are recruiting home-schooled students to take one or more public school classes, because such dual enrollment results in a windfall for the school district in that students enrolled in even one public school course bring state aid allocated for full-time public school students (see Stover, 2001). However, other state school finance systems prorate funds so school districts are compensated only for the portion of time home schoolers actually attend public schools. If these children enroll in the more costly public school courses, such dual enrollment could disadvantage the school district under a prorated reimbursement system.

School leaders will have to deal with home-schooled students reentering the public school system and with requests for these students to participate in selected public school courses and extracurricular activities. The number of home-schooled children is growing and could increase dramatically if states adopt voucher proposals that would allow public funds to flow to parents who educate their children at home. Also, some students already are enrolled in virtual charter schools that cater primarily to previously home-schooled children. State policymakers face difficult decisions in striking the appropriate balance between state interests in ensuring an educated citizenry and parental interests in directing the upbringing of their children. If home schooling continues to become more popular, state and local district regulatory roles may come under increased scrutiny.

COMMERCIALIZATION OF PUBLIC SCHOOLS

The focus thus far has been on opening education to market forces and thereby increasing educational options for parents, but in this section I address using the public schools *as a market* to advance business interests. The mounting commercialization of education is related to marketplace models of schooling since both entail corporate involvement in education, but the two phenomena are distinct. The ultimate goal of some proponents of consumer-based education is to weaken public schools, whereas those seeking to expand commercial activities want to preserve the captive public school market. Private companies increasingly have been capitalizing on the school market with sports and music camps, school jewelry, and attire for athletic teams and performing groups (McLaughlin, 1992).

The most significant recent development has been the use of public schools to advertise products in exchange for money or equipment. Chris Whittle gained national prominence in 1990 when he launched Channel One, a news program with two minutes of advertisements. In return for guaranteeing that students watch the program, schools receive free equipment and other financial incentives. About 12,000 middle, junior high, and high schools serving more than eight million students use Channel One's daily broadcast ("About Channel One," 2001). Advertisers are eager to participate (at twice the price of ads for prime-time network news programs) because of the large audience that even major networks cannot assure on a daily basis (Kozol, 1992).

Channel One critics have vocally denounced use of captive students in public schools for economic motives and have lamented the more than 30,000 commercial messages a year that target children (Consumers Union, 1998). Researchers have reported that student Channel One viewers list more of the advertised brands as ones they would purchase and they have more materialistic attitudes than nonviewers (Greenberg & Brand, 1993/94).

Despite controversy, commercial activities in public schools continue to expand. Similar to the arrangement with Channel One, high schools can receive satellite communications equipment and some advertising revenues in return for piping music and ads into public school hallways and lunchrooms, and elementary schools can receive equipment for showing a multimedia news program including videos and posters as well as ads (Jensen, 1993; McLaughlin, 1992). In addition, gymboards for high school locker rooms and digital display units for school halls can be programmed to carry school messages and advertisements, and school calendars and yearbooks are often financed through advertisements (Consumers Union, 1998). Pepsi and other companies also are making large investments in school facilities, such as gymnasiums, in return for free advertising or vending contracts with the districts (Pipho, 1997).

Moreover, companies are financing learning packets for use in the instructional program. Such packets usually do not carry advertisements, but they might include plugs for specific products and present issues from the companies' perspectives. These free or inexpensive instructional materials include books, work sheets, workbooks, videos, software, or other teaching aids. Schools often welcome these materials, but critics contend that commercialization is at its worse "when it masquerades as educational materials or programs and offers half-truths or misstatements that favor the sponsor of the materials" (Consumers Union, p. 9).

Economic concerns clearly have aligned school districts with these companies; the financial incentives are quite enticing. Having students read, watch, or listen to commercials is the price most school personnel seem willing to pay for equipment, materials, and possibly revenue. School leaders play a pivotal role in establishing the direction that commercial pursuits will take in schools, and they need to be knowledgeable regarding the costs/benefits of such activities and their long-range implications for values transmitted by public schools.

TECHNOLOGICAL ADVANCES

Some of the consumer-based models of education and commercial activities in schools capitalize extensively on technology. Indeed, advances in technology and how technology is used in instruction have major implications for the future of education in the United States. As with efforts to open education to the marketplace, educational leadership preparation programs must address equity and quality concerns in connection with recent changes in technology that are altering the concept of education and where it takes place.

A number of virtual schools are currently operating, and a few states are experimenting with virtual school districts. As noted, cyber charter schools have been controversial in several states because they receive the same per pupil state aid as charter schools operating in traditional settings, which is viewed as a windfall for these cyber schools aimed primarily at home-schooled children (Stover, 2001; Trotter, 2001). Even in traditional school districts, connecting students through technology may replace building new structures as the preferred strategy to expand instructional space. Clearly, this generation of students is being socialized quite differently from those in the past in terms of where they get information and how they interact with others in learning environments.

Technological advances are revolutionizing how pre-K–12 schools and universities operate, but questions remain regarding the ultimate effects of this revolution on our schools and society. The potential is enormous for technology to enhance learning, increase access to information, facilitate domestic and international linkages, and expand our horizons in ways we cannot yet imagine (see *The Technology Source*, 2002). But the rapid pace of the technological changes may signal some dangers as well. A recent report issued by the National Association of State Boards of Education (2001) warned that an ad hoc educational technology system is evolving without sufficient policies, which may increase educational disparities and squander the potential benefits of "e-learning" technologies in our nation's schools.

Educational leaders need to ensure that pre-K–12 students are not disadvantaged because they lack access to particular types of equipment or software. Also, we must not let economic motivations overshadow quality concerns in connection with distance learning. Some companies offering customized instructional programs are advertising that they can identify children's needs and provide appropriate services with guaranteed results solely via the Internet (e.g., eSylvan). When face-to-face interactions are reduced, what is lost in terms of developing social skills, a sense of community, and a commitment to the welfare of the group? Our field should play a leadership role in setting standards for the use of distributed education, establishing policies for acceptable use of the Internet in our schools, designing strategies to assess the merits of materials on the Web, providing professional development activities, and addressing numerous other technology-related issues.

Furthermore, prospective school leaders now have the option of completing their administrative licenses entirely online, and such options are likely to increase significantly during the next decade. A number of institutions are offering graduate degrees in addition to licensure programs via the Internet, where personal interactions with faculty and fellow students are minimal or nonexistent. Few statewide efforts address the quality of learning experiences in these online programs, although professional standards boards in several states do require evidence that licensure candidates have completed standards-based preparation and have passed performance-based examinations. Educational leadership faculty members should be assertive in addressing instructional quality concerns in connection with online degree and licensure programs. If not, as technology-based instruction becomes the norm, the nature of leadership preparation is likely to change in significant, and perhaps undesirable, ways.

AN UNCERTAIN FUTURE

The American citizenry, legislative bodies, and courts have recognized the importance of education in our democracy. The United States Supreme Court has noted that "providing public schools ranks at the very apex of the functions of a state" (*Wisconsin v. Yoder*, 1972, p. 213) and has voiced doubt that any child can succeed in life if "denied the opportunity of an education" (*Brown v. Board*, 1954, p. 493). One of the public school's central purposes in our country has been to inculcate citizenship values in the next generation, but concerns are being raised that these public interests are losing prominence.

The tension between privatization and governmental regulation is affecting many facets of our lives, and education is not immune, even though some people traditionally thought it was. Labaree (1997) has observed that while both equity and efficiency goals treat education as a public good that benefits all members of the community, the social mobility goal, which has become a dominant force in American education, is quite different as it focuses on the individual consumer (rather than the citizen or taxpayer) and treats education as a private good. The market-based school reform strategies discussed in this chapter, such as voucher and charter school programs, favor consumer preferences and individual advancement over the welfare of the group (see Apple, 2000; Goodlad, 1997). Consumer choices also drive instructional consumption in Web-based educational programs, and the consumer is certainly being courted through commercial activities in schools.

Some commentators contend that this emphasis on consumerism and corporate involvement in education will cause the goal of producing a better society to be subjugated to economic motives, consumer preferences, and contractual agreements (see Goodlad, 1997; Houston, 1994; Kozol, 1992; Labaree, 1997). There are concerns about who will champion the collective good in a consumer-oriented education system. Michael Apple (2000) has cautioned that if citizenship is "defined as simply consumer choice," then democracy will be reduced to "selfish individualism," which "may in fact be un-American" (p. 4). Alfie Kohn (2002) has similarly declared that "education isn't one more investment to be justified; it's the foundation of a democracy" (p. 12A).

Others argue just as passionately that opening education to the marketplace supports our national commitment to free enterprise and an entrepreneurial spirit (Doyle, 1994). They further contend that consumer-based models comprise the most powerful strategy to improve public schools, and that only through the marketplace can educational opportunities become better for disadvantaged students, particularly those residing in inner cities who have previously had little educational choice (see Fuller & Caire, 2001; Greene, 2001). Leadership preparation programs must address these value conflicts and implications of the various consumer-based models for schools' instructional and socialization functions.

Many proposals to make education more competitive focus on increasing productivity and efficiency measured by lower costs and improved student performance in basic academic skills. Private companies seeking contracts to operate public schools usually assert that they can produce higher test scores for less money, which is quite enticing to public officials. Virtual pre-K–12 schools and online university degree programs are also designed to reduce instructional costs as well as to ensure ease of educational access for the consumer. Even if not directly tied to market models of schooling, some instructional uses of technology and commercial activities in schools are profit-driven, with satisfaction of stockholders and consumers the bottom line.

Consumer-based strategies also emphasize empowering parents so they can make educational choices in line with their personal beliefs. One area where the research on voucher and charter schools is consistent has to do with parent satisfaction; parents are more satisfied and involved with schools they have been allowed to select for their children (Martinez, Thomas, & Kemerer, 1994; Metcalf, 1999; Weinschrott & Kilgore, 1996). Advocates of home education and vouchers want parents, not the government, to be dominant in directing their children's education, including the values emphasized. And they want parents to be able to select schools that reflect social and ideological homogeneity because such cohesion within schools reduces conflicts about vision and objectives (see Chubb & Moe, 1990). Obviously, a major impetus for home schooling is that parents can ensure that their children are not exposed to values and ideology they find offensive.

As consumer control of education increases, government control is expected to decline. Those applauding such a shift contend that government control of education has led to bureaucratized, ineffective schools (Chubb & Moe, 1990; Doyle, 1994; Fuller, 2000). Advocates of vouchers desire local school autonomy and accountability, and a central feature of most charter school legislation is that state controls are relaxed. Thus, charter schools appeal to many private companies, whose school designs cannot be implemented under restrictive governmental regulations. Also, during the past two decades, home school advocates have been very successful in securing a reduction in state regulations applied to home education.

It remains to be seen whether the movement toward consumer-based models of schooling will be viewed as congruent with the current policy emphasis on educational standards, assessments, and complex education accountability systems that include public reporting and rewards/sanctions for schools. Both movements shift accountability to the school level, so charter and voucher schools may be regarded as a vehicle to support accountability mandates. But the increased regulatory activities accompanying standards-based reforms could be seen as placing an unnecessary government constraint on some consumer-based models. Especially troublesome accountability issues are raised by cyber schools that do not have district or even state boundaries (Snider, 2002).

If the market becomes the primary regulator and government involvement is reduced, this raises significant questions about the state's oversight role in safeguarding individual rights and guaranteeing that all children receive an education necessary for citizenship in a democracy. In carrying out its responsibility to protect the citizenry and advance the common good, must the state ensure that all children are exposed to certain core values and academic content? Or should consumer preferences, with few government constraints, dictate the instructional program and the values emphasized? Assuming that the movement toward consumer-based education means that the purposes, basic structure, and core values of public education in our nation are fundamentally changing, then we need to explore fully the implications of this shift that will reach far beyond public schooling. We must be attentive or may by default embrace policies and ideological positions that perhaps conflict with basic democratic principles (McCarthy, 2000).

Questions about the appropriate government role in a democracy have become even more significant since September 11, 2001. For more than a decade prior to these tragic events, globalism seemed to be thriving on "deregulation and privatization," and there was considerable support for the notion that "markets could encompass more and more social domains" (Sassen, 2002, B12). But in the aftermath of the terrorist attacks, there is less confidence in the market as the answer to everything. In fact, we are witnessing more government regulations, and there are even calls for restrictions on fundamental privacy and expression rights and other personal freedoms (e.g., required Pledge of Allegiance in schools, constraints on expressing unpopular political views). Given the conflicting pressures to expand and reduce government regulations, it has never been more crucial for school leaders to be well versed regarding the basic rights and responsibilities of American citizens and to nurture such understanding among our youth.

Instead of merely reacting to technological advances, pressures from consumers and businesses, global activities, or other external developments that have significant implications for education, school leaders should exert initiative in influencing how these developments affect the direction of education in the United States. As discussed throughout, this may call for school leaders who are prepared to function quite differently than in the past. The stakes are high for our youth and our country, and the changing environment indeed presents awesome challenges for school leaders and for those preparing them.

REFERENCES

"About Channel One." (2001). Channel One Network, Primedia, Inc. www.channelone.com/.

Agostini v. Felton, 521 U.S. 203 (1997).

Apple, M. (2000). *Are vouchers really democratic?* Education Policy Project, Center for Education Research, Analysis, and Innovation (00-08). Milwaukee: University of Wisconsin-Milwaukee. Retrieved from www.uwm.edu/Dept/CERAI/

Berliner, D., Farrell, W., Huerta, L., & Mickelson, R. (2000). *Will vouchers work for low-income students?* Education Policy Project, Center for Education Research, Analysis, and Innovation

(00-37). Milwaukee: University of Wisconsin-Milwaukee. Retrieved from www.uwm.edu/
Dept/CERAI/

Brockett, D. (1998, May 12). Charter laws pave the way for unusual schools. *School Board News,*
pp. 1, 12.

Brown v. Board of Education of Topeka, 347 U.S. 483 (1954).

Buechler, M. (1996). *Charter schools: Legislation and results after four years* (PR-B13). Bloomington: Indiana Education Policy Center.

Bush v. Holmes, 767 So. 2d 668 (Fla. App. 2000), *review denied,* 2001 Fla. LEXIS 952 (2001).

Chittenden Town School District v. Vermont Department of Education, 738 A.2d 539 (Vt.1999),
cert. denied, 528 U.S. 1066 (1999).

Chubb, J. E., & Moe, T. M. (1990). *Politics, markets, and America's schools.* Washington, DC:
Brookings Institute.

Cobb, C., Glass, G., & Crockett, C. (2000, April). *The U.S. charter school movement and ethnic
segregation.* Paper presented at the annual meeting of the American Educational Research Association, New Orleans, LA.

Consumers Union. (1998). *Captive kids: A report on commercial pressures on kids at school.* Washington, DC: Author.

Dare, M. J. (2001). *The tensions of the home school movement: A legal/political analysis.* Unpublished doctoral dissertation, Indiana University, Bloomington.

Doyle, D. (1994). The role of private sector management in public education. *Phi Delta Kappan,*
76(2) 128–132.

Fowler, F. C. (1991). The shocking ideological integrity of Chubb and Moe. *Journal of Education,*
173, 119–129.

Fuller, H. L. (2000). *The continuing struggle of African Americans for the power to make real educational choices.* Milwaukee: Marquette University Institute for the Transformation of Learning.

Fuller, H., & Caire, K. (2001, April). *Lies and distortions: The campaign against school vouchers.*
Milwaukee: Marquette University Institute for the Transformation of Learning.

Gill, B., Timpane, M., Ross, K., & Brewer, D. (2001). *Rhetoric versus reality: What we know and
what we need to know about vouchers and charter schools.* Santa Monica, CA: Rand.

Goodlad, J. (1997, July 9). Making democracy safe for education. *Education Week,* pp. 40, 56.

Green, P. C. (1997). To a peaceful settlement: Using constructive methods to terminate contracts
between private corporations and school districts. *Equity & Excellence in Education, 30*(2),
39–48.

Greenberg, B. S., & Brand, J. E. (1993/94). Channel one: But what about the advertising? *Educational Leadership, 51*(4), 56–58.

Greene, J. (2001, February 15). *An evaluation of the Florida A-Plus Accountability and school
choice program.* New York: Center for Civic Innovation at the Manhattan Institute for Policy Research. Retrieved from www.manhattaninstitute.org/html/cr_aplus.htm

Greene, J., Peterson, P., & Du, J. (1997, March). *The effectiveness of school choice: The Milwaukee experiment* (Harvard University Education Policy and Governance Occasional Paper no. 97-1).
Cambridge, MA: Harvard University.

Houston, P. (1994). Making watches or making music. *Phi Delta Kappan, 76*(2), 133–135.

Jackson v. Benson, 578 N.W.2d 602 (Wis. 1998), *cert. denied,* 525 U.S. 997 (1998).

Jensen, J. (1993). Ad-supported radio rolls into the nation's high schools. *Advertising Age, 64*(31),
22.

Katz, M. B. (1992). Chicago school reform as history. *Teachers College Record, 94*(1), 56–72.

Keller, B. (2001, October 24). Spinoffs from traditional schooling seen as vital to reform. *Education Week,* p. 12.

Klicka, J. D. (1998). *Home schooling in the United States.* Purcellville, VA: Home School Legal
Defense Association.

Kohn, A. (2002, January 24). Measures fall short. *USA Today*, p. 12A.

Kotterman v. Killian, 972 P.2d 606 (Ariz. 1999), *cert. denied*, 528 U. S. 810 (1999).

Kozol, J. (1992), September 21). Whittle and the privateers. *The Nation*, pp. 272, 274, 276–278.

Labaree, D. F. (1997, September 17). Are students "consumers"? The rise of public education as a private good. *Education Week*, 38, 48.

Lockwood, A. T. (2001, November). *Charter districts: Much fuss, little gain*. Arlington, VA: American Association of School Administrators.

Manno, B., Vanourek, G., & Finn, C. (1999). Charter schools: Serving disadvantaged youth. *Education and Urban Society, 31*, 429–445.

Martinez, V., Thomas, K., & Kemerer, F. (1994). Who chooses and why: A look at five school district choice plans. *Phi Delta Kappan, 75*, 578–681.

McCarthy, M. (2000). Privatization of education: Marketplace models. In B. Jones (Ed.), *Educational administration: Policy dimensions in the twenty-first century* (pp. 21–39). Stamford, CT: Ablex.

McCarthy, M. (2001). The legality of home education. *Education Update, VI*(12), 5.

McCarthy, M., Cambron-McCabe, N., & Thomas, S. (1998). *Public school law: Teachers' and students' rights*. Boston: Allyn & Bacon.

McLaughlin, J. (1992). Schooling for profit: Capitalism's new frontier. *Educational Horizons, 71*, 23–30.

McLaughlin, J. (1995). Public education and private enterprise. *The School Administrator, 52*(7), 7–12.

Metcalf, K. (1999). *Evaluation of the Cleveland scholarship and tutoring program, 1996–1999*. Bloomington: The Indiana Center for Evaluation.

Metcalf, K., Muller, P., & Legan, N. (2001). *School choice in America: The great debate*. Bloomington, IN: Phi Delta Kappa.

Michigan v. Bennett, 501 N.W.2d 106 (Mich. 1993).

Mitchell v. Helms, 530 U. S. 793 (2000).

Molnar, A. (2001, May 6). *School vouchers: The law, the research, and public policy implications*. Paper presented at the Hechinger Institute on Education and the Media, Columbia University. Retrieved from www.uwm.edu/Dept/CERAI/documents/publications/cerai-01-17.html

Molnar, A., Morales, J., & Wyst, A. (2000). *Profiles of for-profit education management companies*. Center for Education Research, Analysis, and Innovation. Milwaukee: University of Wisconsin-Milwaukee.

Mueller v. Allen, 463 U.S. 388 (1983).

Murphy v. Arkansas, 852 F.2d 1039 (8th Cir. 1988).

Murphy, J. (1999). New consumerism: Evolving market dynamics in the institutional dimension of schooling. In J. Murphy & K. S. Louis (Eds.), *The handbook of research on educational administration* (2nd ed., pp. 405–419). San Francisco; Jossey-Bass.

Nathan, J. (1996). Possibilities, problems, and progress. *Phi Delta Kappan, 78*, 18–24.

National Association of State Boards of Education (2001). *Any time, any place, any path, any pace: Taking the lead on e-learning policy*. Alexandria, VA: Author.

National Center for Education Statistics. (1999). *Digest of Education Statistics*. Washington, DC: U.S. Department of Education.

No Child Left Behind Act of 2001. (2002). 107 H.R. 1, 107th Congress, 1st Session.

Philadelphia Mayor agrees to state takeover of schools. (2002, January 4). *School Law News, 30*(1), 3–4.

Pierce v. Society of Sisters, 268 U.S. 510 (1925).

Pipho, C. (1995). The expected and the unexpected. *Phi Delta Kappan, 76*(10), 742–743.

Pipho, C. (1997). The selling of public education. *Phi Delta Kappan, 79*(2), 101–102.

Rouse, C. E. (1998). Schools and student achievement: More evidence from the Milwaukee parental choice program. *Economic Policy Review, 4*, 61–76.

Sandham, J. (1999, May 5). Florida OKs first statewide voucher plan. *Education Week*, pp. 1, 21.

Sassen, S. (2002, January 18). Globalization after September 11. *The Chronicle of Higher Education*, pp. B11–12.

Schnaiberg, L. (1998, June 10). Charter schools struggle with accountability. *Education Week*, pp. 1, 14.

Simmons-Harris v. Goff, 684 N.E.2d 705 (Ohio App. 1997), *rev'd*, 86 Ohio St. 3d 1 (1999).

Simmons-Harris v. Zelman, 234 F.3d 945 (6th Cir. 2000), *cert. granted sub nom.* Taylor v. Simmons-Harris, 122 S. Ct. 23 (2001).

Snider, J. H. (2002, January 9). Should school choice come via the internet? *Education Week*, p. 41.

Spring, J. (1997). *The American school 1642–1996* (4th ed.). New York: McGraw-Hill.

Stover, D. (2001, October 30). More public school districts are collaborating with home schoolers. *School Board News*, p. 5.

Strout v. Albanese, 178 F.3d 57 (1st Cir. 1999), *cert. denied*, 528 U.S. 931 (1999).

Supporters of privately financed vouchers tout progress. (1998, May 6). *Education Week*, p. 14.

Task Force on Charter Schools. (2002). *Indiana University's role in the Indiana charter school movement*. Bloomington: Indiana University School of Education.

The Technology Source. (2002, January/February) (bimonthly periodical published by the Michigan Virtual University).

Trotter, A. (2001, October 24). Cyber schools carving out charter niche. *Education Week*, pp. 1, 21.

Tyack, D., & Hansot, E. (1982). *Managers of virtue: Public school leadership in America 1820–1980*. New York: Basic Books.

Walsh, M. (1995, November 29). Sylvan makes quiet inroads into public schools. *Education Week*, pp. 3, 12.

Walsh, M. (1996, February 21). Brokers pitch education as hot investment. *Education Week*, pp. 1, 15.

Walsh, M. (1998, May 27). Edison schools predict "watershed year" ahead. *Education Week*, p. 5.

Walsh, M. (2001, September 12). Lack of profitability spurs school-management shakeout. *Education Week*, p. 8.

Weinschrott, D. J., & Kilgore, S. B. (1996). *Educational choice charitable trust: An experiment in school choice*. Indianapolis, IN: Hudson Institute.

Wisconsin v. Yoder, 406 U.S. 205 (1972).

Williams, L. C., & Leak, L. E. (1996). School privatization's first big test: EAI in Baltimore. *Educational Leadership, 54*(2), 56–60.

Witte, J., Sterr, T., & Thorn, C. (1995). *Fifth-year report: Milwaukee parental choice program*. Madison: University of Wisconsin-Madison.

Witters v. Washington Department of Services for the Blind, 474 U.S. 481 (1986).

Zobrest v. Catalina Foothills School District, 509 U.S. 1 (1993).

Superintendents and Board Members Grappling with Zero Tolerance Policies

Margaret Grogan and Brianne Reck

One of the most serious problems facing administrators is the presence of drugs and weapons in today's schools. Incidents with weapons that were once considered rare and shocking exceptions are occurring more regularly across the country. Sadly, some of these incidents are viewed as commonplace. Newspapers are littered with stories detailing tragedies and close calls because of drugs or weapons on school grounds. Headlines like "Boy Expelled for Bringing Gun to School," "Girl Expelled for Knife in Lunchbox," "Fake Gun, Real Penalty," and "Drug Bust in School Parking Lot" summarize the scope of the problem. America's largest cities as well as its smallest towns are experiencing these concerns increasingly often.

In response to this growing trend of student violence, in 1994 Congress passed the Gun-Free Schools Act and Drug-Free Schools Act, which required states to pass zero tolerance laws to qualify for federal funds under the programs supported by the Elementary and Secondary Education Act (ESEA). Many districts thus adopted policies mandating expulsion for students who violate weapons (not only guns) and drugs regulations under the school code. The general belief was that such policies had made schools safer. Many felt "that the hard line drawn by school officials would be easily understood, rarely challenged, and greatly reduce the number of drugs and weapons incidents" (Vail, 1995, p. 36).

There is some discussion as to whether these policies have been effective. Figures are hard to come by, and record keeping in many districts leaves much to be desired. National Center for Educational Statistics (NCES) data indicate that in 1996–1997, 79 percent of public schools had adopted zero tolerance policies for violence and tobacco use, 87 percent for alcohol use, 88 percent for drug use, 91 percent for weapons other than firearms, and 94 percent for firearms (U.S. Department

Margaret Grogan, University of Virginia
Brianne Reck, Hanover County (Virginia) School District

of Education, 1998). There is certainly a belief that such policies have helped to make schools safer. Proponents of zero tolerance discipline policies justify the need for them by citing increasing societal violence, the breakdown of the family, greater gang activity, and a strong sense of desperation and uncertainty about the future. But violence in schools has its roots in many problems with which educators are very familiar. School violence expert, Dewey Cornell explains:

> all of the attention to school shootings can lead us to overlook more pervasive, but less dramatic, problems. There are everyday problems such as bullying, teasing, and conflicts between rival groups of students. We have many youth who are angry, alienated, and depressed. ("Violence at school," 1999, p. 2)

Regardless of the reasons, school officials now point to an ever-growing number of zero tolerance violations in schools. In 1997, federal figures reveal that approximately 6,276 students were expelled from school for weapons violations (Portner, 1997b). However, not all of these apparently are for legitimate infractions. Horror stories have surfaced about students expelled or suspended unfairly, or even through a case of mistaken identity. There was a 10-year-old boy in Seattle who was expelled for bringing a plastic, one-inch GI Joe gun to class (Norton, 1997). In Fairborn, Ohio, a 13-year-old honors student was suspended for 9 days for possession of Midol tablets (Portner, 1996). Also, an 8-year-old girl in Louisiana who brought her grandfather's antique pocket watch to school for show-and-tell was expelled[1] because there happened to be a small knife on the end of the chain (Portner, 1997a). In instances like these, a kind of hysteria has taken hold of both school officials and the general public. Certainly, post-Columbine America has raised the notion of zero tolerance to new heights. Real or imagined threats to the possible safety of students in schools are now treated with draconian measures in many settings.

One such incident that received wide press coverage occurred in Decatur, Illinois, November 1999. "It was the mother of all bleacher fights, a bleacher fight that would not end. It was a five-star donnybrook that began as a punch-out between teen-age boys in the bleachers at a high school football game" (Page, 1999, p. 51). Reports say that spectators were terrified and some received minor injuries. Under the mantel of zero tolerance disciplinary policies, the school board made the decision to expel seven students for two years—the harshest punishment that had been recorded in that district. The students were not offered alternative placements in an educational setting. Although there was initial media outrage, it might have ended there, as just another example of the overreaction of school officials to student misbehavior, if it were not for the Reverend Jesse Jackson's intercession. When Jackson came to town with his civic group the Rainbow/PUSH Coalition, he managed to persuade the board to reduce the punishment to a one-year suspension with an opportunity for the students to receive alternative schooling. Illinois Governor George Ryan also added his voice to the appeal. Jackson was not satisfied with the reduction; he wanted the students back in school. However, despite Jackson's emotional rallies, his own arrest, and law suits filed with his help claiming that school officials violated privacy laws, the school board remained firm. Some argue that Jackson failed. Yet, a one-year expulsion and a continuation of educational services sounds to most like a much more reasonable response than a two-year separation from school.

The events in Decatur effectively crystallized the emotions and concerns of those who had been growing uneasy about the way zero tolerance policies had come to be applied. At the heart of the matter was not only the excessively harsh punishment, but also the question of race. All seven students were African-American, and the six who were disciplined (one left the state) had varying behavior records. Three were chronic truants, two had been in trouble with the law, but one was captain of the basket ball team (Cohen, 1999; White, 1999). No student was treated as an individual: none's role in the fight was examined nor was his prior record taken into consideration. Ultimately, this incident illustrates two serious trends brought up in earlier discussions of zero tolerance. One is that administrators and school board members are not using appropriate discretion in applying the policies and the other is that a disproportionate number of those penalized are non-white. This chapter focuses on a discussion of the first of these issues: the question of discretion.

THE STUDY

Interested in the moral and ethical implications of zero tolerance policies in K–12 schools in the United States, we designed an exploratory study of school board members and superintendents in Virginia in 1999–2000. The inquiry was designed to find out how board members and superintendents think about zero tolerance policies. What did zero tolerance mean? How did the administrators implement the policies? What purpose did board members and superintendents think the policies served? How effective did decision makers think the policies were? How was discretion used? In 1998, a new state law was passed requiring school boards to expel students who have:

> brought a controlled substance, imitation controlled substance, or marijuana onto school property or to a school-sponsored activity as prohibited by §18.2-255-2. (Virginia School Laws § 22.1-277.01:1)

However, the next sentence in the mandate gave the school board discretion.

> A school board may, however, determine, based on the facts of the particular case, that special circumstances exist and another disciplinary action is appropriate. (Virginia School Laws § 22.1-277.01:1)

Thus, we were particularly interested in what kind of special circumstances might mitigate the compulsory expulsion of students who had violated the weapons and drugs policies.

Qualitative methods were chosen for this study. Since participant perspectives were the focus of the study, interviews were conducted to try to understand how board members and superintendents made sense of the zero tolerance policies they were implementing in their districts. "By learning the perspectives of the participants, qualitative research illuminates the inner dynamics of situations—dynamics that are often invisible to the outsider" (Bogdan & Biklen, 1992, p. 32). The research questions guiding the study were: Do board members and superintendents use discretion in the application of zero tolerance policies? If so, how is discretion applied?

Eleven school board members and five superintendents were interviewed for 60 to 90 minutes. The participants were chosen to represent a variety of school districts. Names of board members were gained through Web pages and telephone contact with central office and personal contact. Superintendent names were also gained from Web pages, personal contact, and Virginia's Public Education Directory. Calls for participants were made purposively. Because the study was exploratory in nature, we sought some diversity in race, gender, size of school district, and location. Each participant in the study represented a different school district. Three researchers, a university professor and two graduate students, gathered data from representatives of 16 school districts in the central and south central regions of the state.

The only two criteria for participation were (1) current board member or superintendent status and (2) more than one year's service on a public school board or in the superintendent's position in that district. Participants were informed of the purpose of the study and chose to participate or not. Only one board member who initially agreed to participate in the study subsequently declined to be interviewed.

Interviews were taped and transcribed. Field notes were kept and shared among the researchers. The interview guides are included in appendix A of this chapter. The interviews were open-ended, allowing the participants to elaborate on areas of most importance to them. LeCompte and Preissle (1993) refer to this method of interviewing as an example of Denzin's nonstandardized interview "in which general questions are to be addressed and specific information desired by the researcher are anticipated but may be addressed during the interview informally in whatever order or context they happen to arise" (p. 169).

The two authors of the chapter coded the data and identified emergent themes. Since the board members were interviewed first, the data from the superintendent interviews were viewed in light of the previous responses. Board members perspectives and superintendent perspectives were thus compared. We used Starratt's (1994) ethic of critique as a theoretical lens to interrogate the data.

There is no attempt to claim broad generalizability of the findings of this study but, in reporting the participants' words, we give rich detail and provide a context for the reader to understand how the findings were developed. Due to the confidential nature of most of the discussions, the study is limited by our inability to cross reference with others involved, board members' and superintendents' perceptions of how the decisions were made.

The rest of the chapter is organized under the following headings: Board members' perspectives; Superintendents' perspectives; Discussion; and An ethic of critique applied.

BOARD MEMBERS' PERSPECTIVES

There were seven male and four female board members interviewed. Nine of the participants in this group were Caucasian and two were African-American males.

Their terms on the board ranged from 24 years to 3 years. Six of the 11 boards were elected boards and 5 were appointed boards. In Virginia, it is a local decision whether to elect or appoint school board members. Most districts now have elected boards but there are several remaining appointed boards. The size of the districts served ranged from 51,000 students to about 2,300 students. Four of the districts were described as rural or suburban/rural, three as suburban, and four as urban.

Board member responses can be categorized under two headings: Board discretion and beliefs about zero tolerance. These two categories provide us with useful insights into how board members interpret their task as public officials upholding the law governing school discipline. From a board member, though, we do not get the whole picture because many infractions of school policy are never considered at board level. On a daily basis, assistant principals, principals, hearing officers, and superintendents decide consequences for student misbehavior. Unless a student is recommended for expulsion or long-term suspension, boards play no role in the deliberations. Yet, the notion of zero-tolerance permeates every sector of the school district as we have seen in the many press articles on administrator overreaction and rigid application of policies. The power of the school board to remove a student from educational services is one manifestation of zero tolerance. Moreover, as many of our participants articulated, school boards have always exercised this power. For some board members, the passage of zero tolerance laws has merely given a name to their board's customary approach. Several argued that "the policy or the legislation has [not] had a significant impact on the way we do business. We have always done business that way" (DC).[2]

Board Discretion

Although the board members gave few details of particular students for reasons of confidentiality, many recalled incidents where the penalty of full expulsion (365 days) was reduced. A participant explained:

> Last year we had a student bring a box opener. . . . He worked in a place where he used one and he brought it to school. . . . We had a weapon search at the school and they found it in his coat. Well, he lied about it, so that was one dealt with on an individual basis and he had a pretty good record. . . . What we wound up doing with him was because he lied we had to kick him out and we ended up giving him homebound [instruction]. (SE)

For this board, the student's prior record, his three-point grade average and the fact that "he wasn't showing [the box opener] to anybody so it wasn't perceived as a weapon" were all factors that they took into consideration. Yet, he was expelled for the rest of the school year. The board member went on to say again that had the student not lied, he would have been fine.

Another example:

> We had a student who pulled out a sheathed knife, a pocket knife, a Swiss knife, . . . and put it in the ribs of his friend at an assembly over a note over a girl. . . . This was a weapon. He was kidding with his friend, but his friend took it seriously enough to tell

his mother and a policeman in the school . . . We can't put him back in school. He has
got potential. He's a young black man who's getting ready to go to high school next year.
A caring mother. He made a dumb mistake here, so we suspended him for the rest of the
year [less than two months] . . . we treated him individually. (OM)

Both board members used the notion of individual treatment to explain that they
did not always follow the spirit of the zero tolerance policies. Although none of the
participants seemed completely aware of the scope of discretion that the mandate allows, all liked the idea that they can "treat [students] individually." Generally speaking, the participants in the group favored the hard line of zero tolerance, but as one
member put it:

> I like . . . being able to show some leeway because there are cases when we can be more
> tolerant and so I think it works to the students' advantage if we're allowed to do that
> from time to time. Every once in a while a kid gets a break. Not that often but it does
> happen. (SE)

Factors that encouraged the board members to favor less severe penalties included: a student's prior discipline record, his or her academic record, his or her attitude, and his or her parent/guardian's attitude. Most of the board members also acknowledged that special education students must not be removed from all services.
Therefore, if the student violator can be seen as someone who has made "a dumb
mistake" or "was in the wrong place at the wrong time" and if he or she is repen-
tant, the chances that he or she will be "kicked out" are reduced. In addition, discretion allows the board to modify the penalty according to the student's good behavior while serving the suspension. Two board members discussed their
approaches.

> If we look at a student and he's making Ds and Fs, [we say] "Why're you making Ds
> and Fs at school?" . . . we do this before we dismiss a student—just to get a feeling. And
> then we look at how cooperative we feel the parent is going to be in the process . . . sup-
> porting the student or is looking for ways out of the situation . . . we weigh all these
> things. . . . and that's the reason we don't just blanket do a 365-day but bring them back
> in and sit down and listen to them again and see how well they've done after we kept
> them out a period of time. We have no problem taking part of the suspension back. (CF)

> [W]e try to give [parents] options if they're bound and determined that their child's in-
> nocent. More than once we give them the option to go to [the city], to the State Police
> and take a lie detector test. One time we had a kid pass the lie detector test and every-
> thing that had been done was rescinded. He was allowed to make up all his work and
> come straight back to school and everything. (SE)

Parent attitudes and tactics counted for or against the student. One board member
observed that: "We often now . . . have lawyers that come along with the family . . .
and if the family only knew, the lawyers sometime get in the way" (OM). He went
on to say that the board would simply rather hear just from the student and his fam-

ily. "What influences us [most] is the sincerity of the student" (OM). If the student offered signs of remorse, the board would be more inclined to offer options.

> We look for honesty and sincerity in what he is telling us. If we feel this incident has impacted him in such a way that he [has] turned a corner, . . . that he understands the seriousness of what he has done. (PM)

On the other hand, if a student is "like blowing up and kind of [has] a hostile attitude, no matter what we can do would be helpful since [the student] is not willing to receive it and admit that they need help to change" (PM).

Embedded in these remarks and in many other board members' statements is an authoritarian tone that reminds us of how students are meant to conduct themselves in the presence of those who have power over their lives. There is no suggestion that the "blowing up" or the "hostile attitude" have legitimate sources. Some of the board members were obviously operating out of very different life experiences than many of the students they were serving. Some board members pictured a certain kind of student who is not welcome in the system regardless of the circumstances he or she finds himself or herself in.

A similar tone emerged in another participant's description of the "habitual offender." The board member explained that zero tolerance policies have allowed his school district to identify "a youngster who doesn't really do one thing that qualifies them to be considered for expulsion but the multitude of things they . . . do [suggests the penalty of expulsion]" (GO). According to this participant, the board has directed principals and teachers to be on the lookout for such students so that if the time were to come, the student would be expelled instead of perhaps suspended. The same board member explained that his board really exercised little discretion in areas he believed are covered by zero tolerance. He put it this way:

> Some will argue that it's not good to enforce zero tolerance policies. They say that circumstances should be considered. If you [commit] one of those offences [here] we don't allow much for circumstances. . . . The board that we've had for the previous four years . . . was very strong and the board that we've got now is even more so. (GO)

However, sometimes community support can play a role in encouraging boards to consider the options for a student as another board member pointed out:

> There have been cases where some teachers have [written] letters in favor of the child saying give them another chance. Sometimes there's letters from ministers and people in the community to support this child and I'll tell you, in most cases that has weighed very heavily in favor of the child. (ZL)

In most cases, there seemed to be a set of conditions that predisposed the board to treat the student more leniently, but few of these cases involved students bringing weapons to school. Lenience did not seem to be an option in many weapons incidents at all. It is interesting to note that not all of the participants had had experiences of weapons violations. Therefore, when some of the board members talked of discretion, they were not referring to events that could be described as safety issues for the school. Nevertheless, one board member did say that she regretted not being able to use discretion where weapons were concerned. She said:

> The kind of things that drive you crazy are when a child picks up something from home which shouldn't be available to the child anyway, but still picks it up and brings it to school to show to his or her friends with no malice, no intention of doing something, but then there is the possibility that . . . another child could be hurt in the process. (DC)

That board member believed that the board could not use its judgment because of the provisions of the code. Boards, are, in fact, allowed discretion under the code, but some district policies do not include it. Moreover, this board member, like many of the others, distinguished cases involving guns and look-alike weapons from all other cases in the interests of the general safety and welfare of the students in the district. After the recent spate of school shootings, it is a mantra that is hard to ignore. Instead, board members used discretion in incidents of drug use (some in cases where there was suspicion of selling) or in cases involving knives or other cutting objects.

Typical of the larger districts in the study, one of the urban participants reported that in his district there was also zero tolerance for fighting and alcohol use:

> We have seen 76 cases since last September. [the interview was conducted in June] . . . and I asked them to give me the breakdown. Fifteen were alcohol related, 9 drugs, 19 assaults, 6 weapons, and we do look-alikes, [there were] 14. (OM)

The same board member continued, "We put probably 10 percent or 15 percent of our students [who violate the code] out of school; the rest we put in an alternative educational system." Another remarked, "Out of 41,000 students, 25 were put out of school for at least a year" (GO). He was referring to those who received no services. In that district, when a student is expelled, his or her parents or guardians are encouraged to find alternative educational opportunities for the student (often private placements), but the school provides no alternative schooling. It was one of the few districts where expulsion was truly synonymous with cessation of educational services.

On the whole, in some drug and a few weapons cases, board discretion revolved around lessening the length of the expulsion or suspension, allowing the student to be placed in alternative arrangements within school district or commuting the "sentence" for good behavior after a student began to serve it. Some districts had more alternative settings than others and, while students do not have a right to alternative education, many of the participants in this group expressed a strong desire to place most of the students who had committed weapons or drugs violations in an educational setting rather than on the street—particularly students who use illegal drugs: "We do have a program that will take those kids in and be able to still service those kids so it's not like we just put them on the street and forget about them" (ZL).

Beliefs about Zero Tolerance

As the forgoing discussion reveals, board members were mainly in favor of zero tolerance for weapons and drugs violations, although some had reservations. One participant had strong reservations, but she had spent the shortest time of all as a board member. She also served in a small district that had not had any weapons violations and only two drug incidents in the past three years. In some ways, this community seemed to be still living in a pre-zero tolerance world. Therefore, when she expressed horror at the treatment of a student, she was probably revealing her worldview—one that has not been shaped by experiences outside her own. She talked of a student who was expelled for his involvement with illegal drugs:

> My thing is this is a child that still has a chance and . . . [it was] the first thing I was involved in, I was so horrified and so upset that I just abstained. It was completely not right. I was a brand new board member and . . . I cried all the way home. . . . I knew he couldn't be in school, but they didn't want to even put him in the alternative school. They just felt that he should not be in school at all. That was a terrifying, just incredibly traumatic thing. (BD)

Living in a quiet, rural community, this board member's attitude towards zero tolerance is certainly colored by the size and location of her district. She says, though, that "we need the zero tolerance policy because . . . that's what the public expects and demands" (BD).

Similarly, the other participants felt that zero tolerance sends a message to the public and particularly to the other students in the district. Indeed, some of the language used betrays an enthusiastic embrace of the approach. One board member talked of bringing dogs in to the school buildings to sniff out drugs. "When they hit . . . a facility, it's a lock down and they hit it sometimes first thing in the morning as the buses are arriving" (GO). He was not the only one to talk in terms of "hit" and "lock down," terms of law enforcement that offer legitimacy to such action. In several cases, the educators seemed able wash their hands of a student once the police or resource officer had taken over. A board member explained:

> It is not only our moral obligation, but our legal responsibility to have law enforcement officials involved, and then the process they take is a totally different way of approaching the situation . . . theirs ultimately goes to the court and the consequences are determined in the court situation . . . sometimes they coincide [with ours] and sometimes they don't. (DC)

All participants believed firmly that the policies served as deterrents; however, none offered comparative figures to back up the claims that there were fewer infractions as a result of the policies. The best informed was the board member from the largest school district of 51,000 students who stated that in the school year 1999–2000, the board heard only 12–16 cases for expulsion. This district offered many interventions and options for students along the way.

Overall, answers to the question of what the participants thought of the zero tolerance approach were unequivocal:

> If we deal with these things swiftly and fairly, we think the word gets back even though we don't publicize it. The kids talk [among] themselves and we think it ends up helping the kids know that it's going to happen to them and they cut back a little bit. We know the first of last year we had several threats. We got rid of some kids and that stuff stopped. (SE)

> [Zero tolerance] is the only thing we have to go on now because we have an obligation to the students and to the teachers and to the parents. . . . I don't see the board veering from our position, making sure that we secure our schools and making sure they're safe. (OM)

However, even amongst those board members who favored the policy in general, a couple of the participants qualified their comments. Most argued that not every case is cut and dried, and that for some infractions, zero tolerance is not in the best interests of the child.

> I'm not 100 percent in favor of zero tolerance for everything. . . . You really don't accomplish a lot when you send a student home, just say go home for 365 days because they've been caught with drugs. A student needs some help. (CF)

> We had almost 50 cases last year with kids that came to us which is a lot. That's almost four a month . . . so if those kids didn't have any leeway at all, . . . out of those 50 at least half of them probably we gave them a penalty less severe than what the administration recommended. . . . So I think it's good that we have some options. (SE)

Even when a board must show zero tolerance for the behavior of a student, it is not a decision that some board members take lightly. A seasoned member who had served several terms as both member and chair of the board had not become inured to the process. "I feel emotionally undone by the time I actually go into open session in the board meeting" (PM). Another participant put it this way:

> When I make the decision [to expel a student], I always wonder how I am affecting the child. What is this going to do to the child and I don't think we make it joyously. We hassle over it and I . . . don't have a problem saying no, [the child is out]. I try when I say no to be sure that I have made the right decision in the process and that I give them some alternatives and options and just don't close the door in their face. (CF)

SUPERINTENDENTS' PERSPECTIVES

In the second phase of the study, five district superintendents were interviewed. The open-ended questions invited the superintendents to discuss their understandings of what was meant by zero tolerance, how their districts implement the policies, the superintendent's role in the decision-making process, what purpose the policies serve, how effective they are, and what circumstances might mitigate the compulsory penalty of expulsion. Four male and one female superintendent were interviewed. All participants were Caucasians. They had served between 20 and 40 years in public education, and had held the position of superintendent between 1 and 10 years. The size of their districts ranged from 25,000 students to 2,300. One of the districts was described as rural, two as suburban, and two as suburban/urban.

The broadening of the language in section 22.1-277.01:1 of the Virginia code in the 1999 Amendments to the Virginia Code provides for district superintendents to be authorized by the school board to conduct a preliminary review of cases covered under the zero tolerance laws "to determine whether a disciplinary action other than expulsion is appropriate" (§ 22.1-277.01:1). This allows a superintendent to exercise discretion in imposing sanctions on students who violate the state-mandated zero tolerance policies for weapons and drugs. Thus, the power to lessen penalties, in instances where the facts of a particular case would indicate that the prescribed penalties are in some way inappropriate, is no longer the sole province of the school board. Now a district may construct its policy so that the superintendent or his or her designee may make determinations about consequences and placement of students in alternative educational programs.

Districts represented by the superintendents in this study have taken one of two approaches. In four of the districts, the school boards retain the power to suspend or expel students, generally basing their decisions on the recommendation of the district superintendent. In the other district, the superintendent is charged with making the determination, and the school board acts as a board of appeal.

Superintendents reported that they were most actively involved in infractions that included recommendations for long-term (more than 10 days) suspensions or expulsions, and less directly involved in short-term (fewer than 10 days). The participants in this part of the study appeared to have extensive contact with building level administrators who make determinations in cases involving lesser offenses and provide information on which the superintendent bases his or her decision or recommendation regarding the disposition of cases where students violate drug or weapons prohibitions. Therefore, these participants have a somewhat different picture of overall student behavior management in the districts than the school board members who are rarely involved until the level of an expulsion hearing.

Among the district superintendents interviewed, little consensus emerged regarding their understanding of what it means to exercise discretion in violations of zero tolerance policies. Almost to a person they commented that in the implementation of zero tolerance policies one must exercise "common sense." What was not so common, however, was an understanding of what each considered sensible. Several related factors appear to influence the superintendent's ability to impose a sanction other than the compulsory expulsion for students who possess weapons or drugs. The way things work in a particular district appears to be a function of the way in which the district's policies define the role and responsibilities of the superintendent and the board, the nature of the relationship between the superintendent and the board, and the public's support and expectations. This section is divided into five parts, the superintendent's role in the decision-making process, his or her relationships with the school boards, the expectations of the public and the media, the ways in which superintendents exercise discretion, and superintendent beliefs about zero tolerance policies.

Roles

First, the roles of the school board and the superintendent as defined in the district's policies affect the ways in which decisions are made. One superintendent, whose school board gives him the responsibility of making determinations in all cases that are subject to a long term suspension or expulsion, indicated:

> The principal recommends to the superintendent that a student be expelled under the policy. The investigation is done at the school level and that suits me just fine. The school board handles any appeals of the superintendent's decision. The school board feels strongly that it is the superintendent's job to suspend long-term, more than ten days. (LB)

Another superintendent explained that:

> We have a process where the building level principal recommends suspension or expulsion. . . . They are going to recommend what they say is right, but they also like to tell us . . . [this student] doesn't read well, and such and such. When we have due process hearings, we go to the bottom of it. We get into everything. Then I make a recommendation to the board and they do the actual suspending or expelling. (HB)

Participants credited a clear delineation of responsibilities and clearly written policies as assets in developing a good working relationship. None, however, framed this discussion in terms of what is of most benefit to students. In fact, the mind-set that was revealed was somewhat reactive and authoritarian in nature. Few talked about preventive programs or the role of the school environment, something over which educators have some measure of control, in cases involving violations of weapon and drug policies. Each characterized his or her role as that of enforcer of policy. The one superintendent responsible for suspending or expelling students in his district indicated that the principals in the district consult him as they prepare a recommendation for long-term suspension or expulsion.

> Sometimes one of them will call me up and discuss what they want to do in a particular situation [long-term recommendation or short-term suspension] and to get my take on whether what they propose to do is consistent with what I think is in the best interests of the district. (LB)

Relationships

The nature of the relationship between the superintendent and the board is critical, and the superintendents all mentioned the need for consistency and support from their school boards. All reported cordial working relationships. Superintendents who make recommendations for the board to act upon, rather than making the determinations themselves, commented more often about the input of the student and his or her parents, and their "hearing" before the board.

> These cases always go in front of the school board because the school board is the agency that has to do the expelling, so the students and the parents also have the opportunity to sit before the school board and to tell them why they would hope that they would not be expelled. (BW)

All of the superintendents felt that the board supported their recommendations. All, in some way, attributed this to having an unambiguous code of student conduct, and "a good working relation" with the board.

> Our policy is rather cut and dried. We let the students know our expectations and we are consistent in our enforcement of the rules. With weapons, there are no exceptions . . . If a student is caught with a weapon, he or she is expelled. (LB)

> The board usually accepts the recommendations I make. We have developed a relationship where they trust my judgment and we [superintendent and principal] always provide enough background and information to explain why we think a particular suspension or expulsion is appropriate. They are free to question us about the case and often do. (FE)

This relationship, however, does not exist in a vacuum, and each superintendent implied that community expectations, pressures, and media scrutiny affect the process on some level.

> On a rare occasion, if there has been a great deal of public attention or a community member has been in contact with a [board] member they might raise the question of a lesser penalty, but by and large they go with my recommendation. (SF)

Perhaps as a recognition of the political nature of their position and that of the board members, these superintendents acknowledged the importance of public interest in student discipline as a factor that has an impact on their ability to gain community support for the overall program.

Public and Media

Community expectations and support appear to encourage superintendents to consider leniency in certain cases; however, school response to highly publicized incidents of school violence have altered public perceptions of the level of safety in schools, and public views toward zero tolerance policies. All five superintendents reported that they had a cordial relationship with the local press and indicated that in general terms that they felt that the press reported and commented on their handling of discipline matters in a supportive manner.

> In both the editorials and in the news articles . . . we have seen a great deal of support for the way in which we handle things. I think the press is generally supportive of us on

discipline issues, and I think that has a great deal to do with the community and its attitudes. (LB)

We were a little apprehensive at first. Neighboring districts have taken a pounding in the press over discipline issues, so we were not quite sure what to expect, but they reported the facts fairly and expressed approval of and support for the way we handled the thing. (HB)

Similar to the cases reported in the national media referenced at the beginning of this chapter, public criticism has followed cases in which superintendents and school boards have imposed harsh penalties when the public perceived that the student deserved a less severe penalty or no penalty. Also, in cases where it appeared that students were not punished as harshly as others who had committed similar offenses, the decisions of the superintendents and school boards were publicly questioned.

Each of the superintendents alluded to a particular event in June of 1999 in which conservative civil liberties activists from the Charlottesville-based Rutherford Institute filed suit to have the record of an 8th grader in a northern Virginia county expunged of a four-month suspension for a weapons violation. The student had taken a knife away from a friend who had threatened to harm herself, and another student had reported that the good Samaritan had the knife in his possession. According to the newspaper, a school spokesperson justified the school board's upholding of the suspension because "students are well aware that possession of a knife is grounds for expulsion. All he had to do was give it to a teacher" (Associated Press Wire Report, June 13, 2000). Four of the five superintendents interviewed suggested that this case was an example of an instance in which a different outcome might have been expected in their district: "In my district that would have been handled differently. You really have to apply some common sense. The public wants safe schools, but they want to know that we are making them safe in a fair and reasonable way" (BW).

In this study, the message these superintendents perceive that the public is sending them is that they are to take a hard line on issues that involve "real" threats to children's safety in schools, but that they should guard against wholesale imposition of zero tolerance. Yet few superintendents could give examples of lesser sanctions in their own districts.

Superintendent Discretion

The intent, the age, and the academic and behavioral histories of the student involved appear to be factors that weigh heavily in making determinations about the appropriateness of penalty guidelines. When asked about mitigating circumstances that might influence his recommendations, one superintendent stated:

Unfortunately sometimes some of our kids see things at home that aren't appropriate. A little kindergartner or first grader . . . picks up a roach or something that dad has left on the coffee table and stick it in their pocket, you know and they have brought it to school to show their friends. Mostly it would have to be age and innocence type of situation. (BC)

With regard to intent, all of the superintendents indicated that situations involving look-alike weapons and drugs are more difficult to address. Again, the perceived intent of the student is a primary factor.

> We've had a situation lately where a young man had a little bit of pot mixed in with some oregano. He had it in small bags trying to push it as a nickel bag, you know, a five-dollar bag. And he was with the intent and the means to sell and receive a profit for it so it was an immediate expulsion. (FE)

Conversely, one superintendent determined that a lesser penalty was appropriate in a situation where a student failed to follow the medications policy and showed fellow students that he had brought his prescription medication to school to give to the nurse. He, therefore, possessed a controlled substance.

> We gave him some short-term suspension for not following our policy for medication. Now had it been that he was trying to give them to somebody, he would have been expelled. You have to one, always maintain what you say you're going to do, and two, you've got to have that common reasoning . . . But sometimes the [prescribed] punishment doesn't fit the crime. (HB)

Similar to the board members, three of the superintendents mentioned a third factor—the student's prior academic and behavioral record. In discussion of cases involving students with no prior violations of school rules and policies, four of the five superintendents agreed that some allowance should be made for students who suffer a lapse of judgment or "just don't think." While they could offer no definitive description of what distinguishes this type of student from others, they all seemed to have a notion of who that student might be.

The superintendents reported that their opportunities to exercise discretion in implementing zero tolerance policies for weapons increased with the rash of bomb threats that followed the events in Columbine, Colorado. In a number of highly publicized cases, including one in an eastern district of Virginia involving a student who made a threat to blow up a school after being harassed by other students, parents and community members in some areas have begun to question whether the implementation of zero tolerance is appropriate although other communities continue to encourage a hard line. Making a decision that fits public expectations appears to be a decisive factor in the minds of these leaders.

> In our case, [the expulsion of a student who threatened to plant explosives in the school] the student had a map indicating where he planned to place the explosives, and there were explosives and other equipment found in the home. In the current atmosphere, the public expects us to act decisively and take no chances. So we had both public and media support. (LB)

Superintendent Beliefs
Four of the superintendents articulated support for zero tolerance policies in theory, but each pointed to difficulties associated with using them as an absolute standard.

Kids need to feel safe, they have to feel secure, they have to know what the rules are if you are going to have a good learning environment, but also you need the support of the community and we need to have that by having good discipline and also by having fair discipline. I don't think you can go off the deep end and take zero tolerance to such a degree that it doesn't really respect situation and respect people. (FE)

The notion of fairness and that of individual treatment are central to the beliefs expressed by these superintendents, but they differ somewhat in what constitutes fair. One respondent indicated that the clarity of the student code of conduct and the fact that students are made aware of the regulations and expectations governing student behaviors make mandated penalties fair.

We are fairly cut and dried in what we do. There are not too many factors or circumstances that mitigate what we do. There could be extenuating circumstances that might be out there, but I can not envision what they might be. Our policy is written with latitude to use discretion, and I think that is appropriate. (LB)

Others, while affirming the need to have policies that deal harshly with certain offenses, believed that there is a need for flexibility so that they might deal with individual cases.

There's times when [zero tolerance] is not the right answer, [but] because there are always some people who are very legalistic and the letter of the law is the letter of the law, for them there's never a time when it's not. . . . [T]hat's why you have the appeal processes and that's why you have appeals to school boards where they can talk to a group of people rather than one person. So, all in all I think for the most part it works. (BW)

One of the superintendents, however, stated unequivocally that he opposed the concept of zero tolerance policies.

I really don't like the term "Zero Tolerance," it sort of sticks in my craw. I don't think we have ever had, nor should we ever have zero tolerance; not even close. I would prefer to say that we have straightforward expectations for student behavior and very strict enforcement of the code. I think that when we start using zero tolerance policies we run the risk of making determinations arbitrarily and unilaterally. . . . I think that the way we manage things is as important as what we do. If we handle discipline situations fairly and firmly, we build community support for our decisions. (LB)

DISCUSSION

The study reinforced, first of all, that while boards must act as single entities when making an official decision, they are comprised of individuals. Superintendents too, though they get advice, are individuals. Although there were some similarities in responses, the 11 board members and 5 superintendents actually represented a range of positions from the toughest to the most flexible. It is easy to imagine that, under certain circumstances, decision makers' own particular opinions might prevail, whereas, in others, they would bow to a majority with whom they might be at odds.

For instance, at least in some of the school board members' minds, one concern is the particularized treatment of students who have violated weapons and drugs policies. They cite the tension between serving both the needs of the community of students and the needs of the one who has violated the policy. In most instances the rights of the many outweigh the individual's.

Critics of zero tolerance policies fear the rigid uniformity with which these policies are applied. Curwin and Mendler (1999) argue:

> What was originally intended as a policy to improve safety in school by ensuring that all children—regardless of race, athletic ability, or parental influence—follow the rules is used now as an excuse to treat all children the same when they are in need of corrective measures. (p. 119)

While several board members and superintendents expressed the belief that he or she was considering the individual, others described Curwin and Mendler's sentiment exactly. Some were adamant that zero tolerance provides an equality of treatment that transcends individualism. However, others cited many factors that would allow them to treat students differently from each other. In the smaller districts, we got a strong sense of a board and superintendent looking very carefully at who the student is and at what would be best for him or her. By contrast, in those districts where there were significant numbers of infractions, options were not always considered for expellable offences. Moreover, when circumstances were taken into account, it was clear some students were plainly not given any options. There were references to students who had a history of trouble, whose parents/guardians were not supportive, whose attitude was defiant, and who were described simply as "out of here." It is hard to define exactly participants' ideas of what kind of student deserves zero tolerance and what kind of student deserves options. But there is no doubt that all had in their minds a profile of an undeserving student. Board members, because they were removed from the school, seemed to prefer a more uniform application of the policies than superintendents did.

School exclusion as a response to student behavior has not shown to be an effective rehabilitative method. Students who drop out of school have often been suspended (Skiba & Peterson, 1999, p. 376). Therefore, there is a distinct possibility that in the interests of the majority (who need to be kept safe at school) a minority of students is "thrown away." The participants spoke of relying on alternative placements and other interventions for most of those who violated drugs and weapons policies. However, none said that all the students would have somewhere to go. More disturbing were the comments of the board members who saw the increase in middle school students expelled for these infractions.

While the study indicated only a few harsh penalties for students who brought look-alike weapons to school or who mistakenly brought weapons to school, there was still a consensus that the policies were designed to be rigid to prevent any potential weapon from being on school premises. Again, some of the superintendents talked of "common sense" mitigating harsh penalties, but most agreed that it would depend on community perceptions. Few will dispute zero tolerance in the interests of safety. However, there were still many indications that students who passed on to others "drugs" such as Advil and Alka Seltzer would be treated just as inflexibly. What seems clear is that, at least at the board level if not before, the circumstances surrounding each incident must be carefully scrutinized. Suspension, even for a day, for young children and alternative placements for older students can have a more far-reaching effect on a student than may be intended.

It is interesting to note the kind of alternative settings that at least one district provided. The board member described this place as "a basic school, which is . . . very intense, very little recreation, very little recess period. It's very structured." He went on to say that even in the regular setting, "We have a person who runs disciplinary hearings . . . resource police officers in uniform in every one of our high schools and middle schools." Indeed, there is a police presence even at the suspension intervention program in that district. "[Suspended students] have to attend classes. Those classes are taught very intense and . . . there is a policeman who teaches part of it, social worker who teaches part of it" (GO).

This board member, like others in the study, spoke as if such students needed reform rather than care and compassion. If the message of zero tolerance is primarily about changing behavior, districts who put resources into building relationships with students are likely to have a better success rate than those that threaten students with the law even at the first sign of behavior that is contrary to the rules of the school. Few of the board members mentioned appropriate use of discretion for offenders whose main crime was ignorance or panic. The case of the student who was suspended long term for lying about the box opener comes to mind. On the other hand, superintendents tended to reason differently. Closer to the students because of their roles as educators and relying on the judgment and information from their principals, superintendents were able to use their discretion more flexibly than board members. Only one superintendent in the study, however, was given full discretion.

In the end, there was little discussion about the moral and ethical implications of decisions. A few participants mentioned what they thought was the "right" thing to do. When probed though, there was little sense of distinguishing what was right for the student from what is right for everyone else. And most often it was argued that "everyone else's" needs must be served at the expense of the offending student. Thus, it is imperative that we consider these policies in moral and ethical terms.

AN ETHIC OF CRITIQUE APPLIED

Starratt (1994) argues that to look at schooling through an ethical lens, we should begin with an ethic of critique, "aimed at [schooling's] own bureaucratic context and the bureaucratic tendency to reproduce the status quo" (p. 46). If we examine the policies from a critical perspective, we cannot miss the participants' efforts to maintain a stance of "business as usual." There was a clear message in the study that students who do not fit school standards need fixing, preferably in a setting removed from the mainstream.

We think many of the board members and superintendents were truly well intentioned. However, there were very few comments suggesting that the regular settings might have contributed to the students' behaviors. Rizvi (1993) captures this sentiment well when he says, "We need to recognize that the educational system not only reproduces inequality it also *generates* it" (p. 205, emphasis in original). Whether it is inequality arising from socioeconomic status or race or gender or life experiences commingling all such factors, two kinds of students emerge from this study: those we wish to keep safe and those we suspect will endanger us—if not in a violent sense, in the sense that they threaten the status quo. And we need to pay attention to the fact that those in the latter category are often disproportionately poor and non-white.

We believe that zero tolerance policies, as they are being implemented in schools in this study, are helping to shape this dichotomous view of students. Thus, an ethic of critique allows us to identify more closely those whom zero tolerance policies benefit and those whom they fail (Starratt, 1994, p. 47). This approach also allows us to problematize the way things are. Many members of the public and many educators themselves support the notion of zero tolerance. Fears of more deaths at school, and belief that taking a hard line sends a message to those who might be tempted to disrupt the schools, have convinced many. But we must "think in oppositional terms, deconstruct the assumptions that limit and legitimate the very questions we ask" (Giroux, 1993, p. 28).

For instance, eliminating zero tolerance laws would not be the same as advocating unsafe schools. Proponents of zero tolerance have bought into the "either/or" mentality that approves of the harsh line as the only alternative to dangerous conditions in schools. The emphasis rather should be on the challenge to design safe learning environments from a perspective that sees safety as a condition to be created rather than endangered. If we accept the idea that safe schools exist and that we can lose them, then we are committed to discovering the threats. This perspective will color our good judgment of students' actions and attitudes. We might then consider student infractions not in terms of whether they pose a threat to the status quo (also read "safety") but in terms of how *much* threat they pose.

Those who framed the law in Virginia included the provision for board and superintendent discretion for good reason. Justice is served only when each case is looked at upon its merits. Therefore, decision makers are meant to take circumstances into account. But zero tolerance thinking distorts this principle. By following zero tolerance policies, educators have lost some of their powers to exercise judgment and sometimes student offenders are punished harshly. The study clearly demonstrated that as soon as the juvenile courts were involved, educators' hands were tied.

An interesting parallel may be found in the way zero tolerance has also been associated with policing, especially in the inner city in the United States. In this context, zero tolerance "focuses on discovering (not deterring) crime by mandating that police stop, frisk and arrest vast numbers of people—many of whom are young black and Hispanic men—for minor offenses" (Rosen, 2000, p. B3). The vain hope is that petty criminals will be found guilty of crimes that are more serious. The parallel becomes clear when we realize that those closest to the individuals to be policed or educated are prevented from using discretion. The police officers are directed to arrest people for every offense rather than to work with them, developing relationships and issuing warnings. The very nature of zero tolerance in both contexts pushes judgment of misbehavior outside the setting in which people operate. Behavior is judged by those with knowledge of the rules rather than with knowledge of the individual. And the emphasis in both contexts is on ferreting out those who really deserve exclusion from our midst.

Finally, an ethic of critique prompts us to consider the world from the perspectives of those students who have been disciplined under zero tolerance policies. What good examples of reasoned adult judgment did they encounter? The authoritarian manner in which many of these life-changing decisions are made certainly does not reinforce the democratic ideals we hold in high regard. When policies are applied rigidly, individual circumstances are often not taken into account and little value is placed on student attempts to challenge the way things are done. By separating students into the two groups that we have identified through this study, proponents of zero tolerance policies effectively demonstrate the power and privilege the mainstream enjoy. Not since segregation has marginalizing students been supported with such zeal.

Instead of educating all students to participate in a democracy whose highest aim is that citizens govern themselves, we are teaching students to accept authority and the need to be governed. Is that what we intend? Educational administrators should rethink zero tolerance policies. This is not to abandon order in the schools or to make them unsafe. It is to clear the way for a more active search for learning environments that live up to our democratic ideals. At the same time, it will allow us to engage in the messy struggle of creating school communities that include all students, all of whom we wish to keep safe.

NOTES

1. According to Skiba and Peterson (1999) this student was actually suspended and sent for one month to a local alternative school (p. 375).

2. Codes have been divised for participants to maintain confidentiality.

REFERENCES

Bogdan, R., & Biklen, S. (1992). *Qualitative research for educators.* Boston, MA: Allyn and Bacon.

Cohen, W. (1999, November 22). Zero tolerance brawl. *U.S. News and World Report, 127*(20), 34.

Curwin, R., & Mendler, A. (1999). Zero tolerance for zero tolerance. *Phi Delta Kappan, 81*(2), 119–120.

Giroux, H. (1993). *Living dangerously.* New York: Peter Lang.

LeCompte, M., & Preissle, J. (1993). *Ethnography and qualitative design in educational research* (2nd ed.). San Diego, CA: Academic Press.

Norton, D. (1997, October 9). Boy expelled from school for showing tiny toy gun. *The Seattle Times* [Online]. Retrieved from www.seattletimes.com/extra/browse/html197/gunn_010897.html

Page, C. (1999, November 19). "Zero tolerance" equates with zero rationality. *Philadelphia Business Journal, 18*(41), 51.

Portner, J. (1996, October 23). Suspensions stir debate over discipline codes. *Education Week on the Web* [Online]. Retrieved from www.edweek.org/vol-16/08react.h16

Portner, J. (1997a, March 26). Zero-tolerance laws getting a second look. *Education Week on the Web* [Online]. Retrieved from www.edweek.org/ew/vol-16/

Portner, J. (1997b, June 25). Gore claims expulsions prove weapons policies working. *Education Week on the Web* [Online]. Retrieved from www.edweek.org/ew/vol-16/

Rizvi, F. (1993). Race, gender and the cultural assumptions of schooling. In C. Marshall (Ed.), *The new politics of race and gender. The 1992 Yearbook of the Politics of Education Association* (pp. 203–217). Washington, DC: Falmer Press.

Rosen, J. (2000, April 23). When good policing goes bad. *The Washington Post*, p. B3.

Skiba, R., & Peterson, R. (1999). The dark side of zero tolerance. *Phi Delta Kappan, 80*(5), 372–382.

Starratt, R. (1994). *Building an ethical school.* Washington, DC: Falmer Press.

United States Department of Education, National Center for Education Statistics, Fast Response Survey System (1998). *Principal/school survey on school violence,* FRSS 63, 1997. Retrieved from http://nces.ed.gov/pubs98/violence/98030008.html

Vail, K. (1995). Ground Zero. *American School Board Journal, 182*(6), 36–38.

Violence at school: An interview with Dr. Dewey Cornell. (1999, June). *VASS News, XI*(10), 1–4.

Virginia school laws. (2000). Charlottesville, VA: Michie.

White, J. (1999, November). Fighting words. *Time Canada, 154*(21), 50.

APPENDIX A
Questions for Interviewing School Board Members on Zero Tolerance Policies in Public Schools in Virginia.

1. What is your understanding of the sanctions for violations of the Zero Tolerance Policy on weapons and drugs in your division?
2. In the past few years, have any students in your division violated the division's policy on weapons and drugs?
3. Please talk a little about how such incidents were handled.
4. The mandate gives school boards and superintendents discretion in the imposition of penalties under these policies. Could you talk about the process used to make these decisions?
5. What is the board role in the process?
6. Who has input in the decision-making process? (principal, student, parent, others?)
7. What were some of the considerations that were taken into account in making the decision to handle this/these incident(s) in that way?
8. Were any of these decisions controversial?
9. How effective do you think Zero Tolerance Policies are? What makes you think that?

Questions for Interviewing Superintendents on Zero Tolerance Policies in Public Schools in Virginia.

1. What is your understanding of the sanctions for violations of the Zero Tolerance Policy on weapons and drugs in your division?
2. In the past few years, have any students in your division violated the division's policy on weapons and drugs?

3. Please talk a little about how such incidents were handled.
4. The mandate gives school boards and superintendents discretion in the imposition of penalties under these policies. Could you talk about the process used to make these decisions?
5. What is your role in the process?
6. Who has input in the decision-making process? (principal, student, parent, others?)
7. What were some of the considerations that were taken into account in making the decision to handle this/these incident(s) in that way?
8. Were any of these decisions controversial?
9. How effective do you think Zero Tolerance Policies are? What makes you think that?

A Call for Professional-Organizational Self-Scrutiny

Seymour B. Sarason

For the purposes of this chapter, I shall begin with the nature and consequences of two kinds of social change. The first kind is initiated by catastrophe, two examples of which are the Japanese attack on Pearl Harbor on December 7, 1941, and the destruction of the World Trade Center on September 11, 2001. In a most general way, in both instances there had been harbingers that we would or might be the object of destructive actions, although no one predicted that those actions would take the form they did: A literally sudden, totally surprising action bearing the hallmark of a catastrophe. But, I must emphasize, there were harbingers which officialdom did not take seriously. That Japan and America were on a collision course was no secret. That the likes of Saddam Hussein and Osama Bin Laden had already made known their goal of destroying American power and influence was certainly not secret. Saddam was developing weapons of mass destruction and Bin Ladan was the force behind bombings of our embassies and the first bombing of the World Trade Center in 1993. The interpretation of these events by officialdom and the general public did not include the possibility that our view of ourselves and the world would or should have to change in ways we never contemplated. Only one country saw it differently—and I would say correctly—several decades before and that was Israel, which preemptively destroyed Iraq's nuclear reactors. Publicly, Israel was criticized for its action although privately officialdom breathed a sigh of relief. Israel was not concerned with social change but with its existence. Today, from the president and the Congress we are told that we may or should take actions identical to what caused Israel to be criticized.

In the case of social change caused by catastrophe we know, or think we know, what our responses should be, however unprepared we are to take appropriate actions. Generally speaking, the social change that may follow such actions is embraced, a

---

Seymour B. Sarason, Professor Emeritus, Yale University

price the public is willing to pay, although there is by no means clarity about possible adverse consequences those changes may have. Problem solving in a context of crisis is always fraught with danger if only because we are compelled to act quickly; time becomes an enemy.

The second kind of social change is wrapped up in the truism that war changes everything and everyone. War may be the result of a catastrophe; it may be described as a necessary and just war; and as in the case of World War II, it may end up in military victory. However, it is not until the war is over and years have passed that we begin to understand that the war unleashed social problems and dynamics, positive and negative, we had not envisioned.

The manifestations of social change, regardless of its initiating causes, is predictable only in a most global way. Its concrete manifestations only become apparent after the social change has begun, by which time its relationships to initiating causes is little cause for reflection except for historians schooled to unravel contexts of causes and effects. So, for example, what we call the sizzling 1960s were years during which it was impossible for people to ignore that a many faceted social change had already occurred and was picking up steam. Generally speaking, that decade came as a surprise to most people—certainly to those 30 years of age or more—as every major societal institution was subject to criticism and attack. It is not an exaggeration to say that as a society we were unprepared for how to think about and react to it. Do you seek to roll back or contain the change? Do you roll with the punch and make essentially cosmetic changes? What was bedeviling was the multiple-faceted nature of the change, involving as it did issues of race, gender, poverty, sexual lifestyle, civil rights, drugs, dress, music, war (Vietnam), generational gulf, and the purposes and content of education in the university and the public schools. Two questions were uppermost in people's minds. How do we explain the social change? What could or should we do about it? The need for explanation was experienced as crucial on the assumption that knowledge of etiology would be a guide to how one should deal with the change. That quest for causation led to very superficial or narrow answers, as if each facet of the change had its own distinctive etiology. The fact is that all the facets had their origins during World War II and not long after that war those facets fed, so to speak, on each other. I have discussed this in my 1996 book, *Barometers of Social Change: Individual, Educational, and Social Transformation*, in 1998, *Political Leadership and Educational Failure*, and in 2001, *American Psychology and Schools: A Critique*. I do not claim to have done justice to the complexity of the issues. But one thing I think I made clear: The failures of the educational reform movement in the post–World War II era are in large part because (a) the educational community had an ahistorical conception of the origins of the social changes with which it was confronted; (b) it publicly adopted the stance that increased expenditures would solve or ameliorate the problems plaguing it; (c) it assumed that the structure and traditions of the system did not require change; and (d) it continued to ignore or reexamine a basic and longstanding problem: What are the distinguishing features and implication of contexts of productive and unproductive learning?

THE NEED FOR SELF-SCUTINY

Societal institutions and professional organizations do not change quickly and willingly, a statement guilty of understatement. Not many individuals willingly start a self-scrutinizing process for the explicit purpose to locate and examine the diverse errors of omission and commission they made in life. My most recent book, *Educational Reform: A Self-Scrutinizing Memoir* (2002), attempted such a task. Predictably, it was not an ego-inflating experience, and I have no doubt that the barriers to insights and candor were operative. It is no different in the case of institutions and the professional organizations with a vested interest in them. In this connection it is interesting to compare education and medicine early in the 20th century. In the medical community there was a small but influential group who regarded medical education and practice as scandalously inadequate, so much so that the Carnegie Foundation for the Improvement of Teaching commissioned one of the two most preeminent educators of the day to study medical education. That person was Abraham Flexner. (The other preeminent educator was John Dewey.) Flexner visited all but a handful of the several hundred medical schools in the United States and Canada. Flexner's report in 1910 did no less than revolutionize medical education and practice. I have discussed that report and its consequences in *The Case for Change: Rethinking the Preparation of Educators* (1993). The change that Flexner's report initiated was accompanied by several interrelated messages to the public. The first was that medical education and practice were in need of radical overhaul. The second was that there was a great deal the medical community did not know about the etiology and nature of major illnesses and disease, an ignorance that could only be reduced by systematic experimentation and research. The third was that the medical community could not say when and to what extent real "breakthroughs" would occur; what could be promised was that the most serious efforts would be made to achieve new and productive knowledge; those efforts would be costly, many of them would be failures, but at some undetermined point new knowledge would be obtained. There were no shortcuts; ignorance is not easily overcome. It could be said that the medical community was candidly proclaiming the virtues of its defects: an extensive ignorance and a grossly inadequate tradition of medical education and practice.

The time of the Flexner report was also the time when public school systems were growing in size, administrative complexity, and in the problems they confronted. But unlike what was happening in the medical arena, there were no messages that seriously proclaimed that there was a most inadequate, untested basis that could serve as guides to dealing with serious problems. There were, of course, a plethora of ideas, plans, fads, and fashions, all well intentioned and passionately defended. Educators were no less concerned with improving the public welfare than the physicians, but there was pitifully little searching self-scrutiny of the actual relationships among schools of education, the realities of the culture of the school, school governance structure and its embeddedness in the political system, and the criteria, process, and forums by which to judge improvement or the need to change. There were many battles (some would say wars) in regard to theory and values, but the fact is that what got changed was cliché-ridden mission statements, the size and differentiation of the administrative hierarchy, and little else. That what we call our educational *system* may be seriously flawed and in need of a major overhaul was for all practical purposes not on the agenda. I italicize system in order to emphasize how little discussion there was about the question: Of what parts was the system comprised? Schools, departments and schools of education, the state department of education, the legislative and executive branches of state and local government, parents—these are parts of the educational system. (This was before the federal government and the unions became players.) Was this a system that could accommodate to and be supportive of educational reform? Why and to what extent were these parts so frequently in an adversarial relationship? Because every system of human relationships, beginning with the family, is characterized by issues of power, what are the positive and negative roles of power in the educational system insofar as efforts to change it are concerned? Is it a system explicitly obligated and given the resources seriously to examine and change its practices, traditions, and relationship to failure and social change, and to do so other than on the basis of personal opinion or data that would not be admissible in a court of evidence? Is it a system in which increasing budgets are correlated with increased quality of output? Is it a system within which there is a consensus about purposes and outcomes and how they are to be evaluated? Is it a system the resources of which are devoted approximately equally to prevention and repair? Is it primarily a reactive or proactive system?

We hear much today about accountability, by which is meant who should be blamed for our educational ills, and it is almost always the case that teachers and administrators are the sitting ducks for potshots. That is a case of misplaced emphasis because those groups are part of a larger system. If you, as one should, take the concept of system seriously, you have to ask: In what ways is that system contributing to our dissatisfactions about level and quality of educational outcomes? One reason the concept of system is not taken seriously is not because people deny the existence of a system but rather that they implicitly rather than explicitly know or believe that the system is, so to speak, so locked in the concrete of tradition that they retreat to the comforts of oversimplifications. In the 20th century there were two notable examples outside of education which illustrates what happens when the concept of system is taken seriously. The first example was set in motion during World War II when it was recognized that the Veterans Administration (VA) was a system of diverse parts utterly inadequate to deal with what was coming down the road: literally millions of veterans who deserved a quality of care and services that agency had not given to pre–World War I veterans. The preexisting VA system was replaced by a new one, a system change which dramatically impacted on medical education, other parts of universities, and the research endeavor. It was by no means an easy, smooth change, but it was successfully accomplished. The second example was in the 1950s when Congress created the Joint Commission on Mental Health to analyze and evaluate the dimensions of mental health problems, and the adequacy of state and local services, especially in regard to the inadequacies of the state hospital system. The result was an essentially new system and rationale for provision of services. One of its accomplishments was to transform state hospitals, really "warehouses," and even dramatically to eliminate many of them. Here again it was not easy because there were many vested interests with a stake in the old system.

SCHOOL ADMINISTRATION AND SELF-SCRUTINY

Let me now turn to what I have learned over the decades from my interactions with school administrators in one-on-one interactions. A fair amount has been written about the phenomenology of school administrators and what they contain is basically similar to what I have learned. Where I may differ with those writings, a matter largely of degree, I attribute to the truly private nature of my interactions. What administrators say publicly or for record can be markedly different from what they think, believe, and feel.

1. Administrators (superintendents, supervisors, principals) early on in that role come to understand the many constraints on utilization of their power to make non-cosmetic changes, let alone system changes. There is no honeymoon period, if by that is meant that school personnel and the board of education willingly (let alone graciously) go along with what they may perceive as a significant change in what they do or how they do it. This is frustrating and more often than not results in a me-they or we-they perception of each other. After World War II Winston Churchill said, "I did not become Prime Minister to preside over the dissolution of the British Empire." Similarly, the new administrator thinks that he or she was not put in the role to preside over and leave unchanged a school system or school with numerous inadequacies.

2. The superintendent has little or no relationship with teachers who, far more often than not, are the ultimate implementers of a proposed change. The superintendent is dependent on administrators lower down in the hierarchy for explaining and overseeing that the spirit and substance of the change become appropriately implemented. Not infrequently, the superintendent has "inherited" administrative associates, some of whom he neither likes, respects, nor trusts. Indeed, one of the first things that may occupy him or her is how it may be possible to remove such associates, a possibility fraught with interpersonal and political conflict. The superintendent comes to respect the adage that winning battles and losing wars should be avoided. What the superintendent tends to be insensitive to is that what he or she experiences and feels is identical to what the administrative staff experience and feel in their relations with principals and teachers. However you define clear, honest communication, it is infrequent in school systems, especially in moderately sized or large school systems. The extreme example is New York City which has 1,100 schools! As is usually the case, what is true of New York City is true in smaller city systems; it is a matter of degree and the frequency of explosions in the media. In any complicated, hierarchically layered organization the psychological distance between those at or near the top and those below them has predictable adverse consequences, and the less that is recognized, the more adverse the consequences.

3. Many administrators, their public rhetoric not withstanding, privately come to see themselves not as leaders but managers, not as educational builders but as firemen putting out fires, not as a justified disturber of an undesirable peace but as a pacifier of potential conflicts, not a chief executive subject to little micro managing but someone who has diverse micro managers looking over his or her shoulders: the board of education, the unions, parent groups, the mayor or city council, the state board of education, field representatives from the federal department of education and its different programs, and community interest groups, aggrieved or not.

4. Boards of education are thorny problems for superintendents. If the board is an appointed one, it says something about the person's connection with and allegiance to political connections. If the board is an elected one, each member frequently has an agenda, which may or may not be good news to the superintendent. In either case the person is almost always not knowledgeable about educational matters. It is beyond the scope of this chapter to describe the different ways the relationship of the superintendent and the board is vexing to both and a source of conflict, articulated or not. From the standpoint of the superintendent, he or she comes to see the board as a group to be coddled, or held at bay, or aversive to innovative changes, or simply lay people in above their heads in matters for which they have little understanding. From the standpoint of the board, the superintendent is one who is not always forthcoming, mires them largely in decisions that are mundane and time consuming, and in subtle and non-subtle ways conveys to the board who is the expert at the meeting; they may personally like the superintendent but only if he or she is appropriately respectful of the board's responsibilities. And what are those responsibilities? As more than a few board members have told me, it may be paraphrased in this way: "With few exceptions our responsibility is to rubber stamp the superintendent's recommendations. And those few exceptions concern fiscal matters and negotiation with the unions, or where we should build a new school or close one down."

5. None of the above is truly comprehensible apart from the problem of time, the superintendent's time. One superintendent put it this way (paraphrased): "I am expected to be at least moderately knowledgeable about child development, the curriculum, teaching, personnel selection, evaluation and standards, preparing a budget and school law. If that were all I was expected to do, it would be a full-time job because each of them presents predictable and unpredictable problems, meetings, planning. When the state legislature in its infinite wisdom passes laws requiring this or that course or practice, or changes standards for graduation or promotion, I have to call and chair staff meetings to determine how we will handle the matter. When our high schools come up for periodic, mandated review for accreditation, it takes numerous meetings to prepare. When the legislature passed charter school legislation and appropriated money for them—which meant reduction of money for our regular schools—we had a series of meetings to apply for some charter schools be-

cause we were under pressure to take advantage of the innovation. So there were more meetings, not uncomplicated ones, and I am not counting the meetings on charter schools with the board, a couple of members of which were dead set against having anything to do with charter schools. And besides all this, I am to represent, talk to, and meet with God knows how many groups in the community in addition to meeting with any politician who has an axe to grind. And when parents want to see me, I have to make time for them. And don't get me started on Washington and its mountains of regulations in regard to programs for handicapped kids. Last week I spent a whole morning with one of their staff in their civil rights division. According to them we are in violation of the law because many of our special students don't spend enough time in regular classrooms, what they call inclusion. And during all of this I can't keep up with the paper work. When we decide to build a new school, I get depressed because I have to make out as if I were an architect so I can ask real architects about the blueprints they show me. Visit schools? I have no time. Get to know teachers and principals? When? In the evening? I spend an average of two evenings a week some place in the community. I don't have time to think and read. I'm on a treadmill. I delegate as much as I can to my top staff and I pray they will do the job well, which happens every now and then. People begrudge me what they think is a handsome salary; they envy me and my presumed power. What would they think if I said out loud that with each passing year the strength of my wish to get off the treadmill increases? Am I painting a too bleak picture? Maybe, but if it is too bleak, it is bleak nevertheless. I never expected to feel this way at age 45."

Superintendents, supervisory staff, principals, teachers—the majority, a large one—articulate two complaints. First, they do not have the time to do justice to their obligations; duties never decrease, they increase, as does the pressure to improve educational outcomes by which they mean higher test scores. The second, implied in the first, is that they are not in control of their working life and destiny.

For the past two decades I have been conducting an unscientific, one item poll. The item is: If you were asked to devise a new plan for our educational system, are you pretty much likely to come up with the system we now have? The immediate reaction is no, usually accompanied by sardonic laughter. If you then ask: What would be a few of the changes you would make, there is a long reaction time usually followed by, "I really would have to think about it." And that response speaks to my point that although the respondents are not in doubt that the existing system is a very flawed one, they have given scant thought to how the system should be changed. In fact, it is my experience that very few educators think in terms of a system of education comprised of parts and their interacting effects. They know there are parts but, nevertheless, when it comes to change they see it primarily in terms of their school or local school system, not as a subsystem in a larger system. You cannot see a system; you have to conceptualize it by identifying its parts and their interrelationships in order to judge how, why, or how well the system functions or malfunctions in achieving its stated purposes. For example, why is it that an apparently tested and successful reform does not spread to other schools within a local school system or to other school systems? That is a crucial question that has hardly been discussed in the educational community. You cannot think about, let alone solve, a question you have not posed. And I submit that the question of lack of spread of an educational reform has not been discussed is largely (not exclusively) because our top educational administrators think in local not system terms; for them the concept of system means the local system over which they preside and all else is background noise.

I am reminded here of a conversation I had with a superintendent of an urban school system in regard to the disparity in emphasis and allocation of resources between prevention and repair. He responded somewhat caustically by saying, "Please don't tell me that in some ultimate sense prevention is more effective than repair. I know that. But what you do not understand is that, like it or not, and I do not like it, I am a fireman spending his days putting out fires, putting bandaids on deep wounds, praying the bleeding will not recur, and dealing with details that send me up a wall. I do not have the time even to fantasize about prevention." That was 40 years ago and I concluded at the time that this superintendent was a very narrow, unimaginative thinker. Today I would say the same thing, but I am infinitely more understanding and sympathetic to his plight because he is embedded in a system inimical to non-cosmetic change that virtually guarantees that the more things change the more they remain the same. Superintendents need more than tea and sympathy.

Any reader familiar with my writings will know that I know that the issues I have barely touched upon in this chapter are mammothly more complicated than what I have said above. And they will also know that I expect that people infected with the quick fix virus will regard me as an octogenarian whose grasp on social realities borders on the pathological. All I can say here in self-defense is that beginning in 1965, orally and in print, I was one hundred percent correct in predicting the downward spiral of our educational system. And with each succeeding book the bases of my prediction became more complex, nuanced, and I would say realistic, which explains the titles of my 1990 book, *The Predictable Failure of Educational Reform,* and the 1998 book, *Political Leadership and Educational Failure.*

So what are possible starting points for actions? But there is a prior question: Who must initiate, put on the table, why radical change is necessary? What must be avoided is the message that the relevant professional communities bear little or no responsibility for the inadequacies of the educational system. The self-protective stance of professional organizations makes it easy to blame sources external to them. In the case of school administrators that means they have to own up to several things: there is a good deal wrong and self-defeating in the selection, preparation, and role of educational leaders; past attempts to deal with these inadequacies have been superficial, a form of tinkering at the edge; radical system change is a must if we seek productive, self-sustaining efforts, which cannot be achieved by silence about what is wrong with the present system. What I say about silence reflects my belief that, in the quiet of their nights, school administrators know, however inchoately, that they are in a failing system, a non-supportive, adversarial system. But it is as if they dare not speak out; they do not want to wash their "dirty linens" in public, thus confusing honesty with weakness. One reason Pope John XXIII is judged so highly in convening the Vatican Council is he said out loud that the church had made mistakes, it needed reinvigoration, and change had to be at the top of the agenda. Another example is the Constitutional Convention of 1787 which recognized that the Articles of Confederation were fatally flawed in regard to forging a unified nation; instead of repairing the Articles they, so to speak, started from scratch. But these examples (and others) point up the absolutely crucial role of far-seeing leadership, however small their number was. It was courageous leadership that sought to bring that message to a wider public. That type of leadership has been absent among school administrators. I have been to and addressed meetings and conventions of school administrators. I have read their journals and books. I came to the conclusion that what the leadership always said unreflectively assumed that the system we now have can be repaired without radical transformation. They know where the fires are, they have proposals for dousing them, but they never explain why they did not and could not work. What school administrators and the educational community generally do not realize is that there are many people who do not want self-serving, self-protective explanations of the deficiencies of our educational system; they have heard those explanations time and again. Likewise, what people want to hear is not the same as what they need to hear, a distinction school administrators have not honored.

I know that many readers of my remarks will not react kindly to what I have said, but consistent with beliefs and experience, I owed it to them to say what I thought they needed to hear. The contents of this chapter were mightily influenced by a book I have just finished and which will be published in 2002 by Teachers College Press. The title is *Educational Reform: A Self-Scrutinizing Memoir*. I looked back on my 55 years in and around educational reform with these questions in mind: What mistakes, practical and conceptual, did I make? What errors of omission and commission did I make? Why was I wrong in being silent about some important issues? Writing that book was quite an experience, a sobering one as well as extremely stimulating.

CONCLUSION

So my suggestion is that a small group of school administrators, self-selected or appointed, be formed, the members of which have several things in common: they are critical of the existing state of affairs; they realize that no transformation of their profession is possible unless seen in the context of the features of the larger school system; they know they are engaged in a task that will meet opposition; they are opposed to vague generalizations and holding out the promise of the quick fix; they must seek ways to put their conclusions to an ever increasing number of people; and they must confront the seriousness of what is at stake, nothing less than the existence of a viable public educational system, or the verdicts of posterity will be cruel. It is predictable that this initial group will not be in agreement on all issues, but if their commitment remains high and they take the long view, they can at least agree that their deliberations should gain currency in their organization. It took the founding fathers four months in hot, steamy Philadelphia to reach agreement and even then it took two years of public discussion and controversy before it was ratified, largely because the Bill of Rights was added to the Constitution. When you read the accounts of the Constitutional Convention, it is no less than amazing that they did what they did despite marked differences of opinion and values. They knew what was at stake and they worked out compromises they could live with. Ironically, there was one compromise that a significant number of the fathers went along with only because if they did not compromise there would be no United States. I refer, of course, to slavery. It was a compromise for which we have paid and will continue to pay a high price. If we continue to tinker at the edges with educational system change, the price we will pay as a society will be very high indeed, as I am sure future historians will surely emphasize.

By professional-organizational self-scrutiny, I do not mean a focus on a school or the local school system but rather on the larger system and the parts comprising it. Tip O'Neil, the legendary Speaker of the House, said that all politics are local. That may pass muster as a quip but it is egregiously misleading; it does not explain why he spent years in Congress and not in Massachusetts. He knew full well that major social problems, far from being local, impact upon other problems near and far. It is precisely because federal, state, and local governments have never recognized—or been helped to recognize—that schools are one part of a larger system that their reform efforts have been fruitless. For example, can you expect schools to undergo non-cosmetic change without similar radical changes in university preparatory programs? Can you expect non-cosmetic changes to occur without changing existing power relationships among the parts in the larger system? Allocation of power is an omnipresent, dynamic aspect of any system or subsystem of human relationships. Any reform effort that does not deal with that aspect is doomed. That is why I judge the Constitutional Convention of 1787 as a remarkable chapter in human history. I can assure the reader that I know that there are other very important aspects.

May I suggest a modest first step school administrators might consider? Select a dozen or so individuals to meet over several days charged with addressing this question: What do we want the public to know about why we have concluded that the existing system is inimical to achieving the goals of reform and, in light of that, what next steps might be taken that will ultimately justify formulating specific concrete proposals? I say long and difficult because the issues are so complicated and will arouse differences in values and opinions. You do not get your house in order by avoiding and remaining silent about an unacceptable state of affairs. You cannot talk about leadership without talking about courage. That explains why I regard Harry Truman with the highest respect because, when he relieved General MacArthur of his post, it was because the general had challenged the tradition of civilian control over the military. Truman knew he would be criticized, vilified, and castigated for his action (and he was) but he knew that his constitutionally defined role left him no acceptable moral alternative. The verdict of history on the general has been negative and that on the president very positive.

Which organizations should assume the responsibility for giving currency to ideas about system change? Certainly the organization of school administrators is one of them and, I believe, a crucial one. If it remains silent, or if it continues to utter clichés, or if it for fear of unfavorable public reaction cannot call a spade a spade, if the imaginativeness of which its members are capable goes unexpressed, the troubling social change of the last half of the last century will continue to pick up steam with consequences for which there is good reason to believe will be more than unfavorable.

REFERENCES

Flexner, A. (1960). *Medical education in the United States and Canada.* Washington, DC: The Carnegie Foundation for the Advancement of Teaching. (Original work published in 1910)

Sarason, S. B. (1990). *The predictable failure of educational reform.* San Francisco: Jossey-Bass.

Sarason, S. B. (1993). *The case for change: Rethinking the preparation of educators.* San Francisco: Jossey-Bass.

Sarason, S. B. (1996). *The barometers of change: Individual, institutional, educational transformations.* San Francisco: Jossey-Bass.

Sarason, S. B. (1998). *Political leadership and educational failure.* San Francisco: Jossey-Bass.

Sarason, S. B. (2001). *American psychology & schools. A critique.* New York: Teachers College Press.

Sarason, S. B. (2002). *Educational reform: A self-scrutinizing memoir.* New York: Teachers College Press.

II

LEADERSHIP PREPARATION

The Impact of Diversity in Educational Administration

Linda C. Tillman

The world of educational administration is not only changing, but also evolving. Epistemological and ontological discussions, as well as discussions about practice, have changed dramatically since the days of theorists such as Cubberly and Griffiths. The changing and evolving nature of these discussions, as well as current scholarship and practice, indicates that educational administration is confronted with both the challenges and the promises of change. These challenges and promises will become increasingly important for the field as it endeavors to develop relevant theory and practice that can be used to more effectively train future leaders who will work for the educational success of *all* children. Changes in focus (leadership versus administration[1]), changes in standards (state standards versus ISLLC[2] versus the knowledge base[3]), changes in program types (educational administration/leadership versus leadership broadly defined[4]), and changes in how we conceptualize issues of race, class, and gender are all themes that have changed the world of educational administration. Another issue, the issue of *diversity*, has also taken center stage in the changing and evolving world of educational administration. The field of educational administration has become more diverse on several levels.

Diversity in the field of education has typically focused exclusively on discussions of race and ethnicity, usually under the umbrella term of multiculturalism. The concept of diversity in educational administration, however, can be expanded to include diversity of theoretical perspectives, diversity of voices, and diversity of the student population in K–12 public education. Each of these issues has become more prominent in the educational literature as well as in presentations at educational conferences. One example of the increased attention to these issues can be found in the 2001 Annual Meeting of the University Council for Educational Administration program which featured 6 sessions on spiritually based leadership, 4 sessions on lead-

Linda C. Tillman, Wayne State University

ership for social justice, and 13 sessions on people of color (K–12 students, teachers and administrators, and graduate students and professors). These numbers represented a dramatic increase in the number of presentations on these topics in previous years. Clearly, the increased attention to these issues in research, scholarship, and conference presentations is evidence of the changing and evolving world of educational administration.

DIVERSITY OF THEORETICAL PERSPECTIVES

Spiritually based leadership theories and leadership for social justice are two theoretical perspectives that are changing the world of educational administration as we know it. A growing number of scholars have offered both theoretical and empirical scholarship on the role of spirituality in educational leadership and leadership for social justice. Work by Capper (1993), Beck and Foster (1999), Murtadha (1999), Sherr (1999), Keyes, Capper, Hafner, and Fraynd (2000), Dantley (2001), and Grinberg (2001) and have made significant contributions to the educational leadership literature. These theoretical perspectives offer legitimate possibilities for new ways of theorizing educational administration in a changing social, political, and economic society.

Spiritually Based Leadership Theories

According to Dantley (2001), "Spirituality is that component of our total selves and community through which we make meaning and understanding of our world. It is our foundation of values, principles, influences and ethics that we exhibit in our interactions with others" (p. 5).[5] Spiritually based leadership theories focus on themes of morality and transformational leadership—leadership that fosters relationships which are both reciprocal and collaborative, and that have the potential to implement significant change in K–12 public education. According to Dantley, this type of transformative leadership transcends traditional theories of positivist paradigms and incorporates leadership theories and actions based on "critical self and organizational reflection" (p. 19). Murtadha (1999) has noted that there is now an increased recognition of the role of spirituality in leadership. Other scholars such as Beck and Foster (1999) have argued that it is imperative that as leaders create a vision for their schools, they consider the importance of moral and spiritual dispositions, language, and practices. Language which includes words like *compassion, forgiveness, wisdom,* and *humility,* and dispositions and practices that attend to issues of power and privilege imply a proactive and a more just and equitable perspective of educational leadership. Additionally, Sherr in the 1999 edition of the *National Council of Professors of Educational Administration Yearbook* challenged educational administration scholars to consider how the field can be improved when the spiritual as well as cognitive aspects of leadership are acknowledged and understood.

Dantley (2001) has argued that "educational leadership is being challenged to engage in a broader conceptualization of its purpose" (p. 2). Dantley uses three principles of Cornel West's (1988) prophetic spirituality to demonstrate how spiritual concepts can be used by educational leaders to change assumptions and behaviors of key actors. Spirituality, transformational leadership, and the notion of leaders as moral agents are linked as Dantley explores West's *deep seated moralism, inescapable opportunism,* and *profound pessimism,* and then uses these principles as a framework for theorizing spiritually based leadership. While West's notions of prophetic spirituality refer to the historical contexts of the lives of African Americans, Dantley's argument is clearly applicable to the changing and evolving world of educational administration. Three of West's principles are applied to three types of leadership in education: principled leadership, pragmatic leadership, and purposive leadership. The three principles inform Dantley's argument for new leadership theories which attend to issues of justice, equity, and fairness in K–12 educational administration.

The first principle, *deep seated moralism,* is used to discuss Dantley's notion of *principled leadership.* Based on idiographic morality (the leader's reflective journey of what is just and right) and nomothetic morality (using this self reflection for systemic transformation),

> Principled leadership begins with a careful and critical reflection of one's position on issues of justice, democracy, and fairness. Principled leadership is initiated when an individual questions the *democratic* (emphasis added) efficacy of administrative decisions and procedures he or she is demanded to implement. (p. 8)

Principled leaders will embrace their spiritual selves (idiographic morality) and will critically examine their own ideologies as well as what they expect from decisions that are made about issues of race, class, gender, and social justice. In addition, teachers and students are co-contributors and co-collaborators in shaping not only the educational setting, but also their individual and collect educational destinies. According to Dantley, the fundamental purpose of principled leadership is "founding the direction of the school on ethical, moral, and socially just postulates" (p. 12).

The second principle, *inescapable opportunism,* is used to discuss Dantley's notion of *pragmatic leadership.* Pragmatic leaders view their leadership role as one that not only promotes the acquisition of skills necessary for successful academic achievement, but one that also emphasizes using those skills to bring about social, educational, political and economic change. A pragmatic leader understands that "schools can either reproduce or challenge the constructions that have been traditionally promulgated through educational institutions" (p. 13). A pragmatic leader becomes a *public intellectual;* that is, the work takes on a spiritual nature where the leader consciously considers the contradictions of espoused philosophies of democratic schools and the reality of schooling today. Dantley considers this approach to be a radical one because it compels schools and school leaders to recognize and act on external factors that affect their work (e.g., poverty, violence, and bureaucracy). Thus, a pragmatic leader considers the implications of what change in teaching and learning in school settings means for the larger society. The links between societal injustices and educational achievement are evident in the pragmatic leadership model, and Dantley points to urban school settings as examples of sites which are particularly in need of this type of leadership.

The third principle, *profound pessimism,* is used to discuss Dantley's notion of *purposive leadership*. Purposive leadership is focused on "transforming school districts or implementing change in local school sites" (p. 17). In the changing world of educational administration then, purposive leadership would become an impetus for innovative changes. The leader engages in spiritual reflection which leads to critical reflection, resistance and reconstruction of the values, norms, and goals at the school site. Again Dantley points to urban school systems and the "intolerable rates of high school student dropouts, the plethora of low achieving schools, and the disaffection especially of the urban public with public schools" (p. 18) as obstacles to the successful educational achievement of all students, and particularly students of color. Indeed, these factors can be considered reasons for profound pessimism. In West's prophetic spirituality model, these obstacles represent challenges that must be overcome by those who practice purposive leadership. These leaders implement and practice leadership that is not only an intellectual undertaking, but also a spiritual one.

Social Justice Leadership Theories

Social justice leadership can be viewed as a movement to investigate and pose solutions for issues that generate and reproduce societal inequities. Social justice theorists focus their inquiry on how institutionalized theories, norms, and practices in schools and society lead to social, political, economical, and educational inequities. According to Larson and Murtadha (in press), researchers in educational administration who work for change under the umbrella of inquiry called "leadership for social justice" do not accept the inevitability of injustices in schools and communities. Evidence of the growing influence of social justice theoretical frameworks can be found in the organization Leadership for Social Justice. This group has gained prominence in the University Council for Educational Administration as well as Division A of the American Educational Research Association. One of the guiding principles of Leadership for Social Justice is to better prepare district and building level administrators for significant issues in schools with regard to race, class, gender, and the marginalization of diverse groups.

Larson and Murtadha (in press) offer a theoretical perspective for the definition, application, and requirements of leadership for social justice. They note that recent shifts in the nature of inquiry regarding just and equitable education have focused on three strands: deconstructing existing logics of leadership, portraying alternative perspectives of leadership, and constructing theories, systems, and processes for social justice. According to Larson and Murtadha it is the third strand that is the least developed, but that holds the greatest possibility for impacting positive change in educational administration.

In the first strand, *deconstructing existing logics of leadership*, Larson and Murtadha (in press) note that researchers have investigated how dominant theoretical assumptions about educational administration have worked to maintain inequities. The deconstruction of these dominant theories have led some social justice theorists to conclude that schools often achieve stability through constraint and coercion rather than consensus. Issues that are prominent in this strand include critical race theory, gender representation, modernist critiques, multiculturalism, and leadership theories for women and people of color. According to Larson and Murtadha, much of the research in this strand points to stable, universal, and difference-blind systems. It is within these types of systems that we find only limited challenges to inequities based on class, race, ethnicity, and gender. Larson and Murtadha's point is significant, since an ambivalence toward *difference-blind systems* (emphasis added) can also be viewed as contributing to and maintaining inequities around these very issues. For example, educational leaders (as well as faculty and graduate students) who insist that they do not see color may consciously or unconsciously reinforce negative stereotypes about the learning styles and abilities of students (both K–12 as well as graduate students) from so-called marginalized groups (for example, African American and Latino/a students). Such stereotypes often are accompanied by the difference blind attitude towards a group's *culture* and *cultural ways of thinking, believing and knowing* as a key factor in the achievement of students.

In the second strand, *portraying alternative images of leadership theory and practice*, the ethics of care, spirituality, love, and leadership are prominent themes. For example, the ethic of care, the ethic of critique, and ethic of justice are viewed as complementary areas of inquiry that can be critical in the development of a more humanly informed practice in educational administration. This strand also places an emphasis on the experiences of people of color in educational administration. That is, the increased numbers for faculty, graduate students, and K–12 students and administrations have led to new frameworks for looking at both old and new areas of inquiry in educational administration research and scholarship. For example, some social justice theorists have focused on the academic achievement of children of color using new frameworks—frameworks that depart from the generalizing and pathology based theorizing and research (Lomawaima, 2000; Tillman, in press) which places children of color in a subordinate position. Thus there is an implication (and an imperative) that researchers and leaders acquire a more informed understanding of the culture and the cultural ways of knowing of specific racial and ethnic groups. Internal educational issues such as the perceptions and expectations of teachers and administrators regarding student success, and external educational issues such as poverty and violence—which can affect a student's opportunity to learn—all have implications for theory, research, and practice in educational administration.

Lomotey (1989), Franklin (1990), Dillard (1995), Pollard (1997), Alston (1999), and Jackson (1999) have provided portrayals of alternative perspectives and images of leadership in their research on African American female superintendents, women of color, and African American principals. These authors found that leaders of color in their studies had a commitment to understanding the community and its cultural norms, and how this knowledge could be used for the educational achievement of their students. For example, Lomotey (1989) found that same race/ethnic affiliation (shared understandings, beliefs, values, culture) enhanced the effectiveness of African American principals in their interactions with teachers and students in the school. Pollard (1997) in her study of African American principals, found that the principal's ethnic identity was key factor in shaping his or her role as an administrator and in developing a mission for the school. Clearly, these and other studies of racial and cultural perspectives on leadership have added to the literature and have given us alternative models for theorizing educational leadership. According to Larson and Murtadha (in press), the third strand, *constructing theories, systems, and processes for social justice,* is the least developed but holds the greatest promise for change in educational leadership theory and practice. As the authors have argued, it is in this strand that researchers will have to go beyond theorizing about social justice leadership to making recommendations for practice. Thus, in constructing theories, systems, and processes researchers must do more than articulate theories that can contribute to change in schools. Educational leadership theorists will be challenged to provide relevant models that can be used to implement meaningful changes that are just and equitable. Prominent themes in this strand include leadership for marginalized school communities, organizing communities and democratic leadership, and developing human capacity and life chances through educational leadership. It is in this strand that leaders for social justice are called upon to promote issues of community. Community-wide initiatives where the purposes of education and the needs of communities of color and communities of poverty are central to the discourses, policymaking, pedagogy, and practice are critical to the meaningful systemic change that is needed in public education today. Like Dantley (2001), Larson and Murtadha (in press) argue that school leaders who want equitable schooling for all children will develop and implement programs and policies that provide opportunities for social, emotional, and academic achievement.

As the preceding discussion indicates, spiritually based leadership theories and leadership for social justice have similar and overlapping themes. Both perspectives emphasize moral values, justice, equity, care, respect, and the imperative for investigations on the impact of race, ethnicity, class, and gender on the educational outcomes of students.

DIVERSITY AND THE IMPACT OF MULTIPLE VOICES

The voices of people of color are also changing the world of educational administration. Professors and graduate students, as well as K–12 administrators, teachers, and students of color, are adding their voices to current theories, research, and scholarship in educational administration. Critical issues that require our attention include the academic achievement of *all* students, particularly those currently classified as minorities or marginalized, diversification of educational administration programs to increase the number of faculty and students of color, and supporting and mentoring faculty and doctoral students of color. Thus, the privileging of voice is now being problematized in theorizing educational leadership.

In her presidential address to the 2001 University Council on Educational Administration convention participants, Maria Louisa Gonzalez discussed current theory and practice in educational administration, and challenged participants to extend the practice of leadership in higher education settings beyond simply preaching, teaching, and researching leadership, but through practice itself. Gonzalez used the concepts of *borders, borderlands*, and *borderlanders* as a framework for her comments. According to Gonzalez, borders function to keep certain groups in a pre-defined space and to prevent, control, or regulate interactions among them. A borderland is a region that lies adjacent to a border, and borderlanders live and function in several different worlds. Applying these concepts to educational administration, Gonzalez used two types of borderlands—*alienated* and *interdependent*—to address the issue of diversity in the professorate. *Alienated* borderlands represent constant friction, the border is functionally closed, and cross-border interactions are non-existent. *Interdependent* borderlands represent stability and engagement in collaborative relationships.

In Gonzalez's analysis, faculty of color can be considered alienated borderlanders: the borders of academe have often functioned to keep them in a pre-defined space, with little interaction with their colleagues. They often experience tension in their work in the academy, and thus they often live in two worlds. Gonzalez pointed to research that concluded that faculty of color often feel alienated, isolated, and excluded in the institutions of higher education where they encounter overt and subtle forms of discrimination. Other factors which contribute to the existence of an alienated borderland for faculty of color include demands placed on their time and energy that are different than what is expected of other faculty members, devaluation of their research on minority issues—particularly if articles are published in non-mainstream journals—and perceptions by their colleagues that they are less qualified for the professorate or less likely to make significant contributions to research. In addition, Gonzalez noted that many borderland faculty of color have noted a pervasive attitude of complacency—the belief that hiring one person of color in a department is sufficient. In a study of African American faculty in predominantly white research institutions, Tillman (2001) reported similar findings. Faculty members felt professionally and socially isolated from their colleagues, and many of these faculty often went outside of their institutions to find colleagues (mentors) who were willing to assist them in their career and personal development. Thus, the recruitment and hiring of faculty of color is important in eliminating these alienated borderlands.

Interdependent borderlands imply that faculty will engage in collaboration and support among themselves. Interdependent borderlands should also apply to faculty interactions with students of color. Embedded in this argument are issues of recruitment of graduate students of color and how they are supported once they enter the program. Gonzalez noted that students of color may be particularly vulnerable to becoming borderlanders, due in part to the lack of faculty who can serve as mentors and role models. Just as the socialization process is important for all faculty, it is also important for graduate students of color. Gonzalez suggests that positive, meaningful interaction with all students, but particularly students of color, goes beyond recruiting them into programs. Rather, the kinds of experiences they are afforded are also critical to their professional and personal growth. Exposure to research and scholarship from a variety of perspectives, recognition of their voices and culture, and opportunities for collaboration on research and publication are necessary and can help eliminate the sometimes uneasy status of borderlander graduate students of color. Their positive socialization is critical to their roles as future leaders, whether as faculty members or as school administrators. The changing world of educational administration necessitates that we must work to create more integrated borderlands for both faculty and students of color.

Integrating the borderland of academe requires that the academy begin putting into practice their new theorizing about the ethics of care, justice, critique, spirituality, and social justice. Clearly Gonzalez's remarks point to the increased attention to people of color and their struggles not only to become participants in discussions of epistemology, theory, and practice, but to become full participants in an integrated academic borderland—a borderland where people on both sides of the border perceive themselves as members of an open and receptive social system. Typically the subjects of the research, people of color are now adding their individual and collective voices and have become more than just the subjects of the research. They are researchers and graduate students who have now become co-constructors of their histories and lived realities.

THE DIVERSE LANDSCAPE OF K–12 EDUCATION

One could reasonably ask whether anyone is paying attention to the changing and evolving world of educational administration. As a field, have we really considered how and to what extent our theory and our practice directly affects children, particularly those children who have been and continue to be under-served and under-educated in U.S. public school systems? The changing demographics of our public school systems have become a critical issue in the field of educational administration as it prepares future leaders. While the educational system in general, and school districts in particular, have historically been designed to serve primarily white, middle-class children (Lewis, 2001), the rapidly changing demographics of schools, and particularly large urban school districts, has necessitated a re-examination of how we train future leaders in our administrative preparation programs.

The landscape of public education is rapidly changing. Johnson and Vladero (2000) report that nationally, African Americans, Latinos/as and American Indians make up one-third of the 54 million children in K–12 classrooms. Currently, Latino/a students represent one of the fastest growing populations in schools. The United States Department of Education (1996) reported that in 1993 the Latino/a student population was 13 percent nationally. It is expected that by the year 2020, Latino/a children will represent over one quarter of all public school students (Reyes, Wagstaff, & Fusarelli, 1999). In addition, in the largest states such as California and Texas, students of color are already the majority. The percentage of students who are from poor families is also increasing. The numbers of children who live below the poverty level increased from one in five in 1984 to one in four in 1990 (Reyes et al.). In addition, Pallas, Natriello, and McDill (1989) have reported that the school age population will be dramatically affected by the expected increase in the number and proportion of disadvantaged students.

According to Skrla, Scheurich, Johnson, and Koschoreck (2002), leadership programs have failed to adequately prepare leaders who will be successful in serving the increasing numbers of poor and minority children. Thus, two questions are critical to a re-examination of our leadership preparation programs and their relevancy for today's society: Are current leadership programs theorized, designed, and intended to prepare leaders who will work toward successful outcomes for *all* children, including low income children of color? Or do these programs continue to emphasize models of leadership which rely more on traditional theories of educational leadership and fail to provide theories (social justice, spiritually based, cultural frameworks), practical application, and experiences that leaders will need in order to meet the social, emotional and academic needs of all children?

Given the changing and evolving world of educational administration, any reexamination of the role of the profession, and the individual and collective roles of professors of educational administration, now must also include the following additional questions: Should we continue to train future leaders using traditional models which are non-inclusive and prepare principals for an "ideal" school? Or, given these changing demographics, should we commit ourselves to bridging theory and practice—that is, training future leaders to work toward the success of *all* children by addressing the problems that plague schools, and particularly those schools that serve large numbers of poor and minority children?

Should the field continue on the first path, an almost exclusive emphasis on traditional models, we are likely to continue to get what we have been getting—too many principals who have not been adequately prepared to address the social, racial, cultural, and economic differences that poor and minority students bring to the educational setting, and the consequent underachievement of many of these students. The continued exclusive use of traditional models will likely continue to produce principals who are either reluctant to, or refuse to implement change because of an over-dependence on theory over practical applications of the knowledge they have acquired. This over-dependence on theory is often at the expense of poor and minority children. For example, many of the current instructional strategies presume that African American children are deficient, thus principals may over emphasize the implementation of strategies and techniques to control low performing African American students (Ladson-Billings, 1998). Traditional theories of educational administration also often reinforce deficit theories that constructs children of color as less interested in and less capable of learning (Scheurich, 2000; Valenzuela, 1999). Thus, an over-dependence on traditional models may limit the opportunities for K–12 leaders to serve poor and minority students who lack the "cultural capital" (Delpit, 1995; Kozol, 1991) which, for the most part, defines success in schools.

Accepting the challenge to take the latter path—committing ourselves to training future leaders to work toward the success of *all* students—will require a willingness to re-think our course offerings, the content of these courses, and more importantly, the ideologies that guide our choices. Will we continue to base all of our teaching on theory and ignore the realities of schooling: violence, racial inequities, and external factors such as poverty? Or will we make the effort to go into the schools, identify critical areas of need, and work with our graduate students in developing courses and course content that is intended to strengthen principal/leadership preparation programs, provide relevant content knowledge, and make our primary goal the preparation of principals who will serve *all* students? The voices and experiential knowledge of our graduate students can and should provide a foundation for some of what is taught in courses. We should not be reluctant to learn from our students who usually come from a variety of school districts—some of which do not provide "ideal" learning environments. In this changing world of educational administration, it is imperative that we avoid teaching an ideal version of leadership. As professors and researchers, we have an obligation to help future leaders conceptualize how they can lead in ways that are equitable rather than in ways that generate and reproduce inequity.

There is no intent here to suggest that we should abandon traditional educational administration theory in total; indeed, it has been useful in the past and continues to be useful in the sense that it allows us to determine how traditional theories and models can be improved given the current needs in our public school systems. However, given the changing demographics as well as the changing imperatives of schools (safe environment, funding, diverse student population, standardized testing), we must re-examine our programs and hold ourselves accountable for the success of *all* children.

CHALLENGES AND PROMISES

The changing and evolving world of educational administration holds both challenges and promises. In this chapter I have explored the impact of diversity of theoretical perspectives, voices, and K–12 public education which have all have brought change to the field of educational administration. These issues are separate, yet connected by a central theme–the imperative for more just, equitable, culturally informed, and culturally engaged forms of educational leadership theorizing, teaching, and practice. We might wish to think of this as a re-positioning of the field to meet the changing and evolving landscape of society and education. Today's leaders face different challenges—challenges which require our individual and collective expertise. Transformative recommendations must necessarily be change to transform our educational system which, in its current form, privileges some groups over others and on many levels is unjust and inequitable. As educational administration scholars, we are being challenged to move beyond the rhetoric that so often dominates our field to a more committed effort to implement meaningful, effective change. Our failing school systems require that we must do more that just articulate theories. Indeed, we must put these theories into relevant practice that addresses issues of race, ethnicity, class, gender, and the marginalization of diverse groups. We are challenged to go beyond our own epistemological musings and give serious consideration to what our roles as professors of educational administration mean for the changing field. We are being challenged to move beyond our theoretical arguments about spiritually based leadership theories and leadership for social justice. The changing world of educational administration now requires us to use these theories to shape discourse, policy, pedagogy, and practice which will lead to success for *all* children.

The changing world of educational administration also holds promises. New possibilities for transformative discourses, theories, and practices do have the potential to change our failing public education system. Leadership for social justice theorists and spiritually based leadership theorists have enhanced our knowledge regarding issues of race, class, gender, equity, justice, fairness, and community. The voices of people of color have presented alternative perspectives and images of leadership — perspectives and images that have increased our knowledge about cultural ways of knowing and cultural forms of leadership. Our field can only grow because of this knowledge. The promises of the changing world of educational administration also hold promises for a changed society.

NOTES

1. I am using the terms *educational administration* and *educational leadership* interchangeably in this paper. However, current discourses on this topic frequently use the term educational leadership rather than educational administration. While it is not within the scope of this paper to enter into a complete discussion of the similarities and differences between the two terms, it is worth noting that much of the focus in field has turned to leadership. For a more extensive discussion of the evolution of and increased use of the term leadership, see Leithwood and Duke (1999).

2. According to Cunningham and Cordeiro (2000), the Interstate School Leaders Licensure Consortium: Standards for School Leaders (ISLLC) were developed to improve policy, practice and research and builds on previous work by professional organizations representing the field of school administration.

3. For more extensive discussions of the knowledge base in educational administration, see Donmoyer, Imber, and Scheurich (1995) and Forsyth (1993).

4. For example, institutions such as Bowling Green State University, the University of Cincinnati, and Wayne State University have structured their leadership programs to offer a broad conceptualization of leadership and draws students from not only the field of education, but from health care professions, social service agencies, and business and industry as well.

5. See Dillard (1995, 2000) and Laible (2000) for discussion of feminist perspectives on the role of spirituality in educational leadership.

REFERENCES

Alston, J. (1999). Climbing the hills and mountains: Black females making it to the superintendency. In C. Brunner (Ed.), *Sacred dreams: Women and the superintendency* (pp. 79–90). Albany: State University of New York Press.

Beck, L., & Foster, W. (1999). Administration and community: Considering challenges, exploring possibilities. In J. Murphy & K. S. Louis (Eds.), *Handbook of research on educational administration* (2nd ed., pp. 337–358). San Francisco: Jossey-Bass.

Capper, C. (1993). *Educational administration in a pluralistic society: A multiparadigm approach.* Albany: State University of New York Press.

Cunningham, W. C., & Cordeiro, P. A. (2000). *Educational administration: A problem-based approach.* Boston: Allyn and Bacon.

Dantley, M. (2001). *Transforming school leadership through Cornel West's notions of African American prophetic spirituality.* Paper presented at the annual meeting of the University Council for Educational Administration, Cincinnati, OH.

Delpit, L. (1995). *Other people's children: Cultural conflict in the classroom.* New York: New Press.

Dillard, C. B. (1995). Leading with her life: An African American feminist (re)interpretation of leadership for an urban high school principal. *Educational Administration Quarterly, 31*(4), 539–563.

Dillard, C. B. (2000). The substance of things hoped for, the evidence of things not seen: Examining an endarkened feminist epistemology in educational research and leadership. *International Journal of Qualitative Studies in Education, 13*(6), 661–681.

Donmoyer, R., Imber, M., & Scheurich, J. (1995). *The knowledge base in educational administration: Multiple perspectives.* Albany: State University of New York Press.

Forsyth, P. (1993). *Educational administration: The UCEA document base.* New York: McGraw-Hill.

Franklin, V. P. (1990). "They rose and fell together": African American educators and community leadership. *Journal of Education, 72*(3), 39–64.

Gonzalez, M. L. (2002). Professors of educational administration: Learning and leading for the success of ALL children. *University Council for Educational Administration Review 64*(1), 4–9.

Grinberg, J. (2001, April). *Practicing popular social justice: Authentic participation and democratic critical leadership in the case of community center in Caracas, Venezuela.* Paper presented at the Annual Meeting of the American Educational Research Association, Seattle, WA.

Jackson, B. (1999). Getting inside history—against all odds: African-American women school superintendents. In C. Brunner (Ed.), *Sacred dreams: Women and the superintendency* (pp. 141–160). Albany: State University of New York Press.

Johnson, R., & Vladero, D. (2000). Unmet promise: Raising minority achievement. *Education Week*, March 15, 2000.

Keyes, M., Capper, C., Hafner, M., & Fraynd, D. (2000, October). *Spiritual justice histories: The lives of two womanist leaders.* Paper presented at the annual meeting of the University Council for Educational Administration, Albuquerque, NM.

Kozol, J. (1991). *Savage inequalities: Children in America's schools.* New York: Crown.

Ladson-Billings, G. (1998). Just what is critical race theory and what's it doing in a nice field like education? *International Journal of Qualitative Studies in Education, 11*(1), 7–24.

Laible, J. (2000). A loving epistemology: What I hold critical in my life, faith and profession. *International Journal of Qualitative Studies in Education, 13*(6), 683–692.

Larson, C., & Murtadha, K. (in press). Leadership for social justice. In J. Murphy (Ed.), *Challenges of leadership.* The 2002 Yearbook of the National Society for the Study of Education.

Leithwood, K., & Duke, L. (1999). A century's quest to understand school leadership. In J. Murphy & K. S. Louis (Eds.), *The handbook of research on educational administration* (2nd ed., pp. 45–72). San Francisco: Jossey-Bass

Lewis, A. (2001). There is no "race" in the schoolyard: Color-blind ideology in an (almost) all-white school. *American Educational Research Journal, 38*(4),781–811.

Lomawaima, K. (2000). Tribal sovereigns: Reframing research in American Indian education. *Harvard Education Review, 70*(1), 1–21.

Lomotey, K. (1989). *African American principals: School leadership and success.* New York: Greenwood Press.

Murtadha, K. (1999). *Spirited sisters: Spirituality and the activism of African American women in educational leadership.* Lancaster, PA: Technomic.

Pallas, A. M., Natriello, G., & McDill, E. L. (1989). The changing nature of the disadvantaged population: Current dimensions and future trends. *Educational Researcher, 18*, 16–22.

Pollard, D. (1997). Race, gender, and educational leadership: Perspectives from African American principals. *Educational Policy, 11*(3), 353–374.

Reyes, P., Wagstaff, L., & Fusarelli, L. (1999). Delta forces: The changing fabric of American society and education. In J. Murphy & K. S. Louis (Eds.), *The handbook of research on educational administration* (2nd ed., pp. 183–201). San Francisco: Jossey-Bass.

Scheurich, J. (2000). Engaging and envisioning the future for educational leadership programs given increased accountability, growing competition, and changing demographics of K–12 students. Paper presented at the annual meeting of the University Council for Educational Administration, Albuquerque, NM.

Sherr, M. (1999). Embracing spirituality: The inner journey of educational leaders. In K. Fenwick (Ed.), *School leadership: Expanding horizons of the mind and spirit.* Lancaster, PA: Technomic.

Skrla, L., Scheurich, J., Johnson, & Koschoreck, J. (2002). *Accountability for equity.* Paper presented at the annual meeting of the American Educational Research Association, New Orleans, LA.

Tillman, L. (2001). Mentoring African American faculty in predominantly white institutions. *Research in Higher Education, 42*(3), 295–325.

Tillman, L. (in press). Culturally sensitive research approaches: An African American perspective. *Educational Researcher.*

U.S. Department of Education, National Center for Education Statistics (1996). *Projection of education statistics to 2006.* Washington, DC: Author.

Valenzuela, A. (1999). *Subtractive schooling: U.S.–Mexican youth and the politics of caring.* Albany: State University of New York Press.

West, C. (1988). *Prophetic fragments.* Grand Rapids, MI: African World Press.

The Need for a Leadership Practice Field: An Antidote for an Ailing Internship Experience

Theodore B. Creighton and Judy A. Johnson

He had just completed a master's degree in education administration from a California university, after many years of classroom teaching at various grade levels. The position confronting him was a principalship in a K–12 district in Central California. He was looking forward to participating in the instructional leadership duties so emphasized in his principal preparation program, along with site-budgeting, curriculum planning, technology implementation, and working with the state's assessment of academic achievement.

First, after three days on the job, was an incident involving three part-time high school employees in the physical education department found drinking gin and tonics while life-guarding elementary students at the pool. Complicating the issue was the fact that one of the high school workers was the daughter of the school's head secretary, a long-standing employee of the district, and who, coincidentally, was a member of a minority population in the district.

Second, after two weeks on the job, was a phone call from an irate parent who demanded the firing of a teacher who supposedly threw a butter knife across the room at a disruptive student. Third, and certainly not the last of unusual decisions faced by this new principal, was the issuance of a grievance filed against him by a classified employee who charged that the principal helped paint parking lot lines on the faculty parking lot the day before school began, which violated district policy stating administrators were not permitted to perform maintenance-related activities.

She had just taken a job as the elementary school principal in a rural Missouri school district. Impacting instruction, enhancing technology, and creating a learning community were her ideals. The war stories told by her professors in the principal preparation program she'd had were helpful, but after 15 years of teaching, she knew the

Theodore B. Creighton, Sam Houston State University
Judy A. Johnson, Sam Houston State University

real needs which should be addressed by the instructional leader. She really *knew* the things that teachers and students expected from their principal. Excitement and anticipation filled her world as she traveled that first day to her new job.

Of course, the first three people in the office asked to see the principal. Obviously, as one of them later stated, they thought she was the *new secretary*—"never imagined to see a lady in the principal's office!" Since the first day was only until noon, it was the second day of the year when reality set in. A mother, angry because she didn't like the teacher to whom her daughter had been assigned, entered that classroom, threw a desk out the window and demanded that her daughter be moved immediately. The third week brought divorced parents having a fist fight in the hallway because each was trying to take the suspended 6th grade daughter home. The finale of that first year came, however, when the young principal did not recommend renewal of contract for a local teacher. Death threats and slashed tires were not something which had been covered in her university administrator preparation program.

Imagine the surprise of these two beginning administrators when the challenges faced during the first year of the principalship were far removed from their expected responsibilities. Somehow, over the next few years, each of these principals managed to deal with incidents and issues such as those mentioned above, but not without much difficulty, stress, confusion, and sleepless nights.

Obviously, the principal preparation programs in their respective universities did very little to prepare them for such unanticipated responsibilities. But are these types of experiences really unexpected? As professors and practitioners alike compare notes, the funny and sad situations such as those described above repeatedly enter the conversations. Challenges, difficulties, and interactions of the most bizarre type are an everyday occurrence in the world of the building level administrator. Being prepared for these events must be just a part of the everyday training perspective for educational leaders. In retrospect, these administrators could have benefited from an opportunity to *practice* some of the skills necessary to handle such issues, both expected and unexpected. These two administrators eventually became extremely proficient at handling irate parent phone calls, angry meetings, and difficult decisions. In each district, budgets were in the black, student performance increased, and test scores were at or above state mandates. Though both became effective school administrators, they continue to ponder even today: "If only I were provided an opportunity to *practice* a bit before being thrown into the actual performance field of the job."

The field of education leadership has long been criticized for the ways in which building level administrators are prepared for school leadership positions (Murphy, 1999). As early as 1960, the American Association of School Administrators (AASA) characterized the preparation of superintendents and principals as a "dismal montage" (p. 84). Farquhar and Piele (1972) used the description of university-based preparation programs as "dysfunctional structural incrementalism" (p. 17). In 1990, Pitner discussed educational administration programs as "zombie programs" (p. 13).

As recently as 1999, McCarthy addressed the issue of change in educational administration by stating, "congeniality and complacency are woven into education administration programs and the majority of faculty do not perceive a need for radical change that would bring about a transformation in education leadership" (p. 209). Now, 40 years after AASA's dismal characterization of leadership programs, Murphy (2001) points to the profession's continued focus on technical knowledge. He places the university in the center of the field, and posits "trying to link theory and practice in school administration has been for the last 30 years a little like attempting to start a car with a dead battery: The odds are fairly long that the engine will ever turn over" (p. 5). Murphy identifies the central problem as our fascination with building an academic infrastructure of school administration, which has produced serious distortions in what is primarily an applied field.

Education leadership has been characterized by a "disconnect between what is taught in university preparation programs and what practitioners need to be able to do in their schools and districts" (Cambron-McCabe, 1999: cited in Young, Petersen, & Short, 2002, p. 11). Though much of the reform movement consistently includes the call for closing the gap between theory and practice, the question still remains: Has any movement toward this goal occurred (Creighton, in press; Creighton & Jones, 2001; English, 2000; McCarthy, 1999; Murphy, 2001)?

The traditional internship presently serves as the vehicle for aspiring principals to practice their problem-solving and instructional leadership skills. There has been recent emphasis from the professional organizations (AASA, NAESP, NASSP, UCEA, NCPEA) for extending the internship experience over more time (e.g., one-year) and weaving the internship throughout preparation coursework. The internship experience is often a set of prescribed activities that basically address *some* of the leadership responsibilities of a building leader. Feedback is provided by a supervising professor and building level administrator. Does the aspiring administrator ever really get a clear perspective on what actions were acceptable, how to improve on some of the responsibilities fulfilled, and where to search for support when difficulties are outside his or her realm of experience? While there have certainly been improvements in the internship experience over past decades, the internship still remains a poor substitute for actual rehearsal experiences and a minimal *practice field* at best.

AN EDUCATIONAL LEADERSHIP PRACTICE FIELD

For some time, it has been argued (Creighton, in press; Creighton & Jones, 2001) that integration and implementation of a leadership practice field is a necessity for preparation programs. The conceptual notion at work here is that of creating a bridge between a *performance field* (working in the system) and a *practice field* (working on the system). This model is based on the work of Daniel Kim (1995), a colleague of Peter Senge (author of *The Fifth Discipline*) and cofounder of the MIT Organizational Learning Center, where he is currently director of the Learning Laboratory Research Project. The central idea is that a *leadership practice field* provides an environment in which a prospective leader can experiment with alternative strategies and policies, test assumptions, and practice working through the complex issues of school administration in a constructive and productive manner.

Kim is fond of using the following scenario as an introduction to the practice field concept:

> Imagine you are walking across a tightrope stretched between two skyscraper buildings in Chicago. The wind is blowing, and the rope is shaking as you inch your way forward. One of your teammates sits in the wheel barrow you are balancing in front of you, while another colleague sits on your shoulders. There are no safety nets, no harnesses. You think to yourself, "one false move and the three of us will take an elevator straight down to the street." Suddenly your trainer yells from the other side, "Try a new move! Experiment! Take some risks! Remember, you are a learning team!" (p. 353)

Kim continues by admitting the ludicrous nature of this scenario, but emphasizes that this is precisely what many companies expect their management teams to do—experiment, and learn in an environment that is risky, turbulent, and unpredictable.

We suggest that this scenario truly resembles the life of beginning school principals, and the concept of a *practice field* is applicable to the field of education administration. Except for a brief experience with some form of internship, considered notoriously weak (Murphy, 1999) and suffering from a lack of quality and relevance (Creighton & Jones, 2001), where do prospective leaders get an opportunity to leave the day-to-day pressures of school administration temporarily and enter a different kind of space where they can practice and learn? Where does the beginning or practicing administrator find an opportunity to discuss, practice, and experiment with leadership skills and techniques before trying it out in the performance field?

Practicing principals in the field continue to tell us that what they do in their daily lives as school administrators has little resemblance to the preparation received at the university level. They also share their frustration with no time to be proactive. They are constantly required to be reactive. Principals have little time and even less opportunity to practice their skills in safe failing places. Even finding time for reflection is difficult in the non-stop hectic pace of a principal's day.

We can think of no other profession that does not value and provide opportunities for new professionals to practice: in a different kind of space where one can practice and learn. The medical profession has a practice field, the legal profession has a practice field, musicians and dancers have a practice field, the New York Knicks have a practice field, pilots and astronauts have a practice field, and on and on . . . but do we have a practice field in school administration? We argue not—and the internship, as we know it, is a sorry excuse for one. Murphy (1999) reported that although supervised practice could be the most critical phase of the administrator's preparation, the component is notoriously weak. Murphy claims that field-based practices do not involve an adequate number of experiences and are arranged on the basis of convenience. The students work in an internship experience that far too often is comprised of supervision, committee work, and reviewing test scores.

Even the experience of student teaching required of prospective teachers offers more opportunity to practice than does the typical administrative internship. First of all, their experience involves full-time participation; typically, one cannot work in any other job or environment during student teaching. At most, additional responsibilities for the teacher candidate include an additional course designed to augment the internship experience. Principal internships, on the other hand, coexist with another job and responsibilities, usually a classroom teaching position. Unless the candidate is a practicing administrator such as a vice-principal (which is very rare), he or she is required to hold down a regular classroom teaching position while *practicing* the roles and responsibilities of a school principal. This situation mostly results in one of two scenarios: (a) the internship experience takes place after hours—before or after the *regular* school day, typically devoid of students and other faculty, or (b) assigned duties and experiences are generally related to bookkeeping tasks (e.g., attendance or program evaluations). These scenarios place our aspiring principals in an environment absent on any opportunity to practice and learn. Demands and expectations begin immediately upon taking the position, however, and there is little opportunity to make mistakes, learn from them, and move forward with a better understanding of the decision-making process. Rather, the beginners are nearly always immediately placed in the front lines in the performance field.

A *practice field* can be viewed as a leader's equivalent to the practice fields of sports teams, doctors, lawyers, artists, and even the military. No musician or professional athlete would dare to immediately, and without an enormous amount of practice, immerse him or herself in a professional performance. No military leader would ask his or her young leaders to take the battlefield without exposing them to the skills, strategies, and dangers of the real war *prior to the battle*. Each of these professions provides strong, significant practice arenas long before the beginning professional ever enters the real production. The goal of the practice field, therefore, is to provide real enough experiences so that the lessons are meaningful. At the same time, the practice field will provide an environment that is safe so that the beginning leader can experiment with policies and programs, test assumed practices, and experiment with alternative strategies. *Try a new move! Experiment! Take some risks! Remember, you're a learning team!*

The Practice Field Further Defined

It has been suggested that we need to view leadership more as a performing art rather than a specific set of scientific skills, competencies, and knowledge (Sarason, 1999; Vaill, 1989). When practicing a symphony, the orchestra has the ability to *slow down* the tempo in order to practice certain sections. A medical student in residence has the opportunity to slow down and practice certain medical procedures or diagnoses. The military or law enforcement charged with the safety of our country *rehearse* their procedures and process *before* they ever encounter the actual situation. The New York Knicks spend most of their time in a *practice field*, slowing down the tempo and practicing certain moves, strategies, and assumptions, long before they take the competition field in a real game. And all of these practice fields exist in an environment with opportunities for making mistakes in a "safe-failing space to enhance learning" (Kim, 1995, p. 353). When and where does the aspiring (or practicing) principal get a chance to *slow down* and practice certain moves or aspects of his or her job in schools?

Similar to a pilot's flight simulator, a leadership practice field puts prospective principals in control of a realistic activity (e.g., an irate parent, a rude phone call, an emergency situation, an incompetent teacher). The purpose is to place the aspiring principals in a simulated environment in which they can learn from experience in a controlled setting. They are in charge of making key decisions similar to the ones they will be making in their leadership positions. New strategies and practices can be tested, followed by reflection on the result or outcome, accompanied by immediate feedback and support from others. Learning is enhanced by shortening the delay between the decision and the result. In the case of "an irate parent," the candidate receives immediate feedback related to issues of sensitivity to the parent's concern, the ability to utilize appropriate listening skills, conflict resolution skills, and handling situations in an appropriate manner. Aspiring principals begin to understand the underlying forces that produce a particular result or outcome.

Argyris and Schon (1978) in their book, *Organizational Learning*, posit that leaders function with a gap between their conceptual belief of the right course of action, and what they actually choose to do in the real situation. Not choosing to narrow or close these gaps can have two effects: (a) prohibit actual learning, and (b) sustain the existing irrelevancy between principal preparation programs and effective leadership in the field. A leadership practice field can help identify and close such gaps. Herein lies one of the most important reasons for the implementation of a practice field construct. Prospective school leaders are provided opportunities to connect what they conceptually believe is the right course of action to what they choose to do under real circumstances. Practicing such behaviors away from day-to-day stresses of the job increases the likelihood of making the right decisions in the real school environment.

LEADERSHIP FIELD PARADIGMS

To fully discuss the concept of a *leadership practice field*, we must have a prototype from which preparation programs can begin. Building upon past experiences, we can use the models below to introduce possibilities for using the practice field concept as an integral part of the university program. That is not to say, by any means, that this would be an adequate resolution to the need for an extensive, ongoing preparation program. Rather, this is just a beginning. Integrating several, diverse styles of engaged learning practice into a comprehensive *practice* arena allows beginning administrators to rehearse the intricacies of their applied art. Leadership, interpersonal relations, decision-making processes, management, technical aspects, and so forth. can all be simulated, practiced, and evaluated. Feedback and support is provided, all within the *safe zone* provided by the practice arena.

University Principal Preparation Component

A leadership practice field was a required component of the principal preparation program at a mid-western university from 1996–1999. The process was used as a required component of a course in the principalship. For this discussion, however, it is suggested that this could be used as a part of the recruitment and selection process.

Students were required to attend a full-day, Saturday session consisting of a variety of behavior-based activities. Individual names were not used during the day at all; students began the day as a hypothetical principal and were identified only by a number (A-1, A-2, A-3, and so forth). Activities were scheduled in several rooms and individual offices and in a manner whereby each student progressed through the activities during the day.

Evaluators and judges were practicing teachers, principals, superintendents, university professors, and students. Each candidate's performance was judged and reviewed by at least three evaluators. Activities included: (a) talking with a student reporting sexual advances by a classroom teacher, (b) reporting to the Board of Education on declining test scores, (c) addressing the teachers' union on budgetary constraints, and (d) meeting an intoxicated parent in the office who was demanding to take his Kindergarten son out of school. Scoring guides and evaluation instruments were developed and discussed prior to the evaluation process. Within the evaluation process, students were given specific feedback and suggestions for addressing and improving their responses and reactions.

Example:

Angry mother's phone call: (Scripted)

Mr. Jones, this is Mrs. Darnell, and WE have a problem. I have tolerated this situation long enough! As you know, my son Joe is going to graduate from the 8th grade this year. He WILL be attending college, and it is VITAL that he do well in school. Learning is what he's there for!

I have watched and listened, and I have determined that he is not learning ANYTHING in Mr. Johnson's class—it is a total waste of time! I want my son transferred to Mr. Lake immediately! Joe liked him; he had him last year in 7th grade and made an A in the class. I am SURE there are other parents who feel the same way, and I would assume you have heard from them also. What are you going to do about this situation?

(Indicate you don't care if the principal denies the request. Your son Joe is a special case and the principal better consider that situation.) The scripting process goes on having the parent suggest that if he (the principal) doesn't transfer Joe, he (the principal) will "hear from you." You mean business, and you intend to talk with the board president and superintendent.

The evaluators listen on a speaker phone to the student's responses. Both the irate parent and the student (principal trainee) are in the privacy of the individual offices, and the student is in no way identified by name. The performance is then rated according to the prescribed assessment instrument. Reflection by the student, the instructor, and the evaluators' remarks then offer the student diverse perspectives from which to begin discussion regarding handling this and similar types of situations.

The School Leaders Licensure Assessment

As a licensure process the Interstate School Leaders Licensure Consortium (ISLLC) developed standards, and an assessment protocol, and a subsequent tool, the School Leaders Licensure Assessment (SLLA). This process addresses six standards, the subsequent knowledge, skills and proficiencies related to those standards, and the procedure by which an administrative candidate is evaluated.

This assessment is divided into three primary parts: (a) Evaluation of Actions, (b) Synthesis of Information and Decision Making, and (c) Analysis of Information and Decision Making. Each section provides the candidate a realistic scenario or documents, information, and so forth. from which to address questions posed about the specific situation. Examples might include issues similar to the following:

A parent has reported that his or her daughter is not allowed to participate in a weight-lifting class. He or she is threatening legal action based on the Title IX legislation if this is not remedied immediately.

An elementary version might address the issue of changing from a traditional 6th grade, self-contained elementary program to a middle school concept with a 5th, 6th, and 7th grade center. The question(s) posed would address areas such as: What actions will you (as the school leader) take with regard to this situation? Or what would be your first steps in addressing this situation?

Other areas in the SLLA process include scenarios and documents related to realistic school settings. Various information such as dropout rates, test scores, parent/ organization concerns, directives from the superintendent, and the like, are developed to simulate accuracy and realism and provided to the candidate. The challenge for the candidate would include determining what information is needed, where to gather that data, and how best to use it in the resolution of this challenge. The SLLA is a constructed-response assessment process; therefore, the evaluation process emphasizes skills such as information/situation analysis, problem identification and determination of informational accuracy, data processing, and integration of personal knowledge into an appropriate response. Additionally, the candidate is expected to be able to observe patterns, demonstrate knowledge of adult learning theory and human relations perspectives, and conceptualize responses in written or presentation form. The shorter versions of the scenarios address one of the six ISSLC standards, with complexity and difficulty of the resolution increasing as information is added in other pieces of the assessment.

The overall purpose of the process, however, is similar to the leadership field practicum discussed above. The purpose is to provide the candidate an opportunity to demonstrate his or her ability and competency in managing the diverse issues inherent in school leadership.

The Administrator Assessment Center

The third variation of a leadership practice field is the concept of an assessment center process. This model presents an opportunity for the beginning school leader to apply his or her knowledge in a realistic situation, thereby demonstrating the ability to lead an instructional program. The potential school leader is placed in a genuine setting very similar to that of the principal candidacy exercise described first in this discussion. Candidates proceed through a variety of settings, leaderless groups, in-basket activities, a pretend school board meeting, and so forth. They are given situations with the expectation of identifying and resolving the problem(s) (obvious and hidden) with the information. The candidates are judged by a panel of experts, university professors, practitioners in the field, trained interviewers, and so forth, to determine their level of ability and proficiency in each of the prescribed areas. Candidates are then provided written and oral feedback on their performance with suggestions for improvement *in the field.*

Areas of Note

It should be discussed at this juncture, however, that except for the first model cited, each of the practice field paradigms mentioned usually take place *at the conclusion of the preparation program.* It is to be hoped that the students are given some opportunities to rehearse their knowledge, skill, and proficiency throughout their preparation programs. The reality, however, is that actual performance, demonstration, and feedback for the necessary competencies are typically provided at the conclusion of formal instruction which is often at the beginning of entrance into the realities of school leadership. Again, let us refer back to the professions of law, medicine, and sports. Is it realistic, or is it ridiculous, to imagine a professional in those arenas evaluated at the conclusion of their training and then immediately taking the professional field to engage in the competition, the medical realities of life or death, or the implications of legal issues?

CONCLUSION

The important issue, as with any professional practice field, is not a perfect performance necessarily, but whether or not the candidate has potential for success and can practice what is required in the handling of a situation such as an irate parent phone call. The practice field observers provide additional comments focused on constructive criticism and allow the candidate to reflect on areas of improvement. The assessment obviously involves subjective decisions by the evaluators. These decisions, however, are based on many years of experience of practicing teachers, administrators, and university faculty. The point is that our profession is currently depending excessively on theoretical and non-behavioral based preparation of school principals. Sarason (1999) argues that preparing teachers and principals with an over-emphasis on non-behavioral based criteria is not justifiable on moral and educational grounds. He continues by making an analogy to the performing arts: "if you want to predict who will make a good actor, you have to see them act, keeping in mind that you are observing an amateur" (p. 99).

The real strength of leadership practice fields is that they provide an opportunity (and perhaps more authentic) for prospective school leaders to practice an actual task from the school administrator's day. Our traditional preparation programs certainly address what a candidate *might do* in a particular situation, but leadership practice fields begin to focus on the issue of what the candidate *will actually do* in a real-life situation.

We are beginning to view leadership less and less as consisting of quantifiable characteristics measured by non-behavioral based activities. Evidence continues to mount indicating educational administration is less objective and "more dependent on the comings and goings of personalities," says Gary Wills (1994) in his best-selling book, *Certain Trumpets*, about the nature of leadership. If we desire to (and we suggest we must) narrow or close the existing gap between what happens in the principal preparation program and what actually happens in the school setting, we must provide more opportunities for prospective school principals to practice their skills where they can *slow down and work on certain sections.*

REFERENCES

American Association of School Administrators. (1960). *Professional administrators for America's schools* (Thirty-eighth AASA Yearbook). Washington, DC: National Education Association.

Argris, C., & Schon, D. (1978). *Organizational learning: A theory of action perspective.* Reading, MA: Addison-Wesley.

Cambron-McCabe, N. (1999). Confronting fundamental transformation of leadership preparation. In J. Murphy & P. B. Forsyth (Eds.), *Educational administration: A decade of reform* (pp. 217–227). Thousand Oaks, CA: Corwin Press.

Creighton, T. (in press). Standards for school administrators: OK, but don't we have the cart before the horse? *Journal of School Leadership.*

Creighton, T., & Jones, G. (2001, August). *Selection or self-selection? How rigorous are selection criteria in education administration programs?* Paper presented at the annual meting of the National Council of Professors of Educational Administration, Houston, TX.

English, F. (2000). Looking behind the veil: Addressing the enigma of educational leadership. *Education Leadership Review, 1*(3), 1–7.

Farquhar, R. H., & Piele, P. K. (1972). *Preparing educational leaders: A review of recent literature.* (ERIC/CEM state of the knowledge series, number 14; UCEA monograph series, number 1). Danville, IL: Interstate.

Kim, D. (1995). Managerial practice fields: Infrastructures of a learning organization. In S. Chawla & J. Renesch (Eds.), *Learning organizations: Developing cultures for tomorrow's workplace* (pp. 351–363). Portland: Productivity Press.

McCarthy, M. (1999). The evolution of educational leadership programs. In J. Murphy & K. S. Lewis (Eds.), *Handbook of research on educational administration* (2nd ed., pp. 119–139). San Francisco: Jossey-Bass.

Murphy, J. (1999). Changes in preparation programs: Perceptions of department chairs. In J. Murphy & P. B. Forsyth (Eds.), *Educational administration: A decade of reform* (pp. 170–191). Thousand Oaks, CA: Corwin Press.

Murphy, J. (2001, September). *Re-culturing the profession of educational leadership: New blueprints.* Paper commissioned for the National Commission for the Advancement of Educational Leadership Preparation. Racine, WI.

Pitner, N. J. (1990, September). *Reinventing school leadership* (pp. 129–131) [Working memo prepared for the Reinventing School Leadership Conference]. Cambridge, MA: National Center for Educational Leadership.

Sarason, S. B. (1999). *Teaching as a performing art.* New York: Teachers College Press.

Vaill, P. B. (1989). *Managing as a performing art.* San Francisco: Jossey-Bass.

Wills, G. (1994). *Certain trumpets: The nature of leadership.* New York: Simon and Schuster.

Young, M., Petersen, G., & Short, P. (2002). *The complexity of substantive reform: A call for interdependence among key stakeholders.* Paper commissioned for the National Commission for the Advancement of Educational Leadership Preparation. Racine, WI.

Small Classes or Accountability?
Using Texas Assessment of Academic Skills,
Class Size Outcomes, and Other Data to
Demonstrate the Necessity of Critique

C. M. Achilles and J. D. Finn

This chapter simultaneously presents: a skill (critique) required by education administrators that best can be addressed in formal education administration (EdAd) preparation; and one current example of the necessity of critique using data from the Texas testing programs.[1] To critique is to obtain and review evidence, weigh the credibility of the data using established criteria, and then to make some informed decision that may be adjusted later when compelling new evidence is available. Educators regularly make decisions about other people's children and money that will affect the lives of students in their charge. The decisions and their consequent actions need to be good.

Educators are continually beset by fads and quick fixes for a myriad of real or presumed problems and crises. Such situations heighten the necessity of critique because pupils rely on others to make their education decisions. Fads often are promulgated by product producers and peddlers, self-professed experts, vanity-press publications, "policy papers" that would not pass peer review, and so forth. Should educators be proud that people are interested enough in education to be this involved? Or should they be wary, even suspicious, of proffered remedies, many of which seem ideology-, power-, or profit-driven?

NON-INDEPENDENT RESEARCH AND THE NECESSITY OF CRITIQUE

There is much rhetoric about "fixing" the schools. Yet, as a recent *New York Times* article explained, folks are skeptical because some recommended "quick fixes" are high-sounding, but seldom based on professional knowledge of schooling. Other remedies are based upon "research" of persons who hardly could be called "disinterested." (Is this advocacy, rather than research?) Archibold (2000) quoted a school

C. M. Achilles, Eastern Michigan University
J. D. Finn, State University of New York, Buffalo

superintendent who noted that he could walk into any store in the community and no one would hesitate to tell him how to run the school system (probably the largest business in town!). "The overriding problem, as he sees it, is a *dearth of independent research* on what actually works. The slightest whiff of apparent success—a limited study . . . yields a headlong, and possibly, misplaced rush of support, he said" (p. v27, emphasis added).

Two Examples of Academic Critique

The *Phi Delta Kappan* has extended a debate started earlier in the less-read *Educational Researcher* over whether or not "Success For All" (SFA) actually provided success for students. Pogrow (2000a; 2000b; 2002), the developer and advocate for Higher Order Thinking Skills, questioned claims made for SFA and whether evaluations done by or commissioned through SFA personnel could be considered independent or disinterested. Slavin (2000, 2002) and Slavin and Madden (2000) summarized findings that SFA was successful. Pogrow (2000b) countered that Slavin and Madden relied only on data from persons closely connected to SFA. Butzin (2000) focused on "disinterested": "I am certainly envious that [SFA and] Robert Slavin's research center have managed to capture $56.14 million in federal grants, plus generating $44 million in program sales" (p. 98). Indeed, SFA is certified as a Comprehensive School Reform Model and is widely supported in schools with Title I funds. Achilles (1998) questioned if SFA's results were equal to grades K–3 small-class results, as long-lasting, and as efficient, and if SFA relied on a small-class effect for its outcomes. Most remedial education projects are expensive and employ "extra" personnel and small groups or tutoring. Some were developed with tax dollars at federal sponsored-research sites. Levin (1998) questioned the cost to local schools of such federally developed programs:

> In fact, I believe that they ought to be made available at low cost and question why they are sold commercially at high prices, given the substantial grants and subsides provided for their development by government agencies . . . presumably to reduce costs and promote their use. (Levin, 1998, p. 9)

Besides the critique and debate over SFA, there is considerable academic critique of the National Reading Panel (NRP) Report (2001) and its antecedents. This critique is manifestly important because reading is a foundation for education. Yet, the federal reading initiative and the support for programs (and research) of the NRP and the phonics-advocating work of the National Institute of Child Health and Human Development (NICHHD) draw an inordinate amount of federal funds (nearly to the exclusion of other approaches). Some titles tell much about the NRP and earlier reading critiques: "The politics of literacy teaching: How 'research' shaped education policy" (Allington & Woodside-Jiron, 1999); "Beyond the smoke and mirrors: A critique of the National Reading Panel Report on Phonics" (Garan, 2001a); "Beyond the smoke and mirrors: Putting out the fire" (Ehri & Stahl, 2001); "More smoking guns: A response to . . ." (Garan, 2001b); and "More smoke and mirrors: A critique of the National Reading Panel Report on Fluency" (Krashen, 2001). Only one critique title, "An open letter to Reid Lyon" (Strauss, 2001), leaves much to the imagination.

Initial Steps to Start the Critique Process

So, how might the educator check on (i.e., critique) ideas offered for education improvement and separate fads from legitimate research or opinions about education? One step is to compare and analyze the ideas by using reasonable and accepted criteria to guide decisions. There are numerous well-established criteria. One recent listing includes the following (Shermer, 2001, p. 36), to which we would add, "Is the research independent?":

- How reliable is the source of the claim?
- Does this source often make similar claims?
- Have the claims been verified by another source?
- How does the claim fit with what we know about how the world works?
- Has anyone gone out of the way to disprove the claim or has only supportive evidence been sought?

The example in table 1 uses criteria to assist the critique process and compares findings of the Student Teacher Achievement Ratio (STAR) large-scale education experiment against guidelines for judging social programs. For persons not familiar with the STAR research (Achilles, 1999; Finn & Achilles, 1999; Mosteller, 1995; Word et al., 1990), appendix A briefly summarizes the STAR experiment.

The STAR results, combined with earlier class-size work such as the Glass and Smith (1978) and Smith and Glass (1979) meta-analyses, Indiana's Prime Time (Chase, Mueller, & Walden, 1986), and other class-size studies emphasize the efficacy of small classes in raising student test scores, in reducing test-score achievement gaps, and in benefiting students in other ways. Robinson's (1990) review of research reported that STAR's small-class effect sizes were about twice as important for minority as for non-minority students, and Wenglinsky's (1997) national study concurred: "fourth graders in smaller-than-average classes are about half a year ahead of fourth graders in larger-that-average classes . . . the largest effects seem to be for poor students in high-cost areas" (pp. 24–25). In addition to immediate small-class benefits, reanalyses of STAR data and case studies show that early small-class students continue to increase their academic excellence after they exit three or four years of small-class experience. (Boyd-Zaharias & Pate-Bain, 2000; Finn & Achilles, 1999; Finn, Gerber, Achilles, & Boyd-Zaharias, 2001).

Blind-Sided: Being Blinded by One Pont of View Strongly Held

Even using independent research and considering only results that meet the criteria of good research can be misleading unless one uses care. Consider the recent interest in the reported increases in test scores in Texas. At first look, the Texas data on

Table 1.   Critique of STAR Results Using Crane's Critera for Social Programs That Work

Crane Criteria and Question	STAR'S Facts
1. Do the benefits outweigh the costs? *YES.*	1. In the short term (K–3), there were no definitive data. In the "follow-up studies," yes; in the STAR reanalysis, yes; in alternative implementations, yes. See Krueger (1997, 1998; Finn & Achilles, 1999; Finn et al., 2001).
2. Does the program have a statistically significant effect on the treatment group? *YES.*	2. Yes. This statistically significant difference was found each year, all years, and in many combinations of analyses done by STAR persons and by others (as far away as London).
3. What is the magnitude of the program's effect? *(Shown in Effect Size or ES)*	3. Effect-size (ES) results were .17–.40 in the early analyses. Effects were about twice as high for minority children as for Anglo children, grades K–3 (each year, all years). Grade-equivalent analyses show continuing growth even after students leave small classes (see #4). (Finn & Achilles, 1999; Finn et al., 2001).
4. How long do the effects of the program last? *(At least into high school and beyond)*	4. Positive academic and social effects of K–3 small classes are highly visible in H.S. and beyond including in college-entrance tests. (Boyd-Zaharias & Pate-Bain, 2000; Krueger, 1997; Krueger & Whitmore, 2000).
5. What is the relationship of the evaluator to the program? *(Independent)*	5. The STAR evaluator was a contracted independent expert. STAR personnel did secondary analyses. The external expert's work is (and was) the primary analysis accepted and published. Others have reanalyzed STAR data with similar results.
6. Can the program and its results be replicated? *(Yes)* 7. Can the program maintain its effectiveness on a larger scale? *(Still being assessed. Yes if well implemented)*	6. & 7. They have been consistently replicated in well-designed class-size analyses. Replications of STAR have been achieved in single districts and in general policy implementations. Reported gains and ES for well-conducted studies are similar. Evaluations of state-wide small-class efforts in CA, and the results in Texas (HB 72, 1984) suggest large-scale benefits, but these results are less definitive than STAR or SAGE in Wisconsin, probably because of less controlled implementations.

Source: Crane, J. (Ed.). (1998). *Social programs that work.* New York: Russell Sage Foundation.

increasing percentages of students passing the 10th grade Texas Assessment of Academic Skills (TAAS) seemed reasonable, especially because of the 1984 passage of Texas House Bill 72 that required small classes in early grades (not more than 22 students in grades K–2 and later, not more than 22 students in grades 3 and 4 with a pupil-teacher ratio or PTR not to exceed 20:1). As data in table 2 show, grade-10 students taking the TAAS in 1995–1996 could have had 2 years of small-class instruction (K–1), the minimum time needed for lasting small-class benefits (Finn et al., 2001). Sophomores in later years could have had 3, 4, and 5 years in early primary small classes; so, based on results of small-class research, we could expect the evident continuing rise in the percent of students passing the TAAS that appears in table 2.

Table 2.   Percentage of Groups of Grade-10 Students Passing All Parts of TAAS by Years

			Percent Passing by Groups. ( ) = Difference from White			
Year	All	White	Hisp*	Af. Am.*	Eco. Dis.*	** Possible years (n) in small class (K–4) ***
93–94	50	64	34 (30)	28 (36)	32 (32)	0
94–95	52	67	36 (31)	31 (36)	34 (33)	1
95–96	57	71	43 (28)	37 (34)	40 (31)	2
96–97	64	78	49 (29)	46 (32)	47 (31)	3
97–98	69	81	57 (24)	52 (29)	54 (27)	4
98–99	75	86	64 (22)	60 (26)	62 (24)	5
99–00	80	89	70 (19)	67 (22)	68 (21)	5
GAIN	30	25	36 (11)	39 (14)	36 (11)	NA
% Gain. Diff from ALL ***		−5	+6	+9	+6	

* Hisp = Hispanic; Af. Am. = African American; Eco. Dis. = Economically disadvantaged.
** *Note.* In 1993–1994 grade-10 students would have had no years of HB 72 small classes. Project STAR analyses showed that 3 years or more in a small class would have lasting benefits into grades 8, 10 and beyond (Finn et al., 2001; Krueger & Whitmore, 2000). Because of time required for full implementation, the years in a small class estimate may be optimistic.
*** The positive gains over All by Hisp, Af. Am. and Eco. Dis. show the equity factor of small classes found in STAR. All students gain from the small-class experience, but students who need more gain, get more gain. From 1993–1994, before sophomore test takers had small classes, until 1999–2000 when they could have had 5 years of small classes, the test-score gap between white and other groups reduced by 19, 22, and 21 percentage points.

Table 2 compares the percentage of 10th grade students passing the TAAS from 1993–1994 through 1999–2000 by four groups: white, Hispanic, African American, economically disadvantaged, and all students. Data seem to show the impact of small classes on the differing groups, with minority and economically disadvantaged students getting larger gains than do white students, results consistent with STAR and other studies (e.g., Robinson, 1990; Wenglinsky, 1997). The largest gains occur after a sophomore could have had at least two years in a small class.

As shown in figure 1, the TAAS pass rates had no clear direction until 1995–1996, when they began, and continued up through 1999–2000. This upward slope could be explained by cohorts of sophomores having increasing small-class exposure in grades K–4 and by other early interventions. Supporters of the TAAS claimed that gains were from testing kids (equivalent to the idea of fattening a hog by weighing it), an accountability measure begun in 1992 and not supported by research, rather than from the *combination* of three strongly research-demonstrated school-improvement processes begun statewide in 1984 with HB 72: pre-school, extended day, and class-size implementations (e.g., Johnson, Treisman, & Fuller, 2000).

The Texas data seem to show both a small-class effect and that small classes reduce the achievement gap over time. The gains shown in figure 1 reflect evidence obtained from STAR. A RAND study (Grissmer, Flanagan, Kawata, & Williamson, 2000), which praised Texas as making progress on the National Assessment of Educational Progress (NAEP), found that states that made progress on the NAEP had,

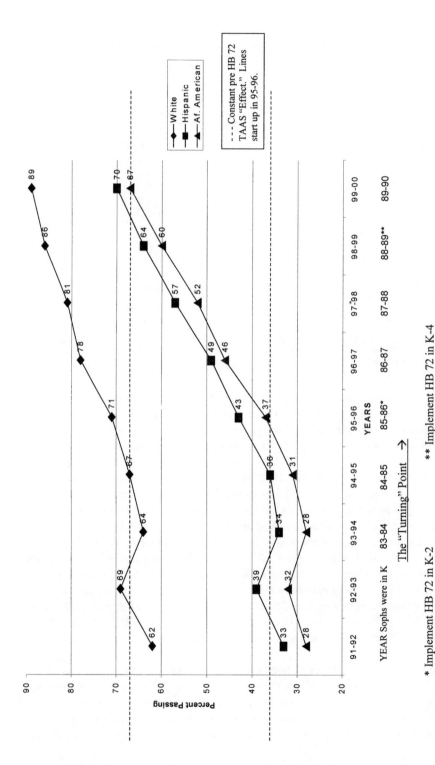

Figure 1. Percentage (%) sophomores passing TAAS by three Groups [Adapted from Cortez (2000)].

* Implement HB 72 in K-2   ** Implement HB 72 in K-4

among other things, small classes in elementary schools, and public pre-kindergarten programs, two components of the Texas education reform started with HB 72 in 1984.[2]

An initial rush to use TAAS data to support the positive benefits of small classes (e.g., Achilles, Finn, Boyd-Zaharias, Gerber, & Pannozzo 2000, 2001) by-passed what an old Appalachian philosopher once opined: "No matter how thin, all shingles have two sides." Recalling this mountain wisdom, and given the un-likely rejection of *three* research-supported interventions in favor of one un-proven "cause" for TAAS gains, along with a tendency to see early small classes as an important basis for school improvement, the necessity of critique became evident. The initial findings in the critique using TAAS and the Texas Assessment of School Progress (TASP) aren't heartwarming.

Another Side of the Shingle: What Critique Has Turned Up (So Far)

Although data presented up to this point make a strong case that the HB 72 (1984) smaller classes are fundamental reasons for the apparent Texas successes and achievement-gap reduction, Haney (2000), an expert witness in TAAS litigation, ex-pressed another side of the shingle. His work attributed much of the TAAS test-score gains to three phenomena other than either a) the HB 72 triad of class size, pre-school, and extended day and b) testing; Haney pointed to retention in grade, dropout, and test-exempted students. Now there are *six* research-based explanations for any gains weighing in against one non-research-based claim.

Besides the TAAS, Texas used the TASP Test to see if Texas secondary school stu-dents were ready to do post-secondary work. Haney (2000, 2001) accumulated data to question the validity of the TAAS and interpretation of TAAS results. For exam-ple, based on NAEP data 1992–1998, Haney (2000) concluded "the magnitudes of the gains apparent on NAEP for Texas fail to confirm the dramatic gains apparent on TAAS," and "The Texas 'miracle' is more myth than real" (Part 7, p. 22). Haney used percentages of students taking the TASP tests and passing all three parts to question TAAS outcomes. Haney (2000) reported taking the following information from the Texas Higher Education Coordinating Board that "describes the TASP test-ing program thus at its website" [http://www.thecb.state.tx.us/]:

> you can find out if you have the reading, writing, and math skills you need to do college-level work through the . . . TASP. The TASP Test, which is part of the TASP program is required—it is not optional. . . . Beginning in fall 1998 you must take the TASP Test . . . before beginning classes at a public community college, public technical college, or pub-lic university in Texas. (Part 7, pp. 22–25)

If the 10th-grade TAAS (reading, writing, and math skills) test results have ac-tually been increasing, one would expect gains in TASP results on the same skills, especially because a student would take the TASP *after* successfully completing the TAAS for graduation from high school. Figure 2 shows a dramatic *decline* in TASP results at the time when the TAAS rates supposedly climbed. Compare the results shown in figures 1 and 2. These differences need careful explanation and critique.

TASP Student Performance Pass Rates by Race/Ethnicity

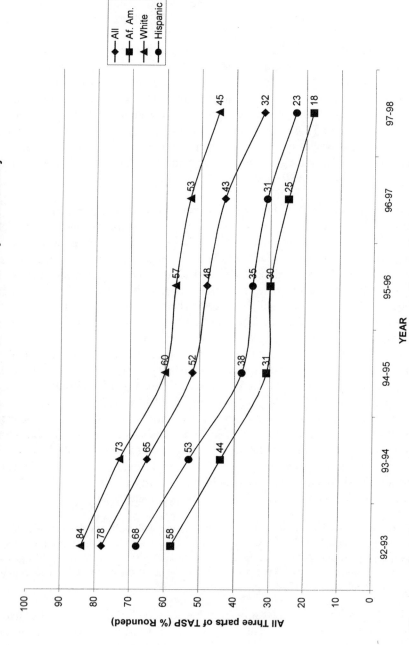

Figure 2.   TASP student performance (1993–1998). Pass rates by race/ethnicity (rounded) (Haney, 2001, p. 20).

Extending the Critique: A Search for Answers

One possible[3] cause of increasing TAAS scores and decreasing TASP outcomes is the current concern among many educators that an undue emphasis on "high-stakes" testing (such as the TAAS exit test) requires educators to teach to the test, providing a restrictive and narrow curriculum. English (2001–2002) raised questions about "dumbing down" schools by relying upon a testing mania to force decisions about curriculum and instruction. English's points had been substantiated elsewhere. In discussing observations in classrooms during the STAR experiment, Evertson and Randolph (1998, as reported in Achilles, 1999, p. 66) noted, "The curriculum in all classes . . . was tightly aligned to achievement of basic skills that could be readily measured by standardized and curriculum-driven criterion-referenced tests." This trend, currently being fueled by testing mandates in other states (e.g., Massachusetts, Michigan, New York), seems to have three predictable outcomes: 1) high retention-in-grade rates, 2) high dropout rates, and 3) fewer of those who pass the basic-skills tests will now have the knowledge and skills to enter and succeed in higher education. Where does that leave the Texas test supporters and the claims of success?[4]

Because the "must pass" TAAS data are mostly from grade 10, what happens prior to 10th grade is important. Haney (2000, Part 5; see also Haney, 2001) reviewed Texas grade retention and dropout data. Students retained in the 9th grade do not take the 10th grade TAAS with their cohort, and if retained in the 9th grade, they may drop out, especially since a student retained in 9th grade may already have been retained at least once. Research shows the strong relationship between retention and dropping out of school; a student retained *twice* is nearly assured of not completing high school (e.g., Roderick, 1995; Texas Education Agency, n.d.) Haney (2000) provided data on retention by grades (K–12) by ethnicity. *Ranges* in percentage retained, grades K–8, for White (.60–4.40), African American (.90–7.0) and Hispanic (1.0–6.6) favor White students, but only moderately. The picture changes dramatically at grades 9 and 10, especially grade 9 the year *before* the TAAS (1996–1997) data). (Part 5, p. 7). Table 3 shows the data. The high 10th grade retention suggests potentially high dropout rates before graduation, something that should support an *increase* (not a decrease) in TASP test outcomes.

Regarding retention in grade and achievement-gap reduction, Haney (2000, Part 5, pp. 3–5) noted the differential in retention for white and other students in Texas:

since 1992 progress from grade 9 to high school graduation has been stymied for Black and Hispanic students *not* after grade 10 when they first take the TAAS exit test, but in

Table 3. Percentage of Students Retained (1996–1997) Grades 9 and 10, Texas

Grade	White	Af. Am.*	Hispanic	Total
9	9.6	24.2	25.9	17.8
10	4.8	11.6	11.4	7.9

*Af. Am. = African American.
(From Haney, 2001).

grade 9 *before* they take the test. . . . Also, in 1998–99 there were 25–30% *fewer* Black and Hispanic students enrolled in grade 10 than had been enrolled in grade 9 in 1997–98. . . . [T]he fact that by the end of the 1990's 25–30% of Black and Hispanic students, as compared with only 10% of white students, were being retained to repeat grade 9 instead of being promoted to grade 10, makes it clear that the *apparent diminution* in the grade 10 racial gap in TAAS pass rates is in some measure an illusion. (pp. 3–4, emphases added)

Texas data seem to show the well-known grade retention and dropout link. "Grade 10 enrollments in 1996–1997 were about 16 percent lower than expected for Black and Hispanic students, but only 8 percent for White students. . . . What happened to these missing students? . . . The grade 9 retention rates in Texas are far in excess of national trends" (Haney, 2000, Part 5, p. 9).

Those 9th grade retention rates, one might surmise, result in increased TAAS exit-test scores at grade 10. They may also contribute to another statistic that accompanies higher TAAS scores and higher retention-in-grade. Reporting on National Center for Education Statistics (NCES) data for 1990–1992, 1993–1995, and 1996–1998, Haney (Part 7, p. 3) concluded: "As can be seen for all three time periods, these data show Texas to have among the lowest rates of high school completion among the 50 states." The NCES data contradict results put forth by the Texas Education Agency (TEA), but they are supported by data provided by the Intercultural Development Research Association (Cortez, 2000). Haney noted that increases in special education–classified TAAS test takers help explain the Texas "Miracle." Special education may "also account for a portion of the closing of the 'race gap' in TAAS scores over this period" (Part 5, pp. 10–11). He noted a change in the passing rates for the General Education Development (GED) test that could influence both students staying in high school and student self-report of completing high school. (Haney, Part 7). In an analysis of data provided by the TEA for the Texas Report Card On Schools, Bobbett, French, and Achilles (1996) had raised questions about missing students and the clear connection of test scores to minority student and low-income student enrollment.

Importance of TAAS-TASP Differentials
The importance of the TAAS (basic skills) and TASP (college-level skill needs) differentials is escalated when a possible increase in basic skills performance is mirrored by a decline in skills students need to be successful in higher education. The decline in TASP performance shown here is being studied in Texas.

The dropout issue is complex. A 1999 report ("Where Have All the Freshman Gone?") issued through the office of Texas State Senator G. Barrientos showed that of the 41,344 freshmen who repeated ninth grade in Texas districts in 1992–1993, 19.5 percent had graduated from high school and another 15.6 percent has received the GED by 1997–1998 (as reported in Haney, 2001, p. 18). Haney (2000) also had noted that, "In other words, for the graduating classes of 1992 through 1999, around 700,000 children in Texas were lost or left behind before graduation from high school" (p. 17).

The dropout-related retention-in-grade issue is complex, also. Haney (2001) reported:

> Whatever the historical cause, the fact that by the end of the 1990s 25–30% of Black and Hispanic students, as compared with only 10% of White students, were being failed in grade 9, instead of being promoted to grade 10, makes it clear that the apparent diminution in the racial gap in TAAS grade 10 pass rates is in some measure an illusion. Through the 1990s, progressively smaller proportions of minority students ever even made it to grade 10 to take the exit level TAAS test. (p. 12)

Johnson, Treisman, and Fuller (2000) argued that achievement increases in Texas were likely influenced positively by the "state's current accountability system, which was initiated in 1992" (p. 20). They did acknowledge "other statewide initiatives over the past decade that have influenced student performances. These include class-size reduction in the early grades, . . . and state funding of extended-year programs and pre-kindergarten" (p. 20). Class size, extended year, and public pre-kindergarten all have strong research bases, something not yet available for testing efforts. The Johnson et al. (2000) claim requires careful critique, as do claims by Skrla (2001), Scheurich, Skrla, and Johnson (2000), Lunenburg (2001), and others who seem to accept the TAAS data and testing explanations uncritically.

Based upon Haney's analyses, early claims that HB 72-generated small classes have contributed substantially to reducing the achievement gap between students of various ethnicities on TAAS results in Texas (1995–2000), may be premature. Additional analyses are required—and thus the necessity of ongoing critique.

Alignment of the increasing passing rates on the TAAS beginning in 1995–1996 with implementation of research-supported improvements (HB 72) in 1985–1986 provides strong (but circumstantial) evidence that testing is not the cause, but this requires further analysis too. One thing seems certain given the increasing retention-in-grade, the decrease in TASP scores, and the dismal high school graduation rates in Texas: Many children were left behind or fell through the cracks in the highly touted Texas education system. There will be a large pool of persons to labor in unskilled occupations in Texas. The testing effort may be education's legacy for large businesses in Texas. Researchers might review the economics of this.

Dropout and grade retention, plus the decline in TASP scores (and questionable interpretations of NAEP scores without considering retention, dropout, test-exempt students, etc.), raise important issues about the *actual* impacts and benefits of "high-stakes" testing in Texas (and elsewhere). As Augustus Caesar would say, "*Festina lente*" (make haste slowly). And for those planning to buy into the testing mania, another Latin expression is apt: *Caveat emptor.* Most of all, the possibility that this new "accountability" is a) just another money-siphoning fad, or b) a new ideological ploy to debase public schooling emphasizes the *necessity of critique.*

NOTES

1. This work was partially supported by a grant from The Spencer Foundation. Portions of this chapter are adapted from three sources: a) Achilles, C. M. (2001, August). *The changing world of*

school administration: Accountability 2001 style, impacts diversity and higher-order thinking. Paper presented at National Conference of Professors of Educational Administration (NCPEA), Houston, TX; b) Achilles, C. M., Finn, J. D., Gerber, S. B., Pannozzo, G., & Boyd-Zaharias, J. (2001, November). *The power of small classes to reduce the test-score achievement gap.* Paper presented at Mid-South Educational Research Association, (MSERA) Little Rock, AR; and c) Achilles, C. M., Finn, J. D., Gerber, S. B., Pannozzo, G., & Boyd-Zaharias, J. (2000, October). *Small classes do reduce the test-score achievement gap.* Paper presented at the Council of Great City Schools, Los Angeles, CA.

2. Forces such as grade retention, dropouts, and exemptions from test taking by qualifying for special education need to be thoroughly considered to see if the "Texas Miracle" is really a "Mirage." (Haney, 2000, 2001). RAND subsequently provided a revision of Texas' education success as reported in Grissmer et al., (2000). These issues became political in the 2000 presidential elections, and continue in "No Child Left Behind," and emphasis on using results from The National Reading Panel's work.

3. We say "possible" because analyses of retention in grade, dropout rates, and who actually is allowed to take the tests may show that the increase is more artifact than fact.

4. In a case-study analysis of Texas testing, Rockstroh (2001) made the following observations (p. 25): "Students who score well on the TAAS, the SAT or the ACT are exempt from taking the TASP. If these students were figured in as having passed the TASP, scores [sic, passing rates] would be significantly higher," and "In effect, only those students who 1) attend a college in-state, 2) attend a publicly funded school, and 3) do poorly on TAAS and/or the SAT and ACT have to take the TASP."

REFERENCES

Achilles, C. M. (1998, April). Small for all. *Phi Delta Kappan, 79*(8), 640.

Achilles, C. M. (1999). *Let's put kids first finally: Getting class size right.* Thousand Oaks, CA: Corwin Press.

Achilles, C. M. (2001, August). *The changing world of school administration: Accountability 2001 style impacts diversity and higher-order thinking.* Paper presented at the annual meeting of the National Council of Professors of Educational Administration, Houston, TX.

Achilles, C. M., Finn, J. D., & Bain, H. (1997–1998). Using class size to reduce the equity gap. *Educational Leadership, 55*(4), 40–43.

Achilles, C. M., Finn, J. D., Boyd-Zaharias, J., Gerber, S. B., & Pannozzo, G. (2000, October). *Small classes DO reduce the test-score achievement gap.* Paper presented at the meeting of the Council of Great City Schools, Los Angeles, CA.

Achilles, C. M., Finn, J. D., Boyd-Zaharias, J., Gerber, S. B., & Pannozzo, G. (2001, February). *Small classes impact the test-score achievement gap positively.* Paper presented at the meeting of the American Association of School Administrators, Orlando, FL.

Achilles, C. M., Finn, J. D., Gerber, S. B., Pannozzo, G., & Boyd-Zaharias, J. (2001, November). *The power of small classes to reduce the test-score achievement gap.* Paper presented at the meeting of the Mid-South Educational Research Association. Little Rock, AR.

Allington, R. L., & Woodside-Jiron, H. (1999, November). The politics of literacy teaching: How "research" shaped education policy. *Educational Researcher, 28*(8), 4–12.

Archibold, R. C. (2000, September 3). Much talk of education on the stump, much skepticism in the schools. *The New York Times*: New York Report, p. v27.

Bobbett, G. C., French, R. L., & Achilles, C. M. (1996, March). *How meaningful are Texas school district report cards?* Paper at the meeting of the American Association of School Administrators, San Diego, CA.

Boyd-Zaharias, J., & Pate-Bain, H. (2000). Early and new findings from Tennessee's Project STAR. In M. C. Wang & J. D. Finn (Eds.), *How small classes help teachers do their best* (pp. 65–98). Philadelphia, PA: Temple University Center for Research in Human Development.

Butzin, S. (2000, September). Iceberg ahead. *Phi Delta Kappan, 82*(1), 98.

Chase, C. I., Mueller, D. J., & Walden, J. D. (1986, December*). PRIME TIME: Its impact on instruction and achievement. Final report.* Indianapolis: Indiana Department of Education.

Cortez, A. (2000, March). Why better isn't enough: A closer look at TAAS gains. *IDRA Newsletter.*

Crane, J. (Ed.). (1998). *Social programs that work.* New York: Russell Sage Foundation.

Ehri, L., & Stahl, S. A. (2001, September). Beyond the smoke and mirrors: Putting out the fire. *Phi Delta Kappan, 83*(1), 17–20.

English, F. W. (2001–2002). Dumbing schools down with data-driven decision making: A deconstructive reading of a popular leitmotif. *National Forum of Educational Administration and Supervision, 18*(2), 3–11.

Finn, J. D., & Achilles, C. M. (1999, Summer). Tennessee's class size study: Findings, implications, misconceptions. *Educational Evaluation and Policy Analysis, 21*(2), 97–107.

Finn, J., Gerber, S. B., Achilles, C. M., & Boyd-Zaharias, J. (2001, April). The enduring effects of small classes. *Teachers College Record 103*(2), 145–183.

Garan, E. M. (2001a, September). More smoking guns: A response to Ehri and Stahl. *Phi Delta Kappan, 83*(1), 21–27.

Garan, E. M. (2001b, March). Beyond the smoke and mirrors. A critique of the National Reading Panel Report on Phonics. *Phi Delta Kappan, 82*(7), 500–506.

Glass, G. V., & Smith, M. L. (1978). *Meta-analysis of research on the relationship of class size and achievement.* San Francisco: Far West Laboratory for Educational Research and Development.

Grissmer, D., Flanagan, A., Kawata, J., & Williamson, S. (2000). *Improving student achievement: What state NAEP test scores tell us.* Santa Monica, CA: RAND Education.

Haney, W. (2000, August 19). The myth of the Texas miracle in education. *Education Policy Analysis Archives, 8*(41). ISSN 1068-2341.

Haney, W. (2001). *Revisiting the "Myth of the Texas Miracle in Education": Lessons about dropout research and dropout prevention.* Paper presented at the Dropout Research: Accurate Counts and Positive Interventions Conference, Cambridge, MA.

Johnson, J. F., Treisman, U., & Fuller, E. (2000, December). Testing in Texas. *The School Administrator, 57*(11), 20–26.

Krashen, S. (2001, October) More smoke and mirrors: A critique of the National Reading Panel Report on Fluency. *Phi Delta Kappan, 83*(2), 119–123.

Krueger, A. B. (1999). Experimental estimates of education production functions. *Quarterly Journal of Economics, 114,* 497–532.

Krueger, A. B., & Whitmore, D. M. (2000, April). *The effect of attending a small class in the early grades on college-test taking and middle school test results: Evidence from Project STAR.* Cambridge, MA: National Bureau of Economic Research. Working Paper 7656. Retrieved from www.nber.org.papers/w7656

Levin, H. M. (1998, May). Educational performance standards and the economy. *Educational Researcher, 27*(4), 4–10.

Lunenburg, F. (2001, August). *Improving student achievement: Some structural incompatibilities.* Walter Cocking Lecture. National Conference of Professors of Educational Administration, Houston, TX.

Mosteller, F. (1995). The Tennessee study of class size in the early school grades. *The Future of Children, 5*(2), 113–127.

Pogrow, S. (2000a, April). The unsubstantiated "success" of Success for All. *Phi Delta Kappan, 81*(8), 596–600.

Pogrow, S. (2000b, September). Success for All does not produce success for students. *Phi Delta Kappan, 82*(1), 67–80.

Pogrow, S. (2002, February). Success for All is a failure. *Phi Delta Kappan, 83*(6), 463–468.

Report of the National Reading Panel: Teaching Children to Read. (2001). Retrieved from www.nichd.nih.gov/publications/nrp/report.htm

Robinson, G. L. (1990, April). Synthesis of research on the effects of class size. *Educational Leadership, 47*(7), 80–90.

Rockstroh, B. (2002). *Texas accountability and preparation for college: TAAS and TASP passing rate disparities.* Unpublished case study for comprehensive examination. South Orange, NJ: Seton Hall University.

Roderick, M. (1995, December). Grade retention and school dropout: Policy debate and research questions. *Research Bulletin.* Bloomington, IN: Phi Delta Kappa.

Scheurich, J. J., Skrla, L., & Johnson, J. F. (2000, December). Thinking carefully about equity and accountability. *Phi Delta Kappan, 82*(4), 293–229.

Shermer, M. (2001, November). Baloney detection. *Scientific American, 285*(5), 35.

Skrla, L. (2001, Spring). The influence of state accountability on teacher expectations and student performance. *UCEA Review, XLII* (2), 1–4.

Slavin, R. E. (2002, February). Mounting evidence supports the achievement effects of Success for All. *Phi Delta Kappan, 83*(6), 469–471.

Slavin, R. E., & Madden, N. A. (2000, September). Research on achievement outcomes of Success for All. *Phi Delta Kappan, 82*(1), 38–40, 59–66.

Smith, M. L., & Glass, G. V. (1979). *Relationship of class-size to classroom processes, teacher satisfaction and pupil affect: A meta-analysis.* San Francisco: Far West Laboratory for Educational Research and Development.

State of Texas (1984). General and special laws of the State of Texas. Sixty-eighth Legislature 6/4/84–7/11/84. Esp. Chapter 28, H.B. No. 72. Austin, TX: Author.

Strauss, S. L. (2001, June/July). An open letter to Reid Lyon. *Educational Researcher, 30*(5), 34–36.

Texas Education Agency (n.d., Est. 93–94). *Closing the gap: Acceleration vs remediation and the impact of retention in grade on student achievement.* Commissioner's Critical Issue Analysis Series, #1. Austin, TX: Author.

Wenglinsky, H. (1997). *When money matters.* Princeton, NJ: ETS Policy Information Center.

Where have all the freshman gone? (1999). Report issued through the office of Texas State Senator, G. Barrientos, Austin, TX. March 18, 1999. (From Haney, 2000, p. 34).

Word, E., Johnston, J., Bain, H., Fulton, B., Zaharias, J., Lintz, N., Achilles, C. M., Folger, J., & Breda, C. (1990). *Student/Teacher Achievement Ratio (STAR): Tennessee's K–3 class size study. Final report and final report summary.* Nashville: Tennessee State Department of Education.

APPENDIX A
A LONGITUDINAL CLASS-SIZE EXPERIMENT

STAR (1985–1989) and the many studies that build upon STAR (See table 1 for a partial listing) benefit from the experiment's tightly controlled, in-school longitudinal design. STAR was conducted by a four-university consortium with external support from consultants, advisory groups, and the Tennessee State Department of Education. Basic design issues are:

(1) Project STAR built on principles recognized in prior research. The intervention began in the primary grades. Small classes had fewer than 20 students. STAR's design enabled researchers to look at the effects on minority as well as majority students. Moreover, the design required a "real" difference in the class sizes, from an average of 24 pupils to an average of 15.

(2) STAR was a controlled experiment that permitted, to the extent possible with empirical data, causal conclusions. Pupils entering K were randomly assigned to a small class (S; 13–17), a regular class (R; 22–27), or a regular class with

a full-time teacher aide (RA). Pupils entering in later years were assigned at random to classes. Teachers were assigned to classrooms at random. Randomization was monitored carefully.

(3) With minor exceptions, students were kept in their class grouping in grades K, 1, 2, and 3. A new grade-appropriate teacher was assigned to the class each year. STAR was a four-year longitudinal experiment.

(4) Norm-referenced tests (NRT), criterion-referenced tests (CRT), measures of self concept and motivation, and other data-collection forms were administered each annually. Researchers used a post-test only design.

(5) The samples were large and diverse. The K year involved over 6,300 students in 329 classrooms in 79 schools in 46 districts. The first-grade sample was larger still. The large samples were maintained throughout the four years, producing an excellent longitudinal database. Total sample = 11,601.

(6) The class arrangement was maintained throughout the day, all year long. There was no intervention other than class size and teacher aides. No special training was provided except to a small sample in second grade; no special curricula or materials were introduced. (Training didn't increase outcomes).

(7) Students were followed and evaluated after STAR ended in grade 3. Most students graduated in 1998. Their college-entrance test results were monitored.

(8) Data have been reanalyzed by non-STAR researchers and original results confirmed and extended.

Learning What They Need to Know:
School Leaders' Lessons of Experience

Lynn K. Bradshaw and Joy C. Phillips

In this chapter we examine the perceptions of principal interns and practicing school leaders regarding how they learned what they needed to know in order to be successful in their leadership roles. Additionally, data analysis examines the extent to which practicing school leaders engage in ongoing professional development activities that enable them to focus on instructional leadership and promote learning for all children. Finally, the paper discusses implications for school leadership preparation programs and the need for additional research to better understand the connections between leadership and learning.

In the past decade, visible changes in leadership preparation programs have included improved course content and delivery (Daresh & Playko, 1997), more substantial clinical experiences and internships (Clark & Clark, 1996; Cordeiro & Sloan-Smith, 1996; Glasman & Glasman, 1997; Murphy, 1999; National Policy Board for Educational Administration, 1995; Short & Price, 1992), and clearer roles for mentors (Crow & Matthews, 1998). Enhanced field-based activities have provided opportunities for future educational leaders to promote teaching and learning as the core activity of the school, to manage change, and to work collaboratively with diverse stakeholder groups (Daresh, 1999). Furthermore, field-based activities have caused students to examine connections between organizational variables and student outcomes in a way that supports school improvement as the "center" for the profession of educational leadership (Murphy, 1999). Although there is a need for more information about "the activities in which students in these longer and improved field experiences are actually engaged" (Murphy, 1991, p. 55), a strong consensus exists among educators and education decision makers that longer internships, approaching full-time status, are preferable to part-time internships, and

Lynn K. Bradshaw, East Carolina University
Joy C. Phillips, University of Texas, Austin

principal interns should be paired with the most successful and experienced principals (Daresh, 1999). Although many believe that such settings are needed to allow principal candidates to be fully immersed in administrative roles under the guidance of positive role models, others have documented that students also learn valuable lessons from examples that are "less than best" (Bradshaw & Wait, 2000).

Even with stronger university programs in educational leadership, the preparation of school leaders is not complete with graduation and licensure, but must be a continuing career-long process. There has been growing interest in and understanding of ongoing, job-imbedded training (Daresh & Playko, 1997; Guskey, 2000; Wood & McQuarrie, 1999) and the roles of formal and informal mentors in continuing administrator development (Barnett, 1995; Crow & Matthews, 1998; Gooden, Carrigan, & Ashbaugh, 1999; Kraus & Cordeiro, 1995; Wood & Killian, 1998). However, important questions remain. How do longer, more carefully selected field experiences impact student learning and their success in administrative roles? What learning takes place on the job? How does learning continue after graduates of school leadership preparation programs are employed in administrative positions? As accountability for preparation programs shifts toward the documentation of graduates' ability to positively impact teaching and learning in their schools, it is important to examine what future and practicing school leaders believe they need to know and how they report learning those lessons.

Studies of the continuing development of corporate executive officers led to a renewed emphasis on continuing employee development (McCall, 1997). While the recommendations for developing leadership skills seemed applicable in business and education settings, the link was based on an untested assumption that the developmental needs of leaders in business and education were similar. There was a need to determine to what extent school leaders and corporate executive officers reported similar experiences "learning what they needed to know" in their leadership roles.

RESEARCH DESIGN AND METHODOLOGY

The purpose of this study was to begin to explore how school leaders reported that learning what they needed to know at different points in their professional careers and to determine whether the strategies used by McCall and others in their studies of corporate executive officers (1988, 1997) were applicable to the study of the development of school leaders.

Conceptual Framework for the Study

A series of studies was conducted at the Center for Creative Leadership to assist corporations in developing a sufficient pool of talented future leaders (McCall, 1997; McCall, Lombardo, & Morrison, 1988). Data were collected through interviews of successful CEOs to determine how they had learned what they needed to know to lead effectively. In four separate studies of career events or episodes that "stood out" and led to "a lasting change" in individuals as managers, McCall, Lombardo, and Morrison (1988, p. 6) found that CEOs' responses could be broadly grouped in three categories: (a) specific assignments that they were given, (b) bosses, and (c) hardships or disappointments.

Interestingly, the results showed that these successful leaders had learned not only from other leaders who were positive role models, but also from leaders who provided poor examples and negative experiences (McCall, 1997). The results of the study were used to strengthen corporate leadership development programs.

Context for the Study

In 1993, the North Carolina Legislature closed existing preparation programs for school leaders on the campuses of the University of North Carolina and invited interested campuses to develop proposals for redesigned programs. Six new Master of School Administration (MSA) programs were approved and implemented in 1996. These new programs were characterized by stronger links between theory and practice and more substantial experiences in the field. At the same time, the North Carolina General Assembly instituted the Principal Fellows Program to support full-time study for selected aspiring principals. Principal Fellows are granted leave from their teaching positions and receive financial support to pursue a two-year Master of School Administration degree.

East Carolina University (ECU), located in Greenville, North Carolina, provides one of the new MSA programs. At ECU, members of the Principal Fellows cohort attend campus classes as full-time students during the first year, and they complete a full-time year-long internship during the second year. During the internship, the Principal Fellows work in their assigned schools four days each week, and they spend the fifth day on campus taking one course and participating in an intern seminar. Early in the internship, all interns assess their knowledge, skills, and professional beliefs against state and national standards for school administrators. Using the self-assessment results, interns develop a growth plan that includes strategies for developing and refining skills during the internship. They develop a Leadership Portfolio containing the internship log, evidence of activities that led to growth within each standard, and reflections about what they have learned. The comprehensive examination is an oral defense of the portfolio.

The University of North Carolina's Doctor of Education Programs, designed primarily to prepare superintendents and other senior level school district leaders, were also redesigned in the early 1990s. Requirements for "residency" status were strengthened, and stronger links between theory and practice were emphasized.

Participants

Participants in this study were 16 principal interns and 12 doctoral students enrolled at East Carolina University during the spring semester of 1996. Principal interns were full-time Principal Fellows completing their full-time administrative internships in the public schools of northeastern North Carolina. Their teaching experience prior to entering the Principal Fellows program ranged from 0 to 8 years. Participating doctoral students were at different stages in their doctoral programs, and they reported from 8 to 27 total years of experience in education.

Research Questions

There were two research questions: (a) How do principal interns and experienced school leaders describe how they learned what they needed to know to be successful? and (b) What are the similarities and differences in the responses of principal interns and experienced school leaders?

Data Collection

A survey was constructed based on the interview guide used by McCall, Lombardo, and Morrison (1988, pp. 191–194) in studies of the development of corporate executive officers. The interview format was divided in three sections: (a) career events or episodes that led to a lasting change in their approach to management; (b) other key events, including the role of other people; and (c) general reflections about career, personal life, and the future (see appendix A). The survey was distributed to Principal Fellow interns and to doctoral students during one of their campus meetings.

Assumptions

Participants in the study were assumed to be "successful" school leaders. Both groups had met requirements for admission to graduate programs. Principal Fellows were serving in full-time administrative internships. Doctoral students were required to document successful administrative experience in order to be admitted to the program, and all were employed in school leadership positions.

The Principal Fellows were completing a redesigned preparation program with stronger links between theory and practice, specific courses in instructional leadership, and expanded field experiences, including a year-long administrative internship that emphasized reflective practice. Because of their years of experience in education and their status as practicing school leaders, it was assumed that the doctoral students had not experienced a redesigned preparation program in school administration and were likely to have completed a more traditional program or obtained add-on licensure in administration.

Limitations of the Study

There were several limitations of the survey methodology. First, it was possible that the survey questions focused responses into certain themes and therefore narrowed the results. Although participants were able to provide meaningful responses to the questions raised, there could have been other important themes that participants were not asked to address. In addition, survey responses were self-reported perceptions of the participants. Although those perceptions were "real," it was not possible to address their accuracy without additional data from other sources. Finally, without follow-up interviews or focus groups, it was not possible to probe responses for explanation, clarification, or elaboration.

Comparable data for the two groups was also limited. Aggregate data regarding gender and years of experience in education were available for both groups, and individual data were available for the doctoral students. However, it was not possible to match individual demographic data with survey responses of the members of the Principal Fellows cohort.

In addition, it was likely that the survey results for the two groups were influenced by a difference in the form of the survey used for the two groups. An additional question regarding the internship was included at the end of the survey for master's students. There was no specific reference to internships in the survey questions for doctoral students.

Analysis of Data

The survey data were analyzed using the computer software program, HyperResearch (ReasearchWare, 1999). HyperResearch is a database-type program into which word processing documents are imported. Responses are then coded, and a variety of reports can be generated. However, this software program is a "work in progress," meaning the full capacity of the intended design has yet to be put into place. Therefore, use of this software requires the researcher to use a combination of manual and electronic analysis strategies.

These survey responses were labeled according to student status—master's or doctoral—and years of teaching experience. The 16 master's responses were numbered M 1–16, and the 12 doctoral responses were labeled D 1–12. Each survey response was entered into a Word file, and each respondent's file was saved as M # or D #. Additionally, each file was saved in both Word format and Text format since HyperResearch will only import files in Text format. HyperResearch considers each of the 28 response files a "case."

The master's and doctoral responses were analyzed separately so that comparisons could be made between the two student groups. The first level of analysis of the responses of the 16 master's students yielded 82 individual codes. The analysis of the 12 doctoral responses yielded 16 more, or 98 individual codes. In the second level of analysis this array of individual codes was reduced to five major categories of responses, or themes.

The remainder of this analysis focuses upon the individual codes within each of the five themes that generated the highest number of responses or were particularly interesting because of differences in the response rates of the two groups.

FINDINGS

Participant responses clustered in five major themes: *Leadership Functions, Community and District Issues, Conflict, Working with Families,* and *Continuing Education.* There were a total of 468 coded responses from both groups of participants. Master's students provided 269 (57 percent) of the total coded responses, and 199 (43 percent) of the coded responses were from doctoral students. Frequencies of responses for both groups according to major themes were shown in table 1. When the themes were ranked by frequency of responses, the results were the same for both groups. *Leadership Functions* received the most coded responses for both groups of students, and *Continuing Education* was second, and *Conflict* was ranked third. *Community and District* and *Working with Families* ranked fourth and fifth, respectively.

Table 1. Frequency of Coded Responses by Themes

	Frequency of coded responses by themes			
Themes	*Master's*		*Doctoral*	*Total*
Leadership functions	111	65%	60	35%	171
Continuing education	75	60%	51	40%	126
Conflict	51	54%	43	46%	94
Community and district	17	33%	34	67%	51
Working with families	15	58%	11	42%	26
Total frequency of coded responses	269	57%	199	43%	468

Frequencies of responses for both groups according to selected first-level codes are shown in table 2. For many themes and first-level codes, the frequency of responses from master's and doctoral students was roughly similar to the pattern for total responses. However, master's students were more likely than doctoral students to address eight issues (see table 3), including six coded responses in the theme *Leadership Functions*. Doctoral students were more likely than master's students to address *Community and District* issues and to provide unique responses in other categories (see table 4). Additional findings for each theme are summarized below.

Leadership Functions

Not surprisingly, focus on experiences related to *Leadership Functions* received high numbers of responses from both master's and doctoral students. Four first-level codes received high response rates in this category: *Discipline* (23), *Implementing New Program* (20), *Building Effective Relationships* (13), and *Teacher Evaluation* (12). However, master's students—who were, after all, in the process of becoming school leaders—seemed most concerned with these experiences. Master's students were also more likely to mention *Implementing Staff Development* and *Leading the Planning Process*. Participants in both groups mentioned *Shared Decision Making*, but this code received a higher response rate from the doctoral students.

Participants reported learning about *Building Effective Relationships* in a variety of ways, including being "upstaged" by a teacher in a meeting and participating in the school improvement planning process. As one respondent stated, "I learned the importance of human relations skills and collaboration. The experience forced me to take a look at group processes and my own individual style." Another respondent reported realizing that he or she was going to be successful as a school leader "when I was accepted and viewed by the school as competent and willing to help and when teachers talked to me about how to make their programs better."

Discipline, a key area of responsibility for assistant principals, was a topic mentioned much more frequently by master's students than doctoral students. Master's students spoke of learning to interact with families, of the importance of not ignoring problems, and realizing they can make mistakes. For example, when one participant met with an irate parent who was intent on reversing the position that had been taken with his child, he reported learning that "As long as I treat every person fairly, I will stand by my actions. But if I am wrong, I have to be man enough to admit my

Table 2. Frequency of Coded Responses by Selected First-Level Codes

Themes	First-level codes	Master's		Doctoral		Total
Leadership functions	Discipline	23	88%	3	12%	26
	Implementing new programs	20	87%	3	13%	23
	Building effective relationships	13	62%	8	38%	21
	Teacher evaluation	12	75%	4	25%	16
	Shared decision making	4	36%	7	64%	11
	Becoming a leader	7	70%	3	30%	10
	Implementing staff development	7	78%	2	22%	9
	Leading the planning process	6	86%	1	14%	7
	Other	19	40%	29	60%	48
Community and district	Proving self	7	58%	5	42%	12
	Public embarrassment	3	33%	6	67%	9
	Public "hot seat"	0	0%	8	100%	8
	Other	7	32%	15	68%	22
Conflict	Managing conflict	18	64%	10	36%	28
	Intervention in conflict	16	76%	5	24%	21
	Personal verbal attacks	3	43%	4	57%	7
	Other	14	37%	24	63%	38
Working with families	Angry parents/family	10	63%	6	38%	16
	Other	5	50%	5	50%	10
Continuing education	Lack of follow-through/mistakes	20	65%	11	35%	31
	Support from an effective mentor	18	67%	9	33%	27
	Positive feedback	8	53%	7	47%	15
	Effective internship	12	100%	0	0%	12
	Expanding knowledge and strategies	6	67%	3	33%	9
	Other	11	34%	21	66%	32
Total coded responses		269	57%	199	43%	468

Table 3. First-Level Codes Addressed More Often by Master's Students

Themes	First-level codes	Master's		Doctoral		Total
Continuing education	Effective internship	12	100%	0	0%	12
Leadership functions	Discipline	23	88%	3	12%	26
	Implementing new programs	20	87%	3	13%	23
	Leading the planning process	6	86%	1	14%	7
	Implementing staff development	7	78%	2	22%	9
Conflict	Intervention in conflict	16	76%	5	24%	21
Leadership functions	Teacher evaluation	12	75%	4	25%	16
	Becoming an administrator	7	70%	3	30%	10
Total coded responses		269	57%	199	43%	468

Table 4. First-Level Codes Addressed More Often by Doctoral Students

Themes	First-level codes	Master's		Doctoral		Total
Community and district	Public "hot seat"	0	0%	8	100%	8
	Other	7	32%	15	68%	22
	Public embarrassment	3	33%	6	67%	9
Continuing education	Other	11	34%	21	66%	32
Leadership functions	Shared decision making	4	36%	7	64%	11
	Other	19	40%	29	60%	48
Total coded responses		269	57%	199	43%	468

mistake, correct it, and move on." Interns reported learning from discipline situations that they took seriously at the time, but were able to "laugh" about later: mistakenly believing that a difficult student had stolen the administrator's walkie-talkie, but learning, after an unsuccessful search of the student, that the principal had the walkie-talkie; running after a student who left campus without permission—and falling down; and learning that the county office "ruled against us in a discipline hearing."

Implementing New Programs and *Implementing Staff Development* were also mentioned much more frequently by master's students than doctoral students. Participants learned that change requires careful strategies and that people need time and support to learn new behaviors. One observed, "I tried to change the Exceptional Children's department too rapidly. The teachers were not ready and things got worse. After Christmas, I looked at things and took a different approach. Things got better." Another intern implemented a hands-on math program "in my very traditional school. As my log shows, it was a very rocky start and just recently has shown major success for all." As a result of the experience, the intern reported, "I learned to slow down. Not to expect everyone to change or believe they could. Change is very slow. Support is needed physically, emotionally, and in other ways from the administrators if change is to occur." Another intern who attempted to work a staff development activity around teachers' planning periods reported, "I learned that it is best to offer staff development with a set schedule (after school hours) and teach those who sign up and show up."

Master's students also mentioned the category of *Teacher Evaluation* more frequently than doctoral students. They talked about the challenges of learning how to effectively observe teachers in their classrooms, to counsel veteran teachers, and to provide constructive feedback. A number of participants reported "their most frightening firsts" in this area. Examples included a post-conference with a 30-year veteran teacher, an observation of a teacher who was "one of my mentor teachers when I started teaching," and a post-conference when the participant had "a lot of positive things to say, but a couple of areas for improvement. I was worried that I might come across too negative, but it actually went quite well." From experiences with evaluation and staff development, students reported learning the differences between the theory and practice of becoming an "instructional leader." For example, one intern described working with a teacher whose lessons appeared to be more "fluff" than depth. "I had to get tough and let her know that her lessons needed improvement. I learned that when getting tough, the best thing is to have examples of how she can better plan her lesson centered around quality learning."

In *Becoming a Leader*, students recounted first experiences with major adminis-trative responsibility: "Being new to the field provided many challenges, but under-standing school operations was the biggest." Another student explained:

> My most frightening first was the first day I had the school alone. Problems have to be thought through carefully. I was left in charge and it really was my defining moment with the administrators at my site. I handled it well, and from that point on they could trust me to handle problems on my own.

The experience of *Leading the Planning Process* also stood out to the master's students, as the following examples demonstrate. Coordinating and writing the school improvement plan from beginning to end was a challenging assignment for one intern. "I was solely responsible for timelines, group team sessions, interpreting data, etc." For another intern, the first meeting of the Student Achievement Com-mittee was a key event. "I was very excited about the year and all I would do. I think I came across too strong." Another intern organized three problem-solving confer-ences to resolve the school's high failure rate. "The results were impressive, effec-tive, and the teachers felt empowered." Although doctoral student responses ad-dressed *Shared Decision Making* more often than master's students, it was striking that only one doctoral response addressed *Leading the Planning Process*.

Community and District Issues

In the second major theme, *Community/District*, master's students most often men-tioned experiences related to *Proving Self* (7). These references related to proving their abilities to teachers and other administrators, to parents and the community, and to themselves. One intern wrote about getting respect from the teachers. "Just re-cently, I have begun to feel as if I've truly earned the respect of the majority of the teachers. I have proven that I can be effective—to the teachers as well as to myself." Another intern reported having to decide how to handle a fight when no other ad-ministrator was on campus. A third intern described the challenge of bringing a di-verse cultural perspective to a rural school site:

> Being viewed by parents as a competent administrator was a challenge for me. When the school year began, the community was not used to seeing a person of African-American descent in a leadership role. As time progressed and interaction occurred, I developed a much better rapport with parents.

While doctoral responses also addressed *Proving Self* (5), they were more likely to involve *Public Embarrassment* (6) or the *Public "Hot Seat"* (8). "Behind-the-back" and untrue accusations, a supervisor who failed to keep a verbal commitment, reassignment to an undesirable position, reprimands for decisions that had been approved beforehand, and learning that staff members could not be trusted were examples of challenging community and district political situations that doctoral students described.

Conflict

Within the theme of *Conflict*, the most frequent responses of both master's and doctoral students addressed the need to *Intervene* (16, 5) and the critical nature of *Managing Conflict* (18, 10). Participants reported examples of major intervention strategies: physically removing a student who had ignored repeated directives to move out of a class where she was causing trouble, issuing a directive that students who received any more bus referrals would not be allowed to go on any field trips, and sending a student home on a plane when he was caught stealing while on Florida field trip. From such an experience, one participant reported learning "to prepare for the unexpected and deal with it calmly."

Survey responses revealed that while *Managing Conflict* was time consuming, it was also an opportunity for learning valuable lessons. For example, when two teachers began yelling at each other in the cafeteria in front of students, one respondent had to separate the teachers and write reprimands. Another participant worried about mishandling a sexual harassment issue by "under-consequencing the male offenders, which created an incensed mother who came to the school three times to scream at me." In one more example, an intern described trying unsuccessfully to talk rationally with an insubordinate teaching assistant.

Working with Families

Another theme of the analysis related to learning to *Working with Families*. Although several types of relationships with parents were mentioned, *Angry Parents* were mentioned most often in the surveys by both groups of participants. A frightening first for one respondent occurred when "I suspended a student whose parent came to school expecting a showdown. We had our showdown. He talked, I listened, and he left. His son remained on the suspension list." Another response highlighted the potential for conflicts to involve students, parents, and other administrators. After a fight on a bus, an intern called parents to make them aware of the incident. "One parent came in and asked that I not deal with her child any more—even though her child was at fault. I was right in what I did. Another administrator was wrong in her decision."

Continuing Education

From the survey responses, both groups of students revealed that they were consciously aware of learning from a variety of types of experiences. In the theme *Continuing Education* the responses of master's students addressed learning from *Lack of Follow-Through/Mistakes* (20), *Effective Mentors* (18), and *Effective Internships* (12). Doctoral student responses also emphasized *Lack of Follow-Through/Mistakes* (11) and *Effective Mentors* (9), but did not mention *Effective Internships*.

Effective Mentors, most often principals and assistant principals, "demonstrated by example," "gave the students room to learn," and "provided helpful feedback."

The following examples illustrate master's students' responses to the survey question asking about the person who taught them the most.

1. "The person who taught me the most was my supervising principal. She took the time to help me grow as an administrator. She shared resources, helped me reflect, and offered suggestions when needed (even if I didn't realize a suggestion was needed!)"
2. "One of the assistant principals. His management style has had the most positive impact on me for growth. He is organized, compassionate but strong, extremely knowledgeable, and has never told me he could not help me with a problem or a concern."
3. "Both principals. Their professionalism, interest, guidance, and direction."
4. "My second principal. She included me, she trusted me, she treated me like I had something to offer. She even got after me for some things the first principal did/didn't do and wouldn't let me do. It hurt to be blamed, but she showed me that my instincts had been right about many things."

Effective Internships (12) were also clearly recognized by master's students as important vehicles for learning. Interns who had opportunities to work at more than one site commented about the value of their potentially difficult assignment.

1. "Although it was uncomfortable at first, I truly believe in having the opportunity to work at two schools at different levels, e.g., elementary and middle."
2. "I was fortunate to know the two principals I chose to work with. They are both highly professional and knowledgeable. They have treated me like a fellow administrator throughout the internship and this has been my biggest growth factor."
3. "Two different schools were great. One school the first semester and the other school the second semester. My two principals got together to make sure I got the experiences I needed."

Finally, *Lack of Follow-Through/Mistakes* offered opportunities for learning. "Forgetting to tell a bus driver she needed to be on duty" and "waiting until Easter break to type the discipline reports" were examples of procrastination that resulted in learning. Participants also revealed they were aware of the need to *Expand Knowledge and Strategies* and the value of *Positive Feedback*. Students wrote about their need to expand their knowledge and strategies in the following comments:

1. "Handling discipline was the biggest challenge that I faced. It concerned me that I might not make the correct choices. However, I have learned how to investigate and follow through in an appropriate manner."
2. "Learning from two different perspectives (by working at two different internship sites) has been very beneficial. I've learned how to do things and how not

to do things. This has been an invaluable experience and I would recommend that all interns experience this."

Positive Feedback was a source of motivation for the students. Survey responses revealed that this feedback was provided in both expected and unexpected ways. For example, one participant noted:

> My principal took the time to thoroughly review decisions of mine both before and after I made them. She was consistently supportive and knew me well enough to deliver her advice in such a way that I nearly always followed it.

An intern was pleasantly surprised "when a group of teachers confronted me and said that they hoped I would be their administrator next year. I have also received this compliment from 'at will' employees."

CONCLUSIONS

Although the data provided interesting information that can be used to improve the preparation of and the ongoing support for the development of school leaders, many important questions remain. In this section we address some of these questions including what the data told us, what the data didn't tell us, and the implications for leadership preparation programs.

What Did the Data Tell Us?

Just as successful CEOs learned what they needed to know from good and bad bosses, challenging assignments, and mistakes or failures (McCall, 1997; McCall, Lombardo, & Morrison, 1988), participants in this study reported that they learned valuable lessons from both positive and negative experiences. Questions that drew the most complete responses were those that asked participants to describe "key events that caused you to change your approach to leadership" and "your most frightening first—something you did for the first time that really had you worried." This research strategy can be used to learn more about the continuing development of school leaders.

Participant responses often reflected the highly interpersonal, political, and sometimes volatile nature of schools. There were many examples of the unique interpersonal challenges inherent in the school setting that involve students, faculty, staff, parents, community members, or other educators and professionals. Responses frequently described interpersonal conflict and safety issues.

There were differences in the responses of the two groups in the area of instructional leadership. For example, interns discussed teaching and learning more than the doctoral students who were practicing school leaders. While neither group mentioned coursework during the preparation program, interns did mention theory and skills that were addressed during the preparation program. Theories of change, strategies for implementing new programs, and techniques for teacher observation and development were mentioned in a variety of master's responses.

Differences between the two groups of student responses suggest a need to consider the relationship of theory and practice. In other words, do full-time master's students relate more to leadership and learning theory because they are immersed more in coursework than in day-to-day life in public school? Similarly, do part-time doctoral students identify more with the pressures of running a campus and responding to community concerns than they do with college coursework? Or do the differences between groups relate to differences in their programs of study? These questions need to be explored further. Both in-depth interviews and periodic surveys of cohorts and graduates should contribute valuable information that can be used to revise programs of study in leadership preparation programs.

What Did the Data Not Tell Us?

Although both groups of students were able to respond to questions similar to those used in the study of the development of leaders in corporations, participants' responses did not reveal whether there were other important factors in their development that were not addressed in the survey questions. Neither group talked much about their preparation programs, but master's students did refer to elements of preparation program content. Opportunities to probe their responses in interviews or focus groups could have yielded more complete information.

If practicing administrators find themselves in roles for which they believe their leadership preparation programs did not prepare them, then university faculty have an obligation to collect practitioner data that will allow universities to more effectively connect program theory to practice. As leadership preparation programs undergo revision, collecting data from cohorts enrolled in distinctly different types of programs becomes a challenge, as this pilot study suggests. For example, doctoral students in this study participated in leadership preparation programs that were significantly different from those attended by the master's students. The master's students attended revised programs that were designed explicitly to link theory to practice and to focus on instructional leadership. Master's students' responses may reflect this explicit program design, whereas doctoral students may not have benefited from such programs of study.

What Are the Implications for Leadership Preparation Programs?

The fact that the master's students were more likely to discuss concepts related to the role of instructional leaders could be promising news for faculty involved in designing and implementing new models of preparation programs for school leaders. The expectations of instructional leaders have continued to expand. Smith and Andrews (1989) identified four categories of instructional leadership behaviors: instructional resource, resource provider, communicator, and visible presence. The concept emerged as part of the effective schools movement and has expanded to include constructivism; facilitative and transformational leadership with a focus on school based management and teacher empowerment; and pedagogy (Carlson, 1996; Murphy & Shipman, 1998; Sergiovanni, 1998; Wiggins, 1994). Redesigned preparation programs have featured knowledge of curriculum and instruction and an expectation that teaching and learning will be the primary focus of the principals' role.

Follow-up studies with participants in this pilot would reveal how these graduates have continued to develop on the job. Specific questions about preparation program components would provide additional information about their perceived value, but it will be important to balance those results with the relative absence of examples from preparation programs in this study. If school leaders, like corporate chief executive officers, continue to value on-the-job experiences more than experiences in preparation programs, it will be important to continue to hear and to address that message.

Additionally, participants in this study reported more negative experiences in the areas of interpersonal communication and conflict than in other areas. Efforts to develop the knowledge, skills, and dispositions required to build effective working relationships and manage conflict must be well integrated across the curriculum for the preparation of school leaders. School leaders have an important public relations role, not only with the parents of student in their schools, but with community leaders and policy makers. Preparation programs must develop the knowledge and skills required to be successful in this sensitive, and highly visible, role. The case study instructional strategy can be used to help students develop conflict resolution skills. Case study has long been used to train future leaders in business schools, and it is increasingly available for use in preparation of educational leaders (e.g., *The Journal of Cases in Educational Leadership*). By examining case studies of realistic school-based leaders, circumstances, and dynamics, developing educational administrators can analyze critically incidents they might personally encounter. Recently, Storey (2001) argued that case studies used as learning tools are particularly appropriate for studying conflict. Storey (p. 7) suggests a five-stage framework for dispute analysis including (1) defining reality, (2) identifying reinforcing events, (3) examining critical incidents, (4) exploring response patterns, and (5) considering output and outcomes of the dispute. Furthermore, case studies have the additional benefit of being equally suitable for use in a wide range of educational leadership courses.

SUGGESTIONS FOR ADDITIONAL RESEARCH

This pilot study opens a window into a critical area in need of further study. In order to more effectively design school leadership preparation programs, much more information is needed regarding what students in these programs and graduates of these programs are currently learning and how they are learning it. Both quantitative and qualitative studies will be helpful. Additional empirical data will help researchers evaluate the learning needs of students in the existing administrator preparation programs and create strategies for addressing ongoing professional development for school administrators.

First, follow-up studies should be designed to address some of the limitations of this study. Interviews and focus groups would enable the researcher to probe for additional information and more complete responses. These data could be used to suggest modifications in the survey instrument for school leaders. Additional data sources, such as 360-degree instruments, documents that illustrated experiences described by participants, and evidence of leader and school effectiveness would provide opportunities for triangulation. More complete data regarding the participants would also allow researchers to explore the effects of such factors as age, gender, education experience, and preparation program characteristics.

Next, the results of this pilot study suggest that there are differences between the two groups in the experiences that were reported. Could this pattern be a matter of time? Are interns somewhat "protected" from the busyness of the school day and therefore more able to engage in activities related to teaching, learning, and school improvement? Are practicing administrators so busy resolving interpersonal crises that they don't have time for important areas such as staying current with best practices in instruction, disaggregating data to monitor academic achievement of all students, or creating a shared organizational vision of high academic achievement based on high standards for all students? Are the patterns a result of differences in preparation programs? Do such patterns result from differences in the level of knowledge and skill or differences in the ability to recognize the importance of the school leader's role in instructional leadership? As school leaders are held more accountable for improved teaching and learning, the importance of these questions has become more urgent for those who prepare school leaders and support their continuing development on the job.

Finally, there were also differences in the responses of the two groups regarding the individuals who "taught you the most" and in references to mentors and bosses when responding to other questions in the survey. The interns generally reported learning most from an individual in the internship situation. The doctoral students, who were practicing school leaders with varying levels of leadership experience, reported looking to bosses, colleagues, and family members. What is the role of mentors in continuing leadership development? Do those new to the profession, in intern and assistant principal positions, tend to focus on their supervising principals while seasoned practitioners look for guidance from a broader array of individuals? Continuing study of the "lessons of experience" of new and experienced school leaders has the potential to provide a foundation for improved classroom instruction and a clearer focus for leadership development activities in internships and on the job.

REFERENCES

Barnett, B. G. (1995). Developing reflection and expertise: Can mentors make the difference? *Journal of Educational Administration, 33*(5), 45–59.

Bradshaw, L. K., & Wait, D. (2000). Learning from practice that is less than best. In F. K. Kochan (Ed.), *The preparation of leaders: Power, policy, and politics* (pp. 51–64). (2000 Yearbook of the Southern Regional Council on Educational Administration.) Auburn, AL: Auburn University, Truman Pierce Institute.

Carlson, R. V. (1996). *Reframing and reform: Perspectives on organization, leadership, and school change.* White Plains, NY: Longman.

Clark, D. C., & Clark, S. N. (1996). Better preparation of educational leaders. *Educational Researcher, 25*(9), 18–20.

Cordeiro, P. A., & Sloan-Smith, E. (1996). Administrative interns as legitimate partners in the community of practice. *Journal of School Leadership, 6*(1), 4–29.

Crow, G. M., & Matthews, L. J. (1998). *Finding one's way: How mentoring can lead to dynamic leadership.* Thousand Oaks, CA: Corwin Press.

Daresh, J. C. (1999). Preparing school leaders to "break ranks." *Connections, 2*, 29–32.

Daresh, J. C., & Playko, M. A. (1997). *Beginning the principalship: A practical guide for new school leaders.* Thousand Oaks, CA: Corwin Press.

Glasman, N., & Glasman, L. (1997). Connecting the preparation of school leaders to the practice of school leadership. *Peabody Journal of Education, 72*(2), 3–20.

Gooden, J. S., Carrigan, J. K., & Ashbaugh, C. R. (1999, October). *Training principal interns: Analyzing the experience.* Paper presented at the annual meeting of the Southern Regional Council on Educational Administration, Charlotte, NC.

Guskey, T. R. (2000). *Evaluating professional development.* Thousand Oaks, CA: Corwin Press.

Kraus, C. M., & Cordeiro, P. A. (1995, October). *Challenging tradition: Re-examining the preparation of educational leaders for the workplace.* Paper presented at the annual meeting of the University Council for Educational Administration, Salt Lake City, UT.

McCall, M. W., Jr. (1997). *High flyers: Developing the next generation of leaders.* Cambridge, MA: Harvard Business School Press.

McCall, M. W., Jr., Lombardo, M. M., & Morrison, A. M. (1988). *The lessons of experience: How successful executives develop on the job.* New York: Lexington Books.

Murphy, J. (1991). The effects of the educational reform movement on departments of educational leadership. *Educational Evaluation and Policy Analysis, 13*(1), 49–65.

Murphy, J. (1999, April). *The quest for a center: Notes on the state of the profession of educational leadership.* Paper presented at the annual meeting of the American Educational Research Association, Montreal.

Murphy, J., & Shipman, N. (1998). The Interstate School Leaders Licensure Consortium: A standards-based approach to strengthening educational leadership. Paper presented at the annual meeting of the American Educational Research Association, San Diego, CA.

National Policy Board for Educational Administration. (1995). *NCATE guidelines: Curriculum guidelines for advanced programs in educational leadership for principals, superintendents, curriculum directors, and supervisors.* Alexandria, VA: Educational Leadership Constituent Council.

ResearchWare. (1999). *HyperResearch.* Newbury Park, CA: Scolari/Sage. Retrieved from www.scolari.com

Sergiovanni, T. J. (1998). Leadership as pedagogy, capital investment, and school effectiveness. *International Journal of Leadership in Education, 1*(1), 37–46.

Short, P. M., & Price, H. J. (1992). Clinical experience in administrator preparation programs: Are we there yet? *UCEA Review, 33*(3), 4–7.

Smith, W. F., & Andrews, R. L. (1989). *Instructional leadership: How principals make a difference.* Alexandria, VA: Association for Supervision and Curriculum Development.

Storey, V. J. (2001, December 3). Dean, judge, and bishop: Lessons from a conflict and implications for school leaders. *International Electronic Journal for Leadership in Learning, 5*(17). Retrieved December 4, 2001, from www.ucalgary.ca/~iejll/volume5/storey.html

Wiggins, R. A. (1994). *The principal as instructional leader: Inducement or deterrent to teachers' personal professional growth?* Paper presented at the 49th annual conference of the Association for Supervision and Curriculum Development, Chicago.

Wood, F. H., & Killian, J. E. (1998). Job-embedded learning makes the difference in school improvement. *Journal of Staff Development, 19*(1), 52–54.

Wood, F. H., & McQuarrie, F. (1999). On-the-job learning. *Journal of Staff Development, 20*(3), 10–13.

APPENDIX A
LEADERSHIP DEVELOPMENT SURVEY[1]

When you think about your experiences as a school leader, certain events or episodes probably stand out in your mind—things that caused you to change your approach to leadership. Briefly describe three "key events" in the space below. Share what happened and what you learned from it—for better or worse.

Now that you have described key events that really stood out for you, the rest of the questions will address some things that may or may not have had a lasting effect on you. Some questions may be more meaningful than others. Please go into depth on the important ones and comment briefly on the others. Some may have been answered in the first section. If so, just make that note.

- What was the biggest challenge you faced?
- What was your most frightening first—something you did for the first time that really had you worried?
- What event (or events) made you realize you would be a successful leader?
- What was a significant near miss—a time when you tried something and failed?
- What was your most significant act of procrastination—a time when you didn't face up to a situation that got steadily worse, resulting in a mess?
- Was there a situation you took very seriously at the time but were able to laugh about later?
- Please describe the person who taught you the most. What did that person do that made him or her so special?
- What was your most significant interpersonal conflict—a situation in which dealing with another person (or persons) was difficult?
- What about being a leader has been fun for you? What are some examples of situations or events you particularly enjoyed? That were the most fun?
- What advice would you give to a younger leader about managing his or her career? What do you need to do for yourself? How much should you let others do for or to you?
- How would you describe your internship experience? Comments?[2]

---

1. Adapted from McCall, Lombardo, & Morrison, 1988, pp. 191–194.
2. This question was included only in the survey for master's students.

Issues That Mentors Share with Proteges

Sandra Harris, Charlene Crocker, and Michael H. Hopson

A recent nationwide survey by Educational Research Service (ERS, 2000) indicated that half the school districts participating had experienced difficulty finding qualified candidates to fill principal vacancies. In fact, even though nearly one half of the teachers in the United States have advanced degrees, relatively few of these teachers are interested in seeking a principalship (Blackman & Fenwick, 2000). Furthermore, a study by Harris, Arnold, Lowery, and Crocker (2000) suggested that complexities of the principalship position frequently cause even students enrolled in principalship preparation programs not to apply for these positions. This has only exacerbated the challenge within the last decade for administrator preparation programs to focus on the need to find more effective approaches for preparing future principals (Lashway, 1998; Milstein, 1993; Young & Petersen, 2002). Several organizations, including the Danforth Foundation, University Council for Educational Administration, and the National Association of Secondary School Principals, have set in motion major initiatives to support innovative principal preparation programs (Daresh, 1997). One of these recommendations to universities is to implement field experience programs which emphasize the importance of collaborative university-school partnerships (Hart & Pounder, 1999; Milstein, 1993). Of these field-based models, one of the most significant is the model of assigning mentors to serve as guides to students as they integrate theory and practice through the field-based learning process (Malone, 2001; Playko, 1991; Stewart, 1991).

Mentoring is a type of scaffolding which provides opportunities for educators to acquire new skills in a social context that allow for internalization of the skills (Feiman-Nemser & Parker, 1993; Vygotsky, 1978). Studies indicate that mentoring

Sandra Harris, Stephen F. Austin State University
Charlene Crocker, Stephen F. Austin State University
Michael H. Hopson, Stephen F. Austin State University

in leadership programs has been mutually beneficial and proteges have developed higher levels of credibility, gained confidence, achieved greater awareness of strengths and deficits, and developed human resource skills and competence in their work (Barnett, 1995; Daresh & Playko, 1990). At the same time, mentors identified sharing ideas, helping others grow in the profession, being inspired, and having an opportunity to analyze what they did, as benefits from participating in the program (Harris & Crocker, 2001). However, collaborative initiatives that include a mentoring component to prepare leaders must also be concerned with implementing mentor training programs (Crocker & Harris, 2002). Therefore, the purpose of this study was to identify the specific types of issues that proteges share with their mentors to enhance mentor training programs.

CHARACTERISTICS OF EFFECTIVE MENTORS

Successful mentors exhibit specific characteristics that include being able to ask the right question rather than always providing the right answer, accepting other ways of doing things, rather than insisting on doing things the same way, a willingness to see people go beyond their own level of performance even when it means the protege does things better than the mentor, and modeling the principle of continuous learning and reflection (Daresh, 1995). Additionally, Southworth (1995) identifies other characteristics, such as being a good listener, acting as a sounding board, encouraging the protege to talk openly, provide an outlet for frustration, offer encouragement, build confidence, clarify roles, maintain sound perspective, and brainstorm strategies for moving forward.

Mentoring is most effective when mentors provide regular time to meet, give immediate feedback and make themselves available to the protege (Jones, Reid, & Bevins, 1997; Monsour, 1998). Thus, mentors emphasize that the learning process is a two-way communication, rather than the "one-way process implicit in the apprenticeship/pedagogic discourses" (Jones, Reid, & Bevins, 1997, p. 259). This two-way communication is built on a foundation of trust which is a major factor in the mentoring experience, so much so, that trust is the pivotal concept on which the mentoring relationship will or will not flourish (Norris & MacGillivray, 1995).

SELECTION OF MENTORS

Because successful mentors exhibit specific characteristics (Daresh, 1995; Southworth, 1995) mentor selection is important; yet, despite the importance of the mentor and the characteristics needed for success, most mentors are selected either by happenstance or by the mentee (Shelton & Herman, 1993). In fact, assigned pairing of mentor and protege does not guarantee success. Frequently, successful relationships grow out of a mutual selection process (Lagowski & Vick, 1995). Southworth (1995) suggests that the pairing of proteges and mentors is "problematic . . . hazardous and challenging" (p. 22). To be effective, both parties must want to participate in the mentoring program. Mentoring cannot be "legislated or forced" (Lagowski & Vick, 1995, p. 80). Although in many cases, women prefer women mentors and men prefer men, it does not necessarily follow that same-gender matching is necessarily more effective (Harris, Crocker, & Hopson, in press). Similarly, the assumption that mentors should be older than the protege does not always hold true. Often, older proteges benefit from being paired with younger mentors (Daresh, 1995; Playko, 1995).

ROLE OF THE MENTOR

The mentoring relationship often extends beyond the professional realm and mentors take on other roles and become significant in a more equal relationship (Lambert, 1995). In fact, Lincoln (1999) suggests that mentor relationships range from competent advising, professional socialization, acquisition of new skills, to a colleagueship and collaboration very much like a friendship relationship. Southworth (1995) recommends several activities for the mentor to aid in helping the protege, including considering and reconsidering recent events and issues, as well as, facilitating the rehearsal of ideas, plans and strategies and allowing individuals to try them out with a colleague whose opinion they trust. The mentor also models and assists the protege in performing the full range of administrative tasks which include supervision and evaluation of teachers, chairing planning committees, conducting staff development, preparing reports, and communicating with parents and students (Gordon & Moles, 1994).

Ubben, Hughes, and Norris (2001) recommend that mentor responsibilities include individual development that focuses on leadership competencies, monitoring and feedback, clinical observations, career strategy advisement, and mediating any conflicts that may arise for the protege. Additionally, Head, Reiman, and Thies-Sprinthall (1992) suggest that the mentor's role includes that of trusted colleague, a developer who encourages protege self-analysis and balances support and challenge, coach, and supervisor.

THE NEED FOR MENTOR TRAINING PROGRAMS

As universities and other entities develop principal preparation programs, they are increasingly seeking better alignment with the actual job of the principalship. Curricula are focusing on standards as well as emphasizing adult learning theory. More and more, principal preparation programs are partnering with school districts to involve principal leaders in mentoring new candidates (Lashway, 1998). Clearly, it is important for leaders to mentor future leaders. In fact, Tichy (1997) states that "The winning leaders I have met all view teaching as one of their major jobs" (p. 44); but in order to influence effectively, mentors must know more than just how to nurture if they are to meet protege needs.

Harris and Crocker (2001) suggest that, while participating in mentoring programs is generally considered positive by mentors, there is a clear implication that the mentor's personal and professional skills and knowledge impact a mentor's ability to serve effectively. Reflective mentoring does not happen automatically; the mentor has the responsibility of helping to make it happen (Crow & Matthews, 1998). Because of this diverse, complex nature of the mentor's role and the wide-range of knowledge and skills needed to be effective, there is a definite need for mentor training to be made available (Barnett, 1991; Crocker & Harris, 2002; Ganser, 1999; Head, Reiman, & Thies-Sprinthall, 1992; Rowley, 1999).

METHODOLOGY
Research Problem
In an effort to improve administrator mentoring programs by providing effective training, this study was designed to explore the kinds of issues that proteges share and do not share with their mentors. Guiding questions focused on who the protege considered his or her most effective mentor and what kinds of issues did the protege share with that individual.

Population
Fifty-seven students enrolled in a master's degree cohort principal preparation program at a regional university in the South participated in this study. Nearly half (49 percent) of the participants were 31–39 years of age; 19 percent were 22–30; 26 percent were 40–45; and 6 percent were older than 45. Forty seven percent were males and 53 percent were females. Participants were all teachers or coaches who had been working in rural, suburban, and urban schools ranging from 3 to 20 years. The school sizes of the participating students ranged from a K–8 rural school of 250 students, to a suburban high school that enrolled over 2,500 students. At the beginning of their university coursework, students selected an administrator on their campus to act as the official mentor and serve as the contact with the university professor who was working with the student. In nearly all cases, the official mentor selected was the principal of the school where the student was teaching.

Data Collection
Based on informal comments from proteges about mentors who were most helpful and what they often discussed with their mentors, we designed a 13-question survey. Participants were asked to identify the position of the individual who served as their "best mentor." They were also asked to identify the types of issues they were most likely to discuss with their "best mentor" on a Likert scale of 1 (*not at all*) to 4 (*very likely*). Issues which participants considered were university coursework, passing the state-mandated certification exam, classroom instruction, classroom discipline, classroom organization, parent relationships, faculty relationships, interpersonal student issues, and their own personal situation. They were also asked to identify what issues they would like to talk about but felt they could not share. Another query focused on what the mentors had done that was most helpful; and, finally, participants were asked to describe what else they would like for the mentors to do to help them more. Surveys were completed at the end of class, so the response rate was 100 percent.

Data Analysis
Frequencies and means were developed using SPSS for Windows 10.0. The survey was pilot-tested with students who were completing their graduate level principal preparation training and revised based on their suggestions. Three university profes-

sors read the open-ended questions separately and coded themes as they emerged. These categories were then compared for consistency (Wiersma, 1995).

FINDINGS

Study findings indicated that most principal preparation students considered a principal or assistant principal on their campus administrator to be their most helpful mentor. Proteges were most likely to discuss school discipline, faculty relationships, instructional procedures, parent relationships, and interpersonal student issues with their mentor. Except for issues that some respondents considered "just too personal," over half of the participants indicated that there were no issues they could not share with their mentor.

Who Is the Best Mentor?

Question one asked respondents to identify the position of the individual who had served as their "best mentor" since entering education. Instructions were given to identify their "best mentor" as one who had helped them with quality help. Only 21 percent of the proteges selected the school campus administrator appointed by the university when they entered the principal preparation program as their "best mentor." However, 47 percent identified their "best mentor" as a principal or assistant principal working at their school or at another school. Table 1 shows the selection breakdown of "best mentors."

What Types of Issues Are Most Likely to Be Shared?

Question two used a Likert-type scale format of 1 (*not at all*) to 4 (*very likely*) to explore what types of issues proteges were most likely to share with their "best mentor." Issues for students to consider were: university coursework, passing the state-mandated certification examination, instruction, school-wide discipline, parent and faculty relationships, student issues and their own personal issues. Participants indicated that all of the issues listed were "likely" to be discussed with their mentor and means ranged from 3.0 to 3.56. Table 2 shows the means of each issue.

What Issues Need to Be Shared, but Are Not Shared?

The third question asked proteges which of the issues listed in table 2 they would like to share with their mentors, but didn't feel that they could. Thirty-one respondents (54 percent) indicated that there were no issues they felt they could not

Table 1. Who Served as the Best Mentor?

Best Mentors	Number
Principal/assistant principal at protege's school or another school	27
University officially selected campus administrator	12
Teacher at protege's school or another school	12
Family member	3
University professor	3

N = 57

Table 2.   Types of Issues Mentors Are Most Likely to
Share with Their Proteges

Issues to Discuss with Mentors	Mean
School-wide discipline	3.56
Faculty relationships	3.42
Instructional procedures	3.30
Parent relationships	3.28
Interpersonal student issues	3.28
University coursework	3.14
Classroom organization	3.12
Passing the State Certification Examination	3.07
Protege's own personal issues	3.00

N = 57

share with their mentors. Generally, issues that proteges felt they could not share with their mentors were personal situations (23 percent), parent relationships (8 percent), faculty relationships (9 percent), and the state-mandated certification exam (10 percent).

Why Can't Some Issues Be Shared with Mentors?

When proteges were asked why they felt they couldn't share certain issues with their mentors, 9 of the 20 proteges who responded to this question focused on privacy issues, such as the need to "keep a confidence" or said that it was just "too personal." Other reasons centered around the mentor's lack of time—"basically, they just didn't have enough time for me"—or the mentor's lack of knowledge—"she is probably not knowledgeable about the subject matter being covered."

What Has the Mentor Done That Has Been the Most Helpful?

The next question asked the proteges to describe what the "best mentor" had done that had been the most helpful to them. The most helpful acts centered around giving advice (59 percent), being supportive (33 percent), listening (24 percent), giving responsibility (10 percent), being a good example (10 percent), and providing opportunities (5 percent).

How Could the Mentor Be More Helpful to the Protege?

The final question explored what issues proteges would like for mentors to consider to help them more. Only 49 percent of the proteges responded to this question. However, of those who responded, 14 (50 percent) indicated that lack of time was a major issue that kept their mentor/protege relationship from meeting their needs adequately. One student said, "There just isn't enough time in the day to communicate about the job!" Another issue that proteges addressed was the area of giving advice. Six proteges commented that they needed "more advice." One said, "I really want to know what my mentor thinks. . . . I get tired of hearing, 'Well, how do you think it should be handled?'" Other issues that were identified by at least one protege included: the need to be more supportive, to be a better listener, to help the protege find a job, to help with discipline within the school, to be more positive, and to help set more specific goals. Several proteges indicated that their mentor needed to meet with the university professor sooner in the semester because, "My mentor really wasn't very available at first, but after my professor visited, he began to take me seriously!" Another said, "My principal expressed a desire to visit with me every time she passed me in the hall. It wasn't until my [university professor] came, though, that she found time to sit down with me."

CONCLUSION

Much of the previous literature on mentoring has focused on the availability of the mentor, the need for the mentor to possess interpersonal skills, the mentor modeling "right" behaviors, and the necessity of the mentor being a good listener (Daresh, 1995; Playko, 1991; Southworth, 1995). While these are important concepts to include in a mentor training program, this study adds an additional component, that of identifying specific issues which proteges need to discuss with their mentors. This has far-reaching implications for principal preparation programs in designing curricula for mentor training programs.

Further analysis of these data clearly emphasizes the important role of the practitioner principal or assistant principal in contributing to the preparation of future principals. When principals in training have concerns about issues from campus-wide discipline to personal issues, it is a practicing administrator that they go to for mentoring help. Of the 57 participants in this study, nearly 70 percent considered their best mentor one who is already in the role of principal or assistant principal either at their campus or at another campus. This suggests, that, in addition to the complex role of the principal in leading the school, helping teachers, and working with students, the principal also plays a major role in the training of these future principals. Thus, the need for mentor training becomes even more vital because this additional principal responsibility must not become the straw "that breaks the camel's back" while, at the same time, the mentor must provide the best training possible for the protege.

Therefore, based on the findings from this study, the following recommendations are made to universities and other principal preparation entities in structuring training programs for mentors to include an issues component that emphasizes identification, training, and support strategies.

1. Identification
   - Notify mentors of the topics that proteges indicate they are most likely to be discussing with them.
   - Include these same topics in the general coursework knowledge-base for principals in training.
2. Training
   - Train mentors in strategies to better respond to these identified issues. For example, our study suggested that student discipline was a major issue of discussion. Preparation programs must structure course content to include

this topic of concern and provide training for practicing principals to be able to adequately discuss this topic with the protege.

- Provide training for mentors in problem-solving strategies to help proteges define their issue, collect information, implement a strategy, and assess the outcome.
- Provide training for mentors that emphasizes building relationships to enhance issue sharing.

3. Support
   - Remind mentors of the importance of keeping a confidence. Obviously when proteges feel that their confidences, as one respondent said, "will be shared with other faculty members," important issues will not be discussed.
   - Provide mentors with ways to build in time for discussion with proteges during the school day. Suggestions to do this include providing release time with a substitute for the protege and mentor to meet on a regular basis and release time from certain duties for the principal serving as a mentor.
   - Provide some means of financial compensation for the mentor. Businesses, as well as grant opportunities, are an excellent source for additional mentor compensation.
   - Involve the university professor as quickly as possible in meeting with the on-campus mentor to establish a collaborative relationship. While a face-to-face meeting should occur early in the program, telephone, and e-mail can enhance communication opportunities.

The principal is critical to the success of the school (Fullan, 1997). Supporting future campus administrators as they practice to become principals in their preparation program will contribute to their confidence in actually applying for and accepting this challenging, complex role. For these programs to be effective, "practitioners must be intimately involved in preparation" (Young & Petersen, 2002, p. 12), and mentoring is one important way to structure this involvement. Providing training programs that include an emphasis on specific issues will support the mentors who are willing and eager to help these future principals by serving as a mentor.

REFERENCES

Barnett, B. G. (1991). School-university collaboration: A fad or the future of administration preparation? *Planning and Changing, 21*(3), 146–157.

Barnett, B. G. (1995). Developing reflection and expertise: Can mentors make the difference? *Journal of Educational Administration, 33*(5), 45–49.

Blackman, M., & Fenwick, L. (2000). The principalship. *Education Week on the Web.* Retrieved February 12, 2002 from www.edweek.org/e...keywords+%22Principal20Shortage%22.

Crocker, C., & Harris, S. (2002). Facilitating growth of administrative practitioners as mentors. *Journal of Research for Educational Leaders (1)*, 2. Retrieved February 1, 2002 from www.uiowa.edu/~jrel/spring01/harris_0107.htm

Crow, G. M., & Matthews, L. J. (1998). *Finding one's way: How mentoring can lead to dynamic leadership.* Thousand Oaks, CA: Corwin Press.

Daresh, J. C. (1995). Research base on mentoring for educational leaders: What do we know? *Journal of Educational Leadership, 33*(5), 7–16.

Daresh, J. C. (1997). Improving principal preparation: A review of common strategies. *NASSP Bulletin, 81*(593), 3–8.

Daresh, J. C., & Playko, M. A. (1990). Mentor programs: Focus on the beginning principal. *NASSP Bulletin, 74*(529), 73–77.

Educational Research Service. (2000). *The principal, keystone of a high-achieving school: Attracting and keeping the leaders we need.* Arlington, VA: Author.

Feiman-Nemser, S., & Parker, M. (1993). Mentoring in context: A comparison of two U.S. programs for beginning teachers. *International Journal of Educational Research, 19*(8), 699–718.

Fullan, M. (1997). *What's worth fighting for in the principalship.* New York: Teachers College Press.

Ganser, T. (1999). Coach, safety net, compass, sculptor: How mentors describe mentoring. *Contemporary Education, 70*(2), 42–44.

Gordon, D., & Moles, M. (1994). Mentoring becomes staff development: A case of serendipity. *NASSP Bulletin, 78*, 66–70.

Harris, S., Arnold, M., Lowery, S., & Crocker, C. (2000). Deciding to become a principal: What factors motivate or inhibit that decision? *ERS Spectrum, 18*(2), 40–45.

Harris, S., & Crocker, C. (2001). *Benefits to mentors: It's like I have a legacy.* Manuscript submitted for publication.

Harris, S., Crocker, C., & Hopson, M. (in press). A study of the influence of gender on mentor selection in a principal preparation program. *Texas Council of Women School Educators Monograph.*

Hart, A. W., & Pounder, D. G. (1999). Reinventing preparation programs: A decade of activity. In J. Murphy & P. B. Forsyth (Eds.), *Educational administration: A decade of reform* (pp. 115–151). Thousand Oaks, CA: Corwin Press.

Head, T., Reiman, A., & Thies-Sprinthall, L. (1992). The reality of mentoring: Complexity in process and function. In T. Bey & C. Holmes (Eds.), *Mentoring: Contemporary principles and issues,* (pp. 5–24). Reston, VA: Association of Teacher Educators.

Jones, L., Reid, D., & Bevins, S. (1997). Teachers' perceptions of mentoring in a collaborative model of initial teacher training. *Journal of Education for Teaching, 23*(3), 253–261.

Lagowski, J., & Vick, J. (1995). Faculty as mentors. *New Direction for Teaching and Learning, 62*, 79–85.

Lambert, L. (1995). *The constructivist leader.* New York: Teachers College Press.

Lashway, L. (1998). *Trends and issues: Training of school administrators.* Eugene, OR: ERIC Clearinghouse on Educational Management.

Lincoln, Y. S. (1999). *Mentoring in the moment.* Paper presented at the meeting of the Southwest Educational Research Association, San Antonio, TX.

Malone, R. (2001). *Principal mentoring.* Clearinghouse on Educational Management. ED 149.

Milstein, M. (1993). *Changing the way we prepare educational leaders: The Danforth experience.* Newbury Park, CA: Corwin Press.

Monsour, F. (1998). Twenty recommendations for an administrative mentoring program. *NASSP Bulletin, 82*(594), 96–100.

Norris, C., & MacGillivray, L. (1995). *Conversations with mentors and their proteges.* Paper presented at the annual meeting of the American Association of School Superintendents, New Orleans, LA.

Playko, M. A. (1991). Mentors for administrators: Support for the instructional leader. *Theory into Practice, 30,* 124–127.

Playko, M. A. (1995). Mentoring for educational leaders: A practitioner's perspective. *Journal of Educational Administration, 33*(5), 84–92.

Rowley, J. (1999, May). The good mentor. *Educational Leadership, 56*(8), 20–22.

Shelton, M., & Herman, J. (1993). Mentoring and shadow consulting: Keys to enhancing novice and veteran school administrator training. *Journal of School Leadership, 3,* 666–678.

Southworth, G. (1995). Reflections on mentoring for new school leaders. *Journal of Educational Administration, 33*(5), 17–28.

Stewart, J. (1991). Priming the principal pump: Interns in Polk county. *Updating School Board Policies, 3*, 1–3.

Tichy, N. (1997). *The leadership engine: How winning companies build leaders at every level.* New York: HarperBusiness.

Ubben, G., Hughes, L., & Norris, C. (2001). *The principal: Creative leadership for effective schools* (4th ed.). Boston: Allyn and Bacon.

Vygotsky, L. (1978). *Mind and society.* Cambridge, MA: Harvard University Press.

Wiersma, W. (1995). *Research methods in education: An introduction* (6th ed.). Boston: Allyn and Bacon.

Young, M. D, & Petersen, G. J. (2002). Enabling substantive reform in the preparation of school leaders. *Educational Leadership Review, 3*(1), 1–15.

Change and Transformation in an Educational Leadership Program

John E. Henning and Victoria Robinson

In this chapter we report on the recent development and delivery of an innovative, practice-based course for preparing future administrators. The course was the result of a collaborative effort between two professors at the University of Northern Iowa to integrate an Educational Leadership course titled "Change and Transformation" with an introductory course in "Educational Research." The purpose of this practice-based course was to address the specific needs of educational leadership students from seven of Iowa's most populated school districts within a distance learning environment. Key components of the course included (a) the integration of course goals and syllabi from two previously distinct courses, (b) the adoption of a practice-based philosophy and the creation of practice-based assignments, and (c) the creation of strategies to support off-site interactions and practicum work in a distance learning environment. Student comments about the course and excerpts from their work are included.

A CHANGING ENVIRONMENT FOR EDUCATIONAL LEADERSHIP PROGRAMS

The paradigm for school leadership is undergoing a profound change, one that has significantly raised expectations for school leaders. In addition to their traditional role as school managers, administrative leaders are increasingly expected to help teachers adopt risky new instructional strategies, to engage stakeholders in change through participatory decision making, and to collect and analyze data as they lead their constituents through the comprehensive school improvement process (Green, 2001). These increasingly high expectations for school leaders have led to increasingly high expectations for preparation programs. According to standards delineated

John E. Henning, University of Northern Iowa
Victoria Robinson, University of Northern Iowa

by the Interstate School Leaders Licensure Program (ISLLC, 1996), building leaders are expected to be visionaries, instructional leaders, ethical role models, collaborators, managers, and politically astute administrators. Each of these roles is reflected in one of the six ISLLC standards.

The new standards add to already existing challenges for current programs, which are often criticized for being removed from school problems and realities. Historically, most educational leadership departments have focused on the managerial side of administration and accordingly have been staffed to offer courses in organizational theory, management, law, or finance, thus making it less likely that Educational Leadership Departments can meet the new standards within self-contained programs (Clark, 1999). Yet few universities offer inter-departmental, integrated courses co-taught by faculty from different departments. Too often courses like "Change and Transformation" are taught without enough emphasis on educational research and courses like "Educational Research" are taught using a theoretical and abstract approach, far removed from school problems and realities.

Unfortunately, the failure of university programs to integrate research skills in the context of practice can send a powerful message to future educational leaders and leave them lacking the knowledge, skills, and dispositions to integrate their decisions with sound research findings. Faculty are criticized for their remoteness and impracticality, and may in fact be completely lacking in practice knowledge (Imig, 2001; Murphy & Forsyth, 1999). The traditional professor's "instincts," perhaps right for research design, may be entirely wrong for a practice-based environment:

> many of the university professors who create and use statistics are more comfortable using them than they are teaching other human beings what they mean. And in all too many instances, statistics are taught in a theoretically rarefied atmosphere replete with hard-to-understand formulas and too few examples relevant to the daily life of education practitioners. (Bracey, 1997, p. 2)

The research skills needed to satisfactorily lead a district through the school improvement process are somewhat different from those needed by university researchers. Whereas university-based research strives to discover generalizable findings that can be widely adapted, the school improvement process is a highly contextualized examination of individual cases for the purpose of improving practice. Therefore, the successful collection and analysis of data in a school setting requires an understanding of the fundamental principles of research, plus a practical sense of how to apply those principles.

> To practice means to apply a body of knowledge to particular cases. It is what separates a scholar from a professional; the former simply masters a body of arcane knowledge, while the latter masters that knowledge and tries to apply it to human problems. (Haller & Klein, 2001, pp. 18–19)

The ISLLC standards have recognized the complexity of professional practice by delineating three different indicators of effective leadership that include performances and dispositions, as well as knowledge. All three indicators are incorporated into each of the six standards. Coursework that addresses only a body of knowledge necessarily excludes the acquisition of dispositions and skilled performances that only come through engagement with particular cases in the field. Shifting to more practice-based instruction has been increasingly recommended over the last 10 years by national organizations, advisory groups, task forces, and accreditation agencies (Murphy & Forsyth, 1999; Shakeshaft, 1999). Yet McCarthy and Kuh have concluded, it is "premature to declare that the majority of educational leadership programs are in the midst of something akin to transformation" (1997, p. 251).

As expectations for administrators have continued to grow, so has the need for new administrators. In the state of Iowa, an estimated 100 superintendents and 350 principals are expected to retire between 2000–2003 (School Administrators of Iowa, 2001, p. 1). Given the current environment, replacing administrators could be a challenge. This is especially true in other states like Iowa, where distances—as well as extended teaching responsibilities, coaching roles, or family commitments— can serve as barriers for potentially excellent future educational leaders. To better serve those desiring educational leadership licensure and in response to a predicted educational leadership shortage in 1997, the University of Northern Iowa's educational leadership department implemented an extensive distance learning course delivery system. Currently, almost all of the educational leadership students at the University of Northern Iowa earn their degrees primarily through distance learning courses, usually in cohorts of students who remain together throughout their degree work. This trend at our university parallels a national trend of increasing demand for distance learning course, as the availability of new technologies continues to grow (Kaufman & Watkins, 2000).

ORIGINS OF THE COURSE

The initial impetus for "Educational Research in School Change and Transformation" came from one of the University of Northern Iowa's educational leadership boards, The Urban Education Network (UEN). The UEN, which is comprised of Iowa's eight most populated school districts, called for a "grow your own" principalship program. Through joint efforts between UEN practitioners and UNI faculty, a 2-year program was designed to include distance learning delivery, quality mentorship, increased practicum experience accompanied by reduced seat-time, a more balanced blend of theory and practice, a special focus on the needs of urban school leaders, and the integration of key courses.

One outcome of this design effort was the integration of an Educational Leadership course titled "Change and Transformation" with "Educational Research," a course offered by the Educational Psychology and Foundations Department. Combining these courses seemed a natural blend to realize the objectives set by UNI faculty and the UEN. Incorporating the use of the research and data would add to the students' understanding of the change process, and using data from the students' home district would embed data collection and analysis in an authentic setting. Consequently, the two departments agreed to merge Educational Research and Change and Transformation and offer it to the UEN principalship cohort in the fall of 2001. Two three credit courses, which would have normally meet twice a week for three hours, were merged into one six credit course that met once a week for three hours. The purpose of compressing students' seat time was to provide more time for them to engage in extensive school improvement projects in their own school districts.

ABOUT THE COLLABORATION

Although the possibility of course collaboration had been considered by the Educational Leadership faculty for many years, budget logistics, scheduling, personnel, and time presented the usual restraints. Recently, however, the integration of the IS-LLC into the Iowa Standards for School Leaders (ISSL) has required that all Educational Leadership programs in Iowa be practice-based, thus encouraging renewed efforts to overcome these roadblocks.

The purpose of integrating the two courses, therefore, was to make the Educational Research course more relevant and more accessible to students, while simultaneously making the Change and Transformation course more data based. Our consequent collaboration was the first for both the course and the two departments. Robinson has been in her current role in the Educational Leadership Department for three years, has taught the Change and Transformation three times previously, and is well familiar with instructional strategies related to the distance learning environment at UNI. Henning has been a member of the Educational Psychology and Foundations Department for two years and taught the Educational Research class three times previously, once in a distance learning setting. Henning also teaches an undergraduate course in Educational Psychology to pre-professional teachers.

We share an extensive experience teaching high school. Robinson taught high school social studies for 20 years, and additionally served as a high school principal for 5 years. Henning taught vocational agriculture for 9 years and English for 12 years. Both remain actively involved with public schools through on-site research and service projects.

The process of integrating the two courses required give and take, honest communication, and much time. To facilitate this kind of course integration, there has to be a willingness to meld, to be selectively eclectic, to take risks, and to engage in new technologies. Collaborators must realize that some of the content or activities in the course they teach might be eliminated or fused. Thus, each must look carefully at what he or she is doing and why. Furthermore, we believe it is very important for both professors to be responsible for all the material taught in the course. Because both of the professors were present for every class meeting and every discussion, the students benefited from a dual perspective on each topic. In a survey administered at the end of the course, a student wrote she liked "having the blend of curriculum, being able to learn from different perspectives, and having double the expertise."

We also agree, however, that the harmonious nature of their collaboration was based at least in part on sharing a common orientation and philosophy of teaching. Both of us believe strongly in a performance-based approach to learning, and both are familiar with the day-to-day operations of public school. This fundamental agreement seemed to eliminate the need for lengthy exchanges about contrasting philosophies and probably accounts in part for the efficient nature of this particular collaborative effort. As a result of our experience, we believe collaborative relationships are more likely to be productive when serious consideration is given to matching individual philosophies and personalities.

INTEGRATING THE COURSE GOALS AND SYLLABI

To integrate the two courses, we examined the current content of their individual courses, selected the elements from both courses that were most relevant to the practice of building principals, and compressed those ideas within the reduced class time format. Previous to this integration, the "Change and Transformation" course in the Educational Leadership program typically examined the comprehensive school improvement process. The completion of a school improvement plan portfolio was the primary assignment. The Educational Research course, a core requirement for all graduate majors in education, typically included the basic principles of both quantitative and qualitative research studies. The course's primary emphasis was to create good consumers of research; thus, an important part of the course was the reading of research studies.

Integrating the two courses caused a shift in emphasis for each course. The Change and Transformation course component was influenced by the adoption of more primary studies, more discussions of research methodology, and the incorporation of extensive data analysis in the school portfolio project. The Educational Research component shifted by emphasizing the study of methods most closely associated with school assessment and improvement, by focusing exclusively on studies related to educational leadership, and by utilizing students' interest to stimulate discussions about the relative merits of various methodological approaches. The result was data-based discussions on the change and transformation process. As one student commented in a survey administered at the end of the course:

> Knowing how to read the research was the first aspect that contributed to my understanding. Then secondly having a *multitude* of research about a single subject (change and transformation) greatly enhanced my understanding. I experienced first hand the relevance of Dr. Robinson's words "Readers are Leaders and Leaders are Readers." I have been guilty of neglecting professional reading in the past and this class really reminded me of the importance of professional reading. Also it helped with the "intimidation factor" that reading research sometimes presents.

THE READING ASSIGNMENTS

Deciding on the reading assignments for the course was one of the our most immediate and practical concerns. Previously, the Change and Transformation course had required *The Example School Portfolio* (Bernhardt et al., 1999). The Educational Research Course had required *Applying Educational Research* (Gall, Gall, & Borg, 1999) to introduce the fundamental principles of research, as well as a coursepak of research studies intended to illustrate a variety of research methodologies. Each study was carefully chosen to illustrate research methodologies typically discussed in an introductory text to Educational Research. (A list of course readings is given after the references.)

The choice of texts for the integrated course reflected the shift in focus of the two courses. To support a school based approach to analyzing data, we adopted Bernhardt's *Data Analysis for Comprehensive School Improvement* (1998) and McMillan's *Essential Assessment Concepts for Teachers and Administrators* (2001). These books replaced the traditional survey of research text typical in an introductory research class. In addition, a coursepak was assembled from research studies selected from two journals from the field of educational leadership, *Educational Evaluation and Policy Analysis* and *The Journal of Educational Administration*. The reading of research studies associated with educational leadership met the dual goal of facilitating the students' reading of research literature, as well exposing them to a number of leadership themes associated with the change and transformation process, for example, accountability and assessment, transformational leadership, and issues and trends in urban schools.

The relevance of the readings to the students' experiences was often revealed during the discussions of these studies, as illustrated below by the following student response to a study, which she posted on the interactive Web site:

> While reading this article I also felt like I was sitting in one of my "at-risk" meetings talking about student attendance and all the issues that deal with it . . . student learning, drop out rates, discipline problems, and suspensions . . . those conversations we all have had especially at the secondary level . . . the same conversations we have year after year. It was nice to see how these professionals put the data to good use instead of having the same ole' conversations that lead to doing the same ole' inadequate approaches in dealing with it. Addressing attendance issues with appropriate and useable data is the way to go.

We felt the decision to incorporate the authentic reading of educational research studies was justified by our practice-based approach to teaching the course. In other words, the skill of reading research can best be acquired by reading the research, and acquiring that skill would not necessarily mean that students need a full introduction from an introductory text in Educational Research. Because the principles of research were introduced through the reading of studies, they were arranged in a very careful order. Initial studies were qualitative in nature to better introduce students to the general format and thinking processes of research methodologies. Qualitative methodology was a good place to begin because it is more closely related to everyday language and every day concepts than quantitative methodology, which requires much more vocabulary and conceptual background.

Accordingly, quantitative analyses were not introduced until the course was well underway, at approximately midterm. By that time, the students were familiar with the general format of research studies and the amount of concentration needed to successfully interpret and draw practical implications from research studies. These qualitative studies were followed by quantitative studies that incorporated the kinds of longitudinal analysis of student achievement associated with school assessment. The following is an excerpt from a student comment about one of these studies on the Web:

> This study was very interesting to me personally since [my] district has come under fire by our community due to a very subjective and negatively written article published by the local paper. It has been a topic now for several weeks and one that I just must air publicly. I believe the backlash of this article will be felt for many months and will have an impact on policymaking and program decisions in the years to come . . . As we have learned and now know, when comparing apples and oranges things will look a bit skewed. For example: Would comparing scores with other urban school districts look different than showing comparisons with all Iowa school districts? Would comparing schools and school districts that have comparable free and reduce lunch numbers look different than using all schools regardless of FR [free lunch] numbers? Also on this same strand, would student mobility numbers look different than students who have not been mobile? Would looking at the growth of a student from year to year look different than looking at the ITBS grade equivalent?

Later studies introduced more complex concepts associated with quantitative data, for example, random sampling, control groups, and significance. These concepts were taught side by side with the studies. In other words, the studies were selected to illustrate a broad array of research in educational leadership and the related instruction addressed the concepts in those specific studies, thus avoiding a separation between the teaching of theory and practice. Student interest in the topics and study findings often sparked their interest in the methodology of the research, as revealed by this Web posting:

> This was an interesting study because it deals with perceptions and not actual factual data. One gap in the study was all the participants were currently involved in continuing education at the time of the study. The results may have been different if it included other teachers not so dedicated to lifelong learning. Did we include all who volunteered or did they randomly select some of the volunteers from a larger number?

PRACTICE-BASED APPROACH

One of the most important challenges we addressed was making the course practice-based; that is, they wanted to assign authentic tasks that were closely connected to the role of building leaders. This was a relatively easy decision, given the call for practice-based curriculum in the Educational Leadership literature, the requirements of the Iowa standards, and the specific request for it by the Urban Education Network. Furthermore, a practice-based approach fit the design of the Educational Leadership program at UNI, which requires a significant number of practicum hours, a relationship with a mentor in their school setting, and the creation of a school portfolio. But the most important reason for a practice-based approach was our strong belief in performance-based assessment. We believe that learning is enhanced in a context rich environment and that performance-based assessment holds students more accountable for the quality of their work and is a better measure of student performance than a traditional paper and pencil test.

The primary course assignment was the creation of a school portfolio. When designing the portfolio, we wanted to incorporate tasks that would require students to collect and analyze data about their schools, encourage them to consult with their mentors, and to facilitate the acquisition of a significant number of practicum hours. The portfolio consisted of the aggregation of a number of individual assignments completed throughout the semester. A brief description of the assignments follows:

1. Analysis of Building Narrative—Students were asked to analyze the narrative that administrators, teachers, students, or parents tell about their building.
2. Contextual Data—Students were asked to report demographic data about their school district, their community, their faculty, and their students. Data were presented both graphically and through written text.
3. Annotated Bibliographies—Students were asked to read and reported on six primary research studies, reporting the purpose, methods, findings, and implications of the studies.
4. Interview—Students were asked to interview stakeholders such as parents, students, or teachers and use a research report format to write up their findings.
5. Climate Survey—Students were asked to create a climate survey, administer it to a class or other sample group in their building, and present their findings in a research report format.
6. An Analysis of Student Achievement—Students were asked to gather at least three years of student achievement data, analyze them, and present their findings in a research report format.
7. An Analysis of Student Achievement and School Demographics—Students were asked to analyze three years of student achievement data in relationship to some other variable such as demographic data and present their findings in a research report format.
8. An Analysis of a School Process—Students were asked to analyze a school process and report their findings in a flow chart or some other medium of their choice.
9. Implementation Plan—Students were asked to use their data and analyses to devise a school improvement plan.

The purpose of the annotated bibliographies (Number 3 above) was to encourage the independent reading of research studies that inform the school improvement process. The other eight assignments involved either the collection or analysis of data gathered from the students' school buildings or districts. This afforded the districts an opportunity to benefit from the students' work in class, as suggested by one student's email message regarding her climate survey.

> Attached is my survey research!! It's a "bit" larger than you requested, as my principal really wanted ALL of the 3rd, 4th, and 5th graders surveyed for data to assist us in the school improvement process . . . so it took me awhile to compile all of the data. (So does that mean I get extra credit?? HA)

The finished assignments were modeled after research reports, with sections for purpose, methods, participants, measures, findings, and discussions. This format is illustrated below by two excerpts from one student's Analysis of Student Achievement from her school building. One excerpt is from the "Analysis" section, and one excerpt is from the "Future Steps" section. Due to space considerations, these excerpts are considerably shortened from the original and do not include the entire analysis.

Analysis. The current trend as identified by the Iowa Test of Basic Skills for all of the grade levels is that there seems to be steady improvement for the past 3 years in vocabulary, comprehension and total reading. The only inconsistency with this is for the 3rd grade. This grade level has shown a slight decline each year. The data gathered from the Scholastic Reading Inventory as well as the Basic Reading Inventory also indicates that the 3rd grade had the smallest percentage reading at their grade appropriate Guided Reading Lexile Level in January and the smallest percentage reading independently at their grade appropriate level.

Future Steps. One of the insights we discovered by looking at the data centers around the 3rd-grade test scores. In response to the slight decline in their test scores, one additional staff member will be funded to provide assistance at this grade level. In addition support from literacy strategists will be provided across all grade levels starting this year, versus grades 1–3 as in the past. The majority of instructional strategies will be aimed at increasing comprehension and vocabulary development by providing consistent and intensive professional development to teachers. New to the building this year, early dismissal on Wednesdays will provide staff with time to learn new strategies to improve comprehension and vocabulary.

As the students completed these assignments, several students commented on the high number of practicum hours they were logging, while others noted that to find sources of data, they often consulted with their mentors. We believe the structural design of the course encouraged this student and mentor collaboration, and they hope this relationship results in continued valuable conversations between the student and the mentor. Near the end of the course one student, who was already serving in a principalship, commented in an email message:

> I wanted to explain why my assignments are a bit tardy. I need to do this for real. I think you should know that what you are asking us to do is exactly what the state is requiring for Schools in Need of Assistance. I need to work with my leadership team in order to get their input on the analysis and SAR etc. so it takes a little longer. Have a great day. You are a kick. I am learning a lot about data . . . This course is so valuable it may be something students should have up front in the program. Perhaps in the second semester. I think comprehensive school improvement is so critical for administrators that they should have it up front. In addition, it really helps with practicum hours.

DISTANCE-LEARNING STRATEGIES TO SUPPORT A PRACTICE-BASED APPROACH

To better facilitate the students' ability to practice these skills, we tried to utilize their existing professional skills. For instance, a number of classroom discussions drew on the professional resources of the students. Two examples are especially salient, a discussion of a recent shooting incident in one of the urban school districts and a discussion of administrative responses to the September 11 tragedy. These discussions occurred among 17 students located at 7 different sites in real time over the Iowa Communications Network (ICN), an important component of the Education Leadership program at the University of Northern Iowa. The ICN classroom can easily link 15 sites from any of the state's 99 counties. Guest speakers—including superintendents, mentors, UEN advisory members, and consultants from places such as the Department of Education in Des Moines or the Educational Testing Service in Iowa City—can join a class with no commute involved. So although students in distance learning courses no longer benefit from the traditional residency model, a new model has emerged. Students now benefit from the network of their cohort group, weekly and lively interactions on the ICN, and lengthy discussion postings on WebCT.

WebCT is university-supported software that serves as an electronic template to support Web-based instruction. The installation of the WebCT component 3 years ago added the means for students to electronically submit papers, access grades, and post comments on a bulletin board. The bulletin board served as a venue for discussions on the research studies, thus giving the students the opportunity to study each other's interpretations. To further stimulate and guide student thinking, we posted questions. Using this electronic tool was an effective way to support teacher-student interaction and facilitate peer learning in a distance environment. The bulletin board was also used to respond to videos, guest speakers, and other issues related to the change and transformation process. Mentors also provided feedback on the WebCT practicum verification forms read by UNI faculty members. Finally, students used it to socialize, to share teaching stories, or for mutual support as they coped with the challenges and pressures of this accelerated program. Over 700 postings were made on the WebCT bulletin board for this the course and each professor received over 300 student e-mails.

In addition, the specific design for this WebCT site further supported student instruction by including the course syllabi, notes brought from the Ed Research class, specific criteria for completing the practice-based assignments, and example papers of those assignments. The technology also permitted all of these to be transmitted directly from the computer screen to remote sites via the television cameras.

Hot links provided quick and easy access to national and state standards, professional organizations and online and electronic journals. The latter made it possible for students to find research studies independently, giving them the potential for future access to research from their home or office without having to come to the university, an important consideration for administrators in Iowa. Previous research classes have relied heavily on mailings and, consequently, less research was actually read.

In sum, the very nature of the course required that students become heavily engaged with technology. Some assignments extended this engagement even further by requiring students to represent data or school processes in charts, graphs, or flow charts. As one student commented: "It was quite interesting trying to figure out how to do a flow chart for school process on the computer . . . my . . . I am learning so much in this class!"

REFLECTING ON CHANGE

Based on student response, the Urban Education Network has recommended offering this course to the next cohort of students in the fall of 2002. We believe that combining our expertise created a synergy that allowed them to more fully address the specific needs of their students. Furthermore, our work together has extended our individual expertise. In a way, each took the other's course, so that both are more sensitive to the issues in the other's field. Both of us are using the assignments from the class in our current courses: Robinson to make the school portfolio assignment in her "Change and Transformation" class more data driven, and Henning in his "Educational Research" class to make his research assignments more relevant. The additional expertise each has acquired will inform our further collaboration next fall.

We also established an important collaborative relationship with our students that reduced the tension between theory and practice. We trusted students to collect relevant data from their school districts; the students trusted us to frame meaningful activities that would cultivate the knowledge, performance, and disposition indicators associated with the six ISLLC standards. This enabled a union between the messy and complex world of practice with the more detached world of scholarship. This experience has led us to conclude that creating an authentic environment requires the academic courage to acknowledge the importance of practice-based learning, insight into the professional knowledge of students, and a willingness to grow through collegial conversations with educational leadership students engaged in practice.

The benefits are potentially substantial. For students committed to assuming an educational leadership role, a practice-based course can generate higher student interest and better learning outcomes. As one student commented at the end of the course:

This course has helped me become comfortable with the educational research component that is essential when engaging in change and transformation. I have a greater understanding of how educational research is used to move forward the change and transformation process.

REFERENCES

Bernhardt, V. L, Blanckensee von, L. L., Lauck, M. S., Rebello, F. F., Bonilla, G. L., & Tribbey, M. M. (2000). *The example school portfolio*. Larchmont, NY: Eye on Education.

Bracey, G. (1997). *Understanding education statistics: It's easier (and more important) than you think*. Arlington, VA: Educational Research Service.

Clark, D. L. (1999). Searching for authentic educational leadership in university graduate programs and with public school colleagues. In J. Murphy & P. B. Forsyth (Eds.), *Educational administration: A decade of reform*. Thousand Oaks, CA: Corwin Press.

Gall, J. P., Gall, M. D., & Borg, W. R. (1999). *Applying educational research: a practical guide*. (4th Ed.) New York: Addison Wesley Longman.

Green, R. L. (2001). *Practicing the art of leadership: A problem-based approach to implementing the ISLLC standards*. Upper Saddle River, NJ: Prentice Hall.

Haller, E. J., & Klein, P. F. (2001). *Using educational research: A school administrator's guide*. New York: Addison Wesley Longman.

Imig, D. (2001). Holding the line on school leader preparation. *AACTE Briefings*, September 10, p. 2.

Interstate School Leaders Licensure Consortium. (1996). *Standards for school leaders*. Washington, DC: Council of Chief State School Officers.

Kaufman, R., & Watkins, R. (2000). Assuring the future for distance learning. *Quarterly Review of Distance Education, 1*, 59–68.

McCarthy, M. M., & Kuh, G. D. (1997). *Continuity and change: The educational leadership professorate*. Columbia, MO: University Council for Educational Administration.

Murphy, J., & Forsyth, P. B. (1999). A decade of changes: Analysis and comment. In P. B. Forsyth & J. Murphy (Eds.), *Educational administration: A decade of reform* (pp. 253–272). Thousand Oaks, CA: Corwin Press.

School Administrators of Iowa. (2000). *Attracting, recruiting and retaining quality school administrators*. West Des Moines, IA: Author.

Shakeshaft, C. (1999). A decade half full or a decade half empty: Thoughts from a tired reformer. In P. B. Forsyth & J. Murphy (Eds.), *Educational administration: A decade of reform*. Thousand Oaks, CA: Corwin Press.

COURSE TEXTS

Bernhardt, V. L. (1998). *Data analysis for comprehensive school wide improvement*. Larchmont, NY: Eye on Education.

McMillan, J. H. (2001). *Essential assessment concepts for teachers and administrators*. Thousand Oaks, CA: Corwin Press.

RESEARCH STUDIES PRESENTED IN THE ORDER ASSIGNED

Danzig, A. B. (1997). Leadership stories: What novices learn by crafting the stories of experienced administrators. *Journal of Education Administration, 35*, 123–137.

Maslin-Ostrowski, P., & Ackerman, R. H. (2000). On being wounded: Implications for school leaders. *Journal of Education Administration, 38*, 216–229.

Firestone, W. A., Mayrowetz, D., & Fairman, J. (1998). Performance-based assessment and instructional change: The effects of testing in Maine and Maryland. *Educational Evaluation and Policy Analysis, 20*, 95–113.

Fennell, H. (1999). Power in the principalship: Four women's experiences. *Journal of Education Administration, 27*, 23–49.

Blase, J., & Blase, J. (2000). Effective instructional leadership: Teacher's perspectives on how principals promote teaching and learning in schools. *Journal of Education Administration, 38*, 130–141.

Hess, G. A., Jr. (1999). Understanding achievement (and other) changes under Chicago reform. *Educational Evaluation and Policy Analysis, 21*, 67–83.

Stecher, B. M., & Klein, S. P. (1997). The cost of science performance assessments in large-scale testing programs. *Educational Evaluation and Policy Analysis, 19*, 1–14.

Weller, L. D. (2000). School attendance problems: Using the TQM tools to identify root causes. *Journal of Education Administration, 38*, 64–82.

Hanushek, E. A. (1997). Assessing the effects of school resources on student performance: An update. *Educational Evaluation and Policy Analysis, 19*, 141–164.

Iver, M. A., & Stringfield, S. (2000). Privatized delivery of instructional services for urban public school students placed at risk. *Educational Evaluation and Analysis, 22*, 375–382.

Geijsel, F., Sleegers, P., & van den Berg, R. (1999). Transformational leadership and the implementation of large-scale innovation programs. *Journal of Education Administration, 37,* 309–328.

Leithwood, K., & Jantzi, D. (2000). The effects of transformational leadership on organizational conditions and student engagement with school. *Journal of Education Administration, 38,* 112–129.

Goldring, E. B. (1993). Choice, empowerment, and involvement: What satisfies parents? *Educational Evaluation and Policy Analysis, 15*(4), 396–409.

Barnnett, K., McCormick, J., & Conners, R. (2001). Transformational leadership in schools: Panacea, placebo, or problem? *Journal of Education Administration, 39,* 24–46.

Henkin, A. B., Cistone, P. J., & Dee, J. R. (2000). Conflict management strategies of principals in site-based management schools. *Journal of Education Administration, 38,* 142–158.

Best Best-Practices: Assessments in Nontraditional Educational Administration Preparation Programs

Gini Doolittle and James Coaxum III

Despite the absence of reliable data supporting the use of state-developed proficiency tests as the primary measure and often sole parameter determining the academic success or failure of a school, demands for public accountability and reform continue to escalate at several different levels. For example, the 2000 presidential election and the media's constant press for school accountability advances earlier calls for vouchers and charter schools at the national level with their increased emphasis on science, math, and technology programs. Eventually, requiring state participation in the National Assessment of Education Progress (NAEP) creates a de facto national policy for academic progress. What has been less obvious on the front page, however, has been a well-publicized critique of these efforts by researchers and practitioners. Although they challenge the current round of rhetoric by asking critical questions about the purposes of such policy initiatives, there has been far too little public debate about such issues. We suggest that such a debate might properly begin with: Do the proposed assessment measures match our goals for teaching and learning (Elmore, 2000)?

Likewise, as we consider the ongoing demands for parallel reform higher education and the programs responsible for preparing school leaders, we should also be raising parallel questions about the purposes and outcomes in nontraditional educational administration preparation programs. With responses to the multiple demands for improving and updating administrative preparation, spawning new genres of university-based efforts to respond to myriad criticisms from the field, claims abound concerning their outcomes. Despite efforts to guide changes in educational administrative preparation programs like those spearheaded by The Interstate School Leaders Leadership Licensure Consortium (ISLLC), National Council for the Accreditation of Teacher Ed-

Gini Doolittle, Rowan University
James Coaxum III, Rowan University

ucation (NCATE), and the National Association of Secondary School Principals' (NASSP) Assessment Center, too few empirical data about how these new practitioners perform as field-leaders have become part of the knowledge base. In fact, even less information is available about how these programs develop and modify their pedagogical practices in order to meet the learning needs of their students.

Currently, the bulk of nontraditional programs are characterized by problem-based learning, field-based learning, and case studies organized around cohort models, although a small number of these new preparation programs utilize more traditional instructional methods within a cohort structure. Regardless of the instructional model, however, the effectiveness of this new genre of preparation programs (Stakenas, 1994) remains largely anecdotal. As a profession, we agree with a growing number of colleagues on the importance of establishing whether this new leadership genus addresses the significant problems associated with the development of new educational leaders. Further, we maintain that the "new knowledge" generated by these programs must be carefully assessed to determine which skills and competencies transfer into the field and, subsequently, how they contribute to improved professional practices (Riehl, Larson, Short, & Reitzug, 2000).

PURPOSE OF THE STUDY

This study examines the process used by members of an Educational Leadership Department who attempted to move toward a more authentic assessment of student learning after the students' first year in the doctoral program. Specifically, the study addresses whether or not students in the doctoral cohort perceived the formative oral examination incorporated as part of the benchmark as authentic and an appropriate assessment of their learning. With critiques emerging from the failure of existing programs to prepare school leaders capable of leading significant change in schools (Young, 2001), the call for more authentic experiences in educational administration preparation programs seem appropriate. Evidencing a balance between theoretical and content knowledge and the practical skills deemed critical to challenge the changing nature of schools, new university programs seek to provide more clearly articulated course structures and articulation between content modules. Thus, students are able to evidence improved learning outcomes and transfer of skills into the workplace through interaction with supportive peer colleagues and additional contact time with course instructors (Scribner & Donaldson, 2000). Intended to create a sense of community, cohort programs have also been viewed recently as "the lesson" of new preparation programs (Barnett, Basom, Yerkes, & Norris, 2000). We argue that if it is critical for educational administration preparation programs to modify and reconceptualize existing strategies for conceptualizing and delivering instruction and content, then it is equally critical to align assessment measures with new instructional strategies and content organization (Wiggins, 1989). In constructing a case for scrutinizing the twin issues of monitoring and evaluation in nontraditional educational administrative preparation programs, we focus on a review of the related literature, the methods used in the study, a summary and analysis of findings, and a discussion of the findings.

LITERATURE REVIEW
Evaluation in Educational Administration Preparation Programs

Corresponding with the current conservative political agenda, no doubt, will be new iterations of the recent calls for scrutiny of both teacher and administrator preparation programs. Starting with William Greenfield's (1995) criticism of educational administration preparation programs for lacking conceptual unity, demands for reform seem to recycle every few years or so. During each of these cycles, other national organizations proffer their own spin on the educational administration reform agenda and, thus, publicize their own criticisms and recommendations for changes in educational administration preparation programs.

Changes such as those advanced by the National Commission on Excellence in Educational Administration (NCEEA), the National Policy Board for Educational Administration (NPBEA), and the Interstate School Leaders Leadership Licensure Consortium (ISLLC) incorporate a variety of strategies purported to improve administrative preparation. For example, citing the lack of attention to carefully sequenced, meaningful, and appropriate academic or theoretical course content, the NCEEA Report (1987), *Leaders for American Schools*, advocates incorporation of field-based experiences for students. Other program modification strategies include understanding the moral choices in leadership (Sergiovanni, 1994, 1999), the importance of understanding the multifaceted aspects of leadership (Greenfield, 1995), and development of consultant-like approaches (Ames & Ames, 1993).

In addition, scholars like Joe Murphy (1992) suggest that preparation reform also needs to include how content is designed and delivered and articulates a need for increased emphasis on topics such as "values, social context, core technology, inquiry, and new forms of leadership" (p. 10). Observing that the context in which principals manage and operate schools might require shifts in leadership style, school organization, and instruction (Jacobson, 1990), Leithwood, Jantzi, and Stainbach (1999) report that some districts even facilitate their own administrative support groups given the absence of systematic professional development supporting these proposed reforms. On the other hand, some preparation programs merely re-title existing courses and programs (Stakenas, 1994) claiming gains in meeting students' changing needs for more relevant preparation. Thus, recent reforms in educational administration preparation programs run the gamut from a return to practice-based knowledge programs popular in the early days of administration preparation to a clearly stated need for preparing future school leaders with the theoretical knowledge base and related craft skills (Milstein & Kreuger, 1993).

Despite repeated demands for meaningful shifts in leader preparation, Willover (1998) recently reported that university preparation programs' responses to these calls for reform promulgated some efforts to improve programs for educational administrators, albeit, very slowly. While these current critics of critics claim that the challenging educational needs of an expanding diverse student body being raised in an increasingly complex and rapidly changing environment are woefully inadequate (Fullan, 1991), the reform efforts continue.

The 1990s: Cohort Programs as Programmatic Innovations

The major component framing the majority of nontraditional university preparation programs has been the almost unrestricted adoption of cohort models. Generated by the Danforth Foundation's support of nontraditional educational administration preparation programs and practitioner level doctoral efforts in the early 1990s, the model and its contribution to the practice of leadership in the field remains largely unexplored by the research community (Barnett et al., 2000; Scribner & Donaldson, 2000). Cohort claims focus on their reported effect in reducing the rate of program non-completion and reducing the excessive number of students remaining "All But Dissertation" (ABD). Further, cohorts are purported to help develop professional learning communities (Barnett & Muse, 1993) by offering a more careful screening of candidates, the inclusion of minority students, authentic instruction, internships, mentoring, substantive peer support, and relevant curricular themes. Also viewed as providing a kind of organizational learning (Schon, 1982; Senge, 1985), cohorts are generally accepted as a practical response to current criticisms, although not all cohorts modify instructional strategies or engage in constructivist learning strategies.

In general, the notion of educational cohorts as both an efficient and effective model for providing practical course sequencing and structure, a supportive peer culture, and an opportunity for more meaningful contact with course instructors appears consistent over time (Barnett et al., 2000; Basom, Yerkes, Norris, & Barnett, 1996; Henkelman-Bahn & Davidson, 1999). Supporters of these programs argue that cohorts serve as an important learning laboratory for modeling community by viewing students as learners and leaders. Such programs are then both content and process driven (Norris & Barnett, 1994) by providing the skills critical for creating collaborative learning environments. Nevertheless, existing studies fail to directly address exactly how learning takes place in this environment (Scribner & Donaldson, 2000; Scribner & Machell, 1999).

Further, cohort studies also report the potential for influencing professional relationships and field practices based on the experiences and strength of the interpersonal relationships developed during the course of these nontraditional programs (Basom et al., 1996; Norris, Barnett, Basom, & Yerkes, 1997). While cohort participants confirm many of these interpersonal benefits, including bonding, community, support, cooperation, sense of belonging, networking, and trust, such self-reports lack evidence of increased academic performance or effective leadership practices in the workplace subsequent to completing the program (Barnett et al., 2000). However, Leithwood, Jantzi, and Coffin (1995) report that teachers perceived their principals as exhibiting successful leadership practices after participating in a cohort program.

More recently, Scribner and Donaldson (2000) report that existing social structures in cohorts may, in fact, constrain individual learning in collaborative student projects. In their study, students often used social mechanism similar to the ones prominent in their professional environments to suppress individual reactions to project elements. By arguing that the press for completing projects within required course time lines needed to be the sole driving force, students were told that getting on with the work must be the sole determiner of their priorities. This silencing not only impeded individual learning, it also provided evidence of gender and class bias.

Instructional Strategies and Their Influence on Learning

Predicated largely on problem-based learning efforts (Barnett, 1993; Bridges, 1992; Bridges & Hallinger, 1995; Clark & Clark, 1996; Hallinger & Bridges, 1996), most cohort programs weave content around problem-solving activities and project-based learning. No "one best" model (Cooper & Boyd, 1988) is advocated, but instead programs are encouraged to utilize "the comprehensive knowledge base" developed by the National Policy Board (NPBEA, 1989, p. 19). Early critiques of this instructional model, suggest that the willingness of university faculty to devote the requisite time for planning, their motivation to share teaching responsibilities with colleagues and field practitioners, and capacity of universities to commit adequate on-going monetary support (Clark & Clark, 1996; Stevenson & Doolittle, 1997) as the only constraints to implementation.

We argue, however, that through the teaching and learning process embedded in these reforms is a need to better understand how the "Praxis, or reflection and action upon the world [in order to transform it]" (Love & Love, 1995, p. 36) occurs. Challenging the conceptual frameworks underpinning existing systems requires critical reflection wherein the student critically examines existing beliefs, assumptions, norms, and practices supporting existing systems. Such critique develops as faculties engage in a critical dialogue with students. Predicated on a profound trust, the dialogue establishes a joint partnership between professor and student for examining existence, roles in the educational process and the subject, and students' own learning (Love & Love, 1995). By reducing the status and power differential, the dialogical process minimizes the distance between professor and student and consequently increases each one's level of consciousness. The process further assists students in understanding that learning often comes from working with others and fosters an awareness of contextual influences and their related impact on individual and group actions.

Defining knowledge as temporary, developmental, and socially and culturally mediated acknowledges the complexity of the world and helps students consciously construct new knowledge by connecting current lessons to previously acquired knowledge and personal experiences (Newmann, 1992). Both a stimulant and motivation for generating interest, critical interaction with peers plays a crucial role in helping students increase long-term retention of course materials, develop higher-level thinking, gain interpersonal communications skills, and encourage growth in self-esteem (Brooks & Brooks, 1993; Bruner, 1971; Johnson & Johnson, 1981; Slavin, 1990) and are consistent with adult learning strategies (Basom & Yerkes, 2001).

With little information available indicating the degree to which such pedagogical strategies remain constant over time, or how these new curricula become realized in practice, Elliot Eisner (1994) argues that attempts to measure, monitor, or evaluate implementation represent a challenging, if not impossible, task. Simply stated, what evidence exists that constructivist notions embedded in these non-traditional programs uniformly supplant more traditional modes of direct instruction and result in improved intellectual outcomes? Likewise, programs advertising alternative assessment processes such as portfolios and educational platforms (Barnett, 1992), have yet to provide sufficient evidence establishing that non-traditional instruction provides empirical evidence of a paradigm shift in the way administrators are being prepared.

DESIGN OF THE STUDY

The Program

Designed for students seeking an Ed.D. in educational leadership, the program's curricular emphasis reflects an instructional approach espousing elements of both transformational leadership and adult learning. Updated and refined several times since its inception in the late 1990s, the program curriculum relies on thematic integrated instruction for delivering course content. Core content is carefully woven around notions of Culture, Organizations, Policy, Change, and Research. With the program's vision of offering a doctoral program for preparing leaders at all levels and in various educational settings, students participate in a learning community environment that continually assesses scholarly research and its relationship to transcending educational institutions through the practice of leadership. Organized around a closed cohort model, the program requires students to enroll in a structured course sequence by registering for nine credit hours of instruction each fall and spring. During the first summer, students complete an in-residence requirement of 10.5 days on campus while enrolled in 11 credit hours of instruction. (See appendix A for course sequence.) In subsequent summers, students enroll in either a seven- or eight-credit-hour sequence.

The Process

Students were interviewed subsequent to their completing the nontraditional program's first benchmark. The benchmark, scheduled after three semesters of coursework, underwent major revisions after field-testing with two previous cohorts. Intended to provide a more authentic measure of student's topical knowledge acquisition in course content including organizations, cultures, and policy, the purpose of the benchmark process was also to assess mastery of each individual's personal theory of leadership, along with the ability to enact it in everyday leadership practice in professional context.

Members of the Educational Leadership Department were anxious to discover if their modifications to the previous benchmark process were more authentic or more accurate measures of students' progress in the program than previous benchmark efforts. The benchmark process is considered critical to maintaining the program's high standards since students are assigned letter grades only during the first summer session and the remainder of the program is graded on a pass/fail basis. Several faculty members cited a need to explore student reactions to the formative oral examination incorporated into the benchmark and whether this assessment was developmentally appropriate for students at this particular point in the program. Faculty also raised questions regarding the previous assessment procedure and its influence on students' negative perception of the program. In general, students believed that the oral examination focused on assessing the development of their leadership theory was an inappropriate measure of their growth and development. They argued that since no two students entered the program with the same understanding of leadership, assessing progress on their development at a fixed point in time did not fit with the program's espoused developmental framework. After reviewing these concerns, a faculty committee was convened to develop an alternative assessment vehicle.

The committee met over a 4-month period and designed a portfolio project for assessing student progress. In a portfolio intended to authenticate their growing fluency between and among the knowledge bases of organizations, policy, and culture taught as core elements of the program, students were asked to synthesize their understanding of the course content in a 20-page paper. The final section of the portfolio was to include a leadership reflection section where students could authenticate their personal growth as leaders by connecting their experiences and learning in the program to their professional practice. Each student would then describe how the knowledge gained from all coursework affected her or his beliefs, values, and how professional performance, therefore, has been shaped by participation in the program. An introduction integrating the various sections of the portfolio was also required. Finally, students were encouraged to place relevant artifacts documenting such growth in an appendix. Faculty provided cohort members with detailed criteria delineating the expectations and criteria for the various tasks embedded in the portfolio process. A scoring rubric was not provided, however.

The Procedures

During the study, both authors served as participant observers and instructors in the doctoral leadership program and both had served on the benchmark revision committee. Data collection for the investigation included classroom observations, field notes, student electronic surveys, and informal discussions with students and other instructors. Surveys, distributed via e-mail, prompted follow-up conversations when student responses were not clear or additional clarification was required. All nine students enrolled in the program were surveyed. The surveys asked students to provide information about the adequacy of the portfolio criteria to convey the assignment, whether the revised benchmark process was an accurate measure of their growth and progress in the program, and whether the program provided them with adequate feedback about their progress and development. One researcher also met with two students subsequent to the completion of their revisions to further assess their reactions to the benchmark process.

All data were analyzed using accepted qualitative research techniques and using the methods advanced by Glaser and Strauss (1967) including both open and axial coding. Electronic surveys were read several times in order to acquire a feel for the data prior to coding. Reducing the coding to common categories resulted in the development of several critical themes. Categories and themes were then matched with the questions guiding the study. Responses were synthesized and returned to the students for what was, in effect, member checking. Subsequent to reviewing student reactions to the member checking, further triangulation of the data was accomplished through informal interviews with both students and faculty. Feedback was forwarded to the department chairperson for dissemination to the faculty.

Scheduled at the close of the six-week summer session, students submitted completed portfolios to one of three panels, each comprised of three faculty members appointed by the department chair. Each panel member was asked to review the portfolios before the oral presentations scheduled the following week. During their presentations, students were required to explicate their theory of leadership and to support their rationale for incorporating the literature and exemplars they chose. All benchmark presentations were videotaped. Faculty responded to the presentation with questions seeking clarification of each student's leadership claims and theoretical explanations. Attempting to be supportive, faculty worked to create a conversation-like atmosphere rather than create a hostile or confrontational environment.

Students could receive a completed or pass grade, needs additional work requiring specific revisions, or Repeat Benchmark I (students might be required to repeat the benchmark totally or in part). Receipt of the Repeat designation required the student to redo the benchmark during the following semester. Failure to successfully complete the benchmark a second time results in the student being dropped from the program. To date, only one student has been dropped from the program's three cohorts, and several students have been required to do minor revisions or incorporate materials from their oral presentation into the written documents.

FINDINGS

Changes in the benchmark process were directly related to student feedback on the previous year's process. Aligned directly with the instructional sequence, the new evaluation package was intended to correspond with and investigate students' mastery of completed coursework and its impact on their professional practice. Faculty hoped that by responding directly to student feedback on the program, a more equitable and appropriate measure was created. One student noted:

> The coursework and program adequately prepared me for the benchmark. They provided me with the theoretical underpinning I needed for the benchmark as well as some opportunities for practical application. Further, they allowed me to articulate my understanding of what I had learned throughout they year and illustrate it with practical examples.

Another followed with "I thought that the coursework prepared me quite well. I appreciated that we were assessed on the material that we covered in our coursework and that we were told exactly what the benchmark would entail." This student reflected the notion that coursework and assessment measures required alignment with program content in order to be considered authentic and was, hence, a reasonable measure of student progress in the program.

Tensions immediately before the benchmark were high; as one doctoral student described, "I know that my brain was 'fried' from preparing for the benchmark and I really had no desire to be in class the night before. I was truly a no factor in the class. . . . I was just there physically." Overall, however, the process appeared to be a vast improvement from earlier attempts to assess student growth.

During this study, the revised benchmark process resulted in one student being required to do revisions in the synthesis paper. Two other students might have received Repeat designations; however, faculty believing that the students did not meet the standards set for mastery by the faculty, instead created a fourth category. This designation required the two students to meet with their respective benchmark committee before revising their benchmark paper. The purpose of this additional meeting was to provide direction and guidance for revisions in the benchmark paper. While this unexpected change created some confusion among faculty and students, faculty members were firm in their belief that the process was intended to be developmental and formative rather than summative and failure-focused. Both students completed the required revisions. A third student also completed requested written revisions.

Analysis of the emergent data themes obviated a number of other critical elements including students' view that the program adequately prepared them for the new benchmark process and concerns about the absence of consistent feedback mechanisms. In contrast from student input obtained the previous year, these students were generally pleased with the revised benchmark, believing it to be an accurate measure of their growth and progress in the program. During member checking, students also acknowledged that things had improved and indicated that some of the issues and concerns they had articulated about the program were improved or had been corrected.

Despite the fact that six of the nine students received a Completed designation, at the same time they also expressed some concerns about the process and, sometimes, offered suggestions for the future. In one case, a cohort member suggested that it would be helpful to obtain feedback before the presentation from the committee. She believed it would then "give you some idea of how to better present." "Having the same committee for all students" might also be helpful, she mused, or perhaps, students might, in "the next cohort see videos, portfolios, and papers . . . so they have the knowledge-base."

Others sought more clarity about what faculty was looking for in the presentation. Concerned about whether the three faculty committees would grade portfolios consistently, one student worried "if they were going to keep to the specificity of the rubric." She went on to state, "in my case, they did." Similarly, another stated her concerns this way, "I thought the rubric needed more. . . . Who knows what each [professor] is looking for among committee or across them. Were we all graded evenly? Consistently?" Someone also made the following request: "I would like to see included in the rubric, how, why, and what the department faculty had to consider in order to determine the assignment [to the committee best suited to them]."

While some felt the rubric was clear, another expressed the thought that "There was just a list of criteria and not a rating scale." Clearly, students, as adult learners, were looking for fairness and what might be described as due process. They wanted clear information about what was expected of them to successfully complete the benchmark process.

For example, another cohort member complained that, in her case, she believed that "there was a discrepancy between two professors. My final revised paper that I turned in was marked 'excellent.' I had to do revisions to complete my benchmark." In contrast, another believed that during the oral presentation, that "the discussion piece lacked substance and did not sufficiently probe my thinking." This observation matched another's complaint that the benchmark oral presentation was regurgitating the portfolio paper and, thus, served little constructive purpose. While this feedback suggests that the new benchmark process represents improvement over previous efforts in monitoring student progress, faculty still need to assess individual students' level of learning, and respond to their apprehensions about the process with clear information about faculty expectations. Data suggest that faculty will also need to attend to what students describe as inconsistencies between and among how faculty actually evaluate student performance.

FEEDBACK

Associated with the issues directly related to the benchmark was the concern that, during their matriculation in the program, students received very little feedback about their performance or progress in the program. Students also expressed concerns about the nature and timing of feedback about their individual progress in the program and several cohort members raised questions about faculty relationships and their possible negative effect on cohort activities and learning.

One student indicated, for example, that she "only received feedback on papers." She agreed with other cohort members that feedback in the ungraded program, in order to be meaningful, had to be "regular" and "consistent." Students expressed a need for more concrete information about their performance. They suggested that it needed to be concrete by citing both weaknesses and strengths. They believed that feedback also needed to challenge them by suggesting ways that they might improve. Citing that much of the feedback she received had not been specific enough, one student complained further that many of the comments received from professors were "not helpful at all." In fact, some comments surfaced "discrepancies between professors." One cohort member noted that "if the guidelines were never clear in the first place, then feedback later loses some value. Ambiguity is *not* always good." Thus, substantial detail about their performance was intrinsic to their understanding of whether or not they "were on track." Students also indicated concern that when feedback was unclear or contradictory, it was related to perceived conflicts or lack of communication between faculty. Given that learning communities function best around an environment evidencing trust, failure to model the behaviors expected of students promotes disaffection with program efforts and impedes student learning. If faculty seek feedback from students and then ignore its implications for their own modeling of behaviors, trust will likely be diminished. Such outcomes then spill over to other aspects of the program, namely recruitment and retention.

DISCUSSION

This study raises some new and important questions about monitoring and evaluation. For example, during member checking, students voiced concerns about whether their responses would be held in confidence and whether individual responses would be identified to faculty. Explaining that she had couched many of her responses in "polite talk," one student believed that obtaining data in this fashion was not nearly as productive as engaging in a direct dialogue. She thought that the responses synopsized in the summary were "clear, but not in color." They did not provide a "clear, precise, picture." Others agreed that there was more to say about the process.

Assured, once again, that the data-gathering process had been constructed in order to protect their individual identities, students went on to emphasize the value of processing the data together with faculty rather than have them review the survey findings from a distance. They cautioned, "otherwise, you could tinker with the wrong thing." Anxious for what they described as a much-needed "dialogue," students then requested that the department chairperson receive copies of their individual responses along with the data summary. They were willing to take the risk of partial exposure of their identity in exchange for what they believed was a better quality method for communicating both their concerns and affinity for the program. "We have invested both time and money in this program. We want to see it succeed," they stated. Each student agreed that each individual's success was directly and inextricably linked to the success of the program. In short, they "wanted their degrees to mean something [after they graduate]." "We are willing to walk our talk as leaders," they proclaimed. They believed that if the program did not succeed, then the value of their degrees might very well be diminished.

As adult learners, students viewed themselves as professionals and expected to be treated with respect. Desiring sufficient structure to guide them in their work, they also sought sufficient leeway to change or modify rules when they are not working. Students wanted clear information about the expectations for coursework and, subsequently, how their work would be valued. Also desiring both the rigor and a match between their learning experiences and the workplace, they expressed the need for coursework that contributed to their professional practice. In order to accomplish this, trust and voice become a critical bridge between student and instructor (Argyris & Schon, 1974; Caffarella, 1994; Daloz, 1999; Zachary, 2000).

Students were, in effect, seeking a space to exercise their voice and, ultimately, to model their own leadership. One student put it this way: "How can I be a leader if I don't practice my leadership in this context?" Simply put, students wanted consistency between what the program advertised about "developing true leaders" (Program Brochure, 2001) and what it delivered. In the process, they wanted respect for the experiences, expertise, and values they brought to the program.

CONCLUSION

Students believed that the revised benchmark process accurately assessed their growth and progress in the program. However, they also expressed concerns about how the process was enacted. Believing that additional consistency was important for program coherence, they expressed a desire for more clarity about faculty expectations for the process. One student noted that the rubric was really a list of criteria since it did not contain a rating scale. Others contended that inconsistencies between professors about what constituted acceptable work led to conflicting assessment of the portfolio pieces, while another student believed the process lacked substance. A second finding pointed to the need for ongoing formative feedback about individual growth and development during the program. Students desired information about their strengths and weaknesses. Expecting that such feedback would help challenge them by identifying areas for future growth, they believed that substantive detail about their performance would help them understand whether or not they were on track.

RECOMMENDATIONS

One of the things missing from the program is a free space (Evans & Boyte, 1992) where such a dialogue might occur. It was acknowledged that the program lacks reciprocal feedback mechanisms might prompt a joint conversation between faculty and students wherein both might explore their respective views of the program. A dialogue might also obviate where student concerns clashed with notions of student commitment, a concern of several faculty. Providing students with a "save harmless" environment would be critical to such an exchange. In addition, the relationships between students and faculty might also benefit by opportunities to engage in a variety of informal social contacts wherein both groups might get to know each other better and subsequently develop better communication and greater levels of trust. Also obvious is the need for faculty to engage in substantive dialogue about their expectations for the program. At some point in these discussions, students might be invited to participate in the process. Yet, these ideas are not as simple to implement as one might imagine.

The most obvious difficulty is that promoting paradigm shifts at the university remains a challenging task for even the most ardent reformer. Simply transferring time-honored traditional practices into new program formats stands to promote dissension as students question fairness when faculty cling to what students believe represents controlling behavior typical of their experiences in traditional administrative preparation programs. Likewise, as traditional programs segue toward new practices, behaviors toward students are likely to undergo challenges as different relationships become established between student and professor (Osterman & Kottkamp, 1993). If program efforts focus on furnishing students with critical skills and competencies that enable them to transfer this knowledge to new settings, then faculty must consider transforming their own practices along with efforts to modify program elements.

Questions of what programs can and should do differently might get underway as faculty examine the need for coherence between their values and beliefs and the pedagogy selected for implementation of new preparation programs. Despite experience in constructing curriculum and new program structures, faculty must set aside adequate time for exploring the overlap between program tenets and their own values and beliefs prior to implementing new programs. Failure to invest in this potentially conflict-ladened process may result in the false clarity (Fullan, 1991) common to many change efforts, or simply result in another round of renaming traditional course offerings.

We posit that new programs need to be lived rather than reflect a patchwork of disparate courses. As professionals, we need to explore the nature of our commitment to developing a cadre of new school leaders. For example, are we willing to invest sufficient time and energy required for creating an ongoing dialogue about the program? Are we willing to discuss both our successes and our failures? What strategies do we need to sustain and grow our own reflective practice? When the going gets rough, will we revert to past strategies of hierarchy and policy? Have we thought through our need to focus students on the acquisition of content? Or have we crafted careful strategies for providing appropriate opportunities for students to experience their new skills and competencies in authentic practice (Spady, 2001)? How can we provide clear and consistent expectations for coursework? Front-loaded guidance on projects? And appropriate strategies for supporting successful adult learning?

The importance of these questions was emphasized recently with Barnett et al. (2000) in their call for additional research giving voice to student perspectives about their cohort learning experiences. The authors, concerned about cohort dynamics, caution about the potential for negative student-faculty relationships, and their subsequent impact on learning as students gain confidence and begin to actively challenge what faculties teach and how they deliver curriculum. They argue that "effective leadership will inevitably lead to power shifts between students and faculty" (p. 272). While emerging student confidence and independence sometimes leads to a sudden reversal in power relations, logically threats to the status quo may generate defensive actions on the part of faculty. Then, with faculty reporting feelings of being overloaded and overwhelmed, power-over responses to student challenges often result with faculty defaulting to top-down strategies for regaining control (Schon, 1987).

Colleagues engaged in nontraditional educational administration preparation programs and their students report that such actions may prompt students to engage in acts of resistance. Unfortunately, such disruptions are detrimental to the cohort experience because "anxious, angry, or depressed students don't learn" (Goleman, 1995, p. 78). Milstein and Cambron-McCabe (personal communication, April 2000) suggest that while faculty might reject, or even ignore the importance of providing adequate planning time, anticipating the amount of energy required to sustain such efforts, and mastering process skills themselves, students almost always reject lip-service and insist on seeing the promised program vision lived. Even more daring, this study suggests a need for faculty engaged in educational administrative preparation programs to engage in an extended careful examination of their own values, beliefs, and theories-in-use (Schon, 1982) prior to program implementation. Acquiring a practice of modeling their own reflective activities as suggested by transformational leadership models (Barnett et al., 2000; Scribner & Donaldson, 2000) help faculty to walk their own talk. Adult learners expect faculty to support their words and expectations with observable, consistent, and predictable behaviors. By being open to take the identical risks required of students, faculty may then be able to construct the necessary bridges for creating a learning community environment

SUMMARY

While the national calls for accountability in educational administration preparation programs move forward, this study argues strongly for beginning that process at the local program level. Without evidence of student engagement in the myriad opportunities and success in engaging in complex learning at the local level, increased support for national measures becomes a moot point at best. Like the popular cliché about charity, student learning must begin at home in our local programs. While it may be seductive to engage in carefully positioned debates about the merits of the ISLLC Standards or the Educational Testing Service's Praxis, if we once again fail to provide students with pedagogy matching our expected outcomes we become increasingly vulnerable to challenges of how we prepare administrators and school leaders. In acknowledging that substantive change in administrative preparation begins at the local level, first, we must as professionals engage in the same rigorous examination of values, beliefs, and professional practices that we demand of our students!

This study also points to several other general, but critical disconnections in the efforts to respond to critiques of educational administration preparation programs. First, it suggests that we need to address: What we really mean by "nontraditional programs" and how are they substantively different from what we offer currently to students seeking to become school leaders? Second, if we modify or transform existing curriculum: What are appropriate measures of student proficiency and how will we know when student have acquired the knowledge, skills, and dispositions underpinning our vision of leadership? Finally, we need to explore: How faculty support or impede program outcomes and to what degree faculty might need to examine their own leadership practices. Without attention to our own values, beliefs, and practices, we run the risk of merely reproducing long-established patterns of behaviors more appropriate to preparation paradigms rejected by our critics.

REFERENCES

Ames, R., & Ames, C. (1993). Creating a mastery-oriented schoolwide culture: A team perspective. In M. Sashkin & M. G. Sashkin (Eds.), *Leadership and culture* (pp. 124–145). Berkeley, CA: McCutchon.

Argyris, C., & Schon, D. A. (1974). *Theory in practice: Increasing professional effectiveness.* San Francisco: Jossey-Bass.

Barnett, B. G. (1992). Using alternative assessment measures in educational leadership preparation programs: Educational platforms and portfolios. *Journal of Personal Evaluation in Education, 6,* 141–151.

Barnett, B. G. (1993). The educational platform: Articulating moral dilemmas and choices for future educational leaders. In B. G. Barnett, F. O. McQuarrie, & C. J. Norris (Eds.), *The moral imperatives of leadership: A focus on human decency* (pp. 129–151). Fairfax, VA: National Policy Board On Educational Administration.

Barnett, B. G., Basom, M., Yerkes, D. M., & Norris, C. J. (2000). Cohorts in educational leadership programs: Benefits, difficulties, and the potential for developing school leaders. *Educational Administration Quarterly, 36*(2), 255–282.

Barnett, B. G., & Muse, I. D. (1993). Cohort groups in educational administration: Promises and challenges. *Journal of School Leadership, 3,* 400–415.

Basom, M., & Yerkes, D. (2001, April). *Modeling community through cohort development.* Paper presented at the annual meeting of the American Educational Research Association, Seattle, WA.

Basom, M., Yerkes, D., Norris, C., & Barnett, B. (1996). Using cohorts as a means for developing transformational leaders. *Journal of School Leadership, 9,* 99–111.

Bridges, E. (1992). *Problem-based learning for administrators.* Eugene, OR: ERIC Clearinghouse on Educational Management.

Bridges E., & Hallinger, P. (1995). *Implementing problem-based learning in leadership development.* Eugene, OR: ERIC Clearinghouse on Educational Management.

Brooks, J. G., & Brooks, M. G. (1993). *In search of understanding: The case for constructivist classrooms.* Alexandria, VA: Association for Supervision and Curriculum Development.

Bruner, J. (1971). *The relevance of education.* New York: Norton.

Caffarella, R. S. (1994). *Program planning for adults.* San Francisco: Jossey-Bass.

Clark, D. C., & Clark, S. N. (1996). Better preparation of educational leaders. *Educational Researcher, 25*(9), 18–20.

Cooper, B. S., & Boyd, W. L. (1988). The evolution of training for school administrators. In D. E. Griffiths, R. T. Stout, & P. B. Forsyth (Eds.), *Leaders for America's schools: The report of the National Commission on Excellence in Educational Administration* (pp. 251–272). Berkeley, CA: McCutchon.

Daloz, L. A. (1999). *Mentor: Guiding the journey of adult learners.* San Francisco: Jossey-Bass.

Eisner, E. (1994). *The educational imagination: On the design and evaluation of school programs* (3rd ed.). New York: Macmillan.

Elmore, R. M. (2000). *Building a new structure for school leadership.* Washington, DC: Albert Shanker Institute.

Evans, S. M., & Boyte, H. C. (1992). *Free spaces: The sources of democratic change in America.* Chicago: University of Chicago Press.

Fullan, M. (1991). *The new meaning of educational change.* New York: Teachers College Press.

Glaser, B. G., & Strauss, A. L. (1967). *The discovery of grounded theory: Strategies for qualitative research.* Chicago: Aldine.

Goleman, D. G. (1995). *Emotional Intelligence: Why it can matter more than IQ.* New York: Bantam Books.

Greenfield, W. D. (1995). Toward a theory of school administration: The centrality of leadership. *Educational Administration Quarterly, 31*(1), 61–85.

Hallinger, P., & Bridges, E. (1996). Developing school leaders who are learning through problem-based leadership development. *Teaching in Educational Administration, 3*(2), 1–4.

Henkelman-Bahn, J., & Davidson, N. (1999). Building a learning community in a doctoral programme in professional development. In J. Retallick, B. Cocklin, & K. Coombe (Eds.), *Learning communities in education: Issues, strategies, and contexts* (pp. 230–246). New York: Routledge.

Jacobson, S. L. (1990). Future educational leaders: From where will they come? In S. L. Jacobson & J. A. Conway (Eds.), *Educational leadership in an age of reform* (pp. 160–180). University Park, PA: University Council for Educational Administration.

Johnson, D., & Johnson, R. (1981). Effects of cooperative and individualistic learning experiences in interethnic interaction. *Journal of Educational Psychology, 73*(3), 444–449.

Leithwood, K., Jantzi, D., & Coffin, G. (1995). *Preparing school leaders: What works.* Toronto, Canada: Ontario Institute for Studies in Education.

Leithwood, K., Jantzi, D., & Stainbach, R. (1999). *Changing leadership for changing times.* Philadelphia: Open University Press.

Love, P. G., & Love, A. (1995). *Enhancing student learning: Intellectual, social & emotional integration.* ASHE-ERIC Higher Education Reports. San Francisco: Jossey-Bass.

Milstein, M. M., & Krueger, J. (1993). Innovative approaches to clinical internships: The University of New Mexico experience. In J. Murphy (Ed.), *Preparing tomorrow's school leaders: Alternative designs* (pp. 9–38). University Park, PA: University Council for Educational Administration.

Murphy, J. (1992). Charting the path. In J. Murphy (Ed.), *The landscape of leadership preparation: Reframing the education of school administration* (pp. 1–12). Newbury Park, CA: Corwin Press.

National Commission on Excellence in Educational Administration (1987). *Leaders for America's schools.* Tempe, AZ: University Council for Educational Administration.

National Policy Board for Educational Administration (1989). *Improving the preparation of school administrators: An agenda for reform.* Charlottesville: University of Virginia.

Newmann, F. M. (1992). *Student engagement and achievement in American secondary schools.* New York: Teachers College Press.

Norris, C. J., & Barnett, B. (1994, October). *Cultivating a new leadership paradigm: From cohorts to communities.* Paper presented at the annual convention of the University Council for Educational Administration, Philadelphia, PA.

Norris, C., Barnett, B., Basom, M., & Yerkes, D. (1997). The cohort: A vehicle for building transformational leadership skills. *Planning and Changing, 27,* 145–164.

Osterman, K. F., & Kottkamp, R. B. (1993). *Reflective practice for educators: Improving schooling through professional development.* Newbury Park, CA: Corwin Press.

Program Brochure. (2001). Leadership Initiative for Tomorrow's Schools. Buffalo: State University of New York at Buffalo.

Riehl, C., Larson, C. L., Short, P. M., & Reitzug, U. C. (2000). Reconceptualizing research and scholarship in educational administration: Learning to know, knowing to do, doing to learn. *Educational Administration Quarterly, 36*(3), 391–427.

Schon, D. A. (1982). *The reflective practitioner.* New York: Basic Books.

Schon, D. A. (1987). *Educating the reflective practitioner: Toward a design for teaching and learning in the professions.* San Francisco: Jossey-Bass.

Scribner, J. P., & Donaldson, J. F. (2000). *An exploratory study of group learning in an instructional cohort.* Paper presented at the annual convention of the University Council for Educational Administration, Albuquerque, NM.

Scribner, J. P., & Machell, J. R. (1999, October). *Interorganizational collaboration in a statewide doctoral program: A lesson in the construction of meaning.* Paper presented at the annual convention of the University Council for Educational Administration, Minneapolis, MN.

Senge, P. (1985). *The fifth discipline: The art and practice of the learning organization.* New York: Doubleday.

Sergiovanni, T. J. (1994). *Building community in schools.* San Francisco: Jossey-Bass.

Sergiovanni, T. J. (1999). *The lifeworld of leadership: Creating culture, community and personal meaning in our schools.* San Francisco: Jossey-Bass.

Slavin, R. (1990). *Cooperative learning theory, research, and practice.* Englewood Cliffs, NJ: Prentice-Hall.

Spady, W. G. (2001). *Beyond counterfeit reforms: Forging an authentic future for all learners.* Lanham, MD: Scarecrow Education.

Stakenas, R. G. (1994). Issues in assessing the outcomes of reforms in principal preparation. *Connections: Conversations on issues of principal preparation, 2*(2), 6–7, 11–12.

Stevenson, R. B., & Doolittle, G. (1997, April). Neglected dilemmas in the new orthodoxy of leadership preparation. Paper presented at the annual meeting of the American Educational Research Association, San Diego, CA.

Wiggins, G. (1989). Teaching to the (authentic test). *Educational Leadership, 46*, 4–9.

Willover, D. F. (1998, Winter). Footnotes, contradictions, and grand expectations (Remarks made on receipt of the Roald F. Campbell Award). *UCEA Review, XXXIX*(1), 6–7.

Young, M. D. (2001, Winter). From the director . . . Building national ties. *UCEA Review, XLII*(1), 6–7.

Zachary, L. J. (2000). *The mentor's guide: Facilitating effective learning relationships.* San Francisco: Jossey-Bass.

APPENDIX A

Course Sequence

YEAR I
Summer   11 semester hours
Research for Educational Leadership I
Leadership Theory
Leadership Challenges
Leadership Seminar I

Fall   9 semester hours
Research for Educational Leadership II
Organizations as Cultures I: Theory
Organizations as Cultures II: Application
Leadership Seminar II

Spring   9 semester hours
Research for Educational Leadership III
Forces of Change in American Society
The Policy Environment
Leadership Seminar III

YEAR II
Summer   7 semester hours
Elective
Leadership Seminar IV

Fall   9 semester hours
Research for Educational Leadership IV
Theories of Change
Changing Organizations
Leadership Seminar V

Spring   9 semester hours
Leadership Problems I
Dissertation Proposal
Leadership Seminar VI

Summer   8 semester hours
Research for Educational Leadership V
Leadership Problems II
Elective

Dissertation 12 semester hours—to be taken prior to dissertation defense

A Journey to Transform Educational Leadership Graduate Programs: The University of South Florida Story

Karolyn J. Snyder

The professional context of our work today offers us the opportunity to shape dramatic changes in education. This is life at the edge of chaos, a place where natural responsive systems thrive and build the energy for sustainable new futures.

This is our life!

The leadership capacities that now are required for schools to prepare students for living in the global age are prompting responses of all kinds among and between universities, school districts, state departments, and social agencies. Educators are faced with the growing complexity of schooling, with increasingly diverse student populations, and rapidly evolving careers for which students must be prepared. These educational demands are set in a context of reduced financial support of schools and a diminishing pool of potential principals and teachers. A rather modest appraisal is that schooling in America is now in a state of crisis.

In the next 5 years, more than 700 new principals and assistant principals will be needed in the Tampa Bay region of Florida. Along with the diminishing supply of principals for existing schools, rapidly growing communities are prompting new school construction and the need for even more teachers and principals. When these conditions are combined with heightened state accountability expectations of schools, there is an urgency for the principalship to be reshaped for changing times. The story shared here is about the power of connections, for new relationships now are being formed between the University of South Florida (USF) and school districts in our region to alter the way in which school leaders are prepared, selected, appraised, and developed over time. As a result of our reaching out as partners with our school districts, we notice that new inter-institutional connections are spawning others in unpredictable ways to shape the future of school leadership in the region.

Karolyn J. Snyder, University of South Florida

An Educational Leadership Advisory Board was formed in spring 2000 with representatives from the County School Districts in Hernando, Pasco, Pinellas, Hillsborough, Sarasota, Manatee, Polk, Hardee, and Highlands. The sixteen faculty, who are housed on four USF campuses, have participated in almost monthly board meetings since that time. Early in our discussions it became apparent that our destinies were necessarily connected: the faculty needed to learn more about the changing realities of school leaders if our graduate programs were to have any current validity, and school districts wanted their future leaders to become not only skilled for new demands, but also grounded in the knowledge bases of learning, leadership, and change. We now perceive that our learning together as faculty and school district leaders holds promise for enhancing the leadership pool and for reframing the ways in which leaders are prepared to influence student-learning patterns. This is a story of a work in progress.

HOW IT BEGAN

In the early Advisory Board meetings, it was clear that we needed a wide assortment of information if we were to be successful in fashioning responsive graduate programs for the times. The faculty began to gather bundles of new information from the social and political arenas, from school districts in our region, and also from our own profession of educational leadership. School district leaders shared with each other and the faculty those qualities and capacities that their districts are seeking in principals, each with a somewhat different philosophical and conceptual orientation. From this complex set of perspectives, trends surfaced that were then shaped over a year by the Advisory Board and faculty into what we call *New Educational Leadership Capacities.* These capacities and their dimensions will provide the foundation for the redesign of the master's, Education Specialist, and Ed.D. programs, as well as the content for a portfolio system in which students document their growth as school leaders.

Our story begins here with what we are learning about the changing social landscape of schooling. The directions provided by professional and governmental agencies are added in our story, for they became lighthouses for our journey. The heart of this report is the set of core values we derived from all reports, which are reflected in the *New Educational Leadership Capacities.* And finally, promising new features are shared about the next stage of our work. This journey has been filled with surprise and hope, along with psychological hurdles that stem from our traditions. Change is never smooth or linear, and it is seldom easy. Nevertheless, we are finding renewed energy and different pathways to the future from our stronger connections with school districts.

CHANGES IN THE CONTEXT OF SCHOOLING

The dramatic shifts we experience in our social, political, technological, and economic environments are illuminating a significant gap between the current practices and patterns of learning found in schools and the requirements for success in adult life. A major national challenge are the *at-risk populations*, which are increasing in number and variety, and are calling for fresh responses. President George Bush reports in his Education Plan (Education Research Service, May 2001) that:

> Nearly 70 percent of inner city fourth graders are unable to read at a basic level on national reading tests. Our high school seniors trail students in Cyprus and South Africa on international math tests. And nearly a third of our college freshmen find they must take a remedial course before they are able to even begin regular college courses. . . . We have a genuine national crisis. More and more, we are divided into two nations. One that reads and one that doesn't. One that dreams, and one that doesn't. . . . After spending billions of dollars a year on education, we have fallen short of meeting our goals of educational excellence. The achievement gap between rich and poor, Anglo and minority is not only wide, but in some cases is growing wider still. (pp. 3–4)

At the other end of the schooling spectrum is the rapidly changing nature of living and working in a world that is simultaneously local and global. Perhaps schools need to view themselves as part of a system that is larger than the local community and its challenges, and to acknowledge the dynamics and features of the emerging global village. The *impact of globalization upon schooling* has not yet been fully felt. World changes are more dramatic than at any other time in human history, largely because the media now are able to transmit information of all kinds both instantaneously and globally (Castells, 2000). A paramount concern for the future of our world is the need for people to understand globalization's impact, to gain strategies to cope with this impact, and to develop a mind-set to thrive in this new world (Held, Goldblatt, & Perraton, 1999; Snyder, Acker-Hocevar, & Snyder, 2000). Castells (2000), a leading scholar in global trends, reports that education lags behind industry and nearly every other form of organization due to its outdated structure and mission.

In order to prepare students for a new century of living and working, education must reconsider its purpose. Is it to prepare youth for the Industrial Age, a period long retired in developed societies (Friedman, 1999; Micklethwait & Wooldridge, 2000)? To simply warehouse youth so that they are kept safe and off the streets (Castells, 2000)? Or is it to prepare students to succeed in an unpredictable, ever-changing, globally connected world (Burbules & Torres, 2000; Snyder, Acker-Hocevar, & Snyder, 2000)? The entire structure of schools and school systems needs to be reworked to respond to changing environments. More important, schools must discover and embrace the emerging trends in workforce competence, which evolved as the centerpiece in a UNESCO international study of schooling for a new century. UNESCO's creed now is that children around the world need to learn how *to know, to do, to be like, and to live with others* in order to succeed in the future (Delors, 1998).

The *changing world of work*, which is now global in its orientation, is another force that will have a dramatic impact on the life chances of high school and adult program graduates. Businesses are becoming increasingly international in production, marketing, development, and distribution. Because of political and financial opportunities that exist through global technological systems, new careers are evolving rapidly (Friedman, 1999). A report on 21st-century skills and jobs was issued by five national agencies (Stuart & Dahm, 1999), which describes how organizations are shifting from hierarchical and rigid systems to those that are flat, flexible, and make use of cross-functional teams. Job designs and employee skills that were formerly specialized are becoming multi-skilled and cross-skilled. In this fast-paced context, management is shifting its patterns from top-down control systems to self-managed teams, with the big picture in mind. Standards that at one time were fixed are now constantly being modified, with worker autonomy and accountability increasing at rapid rates. Major school reforms, such as School-To-Work Transition, Tech-Prep, Career Academies, Work-Based Learning, Career Clusters, and others, are sweeping the country to alter the career paths of youth. One of the dilemmas is that many principals lack an understanding of current workplace realities and career options. If public schools are to survive as viable social institutions, principals and their teachers must become routinely exposed to the realities of the marketplace which 70–80 percent of students will enter following high school graduation.

Not only are new careers and jobs evolving rapidly, but so also is the *personal orientation to work*. Students need to be prepared for careers and jobs in a rapidly changing and dynamic environment where there are few right and wrong answers, and where the challenges require complex and collaborative problem solving capacities across role groups and institutions. A major paradox in this case is that many state departments of education now require students to perform well on tests of established knowledge and traditional skills. When and how will students prepare for a life of rapidly emerging new knowledge, ambiguity, risk taking, and exploration? What is at issue in this paradox is the very nature of schooling itself.

A dilemma lies in the enormous resources that are needed to overhaul schools at all levels while considering the growing disinterest in teaching and school leadership careers to address these challenges. Teaching and leadership are not careers of choice today, and over the last several decades, worker shortages have become more pronounced. *A Report on School Leadership for the 21st Century*, issued by the Institute for Educational Leadership (IEL) (October 2000), documents that in the next 10 years, 2.2 million new teachers will be needed for the new students who will be added to the system, and even more teachers will be needed to replace those who are retiring. To compound the problem, superintendents who were surveyed in 1998 reported a critical shortage of qualified candidates for principal vacancies: over half of their principals will retire without many replacements in the principalship pool (IEL, 2000). The shortage of principals is now of crisis proportions all across America. A wave of retirements is one major cause for the shortage, and a stark reality is that too few teachers are choosing leadership positions in the current climate of criticism, pressure to perform miracles, and accountability for the success of at-risk student populations. The principal's job today is seen as virtually impossible and needs to be reshaped to attract new applicants who are eager to venture into the unknown and face the emerging conditions.

An altogether different approach to schooling needs to be fashioned, one that celebrates learning as natural within a dynamic and rapidly changing and complex environment, and which nurtures the human spirit as well. To survive in a competitive marketplace, schools and districts are likely to shed their control and power orientations over principals, teachers, and students, and instead nurture cultures of learning where risk taking and entrepreneurship become routine for everyone. To attract the next generation of teachers and principals, the work cultures of schools will need a major overhaul, which will, in turn, require a dramatic change in the focus and performance outcomes of Educational Leadership graduate programs. The challenge for us is to prepare leaders who want, and have the capacity, to address the changing conditions of schools.

Emerging Standards of Leadership Excellence

President Bush, in his 2000 Education Report *No Child Left Behind* (Education Research Service, May 2001), calls for school leaders who are accountable for student performance, who focus on what works by reducing bureaucracy and increasing flexibility, and by empowering parents. Bush proposed priorities for leaders that are performance based, and that include attention to disadvantaged students, ensuring teacher quality, advancing English fluency, providing for parental choice and safe schools, increasing funding, and encouraging freedom and accountability.

Within the current context of accountability, a recent report issued by the Southern Regional Education Board (Bottoms & O'Neill, April 2001) noted that for the first time in history, the nation is demanding that middle schools and high schools do for all students what was expected of only one-fourth of students in the past. The report goes on to say that schools must change fundamentally in design and intent so that all students succeed. The authors argue that before schools can change, leaders will need new kinds of preparation and professional development programs. A rather serious problem is that leadership recruitment traditions, preparation, and professional development programs are out of sync with these scaled-up expectations. The question of the hour is: *What do school leaders need to be capable of achieving?* Bottoms and O'Neill (2001) argue that emphasis needs to be given to student learning and success for all, and also to the support of school development goals, refining curriculum, instruction, parent involvement, use of information, faculty development, and the facilitation of change over time.

One of our USF faculty teams examined the literatures that represent emerging practices of the school principal (Mullen, Gordon, Greenlee, & Anderson, in press). Their contribution integrates a discussion of aspects of the school leader's role and major issues vital to principal effectiveness. A portrait of the literature was created by defining leadership capacities that are important for the new millennium, asking, *What do schools need most from their leaders*? The authors focused on school reform and improvement, including applications in disadvantaged settings; successful stories of innovative strategies for comprehensive change (including the empowerment of teachers, students, and stakeholders); and changes in the principalship (including the broader sweep of curriculum leadership) (p. 5). The authors found certain themes to be evident in the contemporary literature. The collective themes that emerged from individual reviews and discussions of the literature are found in table 1.

Table 1. Trends in the School Leadership Literature

1. Facilitating change for school improvement
2. Understanding and reshaping school culture
3. Emphasizing the issue of social justice
4. Facilitating a movement toward systems thinking
5. Providing and stimulating visionary leadership
6. Recognizing the key role of the principal in promoting best practice
7. Defining the assistant principal as a collaborative instructional leader
8. Responding to globalization forces and demographic realities
9. Promoting workforce development and energizing staff
10. Emphasizing democracy and community building with stakeholders
11. Embracing professional development as lifelong learning
12. Establishing mentoring and networking relations and arrangements
13. Facilitating team development and empowering school actors
14. Managing the organization (scheduling, etc.) effectively
15. Providing leadership for continuous curriculum and instruction improvement
16. Developing integrated and inclusive learning environments
17. Building schools as moral communities
18. Developing a technological ethos.

Source: Mullen, Gordon, Greenlee, and Anderson, (in press).

This list of performance indicators is supported by an initiative to provide the content and direction for new national standards of school leadership. An attempt to organize knowledge about emerging educational leadership requirements was made by the Council of Chief State School Officers in partnership with the National Policy Board for Educational Administration. This consortium launched an initiative to cross state boundaries in redefining the principalship—the Interstate School Leaders Licensure Consortium (ISLLC) (Castenell, 2001). Essentially the document calls for standards of strategic visionary leadership, instructional leadership for learning and school cultures, organizational leadership, political and community leadership, and application in the workplace through an internship.

The ISLLC standards, now in use in more than 30 states, have been integrated into the proposed new National Council for Accreditation of Teacher Education (NCATE) standards for educational leadership graduate programs (Castenell, 2001). The National Policy Board for Educational Administration, with representatives from the ISLLC organizations and exemplary educational leadership programs, has worked with NCATE in drafting the standards. A pilot program is now underway to test the standards, which are likely to influence the quality and direction of educational leadership preparation and certification programs throughout the nation.

A study conducted by the Southern Regional Education Board (Bottoms & O'Neill, April 2001) identified features of the changing conditions for preparing a new breed of principals, and urges universities to provide more school-based learning, with attention given to mentoring and internships. Candidates ought to work with real teachers and explore real learning issues and then reflect on these experiences with other candidates in their preparation program. Leaders need to be prepared to improve the core functions of the school curriculum, instruction, and student learning, and become skilled in facilitating school improvement programs.

Barth (2001) reports that many alternative approaches to developing future school leaders are by-passing universities, and many show great promise. Barth himself is working with the State of Rhode Island to design a preparation program for principals that is grounded in what goes on in schools today, with an emphasis on student learning. Initiatives similar to that described by Barth are now being reported in North Carolina, Maine, Texas, and New York. Many university professors are finding themselves engaged institutionally for the first time with school districts in program design efforts, and in marketing ventures to remain in the business of preparing school leaders. Not only are state and traditional private universities competing with aggressive marketing campaigns from new start-up and non-accredited universities, but they are also faced with an emerging parade of certification options to university programs. The future of universities as the primary principal preparation institution is now in doubt, and their continued participation will depend on how well professors respond to changing conditions and connect their work with school districts to reshape a leadership future for schools.

Schooling Changes in Florida
Along with the flurry of national initiatives to reshape the principalship, the state of Florida has generated its own accountability system for student success. Florida schools are focused today on the Florida Sunshine Standards for Student Performance, where students are tested regularly to determine the effects of standards-based instruction. In effect, the State now influences what occurs in all classrooms through a vigorous student testing program. The test results are analyzed, and schools are graded on how well students perform and also on how well they improve in their performance each year. A failing school has three years to improve, and school districts are held accountable by the state for the success of their schools.

The Sunshine Standards and State Tests are only part of the picture. In 1999, the Florida Legislature sponsored a comprehensive review of the 1983 Management Training Act that would recommend the Act's repeal, revision, or reauthorization. The authors of the report (OPPAGA, December 1999) urged the Legislature to require articulation agreements between K–12 systems and universities in order to ensure that leadership programs are current, sufficiently rigorous, readily accessible, and closely aligned with district management training programs. In addition, the certification process needs to encourage greater flexibility through waivers, alternative routes of certification, and the employment of non-certified individuals with strong leadership skills to serve as principals. Florida now is considering a range of options for certifying principals, with university programs being one option.

School District Leadership Requirements
Most school districts in the USF service area are developing vigorous new sets of expectations for school leaders, and most are grounded in a theoretical framework. The Educational Leadership Advisory Board members shared those qualities of

leaders they are seeking. A few are reported here to illustrate the range of core values as well as the similarities in performance capabilities across districts.

1. *Pasco County: A Systems Perspective*. Performance clusters for leaders include continuous improvement of student performance, working with the community, building collaborative work cultures, working on the vision and mission of the school and district, applying systems thinking to school development, and promoting the values of multicultural and socioeconomic diversity.
2. *Pinellas County: A Quality Perspective*. Performance clusters include leadership, information and analysis, strategic quality planning, and a customer focus, with the quality emphasis influencing administration at all levels as well as classroom practice.
3. *Hernando County: A Quality Perspective*. Performance clusters all link with a constancy of purpose and include continuous improvement, communication and facilitation, management, decision making, and critical thinking.
4. *Polk County: Florida Competency Perspective*. Performance clusters include a commitment to vision and mission, organizational and interpersonal sensitivity, information analysis, leadership and management, communications, and high work standards.

Following reviews of the reports on national, state, and local trends, the challenge for the Advisory Board and faculty was to synthesize the findings into a coherent framework for reshaping our graduate programs. What follows is a report of what occurred and its effects on the work of professors and our continued partnerships with school districts.

RESHAPING USF GRADUATE PROGRAMS

To begin the work of redesigning our graduate programs, faculty teams reported their findings to the board on: 1) school reform literatures, 2) changing educational leadership programs, 3) new national standards for leaders, and 4) changing conditions in Florida requirements of school leadership. School district leaders presented their platform for school leaders and the ways in which the district policy links with the recruitment and selection of leaders, certification, professional development, appraisal, and compensation. The themes found in these reports provided the content for identifying a *common set of leadership capacities*, or *core values*, that would become the foundation for redesigning graduate programs.

We have called these core values *New Educational Leadership Capacities*. Ten clusters of ideas emerged as the board and faculty analyzed information reports and documents. For the next several months, the faculty met regularly to discuss, analyze, critique, and finally agree on the ten clusters of ideas for the *New Educational Leadership Capacities*. We confronted our own belief systems and philosophical orientations to our work as professors as we revised continuously "what capacities principals now need to be successful." The Capacities and Dimensions have been adopted by the Advisory Board, and are supported by both ISLLC and NCATE standards. We have added the emphasis on globalization and the emerging world of work and the preparation for careers in a global context.

Why Capacities? The Advisory Board fought continuously for a definition of school and district leadership that is dynamic and transcends the "minimum" orientation to performance that is often reflected in discussions about "standards." The term "capacity" evolved from our discussions and refers to a person's total human and professional qualities, which include an orientation to continuous learning. Thus the term "capacity" is connected to individual performance, while standards typically are viewed as organizational. We now understand that what school districts are seeking, and what USF must help shape, are leaders with the human capacity to do whatever it takes to develop a school where all student populations succeed (see table 2).

We define *capacities* as those personal qualities that drive leadership actions and influence the direction and quality of life for an organization. Personal capacities are built over a lifetime and include intelligence, philosophical orientation, professional knowledge, political and social "savvy," skills for building teams and coalitions, and the drive to do "whatever it takes." In this sense capacities are far more than standards or competencies, which are more finite sets of skills. *Professional leadership capacities represent the total qualities of a person that can in the aggregate drive and influence the performance of an organization and its work units.* We believe that professional capacities can be nurtured and developed, as well as grounded in professional literatures, in social movements of the times, and in school district requirements.

Table 2.   USF's New Educational Leadership Capacities

Candidates who complete the program are educational leaders who promote the success of all students by . . .

Capacity 1:	Promoting student learning as a driving force for curriculum, instruction, and all institutional decision making.
Capacity 2:	Managing workplace financial operations and resources, as well as legal conditions.
Capacity 3:	Understanding, advocating, and continuously adapting to global and local changes consistent with educational beliefs.
Capacity 4:	Developing responsive and adaptive organizational cultures and learning communities within and across organizations
Capacity 5:	Developing and sustaining school-community-university partnerships, coalitions, and networks.
Capacity 6:	Designing and developing a supervisory and professional development system that promotes the learning organization.
Capacity 7:	Creating information systems to guide and facilitate continuous improvement.
Capacity 8:	Providing visionary leadership that establishes common purpose to prepare students for life in the global age.
Capacity 9:	Practicing systems thinking through a system of communication and cooperation to develop the learning organization.
Capacity 10:	Investigating and utilizing technology for developing and sustaining the learning organization.
Capacity 11:	Designing and conducting a major research project as preparation for being a lifelong consumer and producer of research (Ed.D. students only).

DESIGNING A CAPACITY-DRIVEN LEARNING SYSTEM

The next phase of our journey will be to determine the ways in which the *New Educational Leadership Capacities* will influence the design of the three graduate programs, the developmental experiences of our students, the changing role of professors, and the continuing partnership with our school district leaders. Consider a few ideas from this work-in-progress, the master's degree program.

Redesign Task I: The Master's Degree Program

New Courses. The professor's role has been changed from addressing and testing for knowledge, to that of accountability to students for their capacity building. Faculty work teams are now shaping new courses that reflect the capacities. The new courses in this 33-credit-hour program include:

School Development and Change	Budget and Finance
Administration and the Principalship	School Law
Leadership, Power and Policy	Technology and Schools
Curriculum Development	Educational Foundations
Human Resource Development	School Measurement
The Practicum	

The 10 capacities have been assigned to the range of courses with the primary student development emphases. Course goals and objects, as well as knowledge bases and student outcomes, are oriented to the assigned capacities.

As students enter the new master's degree program, they will be given a portfolio system to guide and document their journey. In each course students will be responsible for developing the assigned capacities, and for working under the guidance and quality control of their principal or district supervisor. These district mentors will validate the student's capacity building project. At the end of the master's program, students will enroll in a capstone practicum to assess, share, and be assessed on the quality of their capacity development practice. This course will strengthen and affirm the capacities acquired during the program. For successful graduation purposes, students will present their portfolio of development and, in addition, pass an examination to assess the knowledge base.

Instruction. The new approved courses, with their assigned *capacities* and practicum requirement, will become the cornerstone for any offering on any campus of a particular master's degree course. The delivery of courses will vary from campus to campus, with alternative calendars, and with use of a cohort structure for students becoming the norm. The traditional evening class each week on campus for 14 weeks will become only one of many options available. Already the Lakeland and Sarasota campuses have marketed alternative calendars for new cohorts of students, with differing fee structures. The obligation and accountability of the instructor will be to students by providing a guided practicum experience that links with the designated capacities and real challenges in schools.

Web-Based Courses. Since time has become such a cherished dimension in the life of an administrator, or an aspiring leader, the traditional "seat time" in a university class may be an outdated concept. The president of USF is now recognizing those complete programs that are offered online by granting a stipend of $6,000 to each faculty member who designs for and delivers a course online. The Educational Leadership master's program is one of the recognized programs at USF, and as a result almost all faculty members are now engaged in some form of online instruction with their courses. We are learning not only how to shift our emphasis to "what students need to know and be able to do on the job," but also to transform our delivery systems from instructor-dominated sessions to student responsibilities for learning in the Web environment.

Personal Student Benchmarking. One of our doctoral students, who has supervised principals for many years, is conducting a content validation study of the *New Leadership Capacities*. She will invite a panel of international education experts, along with Florida superintendents, to rate the capacities and their dimensions for relevance and importance. The resulting set of *Capacities and Dimensions* will be shaped into a *self-diagnostic tool* which can be used by our graduate students to benchmark their growth. In addition, school district leaders can use the same tool with principals to benchmark their performance on the job. The university and school districts are building a bridge to each other and to the future. By using the *Capacities* as a self-diagnostic tool, we expect a continuum of support for a common set of values can emerge and grow. We believe a capacity-driven self-assessment system offers hope for the schools of West-Central Florida to be guided by the best knowledge available for creating the conditions for all student populations to succeed.

Recruiting New Graduate Students

The faculty team on the USF Lakeland Campus is working with the Polk, Highlands, and Hardee County school districts, in an area of 3,500 square miles, to distribute brochures and arrange for information sessions to recruit new students for the master's program. In addition, letters have been sent by school district officials to hundreds of principals, asking them to nominate potential leaders for the Educational Leadership program. Already more than 60 new students are enrolled in a new weekend cohort in Polk County. Enrollment in evening classes has also increased because of the new marketing strategies. A new cohort from Highlands and Hardee Counties is expected in fall 2002 with 30 students. Many students are talking now about the high choice environment in which they sign up with a cohort or learning community for weekend, weeknight, or web-based course. These new connections are paying off for both school districts and the USF graduate program.

The university-school district partnership for recruiting a pool of future school leaders is also prompting partnerships for in-service training of current principals. The Wallace-Readers' Digest Funds have awarded a grant to the USF-Polk County partnership to prepare school district administrators to work in a school-based management environment, and discussions are also underway in Highlands and Hardee counties.

The marketing campaign on the Sarasota campus includes district-based information sessions plus an alternative fee structure for extra learning experiences that extend beyond courses. Hernando County hosted an information session for its future school leaders by inviting many universities in the region to showcase their Educational Leadership programs. USF has since started a new cohort of 30 master's students in Educational Leadership in Hernando County. These sample stories provide a new pathway for addressing the "numbers challenge" of the region.

During the fall semester 2001, the faculty and administration of the four campuses which are involved in the Educational Leadership programs met for the first time to explore the potential of viewing ourselves as a regional program, and to share new strategies for the delivery of the master's degree program, marketing and recruitment, and providing alternative delivery calendars. We now envision a system of educational leadership development opportunities for existing and rapidly growing communities in the region.

Figure 1 illustrates the growing complexity of our challenge, which extends beyond delivering courses on four campuses and auxiliary locations. Five clusters of faculty work now include providing information about the master's degree program, student recruitment and selection, course delivery and instruction in cohorts, the student advisement and support system, and the program advisement and continuous improvement process. We are using this model now to create a new Web site for the master's program as a source of information for potential and existing students, and also for leaders across the region and nation.

After the new master's program and its courses have been designed by the faculty and approved by the college, it will be launched officially on all four campuses in fall 2002, using multiple formats and time frames. A portfolio system will provide the quality control for both students and instructors in all locations and conditions. In the process of redesigning the system of professional development for school leaders, professors are exploring various ways to focus on student work and capacity building, along with new delivery systems and alternative time frames. We are learning the power of connections as we journey together to prepare educational leaders for a new age.

How will we know if the new program works for students and school districts? Faculty members will assess and refine the practicum and portfolio elements in each course, and the system as a whole, to review student demonstrations of capacities. An oversight committee of principals and district leaders will address the larger issue of effectiveness by examining a range of data sets that will be gathered each year. The faculty will be accountable for preparing leaders with capacities that have been shaped with district leaders. A partnership in examination of outcomes and effects will ensure the continuous adaptation to changing conditions. We have turned a corner in our work as a faculty and will continue to shape our programs with our school district partners over time.

Educational Leadership Master's Program
Student Support, Quality Control and Accountability System

Campuses: Tampa, Lakeland, St. Petersburg, Sarasota
700 New School Leaders Needed in the USF Region in the Next 5 Years

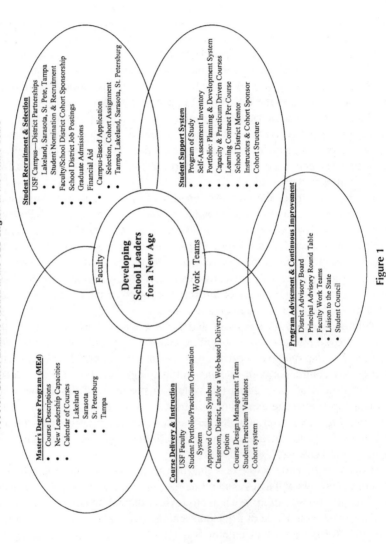

Student Recruitment & Selection
- USF Campus—District Partnerships
  - Lakeland, Sarasota, St. Pete, Tampa
  - Student Nomination & Recruitment
- Faculty/School District Cohort Sponsorship
- School District Job Postings
- Graduate Admissions
- Financial Aid
- Campus-Based Application
  - Selection, Cohort Assignment
  - Tampa, Lakeland, Sarasota, St. Petersburg

Student Support System
- Program of Study
- Self-Assessment Inventory
- Portfolio: Planning & Development System
- Capacity & Practicum Driven Courses
- Learning Contract Per Course
- School District Mentor
- Instructors & Cohort Sponsor
- Cohort Structure

Master's Degree Program (MEd)
- Course Descriptions
- New Leadership Capacities
- Calendar of Courses
  - Lakeland
  - Sarasota
  - St. Petersburg
  - Tampa

Course Delivery & Instruction
- USF Faculty
- Student Portfolio/Practicum Orientation System
- Approved Courses Syllabus
- Classroom, District, and/or a Web-based Delivery Option
- Course Design Management Team
- Student Practicum Validators
- Cohort system

Program Advisement & Continuous Improvement
- District Advisory Board
- Principal Advisory Round Table
- Faculty Work Teams
- Liaison to the State
- Student Council

Developing School Leaders for a New Age

Faculty

Work Teams

Figure 1

REFLECTIONS

We as a faculty have faced many of our own assumptions about the role of universities in preparing educational leaders and have experienced clashes with our colleagues, and even some dead-ends, on our journey to update our graduate programs. In the process some of us have shed many conceptions about our roles as professors and instructors, and about our relationship with schools and school districts. Acting as consultants and becoming involved in partnerships are, for us, fundamentally different ways of influencing practice, and this has forced us to grow. As we prepare for the next phase in our journey, we will begin asking ourselves how well we are functioning as a faculty learning community. After all, that's what we are preparing others to do. Learning how to become a learning community may be the most important challenge of all in transforming our programs. The extent of our commitment to responding to changing requirements has been challenged at every step along the way. Are we ultimately up to the challenge? Only time will tell how strong is our commitment to leadership development for a new time.

REFERENCES

Barth, R. S. (2001). *Learning by heart*. San Francisco: Jossey-Bass.

Bottoms, G., & O'Neill, K. (April 2001). *Preparing a new breed of school principals: It's time for action*. Atlanta, GA: Southern Regional Education Board.

Burbules, N. C., & Torres, C. A. (Eds.). (2000). *Globalization and education: Critical perspectives*. New York: Routledge.

Castells, M. (2000). *End of millennium* (2nd ed.). Malden, MA: Blackwell.

Castenell, L., Jr. (August 27, 2001). Educating new leaders for today's schools. *Briefs, American Association of Colleges of Teacher Education, 22*, 2.

Delors, J. (Ed.). (1998). *Education for the twenty-first century: Issues and prospects*. Paris: United Nations Educational, Scientific and Cultural Organization.

Educational Research Service. (May 2001). *No child left behind: A special reprint of President George W. Bush's education plan, with relevant discussion questions educational leaders should ask*. Washington, DC: Educational Research Service.

Friedman, T. J. (1999). *The Lexus and the Olive Tree: Understanding globalization*. New York: Farrar, Straus, & Giroux.

Held, D., McGrew, A., Goldblatt, D., and Perraton, J. (1999). *Global transformation: Politics, economics, and culture*. Palo Alto, CA: Sanford University Press.

Institute for Educational Leadership. (October 2000). *Leadership for student learning: Reinventing the principalship: School leadership for the 21st century initiative*. A report of the Task Force on the Principalship. Washington, DC: Author.

Micklethwait, J., & Wooldridge, A. (2000). *A future perfect: The essentials of globalization*. New York: Crown.

Mullen, C. A., Gordon, S. P., Greenlee, B., & Anderson, R.H. (in press). Capacities for school leadership: Emerging trends in the literatures. *International Journal of Educational Reform*.

OPPAGA Program Review. (December 1999). Management Training Act should be revised. In *The Florida Monitor Report*. Report Number 99. Tallahassee, FL: Office of Program Policy Analysis and Government Accountability.

Snyder, K. J., Acker-Hocevar, M., & Snyder, K. M. (2000). *Living on the edge of chaos: Leading schools into the global age*. Milwaukee, WI: The American society for Quality Press.

Stuart, L., & Dahm, E. (January 1999). *21st century skills for 21st century jobs*. A Report of the U.S. Department of Commerce, U.S. Department of Education, U.S. Department of Labor, National Institute of Literacy, and the Small Business Administration. Washington, DC.

LEADERSHIP IN PRACTICE

Toward Ethically Responsible Leadership in a New Era of High-Stakes Accountability

Steven J. Gross and Joan Poliner Shapiro

This chapter is an outgrowth of some earlier work that focused on accountability (Gross, Shaw, & Shapiro, 2000). While attempting to deconstruct nine different kinds of accountability, we began to realize that, in most instances, this concept was functioning outside of an educator's control. Additionally, we noticed that, much like an accountant's ledger, accountability, measured by results on high-stakes tests, was functioning as the bottom line in education.

The term "responsibility" is the focus of this chapter. Unlike accountability, responsibility generally comes from within rather than from without. Sirotnik (1995), for example, sees responsibility as a value that belongs at the center of an educator's beliefs. He stated, "Perhaps most important is the word "responsible." Embedded in this word is the moral core that derives from the tacit agreement entered into by educators by virtue of an occupation directed at significantly and profoundly influencing the lives of children and youth" (p. 237).

Agreeing with Sirotnik, Starratt (1994) places responsibility at the center. In fact, when he speaks of the philosophy statement of any school, the first value that he mentions is responsibility. He wrote:

> In such philosophy statements there would be an espousal of core values such as responsibility, honesty, tolerance, loyalty, courtesy, compassion, integrity, fairness, care, and respect. The philosophy statement would then be echoed throughout other institutional support mechanisms, such as the parent-student handbook, the school senate bylaws, the home-school association bylaws. (p. 61)

To provide a theoretical framework for this chapter, we have turned to a number of educational administration scholars in ethics who have described or defined re-

Steven J. Gross, Temple University
Joan Poliner Shapiro, Temple University

sponsibility rather than accountability in their writings. For example, encouraging educators to reclaim their "professional responsibility" (p. 83), Beck (1994) discusses the caring practitioner. What she means by professional responsibility is that educational leaders should believe in all children and consider them to be all worthwhile. Leaders such as these would not "equate worth and achievement," and they would "work to develop a school-wide perspective that views persons (children) as intrinsically valuable and accomplishments as signs or indicators of growth and development" (p. 83).

Greenfield's (1995) approach is not far different from Beck's. He believes that public schools in the United States are "uniquely moral institutions" (p. 63) designed to serve the best educational and developmental interests of children. His explanation as to why public schools are this way includes a focus on the concept of responsibility.

> The dual conditions of involuntary membership and being subjected to socialization processes and purposes not of the children's choosing make the administration of schools a highly moral enterprise.—Unlike administrators in most other contexts, the school administrator thus has a special responsibility to be deliberately moral in conduct. (p. 64)

The special responsibility that Greenfield mentioned is also discussed by Shapiro and Stefkovich (2001). They developed an ethical model for the profession of educational administration that places the best interest of children and young people at the center. In describing the ethic of the profession, they said:

> In sum we have described a paradigm for the profession that expects its leaders to formulate and examine their own professional codes of ethics in light of individual personal codes of ethics, as well as standards set forth by the profession, and then calls on them to place students at the center of the ethical decision-making process. (p. 23)

In his writings, Sergiovanni (1992) has also brought to our attention the importance of the best interests of the children and of the school. Like a number of other educators who emphasize morals and values, he turns to responsibility as a concept, and not the term accountability. In a passage written by Ana Garcia (1988, p. 4), that Sergiovanni highlighted in his book, Steve Johnson, an outstanding educational leader, was described in the following way:

> Things just seem less out of control with Mr. Johnson here. Also, things are communicated more openly. We are given an explanation for why things are done. There is not a mystery behind policy, and if things are not done effectively, we attempt to find a better way. Business as usual is not promoted. Things make more sense, and our philosophy is so much more positive than it was even last year. To Steve Johnson, leadership is not a right but a responsibility. He is always looking after the best interests of the school. (Cited in Sergiovanni, 1992)

Thus, a number of educators who write in the field of ethics in educational administration treat the term *responsibility* seriously. They seem to feel that this concept is an internal belief that can have a powerful effect on the development of outstanding educational leaders. In fact, Sergiovanni (1992) speaks of responsibility when he talks about the heart and head of leadership. To him, the heart of leadership has to do with a person's beliefs, values and dreams, while the head of leadership has to do with reflection combined with a personal vision (p. 7). Starratt (1994) also talks of the heart and the head of a leader when he writes:

> A sense of responsibility urges us to think of others, to help others in need, to honor a contract with another person, to be loyal and trustworthy. . . . The responsibility reminds us that it is not enough to avoid doing harm. We are obliged to do good. (pp. 6–7)

Unlike the advocates of accountability who rely on a bottom line that displays monies in the black, this group of educators place the best interests of students at the center of their educational agenda. In this chapter, then, we ask two key questions: *Should we prepare responsible educational leaders rather than accountable ones? If we did prepare responsible leaders rather than accountable ones, would this make a difference in solving an ethical paradox that arises when standardization and standards clash with the needs of each of our individual students?*

DATA SOURCES

We are turning to five schools that are located in the United States. Three of these schools are part of an ongoing research project begun in 1996 by one of the researchers, Dr. Gross. These schools are in California, Georgia, and New York. An additional two schools from Pennsylvania are included in this study. In particular, for purposes of a case study, we are focusing on an urban high school for non-English-speaking immigrant students that has been studied by Gross for a number of years. This school, called Universal High, serves over four hundred newly arrived non-English-speaking students from all parts of the city which is called Megaburg for reasons of confidentiality. The school has had over a 90 percent graduation rate and an equally high rate of college acceptance. It is one of the first to have charter status in the city. But it has not been all that easy for this school, as it has faced a funding controversy with the city and has done battle with the state department of education. Gross has continued to follow the progress of this school to determine how it has dealt with accountability expectations and still managed to keep its innovative curriculum, instruction, and assessment in place.

While this group of schools constitutes a convenience sample, they nevertheless share a set of common characteristics. All of the schools included in the sample are operating under state-driven accountability systems that include high-stakes testing. All are public and serve urban students. All have a significant percentage of students at risk and, when taken as a whole, will represent elementary and high schools facing significant challenges.

METHODS

In general, semi-structured interviews with school administrators and teachers have been used. Observations of teachers and students in purposively selected classrooms are utilized. Additionally, archival documents and descriptive data on student demographics are examined. Further, semi-structured interviews with state department officials have been carried out. Through the use of this kind of triangulation, recommended by Merriam (1998), and following the steps of phenomenological analysis, described by Kvale (1996), we have identified a number of themes. As described by Yin (1994), cross-case analysis is also used.

In the instance of the case study, which we will present, one of the authors (Gross, in press), carried out hundreds of conversations with a colleague who taught at the school over a 10-year period. Most recently, two visits were made to the school and semi-structured interviews were conducted with a teacher and all administrators. Interviews lasted an average of 30 minutes. Interviewees were asked to describe their approach to curriculum, assessment, and instruction; how the school developed and nurtured a spirit of community for all stakeholders over time; and what leadership behaviors, at all levels, have been experienced at the school. Four classes were observed and short discussions were conducted with students in and out of the classrooms. Students were observed in hallways, in classes, and in administrative offices. Observations were also included of a full faculty meeting. In all cases, observations were analyzed to determine consistency or divergence from interview responses.

Beyond interviews, observations and conversations, a great deal of written material about the school, including research reports from previous studies, were read. Other artifacts included written material from Web sites and newspaper accounts depicting key events in the life of this school.

For the case study, interview tapes were transcribed and attempts were made to identify possible themes. Next, early coding of the data was carried out using the three most useful themes (Glaser & Strauss, 1967). Sub-themes were identified and there was an attempt to look for coherence and a good fit as suggested by Glesne and Peshkin (1992).

FINDINGS: A CASE STUDY

Data from interviews, observations, and school artifacts revealed three core themes which have been central to understanding the course of events at Universal High School, located in Megaburg, over the past 16 years. Universal High is an urban school for non-English-speaking immigrant students. The core themes are: 1) shared values for learning; 2) democratic organization; and 3) strategic moves by the principal. Of the three, the one that relates best to ethically responsible leadership is "shared values for learning." Universal High's mission rests upon a very clear idea of what the future would be for the immigrant students they served.

Here is a quote from the principal of Universal providing a vision for his students.

I think they have a very different vision of the kind of world that they're going to live in and the kind people who are going to occupy positions of power. And it doesn't by and large include the students at this school. So our goal for these kids is very different. I'll give you a concrete example. Some years ago, the president of the regional telephone

company met with the kids and asked: how many of you want to be telephone operators? Of course, not one of them raised their hands. Who in their right mind aspires to
become a telephone operator? Not that it's not honorable work but that's not what people aspire to. Of course he walked into the class, he saw a bunch of immigrants and he
figured their highest aspirations in his company was that they could become telephone
operators. Essentially what we're doing challenges everything that goes into that perception. (Gross, 2001a, p.77)

Teachers and administrators believed these students must be prepared to challenge prevailing stereotypes that they should have a limited future because English was not their first language. They understood that they were doing more
than teaching for impressive test results. They were building a sense of community in this school. Teachers responded in the following ways when asked why
their school was so unusual. Their comments show that community building was
a conscious act developed out of an understanding of students' needs and a sense
of responsibility.

"I think that what is important is a community sense, a family sense. Because teachers
do care about the students. As a team we do work collaboratively together."

The "community sense makes the school unique."

Being a school for immigrants "makes this school very unique because our students feel
better here and they can relate to each other better."

"They work in groups a lot and make lots of public presentations."

(Gross, 2001a, pp. 77–78)

There was not a desire to pit one student against another. But the hands-on, student-
centered, depth-over-breadth quality of instruction at Universal seemed at odds with
mandatory state tests according to many in the school. Over time, there was concern
about moving away from depth and interconnectedness because of the state testing
program. An example of teaching more to cover tests can be heard in the comments
of a teacher:

Well there was this Reformation in Europe and religious fighting going on for a hundred
years, and these Christians were fighting against other Christians and that's why these
pilgrims had to come here. That's how you teach it. You will not have enough time —
The pilgrims came, they came for religious freedom, da, da, da, da, da — the richness is
lost. I mean, you go into the Renaissance — What is the Renaissance doing in American
History? It's everywhere in American History. — I have to cut somewhere, so what do
you cut? — You're being driven. (Gross, 2001b)

Another example of the gap between the state required test and the philosophy of
the school can be seen in the case of a student who could not pass the reading part
of the test. An administrator told Dr. Gross that the student had passed the rest of the
test but failed one question. The student enrolled in college and is already in college-
level English classes:

She's beyond the remedial classes at the university.—She can't [yet] pass [the high school standardized test] so she can't get out of high school but she is already succeeding in college.—It shows you how crazy [this is]. (Gross, 2001a, p. 79)

The core belief in the potential for these students was matched by a concern for their present needs. The school developed a supportive community and the kinds of engaging curriculum, instruction, and assessment strategies that could respond effectively.

Regarding assessment, a teacher describes a student who had a fine portfolio. Here, authentic assessment demonstrated her abilities very well. The teacher felt a test could never show all that she was capable of knowing and understanding. The teacher said:

Because, there's a limit. You can only get A, I mean, assuming you do test that well, well you can only get a hundred on a test where a portfolio. . . . we had a young lady in our early years that I had the privilege of sitting in on her portfolio, I mean she was exceptional. I'm not going to tell you she was an average student, she was exceptional, absolute genius, and accepted at MIT. In four years, she'd gone from zero English to writing science papers that, I'm not stupid, but I had trouble understanding her science papers, and her level of English was just so extraordinary, and for college, she actually developed a computer program that would compare her financial aid packages before she decided to go to MIT. You know, but for her, a test would have been limiting. She might have scored in the top 5 percent on a test, but she was a kid who was capable of going beyond that. Uh, she got involved in doing science stuff with people in the college, she got involved in taking college classes, she went so far beyond what a high school test would [show]. (Gross, 2001a, pp. 78–79)

Serious pressures, however, were perceived in the form of mandatory testing and this concern was also considered to be a clear value affecting future learning.

FINDINGS: FROM OTHER SCHOOLS STUDIED

Beyond the case study, just presented, four other urban schools were included in this study. While this work is ongoing, a major finding thus far is that, in an era of accountability, there are some educational leaders who are willing to act in the best interests of their students even if it means subverting or challenging standards and standardization. Through their actions, these leaders consistently prove that they are responsible educators. Some of the actions appear to be simple and straightforward, while others require considerable energy and boldness.

For example, in one case, a 1st-grade teacher bemoaned the fact that a successful interdisciplinary unit on worms was going to be cut from future plans because the learning outcomes in that unit did not appear on her state's annual tests. This unit involved hands-on science, music, literature-based reading, and other forms of creative, constructivist learning. It could not compete for time, however, with the demands of the testing regimen. In this instance, the principal not only knew of the situation (and many similar instances in the school), but he helped teachers by counseling them and advising them in ways that underscored their professionalism and their right to design an innovative and meaningful curriculum.

A high school principal, in another example, worked to expand her school's shared governance model, especially in the area of curriculum innovation and authentic assessment, even when her state's testing program seemed to run counter to their plans. She helped her faculty understand where the tests might not conflict and where tensions were likely. She also acted as an ambassador for the school and its program at meetings with the superintendent and other district principals. This gave the teachers at her school support and space to continue their efforts.

Unfortunately, this principal eventually resigned because her superintendent did not give her the support she needed to run the school effectively. This resignation could be seen as an example of leaving the field or it could be seen as someone who would rather sacrifice her position than preside over a failing situation.

In addition, both the principal who resigned and her founding principal had entered into a sustained mentor/protege relationship in which they spoke daily and met monthly to help the school sustain its innovation in very difficult times. This is another example of principals (both mentor and protege) taking their responsibilities seriously. No one demanded that they enter into this arrangement. Although there was district monetary support for this, the mentor could easily have found a simpler way to earn her early retirement salary. She insisted on this route because she felt that there were important changes in the school that benefited students and teachers. She not only dedicated herself to sustaining these changes but worked with schools throughout her region to encourage those in other schools. This recently retired principal stopped seeing herself as a leader from one school and started to believe in the generative qualities of leadership that she could exercise on a state-wide stage. This is just the opposite of the accountable worker who merely obeys authority. This is also an example of the power of responsibility; this kind of achievement is not to be expected by those who merely follow dictates from above. This leads to the sense that the accountability movement short-circuits itself by excluding the kind of motivation that comes from within rather than having it externally imposed from above.

In another site, the founding principal had just retired and his replacement was someone who had been at the school for many years. When interviewed, at a time when it was not yet official that she would advance to the principalship, she spoke of the intensive work that she had done to initiate new teachers to this special school. It was not because she was following a state mandate that caused her to organize classes for new teachers. Her careful work (many classes on best practices combined with examples of how all of these played a part in this school) was inspired by her pride in her school and a deep determination that the reforms would continue.

In yet another case, a principal moved his school out of the city system and into charter school status when it appeared that this was the only way to preserve its character, curriculum, and portfolio assessment tradition in the face of high stakes tests. He also brought the state's education commissioner to court (and to appeal) when he felt that making his students take that state's assessments was not in their best interest.

In all of these instances, the leaders believed that they were acting in the best interests of students since they were convinced that the curriculum, instruction, and assessment that their schools had developed were of a higher quality and often more demanding than elements of their state's tests. In some of these cases, leaders were extraordinarily bold and took risks in order to give their students what they perceived to be fine education.

Another major finding has to do with the different degrees of leadership that have emerged in studying responsible educational leaders. What has appeared is a strong connection between the principal and the faculty. This connection is extremely important in enabling the two roles of administrator and teacher to bond. This means that the concept of responsibility is not just what a school administrator must possess, it is also something that a teacher must internalize. With shared responsibility comes the blurring of roles to the point at which teachers are able to act more and more like leaders within their classrooms and their schools. Spillane, Halverson, and Diamond (2001) agree with the concept of expanding leadership from an "individual agency" to the act of leadership itself spread across the school's organization. The shared leadership concept, tied to effective reform efforts, is very much in keeping with the notion of responsibility (since it means greater participation in the larger direction of the school instead of merely fulfilling specific contractual obligations).

DISCUSSION

Purpel (1989) has written about the importance of the ethical concept of responsibility for all educators. He has suggested the following:

> Perhaps the school ought to set itself to the task of helping people to sort out their legitimate responsibilities and contribute to the development of the intellectual, psychological, and spiritual resources required to respond in a way that is fulfilling and meaningful. (p. 45)

In our study, beginning in 1996, we have discovered that the workload of both the teachers and the principal is, by their own measures, far greater in hours on task than they experienced before they took on the significant responsibility of reform. None of them reported external incentives for this work and none of them reported doing this work because of external pressures or threats from controlling agencies, such as state government. They did report, however (and here the number is in the hundreds of individual teachers by now), that they had added extra hours to their work day because they wanted to find more effective ways of teaching their students and they believed in the results that they were achieving.

In thinking about the schools that have been visited and the accountability expectations in the United States we believe that very different metaphors are at work, as discussed by Morgan (1997). He spoke of the metaphor of the *organization as machine*. This is the familiar bureaucratic, command and control operation that one finds at fast-food restaurants. Everything comes out the same, no matter where the restaurant is. McDonald's hamburgers in Beijing taste exactly the same, are served in the same way, and are consumed in the identical atmosphere as they are in Middlebury, Vermont, or in Philadelphia, Pennsylvania. To achieve this kind of uniformity, employees are required to account to specific standards that are easily supervised, quantified, and controlled.

Individual creativity and differences are the enemy of such an organization. This metaphor seems to have much in common with the high-stakes testing regime now a staple of the accountability movement. It is in harmony with these values. Some of the responsible leaders in our study, with their personal obligation to develop a strong ethical code, would be fish out of water in this metaphor. Simply put, the machine is not created to evolve in personal ways.

On the other hand, Morgan (1997) offers other metaphors to consider. One is the *organization as brain*. In this case, it is thinking and reflecting on our actions that matters. In fact, in something that Morgan calls double-looping, organizations think critically about the underlying values that have informed their recent behavior. Power is distributed throughout the organization and there is an assumption that everyone needs to take responsibility for the direction and values of the enterprise. Leading such an organization means being personally responsible and helping everyone in the organization to take responsibility. This is a driving rationale for the development of shared governance. In Georgia and California, the organization as brain caused school leaders to pursue the expansion of their shared governance models to include students, parents, and office and custodial staff.

While no metaphor is sufficient to explain the subtleties of complex organizations and while Morgan reminds us that metaphors obscure reality as they simultaneously reveal new facets of those same organizations, this contrast between the machine and brain metaphor does show important distinctions between accountability and responsibility. Those of us who prepare future educational leaders need to keep these metaphors in mind.

CONCLUSION

To conclude, we return to the two questions stated in the first section of this paper. One question was: Should we prepare responsible educational leaders rather than accountable ones? We believe that the answer to this is "yes." And we say this for the reasons that follow. First, there is a clear set of examples, in both the literature and in our own field research, showing responsible rather than accountable leaders. This give us confidence that such a position does exist and can be aspired to. Second, our research into a number of field-based responsible leadership cases has identified a series of such individuals engaged in the act of responsible leadership relationships. This shows that not only is it possible for a person to be a responsibility-oriented leader (as opposed to merely an accountable one), it is also possible to share these skills and dispositions with a new generation of aspiring leaders.

However, just because such a thing as identifying responsible leaders and educating people to emulate their traits is possible, is it a worthy activity? We feel that the possibility of preparation for responsibility-centered leadership passes this third and most difficult condition. It is worth our while to orient our work toward responsibility rather than accountability for several reasons. First, our examples demonstrate real life cases of leaders who, in Starratt's words, "honor a contract with another person, to be loyal and trustworthy" (1994, p. 6). When a principal thinks enough of his commitment to his students to jeopardize his own future by suing his state's commissioner of education, he is living the contractual commitment. An accountable leader, oriented to obey higher authority, would not consider such a courageous move. In less dramatic but equally meaningful ways, we discovered numerous examples of responsible leaders going far beyond the requirements of accountability. Initiating a work-intensive multiyear mentoring program demonstrates this spirit clearly. Many other options were open to the retiring principal. Her sense of inner purpose, responsibility to her school's development and broader connection to the field of educational leadership in general inspired her decision. We believe that, in this way, responsibility may rekindle the notion of education as a calling, something worth dedicating one's professional life to. Further, we believe that a responsibility-based approach will tap now dormant reservoirs of energy and dedication.

This leaves the second question: *If we did prepare responsible leaders rather than accountable ones, would this make a difference in solving an ethical paradox that arises when standardization and standards clash with the need of each of our individual students?* Our data show that responsible leaders do make a difference in just these circumstances. In Universal's case, the leader's own strategic moves were vital to sustaining powerful, shared values for learning in the midst of a high-stakes testing regime. In another case, the responsible leader played a vital role as she guided her shared-governance structure to discern which accountability programs tended to support their local innovations and which were at odds with these values. In this way, the school governance team could make judicious decisions that had the greatest chance of sustaining important site-based reforms. These leaders exercised Starratt's (1994) model that blends the ethic of critique with the ethic of care and justice. Moreover, we believe that this orientation represents Shapiro and Stefkovich's (2001) model that includes the ethic of the profession as well as the ethics of justice, critique, and care. Finally, such leadership, from our examples shows an ability to use double loops rather than single loops (Morgan, 1997). Double-loop thinking not only includes reflecting on the school's behaviors and making adjustments given predetermined desired outcomes, but it also requires that leaders and their organizations make critical judgments about the meaning, worthiness, and implications of those outcomes. We believe it is exactly this ability that can allow leaders to reap whatever benefits any educational movement may have for their school while simultaneously limiting the excesses of those movements, thereby preventing harm to students.

In our research, then, what has emerged are different approaches educational leaders have used to develop and maintain a "moral core" of responsibility towards their students in the face of accountability, standards, and high-stakes testing. Some of the educational leaders in inner city schools developed coping strategies and even took risks to ensure that their students received a quality education. In dealing with standardization and standards, they still were able to keep much of what is perceived to be good in their current curriculums. Additionally, responsible administrators and teachers worked together to cope with standardization and standards by retaining those parts of the curriculum that they felt met their students' individual needs. They also tended to go beyond what was expected in their contractual obligations. They did this because they cared and because they were working for the good of all their students. Above all, they did this because they were responsible educators.

REFERENCES

Beck, L. G. (1994). *Reclaiming educational administration as a caring profession.* New York: Teachers College Press.

Garcia, A. (1988). *Unpublished case study material.* Department of Education, Trinity University, San Antonio, TX.

Glaser, B., & Strauss, A. (1967). *The discovery of grounded theory: Strategies for qualitative research.* Chicago: Aldine.

Glesne, C., & Peshkin, A. (1992). *Becoming a qualitative researcher: An introduction.* White Plains, NY: Longman.

Greenfield, W. D. (1995). Toward a theory of school administration: The centrality of leadership. *Educational Administration Quarterly, 31*(1), 61–85.

Gross, S. J. (2001a). Navigating a gale: Sustaining curriculum-instruction-assessment innovation in an urban high school for immigrants. *Journal of Research in Education, 11*(1), 74–87.

Gross, S. J. (2001b). [Reactions to standardized testing by a faculty member at Universal high school]. Unpublished raw data.

Gross, S. J., Shaw, K. M., & Shapiro, J. P. (2000). *Deconstructing accountability and democracy for the new millennium.* Paper presented at the annual meeting of the University Council of Educational Administration, Albuquerque, NM.

Kvale, S. (1996). *Interviews: An introduction to qualitative research interviewing.* Thousand Oaks, CA: Sage.

Merriam, S. B. (1998). *Qualitative research and case study applications in education,* (2nd ed.) San Francisco: Jossey-Bass.

Morgan, G. (1997). *Images of organization.* Thousand Oaks, CA: Sage.

Purpel, D. E. (1989). *The moral and spiritual crisis in education: A curriculum for justice and compassion in education.* New York: Bergin and Garvey.

Sergiovanni, T. J. (1992). *Moral leadership: Getting to the heart of school improvement.* San Francisco: Jossey-Bass.

Shapiro, J. P., & Stefkovich, J. A. (2001). *Ethical leadership and decision making in education: Applying theoretical perspectives to complex dilemmas.* Mahwah, NJ: Lawrence Erlbaum.

Sirotnik, K. A. (1995). Curriculum: Overview and framework. In M. J. O'Hair & S. J. Odell (Eds.), *Educating teachers for leadership and change* (pp. 235–242). Thousand Oaks, CA: Corwin Press.

Spillane, J., Halverson, R., & Diamond, J. B. (2001). Investigating school leadership practice: A distributed perspective. *Educational Researcher, 30*(3), 23–28.

Starratt, R. J. (1994). *Building an ethical school: A practical response to the moral crisis in schools.* London: Falmer Press.

Yin, R. K. (1994). *Case study research: Design and methods* (2nd ed). Thousand Oaks, CA: Sage.

The Man in the Principal's Office (Re)Visited by a Woman

Margaret Andrews, Sharon Shockley Lee, and Dorothy James

$\mathbf{F}$eminist researchers contribute rich perspectives on the ways that women in education teach, care for students, and interact with others in schools (Blount, 1998; Dunlap & Schmuck, 1995; Hearn, Sheppard, Tancred-Sheriff, & Burrell, 1989; Maienza, 1986; Marshall, 1992; Shakeshaft, 1989, 1998; Yeakey, Johnston, & Adkinson, 1986). Educational administration literature says little, however, about the daily, perhaps mundane, actions and interactions that routinely characterize the elementary principalship in general and the female principal in particular. Each of us (as women, educators, leaders, and researchers) has a unique understanding of the mundane. We share a common need to critically reflect on what we do, how we do it, and why we do what we do (Bates, 1981). The overlap and intersection of our unique perspectives, our common interest in critique, and our feminism establish the foundation of our study.

Young and Laible (2000) argue that "all research involves crossing (i.e., researching across difference) and all crossings involve problems of understanding, interpretation, and representation, some crossings will be, for different researchers, more difficult than others" (p. 587). Our difficult crossing came when reading Harry Wolcott's *The Man in the Principal's Office* (1973). Our inability to find ourselves and our experiences in its pages impelled this ethnographic study. In this chapter we critically reflect on our crossing: how we understand, frame, and reframe educational administration from Wolcott's point of view and our critical feminist perspective. The differences between Wolcott's findings and ours are less the result of time and gender than of our feminist lenses, the emerging postmodern literature in educational administration, and the slowly shifting paradigm in the field. Even our methodology reflects those changes. Our study is presented as a counterpoint trio, three movements articulated by three distinct voices.

Margaret Andrews (pseudonym), Southern Illinois University
Sharon Shockley Lee, Southern Illinois University, Edwardsville
Dorothy James (pseudonym), Southern Illinois University

FIRST MOVEMENT: CROSSINGS, SHARON'S VOICE

Margaret Andrews and I, both university professors, have known each other for more than 10 years. Our friendship began when we were colleagues at a large, urban university in the Midwest. We were women who crossed the border into a male-dominated department, and we gravitated toward each other for encouragement and support. We shared interests in critical theory, postmodern philosophy, and feminist research. Margaret and I collaborated on ethnographic studies of administrators and other educational leaders. We dreamed of conducting an ethnography of a female principal. We would model it after Wolcott's (1973) classic study, *The Man in the Principal's Office*. Our study, of course, would be *The Woman in the Principal's Office*. But we never got around to it. When Margaret crossed the border from the university to the principalship of "Riverton Elementary School," I suggested she keep a journal, collect artifacts, and conduct an auto-ethnography of herself as principal. Like others before and after her, Margaret found the position of elementary principal all consuming. She crossed to another university 2 years later, and our ethnography of a female principal was again postponed.

I also made a crossing to another university, but we continued to stay in touch personally and professionally. In 1999, Margaret telephoned inviting me to collaborate with her on an ethnography of a woman principal. Her friend, Dorothy James, had just crossed into her first principalship at Riverton Elementary School where Margaret had served as principal 5 years earlier. Dorothy had taught Margaret's daughters and was a teacher and administrative intern in the school when Margaret was principal. It was an intriguing prospect. Comparing Dorothy James and Wolcott's Ed Bell would offer a fascinating crossing—researching across difference (Young, 2000; Young & Laible, 2000).

Margaret and Dorothy met me at an Italian restaurant near my home in a large metropolitan area in the Midwest. We were all dressed comfortably in jeans and sweatshirts. In my field notes, I described Dorothy's appearance: "petite redhead, attractive, younger than Margaret and me, late thirties or early forties." Right away, I saw why Margaret had such high regard for Dorothy. I found her bright, articulate, witty. Over pasta, the three of us discussed possibilities for collaboration and committed to an equal relationship among colleagues. We set a date for me to make the 2-hour drive to Riverton, the small town where Margaret and Dorothy lived and worked. Margaret and I would shadow the principal for the day and conduct interviews of Dorothy and other administrators and teachers. A new crossing had begun.

Riverton

Ed Bell, Wolcott's *Man in the Principal's Office,* was principal of Taft Elementary School located in a suburban community in the Northwest. Riverton, population about 16,000, is a small town in the rural Midwest. A farming and lumbering community with a strong German heritage, Riverton is the county seat of Herman County. Although Riverton residents represent diverse income and educational levels, I noticed no racial diversity as I crossed through town. The Riverton School District includes three schools located on one campus that serve the district's 2,500 students. The district covers an area of about 400 square miles, and students may ride the bus up to an hour to get to and from school.

As we began the study in 1999, both the superintendent and assistant superintendent were male. All of the principals, except one assistant, were female. All administrators were Caucasian. School board policy required that employees reside within the district, an effort to maintain stability, I assumed, and to protect Riverton youth from outside influences.

Dorothy is principal of Riverton Elementary, a K–4 building. At the beginning of the study, all students and staff members were Caucasian; since then, an African-American speech therapist has joined the faculty. All professional staff members were female, but a male 4th-grade teacher was added in 2001.

Riverton Elementary is a one-story, sprawling brick building. As Margaret and I crossed the threshold at the main entrance of the school, medieval banners, plants, wind chimes, and the gentle sounds of Celtic harp music welcomed us. The warm, pleasant atmosphere calmed both children and adults. Dorothy stood in the hallway, quietly talking with a student. The principal wore a striking purple suit. The sleek, well-tailored jacket and ankle-length skirt, slit in front to mid-thigh, seemed more appropriate for Madison Avenue than a rural elementary school. Although modestly dressed, there was something decidedly provocative about Dorothy's appearance. How different Dorothy is, I wrote in my field notes, than Wolcott's principal, Ed Bell.

Qualitative Methodology

As co-researchers, Margaret and I spent 2 years in the field shadowing Dorothy, taking field notes, observing actions and interactions, and interviewing the principal and others. We maintained records of our observations in both written and taped field notes. In addition, both Margaret and Dorothy kept audiotaped journals to record reflections on the practice of a woman in educational administration. Margaret interviewed Dorothy weekly, in open-ended, informal, conversational discussions. Together we selected informants drawn from tenured and non-tenured faculty, staff, central office personnel, and parents. Margaret and I conducted interviews.

Dorothy and Margaret collected artifacts that became part of our database. These included: memos, written and received; the written results of committee work; minutes from meetings, planning documents, school-wide (not individual) achievement test results; videotapes of board meetings broadcast over the local cable channel; newspaper clippings; videotapes of elementary programs, skits, classroom performances, as well as newspaper clippings and cable programming of elementary events. The three of us, both independently and collaboratively, collected and analyzed data. We constructed meaning and confronted the consistencies and inconsistencies of our experiences and interpretations. Shared understandings sometimes emerged from our dialogue. At other times, spirited interactions helped us clarify and strengthen distinct individual perspectives.

Ethical Commitments

We committed to holding each other accountable for conducting responsible, moral, ethical research (Laible, 2000). We would support each other to develop "enlightened" eyes (Eisner, 1998) able to see things differently from others around us and to courageously write and speak about them. We agreed that we would do no harm and guaranteed anonymity to protect study participants. This commitment required that we use pseudonyms for proper names of people and places in the study. Even Dorothy and Margaret's names are coded. Only my name is authentic. We altered or excluded events included from the research report that might violate the anonymity of the district, the informants, or the principal. Margaret, the primary researcher, kept all data secure—interviews, tape recordings, artifacts, reviews and comments on interviews, and journals.

Counterpoint Trio

The principal was the *subject* of Wolcott's (1973) ethnography. Readers hear Ed Bell's words spoken in Wolcott's voice. In our study, Dorothy is a full partner, decision maker, and *co-researcher*, a fundamentally different relationship (Lee, 2000). The relationship between researcher and subject is like the relationship between researcher and laboratory specimen. The specimen has no voice, no real influence on the direction of the research. bell hooks (1990) critiques the violence researchers do to subjects.

> No need to hear your voice when I can talk about you better than you can speak about yourself. No need to hear your voice. Only tell me about your pain. I want to know your story. And then I will tell it back to you in a new way. Tell it back to you in such a way that it has become mine, my own . . . I am still author, authority. I am still colonizer, the speaking subject, and you are now the center of my talk. . . . (p. 152)

As we began the study, we planned to use an iteration of Smith and Geoffrey's (1968) insider/outsider approach. Dorothy, of course, is the insider. I am the outsider. Margaret, as former principal of Riverton Elementary and a resident of Riverton, is both insider and outsider, a border crosser. Although Smith viewed Geoffrey as colleague and coauthor, their research, like Wolcott's was reported in Smith's voice. We found, however, that reporting our collaborative research in unison distorted each of our individual voices. Margaret and I were concerned that as university professors we would drown out, distort, or colonize Dorothy's voice. Determined to avoid inequitable power relationships, disputable representations, and imposing our views on Dorothy, we struggled to design a sensitive, accurate method of presenting our findings (Laible, 2000; Young & Laible, 2000).

We developed a new approach we termed *counterpoint trio*. Our musical metaphor is best represented in the compositions of J. S. Bach, probably the greatest composer of contrapuntal music. His three-part inventions or *sinfonia* are excellent examples of three-part counterpoint. In these compositions, Bach wove three equal melodies together rather than making one melodic voice predominant with subordinate voices as supporting harmony. In reporting our collaborative research, each of us shares stories from her own perspective in her own voice. The counter-point trio expresses a "loving epistemology" (Laible, 2000): independent and collaborative reflection; a deep and enduring respect for each other's uniqueness and common humanity; and a fundamental commitment to one another.

SECOND MOVEMENT: ED BELL AND DOROTHY JAMES—A COUNTERPOINT, DOROTHY'S VOICE

A Woman in the Principal's Office

It has been almost thirty years since Wolcott (1973) conducted his research on a typical principal—the man in the principal's office. At the time of the study, the typical principal was a married, Caucasian family man, between the ages of 35 and 49, with 2 to 9 years of classroom experience. Ed Bell was the archetype of the school principal. He was 45 years old, had three children and a stay-at-home wife. He spent 5 years in the classroom and held minor administrative positions before crossing into the principal's office. Taft Elementary, where Ed spent his last 6 years as principal, had 475 students (p. 58).

I am a Caucasian female, 45 years old, with three adolescent boys and a professional, working spouse. I spent 15 years in the classroom before crossing into the principal's office just over 2 years ago. My school has an enrollment of 753 students and over 100 faculty and staff. There are obvious differences between Ed Bell and me. Most of them are reflected in the current literature on gender and leadership (Schmuck, Charters, & Carlson, 1981; Shakeshaft, 1989). The subtle, mundane differences are more intriguing to me since they capture the important elements of what I really do as principal of Riverton Elementary School.

In my preparation for the principalship, I was introduced to the standard text (Hoy & Miskel, 2001) in education administration, the models, and the theories based on traditional male experiences and understandings (Young & Laible, 2000). Mostly I listened to the "war stories" of my aging Caucasian male professors out of touch with the real world of schools. Mostly, what I "learned" was scientific management. What I eventually came to "know" as a principal was that most of what I "learned" did not survive the crossing from classroom to actual practice.

The Cult of Efficiency

I always understood the necessity of efficient management. Cusick (1992), following Callahan, made sense to me when he explained,

> It is not only, as Callahan (1962) suggested, that schools have to present a business-like efficiency in order to satisfy public expectations; it is that with their size, differentiation, and many more subordinates than superordinates, they have to run smoothly in order to run at all and are, therefore, heavily reliant on a bureaucratic structure. The activities of hundreds of young people engaged in separate activities in separate locations cannot be left to chance, even for a few minutes. The schedule has to be planned and ordered; the routine has to be respected and maintained. (p. 31)

My sense-making emerged as much from my actual experience managing my household and teaching gifted students as it did from anticipation of what administration would eventually be like. In fact, there are many important elements of administration that I wish had been included in the curriculum so I could eventually make sense of them in practice.

Perhaps teaching and learning the "cult of efficiency" worked well for the old patriarchal principal archetype, but I have not found it useful. As principal, I feel compelled to spend time with teachers and students—interacting, reflecting, communicating, brainstorming, sometimes laughing, and sometimes crying. Noddings (1984, 1992) heralded the crossing from the old scientific management paradigm to an emerging feminist perspective when she presented us with the challenge to care. For me, most of the challenge is finding the time to care. It means working 70 hours a week instead of 58, every weekend and most evenings. However, time, or the lack of it, does not explain why I choose not to manage as Ed Bell did. My administrative practice offers a counterpoint to two driving forces of scientific management: hierarchy and routine.

Hierarchy

Ed Bell operated within a hierarchical structure that supported both his personal and organizational lives. Control and authority were not only part of his administrative role, but part of who he was as a man. Ed Bell's public and private lives were separate, and he was at the top of both pyramids. He made decisions, and others, mostly women, carried them out. I cannot separate the public and the private and must manage both of them. My husband, Paul, and I routinely defer to each other's schedules to meet the demands of our jobs, our family, and our public obligations and responsibilities. But the fact is, I am still the one primarily responsible for running our home.

Ed's wife, Alice, organized things like appointments, engagements, meals, schedules, and even Ed's responsibilities at home. Often, she called to remind him of errands he had promised to run. In essence, she attended to almost everything. She even summarized Ed's college readings so he did not have to spend time actually reading the text for class. He admitted, "I took my education by correspondence and Alice did the work for me" (Wolcott, 1973, p. 38). This type of support system literally built into the culture must make a difference in how Ed Bell came to think about his work. Paul does not anticipate my employment needs nor do I expect him to do what Alice did. Consequently, I do not have the luxury of forgetting anything. I am the one responsible for making everything work both at school and at home. In the organizational hierarchy, Ed was dedicated to the administration of Taft Elementary School. In the family hierarchy, Alice too was dedicated to making sure that Ed could administer Taft Elementary School.

Besides having a wife at home to make things easier for him, Ed lived in a world where his male colleagues helped him move up the ladder. The identification of sponsorship exposed an underlying support system, usually for males, that involves "being tapped." Certain leadership traits of male teachers emerge through exhibition of what Wolcott calls GASing (Getting Attention from Superiors) behavior. Male supervisors get to observe the GASers, and support and encourage them to aspire to administration, making suggestions to aid them in their pursuit. Tom Nice "tapped" Ed after he taught just 3 years in the district and was frustrated that an administrative position did not seem imminent. Ed became the latest addition to the "Good Ol' Boys" network. In contrast, am I part of the "Bad Ol'Broads" network? The experience of "being tapped" is not common for women and is unfamiliar to me. The support system for me is not nearly as strong. It is intimate, informal, and I constructed it. I tapped my mentors; they did not tap me. I have not found my experience of tapping mentors critically examined in research and professional literature.

Routine

Ed Bell's routine focused on the managerial/organizational things to be taken care of at Taft Elementary. Because Alice handled the management of the home, family, and other engagements, his normal daily schedule remained relatively unchanged, barring emergencies. He looked forward to a favorite weekend activity—taking a nap on Saturday afternoon. For me, it is the deconstruction of routine, rather than the construction of it, that defines and describes what I do in and out of Riverton Elementary School.

I have a vision for Riverton and I am committed to carrying out that mission with the support, drive, and energy of the faculty and staff. I do not have a routine as much as I have an orientation to administration that includes some routines. My days are filled with walking around, supporting, communicating, and checking on things. I want to establish a certain order and direction which requires all of us to have a connection to teaching and learning and a connection to one another. This notion of connectedness in schools mirrors what Paul and I try very hard to cultivate in our home. It takes a lot of time and a yeoman's effort. Sometimes we fail; more often we succeed.

Wolcott (1973) described Ed Bell as a family man. Am I a family woman? It's just not the same. Ed Bell received credit for being a man with a family. He lived with his young family and participated in activities with them, especially at church. "Being there" made his efforts admirable; "being absent" was understood as part of the difficult work of administration. I am a woman with a family. I chauffeur the boys to extracurricular activities, help with homework, cook, clean, and do laundry. I serve as counselor, advocate, and sounding board at home and at school. I attend every activity that my boys are involved in, selling hot dogs to raise money, and cleaning uniforms. I lead the children's choir at church. I do everything that Ed Bell did and more. Yet the culture regards "being there" as women's work, while "being absent" makes me somehow unworthy.

Luther Gulick (Gulick & Urwick, 1937) coined the acronym POSDCoRB to identify seven functions of management: planning, organizing, staffing, directing, coordinating, reporting, and budgeting. Ed Bell did POSDCoRB *to* or *over* people. In the culture dominated by scientific management, these functions applied only to his professional work. In the emerging feminist leadership frame, I co-construct my life and work, POSDCoRB applies not only to professional responsibilities, but to all aspects of my life. I engage in POSDCoRB *with* people.

My work as principal deconstructs the archetype of patriarchal principal exemplified by Ed Bell and pervasive in educational administration literature. What I learned, I now unlearn and relearn as I co-construct meaning in the daily, even mundane, activities of my personal and professional (non)routines. Administrative coursework did not teach me what I needed to know. The old archetype does not represent my experiences. It leaves its utility at the schoolhouse door. It needs to change (Murphy, 1992).

THIRD MOVEMENT: CROSSING THE BORDER FROM
MODERNITY TO POSTMODERNITY, MARGARET'S VOICE

Crossing Theoretical Borders

There has been a border crossing or paradigm shift, to use an exploited term from the work of Thomas Kuhn (1962), from modernity to postmodernity (Donmoyer, 1995; Foster, 1986, 1998; Greenfield, 1975) maybe even post postmodernity. Some suggest the shift is away from structuralism to poststructuralism, from functionalism to critical theory, from patriarchal to feminist perspectives. I am not so bold as to posit a direction, mostly because I struggle to make sense of the literature that reflects so little of what I know about the actual practice of administration. Rather, I am comfortable with the fluidity of postmodernism and its reluctance to offer alternative archetypes (Foster, 1998). What I do know is that we seem to be moving away from an archetype of educational administration that has been heavily influenced as much by gender, race, and social class as it has by shifts in practice and theory.

I detect these crossings in the assumptions that frame my point of view and guide my practice. Modernist educational administrators, often referred to as scientific managers, view their practice as logical, rational, explicit, and measurable. Given enough time, enough control over variables, and enough technology, they can discover, generalize, and disseminate the "truth" about educational administration as "best practices." It is a search for the best *means* to some educational *ends*. Too often, students and teachers within the schools become the means to the organization's ends. I know. As principal of Riverton Elementary 7 years ago, I participated in numerous attempts to stabilize the organization at the expense of those in it. My evaluations, reflecting how well I did that, were always excellent.

Postmodern administrators make different assumptions (Foster, 1998). They assume that organizations are nothing more than the individuals who constitute them, that all individuals are *ends* not *means* to some other end. Reactionary organizations, like schools, and individuals guided by organizational theory, like administrators, should not be the arbiters of education. The individuals in and around the organizations collectively are the only ones who can make that claim. When postmodern educators deconstruct traditional educational administration, they reconstruct it as a search for the best individual *ends* and the *means* that re-center the individual from the margins of modernist thought. That is why postmodernism is characterized by a sustained critique of the metanarratives that shape education. Postmodernism scratches its head and asks the questions, "Why?" and "Who says?" of current theory and practice. This is Lyotard's (1979) definition of postmodernism, "an incredulity toward metanarratives" (p. ix). Dorothy was incredulous of the old scientific management paradigm that guided her preparation but not her practice. It is this breakdown in theoretical utility that defines postmodern deconstruction. In Dorothy's case, and mine as well, the educational administrative narrative was problematic.

Incredulity, Angst, and Power

Bellah, Madsen, Sullivan, Swidler, and Tipton (1985) write about the angst we face when we suppress the importance of relationships, collectivities. Buber (1958) and Phenix (1964) stress the importance of understanding the power of relationships to make meaning in our world. To know where we stand in relation to others, particularly in a democratic society, is a fundamental end of education. Yet we continuously relegate that type of knowledge to the margins of educational organizations, accept the premise that there is a theoretical reality separate from these relations, and delude ourselves that "individualism" serves to promote democratic ends.

This was evident in Dorothy's attempts to merge her personal and professional lives with some degree of dignity. The old narrative suppressed the existence of an administrator's personal life. An administrator's, indeed any worker's, personal life was either ignored or given perfunctory description. It was seldom considered a variable of significant import and never used to explain how or why administrators did what they did. Theoretically then, the individual received credit for work that was completed on his or her behalf but ignored. The shift from modernity to postmodernity forced us to face our mistake and to reconcile ourselves to the consequences of having alienated our personal lives from our professional ones. The postmodern effort to reconnect is a reaction to the alienation, fear, and slaphappy greed that characterizes a popular culture that disparages connectivity, capitalizes on promoting individualism for corporate gain, and alienates us from essential relationships. Scientific management and the theory that supports it has made such a mistake.

Foucault's analysis of power relations (1977, 1980) complements and advances Buber's writing on the power in relationships. He considers the implications of power in every relationship, not just those between organizations and individuals or superordinates and subordinates. We are forced to recognize the hegemony that pervades current theory and practice. Ed Bell never had problems with his authority, his power, or his relationships, per se. Sure, he chafed at abuses of it by his superiors. He may even have abused his own power on occasion as I certainly did. However, reflecting on it and questioning its legitimacy never seemed to be on Ed's agenda.

His intent was to avoid rocking the boat in an organization that would otherwise keep him afloat. "His freedom was to make no serious mistakes" (p. 307). Wolcott's account offers no evidence of questioning the status quo, no incredulity toward the metanarrative that drove Ed Bell's profession. Today, Dorothy, and most administrators, both women and men, do not have the luxury of perpetuating an unexamined status quo. Too many others are mounting critiques, asking important questions, and confronting the privilege that often accrues to administration. Faced with this paradigm shift, the unease that characterizes education today, administrators and the professors who teach them must respond.

Elkind (1997) describes what it means to shift from modern to postmodern life. First, we cross the border from the nuclear family to more permeable family arrangements. Second, difference supplants progress. Third, particularity rather than universality describes how we think about things. Finally, regularity gives way to irregularity. These shifts mirror not only the differences that we identify between Ed Bell and Dorothy James but also the crossing from the hegemony of the old scientific management era (Reyes, Wagstaff, & Fusarelli, 1999) to postmodern perspectives. We are entering into a confusing polyphony that results when there is an effort to include everyone's voice in the reconstruction of education. Simply put, what worked for Ed Bell will not work for Dorothy James. We need to compose a new narrative that can describe and problematize, not presume to explain, what occurs in schools.

From Hegemony to Polyphony

In the crossing from hegemony to polyphony, it seems to me, we are beginning to recognize the mechanisms that perpetuate hegemony, but we are a far cry from understanding how polyphony might ultimately sound and appear in schools. In Dorothy's story, and in Ed Bell's as well, three constructs emerged that help explain how educational administrators maintain hegemony. They are "cooling the mark out" (Clark, 1960; Goffman, 1952; Parker, 1995), cultural compression (Spindler, 1959), and dysfunctional professional deference.

"Cooling the mark out" was re-introduced by Clark (1960) following Goffman (1952) to describe how an individual becomes a confederate of the con man. The confederate's job is to befriend the mark in order to avoid having the whistle blown on the con game. The principal acts as a confederate of the educational organization, handling those who would otherwise complain about the inevitability of their failure within the constraints imposed by the system. Anger and disappointment are mitigated by the skill of the "instructional leader," often through the provision of support, more often through consolation. Students and teachers are made to feel that they, not the system, are responsible for failure. "Blaming the victim" foils any recognition that it just might be the system that failed, not the individuals within it. We need only read the literature on high-stakes testing and speak to principals in order to understand how they are rewarded for stabilizing the school after the unreasonable demands of testing are foisted upon students and teachers. I certainly did it.

Dorothy did it as well. Given her reputation for putting on "big productions," the superintendent told her to organize a district-wide fete to celebrate an insignificant increase in scores on the statewide achievement test. Reluctantly, Dorothy pulled the staff together and, capitalizing upon the connectedness she had spent the last 2 years cultivating, was able to pull off a respectable after-school meeting. The superintendent literally performed somersaults on the stage which were greeted by incredulity and uncomfortable applause. Such a "show" indicates the level to which administrators will go to mask the damage done in the name of testing. It also hides the general lack of courage among educators to resist, something Greene (1988) suggests is a prerequisite to real freedom.

Sustaining hegemony is the role of principals in a school culture dominated by scientific management. Over the course of the ethnography, Wolcott never reported that Ed reflected on or even asked the postmodern questions, "Why?" and "Who says?" of his own practice. Neither did his staff. Everything was handled; nothing was changed. This is hegemony. Dorothy was never overtly insubordinate, but did get angry about being marginalized. She raised her voice about arcane rules. So did her teachers. She cultivated openness and encouraged thoughtful discussion of educational and organizational issues. The difference was that she felt not only the frustration of recognizing the problems but also the frustration of not being able to do anything about them. Her role was reduced to "cooling the marks out." She did it very well. So did I. How could we sacrifice our professional integrity?

Wolcott used cultural compression (Spindler, 1959) to describe socialization into teaching. I also found Wolcott's analysis useful for examining Dorothy's socialization into administration.

> During the compression process, the boundaries of acceptable behavior for a new teacher [read administrator] become narrower and narrower, starting at the moment he or she receives an initial student teaching assignment. The process continues, and the boundaries tighten, through the progression of taking more and more responsibility for managing the classroom of a supervising (or "master") teacher. Finally, the tyro-teacher is assigned a class of his own. This is a period of teacher's development, to follow Spindler's conceptualization, "when the norms of his group and society bear in upon him with the greatest intensity." ([Spindler] 1959, p. 39) (Wolcott, p. 228)

Cultural compression explains why so many administrators appreciate the importance of being a "team player," as well as dangers of nonconformity. At the Ad team meetings I attended, the superintendent often chastised Dorothy's ideas. He tolerated her colleagues' raised eyebrows, loud sighs, and blatant guffaws when she would describe her plans. This made it safe for them to make fun of Dorothy. "De plan, de plan!" one administrator joked as he mimicked a character from an old TV show. Everyone laughed, even Dorothy, even me. It was not really funny. Eventually, after about 9 months, Dorothy simply quit talking in Ad team meetings unless specifically asked to comment.

Gender added another dimension to the notion of compression. Dorothy was exquisitely sensitive to the thinly veiled sexual innuendo and control (Mills, 1990) used by the superintendent. He would take her hand, touch her shoulder, and hug her. He would make statements like, "I had to come down and see you, Dorothy," "You give me energy," or "Luv ya, doll!" This became such an integral part of Dorothy's compression that we would begin our weekly interviews with an update on the latest suggestive act or comment. Over time, I saw a shift in Dorothy's demeanor. When the superintendent would approach her unexpectedly, she would move into the main office, explain what was on her calendar, pick up the pace, and, on occasion, use my presence as a foil to avoid meeting with him.

I wondered how Dorothy could operate in a role that required her to "cool out" teachers, to facilitate compression, and to tolerate it herself? I wondered why I did it when I was an administrator? It seemed immoral somehow. How can you empower teachers knowing that you will override their pedagogical concerns and questions with economic or structural answers? Why do they defer their professional authority when they know best? Wolcott offered one explanation when he analyzed the evaluation process. Wolcott (1973) described the teachers who were "immune from the negative implications of the socialization process" (p. 272). This means a negative evaluation. They were immune because they were leaving due to pregnancy; because "their careers as teachers were secondary to the careers of their husbands"; or because of their personalities and/or their superb willingness or ability to adapt to the demands of the situation" (p. 272).

In other words, immunity emerged when a teacher had nothing to lose or was able and willing to adapt to demands. Both Ed Bell and Wolcott seemed to think this was a good thing. I think it is dysfunctional professional deference. It is a necessary condition for maintaining a hierarchical system where administrators know less than the teachers about teaching and learning in a specific context. It is an artifact of a system that requires professional deference to minimize important pedagogical issues and maximize control. Those who would challenge the system either have "nothing to lose" or are marginalized as dysfunctional misfits. Let me suggest that it is the other way around. An organization that suppresses expert professional knowledge and privileges administrative control is itself dysfunctional.

Ethic of Polyphony

This brings us to what Sharon, Dorothy, and I call the ethic of polyphony. In homophonic music, one voice, the melody, dominates. Subordinate voices harmonize with and support the melody. In polyphony, however, we hear many equal voices, multiple melodies weaving in and out, creating both consonance and dissonance. The ethic of polyphony requires a shift away from an educational system that demands that individuals adapt, conform, and defer.

Instead, the educational system must necessarily adapt to meet the needs of its members. Administrators cannot socialize organizational members to maintain privilege, to "cool the marks out," and to defer uncritically to authority. Administrators and teachers must find the courage to treat others as ends, challenge others to care, to be just, to think critically, and to include everyone's voice in the discourse on education (Anderson, 2001; Fazzaro, Walter, & McKerrow, 1994).

Noddings' (1984, 1992) work on caring is useful in sorting through the requirements of what it might mean to promote an ethic of polyphony. Engaging all voices assumes that there is a caring relation; one built upon both a caring response and a reciprocal receptivity of that response. This requires a lot of the carer. It suggests the displacement of motivation for anything but caring and the total engrossment of the carer in the relation (Noddings, 1984). This takes a courage that is seldom found in organizations. It is not because individuals within organizations do not care. Rather, the efforts to stabilize the organization against public demands make the ability to care, quite literally, impossible. Caring, by default, loses out to stabilizing the organization (Lyotard, 1979).

Establishing an ethic of polyphony, like ethics of justice, care, and critique (Starratt, 1991), requires far more than recognition of the problem, dissatisfaction with the status quo, or a willingness to critique the organizational structure. Indeed, our colleagues have eschewed the practice of educational administration *sans* some focus on ethical dimensions for quite some time now (Beck & Murphy, 1994; Capper, 1993; Hodgkinson, 1991; MacIntyre,1981; McKerrow, 1997; Raywid, 1986). Border crossings require the courage to change personally (Purpel, 1989). Re-framing the theoretical discourse and the literature is the easy part. (Re)visiting the principal's office compels us to shut the door on the familiar archetype (Sarason, 1996). We must cross the threshold knowing that: we have a moral imperative to care; our practice and research in must reflect lived realities and truths; we are responsible for cultivating the struggle against hegemony; and we must remember that personal courage, transformative action, and social justice are possible.

REFERENCES

Anderson, G. L. (2001). *Promoting educational equity in a period of growing social inequity: The silent contradiction of Texas reform discourse.* Paper presented at the annual meeting of the American Educational Research Association, Seattle, WA.

Bates, R. (1981). *Educational administration, the technologisation of reason, and the management of knowledge: Toward a critical theory.* Paper presented at the meeting of the American Educational Research Association, Los Angeles.

Beck, L. G., & Murphy, J. (1994). *Ethics in educational leadership programs: An expanding role.* Thousand Oaks, CA: Corwin Press.

Bellah, R., Madsen, R., Sullivan, W., Swidler, A., & Tipton, S. (1985). *Habits of the heart: Individualism and commitment in American life.* New York: Harper & Row.

Blount, J. (1998). *Destined to rule the schools; Women and the superintendency, 1873–1995.* New York: State University of New York Press.

Buber, M. (1958). *I and thou.* (2nd ed.) (R. Smith, Trans.). New York: Schribner's Sons.

Callahan, R. E. (1962). *Education and the cult of efficiency.* Chicago: University of Chicago Press.

Capper, C. (1993). Educational administration in a pluralistic society: A multi-paradigm approach. In C. Capper (Ed.), *Educational administration in a pluralistic society* (pp. 7–36). Albany: State University of New York Press.

Clark, B. R. (1960, May). The "Cooling-Out" function in higher education. *The American Journal of Sociology, 65,* 569–576.

Cusick, P. A. (1992). *The educational system: Its nature and logic.* New York: McGraw-Hill.

Donmoyer, R. (1995). *The very idea of a knowledge base.* Paper presented at the annual meeting of the American Educational Research Association, San Francisco.

Dunlap, D., & Schmuck, P. (1995). *Women leading in education.* Albany: State University of New York Press.

Eisner, E. (1998). *The enlightened eye: Qualitative inquiry and the enhancement of educational practice.* Upper Saddle River, NJ: Merrill.

Elkind, D. (1997). Schooling and the family in the postmodern society. In A. Hargreaves (Ed.), *Rethinking educational change with heart and mind* (pp. 20–34). Arlington, VA: Association for Supervision and Curriculum Development.

Fazzaro, C. J., Walter, J. E., & McKerrow, K. K. (1994). Education administration in a postmodern society: Implications for moral practice. In S. Maxcy (Ed.), *Postmodern school leadership* (pp. 85–95). Westport, CT: Praeger.

Foster, W. (1986). *Paradigms and promises: New approaches to educational administration.* Buffalo, NY: Prometheus Books.

Foster, W. (1998). Editor's forward. *Educational Administration Quarterly, 34*(3), 294–297.

Foucault, M. (1977). *Discipline and punish: The birth of the prison* (2nd ed.). New York: Vintage.

Foucault, M. (1980). *Power and knowledge: Selected interviews and other writings, 1971–1977* (C. Gordon, Ed.). New York: Pantheon.

Goffman, R. (1952). On cooling the mark out: Some aspects of adaptation to failure. *Psychiatry, 15,* 451–463.

Greene, M. (1988). *The dialectic of freedom.* New York: Teachers College Press.

Greenfield, T. B. (1975). Theory about organization: A new perspective and its implications for schools. In M. G. Hughes (Ed.), *Administering education: International challenge* (pp. 71–99), London: Athlone.

Gulick, L., & Urwick, L. (1937). *Papers on the science of administration.* New York: Columbia University Press.

Hearn, J., Sheppard, D. L., Tancred-Sheriff, P., & Burrell, G. (1989). *The sexuality of the organization.* Newbury Park, CA: Sage.

Hodgkinson, C. (1991). *Educational leadership: The moral art.* Albany: State University of New York Press.

hooks, b. (1990). *Yearning: Race, gender, and cultural politics.* Boston: South End Press.

Hoy, W. K., & Miskel C. G. (2001). *Educational administration: Theory, research, and practice.* (6th ed.). New York: McGraw-Hill.

Kuhn, T. S. (1962). *The structure of scientific revolutions.* Chicago: University of Chicago Press.

Laible, J. C. (2000). A loving epistemology: What I hold critical in my life, faith, and profession. *Qualitative Studies in Education, 13*(6), 683–692.

Lee, S. (2000). Root out of a dry ground: Resolving the researcher/researched dilemma. In J. Zeni (Ed.), *Ethical issues in practitioner research.* New York: Teachers College Press.

Lyotard, J. F. (1979). *The postmodern condition: A report on knowledge.* Minneapolis, MN: The University of Minnesota Press.

MacIntyre, A. (1981). *After virtue: A study in moral theory.* Notre Dame, IN: University of Notre Dame Press.

Maienza, J. G. (1986) The superintendency: Characteristics of access for men and women. *Educational Administration Quarterly, 22*(4), 59–79.

Marshall, C. (1992). *The assistant principal; Leadership choices and challenges.* Newbury Park, CA: Corwin Press.

McKerrrow, K. K. (1997). Ethical administration: An oxymoron? *The Journal of School Leadership. 7*(2), 210–225.

Mills, A. (1990). Gender, sexuality, and organization theory. In J. Hearn, D. Sheppard, P. Tancred-Sheriff, & G. Burell (Eds.), *The sexuality of organization* (pp. 29–44). Newbury Park, CA: Sage.

Murphy, J. (1992). *The landscape of leadership preparation: Reframing the education of school administrators.* Newbury Park, CA: Corwin Press.

Noddings, N. (1984). *Caring: A feminine approach to ethics and moral education.* Berkeley: University of California Press.

Noddings, N. (1992). *The challenge to care in schools: An alternative approach to education.* New York: Teachers College Press.

Parker, W. C. (1995). The urban curriculum and the allocating function of schools. In E. Stevens & G. Woods (Eds.), *Justice, ideology, and education* (pp. 178–182). New York: McGraw-Hill.

Phenix, P. (1964). *Realms of meaning.* New York: McGraw-Hill.

Purpel, D. E. (1989). *The moral and spiritual crisis in education: A curriculum for justice and compassion in education.* Boston, MA: Bergin and Garvey.

Raywid, M. A. (1986). Some moral dimensions of administrative theory and practice. *Issues in Education, 4*(2), 151–166.

Reyes, P., Wagstaff, L. H., & Fusarelli, L. D. (1999). Delta forces: The changing fabric of American society and education. In J. Murphy & K. S. Lewis (Eds.), *Handbook of research on educational administration* (2nd ed., pp. 183–201). San Francisco: Jossey-Bass.

Sarason, S. B. (1996). *Revisiting "the culture of the school and the problem of change."* New York: Teachers College Press.

Schmuck, P., Charters, W., Jr., & Carlson, R. (Eds.). (1981). *Educational policy and management: Sex differentials.* New York: Academic Press.

Shakeshaft, C. (1989). *Women in educational administration.* Newbury Park, CA: Sage.

Shakeshaft, C. (1998). Wild patience and bad fit: Assessing the impact of affirmative action on women in school administration. *Educational Researcher, 27*(9), 10–12.

Smith, L., & Geoffrey, W. (1968). *The complexities of an urban classroom: An analysis toward a general theory of teaching.* New York: Holt, Rinehart and Winston.

Spindler, G. D. (1959). *The transmission of American culture.* Cambridge, MA: Harvard University Press.

Starratt, R. J. (1991). Building an ethical school: A theory for practice in educational administration. *Educational Administration Quarterly, 27*(2), 185–202.

Wolcott, H. (1973). *The man in the principal's office: An ethnography.* New York: Holt, Rinehart and Winston.

Yeakey, C. C., Johnston, G. S., & Adkinson, J. A. (1986). In pursuit of equity: A review of research on minorities and women in educational administration. *Educational Administration Quarterly, 22*(3), 110–149.

Young, M. (2000). Considering (irreconcilable?) contradictions in cross-group feminist research. *Qualitative studies in Education, 13*(6), 629–660.

Young, M., & Laible, J. (2000). Introduction. *Qualitative studies in Education, 13*(6), 585–589.

Changing Times, Changing Relationships: An Exploration of Current Trends Influencing the Relationship between Superintendents and Boards of Education

Lance D. Fusarelli and George J. Petersen

Historically in the United States, states have delegated much of their authority over educational policy to local school districts. However, reform and restructuring efforts, as well as a weakening economy, have placed enormous political and financial pressure on schools to do more with less, yet continue to demonstrate effective leadership at the district level. Research literature focused on district leadership indicates that the relationship between the superintendent and board of education has a significant impact on the quality of a district's educational program.

In this chapter we explore the implications of three distinct trends on the relationship between superintendents and boards of education: (1) changing demographics; (2) changes brought about by school reform; and (3) changes in superintendents themselves. The heart of this chapter is focused on the impact of these trends on superintendent-board relationships in the future. After examining current research on superintendent-board relations, we examine recent demographic trends and speculate whether changing demographics would alter, in any substantive way, relations between superintendents and boards of education. In a similar vein, how do reforms such as the development of more comprehensive accountability systems (often tied to performance or merit pay for administrators) and changes in school governance models (such as the Chicago model) impact the relationship between superintendents and their school boards? Finally, how do changes in superintendents themselves—in their training and work experiences—affect their relations with school boards? Essentially, we ask whether any of these changes will influence or alter relations between superintendents and school boards and, if so, in what ways? We conclude by investigating three areas meant to stimulate further discussion and research into the relationships between superintendents and boards of education.

Lance D. Fusarelli, Fordham University
George J. Petersen, University of Missouri, Columbia

THE SCHOOL BOARD/SUPERINTENDENT RELATIONSHIP

A superintendent and a board can't sing two different tunes and then expect the public to hum along. Boards of education and superintendents often find themselves targets of criticism in both the professional literature and popular press. Recent reforms and heightened expectations of accountability have created a permanent state of turbulence and pressure. According to Usdan, McCloud, Podmostko, and Cuban (2001),

> District leaders are in an arena that is perpetually besieged by a *potpourri* of often conflicting forces: state laws and regulations, federal mandates, decentralized school management, demands for greater accountability, changing demographics, the school choice movement, competing community needs, limited resources, partisan politics, legal challenges, shortages of qualified teachers and principals and a general lack of respect for the education profession. (p. 26)

These issues, coupled with a growing disenchantment of bureaucratic forms of school management, have eroded the district leader's ability to govern educational institutions effectively (Carter & Cunningham, 1997; Danzberger, Kirst, & Usdan, 1992; Grogan, 1996; Norton, Webb, Dlugosh, & Sybouts, 1996).

Research has clearly articulated that as district leaders attempt to manage these complex changes and pressures, their success hinges on the relationship they have established with their board president (Allison, Allison, & McHenry, 1995; Campbell & Greene, 1994; Lunenburg & Ornstein, 1996; Petersen & Short, 2001) and with their board of education (Berg, 1996; Carter & Cunningham, 1997; Danzberger, 1993; Feuerstein & Opfer, 1998; Hoyle, English, & Steffy, 1998; Kowalski, 1999; McCurdy, 1992; Norton, Webb, Dlugosh, & Sybouts, 1996; Tallerico, 1989). Extant literature in this area has consistently asserted that a poor relationship between the superintendent and the board of education poses a threat to the district's ability to meet its goals. A precarious relationship deters school improvement (Danzberger, Kirst, & Usdan, 1992), affects the quality of educational programs (Boyd, 1976; Nygren, 1992), increases conflict over district instructional goals and objectives (Morgan & Petersen, 2002; Petersen, 1999), weakens district stability and morale (Renchler, 1992), negatively influences the superintendent's credibility and trustworthiness with board members (Petersen & Short, 2001), impedes critical reform efforts, such as district restructuring (Konnert & Augenstein, 1995) and collaborative visioning and long-range planning (Kowalski, 1999), as well as eventually resulting in an increase in the "revolving door syndrome" of district superintendents (Carter & Cunningham, 1997; Renchler, 1992).

While the relationship of the board and superintendent is pivotal in addressing reform and restructuring efforts, a critical component in the superintendent's success is intricately tied to his or her ability to influence critical policy decisions made by the board of education (Blumberg, 1985; Crowson, 1987; Zeigler, Jennings, & Peak, 1974). Recent research points to the fact that superintendents have considerably more control and influence in the establishment of the board agenda than previously thought (Petersen & Short, 2001). However, formal authority for policy articulation and decision making still reside with the board. Therefore, superintendents must, in most instances, attempt to sway the vote of each individual board member (Blumberg, 1985).

School Board Decision Making

Historically, aspiring politicians begin building patronage and payback networks essential to seeking higher office (Bullard & Taylor, 1993), using boards of education as their entry into the political arena. With their ability to create district policy, hire and fire administrators, in this case the superintendent, approve the budget, tenure teachers, and negotiate teachers' contracts, the power of the school board to move the district forward or force it into bureaucratic gridlock is tremendous. Studies that have previously concentrated on issues of school governance and reform have continually emphasized the importance of the school board in the educational process of the district (Bullard & Taylor, 1993; Danzberger, Kirst, & Usdan, 1992; Fullan, 1991; Wirt & Kirst, 1989). While school boards have power, they are usually unpaid, part-time, and untrained and, except for the information presented to them by the superintendent or perhaps what they pick up informally, they know little of the underlying issues for the scores of complex decisions requiring their approval at each board meeting (Cuban, 1976). Therefore, school boards often rely on the professional judgment of the superintendent in many educational matters.

Research has repeatedly articulated that local boards of education are dependent upon an array of external social, economic, and political influences and their decisions are often predicated upon consideration of a host of factors over which they have little or no control (Boyd, 1976; McCarty & Ramsey, 1971; Usdan, 1975). "Although school boards are representative bodies, they are expected to defer to the expertise of the superintendent and choose the 'best' educational policies regardless of community preferences" (Greene, 1992, p. 220). Numerous studies have classified board orientations as either hierarchical or bargaining (Tucker & Zeigler, 1980), and as political or professional (Greene, 1992), in examining their influence on decision making and school district governance. Findings from these, as well as other investigations examining board behavior (Hentges, 1986; McCarty & Ramsey, 1971; Nowakowski & First, 1989; Scribner & Englert, 1977; Zeigler, Jennings, & Peak, 1974) have chronicled the oftentimes conflicting roles, responsibilities, and expectations of boards and their willingness or hesitancy to defer to the expertise of the superintendent in policy decisions. This dynamic continues to generate areas of tension in the margin of control and governance of the school district. Zeigler (1975) argues that because of the conflicting expectations, "school boards behave like typical schizophrenics. On the one hand, they willingly (indeed eagerly) give power away to the experts. . . . On the other hand, they espouse an ideology of lay control" (p. 8). While this may continue to be a tenuous situation in the governance of school districts, research has articulated that the role of school boards in district governance depends primarily on their acceptance of the superintendent's claims to expertise in specific issue areas and secondarily on board orientation (Greene, 1992).

These multiple and frequently competing perspectives and expectations reflect a bewildering array of administrative, legislative, and community priorities that play a major role in the development of local policies (Björk, 2001) and subsequently impact the type and scope of issues faced by a district. Yet, even with the ambiguity of numerous competing pressures, superintendents and board presidents are ostensibly responsible for the content and format of the board agenda and policy decisions. Research and practice support the notion that the superintendent and the board president devote considerable time and thought in working together in developing and setting the agenda for formal board meetings and are recognized as key actors in the decision-making process (Allison, Allison, & McHenry, 1995; Deem, Brehone, & Heath, 1995; Petersen & Short, 2001).

Traditionally the superintendent's role has been characterized as implementer of policies set by the board of education (Konnert & Augenstein, 1995). Typical duties include maintaining the school budget, managing school personnel, and serving as public relations director. Yet, current challenges faced by school administrators, coupled with increasing demands for greater accountability and improved student academic achievement, have added to the already complex nature of school leadership. As a result, the superintendent's role can no longer focus solely on public relations and finance; it must be responsive to innumerable demands including the management of conflicting expectations and multiple agendas (Carter & Cunningham, 1997). As Wirt and Kirst (1997) observe, "Change generates demands in policy-making arenas to which superintendents respond with differing roles and styles of conflict management" (p. 159). We next turn to these change forces and examine their potential impact on relations between superintendents and school boards.

Demographic Changes

"The landscape of public education is rapidly changing" (Tillman, 2001, p. 10). Schools in the United States are becoming increasingly diverse, due in large measure to a massive influx of Latino students into the school system (Fusarelli, 2000). Since 1980, the Latino population "has increased at a rate five times that of non-Hispanic whites, African Americans, and Asians combined" (Howe, 1994, p. 42). Since 1980, the percentage of Anglo students in public schools has steadily declined relative to "minority" youth (Reyes, Wagstaff, & Fusarelli, 1999). Many districts "are still struggling with the challenges of serving these linguistically and culturally different students" (Gonzalez, Huerta-Macias, & Tinajero, 1998, p. xv). As districts across the country become more diverse, they are also becoming less wealthy. Nearly one in four children lives in poverty and the gap between rich and poor is widening.

Complicating these demographic changes are three other trends: one short term and the other two long term. First, after a decade of prosperity, the economy is slipping into a recession. Second, as the nation becomes increasingly non-white, it is also graying, particularly the Anglo majority. As a result, there is increasing pressure to allocate scarce resources toward the care of the elderly (who, among other things, vote in record numbers), leaving fewer dollars available for education. Third, the percentage of households with children is decreasing (20–25 percent nationwide, and as low as 15 percent in some cities) (The Twentieth Century Fund, 1992). This trend does not bode well for school districts heavily dependent on local property tax revenue.

While politics have always been part and parcel of policymaking in education, there are indications that the demographic changes discussed above are contributing to a more divisive, politicized environment than has existed for at least a decade (for example, the 1990s was a decade of relative peace and prosperity). There is a "growing cultural divide among the citizenry" in the United States (Keedy & Björk, 2002). Public education is under attack from both the Left and the Right, and proposals (some radical, some not) covering everything from governance to choice have been adopted in states and locales throughout the country (discussed below; see also Cibulka, 1999). Survey data from the most recent AASA study of the American superintendency revealed that more than 57 percent of superintendents reported the existence of community interest groups actively engaged in debates over property taxes, curriculum issues, and school/community values (Glass, Björk, & Brunner, 2000). Across the nation, "school boards—the traditional linchpin of American educational governance—are facing a serious crisis of legitimacy and relevance" (The Twentieth Century Fund, 1992, p. 1).

School Reform: Reframing Governance and Administration

Throughout the United States, school districts are "constantly undergoing change, stress, and transition, as communities elect new school board members, new demands are made on schools, and key leaders come and go" (Natkin et al., 2001, p. 1). Within the past decade, state regulation and intervention in schools has increased (a growing number of state laws permit state takeover of school districts) and accountability statutes have been strengthened, becoming more comprehensive and sophisticated. The external threat to public education has increased, with the emergence of charter schools, vouchers, tuition tax credits, contracting out educational services to private contractors, and a re-invigorated home-schooling movement. State and federal courts have remained active in education policymaking, and a deepening economic recession has forced districts to do more with less. These forces have had a significant effect on education, including changing the relationship between superintendents and boards of education.

Of particular importance has been an overriding emphasis on educational accountability, often to the exclusion of other purposes of education (Fusarelli, 1999). Accountability reforms offering incentives and rewards to schools and, most controversially, to school personnel (teachers, administrators, and superintendents) have been implemented in several states (Cibulka, 1989). Performance bonuses are now a regular component of superintendent's contracts—some of which are quite substantial.

The Changing Face of the Superintendency

Within the last decade, in an attempt to improve often dismal school system performance, several states passed laws changing their certification requirements for superintendents, effectively permitting anyone—however trained—to become superintendent of a school district. The U.S. Department of Education, the Ford Foundation, the Carnegie Corporation, state governors, and legislators have been discussing and critiquing the training and preparation of school leaders (Olson, 2000). Several states, including Michigan, Tennessee, and Illinois, have either partially or totally eliminated requirements for superintendent preparation. For example, in Tennessee, superintendents need only citizenship and a college degree in any field of study (Kowalski & Glass, 2002). Many policymakers believe that training in business, politics, or the military is sufficient preparation to lead school districts (Maher, 1988; Murphy, 1992).

Although this movement remains small (fewer than two dozen school boards have chosen nontraditional superintendents to lead their districts), these nontraditional leaders are becoming increasingly common in large, urban school systems. Until recently, three of the largest districts in the country—New York City, Los Angeles, and Chicago—with over three million students combined, were being run by superintendents with no significant educational background, no advanced training in an educational administration preparation program, and no certification as a school administrator. Harold Levy in New York was a senior vice president of Citicorp; Ray Romer (Los Angeles) was former governor of Colorado; Paul Vallas (Chicago—recently departed) had extensive experience in public administration and business. This trend of hiring nontraditional superintendents to run school districts reflects the belief that advanced training in educational leadership or administration is unnecessary to lead and manage a school district effectively, although these nontraditional leaders may have extensive training in military or corporate leadership.

INTERESTING QUESTIONS: AREAS FOR FURTHER RESEARCH
How might these trends affect board-superintendent relationships in the coming decade? We pose three areas that we believe merit further exploration.

Non-Educators as Superintendents and the Board of Education
What happens when an individual unfamiliar with the education culture and workings of school boards is chosen to lead a school district? What happens when a board begins to contest policies promoted by the nontraditional superintendent? Or when the board interferes in personnel decisions made by the superintendent? Veteran school administrators are used to such occurrences, having experienced them (and engaged in other board conflicts) throughout their careers. But a nontraditional superintendent may come from a radically different culture, whether it be the military, business, even the public sector—how will the inevitable cultural clash affect relations between such a superintendent and the school board?

If understanding role differences is a major factor contributing to successful superintendent-board relationships, then how easily will nontraditional superintendents unfamiliar with school processes and culture "fit" or meld into the culture of school boards? For example, some board members believe themselves far superior to "mere educators" such as the superintendent (Carter & Cunningham, 1997).

What happens when the superintendent isn't an educator? Conversely, some boards have a history of "passive acquiescence" (Tallerico, 1989, p. 218) whereby board members seldom question the professional expertise of the superintendent. This paradigm is reinforced by superintendents themselves, who since the 1940s have portrayed themselves as professional educators (Glass, Björk, & Brunner, 2000).

Assuming that boards value (to some degree) professional school experience, will they continue to be as acquiescent when the district is under the stewardship of a superintendent lacking that expertise? Or would they be more likely to intervene in district issues such as curriculum and instruction? For example, it is not inconceivable that a school board would hire a nontraditional superintendent for his or her business and management expertise (such as successfully running a multimillion dollar corporation), yet be more likely to intercede in instructional affairs than if the superintendent had extensive school experience (in the classroom and in school administration). These avenues of inquiry are unexplored in the scholarly literature, in part because of the newness and relatively small number of nontraditional superintendents. However, as noted above, the number and visibility of such superintendents is a growing trend in educational leadership and governance, with possibly significant implications for board-superintendent relationships.

Demographic Changes, Reform Initiatives, and the Board-Superintendent Relationship

Although open to dispute among scholars, patterns of board-superintendent interactions follow fairly well established patterns of behavior along a continuum from amicable support to outright hostility. Although the media often portray boards and superintendents as at odds with one another, AASA's latest 10-year study revealed that 69 percent of superintendents reported their evaluations from school boards to be "excellent," and 22 percent were rated "good" (Glass, Björk, & Brunner, 2000). Only 14 percent of superintendents said they left "because of conflict with their school boards" (Glass, Björk, & Brunner, 2000, p. v).

McCarty and Ramsey (1971) classified boards as either dominated, factional, status congruent, or sanctioning, and the role of the superintendent as functionary, political strategist, professional advisor, or decision maker. Tallerico (1989) identified interactions between superintendents and school boards along "a continuum ranging from (a) *passive acquiescence* to (b) *proactive supportiveness* to (c) *restive vigilance*" (p. 218). Wirt and Kirst (1997) conclude that, "Different styles are all versions of the classic 'fight-flight' or 'exit-voice-apathy' characterization of how individuals act when confronted by threatening situations" (p. 166). Regardless of the terminology employed, it would seem as though the dimensions of superintendent-board relations have been fairly well mapped.

Perhaps the study of board-superintendent relations is an intellectual dead end, having been studied and analyzed to the point where there is nothing new to discover and learn. For example, the most recent *Handbook of Research on Educational Administration* contains scant mention of superintendents or school boards (Murphy & Louis, 1999), rather incredible given their responsibility for making and implementing local school policy. Recent studies of board-superintendents relations (See Glass, Björk, & Brunner, 2000; Keedy & Björk, 2002) use McCarty and Ramsey's (1971) model of community power structures, board characteristics, and role of superintendents—a typology that is three decades old. However, recent research using social influence theory explores how district superintendents and school board presidents interact with each other in attending to their respective responsibilities in leading the school organization, specifically looking at their relationship and its influence on issues of agenda construction and board decision making (Petersen & Short, 2001; Petersen & Short, in press).

Additional theoretical and empirical research is needed to examine school board members' and superintendents' views of the current board/superintendent governance model and whether it is perceived as facilitating or impeding the leadership of the district and its ability to respond to the needs of children. Specifically, researchers need to more thoroughly investigate the attitudes and opinions as well as the covariance between boards of education, superintendents, their views of the current board governance model, and its influence on the district's responsiveness to student learning and accountability. Have the pressures and changes discussed in this chapter produced changes in the leadership patterns of districts? Perhaps it has made for more directive, or conversely, more diffuse leadership.

Recently, in New York City, a member of 1 of the city's 32 community school districts was overheard remarking that with the steady erosion of the power of school boards, he did not think they would exist in 5 years—with their governance functions being usurped by the mayor and state government. While we believe the board member's prediction is premature and overly pessimistic, it is true that school boards have been steadily losing power and authority over school governance for decades (Wirt & Kirst, 1997). This raises an interesting question. If the power of school boards has been curtailed in significant, and important ways, then how do these changes impact the relations between superintendents and school boards? If school boards are steadily losing power, are superintendents gaining power and authority over educational leadership and governance?[1]

Changes in the Board-Superintendent Governance Model

In the past decade, school boards and superintendents have come under attack. School boards, in particular, with their preoccupation with patronage and penchant for micromanagement, have been vilified for their ineffectiveness in a series of scathing national reports; see, for example, Danzberger, Kirst, & Usdan (1992) and The Twentieth Century Fund (1992). Included among the host of recommendations for improvement were the establishment of local education policy boards, revision of school board election procedures, improved school board development, contracting out, improved board-superintendent relationships, or abolishing school boards altogether (allowing states to directly run schools).

It is unrealistic to believe that school boards will be abolished any time in the next several decades. No matter how ineffective they appear (and, as many point out, problems with the educational system are not all the school board's fault), locally elected school boards occupy a vital place in American democracy (Wirt & Kirst, 1997). Indeed, if all our representative bodies were threatened with dissolution based on poor performance, our democracy itself might not survive. School boards continue to enjoy widespread popular support, at least when suggestions to abolish the institution are made. School boards "provide local control and an accessible level of government. In a country committed to representative democracy, they provide citizen access that remote state and federal capitals cannot duplicate" (The Twentieth Century Fund, 1992, pp. 6–7).

Another study sharply critical of school boards agreed, stating that boards "enjoyed a great deal of grass-roots support and were viewed as an important mechanism for representative government" because they "dealt with two of the most important elements in citizen's lives: their children and tax dollars" (Danzberger, Kirst, & Usdan, 1992, p. 51). In addition, given the mixed success of state takeovers of failing school districts, there is no concrete evidence that state departments of education could do a better job running local school districts than existing school boards. Thus, despite its shortcomings, it is unlikely that the school board-superintendent governance model will be abolished in the near future. What, then, of the future of local school governance? In an era of significant pressure and change, what will be the roles and responsibilities of school boards and superintendents of the future?

SUMMARY

We have raised three interesting questions that we believe should frame research on board-superintendent relationships in the coming decade. All three avenues of inquiry are important and relevant to practitioners and scholars alike. We are disturbed by the lack of recent theoretical research on school boards and superintendents; the "golden age" of theory building in this area seems to have occurred in the late 1960s and early–mid-1970s. Many of our theoretical constructs are decades old. Recent changes in schools and society necessitate a re-examination of our conceptualizations of school boards, superintendents, and relationships therein. Thus, we conclude with a call for more research in this important area, with particular emphasis on theory building, hypothesis generation, and testing. The world of educational administration is changing; so too must our theories, concepts, and understanding of that world.

NOTE

1. Disagreement exists among scholars on this point. For example, Wirt and Kirst (1997) assert that school boards, superintendents, and central office administrators have been losing power and authority over decision making since 1950 (for more than five decades). However, Glass, Björk, and Brunner (2000) view local policymaking as a pendulum of power swinging back and forth between the superintendent and school board.

REFERENCES

Allison, D. J., Allison, P. A., & McHenry, H. A. (1995). Chiefs and chairs: Working relationships between effective CEOs and board of education chairpersons. In Kenneth Leithwood (Ed.), *Effective school district leadership: Transforming politics into education* (pp. 33–50). Albany: State University of New York Press.

Berg, J. H. (1996). Context and perception: Implications for leadership. *Journal of School Leadership, 6*, 75–98.

Björk, L. G. (2001). *Leadership and the politics of superintendent board relations.* Paper presented at the annual meeting of the American Educational Research Association, Seattle, WA.

Blumberg, A. (1985). A superintendent must read the board's invisible job description. *American School Board Journal, 172*(9), 44–45.

Boyd, W. L. (1976). The public, the professionals, and educational policy: Who governs? *Teachers College Record, 77*(4), 539–578.

Bullard, P., & Taylor, B. O. (1993). *Making school reform happen.* Boston: Allyn and Bacon.

Campbell, D. W., & Greene, D. (1994). Defining the leadership role of school boards in the 21st century. *Phi Delta Kappan, 75*(5), 391–395.

Carter, G. R., & Cunningham, W. G. (1997). *The American school superintendent: Leading in an age of pressure.* San Francisco: Jossey-Bass.

Cibulka, J. G. (1989). State performance incentives for restructuring. Can they work? *Education and Urban Society, 21*(4), 417–435.

Cibulka, J. G. (1999). Ideological lenses for interpreting political and economic changes affecting schooling. In J. Murphy & K. S. Louis (Eds.), *Handbook of research on educational administration* (2nd ed., pp. 163–182). San Francisco: Jossey-Bass.

Crowson, R. (1987). The local school district superintendency: A puzzling administrative role. *Educational Administration Quarterly, 23*(3), 49–69.

Cuban, L. (1976). *Urban school chiefs under fire.* Chicago: University of Chicago Press.

Danzberger, J. P. (1993). Governing the nation's schools: The case for restructuring local school boards. *Phi Delta Kappan, 75*(5), 367–373.

Danzberger, J. P., Kirst, M. W., & Usdan, M. D. (1992). *Governing public schools: New times new requirements.* Washington, DC: The Institute for Educational Leadership.

Deem, R., Brehone, K., & Heath, S. (1995). *Active citizenship and the governing of schools.* Buckingham, UK: Open University Press.

Feuerstein, A., & Opfer, V. D. (1998). School board chairmen and school superintendents: An analysis of perceptions concerning special interest groups and educational governance. *Journal of School Leadership, 8*, 373–398.

Fullan, M. G. (1991). *The new meaning of educational change.* New York: Teachers College Press.

Fusarelli, L. D. (1999). Education is more than numbers: Communitarian leadership of schools for the new millennium. In L. T. Fenwick (Ed.), *School leadership: Expanding horizons of the mind and spirit* (pp. 97–107). Lancaster, PA: Technomic.

Fusarelli, L. D. (2000). Leadership in Latino schools: Challenges for the new millennium. In P. M. Jenlink (Ed.), *Marching into a new millennium: Challenges to educational leadership* (pp. 228–238). Lanham, MD: Scarecrow Press.

Glass, T. E., Björk, L., & Brunner, C. C. (2000). *The 2000 study of the American school superintendency: A look at the superintendent of education in the new millennium.* Arlington, VA: American Association of School Administrators.

Gonzalez, M. L., Huerta-Macias, A., & Tinajero, J. V. (Eds.). (1998). *Educating Latino students: A guide to successful practice.* Lancaster, PA: Technomic.

Greene, K. R. (1992). Models of school board policy-making. *Educational Administration Quarterly, 28*(2), 220–236.

Grogan, M. (1996). *Voices of women aspiring to the superintendency.* Albany: State University of New York Press.

Hentges, J. T. (1986). The politics of superintendent-school board linkages: A study of power, participation, and control. *ERS Spectrum, 4*(3), 23–32.

Howe, C. K. (1994). Improving the achievement of Hispanic students. *Educational Leadership, 51*(8), 42–44.

Hoyle, J. R., English, F. W., & Steffy, B. E. (1998). *Skills for successful 21st century school leaders: Standards for peak performance.* Arlington, VA: American Association of School Administrators.

Keedy, J. L., & Björk, L. G. (2002). Superintendents and local boards and the potential for community polarization: The call for use of political strategist skills. In B. S. Cooper & L. D. Fusarelli (Eds.), *The promises and perils facing today's school superintendent* (pp. 103–127). Lanham, MD: Scarecrow Press.

Konnert, W. M., & Augenstein, J. J. (1995). *The school superintendency: Leading education into the 21st century.* Lancaster, PA: Technomic.

Kowalski, T. J. (1999). *The school superintendent: Theory, practice, and cases.* Upper Saddle River, NJ: Prentice-Hall.

Kowalski, T. J., & Glass, T. E. (2002). Preparing superintendents in the 21st century. In B. S. Cooper & L. D. Fusarelli (Eds.), *The promises and perils facing today's school superintendent* (pp. 41–59). Lanham, MD: Scarecrow Press.

Lunenburg, F. C., & Ornstein, A. C. (1996). *Educational administration: Concepts and practices* (2nd ed.). Belmont, CA: Wadsworth.

Maher, R. (1988). Are graduate schools preparing tomorrow's administrators? *NASSP Bulletin, 72*(508), 30–34.

McCarty, D. J., & Ramsey, C. E. (1971). *The school managers.* Westport, CT: Greenwood.

McCurdy, J. M. (1992). *Building better board-administrator relations.* Arlington, VA: American Association of School Administrators.

Morgan, C., & Petersen, G. J. (2002). The role of the district superintendent in leading academically successful school districts. In B. S. Cooper & L. D. Fusarelli (Eds.), *The promises and perils facing today's school superintendent* (pp. 175–196). Lanham, MD: Scarecrow Press.

Murphy, J. (1992). *The landscape of leadership preparation: Reframing the education of school administrators.* Newbury Park, CA: Corwin Press.

Murphy, J., & Louis, K. S. (Eds.). (1999). *Handbook of research on educational administration* (2nd ed.). San Francisco: Jossey-Bass.

Natkin, G., Cooper, B. S., Fusarelli, L. D., Alborano, J., Padilla, A., & Ghosh, S. (2001). *Predicting and modeling the survival of school superintendents.* Paper presented at the annual meeting of the American Educational Research Association, Seattle, WA.

Norton, M. S., Webb, L. D., Dlugosh, L. L., & Sybouts, W. (1996). *The school superintendency: New responsibilities new leadership.* Boston: Allyn and Bacon.

Nowakowski, J., & First, P. F. (1989). A study of school board minutes: Records of reform. *Educational Evaluation and Policy Analysis, 11*(4), 389–404.

Nygren, B. (1992). Two-party tune up. *American School Board Journal, 178*(7), 35.

Olson, L. (2000). Policy focus converges on leadership: Several major efforts underway. *Education Week.* Retrieved from http://www.edweek.org/ew/ewstory.cfm?slug=17 1lead.h19&keywords=olson

Petersen, G. J. (1999). Demonstrated actions of instructional leaders: A case study of five superintendents. *Education Policy Analysis Archives (7)*18. Retrieved from http://epaa.asu.edu/epaa/v7n18.html

Petersen, G. J., & Short, P. M. (2001). School board presidents and the district superintendent relationship: Applying the lens of social influence. *Educational Administration Quarterly, 37*(4), 533–570.

Petersen, G. J., & Short, P. M. (in press). An examination of the school board president's perception of the district superintendent's interpersonal communication competence and board decision making. *Journal of School Leadership.*

Renchler, R. (1992). Urban superintendent turnover: The need for stability. *Urban Superintendents' Sounding Board, 1*(1), 2–13.

Reyes, P., Wagstaff, L. H., & Fusarelli, L. D. (1999). Delta forces: The changing fabric of American society and education. In J. Murphy & K. Seashore Louis (Eds.), *Handbook of research on educational administration* (2nd ed., pp. 183–201). San Francisco: Jossey-Bass.

Scribner, J., & Englert, R. (1977). The politics of education: An introduction. In J. Scribner (Ed.), *The politics of education. The seventy-sixth yearbook of the National Society for the Study of Education. Part II* (pp. 1–29). Chicago: University of Chicago Press.

Tallerico, M. (1989). The dynamics of superintendent-school board relationships: A continuing challenge. *Urban Education, 24*(2), 215–232.

The Twentieth Century Fund. (1992). *Facing the challenge: The report of The Twentieth Century Fund task force on school governance.* New York: Author.

Tillman, L. (2001). Success for all children: Implications for leadership preparation programs. *UCEA Review, XLII*(1), 10–12.

Tucker, H. J., & Zeigler, L. H. (1980). *Professionals and the public: Attitudes, communication, and response in school districts.* New York: Longman.

Usdan, M. D. (1975). The future viability of the school board. In P. J. Cistone (Ed.), *Understanding school boards: Problems and prospects* (pp. 265–276). Toronto, Canada: Lexington Books.

Usdan, M., McCloud, B., Podmostko, M., & Cuban, L. (2001). *Leadership for learning: Restructuring school district leadership.* Washington, DC: Institute for Educational Leadership.

Wirt, F. M., & Kirst, M. W. (1989). *Schools in conflict* (2nd ed). Berkeley, CA: McCutchan.

Wirt, F. M., & Kirst, M. W. (1997). *The political dynamics of American education.* Berkeley, CA: McCutchan.

Zeigler, L. H. (1975). School board research: The problems and the prospects. In P. J. Cistone (Ed.), *Understanding school boards* (pp. 3–16). Lexington, MA: D. C. Heath.

Zeigler, L. H., Jennings, M. K., & Peak, G. W. (1974). *Governing American schools: Political interaction in local school districts.* North Scituate, MA: Duxbury Press.

Politics and the Socialization of Superintendents

Lars G. Björk, Robert J. Bell, and D. Keith Gurley

During the past several decades, the perception that education had failed the nation's children and jeopardized America's economic well-being has heightened public concern and launched what is arguably the most comprehensive, intensive, and sustained effort to improve education in American history. National commission and task force reports released throughout the reform era (1983–2002) increased expectations for student performance and called for fundamentally changing classroom instruction, how schools are structured and led, as well as the composition and characteristics of school and district governance. Scholars and practitioners learned directly that implementing systemic reforms was complex and, in many instances, depended on community political power configurations, relations among school board members, and the nature of transactions among board members and the superintendent (Björk, 2000b; Blumberg, 1985; Keedy & Björk, 2002; McCarty & Ramsey, 1971). Realization that political conflict can advance as well as destabilize school reform is renewing interest in the politics of superintendent-school board relations (Björk, 2000a; Carter & Cunningham, 1997; Kowalski, 1999). Although scholars and practitioners concur that heightened political activities are changing relationships between superintendents and boards, few studies examine how superintendent roles are changing or may change. Fewer still examine the influence of socialization processes that determine how superintendents enact their roles. In this chapter we report key findings from a nationwide study on the dissonance between superintendent roles and school board political configurations. Then we review literature on organizational, professional, and political socialization to frame a discussion of how superintendents' roles are influenced and may be changed.

Lars G. Björk, University of Kentucky
Robert J. Bell, University of Kentucky
D. Keith Gurley, University of Kentucky

THE POLITICS OF THE SUPERINTENDENCY

The political dimensions of superintendent and board member relations have interested scholars since the late 19th century (Burlingame, 1988; Cistone, 1975; Iannacone, 1991; Scribner & Layton, 1994; Tyack & Hansot, 1982). During the early 20th century, literature described superintendent-board relations as being adversarial, an outcome of political corruption. As a consequence, reformers campaigned for appointed boards and nonpartisan elections to insulate members of boards of education from questionable electoral practices (Cronin, 1973; Iannacone & Lutz, 1995; Tyack & Hansot, 1982). However, by the middle of the 20th century, scholars began to view candidate platforms and debates as an indispensable characteristic of public elections in a democratic society thus legitimizing the study of the politics of education (Burlingame, 1988). Although Morgan (1997) notes that politics and politicking are acceptable ways for individuals and groups to express opinions and advance their interests, Blumberg (1985) observes that educators tend to believe that schooling should remain above the fray of partisan politics, interest group influence, and board of education power struggles. In addition, they tend to view politics as being antithetical to professional behavior (Kowalski, 1999; Malen, 1995; Slater & Boyd, 1999).

Throughout their careers, educators have been socialized to abstain from political activities. Johnson (1996) notes, however, that superintendents have little choice whether or not to enter the political fray; it is becoming a way of life. The nature of superintendents' work brings them into frequent contact with special interest groups, elected public officials, parents, and school board members who, as a matter of course, make multiple and diverse demands on the school system. These exchanges require superintendents to represent the district favorably, possess political acumen to build consensus among competing stakeholders, preserve the integrity of education programs, and gain voter support for future school bond issues (Blumberg, 1985). Fulfilling wide-ranging and often contradictory expectations is becoming increasingly difficult as the ethnic and racial diversity expands, interest group activity increases, and political conflict escalates (Blumberg, 1985; Carter & Cunningham, 1997). In these heightened political contexts, superintendents will need greater acuity and flexibility in working with community interest groups and board power structures (Björk, 2000a; Johnson, 1996).

Research findings support the contention that differing job expectations are often the root cause of conflict in superintendent-board relations (Glass, Björk, & Brunner, 2000) and that chief executives who understand the sociocultural contexts in which decisions are made (Norton, Webb, Dlugosh, & Sybouts, 1996; Pitner & Ogawa, 1981) and have the political acuity to adjust their ways of working with boards tend to be more successful (Björk, 2000a). Although schools historically have been embedded in the political life of local communities, textbooks used to train administrators during the first half of the 20th century espoused that teachers, principals, and superintendents should be apolitical, remaining outside of the influence of partisan politics (Glass, Björk, & Brunner, 2000), a stance endorsed by school boards. At the close of the 20th century, little has changed. Schools are still immersed in local politics, apolitical norms remain institutionalized, and textbooks, professional preparation, and in-service programs for administrators pay little attention to the politics of education (McCarthy & Kuh, 1997). As a consequence, superintendents are placed at a conspicuous disadvantage. For example, Glass, Björk, and Brunner (2000) found that nearly 25 percent of superintendents responding to the American Association of School Administrator's (AASA) nation-wide survey indicated that political conflict contributed to their leaving their last position. Several factors contributed to this state of affairs including conflict with board members (14.6 percent), board elections (9.5 percent) that changed power configurations, and conflict with the community (.4 percent). Further, superintendents indicate that they face significant challenges with regard to relations with their boards (83 percent), interest group activity (57 percent), community involvement in decision making (60.7 percent), and school board decision making (48.8 percent). In addition, 20.6 percent indicate that board micromanagement inhibited their effectiveness. These challenges are clearly political in nature.

During the past two decades (1980–2002), political polarization and ideological divisiveness have increased the intensity of debate over a wide range of educational policy issues in school districts throughout the United States and have contributed to the complexity of superintendent's work (Björk & Lindle, 2001; Gousha, 1981; Keedy & Björk, 2002). Research findings from AASA's recent work, *The Study of the American School Superintendency 2000: A Look at the Superintendent of Education in the New Millennium* (Glass, Björk, & Brunner, 2000), support the notion that broad-based political agendas are being played out at the local level pressing superintendents and boards of education to support their demands. Local residential taxpayer groups bent on reducing property taxes, conservative coalitions interested in reducing waste of public funds, and organized as well as ad hoc pressure groups are challenging a host of administrative decisions, curriculum issues, and policy decisions including vouchers, charter schools, and creationism. The 2000 study found that more than 57 percent of the superintendents confirmed that community interest groups were active in their school districts, with a significant portion engaged in debates around school prayer and property taxes (Glass, Björk, & Brunner, 2000). The study also found that more than 90 percent of superintendents serving in large districts, those with more than 25,000 students, identified attempts by special interest groups to politically influence board policy and district administrative operations. In addition, 95 percent of superintendents serving in these large districts, and 78 percent of those in districts with between 3,000 and 24,999 students, acknowledge that business leaders attempted to exert subtle influence on educational policy through school–business partnerships.

During the past several decades, scholars examined the dynamics of community politics and schooling and observed that superintendents' success and tenure in office are often related to their ability to be aware of community and board of education power structures and understand the politics (Boyd, 1976; Iannacone, 1991; Iannacone & Lutz, 1970; Zeigler, Jennings, & Peak, 1974, 1995) and micropolitics

Community Power Structures	School Board Characteristics	Superintendent Roles
Dominated: Community power structure controlled by a few individuals at the apex of hierarchy in "top down" model. Decision-making group likely to be economic elite in community, but also may be derived from religious, ethnic, racial, or political power structures. Opposition to elite position rarely successful.	Dominated: Board members chosen due to congruence of individual views with those of dominant group (power elite). Individuals take advice from these community leaders. Opposition groups must be organized and strong enough to displace power elite.	Functionary: Superintendent identifies with and takes cues from dominant group; perceives her/his role as implementer rather than developer of board policies. Board selects superintendents willing to work in this context.
Factional: Several groups hold relatively equal power, compete for control over important policy decisions, and may coalesce around economic, religious, ethnic, racial, or political power philosophies.	Factional: Board members represent and act in accordance with community faction groups. Voting more important than discussing issues. If issue is important, majority faction always wins. Board elections hotly contested.	Political Strategist: Superintendent works with majority. When majority changes, superintendent must realign. Superintendent assumes middle course on controversial issues, careful not to alienate minority factions, as majority may shift in the future.
Pluralistic: Power contested by interest groups and dispersed, pluralistic, and diffused. High level of concern for important issues, active involvement of interest groups in decision making.	Status Congruent: Board members active but not rigidly bound to one group or position. Members viewed as equals, discussion of issues important and objective.	Professional Advisor: Superintendent acts as statesperson giving professional advice based on research and experience. Superintendent offers professional opinions, proposes alternatives in open, objective fashion.
Inert: Power in community latent or dominated by status quo. Radical experimentation may not be acceptable.	Sanctioning: Board members' views congruent with pervasive values and views of community. Individual members do not receive overt reinforcement; often follow lead of superintendent, approving proposals without question.	Decision maker: Superintendent initiates action, provides leadership for effectiveness. School board "rubber stamps" proposals. Superintendent leadership constrained by latent community values that emphasize status quo.

Note. From Björk (2002). Adapted from McCarty, D., & Ramsey, C. (1971). *The school managers: Power and conflict in American public education*. Westport, CT: Greenwood.

Figure 1. Types of community power structures, school board political characteristics, and superintendent roles.

(Blase & Blase, 2002; Björk, 2001) of school and district administration. The work of McCarty and Ramsey (1971) made a significant contribution to understanding the relationship among community power structures, political configurations of boards of education and superintendent roles. Research findings generally affirm their assumption that community political structures are aligned with local school board power configurations and those superintendents' roles corresponded to these arrangements. McCarty and Ramsey's (1971) typology of community–school board and school board–superintendent relations and depiction of alignment of community, board, and superintendent characteristics is shown in figure 1.

McCarty and Ramsey's study (1971) presaged a period in U. S. history characterized by heightened political divisiveness and interest in the study of the politics of education. Since the late 1970s, efforts to reform public education in the United States raised fundamental questions about the purpose of education, which constituents were being served, and how well students performed. These and other policy issues were stridently debated and contributed to increasing the level of conflict, political activity, and changes in superintendent-board relations (Björk, 2000a; Carter & Cunningham, 1997; Kowalski, 1999). Findings reported by McCarty and Ramsey (1971) not only made a significant contribution to understanding political dynamics of board-superintendent relations but also identified the propensity of superintendents to enact two dominant roles: professional advisor and decision maker. McCarty and Ramsey's (1971) typology depicting board-superintendent political power configurations framed a series of questions included in AASA's 10-year study and reported initially in *The Study of the American School Superintendency 2000: A Look at the Superintendent of Education in the New Millennium* (Glass, Björk, & Brunner, 2000). Björk's (2000a) analysis of survey data confirmed McCarty and Ramsey's assumptions and raised significant questions as to why over a 30-year period (1970–2000) superintendents persisted in serving as either a professional advisor or decision maker and resisted adopting roles corresponding to demands placed on them by heightened community and board politics. The notions of professional, organizational, and political socialization are presented as frameworks for understanding resilience in superintendent behavior.

RESEARCH METHODS

Beginning in 1923, the Department of Superintendence of the National Education Association (NEA) conducted the first in a series of nationwide studies of the superintendency that have been conducted each decade throughout the 20th century. *The Study of the American School Superintendency 2000: A Look at the Superintendent of Education in the New Millennium* (Glass, Björk, & Brunner, 2000) continues a tradition of longitudinal research on the superintendency. This study provides current information on the superintendency including demographic characteristics, relationships with board members, superintendents' opinions on key problems and issues, participation of women and minorities in the superintendency, as well as professional preparation and superintendents' career patterns. National, state, and local education policymakers, researchers, and the superintendents use these data to

Table 1. Superintendent Sample by District Enrollment Size

	District Enrollment Size			
	>25,000 pupils	*3,000–24,999 pupils*	*300–2,999 pupils*	*<300 pupils*
Sample Size	222	1,175	3,065	874

understand issues and frame solutions. Two primary objectives of the study included (a) maintaining and updating trend data from earlier studies (1960, 1971, 1982, & 1992), and (b) providing an overview of the perspectives of district leaders.

The United States Department of Education provided a stratified random sample from a universe of 12,604 practicing superintendents in regular public school districts in the Common Core of Data Public Education Agency Universe. This database generates summary information for school superintendents by type of district and total enrollment. Table 1 displays the distribution of selected districts within enrollment categories. The sample drawn (*N* = 2,536) of a population of 12,604 was an adequate size and proportion to reflect the diversity of public school districts in the nation as well as gender and race of superintendents. Special attention was paid to ensure that district size, as well as superintendents' gender and racial diversity from previous studies were replicated to meet the objectives of maintaining trend data.

In April 1999, survey instruments were mailed to an over-sampled group of 5,336 superintendents in the United States. By June, AASA forwarded all completed surveys for tabulation and analysis. The number of usable surveys was 2,262, for a return rate of 42.4 percent, that constituted 89 percent of the projected sample or 18 percent of all U.S. superintendents. The greatest number of surveys was returned from the Great Lakes and Plains state regions, which also had the greatest number of school districts.

FINDINGS

McCarty and Ramsey's (1971) typology was used as a framework to investigate superintendent perceptions of board of education power configurations and their corresponding roles in AASA's *The Study of the American School Superintendency 2000: A Look at the Superintendent of Education in the New Millennium* (Glass, Björk, & Brunner, 2000). McCarty and Ramsey (1971) defined dominated communities as elite power structures in which several individuals exert top-down political influence. Elite status is often achieved through economic dominance or historical dominance of a particular ethnic, religious, or racial group and holders of elite status tend to be intolerant of local opposition. As shown in figure 1, McCarty and Ramsey (1971) posit that a dominated community power structure produces dominated school board that in turn necessitates the superintendent to serve a functionary role. A superintendent serving in this capacity identifies with and responds to cues from community elites via their representatives on the board of education, and carries out rather than initiates policy. In communities characterized as elite, boards of education tend to seek out and employ superintendents who are willing to acquiesce to their authority. Findings indicate that very few superintendents (2.6 percent) see their school boards as dominated by an elite community group (see table 2). However, still fewer superintendents (1.2 percent) are willing to serve as functionaries even though not doing so may create conflict with a dominated board. Although serving as a functionary is politically astute, many superintendents, accustomed to being "in charge," may find working in a subordinate position antithetical to their stance as a chief executive officer.

In contrast to elite power structures, communities in which interest groups coalesce around economic, religious, racial, or ethnic concerns and challenge education board policy are regarded as factional (McCarty & Ramsey, 1971). In factional communities, power is distributed somewhat equally among multiple and diverse groups. As a consequence, superintendents must be cognizant of board member linkages with different interest groups and be familiar with their respective stances on routine as well as contested policy issues and administrator decisions. In communities characterized by heightened political activity, superintendents may adopt a political strategist role (see figure 1). This stance calls for aligning their position on issues with those held by a majority of board members while having the acuity to maintain amicable relations with others. Politically astute superintendents are aware that, while a particular group may apply power over time, the characteristics of a particular issue may cause a shift of political power favoring competing factions, thus forming a new majority. Superintendents enacting political strategist roles tend to take a middle course on issues and behave in a manner that does not alienate other factions knowing that the majority may be tentative and shift in the future. *The Study of the American School Superintendency 2000: A Look at the Superintendent of Education in the New Millennium* (Glass, Björk, & Brunner, 2002) found that 19 percent of superintendents indicated that their boards were factional. Even though superintendents are aware that boards are composed of different factions, only 1.6 percent indicated that they adopted a role of political strategist (see table 2). Their reluctance to work in this fashion and adapt to community and board power configurations may help explain superintendent-board conflict and executive turnover.

Table 2. Comparison of Community Power Structure, School Board Characteristics, and Superintendent Roles, 1971 to 2000

Community Power Structure Role Type			School Board Characteristics Power Type			Role of Superintendent Role Type		
	1971	2000		1971	2000		1971	2000
Dominated	16%	—	Dominated	13%	2.6%	Functionary	2%	1.2%
Factional	14%	—	Factional	32%	19.0%	Political Strategist	1%	1.6%
Pluralistic	45%	—	Status Congruent	63%	65.9%	Professional Advisor	33%	47.7%
Inert	25%	—	Sanctioning	3%	12.5%	Decision Maker	64%	49.5%

Note. From McCarty, D., & Ramsey, C. (1971). *The school managers: Power and conflict in American public education.* Westport, CT: Greenwood (p. 200) and Glass, T., Bjork, L., & Brunner, C. (2000). *The study of the American superintendency 2000: A look at the superintendent of education in the new millennium.* Arlington, VA: American Association of School Administrators (p. 25).—Data not available.

Although pluralistic communities also reflect the presence of multiple and diverse interest groups, McCarty and Ramsey (1971) distinguish between pluralistic and factional communities based upon how discourse is carried out. For example, issues tend to galvanize groups of people in both factional and pluralistic communities; however, status congruent boards tend to be issue-oriented, active, and responsive. Consequently, discourse tends to be open and decisions emphasize the common-weal. On the other hand, factional communities facing similar circumstances tend to adhere to rigid ideological positions and stress gaining victory over political opponents. Members of pluralistic communities are characterized as viewing one another as equals and pursue discourse and solutions to problems in an objective manner. As a consequence, superintendents work in a diplomatic fashion with those boards characterized by McCarty and Ramsey (1971) as being status congruent (see figure 1). In these circumstances, superintendents serve as professional advisors offering objective assessments of issues under consideration and alternative policy options for board consideration. Although Glass, Björk, and Brunner (2000) found that 66 percent of superintendents regarded boards as being status congruent, only 48 percent indicated they served as professional advisors (see table 2) suggesting dissonance between alignment of perceived board status and their preferred role.

Inert communities, for all intents and purposes, are conservative and tend to be relatively inactive. Although community interest groups or individuals do not overtly influence members of sanctioning boards, their perspectives are congruent with pervasive values and views of the community. Sanctioning boards tend to follow advice of superintendents and approve or "rubber stamp" their policy proposals. In these contexts, superintendents are allowed to act as decision makers with the proviso that they adhere to latent community values and preserve the status quo (see figure 1). Superintendents serving as decision makers are free to ensure district effectiveness by delineating policies, typically a board prerogative, and making administrative decisions. Glass, Björk, and Brunner (2000) found that 12.5 percent of superintendents characterized their boards as sanctioning; however, nearly 50 percent indicated they acted as decision makers (see table 2). The dissonance between board expectations of superintendents acting as a decision maker (12.5 percent) and their inclination to serve in this capacity (49.5 percent) may lead to conflict.

A comparison of McCarty and Ramsey's (1971) and Glass, Björk, and Brunner's (2000) findings (figure 2) indicate that although some shift in superintendent perceptions of board power configurations and role changes has occurred over the past 30 years, nearly 90 percent of superintendents surveyed in 1971, and 98 percent of those survey in 2000 study, enact two distinct roles: professional advisor and decision maker. Conflict emerges as a result of misalignment between superintendents' preferred roles, such as professional advisor or decision maker, and dominant board power configurations. This lack of congruency between superintendents' roles and board power structures may in part explain why conflict is an enduring problem in the superintendency. These findings suggest that, rather than persisting in two dominant roles, superintendents may find it advantageous to ascertain board power configurations and align their roles to avoid conflict.

PROFESSIONAL AND ORGANIZATIONAL SOCIALIZATION

Superintendents' reluctance to enact roles other than professional advisor and decision maker may be explained by theories of professional and organizational socialization. The term "socialization" has been given a variety of meanings in the social sciences, in part because definitions are informed by different, discipline-based knowledge and traditions that influence how phenomena are viewed and interpreted (Gecas, 1992). Psychologists define socialization as an individual development, although even within psychology various specializations define it differently (Gecas, 1992). Anthropologists define socialization as cultural transmission from one generation to the next, generally calling it enculturation rather than socialization. Among sociologists there is also considerable diversity in the definition of the term, although two major orientations exist. One group, the structural functionalists, views it primarily as the learning of social roles, wherein individuals are integrated into society by learning and then internalizing important roles and statuses of their groups. The second and more prevalent group, symbolic interactionists, views socialization as the formation of the self-concept (Gecas, 1992). They view the development of the self and identity within the context of intimate and reciprocal interaction (Pincus, 1994).

In its most common use, socialization refers to the process of interaction through which an individual (a novice) acquires the norms, values, beliefs, attitudes, and language characteristics of his or her groups. In the course of acquiring these cultural elements, the individual's self and personality are created and shaped (Gecas, 1992). Berger and Luckman (1966) define socialization as "the comprehensive and consistent induction of an individual into the objective world of a society or a sector of it" (p. 130). Etzioni (1975) concurs, stating that:

> primary socialization, which determines the form of the basic personality, takes place as a rule in the family and to some degree within various peer groups. . . . For most actors the main part of socialization is completed with maturity, but learning of specific skills and role orientation continues with every change of status, in particular with membership in new social units, such as organizations. (pp. 245–246)

Boudon and Bourricaud (1989) define "socialization as simply as the assimilation of individuals into social groups" (p. 355). Heisel and Krchniak (1972) suggest that, "Socialization is the process by which individuals acquire orientations requisite to adequate functioning in a social role" (p. 90). Similarly, Merton (1968) conceptualized socialization as the process through which an individual acquires the knowledge base, skills, and dispositions necessary in order to successfully perform a specific role in society. However, Parsons (1951) observes "socialization is the learning of any orientation of functional significance to the operation of a system of complementary role expectations. In this sense, socialization, like learning, goes on through life" (p. 208). In this regard Etzioni's (1975) notion that "socialization refers to the acquisition of requisite orientation for satisfactory functioning in a role" (p. 130) captures the essence of socialization in organizational contexts.

Organizational Socialization

Organizational socialization refers to the process by which one is taught and learns the ropes of a particular organizational role in a specific work setting (Van Maanen & Schein, 1979). Persons entering an organization are continually socialized in formal and informal ways (Dornbusch, 1955). A major outcome of this socialization process is that the culture of the organization is transmitted to new members. Part of the culture of the organization involves folk wisdom and operating rules of thumb that persist over time that define, for example, ways of doing administration.

Organizational socialization is concerned with the process by which the beliefs, norms, and perspectives of the participants are brought into line with those of the organization (Etzioni, 1969). Organization socialization is defined as a process consisting of a series of experiences which result in development of goals, values, norms, and traditions of the organization and its work culture and of a self-image as a member or employee of that organization subject to its practices, rules, and regulations (Etzioni, 1975; Heisel & Krchniak, 1972). So powerful can the effects of organizational socialization be that Merton (1968) has suggested that bureaucratic organizations, with their patent authority systems, are powerful mechanisms for socialization that have the capacity to modify individual personality types. Organization socialization begins upon appointment within the organization and is specific to the educational context (Hart, 1993). Dornbusch and Scott (1975) contend that organizational socialization processes that prepare individuals to be influential begin during the post-appointment period and are focused on creating interactions that legitimize and validate them as the new school leader.

Organizational socialization binds the members of work organizations into communities with far deeper interdependence than those forged through temporary connections with educational institutions (Leithwood, Chapman, Corson, Hallinger, & Hart, 1996). Cosgrove (1986), describes the process of socialization as "resulting in many of the legitimating values of organized community life being passed on to future generations and these are the institutionalized values that sustain and invigorate the external forms of institutions, which without them would be dead skeletons" (pp. 57–58).

Professional Socialization

Professional socialization, on the other hand, is defined as a process composed of a series of experiences that result in the internalization of a certain body of knowledge and skills, as well as a stable identification with commitment to the values, ethics, norms, and traditions of the profession (Heisel & Krchniak, 1972). Merton (1968) observes that "socialization refers to the process through which one becomes a member of a profession and over time develops an identity with that profession" (p. 9). Anticipatory socialization involves an individual adopting and practicing beliefs, values, and attitudes of a group to which they desire to belong (Forsyth & Danisiewica, 1985). Professional socialization in education generally begins in the pre-appointed phase of a school leader's education career and continues into early post-appointment growth and development (Hart, 1993). Although the work of Parkay, Currie, and Rhodes (1992) focuses on principals, their explication of the basic assumptions of the professional socialization process is useful in understanding similar processes for superintendents. These assumptions state that (a) individuals enter a new position at different stages of professional development; (b) individuals move through the stages of professional socialization at different rates; (c) no single factor determines an individual's stage of development; and (d) an individual may operate at more than one stage simultaneously. The notion that individuals are socialized into professions by progressing through distinct stages is an important framework for studying this phenomenon.

Political Socialization

Political socialization has to do with people-oriented explanations of political events. It is a concept directing attention toward the behavior, knowledge, values, and beliefs of the average citizen (Dawson & Prewitt, 1969) and concerns these developmental processes through which persons acquire or develop political orientations (Easton & Dennis, 1969). Kavanagh (1972) reports that the overall effect of the socialization process may be to change or even recreate, as well as sustain, the political culture.

The scholarly work associated with this concept brings with it some potential limitations (Cornell, 1987). Most of the research and theorizing in the field of political socialization, unfortunately, has been based on a narrower conception of politics, one that focuses on public sphere activities in relation to governments and partisan politics. Nevertheless, it seems feasible to draw on the work in this field, while maintaining a broader conception of politics as concerned with both the public and private spheres (Ginsburg & Lindsey, 1995).

There is another potential limitation of the concept of political socialization for our purpose here. It is the tendency for scholars in the field to focus on how political systems remain stable and are sustained through individuals' accommodation to the status quo or to the interest of dominate groups (Cornell & Goot, 1972; Dawson & Prewitt, 1969). In addition, political socialization research has a tendency to rely on an over-socialized conception of human experiences (Wrong, 1961). In the field of political socialization, the passive-reactive model dominates. For example, Baker (1972) suggests that an individual seems to have the imprint of attitudes, values, and behaviors acquired by exposure over time. Gergen and Ullman (1977) note that political socialization practices implant in the individual the particular styles or predispositions that form his or her individual character and that influence, among other things, his or her level of political participation.

School personnel are involved in various processes of political socialization in relation to a range of socializing agents during different periods of their lives (Hirsch, 1971) and there is considerable debate in the literature regarding the relative impact of various agents of political socialization and the relative importance of various stages of the age cycle (Greensburg, 1970). There are political socialization experiences that can occur in formal training of school personnel that can influence development of political identities, orientation and strategies. Such experiences may, to some degree, reinforce or contradict the political socialization messages provided through other experiences (Ginsburg & Lindsey, 1995).

DISCUSSION

Scholars and practitioners concur that during the past 30 years the nature of superintendents' work has become increasingly complex, political, and challenging with regard to board and community relations. These circumstances have contributed to district instability and turnover of superintendents for nearly three decades (Blumberg, 1985; Boyd, 1974, 1976; Burlingame, 1988; Carter & Cunningham, 1997; Cistone, 1975; Cuban, 1976; Iannacone & Lutz, 1970; Johnson, 1996; Kowalski, 1999; McCarty & Ramsey, 1971; Tucker & Zeigler, 1980). Recently, researchers have speculated that superintendents' persistence in serving as either professional advisor or decision maker appears misaligned with their conspicuously political work environments (Björk, 2000a; Björk & Keedy, 2002). Although notions of organizational and professional socialization may help explain the persistence of dysfunctional behavior, these concepts, as well as those research findings on the efficacy of mentoring, provide a framework for the political socialization of superintendents. Developing the acuity and skills as well as the norms, beliefs, and attitudes that enable them to succeed in political contexts are essential to their success and district stability.

Although superintendents are immersed in local politics, they are adverse to political accommodation (Cibulka, 1999; Kowalski, 1995, 1999; Sykes, 1999), preferring to enact roles that fit established professional norms such as professional advisor and decision maker (Glass, Björk, & Brunner, 2000; McCarty & Ramsey, 1971). For example, *The Study of the American School Superintendency 2000: A Look at the Superintendent of Education in the New Millennium* (Glass, Björk, & Brunner, 2000) found that, while assuming a functionary role might be the most politically astute path to take in order to enhance working relationships with dominated (elite) communities and boards, many superintendents working in this context still see themselves as individuals "taking charge" of district affairs rather than "taking orders." Thus, superintendents may be inclined to ignore political context clues, to reject working in a functionary role, and to continue enacting the preferred role of decision maker.

There are other examples of misalignment between superintendents' perceptions of board political power configurations and preferred roles of superintendents (see table 2) that increase the possibility of superintendent-board conflict. For example, although 19 percent of superintendents recognized that their boards were factional, only 1.6 percent adopted a political strategist role. In addition, 65.9 percent of superintendents characterized their boards as being status congruent; however; only 47.7 percent enacted a professional advisor role. Furthermore, while 12.5 percent of superintendents described their boards as sanctioning, nearly half (49.5 percent) preferred to enact the role of decision maker. Thus, the challenge facing the profession, whether it be in the context of university-based preparation programs, professional associations, or state education agencies charged with the responsibility for preparing the next generation of superintendents, is to not only understand social forces that have sustained this dysfunctional behavior over time, but also to understand how to increase superintendents' willingness and capacity to adapt to changing political circumstances in their communities and boards. These notions, derived from literature on professional socialization, learning theory, and mentoring, provide a framework for corrective action.

Professional socialization of superintendents is based on experiences that result in the acquisition of technical skills as well as legitimated norms, values, and traditions of the profession (Heisel & Krchiak, 1972). An examination of different developmental stages of socialization indicate that its influence on behavior is more pronounced during periods immediately preceding or during the time individual is serving in a desired position (Hart, 1993; Parkay, Currie, & Rhodes, 1992). Interactions after an individual is appointed to a position transmit as well as validate norms, values, and attitudes that bind members to the profession and the organization (Dornbusch & Scott, 1975). Literature on political socialization suggests that experiences in school settings can shape their orientation and work strategies. The work of Dewey (1974), Hoberman and Mailick (1994), Lewin (1951), and others support the notion that knowledge acquired through experiences in actual work settings measurably increases recall and transfer to new situations. Research findings on the effects of mentoring suggest that mentoring activities can accelerate the rate at which individuals are socialized into a profession and acquire skills (Bey & Holmes, 1992).

Mentors tend to be senior members of the profession who have been successful in inducting, socializing, and advising aspiring and new chief executive officers (Head & Gray, 1988). Hoberman and Mailick (1994) identified mentoring as an important dimension of field-based learning. Indeed, mentoring is an essential part of medical residencies, judicial clerkships, and internships in educational administration programs. Recent findings by Glass, Björk, and Brunner (2000) indicate that mentoring is a hallmark of the profession and an important factor throughout superintendents' careers. Thus, mentoring can serve as a mechanism through which aspiring and recently appointed superintendents may be introduced to notions of role adaptation and adopting norms, values, and attitudes that reinforce the legitimacy of serving as political leaders (Johnson, 1996). However, selecting mentors is crucial. Those who embrace norms supporting political leadership norms, who perceive the need for adapting their roles to fit community and board power structures, and who are skilled politicians are key to the political socialization process.

Mentors are crucial to the political socialization of superintendents in that they provide useful and immediate feedback that enhances their capacity to observe and analyze their behavior in political work contexts. As a consequence, mentors should be carefully selected to ensure that they are astute observers, provide feedback, nurture reflection, and model appropriate political behavior requisite to superintendent success. Although the characteristics of mentors are important, how they structure their work has varying effects on knowledge transfer. For example, Björk and Keedy

Types of Adult Learning	Mentoring Characteristics	Amount of Transfer
Abstract Learning	Theory	5%
Proposing Application of Ideas	Theory, Practice	10%
Observing Practice	Theory, Practice, Demonstration	20%
Gaining Work Experience	Theory, Practice, Demonstration	20%
Obtaining Feedback	Theory, Practice, Demonstration, Feedback	25%
Reflecting on Actions	Theory, Practice, Demonstration, Feedback, Mentoring	90%

Note. Based on Bridges & Hallinger (1992), Dewey (1974), Gottesman (2000), Joyce (1987), and Joyce & Showers (1983).

Figure 2. Stages of learning, mentoring, and skill transfer.

(2000) citing Joyce and Showers (1983) and Joyce (1987), in their research on mentoring to improve skill performance, found that different types of mentoring configurations produce different outcomes in learners. When professionals learn a new skill or *only theory* in passive training settings, only 5 percent of learners will transfer that new skill into practice. When they learn theory and the skill is *also demonstrated*, 10 percent of participants will transfer what was learned into practice. However the percentage of transfer increases to 20 percent when participants are able to acquire formal knowledge (theory), observe the skill being demonstrated, *and practice* the skill themselves. When *feedback* is added to the theory, demonstration, and practice arrangement, 25 percent of individuals will transfer the new skill to their work setting. Feedback in this context is a literal description of events without opportunity for evaluation, conclusion, or reflection. When *mentoring* is added to the theory, demonstration, practice, and feedback-training configuration, the rate of transfer of new skills increases to 90 percent (see figure 2). Unfortunately, Gottesman (2000) notes most training programs tend to "include only theory and demonstration with some token practice. Almost none include feedback much less [mentoring] on a regular, systematic basis" (p. 22). In sum, the relationship among learning theory, training, and mentoring provides a template for thinking about how aspiring and newly appointed superintendents can acquire political acuity, skills, and norms that can position them to more successfully align their ways of working with the political power configurations of local communities and boards of education.

IMPLICATIONS FOR RESEARCH

Although Glass, Björk, and Brunner (2000) generally confirm McCarty and Ramsey's (1971) findings on the alignment of community and board power structures with superintendent roles, they also found that over a thirty year period superintendents persist in enacting two dominant role types: professional advisor and decision maker. This raises some interesting questions. First, the survey method may not reveal the full scope of superintendents' roles in addressing board and community politics. Although data suggest that the influence of interest group politics on the work of superintendents is increasing, methods reported here are too limited to ascertain its intensity or the capacity of superintendents to work in heightened political contexts. Second, the study focused on ascertaining superintendents' perception of board power configurations and their preferred role. While these data are useful in affirming the value of McCarty and Ramsey's (1971) typology, more dynamic qualities of superintendents' work needs to be examined. In addition, understanding whether or not superintendents adjust their preferred way of working to changes in the political dynamics of board power structures is a gap in the field's knowledge base. Third, although research confirms that superintendents exhibit norms, values, and attitudes that influence how they work, we have little understanding of how and when superintendents are socialized or whether mentoring programs directed towards political socialization of superintendents are viable. Gaining definitive insights into the political work of superintendents and socialization processes will require additional research.

REFERENCES

Baker, D. (1972). Political socialization: Parameters and disposition. *Polity, 3*(4), 586–600.

Berger, P. L., & Luckman, T. (1966). *The social construction of reality: A treatise in the sociology of knowledge.* New York: Doubleday.

Bey, T., & Holmes, C. T. (1992). *Mentoring: Contemporary principles and issues.* Reston, VA: Association of Teacher Educators.

Björk, L. (2000a). Personal characteristics. In T. E. Glass, L. B. Björk, & C. C. Brunner (Eds.), *The study of the American school superintendency 2000: A look at the superintendent of education in the new millennium* (pp. 15–30). Arlington, VA: American Association of School Administrators.

Björk, L. (2000b). Professional preparation and training. In T. E. Glass, L. B. Bjork, & C. C. Brunner (Eds.), *The study of the American school superintendency 2000: A look at the superintendent of education in the new millennium* (pp. 127–309). Arlington, VA: American Association of School Administrators.

Björk, L. (2001). The role of central office in decentralization. In T. J. Kowalski & G. Perreault (Eds.), *21st century challenges for school administrators* (pp. 286–309). Lanham, MD: Scarecrow Press.

Björk, L., & Keedy, J. (2001). Politics and the superintendency in the United States: Restructuring in-service education. *Journal of in-service education 27* (2), pp. 277–305.

Björk, L., & Lindle, J. C. (2001). Superintendents and interest groups. *Journal of Educational Policy, 13*(1), 77–92.

Blase, J., & Blase, J. (2002). The micropolitics of instructional supervision: A call for research. *Educational Administration Quarterly, 38*(1), 6–44.

Blumberg, A. (with Blumberg, P.). (1985). *The school superintendent: Living with conflict.* New York: Teachers College Press.

Boudon, R., & Bourricaud, F. (1989). *A critical dictionary of sociology.* Chicago: University of Chicago Press.

Boyd, W. L. (1974). The school superintendent: Educational statesman or political strategist. *Administrator's Notebook, 22*(9), 1–5.

Boyd, W. L. (1976). The public, the professionals, and educational policy making: Who governs? *Teachers College Record, 77*(4), 539–577.

Bridges, E., & Hallinger, P. (1992). Problem-based learning for administrators. Eugene, OR: ERIC Clearinghouse on Education Management, University of Oregon.

Burlingame, M. (1988). The politics of education and educational policy: The local level. In N. Boyan (Ed.), *Handbook of research on educational administration: A project of the American Educational Research Association* (pp. 439–451). New York: Longman.

Carter, G. R., & Cunningham, W. G. (1997). *The American school superintendent: Leading in an age of pressure.* San Francisco: Jossey-Bass.

Cibulka, J. (1999). Ideological lenses for interpreting political and economic changes affecting schooling. In J. Murphy & K. S. Lewis (Eds.), *The handbook of research on educational administration* (2nd ed., pp 163–182). San Francisco: Jossey-Bass.

Cistone, P. J. (Ed.). (1975). *Understanding school boards: Problems and prospects.* Lexington, MA: Lexington Books.

Cornell, R. (1987). Why the "political socialization" paradigm failed and what should replace it. *International Political Science Review, 8*(3), 215–223.

Cornell, R., & Goot, M. (1972). Science and technology in American political socialization research. *Berkeley Journal of Sociology, 8*(3), 215–223.

Cosgrove, D. (1986). *The effects of principal succession on elementary schools.* Unpublished doctoral dissertation, University of Utah, Salt Lake City.

Cronin, J. M. (1973). *The control of urban schools: Perspectives on the power of educational reformers.* New York: Free Press.

Cuban, L. (1976). *Urban school chiefs under fire.* Chicago: University of Chicago Press.

Dawson, R. E., & Prewitt, K. (1969). *Political socialization.* Boston: Little, Brown.

Dewey, J. (1974). *John Dewey on education: Selected writings.* Chicago: University of Chicago Press.

Dornbusch, S. M. (1955). *A primer on social statistics.* New York: McGraw-Hill.

Dornbusch, S. M., & Scott, W. R. (1975). *Evaluation and the exercise of authority: A theory of control applied to diverse organizations.* San Francisco: Jossey-Bass.

Easton D., & Dennis, J. (1969). *Children in the political system: Origins of political legitimacy.* New York: McGraw-Hill.

Etzioni, A. (1969). *The semi-professions and their organizations: Teachers, nurses, social workers.* London: Free Press.

Etzioni, A. (1975). *A comparative analysis of complex organizations* (2nd ed.). New York: Free Press.

Forsyth, P. B., & Danisiewica, T. J. (1985). Toward a theory of professionalization. *Work and Occupations, 12*(1), 59–76.

Gecas, V. (1992). Socialization. In E. F. Borgatta & M. L. Borgatta (Eds.), *Encyclopedia of sociology: Vol. 4.* (pp. 1863–1872). New York: Macmillan.

Gergen, K., & Ullman, M. (1977). Socializations and characterlogical basis of political activism. In S. Renston (Ed.), *Handbook of political socialization* (pp. 411–442). New York: Free Press.

Ginsburg, M., & Lindsey, B. (1995). *The political dimension in teacher education: Comparative perspectives on policy formation, socialization, and society.* Washington, DC: Falmer Press.

Glass, T. E., Björk, L. B., & Brunner, C. C. (2000). *The study of the American school superintendency 2000: A look at the superintendent of education in the new millennium.* Arlington, VA: American Association of School Administrators.

Gottesman, B. (2000). *Peer coaching for effectiveness* (2nd ed.). Lanham, MD: Scarecrow Press.

Gousha, R. P. (1981, February). *What's happening to superintendents?* Paper presented at the annual meeting of the American Association of School Administrators, Atlanta, GA. (ERIC Document Reproduction Service No. ED204845)

Greensburg, E. (1970). *Political socialization.* New York: Atherton.

Hart, Q. W. (1993). *Principal succession: Establishing leadership in schools.* Albany: State University of New York Press.

Head, M. S., & Gray, M. (1988). The legacy of mentor: Insights into Western history, literature, and the media. *International Journal of Mentoring, 2*(2), 26–33.

Heisel, A. R., & Krchniak, S. P. (1972). Socialization in a heternomous profession: Public school teaching. *Journal of Educational Research, 66*(2), 89–93.

Hirsch, H. (1971). Political socialization: Review of the literature. In H. Hirsch (Ed.), *Poverty and publication.* New York: Free Press.

Hoberman, S., & Mailik, S. (1994). Some learning theory. In S. Hoberman & S. Mailik (Eds.), *Professional education in the United States: Experiential learning, issues, and prospects.* Westport, CT: Praeger.

Iannacone, L. (1991). Micropolitics of education: What and why. *Education and Urban Society, 23*(4), 465–471.

Iannacone, L., & Lutz, F. W. (1970). *Politics, power and policy.* Columbus, OH: Merrill.

Iannacone, L., & Lutz, F. W. (1995). The crucible of democracy: The local arena. In J. D. Scribner & D. H. Layton (Eds.), *The study of educational politics: The 1994 commemorative yearbook of the Politics of Education Association (1969–1994).* Philadelphia: Falmer Press.

Johnson, S. M. (1996). *Leading to change: The challenge of the new superintendency.* San Francisco: Jossey-Bass.

Joyce, B. R. (1987). *Staff development awareness.* Unpublished manuscript, University of South Carolina, Columbia.

Joyce, B. R., & Showers, B. (1983). *Power in staff development through research on training.* Alexandria, VA: Association for Curriculum and Staff Development.

Kavanagh, D. (1972). *Political culture.* London: Macmillan.

Keedy, J. & Björk, L., (2002). *Superintendents and local boards and the potential for community polarization: The call for use of political strategist skills of education.* In B. Cooper & L. D. Fusarelli (Eds.), *Reconceptualizing leadership: The superintendency in transition.* (pp. 103–127). Lanham, MD: Scarecrow Press.

Kowalski, T. J. (1995). *Keeper of the flame: Contemporary urban superintendents.* Thousand Oaks, CA: Corwin Press.

Kowalski, T. J. (1999). *The school superintendent: Theory, practice, and cases.* Upper Saddle River, NJ: Merrill.

Leithwood, K., Chapman, J., Corson, D., Hallinger, P., & Hart, A. (1996). *International handbook of educational leadership and administration.* Dordrecht, The Netherlands: Kluwer Academic.

Lewin, K. (1951). *Field theory in social science.* New York: Harper & Row.

Malen, B. (1995). The micropolitics of education. In. J. D. Scribner & D. H. Layton (Eds.), *The study of educational politics: The 1994 commemorative yearbook of the Politics of Education Association (1969–1994)* (pp. 147–167). Philadelphia: Falmer Press.

McCarthy, M., & Kuh, G. (1997). *Community and change: The educational leadership professorate.* Columbia, MO: University Council for Educational Administration.

McCarty, D. J., & Ramsey, C. E. (1971). *The school managers.* Westport, CT: Greenwood.

Merton, R. K. (1968). *Social theory and social structure.* New York: Free Press.

Morgan, G. (1997). *Images of organization* (2nd ed.). Thousand Oaks, CA: Sage.

Norton, M. S., Webb, L. D., Dlugosh, L. L., & Sybouts, W. (1996). *The school superintendency: New responsibilities, new leadership.* Boston: Allyn & Bacon.

Parkay, F. W., Currie, G. D., & Rhodes, J. W. (1992). Professional socialization: A longitudinal study of first-time high school principals. *Educational Administration Quarterly, 28*(1), 43–75.

Parsons, T. (1951). *The social system.* Glencoe, IL: Free Press.

Pincus, A. (1994). *Professional and organizational socialization and the role of the school psychologist in the New York Public Schools.* Unpublished doctoral dissertation, St. John's University, New York City.

Pitner, N. J., & Ogawa, R. T. (1981). Organizational leadership: The case of the school superintendent. *Educational Administration Quarterly, 17*(2), 45–65.

Scribner, J. D., & Layton, D. H. (Eds.). (1994). *The study of educational politics: The 1994 commemorative yearbook of the Politics of Education Association (1969–1994).* Philadelphia: Falmer Press.

Slater, R. O., & Boyd, W. L. (1999). Schools as polities. In J. Murphy & K. S. Louis (Eds.), *The handbook of research on educational administration* (2nd ed., pp. 323–336). San Francisco: Jossey-Bass.

Sykes, G. (1999). The "new professionalism" in education: An appraisal. In J. Murphy & K. S. Lewis (Eds.), *The handbook of research on educational administration* (2nd ed., pp. 163–182). San Francisco: Jossey-Bass.

Tucker, H. J., & Zeigler, L. H. (1980). *Professionals versus the public.* New York: Longman.

Tyack D., & Hansot, E. (1982). *Managers of virtue.* New York: Basic Books.

Van Maanen, J., & Schein, E. (1979). Toward a theory of organizational socialization. *Research in Organizational Behavior, 1,* 209–264.

Wrong, D. H. (1961). The oversocialized conception of man in modern sociology. *American Sociological Review, 26*(2), 183–193.

Zeigler, L. H., Jennings, M. K., & Peak, G. W. (1974). *Governing American schools: Political interaction in local school districts.* North Scituate, MA: Duxbury Press.

Zeigler, L. H., Jennings, M. K., & Peak, G. W. (1995). *Governing American schools: Political interaction in local school districts* (2nd ed.). North Scituate, MA: Duxbury Press.

Unrestricted Reemployment of Retired Administrators: Effective Policy or a Cause for Concern?

Theodore J. Kowalski and Scott R. Sweetland

Rehiring retired school administrators is not a new practice. In the past, however, principals and superintendents had to accept employment in another state or in a different profession in order to avoid retirement income penalties. Today in the midst of reported administrator shortages, policymakers in some states have been persuaded to pass a rehire policy permitting individuals to retire (usually under an early retirement provision) and continue working in a covered position (i.e., a position that requires participation in the same pension fund). These policies have not been uniform, especially with respect to placing an earnings ceiling on rehired employees. The broadest rehire policies have no earnings restrictions; thus, they allow administrators to retire and be rehired by their employers—typically in the very same position. Depending on a state's pension program, a rehired administrator would increase his or her annual income by 50 to 85 percent.

At first glance, rehire policies appear to be an economical alternative for dealing with an undersupply of qualified administrators. In addition, education special interest groups almost always support a rehire policy enthusiastically—a fact that has not gone unnoticed by state legislators. Experiences with these programs, however, expose the possibility of unanticipated problems, both for public education and for the school administration profession. The purposes of this chapter are (a) to explore the intent of rehire policies, (b) to compare policies that have different levels of earnings restrictions, (c) to identify possible problems with an unrestricted policy, and (d) to recommend an agenda for research on this topic. First, early retirement programs and supply and demand conditions are discussed. Then, three state pension programs with rehire provisions are summarized: Indiana (a high restriction state), South Carolina (a moderate restriction state), and Ohio (a low restriction state). The

Theodore J. Kowalski, Kuntz Professor of Education, University of Dayton
Scott R. Sweetland, Ohio State University

argument is made that an unrestricted policy has the potential to damage public education and the school administration profession. The need for research is stressed and a possible agenda for such inquiry is outlined.

PERSPECTIVES
Before examining specific rehire policies, the strategy of allowing school administrators to retire and continue working needs to be put in context. Three topics are briefly discussed for this purpose. The first is inclusion of early retirement provisions in state pension programs; the second is prevailing supply and demand issues; the third is the effects of early retirement in public education.

Adoption of Early Retirement Programs
Between the 1970s and the early 1990s, the most common change made to state educator pension programs was the inclusion of an early retirement option (Auriemma, Cooper, & Smith, 1992). The inclusion of this benefit was prompted by prevailing conditions including:

- *Producing cost savings for taxpayers*—Policymakers calculated that replacing experienced educators with less experienced and less educated individuals would reduce personnel costs.
- *Reducing reduction-in-force decisions*—During the 1970s and 1980s, many districts experienced declining enrollments and school boards were faced with the prospect of eliminating jobs in order to balance budgets. Lobbyists for education special interest groups took the position that early retirement could avoid such action and the potential litigation costs that might be associated with it (Natale, 1991).
- *Creating a benefit for educators*—Although often on opposite sides of policy initiatives, teacher unions and administrative associations have tended to unite when pursuing matters mutually beneficial to their members (Wirt & Kirst, 1997). Early retirement programs clearly fall into the category of mutually beneficial programs. Promulgating such legislation constituted a "no lose" situation for state officials; virtually no one opposed the establishment of early retirement benefits and the action generated approval from the entire education community.
- *Increasing the demand for educators*—Many states were experiencing a significant imbalance between the number of licensed educators and the number of jobs available. Early retirement presented a vehicle for increasing demand by moving individuals out of public schools prior to the customary retirement age.

Largely because tax revenues subsidize pension plans for public school educators, policies governing them are basically developed in political arenas—a context where self and group interests often compete with the general public's interests. For instance, education special interest group lobbyists and taxpayer association lobbyists typically have had very different interests with regard to early retirement provisions. Education lobbyists have supported early retirement largely because it is a fringe benefit; taxpayer lobbyists have supported the idea largely because it is considered economically efficient. Therefore, early retirement presented a rare situation in which policymakers could mollify two important pressure groups with a single policy.

Supply and Demand for Administrators

Rehire policies are rooted in the assumption that there is an undersupply of qualified educators. Verification of shortages is a difficult task for at least two reasons. First, supply and demand conclusions can be based on different types of criteria. For example, the claim that a shortage of qualified administrators exists in Ohio is widely accepted even though it appears to be based primarily on complaints from employing officials (school boards and superintendents). Yet, one could draw a very different conclusion about shortages from data reported by the Ohio Department of Education—data that show that there were 3.5 licensed principals for every principal position in 1999 (Ohio School Boards Association, 1999). Second, the term "shortage" is relative because definitions are frequently influenced by personal philosophy and bias. Emily Feistritzer (1998), for example, refutes claims of teacher shortages on the grounds that supply and demand studies rarely consider persons she considers to be competent but unlicensed (e.g., retired military personnel). Thus, opinions about shortages are affected by opinions about occupational qualifications.

Claims of a shortage of elementary and secondary school educators have been influenced by employment forecasts. For example, Fideler and Haselkorn (1999) forecast that the number of new teachers hired during the 1980s will nearly double during the first decade of the 21st century. Immigration, resulting in enrollment increases, and early retirements, resulting in added vacancies, are the major variables affecting such projections (Gerald & Hussar, 1998; Ingersoll, 1997). With respect to school administration, the Bureau of Labor Statistics estimates that there will be a 10 percent employment increase in these jobs between 2000 and 2008 (McCreight, 2001). Forecasts indicating an increased demand within an occupation, however, do not necessarily equate to an occupational shortage.

From the economist's perspective, a shortage exists when the demand for persons in a particular occupation exceeds the supply of individuals *qualified*, *available*, and *willing* to do that job (Veneri, 1999). These criteria, however, are subject to interpretation. More specifically, economic criteria (e.g., prevailing or recent wage scales), social criteria (e.g., role expectations based on evolving needs such as reform), and institutional criteria (e.g., licensing, resources) influence conclusions (Blank & Stigler, 1957; Franke & Sobel, 1970). Employers, for instance, may incorrectly declare an occupational shortage as a result of being displeased with the caliber of applicants—especially when they demand high quality but are unwilling to improve compensation or working conditions to attract the level of candidates they desire (Veneri, 1999, p. 15).

Two facts need to be considered in relation to an occupational shortage in school administration. After 1960, the supply of administrators (measured by the number of individuals who hold a license or who are license eligible) consistently exceeded demand in virtually all areas of school administration (McCarthy, Kuh, & Zent, 1981). As a result, many school boards experienced large applicant pools, especially for superintendencies. Although these pools have declined in recent years, they appear to remain relatively large in most sections of the country. For example, recent studies of superintendent search consultants revealed that their average applicant pools still contained 20 or more applicants (e.g., Glass, 2001; O'Connell, 2000). Second, the value placed on professional preparation and state licensing for administrators by employers typically has been very low. As far back as the early 1970s, noted historian David Tyack (1974) characterized the preparation of school administrators as being in intellectual disarray because of low admission standards and a curriculum consisting of sporadic and uncoordinated graduate study. He argued that while licensing had enhanced legitimate authority of administrators (e.g., school boards had to abide by licensure laws), it had failed to persuade policymakers and the general public that school administration was a true profession. In essence, school board members who considered professional preparation to be only marginally important felt more comfortable when they had huge applicant pools permitting them to hire a person of high caliber at their salary level.

When one considers the recent history of administrator preparation, licensing, and applicant pools, and when one uses an economic definition of an occupational shortage, there is reason to question the validity of a shortage of school administrators. In most other professions, applicant pools as low as 10 would not constitute an undersupply. However, in school administration, many employers reject professional preparation and licensure as qualifications to enter practice. Faced with dwindling applicant pools, the true concern of these employers is a combination of quality and quantity—that is, they are unable to find an adequate number of applicants who meet their criteria at their predetermined level of compensation (Kowalski, in press).

Effectiveness of Early Retirement Policy

Monitoring, forecasting, and evaluation are three common approaches that have been used to analyze public policy (Fowler, 2000). None of them appears to have been employed systematically and uniformly to determine if early retirement provisions have achieved their economic objectives. For example, virtually no empirical evidence is available to determine if replacing higher paid employees with lower paid employees has resulted in savings for taxpayers or a productivity increase in local school districts. Even so, many local district school boards took for granted that early retirement programs achieved their primary economic goal and they adopted such programs to augment state pension plans. Some of these district programs have already resulted in financial crises, largely because they were poorly conceived and based on gross underestimates of long-term costs (Brown & Repa, 1993). The achievement of the political objective of these programs (responding to education's special interest groups), however, is axiomatic; no educators' association or local union has lobbied to rescind early retirement programs.

The potential effects of administrator early retirement provisions on local school districts and on the welfare of the profession rarely have been discussed. This inattention became more disconcerting in the 1990s because of reported shortages of principals (e.g., Moore, 1999) and superintendents (e.g., Cooper, Fusarelli, & Carella, 2000). Expectedly, limited data that are available reveal a nexus between early retirement programs and supply/demand concerns. A recent Indiana study (Kowalski & Rausch, 2001), for example, found that two-thirds of the superintendents who exited the position in that state (i.e., individuals who stopped practicing as a superintendent for at least a year) opted to retire prematurely. An Alaska study, reporting that the demand of educators in that state was at an all-time high, cited the state's early retirement program as the primary cause of this condition (LaBerge, 1999). Neither such findings nor a lack of evidence about economic effectiveness has resulted in early retirement programs being rescinded. Instead, education lobbyists and policymakers have pursued ways to increase supply or decrease demand within the context of existing retirement policies.

THREE STATE PROGRAMS

State pension plans reflect a mix of political philosophies, laws, and supply-demand conditions. In addition, state pension plans are configured differently with respect to participation; some states have a separate plan for educators and some have a single plan for all state employees. Consequently, there are considerable structure and policy differences across the states, including differences in allowing retirees to work in covered positions. Three state pension programs—Indiana, Ohio, and South Carolina—were selected for analysis. The basic elements of each program cogent to rehiring retirees are summarized.

Indiana's Retirement System[1]

Indiana school administrators participate in the state's Teacher Retirement Fund (TRF), a program that does not include state employees outside of education or most state university faculty.[2] Members in the TRF also are required to participate in Social Security. The TRF has two primary components. The first, called the employee's annuity savings account, has the following parameters:

- Employers are required to contribute 3 percent of an employee's salary.
- Employees are required to contribute a minimum of 3 percent of their salaries.
- Employees may increase their contribution up to 10 percent in 1 percent increments.
- Employers may elect to pay the employee's share.

The annuity savings account is subject to taxation either when the member withdraws it after retirement or when it is expended (either by rolling into monthly retirement benefits or by converting it in some other manner). Members are given five choices for investing the principal in their accounts (e.g., bonds, stocks, and money market funds).

The second component is known as the state's pension portion. A mix of salary history, years of service, retirement age, and retirement options determines benefits in this component. The following provisions are especially pertinent to this portion of the program:

- A person's mean salary for retirement purposes is determined by averaging the five highest annual salaries during a person's career.
- Persons must have a minimum of 10 years of credible service to be "vested" in the system.
- One can retire without penalty under the following three circumstances: (a) at age 65 with 10 or more years of credible service; (b) at age 60 with 15 or more years of credible service; (c) at age 55 if age and years of credible service at least equal 85.
- One can retire with reduced benefits at age 50 and at least 10 years of credible service; the amount of reduction depends on age.
- Military service and out-of-state service may be used to increase years of service in the system; this provision, however, is restricted.

Members who retire may return to work in a covered position (i.e., a position participating in TRF) provided that: (a) the person has been retired for at least 90 days, and (b) the person does not earn more than $25,000 annually. Thus, this limited re-hire provision prevents retired administrators from continuing to be employed in Indiana public schools on a full-time basis. Administrators receiving early retirement benefits typically have accepted an administrative position in another state or a job not covered by the TRF if they continued to work. Recently a few administrators have found a way to circumvent the intention of the earnings ceiling; they have accepted administrative jobs in Indiana not requiring an administrative license. The most common have been business manager, director of facilities, and director of transportation services.

Ohio's Retirement System[3]

Ohio school administrators participate in the State Teachers Retirement System (STRS), a system that covers public-sector educators, including those in higher education. However, a few other public employee groups also are included. The STRS operates in lieu of Social Security, but participants are required to contribute to Medicare.

The STRS is a defined benefit rather than defined contribution program. Even though law defines required contributions, participants acquire the right to benefits that are not directly associated with their individual contributions. The following provisions apply to this program:

- Employers are required to contribute 14 percent of their total employee payroll to the program.

- Employees are required to contribute 9.3 percent of their gross earnings to the program.
- Employees are not allowed to increase their contributions to the program.
- Employers may pay an employee's share to the program (commonly referred to as "pick up" provision).

Participants in the program do not choose among investments or other options; rather, the program is professionally managed centrally for membership benefit. Retirement distributions are generally taxable to individuals as income.

Upon retirement from the system, a mix of salary history, years of service, retirement age, and retirement options determines the benefits received. The following provisions are especially important to understanding the program:

- A person's mean salary for retirement purposes is determined by averaging the three highest annual salaries during a person's career.
- Persons must have a minimum of 5 years of credible service to be "vested" in the system.
- One can retire without penalty under the following three circumstances: (a) at age 60 with 5 or more years of credible service; (b) at age 55 with 25 or more years of credible service; (c) at any age with 30 or more years of credible service.
- One can retire with less than 30 years of credible service and before age 65, but there is an actuarial reduction in benefit.
- Individuals can purchase additional credible service to make up for years of education or public service not otherwise recognized by the program.

An inherent assumption of the program was that calculating lifelong benefits based on the 3 highest earnings years would induce administrators to continuously peak their salaries by remaining in the workforce and pursuing higher paying positions. Some administrators, however, leveraged their incomes by accepting positions with organizations that did not participate in the STRS program or by working in school districts in other states.

Advents in early retirement incentives caused some persons to retire as early as age 50, an extremely early age when one considers the average life expectancy of about 80. Moreover, as workforce demographics changed, some school districts complained that early retirement incentives worked too well. Coupled with increasing student enrollments and limited numbers of teachers who were prepared to go into administration, early retirement incentives were thought to contribute to labor shortages.

Until September 15, 2000, educators covered by the STRS program were subject to a pension plan penalty for working more than 85 days during the first 18 months of retirement. By eliminating the 85-day ceiling, the Ohio legislature more closely aligned the STRS retirement provisions with those existing in pension plans covering other state employees (Switzer, 2001). In addition to justifying the change in the back-to-work provision on the basis of equal treatment of state employees, policy-makers pointed out that rehiring retired administrators could result in savings for local districts. Specifically, these savings could be realized in the following areas:

- If a district has an administrative salary schedule, the board is not required to grant service credit. Thus, an administrator could be rehired at a salary lower than he or she was previously receiving or the salary could be frozen for a specified period of time.
- A rehired administrator would not sustain accumulated sick leave (because accepting severance pay eliminates accumulated days).
- The board would not have to provide health insurance since the individual would be covered by the STRS's health insurance program.

Because the revision in the back-to-work provision is so recent, there have been only a limited number of cases in which the same employer has rehired a retired administrator. Under the current program, an administrator at any age with at least 30 years of credible service (but fewer than 35 years) receives 66 percent of salary; an administrator with 35 or more years receives 87.5 percent.

South Carolina's Retirement System[4]
South Carolina's rehire provision falls between Indiana and Ohio. The South Carolina Retirement Systems (SCRS) is made up of four distinct retirement programs:

- The Police Officers' Retirement System
- The General Assembly Retirement System
- The Judges' and Solicitors' Retirement System
- The South Carolina Retirement System, serving state employees, teachers, and other government employees

Placing educators with most other state employees in one pension program makes it difficult for policy to be tailored to any specific employee group. Prior to 2001, those in the SCRS, including school administrators, were allowed to retire and return to employment in a covered position after 60 days without suffering a loss of annuity payments, regardless of the compensation involved. This option, however, was deleted and effective July 1, 2001, a retiree may return to work in a covered position without penalty provided that he or she has been retired for at least 60 days and the annual income during the fiscal year does not exceed $50,000. An exemption may be obtained from the earnings limitation for certain teachers hired in a geographical need or a critical academic need area. Such exemptions are approved on an annual basis by the South Carolina Department of Education.

Although there are differing opinions regarding the reasons why state policymakers decided to impose an earnings ceiling on the rehire provision, South Carolina administrators tend to believe that a political backlash from taxpayers was responsible.

The backlash may have been initiated by media reports of school superintendents receiving both a pension and a full salary from a local district. The combined income issue also captured the attention of state legislators. Given the level of the income ceiling, administrators tend to believe that the ceiling was targeted at them. Whereas most school administrators in the state earn more than the ceiling, many of the others pension plan members do not. Thus, the judgment that the ceiling was imposed largely for political reasons (i.e., to diminish a backlash from taxpayers) may indeed be accurate.

DISCUSSION

The summary of policies in Indiana, Ohio, and South Carolina illustrates how restrictions on earnings may vary, and thus, why it is precarious to discuss rehire policies generically. An unrestricted earnings policy clearly has the greatest potential to decrease the demand for school administrators by enticing experienced school and district administrators who opt for early retirement to continue working in the same position. However, an unrestricted policy also has the greatest potential to spawn political conflict. A negative reaction to recent superintendent rehires in Ohio and South Carolina's decision to add an earnings ceiling support this conclusion. By comparison, Indiana's highly restrictive policy has been rarely used and rarely discussed.

For many legislators, adopting an unrestricted rehire policy is a rational and politically advantageous decision, especially in light of the increasing demand for administrators and the overwhelming support of education special interest groups. This strategy, however, has a potential dark side that needs to be debated. The following are the more prevalent concerns:

- In states with unrestricted policy, taxpayers often react negatively when they discover that superintendents or other educators are receiving dual incomes. The nature of their disapproval may be political (e.g., they simply resent a public employee making so much money) or economic (e.g., they resent the arrangement because tax dollars were already expended to support pension plan payments). In an environment where many taxpayers are already reluctant to increase public school funding, dissatisfaction with a rehire policy could have a negative systemic effect on critical matters such as bond referenda and school board elections.
- Faced with potential taxpayer criticisms, school boards are likely to seek concessions from rehired administrators. In Ohio, for example, several superintendents who took advantage of this provision agreed to have their salaries frozen. Compensation concessions may produce two troubling outcomes. First, they may restrict compensation packages subsequently approved for other district employees since, either formally or informally, salaries in most districts are indexed to the superintendent's salary (Kowalski, 1999). Second, such concessions may affect the compensation of the next superintendent; without increases

over a period of 2 or more years, the salary of the position will actually be reduced (assuming some level of inflation).

- Initially, superintendents are the most likely employees to be rehired. But as a precedent is established, other administrators and teachers are likely to demand equal treatment. In Ohio, for instance, several local teacher unions have already negotiated rehire policy even though the law is less than 2 years old. Picking and choosing which employees get to be rehired may prove to be a political and legal dilemma for local boards.
- Ironically, rehire policy could end up affecting the supply of school administrators negatively. Educators are attracted to this specialization by a number of intrinsic and extrinsic motivators, including the possibility of providing leadership in a supportive environment and the opportunity to make more money. Rehire policies could dramatically reduce the demand for administrators in districts having the most attractive positions. In addition, they create an option for teachers to remain in classroom while substantially increasing their income.
- The long-term financial implications of rehire policies are still unknown. As an example, a recent editorial in the *Columbus Dispatch*, a major newspaper in Ohio, warned that the $3.25 billion Health Care Stabilization Fund in the State Teachers Retirement System would be depleted by 2016 if the current rehire policy remained in effect (Back to school, 2001). Under Ohio policy, the cost of health care for rehired employees is transferred from local employers to the pension program. In addition, little thought has been given to possible repercussion if unrestricted rehire policies are rescinded. Such action could trigger a mass exodus of administrators in a single year.

Unfortunately little effort has been made to examine the effectiveness of unrestricted rehire policies, the conditions that have contributed to their political acceptance, and the unanticipated outcomes that they may produce. School administration scholars have the responsibility of developing a research agenda for this topic. The following are some of the topics that should be included:

- *The supply and demand for administrators*—The concept of rehiring is premised on the assumption that a critical shortage of school administrators exists. Yet, research on this matter has largely consisted of opinions articulated by administrators, school board members, and search consultants. As previously noted, there are more than three times as many Ohio educators holding a principal's license as there are principalships in the state; yet, the claim of a shortage is widely accepted. So the most fundamental research question is: Are claims of administrator shortages valid?
- *The role of education special interest groups*—Lobbying for early retirement was one of the rare instances when education special interest groups joined forces. The extent to which this occurred in relation to rehire policy is basically unknown. Differences in policy restrictions may be associated not only with

collaboration among education special interest groups but also with the individual and collective political power of these groups. For example, is there an association between the political strength of education special interest groups in a state and the adoption of unrestricted policy?

- *The scope of the pension program in terms of membership*—Pension programs are not uniform across states with respect to membership. Some plans cover all state employees; others cover only elementary and secondary public school educators. Possible connections between the membership scope and rehire policy restrictions need to be examined. For example, are unrestricted policies more likely to be adopted in pension plans that include state employees other than teachers and administrators?
- *Policies in other public employee pension plans*—The status of rehire policy for educators should be studied in relation to other state employee pension plans. For example, are states with unrestricted policy for other state employees more likely to adopt the same or similar policy for educator pension plans?
- *Effects of rehire policy at the state level*—Rehire policies have statewide implications. Subjects that merit study in this category include possible effects on (a) the supply and demand of administrators, (b) enrollments in school administration programs, (c) the economic stability of state pension programs, and (d) general support for public education. For example, do unrestricted rehire policies actually decrease the demand for administrators without affecting supply?
- *Effects of rehire policy at the local district level*—Rehire policies also have the potential to generate concerns at the local district level. Subjects that merit study in this category include possible effects on (a) long-term salary trends for administrative and teaching personnel, (b) litigation related to personnel decisions, (c) taxpayer opinions and attitudes, and (d) conflict with individual employees or employee groups. For example, have districts negotiated provisions on rehiring practices? To what extent have rehire policies resulted in economic, legal, or political conflict for local school boards?

Until more is learned about the potential consequences of unrestricted rehire policies, caution is in order. This is especially so given the possibility that the issue generating this policy, the purported undersupply of educators, may have been misconstrued.

NOTES

1. Data for Indiana were obtained from the *Active Member's Handbook 2001* published by the Indiana State Teachers' Retirement Fund.

2. Professors at Ball State University and Indiana State University may participate in the TRF or in another approved retirement system; only a small percentage opts to be in the TRF.

3. Most data for Ohio were obtained from the *Service Retirement and Plans of Payment, 2000–2001* published by the State Teachers Retirement System of Ohio.

4. Data for the South Carolina system were retrieved August 15, 2001, from World Wide Web: www.scrs.state.sc.us and from discussions with several school administrators in the state.

REFERENCES

Auriemma, F., Cooper, J., & Smith, T. (1992). *Graying teachers: A report on state pension systems and school district early retirement incentives.* (ERIC Document Reproduction Service No. ED347 620)

Back to school. (2001, December 28). Editorial. *The Columbus Dispatch*, p. A18.

Blank, D. M., & Stigler, G. J. (1957). *The demand and supply of scientific personnel.* New York: National Bureau of Economic Research.

Brown, H. R., & Repa, J. T. (1993). Do early outs work out? Teacher early retirement incentive plans. *School Business Affairs, 59*(8), 12–16.

Cooper, B. S., Fusarelli, L. D., & Carella, V. A. (2000). *Career crisis in the school superintendency? The results of a national survey.* Arlington, VA: American Association of School Administrators.

Feistritzer, C. E. (1998, January 28). The truth behind the "teacher shortage." *The Wall Street Journal*, C3.

Fideler, E., & Haselkorn, D. (1999). *Learning the ropes: Urban teacher induction programs and practices in the United States.* Belmont, MA: Recruiting New Teachers, Inc.

Fowler, F. C. (2000). *Policy studies for educational leaders: An introduction.* Upper Saddle River, NJ: Merrill, Prentice Hall.

Franke, W., & Sobel, I. (1970). *The shortage of skilled technical workers.* Lexington, MA: Heath-Lexington Books.

Gerald, D. E., & Hussar, W. J. (1998). *Projections of education statistics to 2008.* Washington, DC: U.S. Department of Education, Office of Education Research and Improvement.

Glass, T. E. (2001). *The superintendent crisis: A review by search consultants.* Denver, CO: Education Commission of the States.

Indiana State Teachers' Retirement Fund. (2001). *Active members handbook 2001.* Indianapolis: Author.

Ingersoll, R. M. (1997). Teacher turnover and teacher quality: The recurring myth of teacher shortages. *Teachers College Record, 99*(1), 41–44.

Kowalski, T. J. (1999). *The school superintendent: Theory, practice, and cases.* Upper Saddle River, NJ: Merrill, Prentice Hall.

Kowalski, T. J. (in press). Superintendent shortage: The wrong problem and wrong solutions. *Journal of School Leadership.*

Kowalski, T. J., & Rausch, J. (2001, February). *Exits from the superintendency in Indiana: Frequency and causes.* Paper presented at the Annual Meeting of the American Association of School Administrators, New Orleans.

LaBerge, M. (1999). *Statewide educator supply and demand report, state of Alaska, 1998.* (ERIC Document Reproduction Service No. ED 441 622)

McCarthy, M., Kuh, G., & Zent, A. (1981). *Investigation of supply and demand of school administrators in six states between 1975–76 and 1979–80.* (ERIC Document Reproduction Service No. ED 014 280)

McCreight, C. (2001). *Solutions to securing qualified principals.* (ERIC Document Reproduction Service No. ED 452 613)

Moore, D. H. (1999). *Where have all the principals gone?* (ERIC Document Reproduction Service No. ED429 368)

Natale, J. A. (1991). Early retirement plans blow in on the recession's ill wind. *American School Board Journal, 178*(8), 30.

O'Connell, R. W. (2000). *A longitudinal study of applicants for the superintendency.* (ERIC Document Reproduction Service No. ED 452 590)

Ohio Schools Boards Association (1999). *Principal searches.* Retrieved August 15, 2001, from www.osba-ohio.org/PrincipalSearch.html

South Carolina Retirement System. (2001). *Defined benefit plan details*. Columbia, SC: Author. Retrieved August 15, 2001, from www.scrs.state.sc.us

State Teachers Retirement System of Ohio. (2001). *Service Retirement and Plans of Payment, 2000–2001*. Columbus: Author.

Switzer, K. (2001). *Administrative and certificated staff retirement and re-employment*. Retrieved August 15, 2001, from www.nsba.org/nepn/newsletter/0201.html

Tyack, D. B. (1974). *The one best system*. Cambridge, MA: Harvard University Press.

Veneri, C. M. (1999, March). Can occupational labor shortages be identified using available data? *Monthly Labor Review*, 15–21.

Wirt, F. M., & Kirst, M. W. (1997). *The political dynamics of American education*. Berkeley, CA: McCutchan.

Addressing Mentor-Principals' Lifelong Learning Needs in the Preparation of Principal Candidates

Lawrence T. Kajs, John M. Decman, Chris Cox, Edward Willman, and Ramon Alaniz

School reform agendas can create new role changes for school administrators (Crow & Matthews, 1998; Jean & Evans, 1995; Marsh, 2000); consequently, educational administration programs must be responsive to the changing needs of principal preparation. For example, Weiss and Cambone (2000) have identified shared decision making (SDM) as a school reform of major proportion having the potential to alter the balance of power within a campus setting (p. 366). Thus, it would be expected that principal preparation programs would address the campus leader's role and responsibility in developing the SDM process. A central criticism about preparation programs is that principal candidates are not being sufficiently prepared to handle the ongoing "real-life" issues of a school.

A strong mentoring program for principal candidates has the potential to be one of the most effective ways of preparing new school administrators for the changing issues of schools (Crow & Matthews, 1998; Daresh & Playko, 1997; Muse, Thomas, & Wasden, 1992; Walker & Stott, 1994). A successful mentoring program can provide rich opportunities for principal candidates to expand their administrative abilities through the acquisition of knowledge and the development of skills and dispositions in their preparation for campus leadership. This is especially important since principal leadership is vital to the improvement of schools (Barth, 2001; Lunenburg & Ornstein, 2000; Sergiovanni, 2001).

While principal mentoring is highly valued in candidate preparation (Ashby, 1993; Capasso & Daresh, 2001; Schmuck, 1993; Shelton, 1991) and educational leadership guidelines call for trained mentors (National Council for the Accredita-

Lawrence T. Kajs, University of Houston, Clear Lake
John M. Decman, University of Houston, Clear Lake
Chris Cox, Alvin Independent School District, Alvin, Texas
Edward Willman, Texas A&M International University
Ramon Alaniz, Texas A&M International University

tion of Teacher Education, 1998), data indicate that lifelong learning (professional development) is not necessarily required for the mentoring role (Kajs, Weise, Baitland, & Cox, 1998). A challenge for educational administration faculty is to provide opportunities for lifelong learning to principals who serve as mentors. Little research exists on the type of lifelong learning needs, i.e., educational program areas, principals find essential to serve as mentors.

In this chapter we will first discuss the forces of change in the preparation of future campus administrators that lead to the need for mentoring. Secondly, we will describe the need, benefits, structure, and effectiveness of mentoring programs for principal candidates. Thirdly, we will underscore how lifelong learning (professional development) can strengthen mentor-principals' mentoring abilities in working with principal candidates, including a discussion about the growing institutional support for school administrators' continued professional development. Fourthly, we will discuss the research findings of 100 school principals, covering 23 South Texas school districts, who were asked to identify and to rank, on a Likert-type scale, the lifelong learning needs to serve the role of mentor-principal. Lastly, we will address the implications of the research results in addressing the lifelong learning needs of mentor-principals.

FORCES OF CHANGE

Major forces behind the recent increased popularity of mentor programs for principal candidates have been a result of several national and state educational reform reports. *A Nation at Risk* (United States National Commission on Excellence in Education, 1983) and *Turning Points 2000: Educating Adolescents in the 21st Century* (Jackson, 2000) are examples of two major reports. These studies, among others, critiqued schools as failing in their duty to prepare students for the many expectations and demands they may experience as adults.

During the last decade, standards-driven reform efforts have sought to increase student achievement (Shanker, 1994), restore public confidence in schools (Edmundson, 1993), and create educational environments in which all children are successful (*What Goals 2000 Means for You*, 1994) in educational communities across the United States. In this national quest for educational excellence, the school campus administrator plays a crucial role in achieving these goals (Barth, 1990, 2001; Brookover, 1981; Griffiths, Stout, & Forsyth, 1998; Sergiovanni, 2001). "Every educational reform report since the 1980s has concluded that schools are only as good as their administrators" (Lunenburg & Ornstein, 2000, p. 575).

Criticizing the perceived lack of quality of leadership found in most educational communities, the most common recommendation of these reports was that, if schools were to improve, principals would have to become more effective instructional leaders. Successful leadership by principals is viewed as critical for schools to effectively prepare students (Brookover et al., 1982; Sergiovanni, 2001). Effective Schools Research (Brookover & Lezotte, 1979; Edmonds, 1979) laid the groundwork by "introducing the profile of an effective principal as an instructional leader whose vision of excellence permeates every dimension of a school's character" (Weise, 1992, p. 7). This leader is one who is capable of providing a clear sense of mission and fostering high agreement among staff as to goals and purposes.

Lemley (1997) indicates that new models of educational leadership have addressed the need to develop the school as a community of learners. The advent and integration of site-based management and building level decision making has created an increasing demand on the role of the principal. For the principal, change is a constant reality of leadership with the dynamics of leadership revolving around how one creates, facilitates, embraces, and builds meaningful change in schools.

The increasingly accepted view of the effective principal has led to widespread criticism that universities are not preparing prospective administrators to deal with the "real-life" aspects of their positions. Lunenburg and Ornstein (2000) noted:

> The prospect of inadequately trained school leaders is serious when one considers the public schools' struggle with such problems as drug abuse, school violence and vandalism, at-risk youngsters and AIDS. It is not surprising therefore that calls for reforms of university programs for the preparation of school administrators have resounded through the nation. (p. 575)

Recognizing that the clinical field experience in which principal candidates engage is pivotal to their future success as effective leaders, many universities across the nation began implementing an internship course in their principal preparation programs during the 1960s. It was during the 1960s that the American Association of School Administrators (AASA) fervently supported the need for internships in the preparation of school administrators (Ovando, 1998). This trend continued throughout the 1980s, at which time the internship experience became a crucial element of the principal certification program (Ovando, 1998). Universities are again evaluating their principal preparation programs to ensure that principal candidates undergo sufficient and appropriate internship experiences that will prepare them for meeting the challenges related to the current view of leadership—that of a visionary leader (Weise, 1992).

Hoyle, English, and Steffy (1998) provide direction and guidance for universities in examining their principal preparation programs, specifically the internship component. Drawing upon the standards created by national educational organizations including the American Association of School Administrators (AASA), the National Association of Secondary School Principals (NASSP), the National Association of Elementary School Principals (NAESP), the National Policy Board of Educational Administration (NPBEA), the Association for Supervision and Curriculum (ASCD), Council of Chief State School Officers (CCSSO) and National Council for Accreditation of Teacher Education (NCATE), Hoyle, English, and Steffy (1998) provide an extensive profile of the knowledge and skills the contemporary campus administrator must possess to inspire leadership for excellence (pp. 7–8).

NEED, BENEFITS, STRUCTURE, AND EFFECTIVENESS
OF MENTORING FOR PRINCIPAL CANDIDATES

Need for Mentoring

As university faculty members across the nation reevaluate their graduate educational leadership programs to ensure that principal candidates participate in relevant experiences for the challenges of campus leadership, a strong mentoring component should be addressed. Taking the lead from successful teacher education programs that incorporate strong mentoring elements, principal certification program professors need to assess the effectiveness of the mentoring process in their internships. This would include studying the characteristics of effective mentor-principals as well as the responsibilities of mentor-principals (Capasso & Daresh, 2001), which in turn would impact mentor selection, mentor preparation, and accountability (Geismar, Morris, & Lieberman, 2000; Kajs et al., 1998).

Benefits of Mentoring

The benefits associated with successful mentoring programs for prospective principals are considerable. Crow and Matthews (1998) assign three types of development to the role of mentoring: professional, psychosocial, and career (p. 25). Successful mentoring programs allow for the identification of appropriate role models as well as assist principal candidates in refining their personal philosophies of educational leadership and developing commitment to their administrative careers through personalized coaching and feedback (Capasso & Daresh 2001; Daresh & Playko, 1992). Learning is experiential and, therefore, problem-centered rather than subject-centered. Because of "hands-on" types of experiences, principal candidates are able to observe and learn proven techniques and strategies that their mentors have used successfully in varying settings. Multiple opportunities to reflect, discuss, and interact with administrators help principal candidates improve communication skills as well as increase the sense of connection that comes from working with mentor-principals. In a study to determine what occurred in mentor relationships, Ashby (1993) reported that decreased feelings of isolation as well as expanded informal networks were benefits to both principal candidates and mentor-principals. Mentoring can positively influence career advancement for principal candidates because of the special help, encouragement, and attention given by a mentor, including the opportunities to team and be visible with the mentor (Capasso & Daresh 2001; Luebkemann & Clemens, 1994; Schmuck, 1993).

The mentoring process can provide benefits to mentor-principals as well. Crow and Matthews (1998) outline multiple benefits provided to mentors that include approval of their work performance, recognition of their value to the organization, and learning opportunities, e.g., self-assessment of their philosophies underlying their administrative actions. Daresh and Playko (1992) also indicate that mentors can achieve a high degree of satisfaction in helping other individuals. Principals carry with them "extraordinary insights about their work" which they can share in their mentoring relationships (Barth, 1990, p. 78). This exchange process sets the stage for fostering reflection, cooperation, and friendship for both mentor-principals and principal candidates (Crow & Matthews, 1998). Moreover, the process of mentoring accelerates learning and leadership development for the principal candidates and mentor-principals alike (Hopkins-Thompson, 2000). Cordeiro and Smith-Sloan (1995) point out that mentor-principals become co-learners through the relationship with their principal candidates in three ways, by (1) examining their own ideas, (2) learning new content knowledge, and (3) exchanging ideas in collaboration on projects (p. 15).

Structure of Mentor Programs

Although the structure of the majority of mentor programs for principal candidates closely parallels that of mentor-teacher programs, Daresh and Playko (1989) caution that mentorship practices for beginning teachers and administrators, while sharing some common features, have important differences that necessitate a different type of mentoring program for principal candidates. Daresh and Playko (1989) identify key issues that cause this differentiation. First, while a substantial amount of research exists on effective teaching, the same does not hold true for research on effective principalship. Principals who want to mentor an aspiring or beginning administrator, especially for the first time, find a lack of research to guide them. Second, the close contact that exists between mentor-teacher and protégé by virtue of proximity, allowing for timely feedback, is usually absent in the mentor-principal and principal candidate relationship. The variability and unpredictability of the principal's job does not always provide opportunities for regular feedback. Third, while mentor-teachers may focus more on orientating preservice and beginning teachers to the teaching profession, mentor-principals assume that principal candidates already have this prospective because of previous school experience. Thus, the mentor-principal's role is not one of orienting the principal candidate to the workings of a school, but one of developing responsibility in becoming a formal leader of a campus community. Daresh and Playko (1989) indicate that mentor-principals are to serve as "translators" helping their protégés to "learn a new dialect that is spoken in the same familiar land" (p. 92). While mentor relationships at the administrative level are not totally akin to those of the mentor-teacher and protege, fundamental learning must take place through the process of the mentorship. Crow and Matthews (1998) identify and briefly explain four content areas viewed essential in the structure of mentorship programs for teachers and principals that include knowledge, skills, behaviors, and values (p. 26). They explain:

> Knowledge content involves theoretical, community, and personal information. Interpersonal relationships, communication, and supervision are examples of skill content. Content related to behavior includes teacher selection, networking, and discipline. Value content includes cultural and professional norms, beliefs, and assumptions. (p. 26)

Addressing these content areas in a meaningful and functional way underscores the importance of mentor-principals being lifelong learners.

Effectiveness of Mentoring Programs

Although a paucity of empirical data exists that verifies the effectiveness of mentoring principals, studies are noteworthy for their support of the mentoring process. A study conducted by Shelton in 1991 examined the perceptions of 377 elementary school principals with regard to mentoring. Over 80 percent perceived mentoring to be helpful. These principals also shared the belief that mentoring should play an integral role in training principal candidates.

Ashby's (1993) study of principals in the Illinois Administrators' Academy examined changes in instructional leadership of new principals to determine whether mentoring relationships significantly impacted principals' behaviors. She found that all principals reported changes, to some degree, in behavior associated with the leadership dimensions of effective schools. In short, mentors appear to be crucial in changing perceptions and behaviors of entry-level administrators by helping them connect their knowledge base of instructional leadership to their behaviors.

A study of a 2-year experimental administrator preparation program in Oregon, in collaboration with the National Association of Secondary School Principals (NASSP) Assessment Center program, produced comparative results between experimental programs and traditional ones. Schmuck (1993) found that principal candidates developed more favorable attitudes toward their training program and acquired a deeper understanding of leadership than did students in more traditional preparation programs. Also, principal candidates in the experimental program were able to more successfully negotiate their first year as an administrator than those in the traditional program. In a Montana study, Jean and Evans (1995) concluded that educational administration programs should include an internship with mentoring for principal candidates to be better prepared to handle the critical tasks of schools, e.g., team building and teacher evaluations.

In the study of a Kentucky program, Ricciardi (2000) found that novice administrators who were being mentored were far more involved in school management and interpersonal issues rather than on developing competencies in instructional leadership. These findings reflected research by Doud and Keller (1998) in a National Association of Elementary School Principals (NAESP) study. If school principals are going to lead schools in an era of retrenchment and accountability, their preparation and their lifelong learning activities, including those in the mentoring program, must be more balanced.

LIFELONG LEARNING FOR MENTOR-PRINCIPALS

The increasing involvement of principals in mentoring programs requires school leaders to participate in lifelong learning to prepare them for their mentoring responsibilities. Lifelong learning can be described as the continuation of learning throughout one's life that contributes to a person's social well-being, and personal and professional development (Knapper & Cropley, 1985). Professional development provides leaders information to construct knowledge, think creatively and function productively (Cross, 1991). The process of lifelong learning can transform a leader into becoming a self-renewing individual—one who continually seeks out new knowledge and alternative solutions to problems (Collinson, Sherrill, & Hohenbrink, 1994, pp. 5–7). "The most noble and distinguishing characteristic of human life is the capacity to learn. Learning is a sign of life and the lifelong expression of our sense of wonder and worth" (Barth, 1990, p. 78). Thus, lifelong learning can assist school administrators to better understand the ever-changing educational environment and to broaden their knowledge and skills development, strengthening their ability to serve as mentors.

Institutional Support for School Administrators' Lifelong Learning

Due to advances made in educational research concerning effective schools, as well as public demands for accountability, the number of states that require continuing education for many professions has significantly increased in the last 10 years (Queeney & English, 1994). Recognizing that school administrators are in a pivotal position to effectively address growing student diversity, societal expectations, and new technologies, state department initiatives and state legislation have helped to maintain a role in the professional development of the school administrator through technical assistance and support. For example, a major piece of legislation in Missouri, the Excellence in Education Act of 1985, provided for the establishment of a Leadership Academy administered by the Missouri Department of Elementary and Secondary Education (Stone & Heard, 1995). The program's purpose is to provide school leaders preparation on current and relevant issues in leadership education. Similarly, South Carolina's Plan to Reach the National Education Goals 1994, a major statewide initiative, provides for teams of education consultants who are responsible for providing administrators with effective leadership and managerial skills (Stone & Heard, 1995). The Minnesota Administrators' Academy began a mentoring program in the early 1990s to improve the professional development for beginning principals (Monsour, 1998). Likewise, the state-mandated Kentucky Principal Intern Program (KPIP) provides job development education for new campus administrators in a 1-year mentoring program (Ricciardi, 2000). Other state departments of education, including those in Georgia and Colorado, have established programs that target leadership development (Stone & Heard, 1995).

Besides state support for lifelong learning opportunities, foundational assistance also exists. The Danforth Foundation, which awards grants to universities to encourage greater university-school district collaboration, has given support in developing the interaction between mentor-principals and principal candidates (Weise, 1992). During the late 1990s, the Bill and Melinda Gates Foundation has provided resources to the Technology Leadership Academy for Superintendents and Principals in Texas to develop school administrators' competencies in the leadership roles. Information about this program can be found at Texas Education Agency (2000), www.tasanet.org/depserv/profdev/Techacademy.pdf.

Principal Input

Increased interest and support of mentor programs as a critical component of graduate administrative preparation programs necessitate increased cooperation between schools and universities to develop an effective field-based approach to learning. In developing successful mentoring programs, a critical component is to identify the knowledge and skills school administrators need to serve as successful mentors. Research alludes to essential knowledge and skills of administrators (Hoyle, English, & Steffy, 1998; Schmieder & Cairns, 1996; Weise, 1992). For the school-university relationship to be truly collaborative in creating and sustaining effective mentoring programs, school administrator input is vital, especially since this information can serve as topics of lifelong learning for mentor-principals. Toward this end, we developed and piloted a questionnaire that asked 100 schools principals from 23 South Texas school districts to identify and to rank, on a Likert-type scale, the knowledge and skills essential for a principal to serve as a mentor-principal to a prospective administrator in a principal certification program.

RESEARCH STUDY ON KNOWLEDGE AND SKILLS FOR THE ROLE OF MENTOR-PRINCIPAL

Research Methodology

The questionnaire sought demographic and experiential information about principals, the respondents, in the study. These questions provided variables of three levels of measurement: nominal (e.g., campus name), ordinal (e.g., 5 or less years of experience as a principal), and ratio (e.g., the number of years as a principal). The Frequencies and Descriptives modules of the Statistical Package for the Social Sciences (SPSS) were used for statistical data analysis.

Secondly, we asked principals to identify the knowledge and skills that are essential for a principal to serve as a mentor to a principal candidate in the principal certification program. The questionnaire included a list of 31 professional program components or areas that listed knowledge and skills, as well as three blank spaces for principals to add any other program components not included on the list. This selection of professional program components was not intended to be an exhaustive list of knowledge and skills, but a comprehensive one. Respondents ranked the program components from least essential (1) to most essential (5) on a Likert-type scale. A staff development specialist reviewed the list of knowledge and skills, and three principals piloted the study, providing comprehensiveness of program components and suitability of program design.

This study used judgment and convenience sample approaches instead of random sampling in soliciting principals' participation (Pfaffenberger & Patterson, 1987). These methods were used since the primary purpose of the study was to identify trends and not necessarily draw conclusions for all principals.

After 100 respondents ranked on an ordinal scale the program components from least essential (1) to most essential (5), the data were analyzed using the median, mode, and quartiles. For purposes of analysis, pie charts and box plots were also used to investigate and graphically portray the data. The arithmetic mean and standard deviation were not deemed appropriate statistics for ordinal variables.

Demographic Results of Respondents

Questionnaires received from 100 principals representing 23 school districts in South Texas were analyzed. As shown in table 1, forty-six percent (46 percent) of the respondents were female and fifty-four percent (54 percent) of the principals were male. Ninety-two percent (92 percent) of the participants held a master's degree and eight percent (8 percent) had earned a doctorate. Forty-four percent (44 percent) had previous experience mentoring a principal intern and twenty-nine percent (29 percent) had previously mentored only a teacher. The majority of these principals, eighty-one percent (81 percent), had held other campus level administrative positions. The percentages of the 100 participants based on years of experience as a principal were: (a) forty-seven percent (47 percent) had 5 or less years of experience; (b) twenty-four percent (24 percent) had 6 to 10 years; (c) ten percent (10 percent) had 11 to 15 years; (d) six percent (6 percent) had 16 to 20 years; (e) six percent (6 percent) had 21 to 25 years; and (f) seven percent (7 percent) had 26 or more years of experience. The median number of years of experience as a school administrator was 7.5 years. Fifty-one percent (51 percent) of the principals managed an elementary campus, twenty-nine percent (29 percent) were responsible for a middle school campus, and eighteen percent (18 percent) were responsible for a high school campus. Two percent (2 percent) managed a combined elementary and middle school campus. The campus populations of surveyed principals ranged from 300 to 3,200 students with a median student population of 760. The teachers on campus ranged from 20 to 200 with a median of 50. The size of their support staffs ranged from 0 to 225 with a median staff size of 15. Twenty-one (21 percent) percent of the principals did not indicate having an assistant principal. Fifty-four percent (54 percent) of the respondents had one assistant principal, and twenty-five percent (25 percent) had two assistant principals. (See table 1.)

Results of Study on Knowledge and Skills

To identify what knowledge and skills are essential for a principal to have in order to serve as a mentor to a principal candidate, 100 responding South Texas principals ranked the 31 professional components from least essential (1) to most essential (5). The rankings were created using the median as the first ranking criterion. Intra-rankings within the various categories of "Most Essential," "Very Essential," and "Essential" were established using the values of the first, second, and third quartiles. Therefore, a component with quartiles of 4, 4, and 5, respectively, is considered more essential than a component whose quartiles are 3, 4, and 4. (See table 2.)

The results indicated that principals ranked seven program areas (1) conflict resolution strategies, (2) interpersonal and social skills, (3) communication techniques, (4) school leader as change agent, (5) time management techniques, (6) curriculum design and development, and (7) appropriate school law issues as the most essential, with a median of five. For purposes of intra-ranking within this most essential category, the first three program components, i.e., conflict resolution strategies, interpersonal and social skills, and communication techniques, all had first, second, and

Table 1. Demographic Information of 100 Principals from 23 South Texas School Districts

Gender, Academic Degree, and Experience	Percentage
Female	46
Male	54
Master's	92
Doctorate	8
Previous Experience Mentoring Principal	44
Previous Experience Mentoring Teacher Only	29
Held Other Campus Level Administrative Positions	81

Years of Experience as Principal	Percentage
(a) Five (5) or Less	47
(b) Six (6) to Ten (10)	24
c) Eleven (11) to Fifteen (15)	10
(d) Sixteen (16) to Twenty (20)	6
(e) Twenty-one (21) to Twenty-five (25)	6
(f) Twenty-six (26) or More	7
7 Median Years Experience as School Administrator	7.5

Types of Campus Managed	Percentage
Elementary	51
Middle School	29
High School	18
Combined Elementary and Middle School	2

Populations	Range	Median
Students	300–3,200	760
Teachers	20–200	50
Staff	0–225	15

	Quantity	Percentage
Assistant Principals	0	21
Assistant Principals	1	54
Assistant Principals	2	25

third quartile of 5; while the remaining four program areas, i.e., school leader as change agent, time management techniques, curriculum design and development, and appropriate school law issues had a first quartile of 4, second and third quartile of 5.

The 100 principals ranked program components, numbered 8 to 28, as very essential with a median of 4. However, program components, numbered 8 to 22, each had a first and second quartile of 4, and a third quartile of 5. These program components included (8) appropriate task assignments for interns, (9) leadership styles, (10) responsibilities of the mentor, (11) motivational techniques, (12) community relationship development, (13) critical thinking/higher order questioning processes, (14) problem-solving processes, (15) planning techniques, (16) parental involvement techniques, (17) long-term planning strategies, (18) human resources management, (19) financial planning and budgeting procedures, (20) risk and safety man-

Table 2.   Ranking of the 31 Program Components from Most Essential to Essential

Program Components	Rank	Median	First Quartile	Second Quartile	Third Quartile
1. Conflict Resolution Strategies	Most Essential	5	5	5	5
2. Interpersonal and Social Skills	Most Essential	5	5	5	5
3. Communication Techniques	Most Essential	5	5	5	5
4. School Leader as Change Agent	Most Essential	5	4	5	5
5. Time Management Techniques	Most Essential	5	4	5	5
6. Curriculum Design and Development	Most Essential	5	4	5	5
7. Appropriate School Law Issues	Most Essential	5	4	5	5
8. Appropriate Task Assignments for Interns	Very Essential	4	4	4	5
9. Leadership Styles	Very Essential	4	4	4	5
10. Responsibilities of the Mentor	Very Essential	4	4	4	5
11. Motivational Techniques	Very Essential	4	4	4	5
12. Community Relationship Development	Very Essential	4	4	4	5
13. Critical Thinking/Higher Order Questioning Processes	Very Essential	4	4	4	5
14. Problem-Solving Processes	Very Essential	4	4	4	5
15. Planning Techniques	Very Essential	4	4	4	5
16. Parental Involvement Techniques	Very Essential	4	4	4	5
17. Long-Term Planning Strategies	Very Essential	4	4	4	5
18. Human Resources Management	Very Essential	4	4	4	5
19. Financial Planning and Budgetary Procedures	Very Essential	4	4	4	5
20. Risk and Safety Management	Very Essential	4	4	4	5
21. Organizational Behavior	Very Essential	4	4	4	5
22. Technology Education/Training	Very Essential	4	4	4	5
23. Marketing of Services	Very Essential	4	3	4	4
24. Research Procedures to Conduct Collaborative Inquiry	Very Essential	4	3	4	4
25. Reflective Practice	Very Essential	4	3	4	4
26. Learning/Personality Inventories	Very Essential	4	3	4	4
27. Alternative/Authentic Assessment Practices for Assessing the Intern	Very Essential	4	3	4	4
28. Policymaking Procedures	Very Essential	4	3	4	4
29. Adult Learning Theories	Essential	3	3	3	4
30. Grant Writing Ability	Essential	3	3	3	4
31. Fund-Raising Techniques	Essential	3	2	3	3

agement, (21) organizational behavior, and (22) technology education/training. The program components, numbered 23 to 28, had a first quartile of 3, and a second and third quartile of 4. These program components included (23) marketing of services, (24) research procedures to conduct collaborative inquiry, (25) reflective practice, (26) learning/personality inventories, (27) alternative/authentic assessment practices for assessing the intern, and (28) policymaking procedures.

The principals ranked the remaining three program components, numbered 29 to 31, as essential with a median of 3. Two of the three program components, (29) adult learning theories and (30) grant writing ability, had a first and second quartile of 3, and a third quartile of 4. The final program component, (31) fund-raising techniques, had a first quartile of 2, and a second and third quartile of 3. None of the 31 professional program components received a median ranking below 3.

IMPLICATIONS OF THE RESEARCH

Questionnaire results indicated that South Texas principals find some knowledge and skills more essential than others for service to the mentoring role of principal candidates. The top seven lifelong learning program components of mentor-principals, with a median of 5, were conflict resolution, interpersonal and social skills, communication techniques, school leader as change agent, time management techniques, curriculum design and development, and school law issues. These results are not surprising, considering the school principal's multifaceted position. Each of the top seven components will be briefly discussed.

As managers, principals are involved in handling conflicts. Conflicts in schools are inevitable since schools operate as open social systems (Green, 2001). Mentor-principals need to be familiar with the types and sources of conflict resolution strategies, e.g., Situation-Target-Path (S-T-P), to address problematic issues (Schmuck & Runkel, 1994). Conflict management strategies could include taking a preventive approach to problems by establishing relationships with people to reduce the potential for future conflicts (Razik & Swanson, 2001, p. 182). In the State of Texas, the *Texas School Law Bulletin* (1998) highlights the importance of conflict resolution education for school professionals, requiring annual professional development in this area.

As a campus leader, principals need to demonstrate strong interpersonal communication skills. The level of relationship between the mentor-principal and principal candidate is based in large part by their interactions, e.g., coaching. The ability to exchange information in an effective and respectful manner is especially critical in carrying out the learning process. These skills have greater value than given to professional experience, personal qualities, and subject-specific expertise (Hawkey, 1997).

The third program component, communication techniques, which includes verbal and written approaches, serves to transmit information to members of an organization. It is estimated that principals can spend up to 80 percent of their time communicating with staff, students, parents, and the community at large (Green, 2001, p. 96). Hanson (1996) states "Communication is the glue that holds an organization together and harmonizes its parts" (p. 224). An effective communication system can establish a strong foundation in developing a school culture responsive to addressing a people's needs (Clarke, 1999; National Education Association, 1997).

The school leader functioning as a change agent reinforces the principal's role of being a visionary leader who can guide and collaborate with the school community to develop clear goals and to organizationally work toward them. Nelson and Quick (1997) indicate that effective change agents possess technical and interpersonal communication skills, and exercise multiple leadership styles to achieve results. Razik and Swanson (2001) note:

> Effective principals initiate change by using teacher leadership, Golding and Rallis said (1993). They do this through motivating teachers by creating a problem-solving climate, using participatory decision making, establish collegial communication, providing for recognition and rewards, and obtaining the resources necessary to make and maintain change. (p. 335)

The fifth program component, time management techniques, is the recognition that the principal's job requires prioritization of time and talent, as well as the ability to delegate responsibilities. Time management techniques incorporate planning strategies to "valutize" work objectives in order to make choices about priorities (Roesch, 1998). Glatthorn (2000) points out that effective school leaders possess the ability to plan systematically and efficiently manage their time to fulfill set goals (p. 152). In two studies of school leadership internship programs, in Connecticut and Texas, time management was identified as a key element in carrying out a school administrator's organizational responsibilities (Cordeiro & Smith-Sloan, 1995; Ovando, 1998).

Curriculum design and development, the sixth program component, addresses the principal's central role of instructional leader. This program area is especially essential considering the research by Doud and Keller (1998) and Ricciardi (2000) that school principals tend to dedicate little time to curriculum and instruction issues, although principals are being held more accountable for schools' instructional successes. McEwan (1998) states that the principal, as an instructional leader, must be able to articulate and represent (symbolize) to the campus faculty and larger community the value of schooling.

Lastly, the seventh program component is school law issues. Given the litigious nature of society, the number of state and federal mandates in education, and the complexities of a pluralistic society, principals need a strong foundation and continuous update in changing education laws (McCormick & Kajs, 2001). Principals must be familiar with laws governing due process, sexual harassment, and school safety, to name a few. Unfortunately, principals may not be sufficiently prepared in school law. In their research on the legal knowledge of school officials in Texas, Higham, Littleton, and Styron (2001) found that teachers and school administrators lacked sufficient knowledge of legal issues impacting public schools. They went on to mention that these results were consistent with findings in other states, as well.

These top seven program components have knowledge and skills guidelines directly or indirectly stated by NCATE (1998) in its Advanced Programs in Educational Leadership for Principals, Superintendents, Curriculum Directors, and Supervisors. The seven elements and their corresponding NCATE guideline numbers are: conflict resolution strategies (NCATE 7.5), interpersonal and social skills (NCATE 7.1), communication techniques (NCATE 7.2, 7.3, 10.3), school leader as change agent (NCATE 1.4), time management techniques (not specifically mentioned, but implied in NCATE 6.1, 6.3), curriculum design and development (NCATE 3.1 to 3.9), and appropriate school law issues (NCATE 11.1, 11.2). (See appendix A: Seven Top Program Components and Corresponding 1998 NCATE Guidelines.)

The results of this South Texas study indicate a need for university leadership and public school administrators in this geographical area, and probably other regions of the country as well, to collaborate in developing lifelong learning programs for mentor-principals, as well as in strengthening principal certification components. For instance, Muse and Willardson (1998) indicate that three Utah universities have addressed mentor-principals' lifelong learning needs by providing workshops each year, as well as a handbook for mentoring principal candidates. They reported, after a 5-year period, that this program has been effective.

Since forty-seven percent (47 percent) of the participants in this study have been principals for 5 years or less, educational administration faculty can use this study in reviewing and redesigning their principal preparation programs to better address the needs of campus administrators. For example, a course on negotiations could incorporate four of the top program components: conflict resolution strategies, communication techniques, interpersonal and social skills, and time management techniques. These four components were identified as key abilities of school leaders to effectively handle the organizational responsibilities of schools (Cordeiro & Smith-Sloan, 1995; Ovando, 1998). Principal preparation programs need to develop energetic school leaders who can create and nurture communities of learners, empowering other leaders, faculty, staff, as well as students and parents (Crow & Matthews, 1998; Sergiovanni, 2000).

Situations may exist where a principal may wish to serve as a mentor to a principal candidate, but may not be able to handle the many responsibilities of the mentoring process because of time constraints and lack of proficiency with certain knowledge and skills, e.g., technology. A viable option could be the use of the support team approach in the mentoring of the principal candidate (Kajs, Cox, Willman, Alaniz, & Gomez, 2001).

The Support Team Approach in Mentoring Principal Candidates

In preparation programs the assigned mentor tends to be the sole person at the campus level accountable for mentoring (Kajs, Alaniz, & Willman, 1998). These responsibilities are usually added on to the mentor's current chores. Hence, the mentoring process may be affected by time constraints considering the situational character of the mentor-principal's job (Hanson, 1996). Moreover, mentor-principals may also have shortcomings in some knowledge and skills areas valuable to the mentoring process that could cause frustration for mentors and disappointment for principal candidates. Another potentially problematic issue is the compatibility between mentors and principal candidates. If the two lack compatibility, it could strain the relationship, creating a negative climate for learning (Cline & Necochea, 1997; Hawkey, 1997).

The issues of time constraints, knowledge and skill limitations, and possible compatibility conflicts in a mentoring arrangement can be addressed by using the support team approach process (Kajs et al., 1998). The support team should comprise the mentor-principal and campus educators, as well as school district administrators and university faculty, who bring special knowledge and skills to the mentoring process. Team members should also possess communication skills since they are valuable in establishing a successful exchange process of ideas (Hawkey, 1997). Principals overwhelmingly indicated preference for the support team approach in mentoring principal candidates (Kajs et al., 2001).

The support team model demonstrates a concerted effort to address principal candidates' content and skill needs. This team approach reduces time commitments of mentor-principals as well as sharing mentoring tasks with other educators. If a personality conflict occurs between the principal candidate and mentor-principal, or any other team participant, then other members can help the aspirant. Moreover, the variety of support members' expertise can alleviate mentor-principals' shortcomings in meeting principal candidates' variety of needs. The support team approach demonstrates that school district leadership views the preparation of principal candidates not only a campus responsibility, but also a school district one (Ganser, 1995). The collaborative nature of the support team approach demonstrates to principal candidates the value of interpersonal and inter-institutional relationships (Rubin, 1998).

Since the support team consists of a variety of educators with multiple assignments and work locations, coordination of participants is crucial to an effective mentoring process. Consequently, a coordinator for the support team should be selected to organize team members' responsibilities and tasks following a well-formulated schedule. Using a computer-based project management software package, e.g., Microsoft Project 2000, can be a valuable tool in developing schedules and in providing accountability. Since this software can make scheduling accessible on the Internet, team members are able to communicate with one another more readily. Moreover, communications can take place among participants via "telementoring" (e.g., conferencing or e-mails via the Internet), as well as the customary face-to-face approach.

While principals view the support team approach as a viable approach to mentoring principal candidates (Kajs et al., 2001), its lack of use at the campus level can be due to a number of reasons. First, this team approach requires the selection of a group of talented people who may already have multiple assignments with extensive time commitments. Second, resources would be needed to provide for a coordinator to schedule and monitor the support team members' activities. Lastly, the mentor-principal and the other team participants may bring different or competing philosophies and views on campus leadership, which could have an adverse affect on the principal candidate. With the mentor-principal being solely responsible for mentoring at the campus level, certainty exists about whom is accountable for preparing the principal candidate.

CONCLUSION

Principal preparation programs must be poised to address the role expectations of school administrators, especially those expectations brought on by school reform agendas. Mentoring is a viable and effective approach to address these expectations in a principal preparation program (Daresh & Playko, 1997). Through the mentoring experience, principal candidates receive guidance and support as they become familiar with the roles of campus leader and manager. Mentor-principals benefit from the experience as well. Mentors have the opportunity to be co-learners in the exchange of ideas about principalship and to find satisfaction in transmitting and sharing the knowledge, skills, behaviors, and values of a campus administrator (Crow & Matthews, 1998, p. 26).

This research study provides foundational information for further research and guidance for educational leadership professors in developing meaningful lifelong learning programs for principals who serve as mentors and for school leaders in general. Principals are expected to participate in lifelong learning to update knowledge and skills in school administration and to serve as a model to others in affirming the value of learning. The research information can also assist in the development of key educational components of a principal certification program to prepare campus leaders "whose vision of excellence permeates every dimension of a school's character" (Weise, 1992, p. 7).

REFERENCES

Ashby, D. (1993). On the job mentoring for administrator renewal. *Planning and Changing, 22*(3–4), 218–230.

Barth, R. S. (1990). *Improving schools from within: Teachers, parents and principals can make a difference.* San Francisco: Jossey-Bass.

Barth, R. S. (2001). *Learning by heart.* San Francisco: Jossey-Bass.

Brookover, W. B. (1981). *Effective secondary schools.* Philadelphia: Research for Better Schools.

Brookover, W. B., Beamer, L., Efthim, H., Hathaway, D., Lezotte, L., Miller, S., et al. (1982). *Creating effective schools.* Holmes Beach, FL: Learning Publications.

Brookover, W. B., & Lezotte, L. W. (1979). *Changes in school characteristics coincide with changes in school achievement.* East Lansing, MI: Institute for Research on Teaching, Michigan State University.

Capasso, R. L., & Daresh, J. C. (2001). *The school administrator internship handbook.* Thousand Oaks, CA: Corwin Press.

Clarke, J. H. (1999). Growing high school reform: Planting the seeds of systemic change. *NASSP Bulletin, 83*(606), 1–9.

Cline, Z., & Necochea, J. (1997). Mentoring for school reform. *Journal for a Just and Caring Education, 3*(2), 141–159.

Collinson, V., Sherrill, J., & Hohenbrink, J. (1994). *The best kept secret . . . self-initiated change: Veteran teachers' catalyst for renewal.* East Lansing, MI: National Center for Research on Teacher Learning. (ERIC Document Reproduction Service No. ED373061)

Cordeiro, P. A., & Smith-Sloan, E. (1995, April). *Apprenticeships for administrative interns: Learning to talk like a principal.* Paper presented at the annual meeting of the American Educational Research Association, San Francisco. (ERIC Document Reproduction Service No. ED385014)

Cross, K. P. (1991). The roads to a learning society. In L. Lamdin (Ed.), *Roads to a learning society* (pp. 133–140). Chicago: Council for Adult and Experiential Learning.

Crow, G. M., & Matthews, L. J. (1998). *Finding one's way: How mentoring can lead to dynamic leadership.* Thousand Oaks, CA: Corwin Press. (ERIC Document Reproduction Service No. ED414263)

Daresh, J. C., & Playko, M. A. (1989). Teacher mentors and administrator mentors: Same track, different stations. *Planning and Changing, 20*(2), 89–96.

Daresh, J. C., & Playko, M. A. (1992). Perceived benefits of a preservice administrative mentoring program. *Journal of Personnel Evaluation in Education, 6*(1), 15–22.

Daresh, J. C., & Playko, M. A. (1997). *Beginning the principalship: A practical guide for new school leaders.* Thousand Oaks, CA: Corwin Press.

Doud, J. L., & Keller, E. P. (1998). *A ten-year study: The K–8 principal in 1998.* Reston, VA: National Association of Elementary School Principals.

Edmonds, R. (1979). Some schools work and more can. *Social Policy, 9*(2), 28–32.

Edmundson, P. (1993). Renewal agendas and accreditation requirements: Contrasts and correspondence. *Journal of Teacher Education, 44*(3), 170–175.

Ganser, T. (1995). What are the concerns and questions of mentors of beginning teachers? *NASSP Bulletin, 79*(575), 83–91.

Geismar, T. J., Morris, J. D., & Lieberman, M. G. (2000). Selecting mentors for principalship interns. *Journal of School Leadership, 10*(3), 233–247.

Glatthorn, A. A. (2000). *The principal as curriculum leader* (2nd ed.). Thousand Oaks, CA: Corwin Press.

Green, R. L. (2001). *Practicing the art of leadership: A problem-based approach to implementing the ISLLC standards.* Columbus, OH: Merrill Prentice Hall.

Griffiths, D. E., Stout, R. T., & Forsyth, P. B. (Eds.). (1998). *Leaders for America's schools: The report of the National Commission on Excellence in Educational Administration.* Berkeley, CA: McCutchan.

Hanson, E. M. (1996). *Educational administration and organizational behavior.* Boston: Allyn & Bacon.

Hawkey, K. (1997). Roles, responsibilities, and relationships in mentoring: A literature review and agenda for research. *Journal of Teacher Education, 48*(5), 325–335.

Higham, R., Littleton, M., & Styron, K. (2001). Analysis of legal knowledge of school officials in Texas. In *2001: A legal odyssey, education law conference papers* (pp. 327–341). Dayton, OH: Education Law Association.

Hopkins-Thompson, P. A. (2000). Colleagues helping colleagues: Mentoring and coaching. *NASSP Bulletin, 84*(617), 29–36.

Hoyle, J. R., English, F. W., & Steffy, B. E. (1998). *Skills for successful 21st century school leaders.* Arlington, VA: American Association of School Administrators.

Jackson, A. (2000). *Turning points 2000: Educating adolescents in the 21st century.* New York: Teachers College Press.

Jean, E. W., & Evans, R. D. (1995). *Internships/mentorships for first-year principals: Implications for administrative certification and graduate program design.* East Lansing, MI: National Center for Research on Teacher Learning. (ERIC Document Reproduction Service No. ED390805)

Kajs, L. T., Alaniz, R., & Willman, E. (1998, February). *The selection and preparation of mentor educators.* Paper presented at the annual meeting of the American Association of Colleges for Teacher Education, New Orleans, LA.

Kajs, L. T., Alaniz, R., Willman, E., Maier, J. N., Brott, P. E., & Gomez, D. M. (1998). *Looking at the process of mentoring for beginning teachers.* Retrieved September 9, 2001, from www.altteachercert.org/

Kajs, L. T., Cox, C., Willman, E., Alaniz, R., & Gomez, D. M. (2001). *Organizational designs to promote effective mentoring of prospective/beginning campus administrators: The support team approach.* Unpublished manuscript, University of Houston-Clear Lake.

Kajs, L. T., Weise, K. R., Baitland, B., & Cox, C. (1998, October). *Aligning the principal certification internship program with the NCATE standards: A plan of action.* Paper presented at the annual meeting of the University Council for Educational Administration, St. Louis, MO.

Knapper, C. K., & Cropley, A. J. (1985). *Lifelong learning and higher education* (2nd ed.). Dover, NH: Croom Helm.

Lemley, R. (1997). Thoughts on a richer view of principals' development. *NASSP Bulletin, 81*(585), 33–37.

Luebkemann, H., & Clemens, J. (1994). Mentors for women entering administration: A program that works. *NASSP Bulletin, 78*(559), 42–45.

Lunenburg, F. C., & Ornstein, A. C. (2000). *Educational administration: Concepts and practices* (3rd ed.). Belmont, CA: Wadsworth.

Marsh, D. D. (2000). Educational leadership for the twenty-first century: Integrating three essential perspectives. In *The Jossey-Bass reader on educational leadership* (pp. 126–145). San Francisco: Jossey-Bass.

McCormick, L. M., & Kajs, L. T. (2001, November). *Computer database model to strengthen education law preparation of principal candidates.* Paper presented at the annual meeting of the Education Law Association, Albuquerque, NM.

McEwan, E. K. (1998). *Seven steps to effective instructional leadeship.* Thousand Oaks, CA: Corwin Press.

Monsour, F. (1998). Twenty recommendations for an administrative mentoring program. *NASSP Bulletin, 82*(594), 96–100.

Muse, I. D., Thomas, G. J., & Wasden, F. (1992). Potential problems (and solutions) of mentoring in the preparation of school administrators. *Journal of School Leadership, 2*(3), 310–319.

Muse, I., & Willardson, J. D. (1998). Mentor principal preparation program. In L. L. Oldaker (Ed.), *Proceedings of the National Council of Professors of Educational Administration 52nd annual conference.* Juneau: University of Alaska Southeast.

National Council for the Accreditation of Teacher Education. (1998). NCATE curriculum guidelines. Washington, DC: Author.

National Education Association. (1997). *Hard lessons about educational change.* Paper prepared by the Center for Innovation. Washington, DC: Author.

Nelson, D. L., & Quick, J. C. (1997). *Organizational behavior* (2nd ed.). New York: West.

Ovando, M. N. (1998, August). *Assessment of intern's performance: A key to enhance school leadership preparation programs.* Paper presented at the annual meeting of the National Council of Professors of Educational Administration, Juneau, AK. (ERIC Document Reproduction Service No. ED426982)

Pfaffenberger, R. C., & Patterson, J. H. (1987). *Methods for business and economics.* Homewood, IL: Richard D. Irwin.

Queeney, D. S., & English, J. K. (1994). *Mandatory continuing education: A status report,* Columbus: ERIC Clearinghouse on Adult, Career, and Vocational Education, Center on Education and Training for Employment (CE067218), The Ohio State University. (ERIC Document Reproduction Service No. ED372306)

Razik, T. A., & Swanson, A. D. (2001). *Fundamental concepts of educational leadership* (2nd ed.). Columbus, OH: Merrill Prentice Hall.

Ricciardi, D. (2000). *Experiences of Kentucky principal intern program participants: Job assistance provided in the entry year.* Paper presented at the annual meeting of the American Educational Research Association, New Orleans. (ERIC Document Reproduction Service No. ED451597)

Roesch, R. (1998). *Time management for busy people.* New York: McGraw-Hill.

Rubin, H. (1998). *Collaborative skills for educators and nonprofit leaders.* Chicago: Lyceum.

Schmieder, J. H., & Cairns, D. (1996). *Ten skills of highly effective principals.* Lancaster, PA: Technomic.

Schmuck, R. A. (1993). Beyond academics in the preparation of educational leaders: Four years of action research. *OSCC Report, 33*(2), 1–10.

Schmuck, R. A., & Runkel, P. J. (1994). *The handbook of organizational development in schools and colleges.* Prospect Heights, IL: Waveland.

Sergiovanni, T. J. (2000). Leadership as steward. In *The Jossey-Bass reader on educational leadership* (pp. 269–286). San Francisco: Jossey-Bass.

Sergiovanni, T. J. (2001). *The principalship* (4th ed.). Boston: Allyn & Bacon.

Shanker, A. (1994). *Standards for all: A vision for education in the 21st century.* East Lansing, MI: National Center for Research on Teacher Learning. (ERIC Document Reproduction Service No. ED367665)

Shelton, M. M. (1991). Mentoring: Lending a hand to tomorrow's principals. *Principal, 70*(4), 16.

Stone, F., & Heard, G. (1995). Staff development policy making in the states. *Journal of Staff Development, 16*(2), 815.

Texas Education Agency. (2000). Technology leadership academy for superintendents and principals. Retrieved October 1, 2001, from www.tasanet.org/depserv/profdev/Techacademy.pdf

Texas school law bulletin. (1998). Austin, TX: Texas Education Agency.

United States National Commission on Excellence in Education. (1983). *A nation at risk.* Washington, DC: Author.

Walker, A., & Stott, K. (1994). Mentoring programs for aspiring principals: Getting a solid start. *NASSP Bulletin, 78*(558), 72–77.

Weise, K. R. (1992). *Through the lens of human resource development: A fresh look at professional preparation programs.* East Lansing, MI: National Center for Research on Teacher Learning. (ERIC Document Reproduction Service No. ED355667)

Weiss, C. H., & Cambone, J. (2000). Principals, shared decision making, and school reform. In *The Jossey-Bass reader on educational leadership* (pp. 366–389). San Francisco: Jossey-Bass.

What goals 2000 means for you. (1994). *The ERIC Review, 3*(2), 10–11. (ERIC Document Reproduction Service No. ED376795)

APPENDIX A
Seven Top Program Components and Corresponding 1998 NCATE Guidelines

Program Components	NCATE Guidelines	NCATE Guideline Descriptions
(1) Conflict Resolution Strategies	7.5	• Apply counsel and mentoring skills, and utilize stress management and conflict management techniques.
(2) Interpersonal and Social Skills	7.1	• Use appropriate interpersonal skills (e.g., exhibiting sensitivity, showing respect and interest, perceiving needs and concerns, showing tact, exhibiting consistency and trustworthiness, etc.)
(3) Communication Techniques	7.2	• Use appropriate written, verbal, and nonverbal communication in a variety of situations.
	7.3	• Apply appropriate communications strategies (e.g., identifying audiences, determining messages,

		selecting transmission mediums, identifying reaction of receivers, soliciting responses.
	10.3	• Communicate effectively with various cultural, ethnic, racial, and special interest groups in the community.
(4) School Leader as Change Agent	1.4	• Initiate, manage, and evaluate the change process.
(5) Time Management Techniques	6.1	• Establish operational plans and processes to accomplish strategic goals using practical applications of organizational theories.
	6.3	• Implement appropriate management techniques and group processes to define roles, assign functions, delegate effectively, and determine accountability for attaining goals.
(6) Curriculum Design and Development	3.1	• Create with teachers, parents, and students a positive school culture that promotes learning (e.g., holds high expectations, focuses on accomplishments and recognition, and promotes a supportive climate).
	3.2	• Develop collaboratively a learning organization that supports instructional improvement, builds an appropriate curriculum, and incorporates best practice.
	3.3	• Base curricular decisions on research, applied theory, informed practice, recommendations of learned societies, and state and federal policies and mandates (e.g., cognitive development, human development, learning styles, contemporary methodologies,

content priorities, special needs legislation on topics such as least restrictive environment, etc.).

3.4 • Design curriculums with consideration for philosophical, sociological, and historical foundations, democratic values, and the community's values, goals, social needs and changing conditions.

3.5 • Align curricular goals and objectives with instructional goals and objectives and desired outcomes when developing scope, sequence, balance, etc.

3.6 • Develop with others curriculum and instruction appropriate for varied teaching and learning styles and specific student needs based on gender, ethnicity, culture, social class and exceptionalities.

3.7 • Use a variety of supervisory models to improve teaching and learning (e.g., clinical, developmental, cognitive, and peer coaching, as well as applying observation and conferencing skills).

3.8 • Use various staffing patterns, student grouping plans, class scheduling forms, school organizational structures, and facilities design processes, to support various teaching strategies and desired student outcomes.

3.9 • Assess student progress using a variety of appropriate techniques.

| (7) Appropriate School Law Issues | 11.1 | • Apply knowledge of federal and state constitutional, statutory, and regulatory provisions and judicial decisions governing education. |
| | 11.2 | • Apply knowledge of common law and contractual requirements and procedures in an educational setting (e.g., tort liability, contract administration, and formal hearings). |

School Leaders' Perceptions of Multicultural Competencies: Implications for School Leadership

Martha N. Ovando

Predictions of demographic shifts have become a reality, and school leaders must respond to the challenge of providing educational excellence to all students who may come from diverse "racial and cultural origins that are neither white nor European" (Gough, 1993, p. 3). As a result, principals across the country are facing dramatic changes in student populations, and they need to understand their cultural values, beliefs, experiences, and motives. Schools that have served a single predominant student population are witnessing changes in racial and ethnic diversity. According to Diegmueller:

> as children who were once considered the minorities in American society become the majority in the nation's classrooms, more teachers and administrators and other members of the education community are discovering they must adapt to their diversified student body if they are to provide a quality education for all children. (1992, p. 8)

Furthermore, recent research supports the notion that a principal plays a key leadership role in creating and facilitating a school culture that is conducive to learning for all students (Jason, 2000; Lucas, 2000; Mercer, 2000). However, to be effective in influencing school culture, a principal needs to develop an enhanced comprehensive understanding of the diverse cultures which are represented in the school. Additionally, principals must develop productive working relationships with teachers and other personnel who may also come from diverse backgrounds (Sergiovanni & Starratt, 1995).

In an effort to enhance the preparation of school administrators, professional associations have prompted the development of standards of performance (Lauder, 2000). These standards reaffirm the notion that principals should have a clear understanding of the school context and become familiar with the diverse needs of

Martha N. Ovando, University of Texas, Austin

students; however, few researchers have focused on the multicultural competencies needed to lead schools that serve students with biracial, multiethnic identities (Wehrly, Kenny, & Kenny, 1999). Furthermore, understanding such entities becomes a priority for school leaders who aspire to be celebrants and mediators as they attempt to create a collective unity of purpose. As Hart and Bredeson affirm, "as a celebrant, the principal focuses on legitimating the value of differences to enrich educational experiences of all learners. However, the principal is also a mediator who reconciles sources of conflict embedded in coexisting values, traditions, and mores" (1996, p. 281).

Previous research found that experts in the field of multicultural education and experienced superintendents agree that school superintendents should possess multicultural competencies and that the "emerging tapestry of diverse cultures in schools requires that superintendents' leadership development be enhanced to include multicultural knowledge, skills and attitudes" (Ovando & Troxell, 1997, p. 410); however, few studies have focused on the multicultural competencies perceived to be important for school leadership at the campus level.

In this chapter I present the results of a study examining school principals' perceptions relative to the importance of multicultural competencies needed to lead schools with a multicultural student population. I begin with the background of the study, followed by the methodology and a summary of findings, and conclude with an examination of implications for school leadership.

BACKGROUND OF THE STUDY
The 1990s have been filled with predictions of dramatic demographic changes. Today, those changes are here and school personnel, including principals, are faced with the imperative to respond to a changing school population. Thus, it seems relevant to examine the trends in demographic changes, principal leadership and school culture, standards of performance for school principals, and multicultural competencies needed to address the multicultural needs of today's students.

Demographic Changes
Recent national census data reveal demographic changes never before witnessed. The increase in the numbers of minority populations has led to demographic shifts which deserve the attention of policymakers, school leaders and researchers. It is reported that "nationwide, about 40 percent of children belong to racial or ethnic minority groups" (Bahadur, 2001, A1). This national trend is also reflected in several states, particularly among teens and children. Mirroring this trend, Texas has experienced an increase in its minority population (18 year olds and younger), from 49 percent in 1990 to 57 percent in 2000. Moreover, specific cities appear to be witnessing a major overall minority increase. For instance, Austin, the capital of Texas, is clearly becoming a minority/majority city. Recent census data show that the minority population under 18 has increased from 52 percent in 1999 to 62 percent in 2000 (see table 1). This trend has profound implications for schools and school leaders. As Bahadur puts it:

the rising number of young Hispanic, African Americans and Asians will soon strip the word "minority" of its dictionary meaning. This growing diversity is fertile ground for a crop of Texans who are less race conscious than their forebears. But it also poses a challenge to school districts and lawmakers because many minority children face barriers to success such as poverty and limited English skills. (2001, A1)

The recent demographic changes, indeed, support Lucas's (2000) assertion that "the expression 'minority students' will not be statistically significant" (p. 2). Others predict that "Hispanic and Asians will constitute 61 percent of the nation's population growth by 2025, which in turn will dramatically change the makeup of the school-age populations" (Tirozzi, 2001, p. 434). Further, several schools in the nation are already becoming majority/minority contexts, creating what some call a "multicultural generation" (Bahadur, 2001, p. A1), bringing great cultural diversity and challenges which require a different kind of school leadership. As Smith affirmed, "The vision and responsibility for maintaining ideals and programs that are responsive to racial, ethnic, linguistic, cultural, religious, and gender diversity has become one of the leadership challenges of the coming century" (1996, pp. 33–34). Consequently, school principals who wish to meet the many challenges of the 21st century need the kind of school leadership that will enable them "to provide a positive learning environment for a highly diverse student population" (Ferrandino, 2001, p. 441), in addition to creating a school culture that embraces diversity and is conducive to successful learning for all students.

Leadership and School Culture

The notion that principals play a key leadership role in creating a school culture that is conducive to learning for all students has been recognized in prior studies. For instance, Mercer (2000) discovered that "no one occupies a more influential position from which to influence the shaping of a school's culture than the principal" (p. 217). In building a strong school culture, school leaders must also attend to the different needs of teachers, creating the right conditions to address them. According to Sergiovanni and Starrartt (2001), the right conditions "are those that support both the psychological and symbolic needs of teachers; needs that are the subject matter of school climate and school culture" (p. 331).

Table 1. Demographic Changes in Teens and Children in Texas and Austin, 1990–2000

	Texas		Austin	
Year	1990	2000	1990	2000
Population				
White	51%	43%	48%	38%
Hispanic	34%	41%	33%	43%
Black non-Hispanic	13%	12%	16%	13%
Other non-Hispanic	2%	2%	3%	6%

* From: Bahadur, G. (2001, March 23). Minorities constitute majority of area youth. *The Austin American-Statesman*, pp. A1, A6. Some totals may not equal 100 because of rounding.

According to Schein (1992), school administrators and teachers need to develop an understanding of the school's organizational culture and an increased awareness about the relationship between that culture and student success. Experts in the field suggest that school culture is inclusive of norms, values, beliefs, traditions, artifacts, symbols, espoused values, rituals, and basic underlying assumptions of people within the school (Schein, 1992). Others affirm that a school culture may include the school's history, beliefs, values, norms and standards, and patterns of behavior (Sergiovanni & Starratt, 2001, p. 321). It is critical, then, that a school culture celebrates and honors the increasing multicultural diversity in today's schools and classrooms. As Goleman (1995) suggests, it is imperative that an organization's culture nurture tolerance for a diverse work environment.

Furthermore, Banks (1994a) reminds us that a school culture should facilitate educational empowerment and progress for all ethnic groups represented in the school. Therefore:

> learning how students and teachers from different backgrounds see the work of the school becomes a leadership priority. Without understanding the values, norms, beliefs, and experiences from which perceptions are formed, the clash between educators and those they educate is inevitable. (Jason, 2000, p. 9)

However, it is relevant to affirm that to be an effective leader and create a school culture that recognizes and honors the diverse values of all students, a principal must first understand the diverse cultures which are represented in the school. As Jason states, "A monocultural approach is simply not adequate for solving problems and resolving issues involving equity and excellence in educating students from various backgrounds for democratic citizenship in the 21st Century" (2000, p. 8).

Recognizing the imperative to meet the multicultural needs of an increasingly diverse student population, school leaders must prepare to rise to the challenge. The current demographic shifts and the increase in diversity have created calls for more comprehensive school leadership standards which may be used as guidelines for school leadership practice and development.

Standards for School Leaders

As demands for quality education for all students have resulted in calls for professional accountability at all levels, professional organizations have engaged in the development of professional standards of performance for all school personnel, including school leaders at the campus level. However, standards should not be taken as absolute measures of performance but as frameworks that guide school leadership development. It is reported that standards for school leaders "present a common core of knowledge, dispositions and performances that will help link leadership more forcefully to productive schools and enhanced educational outcomes" (Council of Chief State School Officers [CCSSO], 1996, p. 3). The interest in the development of standards for performance has been widely recognized at both national and state levels. For instance, at the national level, the Interstate School Leaders Licensure

Consortium (ISLLC) has adopted a set of standards in an effort to "raise the bar for the practice of school leadership. Thus the standards and indicators reflect the magnitude of both the importance and the responsibility of effective school leaders" (CCSSO, 1996). These standards are stated in terms of three indicators, knowledge, disposition and performance, and include:

Standard 1. A school administrator is an educational leader who promotes the success of all students by *facilitating the development, articulation, implementation, and stewardship of a vision of learning that is shared and supported by the community.*

Standard 2. A school administrator is an educational leader who promotes the success of all students *by advocating, nurturing, and sustaining a school culture and instructional program conducive to student learning and staff professional growth.*

Standard 3. A school administrator is an educational leader who promotes the success of all students by *ensuring management of the organization, operations, and resources for a safe, efficient, and effective learning environment.*

Standard 4. A school administrator is an educational leader who promotes the success of all students by *collaborating with families and community members, responding to diverse community interests and needs, and mobilizing community resources.*

Standard 5. A school administrator is an educational leader who promotes the success of all students by *acting with integrity, fairness, and in an ethical manner.*

Standard 6. A school administrator is an educational leader who promotes the success of all students by *understanding, responding to and influencing the larger political, social, economic, legal, and cultural context.* (CCSSO, 1996, pp. 10–21, emphasis in original)

These standards emphasize that school leaders must address the needs of all students including the growing diverse groups reflecting the national demographic changes. As Wehrly, Kenny, and Kenny (1999) affirm, individuals with biracial, multiethnic/multicultural/multiracial identity are the largest growing population in the United States. The new make up of schools' student populations has also prompted other professional associations to take a new look at preparation programs to develop performance-based standards (Lauder, 2000). For instance, clear performance-based standards have been developed by the National Policy Board for Educational Administration. These standards contain "21 Performance Domains." These performance domains are grouped in four categories: the functional domain, the programmatic domain, the interpersonal domain, and the contextual domain. The contextual domain includes philosophical and cultural values, legal and regulatory applications, policy and political influences, and public relations (Lauder, 2000).

The national emphasis on the need for school leadership to understand the school context requires that principals become cognizant of the multicultural needs of students. School leaders should not only understand the new multicultural makeup of schools but should develop their capacity to address the learning and social needs of students in order to make a difference in the education of all students. Following the national trend, some states have also taken the initiative to focus on the preparation of school leaders by establishing professional standards which highlight the leadership proficiencies needed to lead schools. Texas, for instance, has adopted Learner-Centered Administrator Proficiencies with the primary focus being on the success of all learners. These include Learner-Centered Leadership, Learner-Centered Climate, Learner-Centered Curriculum and Instruction, Learner-Centered Professional Development, Equity in Excellence for all Learners, and Learner-Centered Communication (Texas Education Agency, 1994).

Most recently, Texas has approved a set of standards for the preparation and assessment of school principals. These include:

1. Learner-Centered Values and Ethics of leadership
2. Learner-Centered Leadership and Campus Culture
3. Learner-Centered Human Resources Leadership and Management
4. Learner-Centered Communications and Community Relations
5. Learner-Centered Organizational Leadership and Management
6. Learner-Centered Curriculum Planning and Development
7. Learner-Centered Instructional Leadership and Management

(State Board for Educator Certification, 1999, pp. 2–6)

The aforementioned illustrations of standards clearly reinforce the notion that school leaders have the responsibility to assure that "all students" achieve success. While the trend in demographic changes was recognized during the 1990s, educational institutions and other social organizations are only now beginning to engage in systematic efforts to become more knowledgeable, proficient, and culturally responsive. One avenue to achieve such a proficiency and to be able to respond to the needs of today's children from multiple cultural backgrounds may involve developing the multicultural knowledge, skills, and attitudes found to be relevant for other levels of school leadership (Ovando & Troxell, 1997) and to determine how important these are perceived to be for school leadership at the campus level.

Multicultural Competencies
Multicultural education has become a discipline that has been integrated in the preparation of teachers, counselors, and, to some extent, of school administrators. It is no longer uncommon to find descriptors such as multicultural values, multicultural sensitivity, multicultural awareness, and the like. Banks affirms that the main goal of multicultural education is "to restructure curricula and educational institutions so that students from diverse social classes, racial and ethnic groups, and both gender groups experience equal educational opportunities" (1994a, p. 102). Further-

more, addressing the needs of today's children will involve restructuring the culture and organization of schools so that "students from diverse racial, ethnic, and gender groups will experience equality" (Banks, 1994b, p. 14). While the major tenets of multicultural education have been integrated into the curriculum, and into teacher sensitivity development efforts, it has also been advocated that school leaders "acquire the multicultural competencies necessary to value and work with children with multiple cultural backgrounds" (Ovando & Troxell, 1997, p. 413).

More recently, it has been emphasized that "inadequate understanding of cultural perspectives results in education in which students' potential is not realized because communication so necessary to the teaching-learning process is lacking" (Jason, 2000, p. 9). Similarly, the new demographic changes highlight the "diverse challenges of multiculturalism" faced by teachers (Franklin, 2001, p. 1). Further, "the blend of ethnicities and value systems often places teachers in a 'cultural minefield' where they must navigate a careful path to trying to respect the sensibilities of many different groups" (Franklin, 2001, p. 1). The school principal is in a similar situation as he or she attempts to build a school culture that embraces the myriad of differing and sometimes conflicting diverse cultural values represented in schools today.

One way for school leaders to respond to the multiculturalism challenges of today could be to develop the competencies that might enable them to better understand, respect, honor, and meet the needs of all children. According to Norton, Webb, Dlugosh, and Sybouts, a:

> competency refers to the ability to accomplish a task at a satisfactory level of performance. To be competent is to possess sufficient skill and knowledge to meet a stated purpose or to have the capacity equal to the requirements of the task. (1996, p. 305)

Thus, it can be asserted that a multicultural competency includes the knowledge, skills, and attitudes (Ovando & Troxell, 1997) which enable a school leader to create a learning community in a multicultural setting where all students experience success. As Shields affirms, "The true potential of a learning community is that it holds the promise of uniting people of different backgrounds, cultures, languages, and beliefs, in an ethical, just, and caring educational community" (1996, p. 72).

While there is consensus about the need for superintendents, teachers, and school principals to be responsive to their changing school contexts as they attempt to build strong learning communities, limited field-based research focusing on principals' perceptions of multicultural competencies exists. Consequently, several questions remain to be answered as school leaders attempt to make sure that there is congruence between what they say they value and what they actually do as they work with students, teachers, and parents from multicultural backgrounds. For instance, what competencies do practicing school principals perceive to be important to lead diverse schools? To what extent do they use these competencies? How do principals prepare to respond to the multiple needs of students? How could principal preparation institutions equip aspiring school principals to respond better to their multicultural settings?

METHODOLOGY

The purpose of this study was to determine principals' perceptions about the importance of multicultural competencies (knowledge, skills, and attitudes) to lead schools serving diverse student populations. It further focused on the extent to which school principals report using these competencies, on how principals prepare to address the diverse needs of students, and how administrator preparation institutions may contribute to the development of multicultural competencies of aspiring school principals. However, this study did not focus on principals' actual leadership behaviors.

This study was conducted following descriptive studies guidelines. A survey approach was used to examine principals' perceptions (Sprinthall, Schmutte, & Sirois, 1991). The instrument consisted of a questionnaire containing the multicultural competencies (knowledge, attitudes, and skills) identified by Ovando and Troxell (1997) with slight modifications to fit campus-level school leadership.

Participating principals were selected using reputation references and snowball sampling techniques (Gay & Airasian, 2000). Initially, principals were identified with assistance from district office personnel from an urban school district. The area superintendent was asked to nominate a principal who served in multicultural settings, had at least 3 years of experience as principal, and was effective in working with students from diverse backgrounds for each school level. The initial group included one principal from each level. Once the first three principals were identified, they were mailed the questionnaire including a self-addressed and postage-paid envelope. These in turn recommended other principal colleagues and only those who met the criteria were asked to participate. A total of 14 principals completed the survey questionnaires. Of these, three were high school principals, four were middle school principals and seven were elementary school principals. Respondents' principal experience ranged from 3 to 27 years. Table 2 presents other characteristics.

The district chosen for the study, Austin, Texas, serves approximately 80,000 students. Of these, about 67 percent are minority students representing Hispanic, African American, Asian, and Native American students (see table 3).

Table 2.   **Participating Principals' Demographic Characteristics**

Characteristic	Number	Percentage
Gender		
Male	6	43
Female	8	57
Ethnicity		
White	5	35
African American	3	21
Hispanic	6	43
Highest Degree		
M. A.	10	71
ABD	2	14
Doctorate	2	14

Table 3. Student Demographics for Participating District

Ethnicity	Percentage
African American	17
Asian	3
Hispanic	46
Native American	1
White	35

Note: Total is more than 100 percent because of rounding.

Participants were asked to check the perceived importance of each statement of the first part of the questionnaire. The questionnaire was structured according to Thurstone's (1945) four-point scale as follows: 1) Very Important (VI), 2) Important (I), 3) Somewhat Important (SI), and 4) Not Important (NI). It included three dimensions of competencies: multicultural knowledge, multicultural attitudes, and multicultural skills. Further, the second part of the instrument included open-ended questions. These questions focused on the extent of use of multicultural competencies, preparation to respond to the diverse needs of students, and ways that preparation programs could prepare prospective school principals.

Data analysis was completed using basic quantitative measures as well as qualitative techniques. Thus, the importance of each multicultural competency was analyzed by computing overall means. Each competency was then ranked according to the overall mean. Participants' responses to open-ended questions were analyzed inductively, coding and sorting verbatim to "isolate patterns, process, commonalities and differences, and to gradually elaborate a set of generalizations" (Miles & Huberman, 1994, p. 9) regarding the focus of the study. Finally, responses to the question relative to preparation institutions' contributions were analyzed computing percentages of responses.

RESULTS

The results of this study are reported according to the areas addressed in this study. These include the perceived importance of multicultural competencies, extent of use of multicultural competencies, preparation to respond to the diverse needs of students, staff, and parents, and preparation of aspiring school leaders.

Perceived Importance of Multicultural Competencies

According to the participating principals, most of the multicultural competencies are important to lead schools serving diverse populations. These results show that the most important multicultural knowledge was seen as "having knowledge of the cultural background, traditions, and needs of the school's local community." The least important appeared to be "knowledge of the various religious beliefs and traditions of individuals" (see table 4).

Results also revealed that "promoting standards for action based upon the belief in the educability of all children" was seen as the most important multicultural

Table 4. Participants' Perceptions of the Importance of Multicultural Knowledge

Competency	Mean	Rank
1. The school leader has knowledge of the cultural background, traditions, and needs of the school local community.	1.38	1
2. The school leader possesses a broad perspective of multicultural education and the science and art of instruction.	1.47	3
3. The school leader has knowledge of the unique and common cultural experiences of all school stakeholders.	1.70	4
4. The school leader has a knowledge base about verbal and nonverbal communication patterns of diverse cultural groups.	1.43	2
5. The school leader has knowledge of the various religious beliefs and traditions of individuals.	1.84	5

attitude, whereas "possessing a philosophy of action which gets others to accomplish objectives" was perceived as least important (see table 5).

Finally, results revealed that "creating a nurturing school environment which is inclusive of all individuals regardless of their cultural background" was seen as the most important skill, whereas "creating an inclusive organization entity and working with the different local cultural groups" appeared to be least important (see table 6).

Extent of Application of Multicultural Competencies

According to the results of this study, all respondents agreed that they apply all the multicultural competencies to a large extent. However, they also recognized that there is room for improvement and that at times it can be challenging to be responsive to all students' heterogeneous needs. The following principals' comments reflect their thinking.

> I do to an extent. I especially recognize that we must honor cultural diversity within the school both as a learning tool and as an avenue not to offend someone if we don't.

> On a 1–10 scale (10 being a large extent), I would rate myself as an 8. With an extremely active, vocal Anglo parental population (60 percent), it's easy to forget the cultural needs of our less-involved, quieter Hispanic (30 percent) and African American (10 percent)

Table 5. Participants' Perceptions of the Importance of Multicultural Attitudes

Competency	Mean	Rank
1. The school leader possesses a willingness to lead a diverse group towards consensus.	1.25	3
2. The school leader promotes standards for action based upon a belief in the educability of all children.	1.02	1
3. The school leader possesses a philosophy of action which gets others to accomplish objectives.	1.34	4
4. The school leader possesses a genuine disposition which leads others to value human diversity.	1.12	2

Table 6.   Participants' Perceptions of the Importance of Multicultural Skills

Skills	Mean	Rank
1. The school leader possesses the ability to form positive relationships with groups from diverse cultural backgrounds.	1.32	2
2. The school leader possesses the ability to create an inclusive organizational entity.	1.33	3
3. The school leader possesses the ability to work with the different local cultural groups.	1.33	3
4. The school leader possesses the ability to create a nurturing school environment which is inclusive of all individuals regardless of their cultural background.	1.23	1

populations. Although, philosophically, I strongly agree with the multicultural competencies, it's an ongoing struggle to get the dominant Anglo population to expand their cultural awareness.

On a scale from 1 (low) to 10 (high), I would rate myself as an 8 1/2. Each of the competencies listed are of utmost importance and highly valued; however, personally speaking, there is room for growth. As a school leader, I try to model these competencies with my community.

Being principal of a diverse racial and ethnic population, I have to apply all three competencies. There are different levels to be aware of—working with teachers, understanding the children's background and interacting, reaching and educating parents and the community. It is not easy, but it is doable. You must learn how to set goals and have patience to see them through. Since I have a diverse background myself, it was easier to come to this school and work with the multiculturalism. The biggest hurdle is reaching out to parents and assisting them in becoming active partners in their children's education. Reaching out to a diverse population with so many needs is challenging.

Preparation to Respond to the Diverse Needs of the School Community

It appears from the results that principals prepare in a variety of ways. These may include personal experience, surveys, reading, developing a shared vision, training, data gathering, creating ethnically diverse committees, neighborhood walks, listening to various groups, formal and informal meetings, administrative preparation programs, recruitment efforts, keeping open lines of communication with all, school-wide multicultural presentations, and involving parents, staff, and influential community members in decision making on campus.

As principals stated:

The administration preparation program I attended focused on cultural differences and preparing principals to work in areas that have heavy concentration of Mexican-American and Indian.

Mainly through my experiences at the university. One experience in particular influenced me. I was required, along with other graduate students, to survey families in a predominantly African-American and Hispanic community. Sitting in their homes and listening to their concerns related to the schooling of their students was powerful. In addition, I read and studied multicultural research and literature. I engaged in honest, substantive conversations with people of color. I sought out colleagues of color and chose them to be my mentors.

I feel I spent a lifetime preparing to respond to the diverse needs of students. As an administrator, I hold individual meetings with all staff members at the beginning and end of each school year to listen to "their story" and discover the passion/energy that drives them. I meet regularly with parents, establish a "parent room" on campus, conduct neighborhood walks and house meetings to let parents know I want to be part of the community—not just work in the community. I also work with Austin Interfaith to build community relationships and promote a common vision.

First, I gathered data on the students and community. Then, I funded positions to help me reach out to our population. That involved instructional specialists, counselors, parent involvement representatives, and community partners. Training faculty and staff on the needs of our specific population was paramount. We deal with social, economic and lack of education opportunities. Understanding these issues were and continue to be important to us.

Development of Multicultural Competencies of Aspiring School Leaders

All respondents offered specific suggestions to prepare aspiring school leaders. While a variety of suggestions emerged from the data, field-based experiences, visits to diverse schools, multicultural courses, and reading of pertinent literature were the most frequently suggested strategies to prepare aspiring school leaders (see table 7).

Table 7. Participants' Perceptions of the Importance of Strategies to Prepare Aspiring School Leaders

Suggestions	Percentage	Rank
Field-based experiences in diverse schools	42	1
Visits to real diverse schools	42	1
Courses which include the multicultural competencies	28	2
Reading pertinent literature	21	3
Recruitment of individuals with cultural sensitivity	14	4
Heterogeneous grouping of students	14	4
Exposure to social service agencies	14	4
Guest speakers (minority school leaders)	14	4
Shadow successful school leaders	14	4
Recruit culturally diverse professors	7	5
Provide Web sites	7	5
Research of best practices	7	5
Open, honest discourse	7	5
Development of responsive leadership	7	5

Note. Total is more than 100% because respondents listed more than one suggestion.

Furthermore, according to at least one respondent, all education students need to be prepared to understand issues of cultural pluralism, to open an honest dialogue on what it means, and what it will take to respond to the multiple needs of all students. As a principal affirmed:

> Most teachers come from middle-class backgrounds with very little understanding on how to work with children of poverty, disadvantaged backgrounds or different ethnicities/races. Teacher preparation programs must train future educators on the reality of the society we live in. Having misconceptions and little interactions with urban school populations is not conducive to success in the classroom (i.e., lack of understanding of how to discipline or manage students, lack of understanding of how different cultures react to children and why.

CONCLUSION

This study attempted to determine principals' perceptions about the importance of multicultural competencies to lead schools serving diverse student populations. It further explored to what extent school principals apply these competencies, how school principals prepare to address the diverse needs of students, and how administrator preparation institutions can contribute to the development of multicultural competencies of aspiring school principals.

Results suggest that most participants agree that the multicultural competencies included in this study are important for leading schools that serve students who come from different cultural backgrounds. This supports Jason's assertion that:

> a principal's leadership actions that are not grounded in understanding the perspectives of different client populations and communities served by the school will be rendered less effective by the stronger phenomenological influence in which different cultures and groups view their world and act accordingly. (2000, p. 8)

The three most important competencies were perceived to be: 1) knowledge of the cultural background, traditions, and needs of the local school community, 2) attitude that promotes standards for action based upon the belief in the educability of all children, and 3) skill to create a nurturing school environment which is inclusive of all individuals regardless of their cultural background.

Furthermore, results also suggest that principals apply the different multicultural competencies to a large extent and on everyday communications and interactions with students, faculty, parents, and community. Application of multicultural competencies allows school leaders to better understand, and honor cultural diversity within the school setting, and to better respond to the multiple needs of students. This finding supports Herrity and Glasman's assertion that

> Since differences in language and culture of students and their families are often subtle, principals must have the knowledge of the manifestation of those norms in the classroom and in social situations. They must also have a knowledge of the pragmatics related to diversity and culture to know when and how to apply that knowledge in real-life meaningful situations. (1999, p. 244)

All principals reported enhancing their preparation in unique and creative ways to address adequately the multicultural needs of the students they serve. They take an active role in learning about the different groups represented in their campuses and they also offer training to the campus faculty. This suggests that preparation to respond to the multiple needs of all students is an ongoing process that starts with university preparation programs and becomes a lifelong commitment to ensure that all students are successful. Furthermore, principals should also strive to prepare teachers to better respond to the varied needs of students in the classrooms.

Further, results suggest that preparation programs may develop multicultural competencies of aspiring school leaders by purposefully designing field-based experiences within diverse settings, arranging visits to multicultural schools, and offering multicultural courses that include both the theoretical foundations of leadership, multicultural education, and the implication for school leadership practice. Consequently, preparation institutions should adopt a more integrated approach to prepare future school leaders. As Taylor asserts, an integrated approach "combines leadership, cultural pluralism, and critically reflective inquiry to form an organizing principle. It seeks to prepare leaders as agents in pluralistic and democratic schools who understand the complex relationship between the culture of the school and society" (1995, p. 66).

Similarly, field-based experiences should afford prospective school leaders opportunities to enhance their awareness of the multiple needs of students and to apply multicultural knowledge, skills and attitudes as they learn to create schools that are culturally responsive. This is congruent with Banks' (1994) suggestion about the need to create multicultural, learner-centered schools. It is imperative that preparation programs expand leadership preparation to include relevant multicultural competencies. As Herrity and Glasman affirm "universities are in the best position to apply the latest theoretical knowledge and research information on effective models of instruction and instructional leadership for diverse student populations" (1999, p. 245). Others also report that a relevant and well-designed field-based experience is one of the critical components of "a tridimensional foundation for school leader preparation" (Ovando, 2000, p. 148), with the other two being theoretical knowledge and reflection. Therefore, preparation institutions must strive to afford aspiring principals field-based experiences in either multicultural settings or in schools that are undergoing significant changes in student population so that administration students are exposed to the everyday challenges of meeting the increasingly heterogeneous needs of all students.

While findings of this study support the importance of the multicultural competencies included in the study for the practice and preparation of school leadership, it is relevant to remember that only school leaders who embrace an inclusive thinking paradigm and become lifelong learners will be in a position to make a difference in the lives of our changing student population. Administrator preparation institutions may contribute to their preparation; however, it takes a visionary school leader to stand up to the challenges associated with serving all students and creating nurturing school environments to ensure that all students experience success.

REFERENCES

Bahadur, G. (2001, March 23). Minorities constitute majority of area youth. *The Austin American-Statesman*, pp. A1, A6.

Banks, J. A. (1994a). *An introduction to multicultural education*. Boston: Allyn & Bacon.

Banks, J. A. (1994b). *Multiethnic education: Theory and practice* (3rd ed.). Boston: Allyn & Bacon.

Council of Chief State School Officers. (1996). *Interstate School Leaders Licensure Consortium: Standards for School Leaders*. Retrieved February 27, 2002, from www.mcpa.cc/isllc.pdf

Diegmueller, K. (1992). Schooling staff in the ways of the world. *Journal of Staff Development, 13*(2), 8–11.

Ferrandino, V. L. (2001). Challenges for the 21st-century elementary school principal. *Phi Delta Kappan, 82*(6), 440–442.

Franklin, J. (2001). The diverse challenges of multiculturalism. *Educational Leadership, 43*(2), 1–8.

Gay, L. R., & Airasian, P. (2000). *Educational research: Competencies for analysis and application*. Columbus, OH: Merrill, Prentice-Hall.

Goleman, D. (1995). *Emotional intelligence: Why it can matter more than IQ*. New York: Bantam Books.

Gough, P. B. (1993). Dealing with diversity. *Phi Delta Kappan, 75*(1), 3.

Hart, A. W., & Bredeson, P. V. (1996). *The principalship*. New York: McGraw-Hill.

Herrity, V. A., & Glasman, N. S. (1999). Training administrators for culturally and linguistically diverse school populations: Opinions of expert practitioners. *Journal of School Leadership, 9*, 235–253.

Jason, M. H. (2000). The role of the principal as transformational leader in a multicultural community. *High School Journal, 83*(3), 1–10.

Lauder, A. (2000). The new look in principal preparation programs. *NASSP Bulletin, 84*(617), 23–29.

Lucas, L. (2000). Facilitating the transitions of secondary English language learners: Priorities for principals. *NASSP Bulletin, 84* (619), 2–13.

Mercer, D. C. (2000). *Understanding the culture of an academically improving elementary school with a majority of students of color*. Unpublished doctoral dissertation, University of Texas at Austin.

Miles, M. B., & Huberman, A. M. (1994). *Qualitative data analysis: A sourcebook of new methods*. Newbury Park, CA: Sage.

Norton, M. S., Webb, L. D., Dlugosh, L. L., & Sybouts, W. (1996). *The school superintendency: New responsibilities, new leaderships*. Boston: Allyn & Bacon.

Ovando, M. N. (2000). Assessment of interns' performance: A key to enhance school leader preparation for the new millennium. In P. M. Jenlink & T. J. Kowalski (Eds.), *Marching into a new millennium: Challenges to educational leadership* (pp. 140–159). Lanham, MD: Scarecrow Press.

Ovando, M. N., & Troxell D. (1997). Superintendents' multicultural competencies. *Journal of School Leadership, 7*, 409–431.

Schein, E. H. (1992). *Organizational culture and leadership,* (2nd ed.). San Francisco: Jossey-Bass.

Sergiovanni, T. J., & Starratt, R. J. (2001). *Supervision: A redefinition*. New York: McGraw-Hill.

Shields, C. M. (1996). Creating a learning community in a multicultural setting: Issues of leadership. *Journal of School Leadership, 6*, 47–74.

Smith, S. (1996). Leadership training for cultural diversity. *Multicultural Review, 5*(1), 33–38.

Sprinthall, R. C., Schmutte, G. T., & Sirois, L. (1991). *Understanding educational research*. Upper Saddle River, NJ: Prentice Hall.

State Board for Educator Certification. (1999). *Chapter 245: Principal certificate*. Austin, TX: Author.

Taylor, E. (1995). Talking race in concrete: Leadership, diversity, and praxis. *Journal of Professional Studies, 3*(1), 61–68.

Texas Education Agency. (1994). *Learner-centered proficiencies for administrators*. Austin, TX: Author.

Thurstone, L. L. (1945). *Multiple factor analysis*. Chicago: University of Chicago Press.

Tirozzi, G. N. (2001). The artistry of leadership. *Phi Delta Kappan, 82*(6), 434–439.

Wehrly, B., Kenny, K. R., & Kenny, M. E. (1999). *Counseling multicultural families*. Thousand Oaks, CA: Sage.

Women in School Leadership:
Taking Steps to Help Them Make the Leap

Sandy Hutchinson

Throughout history, the role of women in education has evolved. Family structures and economic need have resulted in a shift in women's roles in society, and the roles of women have also changed in the field of educational administration. But while women have an interest in securing positions in educational administration, they are underrepresented in the superintendency in the state of Missouri, as they are throughout the nation (Blount, 1998).

In the first half of the 1800s, most teachers were still men, especially in the urban areas. However, the need for teachers grew throughout the states and territories. Blount (1998) suggested that since men were unwilling to relocate to the remote areas and work for low wages, women were hired to fill these positions. Women fulfilled their obligations so well that Horace Mann, the first state secretary of education in Massachusetts, stated in 1837 that women were natural teachers (Blount, 1998).

The numbers of women in education continued to grow and, after the Civil War, the majority of teachers were women. By the turn of the century, women accounted for over 70 percent of all teachers, and in 1920 women held 86 percent of all positions in education, including supervisory and administrative (Blount, 1998). Gribskov (1980) reported that in 1928, 55 percent of all elementary principals in the nation were women, and approximately 25 percent of all county superintendents were women.

The mid-1900s saw a decline in the number of women in school administration (Shakeshaft, 1987). Blount (1998) reported that in 1950, 56 percent of all elementary principalships were held by women, but 10 years later, that number dropped to 4 percent. Similarly, in 1939, there were 765 women school superintendents, but by 1962 that number had dropped to 222, a 70 percent decline in 23 years. This drop in

Sandy Hutchinson, Central Missouri State University

numbers might, in large part, be attributed to the consolidation of small rural districts and the resulting decline in county superintendencies (Shakeshaft, 1987).

According to Shakeshaft (1987), World War II transformed many of America's social and economic conditions. While men were called to military service, women took over many of the jobs vacated by men. After the war, men returned home and the effort to recruit more men into the teaching profession ultimately lessened women's chances of attaining superintendencies. With more male teachers in the classrooms, the pool of men for administrative positions increased. Many school systems preferred men for administrative work. This, coupled with the idea that many men were recruited with the promise of quick promotions, made the odds for advancement much greater for men than women (Blount, 1998).

By 1970, the number of women superintendents declined to its lowest level of the century (Blount, 1998). Since 1970, however, women have achieved modest gains in district superintendencies, with Glass (1992) reporting 6.7 percent of the nation's superintendents being women. In their AASA study, Glass, Bjork, and Brunner (2000) surveyed 2,262 superintendents and found 13 percent of their total were women.

Blount's (1998) studies of 20-year increments have shown the number of women administrators in the state of Missouri rose from 1910 until 1930, and then stayed consistent until 1950. Between 1950 and 1970 the number of women administrators dropped drastically with the decline in the number of county superintendents. Blount found that in 1910, women headed 3 of 146 local districts, and 11 of 114 county superintendents were women. By 1930, according to Blount, only 2 of 201 local districts were governed by women, though the number of women county superintendents rose to 30 of 114. Blount's 1950 statistics showed no women local superintendents in the 204 local districts, and 27 of 114 county superintendents were women. Blount also found that by 1970 the number of local school districts had more than doubled to 466, but none of these local districts were headed by women. The number of county superintendents had dropped to 34, with 7 of them being women. By 1990, according to Blount, women superintendents headed 10 (2.2 percent) of the 450 K–12 school districts, and there were no longer county superintendents in the state of Missouri. The Missouri School Directory (1999–2000) reported that women superintendents governed 48, or 10.6 percent, of the 451 K–12 school districts in Missouri.

A review of the research revealed notable differences between men and women who served in positions of educational administration. These differences were not only found in the disparity between the numbers of men and women serving in leadership positions, but also in various other areas, including personal characteristics, professional preparation, and career paths. Differences were also noted in the effect of mentors, networking, gender-related myths, and career aspirations.

Glass' (1992) study of 1,734 superintendents nationwide netted responses from 115 women. He concluded that women superintendents, on the average, are younger than their male counterparts. Glass calculated the mean national age for all superintendents to be 49.8 years, but nearly 70 percent of the women respondents were younger than the mean. It is interesting to note, however, that men usually gained their first administrative position at an earlier age than women.

Glass et al.'s (2000) study of 2,262 men and women superintendents also revealed several significant differences between the men and women studied. According to this study, only 76.9 percent of the women were married, compared to 94.7 percent of the men. Glass et al. revealed that 91.5 percent of the women in their study were 41–60 years old, compared to 89.3 percent of the men.

In the area of professional preparation, Glass et al. (2000) reported that 56.8 percent of women superintendents had earned doctorates, compared to 43.7 percent of the men. Education specialist degrees had been earned by 23.7 percent of the men, while 10.5 percent of the women had earned specialist degrees.

Glass et al. (2000) found that 40.5 percent of the men they surveyed spent 5 years or less in the classroom prior to their first administrative position, compared to 20.2 percent of the women. Their study also revealed 37.5 percent of the men, compared to 40.4 percent of the women, spent 6 to 10 years in the classroom, while 22 percent of the men, compared to 39.4 percent of the women, spent over 10 years in the classroom. According to Glass et al., 43.8 percent of the women and 17 percent of the men were elementary teachers. More male superintendents (65 percent) had coached athletics, compared to 12.6 percent of the women superintendents.

In the study conducted by Glass et al. (2000), 71 percent of the women acknowledged having a mentor, compared to 56.3 percent of the men. Glass et al. further noted that greater numbers of both men and women acknowledged having mentors than those in Glass' 1992 study.

Interviews conducted by Grogan (1996) revealed that many women superintendents expressed the need to become visible to others through professional organizations. Through involvement in professional organizations, the women in Grogan's study became visible to members of the male network and then gained approval of some of the members. This approval and subsequent sponsorship provided extra credibility for the women, aiding them in their pursuit of the superintendency.

Myths about women may sometimes be barriers to the career advancement of women in school administration. Pigford and Tonnsen (1993) suggested that the process of socialization prepares men to be leaders and women to be helpers. Given the fact that leaders are generally expected to have masculine traits, women who are aspiring to leadership positions sometimes find themselves in a quandary. Do they want to be women or do they want to be leaders? To be both is often viewed as contradictory. Thus, women often find themselves in no-win situations. If women are accommodating, polite, and passive, as society expects women to be, they lose their credibility as leaders. On the other hand, if they are competitive, aggressive and tough, they may have to deny their identity (Pigford & Tonnsen, 1993).

In her study of 54 Missouri superintendents, Burns (1995) concluded that approximately 30 percent of her respondents had not earned their administrative certification to get an administrative position, but rather to further their education. The administrative training fit into a program of graduate study, and their career evolved from that point.

The purpose of this study was to gain an understanding of the personal character-istics, educational background, support systems engaged in, obstacles encountered by, and aspirations of the women who had been granted certification for the super-intendency in the state of Missouri during the 10 years of 1990–2000. The follow-ing research questions provided the original focus of the investigation:

1. What are the personal characteristics and educational background of the women in Missouri who have earned their superintendent certification between the years 1990–2000?
2. What, if any, support systems were experienced by the women aspiring to the superintendency?
3. What, if any, obstacles were encountered by the women?
4. What are the professional aspirations of the Missouri women who have earned their superintendent certification?

DATA COLLECTION AND INSTRUMENTATION

This study was designed to include both qualitative and quantitative components. A demographic survey was used to gather data. In-depth interviews were used to col-lect qualitative data that were "rich in description of people, places, and conversa-tions not easily handled by statistical procedures" (Bogdan & Biklen, 1998, p. 2).

Data collection efforts were focused on answering four research questions through the use of the quantitative and qualitative methods. A data coding system was de-veloped to assist in identifying themes that emerged through this process. Issues of reliability and validity were addressed through the use of multiple data sources, a chain of evidence in the form of written transcriptions and survey responses, and through the use of a second researcher who independently analyzed interview tran-scriptions for themes.

Population and Sample

Superintendents in the state of Missouri must be licensed through the Missouri De-partment of Elementary and Secondary Education. Licensure requirements include the successful completion of the District-Level Administrator's Assessment Center, administered through the Leadership Academy of the Missouri Department of Ele-mentary and Secondary Education.

A list of the 116 women who had successfully completed the District-Level As-sessment Center since its inception in 1990 until 2000 was obtained from the Lead-ership Academy. This list included all of the women, representing 32.6 percent of the total number of educators, who had earned their Missouri superintendent's certifica-tion between the years 1990–2000.

Demographic surveys with a cover letter were mailed to the 116 women on the list. (A copy is included in appendix A.) The literature on superintendents suggested women superintendents possessed particular personal characteristics and followed common career paths. These trends guided the formation of the research questions used in this study. Personal characteristics, educational background, and career paths of the Missouri women in this study were gathered through the use of these preliminary demographic questionnaires. The questionnaires also sought to determine which respondents would agree to a personal interview if selected. Of the 116 mailed surveys, 66 (56.9 percent) were completed and returned, 9 were returned "undeliverable" due to a lack of a forwarding address, and 1 woman was confirmed as deceased.

A purposeful sampling of participants was selected from those that indicated they would agree to an interview. In purposeful sampling, the researcher chooses particular subjects "because they are believed to facilitate the expansion of the developing theory" (Bogdan & Biklen, 1998, p. 65). The 66 respondents were divided into three groups. The first group consisted of 25 women currently serving as superintendents. The second group included 19 women who were currently serving in central office positions, either as a director or assistant superintendent. The third group consisted of the remaining 22 women who were not currently serving as a superintendent or in a central office position. This group included women who were building level administrators, teachers, and those who were no longer in public K–12 education settings. Eight women from each of these three groups were selected for personal interviews, for a total of 24 interview participants. To assure a representative sampling of the respondents, participants were selected based on the geographic locations, district size, and the positions held of all women who responded to the demographic questionnaire.

Eight superintendents were selected for personal interviews. These superintendents were from school districts with student populations ranging between 110 and 1,800. Two women were selected from the central and two from the southern regions. One superintendent each was chosen from the northwestern, eastern, western, and southeastern regions of the state.

Of the eight central office administrators, six were assistant superintendents and two held director positions. Three were chosen from the western region, as were three from the eastern side of the state. One was selected from the southeast and one from the southwest regions. School district populations for these eight women ranged from 3,400 to 25,000.

The remaining eight participants included four elementary principals, one assistant principal, and one teacher who formerly held a director position. Also included in this group were a former elementary principal who currently was employed in higher education, as well as a retired assistant superintendent who was currently employed in the private sector. Five of these women were from the eastern region of the state, and one each was from the western, southwestern, and southeastern regions.

Overall geographical representation of the participants included nine interviewees from the eastern, five from the western, three from the southeastern, two each from the southwestern, central, and southern regions, and one from the northwestern region. There was only one respondent from the northeastern region. Therefore, no interviewees were chosen from that region of the state.

The interviews, which lasted approximately 45 minutes, consisted of open-ended questions, allowing the interviewer to probe for in-depth information. Such interviews allowed the participants to answer the questions from their own frame of reference, allowing them to freely express their thoughts (Bogdan & Biklen, 1998). A copy of the interview questions is included in appendix B.

SUMMARY OF FINDINGS

Major themes emerged through the process of data collection. These themes are organized and presented by the topics of support systems, gender myths, career aspirations, and women's perspectives.

Support Systems

When asked if there had been administrators or mentors who had influenced them, most of the 24 interview participants indicated there had been influential people in their careers. Most of these individuals identified as mentors had served as building principals while the women were teaching, superintendents while they were principals, or university professors while they were students. Of the 24 participants, 18 (75 percent) spoke only of men who had mentored them. Five women (20.8 percent) mentioned other women who had served as mentors to them. Four participants (16.7 percent) talked of the need for women to support each other more, as they felt other women had previously been unsupportive of them.

All participants agreed it was important to network with others. Most women spoke of networking with the other administrators in their county, activity conference, as well as their district administrators' organizations.

Gender Myths

The 24 interview participants were asked to list various gender myths and describe any effect they believed those myths might have had on their career. The most common myth, mentioned by 14 women (58.3 percent), was that women were too weak to handle the superintendency, and if they were assertive they were considered to be too harsh. Nine women (37.5 percent) discussed the myth that women cannot handle the finances as well as men. Eight participants (33.3 percent) discussed the myth that women are too emotional to be superintendents. While the participants acknowledged that women are usually more emotional than men, most did not view it as a reason why women could not be effective school leaders.

Career Aspirations

The 66 survey respondents were asked to indicate their career goal, with 33 (50 percent) indicating that their current title within the K–12 arena was their ultimate career goal. Of those 33 women, 21 were superintendents, 9 were directors or assistant superintendents, and 3 were building level administrators. Ten women who were not currently serving as superintendents, including 8 directors/assistant superintendents and two building level administrators, indicated that the superintendency was their ultimate career goal. A total of 31 respondents (47 percent) considered the superintendency to be their ultimate career goal.

Of the remaining 35 respondents, 15 (22.7 percent) listed the assistant superintendency as their career goal. Eight women (12.1 percent) wanted to teach at the college level or publish in the future. Two (3 percent) hoped to work at the state department of education, two (3 percent) were undecided, and one (1.5 percent) was currently unemployed and articulated no clear career goal specific to an administrative position.

As mobility can be a factor in women's achievement of their career goals, the 24 interview participants were asked if they were mobile or placebound. Eight (33.3 percent) stated they were placebound, while 16 (66.6 percent) considered themselves mobile. Of those considering themselves mobile, several stated they were highly mobile, while others considered themselves selectively mobile.

The 66 women responding to the demographic survey were asked if they had applied for administrative positions but not been offered the position. A total of 49 (74.2 percent) replied that they had applied for positions that they were not offered. The remaining 17 (26 percent) had never applied for an administrative position they were not offered.

The 24 interview participants were also asked the same question, to which 6 (25 percent) responded they had never applied for an administrative position they were not offered. The remaining 18 (75 percent) cited a variety of reasons why they believed they had not been offered positions. Gender, lack of experience, the lack of a proper fit between the candidate and the district, and lack of certification were listed as possible barriers. Six (25 percent) did not believe there were any significant factors involving their consideration for administrative positions.

Of the 9 participants who were currently serving, or who had served, as superintendents, 6 indicated they had not searched for the position, rather they had been sought out. The 3 women who actively searched for a superintendency reported they had spent between 1 month and 2 years seeking the position.

When asked if any extenuating circumstances had prevented them from seeking an administrative position, 44 (66.7 percent) of the 66 survey respondents replied that there had not been. The remaining women cited family obligations, being placebound, as well as their gender, as extenuating circumstances.

The 24 interview participants were asked if they had encountered obstacles as they pursued their career goals. Eight women (33.3 percent) did not believe they had encountered any serious obstacles. Seven (29.2 percent) mentioned gender issues, while 4 (16.7 percent) believed their only obstacles had been their own attitudes and personalities.

Of the 66 women responding to the demographic survey, 35 (53 percent) believed their gender had hindered their career advancement. Twenty (30.3 percent) believed their gender had neither helped nor hindered them. Six women (9.1 percent) believed that being a female had helped them advance in their career, while 5 (7.6 percent) believed it had both helped and hurt them.

When asked if their gender had affected their career, 8 (33.3 percent) of the 24 interview participants believed it had affected their career negatively. Seven (29 percent) felt their gender had possibly created some problems, but they did not make an issue of it. Five (20.8 percent) believed that being a woman had helped them in their career, and 4 (16.7 percent) did not believe their gender had affected their career.

The 24 interview participants were asked to share their views of why 10–12 percent of the superintendents in Missouri and across the nation were women. Mentioned by 13 women (54.2 percent) was the idea that the superintendency has traditionally been a man's job. Ten women (41.7 percent) believed that women were not willing to deal with the problems associated with the superintendency. Other reasons cited by the participants included the notion that communities and school boards were not ready to accept women as superintendents, that the superintendency is time consuming, women limit themselves in what they are willing to try, and women fear being rejected. However, 5 women (20.8 percent) expressed optimism with the belief that the numbers of women in the superintendency have grown, and will continue to do so.

Women's Perspectives

Interview participants were asked to reflect on what it was like to be a woman school leader. Nine (37.5 percent) expressed very positive thoughts, while 7 (29.2 percent) talked about the nurturing, caring traits that women bring to leadership positions. Six women (25 percent) tended to look past the gender issue in their careers. Other thoughts included the idea that women must work harder than men, there is a great deal of responsibility associated with school leadership, and that women often do not support other women.

When asked if they believed they had made sacrifices to achieve their position in their career, 20 (83.3 percent) of the 24 interview participants believed they had. The most frequently mentioned sacrifice was the loss of time with their families, friends, and self, cited by 14 (58.3 percent). Four women (16.7 percent) did not feel they had made sacrifices because they had made the choice to pursue their career.

Interview participants were asked to finish the statement: "If I had it to do all over again, I would _____." Twelve (50 percent) said they would probably follow the same career. Four (16.7 percent) would have gone into administration sooner, and three (12.5 percent) would not have let their careers interfere with their family as much as it had.

When asked what advice they would offer other women considering careers in educational administration, 16 (24.2 percent) of the 66 survey respondents encouraged women to persevere. Eight (12.1 percent) wrote of the need to be prepared to work hard. Other advice included networking and finding mentors, as well as finding a balance between family and work.

When asked to share advice, 10 (41.7 percent) of the 24 interview participants stressed the importance of knowing one's self and being strong. Seven (29.2 percent) spoke of the importance of having support systems, while 4 (16.7 percent) encouraged other women to pursue their career goals.

IMPLICATIONS FOR PRACTICE

Instructors in graduate programs preparing women for the superintendency should be held accountable in a number of areas. However, results of this study would suggest the following areas in particular.

First, women should have a clear understanding of the challenges facing them. These challenges would include a loss of time with families, the possible need to be mobile, the idea that some communities are biased against women in administration, and that administrative positions can create a feeling of isolation. Therefore, prior to pursuing careers in educational administration, women should have a clear understanding of their own personal beliefs toward education and be sure that their families understand the time factor and emotional stress inherent in the field of educational leadership. Conscious efforts should be made by women to identify mentors and to network with others in the field of educational administration. If, after careful consideration, women aspire to positions of educational administration, they should be encouraged to pursue their career goals.

Second, universities should play a vital role in informing others of the growing number of potential superintendency candidates who are women. This could be achieved through presentations to administrator, school board and parent/teacher organizations, as well as through articles in the various publications supporting these organizations.

Superintendent organizations should be made aware of the importance of mentoring aspiring school administrators. This could be accomplished through the establishment of programs in which experienced superintendents serve as mentors for beginning administrators.

Through presentations, university personnel should inform state and national school board organizations and the general public of the growing number of female candidates for the superintendency. These same organizations should also learn about the various strengths women bring to the superintendency, as well as the various obstacles women face as they pursue the superintendency.

SUMMARY

Although women are underrepresented in the superintendency in the state of Missouri, as they are throughout the nation, women have an increasing interest in securing positions in educational administration. This study was undertaken to provide information about those women who aspire to the superintendency.

Throughout this study, several themes emerged regarding the experiences and attitudes of women who have been certified as superintendents. These themes should serve as a guide to women considering a career in school administration, as well as to those instructors in administrator preparation programs.

First, being a school administrator had a large impact on the women administrators and their families. While most women acknowledged a great deal of support from their families, they also believed their careers took much time away from their families.

Next, an increasing number of women are interested in school administration. While the number of women in the superintendency in the state of Missouri is increasing, gender issues are still a factor in some school districts. Women's personalities and leadership styles are often different from men's. However, women in this study suggested that other women should consider themselves school administrators first and women second, and not make an issue of their gender.

Prior to entering the field of school administration, women should have strong support systems. Those support systems come from families, mentors, and through networking with others in the field. Although many women in this study did not feel support from other women in school administration, they believed it was important for women to support each other.

The women in this study were pleased with their choice of career. Although it was a stressful and time-consuming profession, they found it to be a rewarding career. Their advice to other women aspiring to positions in school administration was to go for their goals.

In conclusion, women may experience unique obstacles as they strive to gain access to the superintendency and other positions in school administration. Universities providing training programs for school administrators should be held accountable for helping to ensure the success of quality candidates as they pursue their career goals. With hard work, persistence, and an understanding of the barriers facing them, women can overcome the difficulties and become successful school administrators.

REFERENCES

Blount, J. M. (1998). *Destined to rule the schools: Women and the superintendency, 1873–1995.* Albany: State University of New York Press.

Bogdan, R. C., & Biklen, S. K. (1998). *Qualitative research for education: An introduction to theory and methods.* Boston: Allyn & Bacon.

Burns, B. D. (1995). *Women superintendents: A study in public schools in Missouri.* Unpublished doctoral dissertation, University of Arkansas.

Glass, T. (1992). *The 1992 study of the American school superintendency.* Arlington, VA: American Association of School Administrators.

Glass, T., Bjork, L., & Brunner, C. C. (2000). *The 2000 study of the American school superintendency.* Arlington, VA: American Association of School Administrators.

Gribskov, M. (1980). Feminism and the woman school administrator. In S. K. Biklen & M. B. Brannigan (Eds.), *Women and educational leadership* (pp. 77–91). Lexington, MA: D. C. Heath.

Grogan, M. (1996). *Voices of women aspiring to the superintendency.* Albany: State University of New York Press.

Missouri school directory. (1999–2000). Jefferson City, MO: School Core Data Section, Missouri Department of Elementary and Secondary Education.

Pigford, A. B., & Tonnsen, S. (1993). *Women in school leadership: Survival and advancement guidebook.* Lancaster, PA: Technomic.

Shakeshaft, C. (1987). *Women in educational administration.* Newbury Park, CA: Sage.

APPENDIX A
DEMOGRAPHIC SURVEY

Your participation is voluntary and you may refuse to answer any questions(s).

1. Age_____

2. Please indicate your marital status:

   Single____Married____Divorced____Engaged____Separated____Widowed____

3. If you have children, please list their ages: _____

4. Please outline your education, beginning with your bachelor's degree:

Degree   Major   University   Date Completed

_____

_____

_____

5. Please list your educational certifications and the dates received, including your superintendent certification:

_____

_____

_____

6. Please outline your career path as an educator, beginning with your first teaching position and proceeding through your current position.

Position & approx. size of district Age Start date End date Reason for changing

_____

_____

_____

_____

_____

_____

_____

_____

7. What is your current position?

How long have you been in this position? _____

What is the size of the district, if it is a position in education? _____

What is your annual salary? _____

8. If you have been an administrator, how many years did you teach prior to your first administrative position? _____

9. What are your career aspirations in terms of job title (ex. Superintendent, Asst. Superintendent, Principal)?

_____

10. Have you applied for administrative positions and not been chosen? If yes, please briefly describe.

_____

_____

_____

11. Do you feel that being a woman has either helped or hindered you in your career? Please describe.

_____

_____

_____

12. Have there been any extenuating circumstances that have prevented you from seeking or holding a specific administrative position?

_____

_____

13. Please briefly describe your family's role in your career.

_____

_____

14. Are there any other thoughts you would like to share with me concerning your career in education?

_____

_____

_____

_____

15. What advice would you like to share with other women who might be aspiring to positions in educational leadership?

_____

_____

16. Would you be willing to meet with me for a personal interview to be held at a place and time convenient for you? _____

If yes, please supply your name, telephone number, e-mail address and mailing address on the enclosed form.

Thank you very much for completing this survey!

APPENDIX B
INTERVIEW QUESTIONS

1. Could we begin with you telling me a little about your background and how you reached this position in your career?
2. Please describe the characteristics of your family. What effect has your family had on your career, and what effect has your career had on your family?
3. Please describe your academic preparation for the superintendency, and what prompted you to pursue that training and certification.
4. Were there administrators or mentors who have influenced or assisted you in any way? If so, please describe them and their influence on your career.
5. Do you network with other administrators? If so, how has this affected your career?
6. What are your career goals?
7. Have you applied for positions and not been offered the job? If so, how far did you make it in the application process?
8. If you have been a superintendent, how long did you search for the job?
9. What effect do you feel your gender has had on your efforts to become a school administrator?
10. There are some gender-related myths. Can you describe your feelings toward those myths and any effect they might have had on your career?
11. What is it like to be a woman superintendent/educational administrator/or aspirant to the superintendency?
12. Do you feel you have made sacrifices to achieve your position in education?
13. Statistics show that approximately 10–12 percent of the superintendents are women. Why do you think there are so few women superintendents in the United States and Missouri?
14. Have you encountered particular obstacles as you have pursued your professional goals? If so, please describe.
15. Please finish this statement: If I had it to do all over again, I would _____.
16. What gives you satisfaction as an educational administrator?
17. What advice would you give to women who are aspiring to the superintendency/positions of educational leadership?
18. Do you have any closing thoughts you would like to share?

Administrator Entry Year Programming:
A Cross-Institutional Pilot Program—
Process, Program Descriptions, and
Lessons Learned

Louis Trenta, Robert Beebe,
Patrick Cosiano, and Harry Eastridge

In 1999 the state of Ohio established five groups to develop and pilot test entry year programs for administrators. The northeast Ohio group took as the primary objectives of the project to develop, operate, and evaluate an entry year program for principals designed to reflect its own vision of what such a program should be. Since the group was created to assist the Ohio Department of Education in preparing to administer the state's new administrators' licensing law, which will be effective in July 2002, the members were somewhat constrained by the requirements of the law. Nonetheless, the participants, as university professors and district administrators, possessed, and sought to apply, experience with past and current induction efforts for new administrators. While each participant's experience and grasp of the literature related to administrator induction programs would naturally vary, the various ideas expressed in recent literature on the topic were brought forward in the course of the discussions and activities of the coordinating committee.

One key idea related to the relationship between the educational administration preparation program and the first job as an administrator. Mosrie (1990) in writing about a principal training and development program stated that graduate school alone was not an adequate preparation for the principalship and reviewed a principal support program in which the new principals had a support team working with them for their development during their first year (pp. 14–15). While writing specifically about mentoring new school leaders in the United Kingdom, Southworth (1995) made an applicable point when he noted that mentoring could be a vehicle for stimulating reflective leadership or a simply a means to preserve the current accepted

Louis Trenta, University of Akron
Robert Beebe, Youngstown State University
Patrick Cosiano, Baldwin-Wallace College
Harry Eastridge, Cuyahoga County Educational Service Center

views of the school leader's role. He argued for the stimulation of reflection and noted that the passing on of current role assumptions would not prepare school leaders for the challenges of schooling over the next century (pp. 26–27). Zachery (2000) recently noted that the focus of mentoring has shifted "from a product oriented model, characterized by the transfer of knowledge, to a process-oriented relationship involving knowledge acquisition, application, and critical reflection" (p. 4).

Over the years, John Daresh has consistently noted that new principals needed support in "responding to problems with role clarification, limitations on technical expertise, and difficulty with socialization to the profession at large and to the norms of specific school systems" (1987, p. 21). In a May 1990 article, he added to that list "a deep sense of professional isolation and a lack of feedback concerning the extent to which . . . [they] are performing their jobs effectively" (1990, p. 2). Hartzell et al. (1994), writing about new assistant principals, spoke of lost support systems as well as isolation and lack of feedback (p. 29). Writing in the United Kingdom, Kirkham (1996) also noted the need of "a secure environment where they [new heads of schools] can explore ideas and possible change with colleagues who understand their words and the issues they regularly face" (p. 82).

At the heart of the efforts to help new administrators is the mentor. Geismar, Morris, and Lieberman (2000, May) provide an extensive review of the characteristics of mentors suggested in the literature (pp. 235–236). Among the characteristics they and others have mentioned as needed by an effective mentor are experience regarded as effective in the administrator role, ability to ask the right questions rather than giving the right answers, acceptance of alternative ways of carrying out the role, an expressed desire to help people surpass them, knowledge of models of continuous learning and reflection, awareness of the political and social realities of administrative life (Capasso & Daresh, 2001, p. 103; Daresh & Playko, 1990, p. 74), and a personal style with which the new principal feels comfortable and secure (Wilmore, 1995, p. 93). A study of a British headteacher mentoring program had the new headteachers and mentors rank order the characteristics and skills desired in the mentor: listening skills; open, warm, and enthusiastic behavior; experience of headship; providing feedback; being non-judgmental; and counseling skills (Bolam, McMahon, Pocklington, & Weindling, 1996, p. 39). Whatever the characteristics and skills, the matching of mentor and mentee is best done collaboratively with the mentor, mentee, and the organizing body each having input (Walker & Stott, 1994, p. 73).

Beyond the characteristics of the mentor is the nature of the contacts between the mentor and the mentee (new administrator). Richardson and Prickett (1991) in their evaluation of a beginning principals intern program recommended that the principal interns have multiple group meetings at regional sites (p. 67). Bolam et al. (1996) suggest a minimum of five to six meetings over a 12–15 month span (p. 38). Zachery (2000) suggested a relatively short duration for the relationship with the length of time controlled by the accomplishment of specific learning objectives (p. 3). She also noted that current technology allows the relationship to be less face-to-face than was true in the past (p. 4).

The content of the interactions has also changed. Coleman et al. (1996) noted that almost all mentors in England reject the transmission of expertise concept in favor of a two-way relationship (p. 11). Daresh (1987) said some of that when he wrote about mentors' not telling new principals what to do but rather guiding them to make their own choices (p. 20). Southworth (1995) argued against the expert-novice enactment of mentoring in favor of a stimulating, reflective leadership oriented to the learner and critical and developmental in nature (p. 26). Zachery (2000) took this a step further and wrote that the mentee shares responsibility for the learning process with the goal of becoming self-directed (p. 3).

Recommended starting points might appear to vary and yet they seem to coincide on a need to begin by building the relationship. Trust, openness, and respect must be established (Bolam et al., 1996, p. 41; Walker & Stott, 1994, p. 74). In terms of the work to be done, running a school, Bolam et al. (1996) suggest beginning with practical, short-term concerns and technical advice as best fitting the needs of the new administrator and a later move into more fundamental issues (p. 41). Walker and Stott (1994) wrote about the benefits of a supportive structure for the mentor-mentee relationship, recommending competent, trained facilitators to work with the mentor-mentee pairs (p. 75).

Wilmore (1995) suggested using logs of activities as a way for new administrators to document continued growth. These are kept in a professional portfolio that, along with the logs, helps keep the mentees focused on their development plans (p. 95). Shipman and Murphy (2001, February), writing about a development program for current administrators, spoke both of portfolios being for professional development—addressing specific needs or challenges—and of a prototype portfolio developed primarily for relicensure (p. 2).

This chapter will review the process used in developing the pilot, a description of the program as implemented, and the lessons learned from this pilot.

BACKGROUND: PROGRAM DEVELOPMENT
Cross-Institutional Structure

Two university professors were asked to coordinate the effort in northeast Ohio. They solicited participation from the superintendents of the region, practicing principals, and faculty member/representatives of the other universities in the region that have administrator preparation programs. In the process of organizing, the superintendent of a county Educational Service Center agreed to be a third coordinator and act as fiscal agent for the project.

A coordinating committee was formed and included active and retired public school administrators and one or two representatives from each of the colleges and universities in northeast Ohio that have programs to prepare educational administrators. It created a program pilot that featured four clusters of mentors and mentees facilitated by a member of the Coordinating Committee.

Basic Considerations in Designing the Program

The goals of this program as put forward by the Ohio Department of Education (2000) were to:

1. Provide leadership and learning support systems for first- and second-year principals.
2. Assist in further development of Ohio's administrative portfolio, with articulation to the Ohio Administrative Competencies passed by the Ohio State Board of Education in January 1998.
3. Provide a collaborative learning community to share best practices and best ideas between higher education institutions and principal preparation programs.
4. Create a statewide community of learners to best assist in reshaping the role of the principal to meet the challenges of the 21st century.

As the Coordinating Committee shaped up and began discussing the pilot program, the basic considerations the Committee accepted as underlying the pilot were to:

1. Create an enriched initiating experience for beginning school principals.
2. View this as a hand-off from university training to in-the-field induction/ training.
3. Value the capabilities and right of participants to make decisions within the cluster.
4. Limit regional educational experiences to universal needs of participants.
5. Rely on the cluster as the level in which it was best to provide for or develop
   • Mentor-mentee relationship,
   • Networking among like professionals, and
   • A portfolio for submission to the Educational Testing Service.
6. Ensure that the Coordinating Committee had direct knowledge of the activities of the clusters.

Program Description

The Coordinating Committee generated the structure of the program (see figure 1) and provided the planning and implementation of the large group (all the facilitators, mentors, and mentees in the pilot program) meetings. The facilitators reported to the Coordinating Committee the activities, results, and problems experienced in the small groups and obtained advice. The facilitators also met together to discuss their various activities, expectations, and alternatives. In facilitating the small groups the facilitators organized the groups' meetings, provided motivation to carry out the program activities, and gave suggestions and advice to both mentors and mentees as needed on an individual basis. In creating the mentor-mentee pairings two strategies were used. First, those mentors and mentees who had been recommended together by their superintendents were accepted as "given" or "natural" pairs. Second, others selected for the program were assigned to small groups in balanced numbers and in rough geographic proximity. At the initial large group meeting and after some group development activities, these unpaired mentors and mentees were invited to make their own matches from those in their small groups.

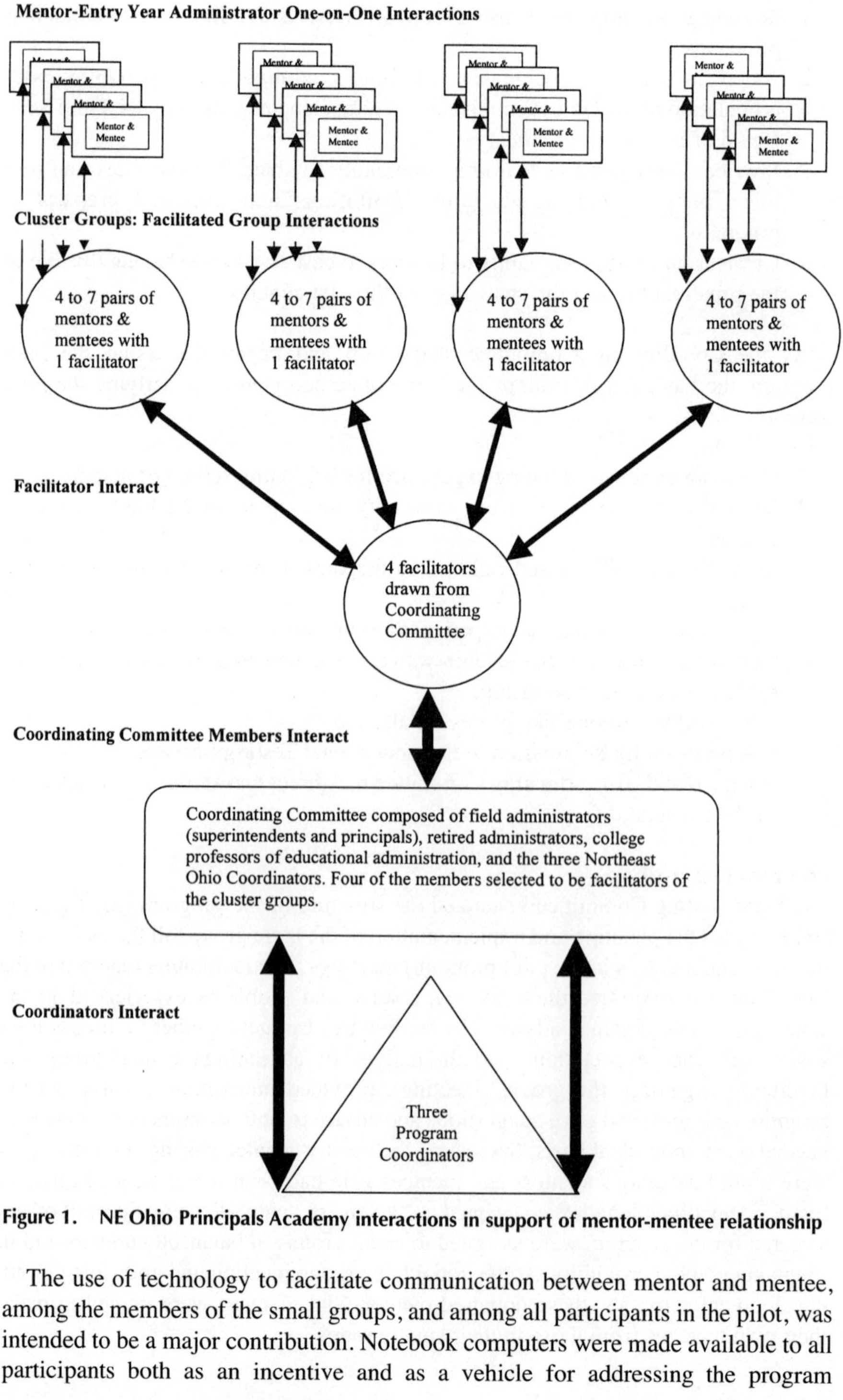

Mentor-Entry Year Administrator One-on-One Interactions

Figure 1.   **NE Ohio Principals Academy interactions in support of mentor-mentee relationship**

The use of technology to facilitate communication between mentor and mentee, among the members of the small groups, and among all participants in the pilot, was intended to be a major contribution. Notebook computers were made available to all participants both as an incentive and as a vehicle for addressing the program objectives. A Web site was created that enabled e-mail communications and bulletin board–type sharing and responding to information.

The initial large group meeting provided an overview of the program, its goals, and its structure. There was some presentation and discussion of the mentor-mentee relationship in the large group, but once the smaller groups were defined and mentors and mentees paired up, the continuing development of role expectations and group ground rules was left up to the facilitators and the small group members. Within the small groups the personal relationships were fostered and the work begun on the portfolios. As the pilot ended, 48 of the initial 55 mentors and mentees had stayed with the voluntary program for the 2-year experience.

PROGRAM EVALUATION

As part of the pilot, one member of the Coordinating Committee and an outside person were asked to evaluate the program's first year for the purpose of improving the program in the second year. In the second year they were asked to undertake a second evaluation. This second evaluation was to determine the workability of the program as a whole and the differential effectiveness of its major components in developing portfolios and as a contributing factor to school improvement. The first year's evaluation was not put into place until nearly 9 months into the program. This restricted evaluation of activities from the early months to data collected for other purposes and the recollections of the participants looking back in time.

The First Year

Four questions focused the first year's evaluation. First, what were the views of the Coordinating Committee and facilitators (those delivering the program) about the program—what worked and what could be improved? Second, what were the views of the mentors and mentees (those receiving the program) about the program—what worked and what could be improved? Third, how did the major components of the program compare with independent standards for those types of components? And, fourth, what was the worth of this Entry Year Program as a means for the entry year principal to fulfill the requirements for the 5-year license, develop his or her portfolio as an assessment device, and develop a support program for professional growth and successful entry into educational administration?

The major information sources were the minutes and documents of the program, evaluations of the two regional meetings held prior to authorizing the evaluation, an open-ended survey of the Coordinating Committee, interviews with the facilitators, and a survey of the participants—mentors and the entry year administrators. The information gathered was analyzed and summarized according to the major components of the pilot program and identified benchmarks related to mentor programs and effective meetings.

The data were then interpreted to respond directly to the four focusing questions. General evaluative comments were prepared. Finally, conclusions in the form of identified strengths, weaknesses or problem areas, and recommendations were developed.

The Second Year

The second year was 3 months underway when the Coordinating Committee authorized the second year evaluation. Over the next 2 months the proposed focus of the evaluation shifted from an evaluation paralleling that of the first year to one that would result in recommendations from all those engaged in the project to the Ohio Department of Education and other interested parties.

The evaluators worked with a subcommittee of the Coordinating Committee to identify the significant components and functions of the pilot entry year program. Seven were identified: introductory informational work and meetings, the mentor-mentee relationship, personal and interpersonal aspects of the program, the portfolio, organization including time and expectations, the use of technology, and training. All participants in the program were surveyed for their comments on each of these seven plus an open-ended "other."

The responses were coded by content, regrouped, and send back to the participants for additional confirmation or comment. There were six groups of comments centering around mentoring, meetings, portfolio, organizational aspects, technology, and miscellaneous. A summation of the comments was prepared for each of the topical areas and the second round comments were added separately to the summation.

The Coordinating Committee reviewed the initial responses and noted that school improvement and student achievement had not received many comments. It determined to make this a major aspect for the recommendations and seek more input on it at a general meeting of the participants. The general meeting was organized so that there were seven centers of topical interest, each led by a facilitator and a scribe. The participants rotated through the seven centers, considered the data from the surveys, and made suggestions for recommendations related to that aspect. The scribes and facilitators then wrote a statement intended to capture the consensus of the participants. These statements were reviewed by the full group and assented to as representative of the opinion of the group on the topic.

LESSONS LEARNED

The participants in this program—Coordinating Committee members, mentors, and mentees—reviewed the successes and problems in this pilot and prepared recommendations about the structure and operation of the entry year program that will be required by the state in 2002. With the assistance of the program evaluators, they structured these ideas into six topical areas: the mentor-mentee relationship, the meetings, the organizational structure, the portfolio requirement, the use of technology, and the relationship of the entry year program to school improvement. After a review of the participants' findings, the three coordinators provided additional insights. Finally, the evaluators added several comments based on their review of the program and the evaluation reports prepared for the Coordinating Committee.

Mentor-Mentee Relationship

The participants identified four key themes as important for constructing a mentoring program and for relationship building for the entry year principal: training, proximity, the first year, and networking. They saw a critical need for training the mentors particularly about portfolio development, since this is the evaluative product for the Ohio entry year administrator. In addition, the participants recommended training about how to mentor using sound coaching and socializing skills.

The participants identified as a key aspect the proximity of the mentor-mentee pairs with consideration for the pair working at the same education level and in communities having comparable socioeconomic demographics. Geographic proximity was viewed as making frequent contact easier and demographic proximity would increase the likelihood of common issues to discuss.

Concerning the first year, the participants' recommendation was that the first year be one of "getting to know" one another personally, each other's communities, and each other's talents and needs. To aid in this process both mentor and mentee should write reflections. During this first year, the mentors should be engaged in professional development as mentors. The participants also recommended there be no portfolio work the first year other than that provided for mentors as part of their training.

Two other mentor-mentee related issues were support by superintendents and the cluster groups. Supportive superintendents who authorize and encourage blocks of time to be devoted to this experience were judged crucial to building the support networks for the entry year administrators. The use of cluster groups increased the networking capabilities of the participants and was recommended for inclusion in the state's program.

The Program Coordinators had additional observations related to the mentor-mentee relationship. They noted that a program such as this should initiate and maintain efforts to recruit a diverse and highly qualified cadre of persons to be assigned as mentors to entry year principals. The selection by solicitation of superintendents' recommendations was accepted as necessary for a start-up pilot program. Considering the need for experiences in diversity and the strong recommendations for training of the mentors, it was the judgment of the Coordinators that mentor recruitment not be left to chance or even simple recommendation. The program should actively seek out and recruit mentors to reflect the broader diversity of our society. Once identified as potential mentors, superintendents and boards of education should be asked to provide time for them to be trained and to participate in entry year relationships even for new administrators not in their districts. It also was seen as imperative that the new administrators participating in entry year programs receive a satisfying experience as mentees, an experience that, we hoped, would develop into a co-mentoring or mutually beneficial relationship with their mentors, so that the new administrators would be willing and ready to take on the role of mentor in subsequent years.

Meetings

An introductory meeting that gives a very clear picture of the goals of the program is important. In this pilot program, aspects of the program were still being formulated at that time by the state and consequently by the local coordinating committee. The lack of clear, concise directions and expectations received significant criticism from the participants in all roles.

The participants also endorsed the regional and cluster structure of this program with particularly strong support for maintaining the small group and cluster meetings involving four to six pairs of mentors and mentees. Indeed, the participants called the cluster group meetings "the engine that drives the entire entry year process" (Trenta & Covrig, p. 11). While the participants did not recommend changes in the structure of the cluster group meetings, they did recommend more structure, in the form of time lines, for the completion of parts of the portfolio.

Participants found that the regional meetings should be fast paced and organized in ways supportive of the cluster group meetings. Several cluster groups tagged cluster meetings onto the regional meetings, extending their day, and eventually sought to have them built into the regional meeting.

State level meetings were not particularly valued. These were meetings of participants from all five pilot programs and were viewed as not well organized in support of what were perceived to be the goals of this local pilot program.

Organizational Structure

The participants gave broad support to maintaining the regional, cluster, and mentor-mentee structure. Each level of the structure was seen as fulfilling a function that contributed to the success of the pilot. Even so, there were some criticisms. One was a definite call for much clearer direction and goal statements from the state during the beginning of the program. The state's time line for portfolio preparation was strongly criticized. But these criticisms were not so much about organizational structure as about process. The participants objected to being required to prepare portfolios without knowledge of the evaluation process let alone the rubrics by which the quality of their work would be determined.

The local Coordinating Committee structure involving a university–field administrator collaboration was deemed a strength. Having representatives of all the region's university educational administrator preparation programs represented along with current and recently retired field administrators added value to the program. One recommendation from the participants was that the Coordinating Committee should generate more suggestions for cluster group discussions.

The program coordinators offered an additional observation about the program's structure. They noted that this entry year program generated a complexity of relationships. As can be seen in figure 1, there were five levels of relationships evident in this pilot. First there was the mentor-mentee relationship—a one-on-one relationship. Second was the small, geographic group relationship involving from four to seven sets of mentors and mentees with a facilitator. Third was the relationship of the facilitators with each other as they supported and educated each other. Fourth were the interactions among the members of the Coordinating Committee as oversight and resource to facilitators and small groups, and as a provider of experiences through the large group meetings. This relationship included the additional complexity for the facilitators of serving as intermediaries between the small groups and the Coordinating Committee. Finally, there were the interactions among the three Program Coordinators, including their liaison role with the state.

The program evaluators noted that within this program structure—with facilitators linking the Coordinating Committee and the small groups—the facilitators proved to be topically well-informed of the attitudes, opinions, and concerns of the mentors and mentees, more so than was the Coordinating Committee. However, even though the facilitators did effectively communicate the topics, they were not as effective in communicating the intensity or priorities of those attitudes, opinions, and concerns.

Another observation made by the evaluators was that mentors and mentees tended to focus more on the here-and-now while Coordinating Committee members tended toward a more global perspective. The planners may have recognized that this was a pilot with limitations of information and procedures, and the mentors and mentees probably saw this program as happening to them and making demands on their time and energy for work products with nebulous or non-existent standards for measuring progress or success. Reactions and feedback varied accordingly.

Portfolio Requirement

Interestingly, the participants saw portfolios as another strength of the program, although with frequent, pointed comments about making portfolio development a 2- or 3-year project with refined time lines and improved alignment to the ISLLC standards. More specifically, the mentors and mentees recommended work on the portfolio really should not commence until the second year of the entry program, and some believed that 2 years from then ought to be allowed for its completion—a total of 3 years.

Two modifications were commonly recommended to the portfolio requirement. First, it appeared critical that the rubrics and procedures for evaluation must be clearly and completely spelled out at the very beginning of the program. The favored idea was to discuss the rubrics and procedures at the introductory general meeting and during the cluster meetings. In this pilot, the rubrics for evaluating the portfolios were never provided. This lack may have influenced the strength of the calls for such disclosure. The second criticism of the portfolios was directed toward making the portfolio content requirements be more practical, that is, more closely parallel to the work functions of principals in their first years.

The Program Coordinators made several observations about the portfolio requirement. The Coordinators stated that if the portfolio is to be used to provide screening of entry year principals for licensure or other high-stakes decision making, it is essential that a thorough validation be conducted, both of the portfolio assessment procedures and of the applicable cut-off scores. They also believed intensive assessor training should be provided to ensure the validity of these assessments. Additionally, they believed responsibilities and processes should be defined for dealing with individuals who do not meet or exceed the cut-off scores for the portfolios.

The Coordinators spoke to both the portfolio requirement and mentor training in recommending that a clear definition of the portfolio, both operationally and in terms of purpose, should be provided to mentors along with intensive training in portfolio preparation. They believed that consideration should be given to the expansion of portfolio content to include all core areas of principal performance, for example, all state-adopted administrative competencies, interpersonal relations, and so forth.

The Coordinators further recommended that consideration be given to the use of alternative or supplemental methods for the screening of entry year principals for licensure, to include the assessment of reflective writings, state-sponsored panel interviews, traditional superintendent recommendations, and paper-and-pencil tests.

Use of Technology

The provision of a laptop computer was highly endorsed and not just as an incentive. Rather, the participants saw computer technology as an important tool for administrator effectiveness. The program Web site was judged valuable although there were some difficulties in accessing it. The use and potential of technology for communications was accepted even as emphatic calls for better training in the use of the computer and the Web site were made by participants.

The Coordinators believed that a stable, statewide Web site with e-mail, chat, and links to professional resources and discussion lists might further improve the use of technology for communication.

Focus on Student Achievement

The participants did not find that the program as presented provided a strong connection to school improvement and student achievement. Although few commented on this aspect initially, when it was pointed out the participants emphasized this focus as an essential focus of the entire program and recommended that cluster group discussions have this as a common theme, using research and journal articles to inform the discussions.

Limitations

In considering the reflections of the Program Coordinators, it must be noted that they did not interject themselves in the development of the total group's comments and recommendations, although they did support them as they were adopted by the group. The comments or lessons put forth in this paper as from the Program Coordinators were more individual in origin and status than those of the total participant group. Nonetheless, they are significant in that the Program Coordinators were responsible for starting and supporting the process that developed the program and recommendations described above.

While this pilot did include representatives from the administrator preparation programs on an ongoing basis, superintendent participation was more difficult to come by in terms of developing and coordinating the program. Yet, as it moved into the second year, several superintendents joined the Coordinating Committee and took an active role in the program. The types of support individual mentors and mentees received from their superintendents with regard to this program were not at all clear. Incidental comments passed along were indicative of significant variations in awareness and support of the activities of the participant-administrators on the part of superintendents.

During the exercise intended to bring about a convergence of ideas for recommendations about entry year programs, Coordinating Committee members were used as table facilitators and scribes. This left very few Coordinating Committee members to rotate through the seven tables and to provide topic-by-topic input. The resultant recommendations might have been different to some degree if a means had been devised for the Committee members to react to the data related to each of the aspects or if the facilitator and scribe roles had been spread out among all the participants.

In this study the issue of necessary or appropriate characteristics of mentors was not directly considered. Superintendents recommended all the mentors, and all were volunteers for the project. Thus the trait identified by Wildman, Magliaro, and Niles (1992) as the prime trait for supporting and maintaining the mentor-mentee relationship, the willingness of an experienced person to be a mentor, was present as a given.

This study focused narrowly on the single pilot program in northeast Ohio. While the politics of state sponsored mentoring and screening of entry principals should be examined, that issue was not part of this study. Funding issues, the support of state-level professional organizations, and the degree and types of support provided by school districts and administrator preparation institutions were not dealt with in this study.

DISCUSSION AND CONCLUSION

The fact that 48 of 55 of the initial mentors and mentees stayed with the program from the initial meeting to the end of the pilot, an essentially voluntary program, is perhaps the best indicator of the perceived value and success of this particular program. Another is that the Coordinating Committee maintained a collegial relationship between the northeast Ohio graduate programs that prepare educational administrators somewhat in competition with each other. Thirdly, the Coordinating Committee did grow over the term of the pilot, attracting more superintendents into an active role.

This pilot utilized many of the ideas noted in the literature review and went beyond it in its attention to the complexity of relationships that this collegially developed and operated program generated. The importance of trust, respect, and caring—at all levels of the various relationships—just may have been the greatest lesson learned and confirmed by this pilot entry year program.

Some areas of further study with regard to entry year programs for administrators include the funding issue. If the state mandates the program without providing funds and training for mentors, will it reach the goals intended by the legislature? What level and types of support and commitment from the State, the universities, and the districts would offer the best chance for both successful entry and successful screening of new administrators?

Within such programs, there is a need to identify the how the program changes when the mentors are administrators who themselves have gone through such an entry year program. In a sense, the first generation to experience entry year can reasonably be expected to have a context different from that for all subsequent generations.

REFERENCES

Bolam, R., McMahon, A., Pocklington, K., & Weindling, D. (1996). Mentoring for new headteachers: Recent British experience. *Journal of Educational Administration, 33*(5), 29–44.

Capasso, R. L., & Daresh, J. C. (2001). *The school administrator internship handbook: Leading mentoring, and participating in the internship program.* Thousand Oaks: Corwin Press.

Coleman, M., et al. (1996, April). *Re-thinking training for principals: The role of mentoring.* A paper presented at the annual meeting of the American Educational Research Association, New York. (ERIC Document Reproduction Service No. ED397479)

Daresh, J. C. (1987). *The highest hurdles for the first year principal.* Paper presented at the annual meeting of the American Educational Research Association, Washington, DC. (ERIC Document Reproduction Service No. ED280136)

Daresh, J. C. (1990). Formation: The missing ingredient in administrator preparation. *NASSP Bulletin, 74*(526), 1–5.

Daresh, J. C., & Playko, M. A. (1990). Mentor programs: Focus on the beginning principal. *NASSP Bulletin, 74*(527), 73–77.

Geismar, T. J., Morris, J. D., & Lieberman, M. G. (2000). Selecting mentors for principalship interns. *Journal of School Leadership, 10*(3), 233–247.

Hartzell, G. N., et al. (1994). *Addressing the problems of first-year assistant principals.* Paper present at the annual meeting of the National Association of Secondary School Principals, New Orleans, LA. (ERIC Document Reproduction Service No. 369179)

Kirkham, G. (1996). Headlamp and the need for an enlightened view of mentoring for new school leaders. *Journal of Educational Administration, 33*(5), 74–83.

Mosrie, D. (1990). An effective principal training and support system. *NASSP Bulletin, 74*(526), 12–15.

Ohio Department of Education. (2000). *Request for proposals: Entry year principals' program, fiscal year 2000.* Columbus, OH: Author.

Richardson, M. D., & Prickett, R. L. (1991, April). *A comprehensive evaluation of Kentucky's beginning principal intern program.* A paper presented at the Annual Meeting of the American Educational Research Association, Chicago. (ERIC document Reproduction Service No. ED331159)

Shipman, N. J., & Murphy, J. (2001). Standards for school leaders: Gaining momentum. *Principal Leadership, 1*(6), 69–70. Retrieved September 28, 2001, from http://proquest.umi.com/pqdweb?TS=1001707...C=1&Dtip=1&Did=000000069698811&Mtd=1&Fmt=3

Southworth, G. (1995). Reflections on mentoring for new school leaders. *Journal of Educational Administration, 33*(5), 17–28.

Trenta, L. S., & Covrig, D. (2001). *Evaluation report Northeast Ohio Principals Academy entry year program: Year II.* Cleveland: Northeast Ohio Principals Academy.

Walker, A., & Stott, K. (1994, January). Mentoring programs for aspiring principals: Getting a solid start. *NASSP Bulletin, 78*(558), 72–77.

Wildman, T. M., Magliaro, S., & Niles, R. A. (1992). Teacher mentoring: an analysis of roles, activities, and conditions. *Journal of Teacher Education, 43*(3), 205–213.

Wilmore, E. L. (1995, April). It's not easy being green: Mentoring for the first year principal. *NASSP Bulletin, 79*(570), 91–96.

Zachery, L. J. (2000). *The mentor's guide: facilitating effective learning relationships.* San Francisco: Jossey-Bass.

Author Index

About the Editors

George Perreault teaches in the Department of Educational Leadership at the University of Nevada. He previously served as a principal and superintendent in Florida and New Mexico, as well as on the faculty of New Mexico Highlands University, Gonzaga University, and East Carolina University. Professor Perreault has published numerous professional articles and authored or coauthored seven books, including the 2001 NCPEA Yearbook, *21st Century Challenges for School Administrators*. In addition, he is associate editor of the *School Public Relations Journal* and serves on the editorial board of two other national journals.

Fred C. Lunenburg is professor and research fellow in the Center for Research and Doctoral Studies in Educational Leadership at Sam Houston State University. He was previously on the faculty in educational administration at the University of Louisville, distinguished visiting professor at the University of Utrecht, and professor and dean of the College of Education at Southern Utah University. Prior to moving to the university level, he served as a principal and superintendent in Minnesota and Wisconsin. Professor Lunenburg has authored or coauthored 12 books and more than 100 articles in education.